STANTON: THE LIFE AND TIMES OF LINCOLN'S

SECRETARY OF WAR

Edwin McMasters Stanton in 1866.

STANTON

*The Life
and Times
of Lincoln's
Secretary
of War*

BENJAMIN P. THOMAS
AND HAROLD M. HYMAN

ALFRED · A · KNOPF · NEW YORK 1962

L. C. catalog card number: 61–17829

THIS IS A BORZOI BOOK,
PUBLISHED BY ALFRED A. KNOPF, INC.

FIRST EDITION

TO JAMES G. RANDALL

"the memory be green"

PREFACE

I DID NOT KNOW Benjamin P. Thomas except through his writings. When he died, he was at work on a biography of Edwin McMasters Stanton, and I undertook to complete it. I soon learned that my task was more difficult in some ways than initiating a book alone. A man who was not at hand to counsel me or to argue with was my co-author.

But co-author he has been. In the notes, outlines, and chapter drafts that he had assembled, Mr. Thomas had partially shaped elements of the story he wanted to tell. He had built from the rich resources of his prodigious research, drawing from the years of thought and study that he had devoted to the Lincoln theme, enlivening all with the warmth of his large heart and brave imagination.

To be sure, we disagreed on many matters. He had touched on themes that I decided to pass over, just as I opened up channels of inquiry that he might have ignored. As this work progressed, however, I found to my pleasure that Mr. Thomas and I had achieved a partnership, and I received an education at his gentle hands.

I am honored at this association with Ben Thomas, and I hope that he would have approved of what I have done with our Stanton. Of course I accept full responsibility for this book, but I gratefully acknowledge his contributions to its conception and completion.

Across the country, busy librarians and archivists searched their collections for useful material and made it available to us. The footnotes will indicate the extent of our obligations to university and private libraries and historical societies, and agencies of the states and of the national government. They will not, however, note the many persons who spent time and energy checking leads that did not bear fruit but whose efforts were nonetheless important. To all these men and women, to the personnel of the Interlibrary Loan office at

UCLA, and to the staff of the Huntington Library, who among other services made the S. L. M. Barlow Papers quickly available for use, I offer heartfelt thanks.

Stanton descendants who with openhanded generosity provided manuscripts include William Stanton Picher, Gideon Townsend Stanton, and Mrs. E. K. Van Swearingen, who added hospitality to her contributions to research. Important manuscripts were also produced by George Bonaventura, Professor Edward S. Corwin, W. V. Houston, Willard King, Mrs. K. McCook Knox, the estate of Foreman M. Lebold, Hugh McCulloch (grandson and namesake of Lincoln's Secretary of the Treasury), Ralph Newman, Milton Ronsheim, Carl Sandburg, Miss Alexandra Sanford, William Selden, Mrs. Henry D. M. Sherrerd, Justin Turner, and Craig Wylie. Professor Robert V. Bruce assisted Mr. Thomas in the early stages of his research, and I benefited substantially from his efforts. My colleague Professor Brainerd Dyer added the reading of this manuscript to the heavy professional burden he bears. His criticisms and encouragement were of great value, and I am grateful for his gracious aid. As this book progressed toward its present form, Alfred A. Knopf and Henry Robbins offered firm, patient editorial guidance.

A grant from the Social Science Research Council made it possible for me to enlarge my understanding of Stanton as Secretary of War and of the politics under President Johnson that involved the war office, and UCLA provided funds and free time to assist me in this work. I know how much I owe to my wife, Ferne, and to our children, Lee, Ann, and Billy.

HAROLD M. HYMAN

CONTENTS

CONTENTS

PLATES

ILLUSTRATIONS

INTRODUCTION

"AT PRESENT," Theodore Tilton wrote of his friend Edwin McMasters Stanton in 1870, "he is, perhaps, the least popularly understood and appreciated of any of our first-class statesmen." [1] The same is true today.

This misunderstanding and lack of appreciation do not mean that Stanton has been ignored for ninety years. No one dealing with the vital political center of the nineteenth century has failed to consider his career. As Tilton said, Stanton was of "first-class" importance. He fought on the front lines of the party battles in the age of Jackson. Secession raised Stanton's significance to a higher level. He entered Buchanan's cabinet and helped to inspire that President with an enhanced sense of the powers of his office and of the dignity of the nation.

Then, as War Secretary under Lincoln, Stanton worked to guide the Union's search for the men and measures adequate to crush the rebellion. Partly due to his efforts and ideas, the North by 1865 had come to something remarkably like modern concepts of total war. In our current concern with increasing the fighting strength of the military forces while retaining civilian direction over the military establishment, there are lessons we may learn from Stanton's successes and failures. [2]

Continuing in the war office under Lincoln's successor, Stanton found that issues almost as disruptive as those that had ruptured the Union in 1860 had come to the fore. His decision to defy Andrew Johnson helped to bring on the only impeachment a President of the United States has suffered.

Considering the exacerbating nature of the controversies in which Stanton played a part, it is little wonder that disagreement should exist among those who deal with him. But the large literature on Stanton

[1] *Sanctum Sanctorum* (New York, 1870), 217.
[2] T. Harry Williams, *Americans at War: The Development of the American Military System* (Baton Rouge, 1960), 47–81; General Sir Frederick B. Maurice, *Governments and War: A Study of the Conduct of War* (London, 1926), 118–23.

has transcended the limits of constructive disagreement. For example, Stanton's three biographers have been his frank champions, finding few faults that marred their subject and fewer virtues to attribute to his enemies and critics. On the other side, a more numerous phalanx of Stanton's contemporaries and subsequent commentators have condemned Stanton in terms of unqualified derogation.

There can be no question that for the general public, as well as for most scholars in the field, Stanton's critics have won the battle. Despite the eulogistic judgments of his biographers, Stanton's place in our history has descended ever lower. This downward drift has gone so far that he has been implicitly accused of conniving in Lincoln's murder.[3]

Stanton's supporters and detractors share responsibility for the descent of his reputation. Setting out either to praise or to pillory their subject, these authors permitted their prejudgments to determine their conclusions and exceeded the allowable limits set by the nature of the evidence at their disposal. The defenders depended on the conclusions of Stanton's intimates and political helpmates; indeed, his first biographer, George C. Gorham, was an important Republican politician as well as a warm personal friend during the time Stanton held the war portfolio. On the other hand, such men as Gideon Welles and Jeremiah Black, who hated Stanton personally and who bitterly opposed his politics, set down their opinions on him in order to express partisan convictions.

With a surprising lack of critical caution, "revisionist" historians during the past thirty years accepted this latter body of writings as valid guidelines to the past. The "new look" that revisionists offered of the Reconstruction years resulted in a lofty rise in Andrew Johnson's stature. As Johnson rose, Stanton fell. Despite the revisionists' impressive contributions to our understanding of the events they described, their conclusions need to be reconsidered.

The authors in both camps could have benefited from a statement by John T. Morse, Jr., who helped to prepare the invaluable, partisan "diary" of Gideon Welles for publication. Morse, bemoaning the fact that Stanton had not kept an equivalent record, warned that Welles's

[3] George C. Gorham, *Life and Public Services of Edwin M. Stanton* (Boston, 1899); Frank A. Flower, *Edwin McMasters Stanton, Lincoln's Great War Secretary* (New York, 1905); Fletcher Pratt, *Stanton: Lincoln's Secretary of War* (New York, 1953). Hereafter these will be cited as Gorham, *Stanton;* Flower, *Stanton;* and Pratt, *Stanton.* The accusations involving Stanton in Lincoln's murder are in Otto Eisenschiml, *Why Was Lincoln Murdered?* (Boston, 1937); and Theodore Roscoe, *The Web of Conspiracy* (Englewood Cliffs, 1959), which are unsound in method and untrustworthy in conclusions, as is Milton Lomask, *Andrew Johnson: President on Trial* (New York, 1960), concerning Stanton's role in the impeachment crisis.

account of events "is too much like sitting at the prize-ring and seeing only one pugilist." [4]

It is in part Stanton's own fault that his critics have hit with more effect than his champions. He refused to become a contender on his own behalf. Stanton told Tilton that he despised the "common arts" by which men keep their names "green and fragrant before the people," and he ignored the suggestions that came to him from John W. Draper, Francis Lieber, George Bancroft, and John C. Ropes that he keep a diary and arrange his personal papers in an attitude of polemical defense. In addition, Stanton's biographers, however anxious to extol their subject, failed in their task of re-creating a personality. In their lives of Stanton they failed to build a live Stanton. Yet one of Stanton's friends, the scholar Lieber, thought of him as a man so warm and complex that a Plutarch would have delighted in the task of describing him. [5]

A better balance has recently been emerging in our approach to the Lincoln-Johnson years. Stanton—like Welles, Chase, and Seward among his cabinet colleagues and Grant, Sherman, and Halleck of the army galaxy—is beginning to stand forth out of the shadow cast by Lincoln's overtowering figure. There is increasing recognition of the complex nature of the Civil War and Reconstruction. Historians are accepting the need for fresh approaches to the era's problems and personalities. As the inadequacies of oversimple theses on the period become apparent, and new bodies of evidence come to light, the awareness of the need for re-evaluation has grown markedly.

The opportunities for a fairer evaluation of Stanton's life are greater today than ever before. A century of scholarship is at hand to be exploited, and revealing manuscript sources are available for use as never before. As an example, a sharp beam of light is cast on Stanton in an unpublished sketch prepared by his sister, which contains many letters he wrote to her and to others. In addition, a substantial body of letters brought forth by Stanton descendants, collectors, and archivists offers new insight. Perhaps we are ready for the "realistic" study of Stanton that Professor James G. Randall called for two decades ago. [6]

[4] Morse, *The Diary of Gideon Welles* (Boston, 1911), I, xxxi–xxxii (hereafter cited as Morse, *Welles Diary*). The 1960 edition by Howard K. Beale (henceforth cited as Beale, *Welles Diary*) in I, xxi–xxxiv, offers guidance in using the earlier set. The Morse version will be employed except as Beale corrects errors or adds new data.

[5] Tilton, *op. cit.*, 217; Lieber to "My Dear Sir" (probably Benson J. Lossing), Dec. 25, 1865, Lieber Papers, LC.

[6] Randall, "The Civil War Restudied," *JSH*, VI, 455–6; "Edwin M. Stanton: A Biographical Sketch by His Sister, Pamphila Stanton Wolcott" (hereafter cited as

In 1885, John P. Usher, who worked alongside Stanton in the cabinet, bemoaned the fact that contemporary writing on Lincoln was "the d—dest trash and fiction . . . lies respecting things possible and impossible." To this, Judge David Davis replied: "Yes, but what is the use of correcting it."

There is always a use in correcting it. But correctives should follow an injunction that Hay set down seventy-five years ago when he and Nicolay were preparing their great history of Lincoln: "We must not write a stump speech. . . . We will not fall in with the present tone of blubbering sentiment, of course. But we ought to write the history of those times like two everlasting angels who know everything, judge everything, and don't care a twang of the harps about one side or the other . . . [L]et us look upon men as insects and not blame the black beetle because he is not a grasshopper." Then Hay reminded Nicolay that there was one exception to his admirable injunction to objectivity: "We are Lincoln men through and through."

We are not "Stanton men through and through." But we agree with another admonition of Hay's, in which he warned Nicolay that Stanton "is going to be a nut to crack." [7]

It has defied cracking for ninety years, but the kernel is worth another effort.

Wolcott MS), The Rice University, Fondren Library, used by permission of W. V. Houston.

[7] Usher to Ward Lamon, Oct. 13, 1885 (including Davis's statement), HL; William R. Thayer (ed.), *Life and Letters of John Hay* (Boston and New York, 1908), II, 33 (cited henceforth as Hay, *Life and Letters*).

ABBREVIATIONS

AGO	Adjutant General's Office
AHA	American Historical Association
AHR	*American Historical Review*
ALA	Abraham Lincoln Association
ALQ	*Abraham Lincoln Quarterly*
AM	*Atlantic Monthly*
ANJ	*Army and Navy Journal*
BPL	Boston Public Library
BU	Brown University Library
CalHS	California Historical Society
CFL	Calais Free Library
CG	Commanding General
CHS	Chicago Historical Society
CM	*Century Magazine*
ColHS	Columbia Historical Society (Washington, D.C.)
CU	Columbia University Library (Special Collections)
CWH	*Civil War History*
DU	Duke University Library
GI	Gilcrease Institute
HL	Huntington Library
HML	Hayes Memorial Library
HQA	Headquarters of the Army
HSP	Historical Society of Pennsylvania
HU	Harvard University Library
	(Houghton Library unless otherwise specified)
IGO	Inspector General's Office
IndHS	Indiana Historical Society
ISHL	Illinois State Historical Library
ISHS	Illinois State Historical Society
IU	Indiana University Library
JMSI	*Journal of the Military Service Institute*
JSH	*Journal of Southern History*
LC	Library of Congress (Manuscripts Division)
LMU	Lincoln Memorial University Library
LNLF	Lincoln National Life Foundation
MA	*Military Affairs*
MAH	*Magazine of American History*
MdHS	Maryland Historical Society
MH	*Magazine of History*
MHM	*Michigan Historical Magazine*
MHS	Massachusetts Historical Society

xvii

MHSM	*Military Historical Society of Massachusetts*
MoHR	*Missouri Historical Review*
MoHS	Missouri Historical Society
MVHR	*Mississippi Valley Historical Review*
NA	National Archives
NAR	*North American Review*
NCHR	*North Carolina Historical Review*
NEQ	*New England Quarterly*
NHB	*Negro History Bulletin*
NHSP	*Naval Historical Society Publications*
NYHS	New-York Historical Society
NYPL	New York Public Library
OAHS	Ohio State Archaeological and Historical Society
OHS	Ohio Historical Society
OSAHQ	*Ohio State Archaeological and Historical Quarterly*
PHR	*Pacific Historical Review*
PU	Princeton University Library
QMG	Quartermaster General
RG	Record Group (in National Archives)
SAQ	*South Atlantic Quarterly*
Sec. War	Secretary of War
SHA	Southern Historical Association
TQHGM	*Tyler's Quarterly Historical and Genealogical Magazine*
UCB	University of California, Berkeley (Bancroft Library)
UCLA	University of California, Los Angeles (Special Collections Library)
UR	University of Rochester Library
USC	University of Southern California Library
UW	University of Washington Library
VMHB	*Virginia Magazine of History and Biography*
VSL	Virginia State Library
WD	War Department
WLCL	William L. Clements Library, University of Michigan
WPHS	Western Pennsylvania Historical Society
WSHS	Wisconsin State Historical Society
YU	Yale University

STANTON: THE LIFE AND TIMES OF LINCOLN'S

SECRETARY OF WAR

CHAPTER I

A FAIR PROSPECT

CHRISTMASES during Edwin Stanton's childhood were high-lighted by visits from relatives from all over Ohio. When the onset of dusk ended the day's play, the tired children gathered with the adults by the warm hearth in the front parlor. His father would read from the Bible. Then, with little difficulty, an aunt or uncle could be cajoled into reminiscing about how the family came to Ohio.

The children wanted especially to hear about grandmother Abigail Macy Stanton. She had been a tiny woman, but a strong-willed one. Once, after falling from a horse and breaking her arm, she had walked alone through miles of hilly woods in order not to miss Quaker meeting. Grandfather Benjamin Stanton had been a massive, powerful man, as stubborn as his wife. During the American Revolution he was Quaker enough to stay out of the Army, but as a fervent rebel, he fitted out privateers. Along with the varied business interests near Beaufort, North Carolina, which his father had bequeathed to him, had come numerous Negro slaves. Benjamin refused to set them free, though Abigail and other Friends preached at him for years to do so. He did, however, free them in his will. But by 1799, the year of his death, North Carolina law forbade manumission.

Abigail set forth with her children and "the poor black people" for land where no slavery existed. By schooner, oxcart, raft, and foot, this courageous woman led her charges across the mountains to Jefferson County, Ohio, where in 1800 she purchased a 480-acre tract one mile west of Mount Pleasant.[1]

[1] Reminiscences concerning childhood in Edwin M. to William Stanton, *ca.* Dec. 25, 1865, copy owned by the estate of Benjamin P. Thomas; and Wolcott MS, 1–19. For genealogical data, see William Henry Stanton, *A Book Called Our Ancestors: the*

Of such stock was David Stanton, Edwin's father, one of the four sons of Benjamin and Abigail. When he was twenty-four years old, David married Lucy Norman, "a plump, substantial, vivacious" young woman of Culpeper County, Virginia. Her father was a wealthy miller and planter, much given to lawsuits against his neighbors. Lucy's disposition was as unbending as her father's. She left home at sixteen because he had taken a third wife, of whom she disapproved, and went to live with her godfather, David McMasters, a Methodist preacher, and his wife. With them, Lucy moved to Mount Pleasant, and here she met David Stanton.

Silhouettes of Edwin Stanton's parents, Lucy and David Stanton, probably made on their honeymoon in 1814.

They married on February 25, 1814, and the Reverend McMasters performed the ceremony. A son was born to them in Steubenville on December 19 that year; they christened him Edwin McMasters Stanton.[2]

Stantons (Philadelphia, 1922), 1–82. The first ancestor on Edwin's father's side to come to America was Robert Stanton, born in England in 1599. Benjamin was his great-grandson. Robert Stanton settled in Virginia and became a Quaker. Benjamin's father, Henry, moved to North Carolina.

[2] For more than a century, unfriendly accounts have insisted that Edwin was born

David Stanton began medical studies when Edwin was five months old. Because of the novelty and scarcity of medical books, almost all doctors studied with a qualified physician and submitted to an examination by a board of local officials when they felt ready. On May 9, 1818, David was found "duly qualified to practice Physic and Surgery." He soon became known as a benevolent, devoted, and industrious physician. David also had his share of the headlong streak that marked the Stantons. Expelled from Quaker meeting because of differences of opinion concerning Biblical interpretation, he joined his wife in the Methodist Church, only to defy its opposition to antislavery agitation.[3]

Edwin's parents contributed small amounts of money to aid Benjamin Lundy, whose abolitionist newspaper was printed in Steubenville. Edwin later remembered the antislavery discussions which his father and Lundy enjoyed, and that the doctor once sought to "make it a matter of conscience not to use an article of medicine that may be the product of slavery."

Concerns for social problems did not, however, dampen the congeniality of the Stanton home. There was never much money, for a village doctor's fees were small and payment in produce rather than cash was the rule. There was, on the other hand, no want.[4] An atmosphere of happiness and service pervaded Edwin's childhood, and as the family increased—another son, Darwin, and daughters Oella and Pamphila followed Edwin—the oldest child lived happily in the warm security it afforded him. Edwin quickly sensed the respect in which his father, a skilled physician by the standards of that day, was held by the community. Dr. Stanton assembled a "cabinet of curiosities" that impressed his neighbors, and Pamphila always remembered the pretty sight of Edwin and Darwin stalking snakes, frogs, and insects in order to add them to their father's collection.

"too soon." See, for example, Rev. Thomas Forbes to J. M. Grinnan, Jan. 12, 1931, quoting a memorandum by his grandfather, John Murray Forbes, written early in 1862 on the margins of a then popular history of the United States, in Forbes Papers, LC. The marriage certificate, located in the Jefferson County Courthouse, Steubenville, through the aid of Miss Lydia M. Miller, should put this canard to rest for all time. See also Wolcott MS, 25–7.

[3] Wolcott MS, 27; letter of Dr. John Andrews in Columbus (Ohio) *Morning Journal*, May 24, 1866; Frederick C. Waite, "The Professional Education of Pioneer Ohio Physicians," *OSAHQ*, XLVIII, 189–97.

[4] David to Benjamin Stanton, April 28, 1821, owned by William Stanton Picher; Henry Wilson to William Lloyd Garrison, Feb. 11, 1864, Anti-Slavery Papers, BPL; Wilson, "Jeremiah S. Black and Edwin M. Stanton," *AM*, XXVI, 469–70; Francis P. Weisenburger, *The Passing of the Frontier, 1825–1850* (Columbus, 1941), 209.

Darwin had his father's blue-gray eyes, fair complexion, light-brown hair, and elastic step. Edwin, with his dark skin, brown eyes, and erect carriage, resembled the mother, though Pamphila thought that he had a "more self-assertive nose." All the Stanton children participated in the devout religious life that parental piety enforced. Methodist ministers and elders crowded their home when quarterly meetings were held in Steubenville, and notwithstanding Dr. Stanton's separation from the Quaker faith, many Friends visited him socially and as patients.

At seven, Edwin attended Miss Randall's private school. The next year he attended a seminary taught by Henry Orr, then the "Old Academy" on High Street, and last the Reverend George Buchanan's Latin School, perhaps the first classical school in the West. William Dean Howells's father was Edwin's seatmate at one of these schools and shared with him the use of a *United States Speller*, a *Western Calculator*, and a *Murray's Reading Lessons*. Howells remembered Edwin as a physically delicate, grave and studious youth.

Before he was ten years old, Edwin worked part time on a neighbor's farm. But such a schedule, in addition to required household chores, proved to be more than his constitution could stand, and he returned to a more normal routine.[5] Perhaps too late, for in his tenth year Edwin suffered an asthmatic seizure. This disease would continue to torment him for the remainder of his life, sometimes to the point of convulsions. Edwin found solace in religion. He organized prayer meetings for children at which he presided and led the hymns, was a member of a Bible class, and at thirteen was admitted to fellowship in the Methodist Church.

Steubenville residents remembered him as a frank and manly boy. He and Darwin liked to horrify neighbors by dropping in on them with pet snakes coiled around their necks. Having a doctor as a father provided further opportunities for deviltry. A favorite nighttime prank involved placing a lighted candle inside the skull of one of the doctor's skeletons to frighten strollers. On one occasion, Edwin's father left him detailed instructions for attending to patients. Edwin mischievously gave a woman with foot trouble some apple butter. She later thanked the doctor profusely, claiming it had done her corns more good than anything else she had tried.

[5] Wolcott MS, 29–30; reminiscence of A. D. Sharon, Washington *Evening Star.* March 16, 1900; William Cooper Howells, *Recollections of Life in Ohio from 1813 to 1840* (Cincinnati, 1895), 42. Three other Stanton children died before 1825; see Stanton, *op. cit.*, 568.

Most of Edwin's contemporaries regarded him as an unusually mature and self-reliant youth, and somewhat imperious in demanding his own way in boys' games. But he was never, according to Pamphila, "combative or abusive." Such accounts contrast with the one narrated by James Gordon Bennett, editor of the New York *Herald*, who later claimed to have investigated Stanton thoroughly and stated "that his whole characteristics were exhibited in this, that when a youngster going to school he kissed the —— of the big boys and kicked those of the little ones." [6]

Edwin's asthmatic affliction may explain some of his personality traits. He could not participate in the rougher games of boyhood. A belligerent pose may have forestalled the dread taunt of "sissy." Like many victims of asthma, Edwin had a strong craving for affection and a constant sense of dependency, but he hid these feelings behind a brusque exterior. As he grew older he increasingly exhibited the irritability that is another common manifestation of his ailment. It may also have been part of his character, merely magnified by the asthmatic condition.[7]

On December 30, 1827, Stanton's father died. The thirteen-year-old boy left school four months later to serve as apprentice to the bookseller James Turnbull. He was paid $50 for the first year, $75 for the second, and $100 for the third. Lucy Stanton needed even this meager financial aid, for the general store that she opened in April 1828 in the front room of the Stanton home on Third Street failed to provide a living for the family.

As clerk and handyman at Turnbull's, Edwin found time to read, sometimes becoming so absorbed in a book that he neglected customers. But his employer thought well of him, allowing him time off in the evenings for his studies at the Latin School and forgiving his frequent illnesses. Edwin's work at the bookstore increased his sense of isolation from his fellows. He could not often join them on the picnics held

[6] Bennett's memorandum in Schuckers Papers, LC; Pamphila's and other recollections in Wolcott MS, 1–27. Other data in District of Columbia, Supreme Court, *Eulogies on the Death of Hon. Edwin M. Stanton* (Washington, 1870), 9 (henceforth cited as Supreme Court, *Eulogies*); Gorham, *Stanton*, I, 9–10; Flower, *Stanton*, 23; Edward T. Heald, *Bazaleel Wells: Founder of Canton and Steubenville, Ohio* (Canton, 1948), 182, and Henry Howe, *Historical Collections of Ohio* (Cincinnati, 1904), II, 265–6.

[7] Alan James Glasser, *Personality Attributes Related to Bronchial Asthma in the Adult Male* (Ph.D. thesis, Boston University, 1953); J. W. L. Doust and D. Leigh, "Studies on the Physiology of Awareness: the Interrelationships of Emotions, Life Situations, and Anoxia in Patients with Bronchial Asthma," *Psychosomatic Medicine*, XV, 302.

in the fields or deep woods, or in the raids on apple and peach orchards which contemporaries recalled. Edwin could only watch through the window of his employer's shop when on winter days his friends built roaring bonfires in the street, yelling loudly at the explosions of the buckeye nuts they had tossed into the flames.[8] Forced into solitude because of his job and his asthma, the youth spent most of what free time he had alone. He found a lofty, rocky perch on the hills overlooking the Ohio River. Here, with only the tall trees for company, he watched the busy drama always unfolding on the water four hundred feet below; later he described to A. D. Sharon how he used to daydream of one day becoming a great success.

Even as an adolescent, Edwin's vision of success was expressed in material terms. The glamorous age of the steamboats was just beginning; the arrival at Steubenville of one of these wonders, with its puffing stack and thrashing paddles, drew him from his hideaway to join his excited friends on the busy waterfront. A ceaseless panorama of river craft laden with goods and people passed by, linking the northeast and southwest of the burgeoning country. Movement, change, and growth were the postulates of the period. Edwin's grandmother had heard wolves howl near Mount Pleasant and had worried over Indian marauders. Now Steubenville was a bustling town with neat houses of brick, wood, and stone, clustered beside the river in a natural amphitheater. Its 3,000 residents worked in foundries, boatyards, two cotton factories with a thousand spindles each, a paper mill of high quality, and small shops. Fertile land rewarded the farmer's labor well, and the rolling hills provided fine grazing for sheep and cows.

Dr. Alexander M. Reid, a lifelong intimate of the Stanton family, remembered young Edwin's observation to him that in order to get a share in this richness a man had to scramble. To the fatherless boy, the prizes of the struggle seemed worth the effort.[9]

Three years in Turnbull's bookshop convinced Edwin that, in view of his health, the quickest way to the things he wanted was through

[8] Howells, *op. cit.*, 45–6, 73–5, 84–5; recollection of Rev. John Lloyd to Stanton, April 10, 1865, Stanton MSS, LC (hereafter this collection will be identified as Stanton MSS); Steubenville *Republican Ledger*, April 9, 1828, on Mrs. Stanton's store.

[9] Sharon in Washington *Evening Star*, March 16, 1900; Reid, "People of Distinction I have met," ms, owned by Alexandra Sanford. See also Howe, *op. cit.*, I, 972, II, 262; Heald, *op. cit.*, 181–2; Supreme Court, *Eulogies*, 7; Flower, *Stanton*, 23; J. H. Hunter, "The Pathfinders of Jefferson County," OAHS *Publications*, VI (1898), 249; Harold E. Davis, "Economic Basis of Ohio Politics, 1820–1840," *OSAHQ*, XLVII, 296–7; William T. Utter, *The Frontier State, 1803–1825* (Columbus, 1941), 166, 245.

education. He decided to attend college. Impressed with his intensity and obvious intelligence, Turnbull agreed to suspend the apprenticeship agreement, which had been renewed, and Daniel L. Collier, Mrs. Stanton's lawyer and Edwin's guardian, began a series of loans to him which he continued for four years, and which finally totaled almost $850. Decently clad in a new suit, sixteen-year-old Stanton left Steubenville for the first time in his life, in April 1831, bound by stagecoach for Gambier, Ohio, to attend Kenyon College.[1]

Kenyon was one of the four colleges which Ohio then boasted. In all, there were fewer than 600 students in the thirteen colleges west of the Alleghenies at that time. Edwin Stanton was about to enter a small and privileged group. When he first saw Kenyon, it was still a college in the wilderness. On every side the grounds descended into dense primeval woods. Deer, raccoons, squirrels, and rattlesnakes were common.

By modern standards, Kenyon required a great deal of its students. The rising bell sounded at 5 a.m. Within twenty minutes young Stanton had washed and dressed, made up his bed (students slept in three-decker, built-in bunks on loose straw mattresses), cleaned his share of the room, and built his fire in cool weather. In addition to prayers and classes, students took an occasional turn at working in the college fields and on the campus roads. Salmon P. Chase recalled that the founder of the college, Bishop Chase, his uncle, expected every boy to do "most of whatever a boy could do on a farm." Annual charges were $30 for instruction, $40 for board, $4 for a room with a stove, and $6 for one heated by a fireplace. Henry Winter Davis, two classes below Stanton at Kenyon, remembered that the ground was often so muddy that it was common to see forty or fifty students strung single-file on a fence top, going to their meals.[2]

Kenyon was an outpost of Episcopalianism, and Stanton, along with the other students, attended morning and evening prayers on weekdays and two church services on Sunday. Spontaneous religious revivals among the students were frequent, and classes often had to be suspended. Theological students held prayer meetings in the barnlike dormitory to buoy up the faith of weaker brethren and to enlist recruits

[1] Account with Collier owned by Gideon Townsend Stanton; Walter G. Shotwell, *Driftwood: Being Papers on Old-Time American Towns and Some Old People* (London, 1927), 70.

[2] Ms "Autobiography of Henry Winter Davis," 27–8, MdHS; Flower, *Stanton*, 27; Gordon Keith Chalmers, *The College in the Forest, 1824* (New York, 1948), 21; William B. Bodine, *The Kenyon Book* (Gambier, 1891), 44, 206, 219–21, 234–5, 317; Rev. C. W. Leffingwell, "Bishop Chase and Jubilee College," ISHS *Transactions* (1905), 87.

for the ministry. The first purpose of Kenyon was religion, and secular studies were an afterthought. Faculty and students fanned out from the college each Sunday to minister to congregations in isolated forest hamlets. Religious concerns so dominated college life that a Temperance Society boasted of almost 100 per cent student membership.[3] Though Stanton joined this association, he held aloof when it extended its efforts against the use of tobacco. He had begun to smoke cigars, and in other ways was growing up quickly.

Three months after he came to Gambier, Stanton wrote to a Steubenville friend: "I am in chase of a petticoat, what success I may have God only knows—but if I fail, it will not be for want of exertion on my part." He recounted how he had spent an evening with the girl so enjoyably "that I took no note of time," and at 1 a.m. started back to the campus but lost his way in the woods. Finally, just before dawn, "cold, wet, and tired," he crawled into his bunk. He had still to pay the price for the chill and fatigue of his adventure resulted in a fever and confinement to his bed for several days. "So much for love," he wrote, "rather expensive, don't you think so?"

With a similar adolescent bravado, he went on to tell of attending a Fourth of July celebration where "every man, woman and child were drunk as a fidler's [*sic*] bitch." He added further: "Our Faculty, through fear of cholera, have prohibited bathing, and almost everything else but studying—would to God they would prohibit that shortly."

Stanton's romantic impulses got him into more trouble when he and S. A. Bronson, a sophomore who later became professor of theology and president of Kenyon, borrowed Bishop Chase's prize horse one night and rode tandem into the country to call on two young ladies. They returned quite late and hurriedly. The next morning the bishop became irate at finding his horse in a lather. Knowing that Chase would stop at nothing to ferret out the culprits, Heman Dyer, a theological student who was also principal of the college grammar school, advised Stanton to confess. Stanton went to see the bishop. An emotional display took place, with Stanton and the dignified churchman in tears, until the youth's pleas for forgiveness succeeded in weakening the bishop's resolve to expel him. The incident was passed over.

One escapade, however, went beyond the bounds of adolescent

---

[3] George F. Smythe, *Kenyon College, Its First Century* (New Haven, 1924), 79, 86, 113n., 171; Wyman W. Parker, "Edwin M. Stanton at Kenyon," *OSAHQ*, LX, 237–8; Heman Dyer, *Records of an Active Life* (New York, 1886), 55–62; John James Piatt, *Pencilled Fly-Leaves* (Cincinnati, 1880), 169–98.

adventure. Stanton and other students believed that a certain young tutor had betrayed their confidences, and one day at mealtime, at a signal, they rose and pelted the poor man with edibles and crockery. Someone snuffed the lights, and amid a riot of jeers, hoots, and cackles, the victim was cuffed to the door, and he never returned to Kenyon. It was Dyer's overly lenient judgment that Stanton "was determined that the offender should be punished, law or no law, and was willing to suffer the consequences." There were, apparently, no consequences for Stanton or the other student conspirators to suffer.

Though Stanton was at first outwardly indifferent to the religious life of Kenyon and did perhaps more than his share of carousing, he was also an avid student and a voracious reader. His sister recalled that he had written in the first books he owned: "I am going to read these books through," and love of books remained part of his life at college and later. He was frequently sick and rarely could sleep through a night because of his asthmatic affliction, but he did not spare himself.[4]

Part of the life at Kenyon which Stanton found most congenial and constructive was his participation in the activities of the Philomathesian, a literary society. He was active on its committees, took part in several debates, in one of which he derided professional soldiers, was finally elected secretary, and won the society's vellum diploma for commendable service, which he prized enough to hang in his law offices in later years. Markedly more aware of current events than many of his fellow students, Stanton joined enthusiastically in a Philomathesian debate in 1832 on the burning issues of nullification and slavery. The exchange became so heated that eleven students from Southern states withdrew from the Philomathesian and formed a new society.

Stanton's sympathies were clear. He avidly read all the numbers that he could obtain of the new abolitionist newspaper, the *Liberator*, printed in Boston by William Lloyd Garrison, years later writing to the crusader that "from earliest youth [you] have been an object of my respect and admiration." Stanton recalled with a fellow student: "We fought the South together at Kenyon, and whipped."[5]

[4] Parker, "Edwin M. Stanton at Kenyon," *loc. cit.*, 235, 238, 243–5; Wolcott MS, 40; Dyer, *op. cit.*, 71–3.

[5] Philomathesian Minute Book, Kenyon College Library; Parker, "Edwin M. Stanton at Kenyon," *loc. cit.*, 239–42; Smythe, *op. cit.*, 323–4; Wendell P. and Francis J. Garrison, *William Lloyd Garrison, 1805–1879* (New York, 1885–9), IV, 152; Gorham, *Stanton*, I, 16; Willard L. King, *Lincoln's Manager, David Davis* (Cambridge, 1960), 10–14 (hereafter cited as King, *Davis*).

Then, in the beginning of his sophomore year, just as he was immersing himself fully in the serious intellectual and religious life of the college, he had to leave. Reports from home had warned him that the family's financial situation was worsening, but he had not realized the full seriousness of the problem until he returned to Steubenville for the 1832 summer recess. While he was home the family's legal adviser convinced Mrs. Stanton that Edwin must forgo the luxury of further college education in order to return to gainful employment. Turnbull was willing to renew with improved terms the suspended apprenticeship agreement. "I abandoned all hopes," Stanton confessed to a Kenyon classmate, A. J. McClintock, "renewed my engagement, and shall set out next Monday for Columbus," where he would work in another bookstore owned by Turnbull and managed by the merchant's brother.

Stanton assumed a nonchalant air. "The fact is," he wrote, "I believe in the maxim that says a short life and a merry one is the better." [6] Despite his boastful flippancy, he took from Kenyon a fair share of the history, mathematics, chemistry, geology, political economy, Latin, and Greek that he had studied, and much more than he had learned in class. The months there had inspired him to hope for a professional career, fixed his religious affiliation in the Episcopal denomination, fashioned his views on federal-state relations, and confirmed the abhorrence of "the slave power" which his parents had set in him. He kept abiding friendships with Kenyon students and faculty and an enduring love for the school, seeing to it that his son and nephews attended there and aiding Kenyon graduates as much as he could. In later years Pamphila lived in Gambier, and Stanton loved to visit her there and to wander through the lovely campus of the school. [7]

Late in September 1832, Stanton boarded the stagecoach for Columbus. By the terms of a new contract with Turnbull he was to receive $250 a year, and his immediate needs would be met by the $50 in cash which he had obtained as another loan from Collier. With youthful resiliency, he rebounded from the depression occasioned by his forced departure from Kenyon, in anticipation of the novelties and opportunities that Columbus promised.

[6] Parker, "Edwin M. Stanton at Kenyon," *loc. cit.*, 242, 245–7; Wolcott MS, 36, 41–4; Bodine, *op. cit.*, 288–9.

[7] Stanton to McClintock, June 5, 1834, CHS; McClintock to E. L. Stanton, Dec. 5, 1869, Stanton MSS; Bodine, *op. cit.*, 286; *The Kenyon Collegian*, XXXII, is devoted to Stanton's continuing support of the college, which granted him an LL.D. in 1866.

Situated on low ground along the Scioto River, Columbus, now the state capital, was a rapidly growing town of almost 2,700 people when Stanton arrived there. High Street, the main thoroughfare, had broad sidewalks paved with brick, and more than seventy coaches brought passengers into the city each week. Horsemen, carriages, and wagons moved along it constantly. Two blocks of the business district had three-story brick store buildings; most of the houses were also of brick with arcades of wood in front shading the sidewalks. The state buildings had already become dilapidated, and cows grazed on the Capitol grounds.

Stanton settled quickly into his new life. "I have a great deal of time for reading," he informed his friend McClintock, "and board in a family with which I am highly pleased." This was the family of Dr. H. Howard, of whom Stanton wrote: "The old folks are intelligent, hospitable, kind and in short just such folks as you would like. Their daughters—they have four—though not handsome are very agreeable," and he singled out young Ann Howard for avuncular regard.

He soon gained a wide acquaintance among Columbus's younger set, finding the females modest, sensible, and well informed, though plain, but the young men "impudent, ignorant, self-sufficient counter jumpers." Professing his boredom with trade, Stanton wrote that he was "becoming acquainted with the proper method of doing business, learning how to cheat and avoid being cheated, besides the various usages of the world." [8]

Then, during the spring and early summer of 1833, the cholera, which had struck heavily in eastern Ohio, moved menacingly westward along the route of the National Road. The epidemic began raging in Columbus during the unusually hot summer months. On August 9, Stanton was served his midday dinner by Ann Howard, and then he returned to the bookstore. An hour later Ann collapsed. At 4 p.m. she was dead. As a precautionary measure to keep the plague from spreading, her family buried her at once. When Stanton learned of the horrible event, he experienced a morbid conviction that she had been buried alive. Persuading a young medical student and another boarder to help, he hurried to the burial ground and by lamplight exhumed and opened the casket. At the risk of contamination he made certain that the girl's body gave no sign of life, an act which his neighbors applauded for its courage, however questionable by modern standards.

[8] Parker, "Edwin M. Stanton at Kenyon," *loc. cit.*, 245, 247-8; ms account with D. L. Collier, owned by Gideon Townsend Stanton; Jonathan Forman, "The First Cholera Epidemic in Columbus, Ohio (1833)," *Annals of Medical History*, n.s., VI, 413-5; Weisenburger, *op. cit.*, 21-4.

He exhibited the same bravery while the epidemic continued its grim course, and sat nightly with stricken friends at the peril of his life. Such deeds took courage of a high order, for Stanton knew enough medical lore from his father's practice to understand the consequences of contagion. He hid his fears in the youthful guise of bravado. "My own health has been good," he wrote to McClintock, "saving that I nearly died a week since in debauch. . . . The following night I was attacked with very alarming symptoms—of cholera; from that I also escaped, by strong and timely measures. From these circumstances, I have been induced to 'forswear sack and live cleanly' —for the present." [9]

Stanton's debauches seem to have been more callow fiction than fact. His Columbus neighbors and friends, many of whom later became violent enemies of his politics and actions, attest only to his sobriety and application to his reading during this period. And now he had a new reason to inspire his search for success. He had fallen in love.

In Columbus he had attended the Trinity Episcopal Church, where William Preston, a Kenyon trustee, was rector. At Sunday school he met Mary A. Lamson, the rector's sister-in-law. She was a year younger than Stanton, of average height, with a slim, attractive figure; in his words: "Her hair was soft and brown; her eyes dark; her brow and forehead beautiful. Her teeth, white and regular, were the finest I ever beheld; and . . . a full red lip gave to her mouth, especially when she smiled, surpassing sweetness." Mary's intellect and literary interests also impressed the smitten youth.

So, in mid-September 1833 he asked his guardian for help so that he might return to Kenyon for a year to finish his course, then to study law, and thus advance himself. Turnbull had treated him unfairly, he complained, for although Stanton had assumed the management of the Columbus store, he had been refused an increase and thus had been able to save very little money toward his education. But, mindful of his obligation to his family's support, he was willing to manage the store for another year if Turnbull granted him the raise.

Collier consulted the bookseller, who again refused the increase. Stanton thereupon abandoned his hopes of completing college and urged his guardian to allow him to study in Columbus under the preceptorship of a practicing lawyer. His persistence impressed Collier, who secured Turnbull's reluctant agreement to cancel the apprentice-

---

[9] W. Pinckney to Edwin L. Stanton, *ca.* Jan. 1870, Stanton MSS; Parker, "Edwin M. Stanton at Kenyon," *loc. cit.*, 250; Wolcott MS, 46, 112–3; Forman, "First Cholera Epidemic . . . ," *loc. cit.*, 419–20; Flower, *Stanton*, 30.

ship contract. Collier, however, correctly pointed out to Stanton that he would be much better off studying law in Steubenville at Collier's office than in Columbus. Steubenville's lawyers had worked out a regular system of instruction for their students, and Stanton would join five neophyte attorneys already enrolled there.

Mary Lamson helped him make the difficult decision to accept Collier's offer and to give up hope of returning to Kenyon by promising to wait for him even though it meant an indefinite separation. In November 1833, Stanton began the unhappy journey back to Steubenville. There he found his family in pitiable straits. They had rented a small, decrepit three-room house further up Third Street from the comfortable residence in which he had spent his childhood. At first Stanton found it difficult to adjust, and wasted his days and evenings renewing acquaintanceships and putting on the airs of a sophisticate who had listened to debates at the state capital and attended college. But he soon assumed the labors of a student of law and the duties of the head of his family. During the winter his mother suffered from erysipelas and Pamphila had whooping cough. Since he wanted his other sister, Oella, to continue her studies at Beatty's Seminary, he brought his lawbooks home and mixed elementary law with nursing the sick women.[1]

By the turn of the year 1834, Stanton was in a better frame of mind; his family's health was improved and he was encouraged by his progress in his studies. He thanked God that he had failed in his earlier purpose of remaining in Columbus. "My guardian was wiser than I," he admitted to McClintock, "so here my term of probation will be passed." Stanton borrowed still more money from Collier and other Steubenville residents, and moved his family into a more comfortable house on High Street, near the Seminary.

Pamphila remembered these months as a happy time. Darwin was always fun-loving, and Edwin, though more serious, applauded his jests with an easy, hearty laugh. Well informed on politics, Stanton discoursed to the family on current happenings. Detesting idleness, he took advantage of every cultural advantage the town afforded. Monday evening found him at the Atheneum for debates. Examinations for all Steubenville law students took place on Tuesday and Friday nights, and on Saturday night the Lyceum provided lectures on literature, science, and history. Mary Lamson's influence was reflected in his reawakened interest in religion, and in his confession to Pamphila of a Quakerish

[1] Parker, "Edwin M. Stanton at Kenyon," *loc. cit.*, 249–52; Wolcott MS, 40–3, 46–7, 112–13.

disgust at all military pomp. He led his family in morning and evening prayers and taught a class at the Methodist Sunday school.

What made him happiest was the high quality of the instruction he was receiving. The Steubenville bar, he claimed, was the equal of that of Columbus, and its regular curriculum for students was attracting state-wide attention. Stanton particularly welcomed the fact that the large-scale business that Steubenville's lawyers enjoyed forced more practical work on their students than was usual. In June, Stanton wrote McClintock that he had assisted his mentor in every principal settlement in Ohio.[2]

A year passed by quickly for young Stanton. Then, during the spring of 1835, Ohio was thrown into turmoil as Theodore Dwight Weld and other students who had incurred disfavor at Lane Seminary in Cincinnati for antislavery agitation, carried their preachments throughout the state. They advocated racial equality, a doctrine that few persons were willing to embrace, and endeavored to organize abolition societies.

Weld offered a series of lectures in Steubenville. Years later, he recalled that he had been told that a young lawyer named Stanton intended to challenge his thesis at the meeting. The traditional account of this incident, by Weld, and another version, by Henry Wilson, had it that Edwin was so struck by the force of Weld's arguments that he remained dumb, then went privately to see Weld and, confessing that "my guns are spiked," announced his conversion to the doctrine that "all men hold their rights by the same title deed." But Allyn E. Wolcott, for whom Stanton had secured a place as a student in Collier's office after an introduction by their mutual friend McClintock, and who later became related to Edwin by marriage, recalled only that he and Stanton went together to hear Weld lecture at the Methodist church. "We both called on Weld the next day," he recalled, "and had a very pleasant conversation with him. I never heard that Edwin intended answering [Weld] . . . or was expected to answer said lecture. If he had thought of such a thing, he certainly would have informed me of it."[3]

Stanton was busy enough readying for his imminent bar examination

[2] To McClintock, June 5, 1834, CHS; Wolcott MS, 47, 53–4; Parker, "Edwin M. Stanton at Kenyon," *loc. cit.*, 249, 251–2.

[3] Wolcott MS, 51; Wilson, "Jeremiah S. Black and Edwin M. Stanton," *loc. cit.*, 469; Benjamin P. Thomas, *Theodore Weld: Crusader for Freedom* (New Brunswick, N. J., 1950), 70–121; F. Fowler to Weld, Feb. 19, 1887, Weld MSS, WLCL.

and too ambitious to entangle himself in the pitfalls of the growing abolition controversy. In August 1835, he went to St. Clairsville for his bar examination and passed it. Still under age, he could not be licensed, though Collier thenceforth allowed him a large measure of responsibility in preparing cases for court. Soon after passing his examination, he was arguing a slander suit while Collier watched from the rear of the courtroom. One of the opposition attorneys asked the court to oust Stanton from the case for being under age and not entitled to practice. Collier rose and defended the qualifications of his student. Stanton had cheek enough to remain standing during Collier's speech and resumed pleading the instant his guardian finished, without waiting for the judge to rule.

During the three years that Stanton spent in Collier's office, he and Mary Lamson corresponded faithfully. While he tried to master his lawbooks, she continued her own schooling, studying French and Latin and hoping to go on into chemistry, geometry, and arithmetic. "Arithmetic I like," she wrote to her fiancé. "As females often have the character given them, perhaps justly, of being irresolute and unsettled in purpose, mathematical studies should be considered of the highest importance to them." Mary felt that women would never be able to exercise their rightful place in the world until they were better educated. Obliged to quit school soon after this, she asked Edwin to advise her in her reading. She had enjoyed Felicia Hemans's romantic poems, she wrote, but she found Thomas Moore's *Journals and Letters of Lord Byron* in questionable taste, since it revealed Byron's "censurable" as well as his admirable traits.

Stanton replied that he was not fit to advise her, as his own reading had become so specialized. Her own good taste and the advice of her sister would set proper standards. He believed, however, that she was wasting her time with Moore. Byron's poetry was fine but his character was abhorrent, and though knowledge was desirable, it should not be knowledge of evil. There was enough evil in life without seeking it in books. Love had changed Edwin Stanton. The free and easy moral attitude that he had at least assumed at Kenyon and during his first months in Columbus now gave place to prudery.[4]

"I am twenty-one, a free man, and admitted to practice law," he exulted in December 1835. A few weeks after the turn of the year 1836 he moved to Cadiz, an Ohio village of 1,000 inhabitants, the seat of

[4] Wolcott MS, 103–5, 108–9; Flower, *Stanton*, 31; Shotwell, *op. cit.*, 72.

Harrison County, where Chauncey Dewey, a wealthy lawyer with an established practice, had offered him a partnership. Slow in speech and in methods, the forty-year-old Dewey disliked the rough and tumble of the courtroom. Stanton immediately took over much of the firm's trial work with Dewey as mentor. The younger man learned much from this association, for the firm handled a large proportion of the cases in Harrison County and enjoyed an extensive practice in neighboring counties.

People in Cadiz called him "Little Stanton," although he was five feet eight inches tall and stocky in build. Though extremely near-sighted, so that he peered intently through thick-lensed spectacles, he was an attractive youth, taken together: clean-shaven, with thick, dark, disheveled hair, and friendly and good-natured when not battling to win a case.

He brought system to Dewey's office; papers were now in perfect order. After a full day of pleading in court, Stanton would return to the office and labor for hours more. He was known, more than once, to climb into his buggy after midnight, drive the twenty-five miles to Steubenville for a document or a book, and be back in court the next morning ready for another full day of work.[5]

Stanton's evident talent and capacity for work soon widened his practice and his reputation. He received frequent compliments from other lawyers and from judges for his courtroom pleadings and his legal researches. Although some of his contemporaries envied his "intuitions that made effort easy and effect startling," his quick success came as a result of vast effort. Stanton "worked terribly," according to a young lawyer who shared quarters with him at this time. Such application took its toll. His health suffered, and though he had become extremely religious his church attendance now fell off.

He had good reason for this attention to his career. In addition to his own ambitions, his family continued to cause him worry. Stanton helped send his brother Darwin to Harvard University to study medicine, despite the opinion of Steubenville residents that Darwin would never be much of a doctor. In the spring of 1836 the home that Edwin had been renting for his mother and sisters in Steubenville was sold, and they were obliged to move. His mother was severely ill that summer, and Oella left school to serve as housekeeper. Stanton hurried home despite a severe illness of his own and decided to send the family to grandfather Norman's in Virginia until he had a home in Cadiz to

[5] Wolcott MS, 55; Shotwell, *op. cit.,* 72–7; Howe, *op. cit.,* I, 896, 976, II, 177.

bring them to. He and Mary had decided to wait no longer to marry.

Stanton arranged with Joseph Hunter, of Cadiz, a cabinetmaker and later mayor of the town, for the use of the room over his shop as a law office, for Stanton intended to set up a separate practice while maintaining a limited association with Dewey. In lieu of rent, Stanton instructed Hunter in law and took some of his meals at the Hunter home, although the latter part of this arrangement ended when he brought Mary to Cadiz.

On the outskirts of the town Stanton found a house to suit him and his bride. Five days before his twenty-second birthday, he set out for Columbus and his wedding. He and Mary had planned to hold the ceremony in the church where they had first met, but Stanton fell ill, and it was performed in the Reverend Preston's home on December 31, 1836. The honeymoon was a ride of 125 miles to Cadiz in a stage sleigh, which Stanton recalled as the "brightest, sweetest journey of all my life," and then a visit at Benjamin Tappan's home in Steubenville.

Stanton had known Judge Tappan since boyhood. Benjamin Tappan, Jr., had been one of his schoolmates, and over the years a close relationship had developed between the judge and the fatherless boy. A few months after Edwin's marriage, in which the Tappan family rejoiced out of fondness for him and enthusiastic liking for Mary, he and Judge Tappan formed a partnership to practice law in Steubenville, though Stanton continued to live in Cadiz and kept his association with Dewey.[6]

A member of a devout New England family and one of Ohio's early settlers, Tappan, now sixty-four, had served in the state senate, on the Ohio canal commission, and as chief judge of the circuit court of common pleas. His support of Andrew Jackson for President earned him an appointment as a federal district judge, but the Senate had refused to confirm him. The judge's brothers, Arthur and Lewis, both clamorous abolitionists, were the chief financial supporters of the American Antislavery Society. Judge Tappan, too, disliked slavery; but he also distrusted agitators and preferred to keep silent on the subject, a practice which impressionable young Stanton later emulated.

[6] Wolcott MS, 52–5, 105–6; John L. Miner to Stanton, Nov. 18, 1835, Benjamin Tappan, Sr., to Jr., Dec. 28, 1836, March 8, 1837, Tappan, Jr., to Stanton, Feb. 26, 1837, Tappan Papers, LC; Flower, *Stanton*, 32; Dard Hunter, *My Life with Paper: An Autobiography* (New York, 1958), 16; Parker, "Edwin M. Stanton at Kenyon," *loc. cit.*, 242–3; Hunter, "Pathfinders of Jefferson County," *loc. cit.*, 219; Howe, *op. cit.*, I, 972, II, 265; Steubenville *American Union*, May 31, 1837; T. B. Thorpe, "Edwin M. Stanton," *Harper's*, XLV, 375.

Soon after forming the partnership with Tappan, Stanton went to Virginia to bring his mother and sisters to Cadiz. He showed the women the sights of Washington on the way home and shared the thrill of their first ride on iron rails, in what Pamphila described as "the wonderful new cars," from the capital to Baltimore, thence to Frederick, where they transferred to a stagecoach. Once back at Cadiz, he proudly introduced his new wife to his mother and sisters and guided them through the home that they would all share. It was more than a mile from the town, a square brick house of a story and a half. A large porch shaded the front, and there was a wide center hall separating two large rooms on either side. Dormer windows projected from the roof. There was an orchard, a grove of maples, and a pasture with a brook. Stanton discovered that he was skillful with tools; he installed a furnace, then a new contrivance, in the basement. Before setting out for his office in the mornings, he hoed and raked the garden, sometimes singing aloud.

When he returned home in the evening, he liked to recount the day's experiences or read aloud to the family. Oella was unable to return to school, as their mother was so often ill, and Stanton encouraged her and Pamphila to read Plutarch's *Lives* and other classics, Whittier's "The Yankee Girl," and Bryant's "Thanatopsis," which he considered "the finest piece of poetry he had ever seen."

To Pamphila her beloved brother was always patient and forbearing under his many responsibilities. "But he was imperative where a duty was to be performed," she wrote, "for with him, where duty and obedience were involved, he knew no dallying, no turning aside." She remembered, too, how quick he was at repartee, and how his words sometimes cut, although she did not think he meant them to. Pamphila rejoiced at the clear indications that Edwin and Mary were very much in love. Mary made herself part of his family, and his friends were as smitten by her angelic disposition as he was. Her influence on him was immediately noticeable; he completely stopped drinking, cut down on his cigars, and established regular eating habits. Stanton later declared that his reprehensible qualities had been repressed by her presence. He was very happy.[7]

Interests apart from his office and home increased in importance in Stanton's life. He became active in the Cadiz Antislavery Society and

[7] Stanton to Salmon P. Chase, Dec. 2, 1847, Chase Papers, HSP; Wolcott MS, 60–70, 119–20; Weisenburger, *op. cit.,* 218, 279–80; James Thompson to Stanton, Nov. 23, 1838, Tappan Papers, LC.

helped edit as well as write articles for the Cadiz *Sentinel.* In 1837 he ran successfully on the Democratic ticket for prosecuting attorney of Harrison County. The salary was only $200 a year, but adding this to fees from his private practice, and a legacy from his grandfather who died early in 1838, Stanton was able to speculate in real estate in Washington County and Cadiz.

His increasing professional and political stature won him a place on the county central committee of his party, and he supported the successful movement to name Tappan for United States senator. Tappan needed someone to attend to his extensive practice, and his natural choice fell on Stanton. Their ties had been drawn closer by Oella's marriage to Tappan's son, who was now practicing medicine in Steubenville.

In October 1838, Stanton moved back to Steubenville, where he bought a house on Third Street a few doors north of Market, near his office. This time he and Mary set up housekeeping alone. Darwin had finished his medical training and took up residence just across the river from Steubenville, at Hollidays Cove, Virginia. The elder Mrs. Stanton and Pamphila moved there to make a home for him. In July 1839, however, Darwin married Nancy Hooker, of Brook County, Virginia, and once again his mother and Pamphila became part of Edwin and Mary's household.

The early months of 1840 were a time of celebration for Stanton. In February he settled his debts with Collier, receiving the grand sum of $4.18 as his share from his father's estate, after deductions for funds advanced from the family counselor. On March 11, the Stanton's first child was born at Columbus, where Mary had gone to stay with her sister through the winter. They named the baby Lucy Lamson Stanton.

Stanton adored the baby, loved his wife, was advancing in the profession he wanted to practice, and was overcoming the financial problems that had beset the family for so many years. He wrote to Mary shortly before their sixth wedding anniversary and reviewed their life together in ecstatic terms. "We six years ago were but lovers, . . . we are now parents; . . . I loved you first for your beauty, the grace and loveliness of your person. I love you now for the richness and surpassing excellence of your mind. One love has not taken the place of the other, but both stand side by side."

In later years he looked back on this period as the happiest time of his life. Now in his middle twenties, he faced the future with confidence.[8] Surmounting the handicaps of early poverty, he had achieved the profession for which he had labored so long, and had proved his proficiency in it. His marriage was successful and his family life was harmonious; he took pride in his support of his mother and sisters and his subsidizing of his brother's medical career. Edwin Stanton was a young man on the way up, and he was determined that nothing should stand in his way.

[8] Stanton to Benjamin Tappan, Sr., July 24, 1837, Tappan Papers, LC; Wolcott MS, 71–3; Steubenville *American Union,* June 26, 1838; Stanton to Mary, *ca.* Dec. 1842, owned by Edward S. Corwin; same to William Stanton, March 13, 1859, owned by William Stanton Picher; ms account with Collier, owned by Gideon Townsend Stanton; Thomas Norman will, Culpeper County Will Book O, 1836–9, VSL.

CHAPTER II

JACKSONIAN REFORMER

In HIS partnership with Tappan, Stanton was allied with a man of keen legal judgment and potent influence. The young lawyer plunged into greater activity in Democratic politics. It was the height of the Age of Jackson, and the doughty old President's attack on the Bank of the United States was being carried forward under his successor in the White House, Martin Van Buren. Wages, working hours, corporation charters, the tariff, taxes, and qualifications for voting were coming under scrutiny as the Jacksonians assailed all forms of special privileges.[1]

Ohio Democrats centered their assault on privilege on the private banks, chartered by the state legislature, and their control of credit and the currency. The radical Democrats insisted that these banks had recklessly issued paper money, causing a ruinous inflation that resulted in the panic of 1837 and the hard times that followed it. They heartily applauded President Van Buren's establishment of an "independent Treasury" in which government funds formerly entrusted to state banks were now deposited, and insisted that the Ohio legislature curtail the financial and political power of the state banks.

Many conservative Democrats, on the other hand, advocated caution, and wanted merely to regulate the amount of notes a bank might issue. The bank question created such factional bitterness within Democratic ranks that Stanton predicted in 1839: "If the Whigs had a thimble full of sense or honesty they would carry this state next fall. And as matters stand now it is by no means certain that Ohio will not be lost to Mr. Van Buren."

[1] Arthur M. Schlesinger, Jr., *The Age of Jackson* (Boston, 1946), 190–209.

Under Ohio law, each bank in the state had been chartered by a special act of incorporation passed by the state legislature. This practice led to confusion in banking standards, as well as corruption in granting charters, and caused the banks to regard their corporation charters as contracts enforceable in the courts and beyond the power of lawmakers to modify. A major purpose of the radical Democrats was to enact a general banking law which would, it was hoped, break the corrupt favoritism practiced at Columbus, so that any bank which could qualify might be incorporated.

The rift within the Democratic party made it impossible to enact such a sweeping law, but in February 1839 a compromise measure passed providing for strict limitation of note issues and for closing any banks which failed to redeem its notes in specie on demand. Ohio Whigs interpreted the bank law as a radical attack on property in general and planned to make the state election of 1839 a referendum on Democratic policy. The Whigs knew, however, that most Ohioans retained their frontier prejudices against banks and bankers, and that their sole hope of victory lay in Democratic disunity, against which Tappan and Stanton fought vigorously and successfully.

Stanton's political star was rising; he impressed listeners with his frequent speeches and continually delighted Judge Tappan as a partner, friend, and political legman.[2] During the campaign Stanton hewed to the radical Democratic line of antipathy to paper money, accusing the financial interests of oppressing the people. Whig opponents blamed Democratic ignorance in matters of finance for causing the panic. Despite the intensity of the Whig campaign, the Democrats held together and retained control of the state legislature.

Shortly after the election, however, cleavage threatened them again. Democratic Governor Wilson Shannon, who had been elected in 1838 on an anti-bank platform, recommended mere limitation of bank powers rather than the stringent general banking law favored by Tappan and Stanton. When Shannon in 1840 gained renomination for governor against radical Democratic opposition, Stanton asked Tappan if he should work for the heretic's election. Tappan agreed that Shannon should be "politically damned" for compromising on the banks, but as he had been nominated by the party, they would have to add their support. Stanton accepted Tappan's decision and the code of party regularity that it embraced.

---

[2] Stanton to ?, probably Tappan, Jan. 14, 1839, Stanton MSS; Edgar Allan Holt, *Party Politics in Ohio, 1840–1850* (Columbus, 1930), 6–24.

Besides renominating Shannon, the Democratic state convention endorsed Van Buren's candidacy for a second term as President. Stanton, as a member of the committee on resolutions, helped frame a platform approving the Independent Treasury and endorsing such features of the Democratic program as opposition to a protective tariff as an adjunct of monopoly, and to internal improvements at federal expense.[3]

The Whigs chose to avoid issues and named as their candidate for President William Henry Harrison, a military hero, innocent of known political views. When a Democratic newspaper derided Harrison as a man who would be entirely happy with a barrel of cider and a back-woods cabin, the Whigs adopted the squib and extolled these symbols of purity and simplicity. Parades, rallies, and barbecues created wild excitement. Tempers grew short as election day approached. Ohio's Whigs and Democrats convened in Steubenville in July. Stanton made a public speech in which he demanded that more than $5,000 in the notes of the defunct local bank be honored. The officers of that bank were Whigs. Their supporters, passing Stanton's office, were enraged when they saw a tombstone he had set up, plastered with the bank's worthless notes. Angry Whigs rushed the grandstand where Stanton was holding forth. A free-for-all followed in which several persons were injured. Stanton escaped unhurt, and thereafter during the campaign was more circumspect. He impressed his audience at Wintersville soon after, when he debated the issues with John A. Bingham, a forceful lawyer from Cadiz who in later years as a congressman would become Stanton's firm friend.

Harrison carried the nation. Ohio Whigs elected Thomas Corwin governor and won control of the lower house of the state's legislature. Stanton took no comfort from the fact that the Whigs had been obliged to assume Democratic trappings in order to win, and he did not trouble to conceal his contempt for Harrison. Soon after the President-elect visited Steubenville on his river voyage to Washington, Stanton advised Tappan that "he is regarded even in his own party as an old imbecile." [4]

As a matter of course, Harrison promised to replace Steubenville's Democratic postmaster with a Whig, and Stanton acidly noted that the

[3] Tappan to Stanton, Feb. 8, 20, 25, March 3, 1840, Dr. John K. Wright Collection, LC; memo, Jan. 8, 1840, Stanton MSS; Holt, *op. cit.*, 20–1.

[4] Stanton to Tappan, March 7, 1841, Stanton MSS; Tappan to Stanton, May 12, 1840, Wright Collection, LC; Holt, *op. cit.*, 56; Steubenville *Log Cabin Farmer*, July 23, 1840; Shotwell, *op. cit.*, 81–2; Flower, *Stanton*, 36.

"hungry crew are all agape," with six vying for the office. A local Whig leader, Jim Collier, got the inside track. He spirited off Harrison's granddaughters, who attended school in Steubenville, and drove them to Wheeling to join their grandfather. Collier thus reached Harrison before any other aspiring Steubenville Whig could, and he received the promise of the post office.

Stanton then conceived a scheme to capitalize on the chagrin of Collier's outmaneuvered Whig rivals. He hoped to persuade the incumbent Democratic postmaster to resign immediately, as he would in any case soon be ousted. Then the county Democratic committee would replace him by a pliant anti-Collier Whig and let the incoming Whig administration wrestle with the problem of supplanting a Whig postmaster with Collier. He was sure that if Senator Tappan would convince outgoing President Van Buren to approve the plan, the results would please all Democrats. "It will breed a deadly strife in the Whig ranks," he predicted.[5]

He went so far in anticipation of Tappan's approval as to prepare the principals for the scheme, when Tappan rejected it. It was incredible, Tappan wrote, that Stanton should think he would ever appoint a Whig to office. And if Tappan had recommended him, Van Buren would not appoint him, nor would the Senate confirm him, regardless of the benefits that Democrats of Jefferson County might obtain.

Stanton answered lamely that he had not intended to embarrass Tappan and that similar strategy had been employed elsewhere. His plan had only one purpose—to divide Whig ranks as Democrats had been divided. He had no desire to benefit a Whig; "I acted to mortify the whole Whig party—and some of its leaders in chief."

Political efforts combined with court work to keep Stanton busy in Steubenville and in a half dozen other county seats across Ohio. He served as secretary of the Democratic Central Committee of Jefferson County and in 1840 attended the county and district conventions. As hard times continued and bank after bank suspended specie payments, the Democrats took full advantage of the general discontent. "A merry time we are likely to have for the next few years," wrote Stanton.[6]

Though political events bore him out, Stanton could not celebrate. He had spent the summer months of 1841 in anxiety that grew ever

[5] Stanton to Tappan, Feb. 6, 12, 22; James Means and Stanton to Tappan, Feb. 22, 1841, Tappan Papers, LC.
[6] Tappan to Stanton, Feb. 22, 1841, Tappan Papers, LC; Stanton to ?, probably Tappan, Feb. 6, same to Tappan, June 27, Tappan to Stanton, Feb. 16, 1841, Wright Collection, LC; Steubenville *American Union*, July 31, Aug. 7, 28, 1841.

more fearful as his daughter Lucy sickened, weakening from some undiagnosed ailment as the long weeks passed. He abandoned politics, transferred office matters to the six student lawyers he now employed, and kept constant watch by her tiny bed. Stanton and his wife prayed, and felt an answering improvement in the baby's condition; then, late in August 1841, Lucy died.

Both parents bore their heartache bravely to others, but to each other the blow seemed beyond enduring. Mary, who had recently lost her sister, became ill in turn, and Stanton seemed almost distracted. Pamphila and Mary urged him to return to the beneficent distractions of his practice and politics, and the new year saw him active once again.[7]

The bank issue continued to divide the Democrats; early in 1842 Stanton encountered open revolt. Many Democrats were signing pro-bank petitions which Whigs had inspired, and former political friends were openly denouncing Tappan, Stanton himself, "and anyone who would not bow down to Bank influence."

With other county leaders, Stanton quelled the revolt. The leaders then fell out over the question of punishing the pro-bank seceders. Stanton took the view that they should be severely punished, "coming square out and exposing them to the people denouncing them openly as unworthy of confidence and through the newspaper cut them off from the Democratic party." The opposite view temporarily won, however, and the dissenters, from fear that they might go to the Whigs entirely if treated rigorously, were welcomed back into Democratic ranks. Stanton bided his time, still determined on punishment for the bolters.

Ohio's radical Democrats, now in full control of local party units and of the state legislature, pushed through a general banking law, to which all future charters had to conform, and which opened incorporation to

---

[7] Wolcott MS, 73–5; Christopher P. Wolcott to Tappan, Sr., Aug. 27, 1841, Tappan Papers, LC. W. S. Buchanan, a student in Stanton's office, recorded that Stanton once again gave way to the morbid instability that he had exhibited when Ann Howard died of cholera; Stanton allegedly exhumed Lucy's body more than a year after she died and sealed the ashes in a metal box made for the purpose. He was supposed to have kept this box in his own room; Flower, *Stanton*, 38. This is highly questionable, however, for Stanton wrote to Lewis Tappan (March 20, 1844, Lewis Tappan Papers, LC) describing Mary's wish to have a monument "placed over the grave of our child." This monument was never erected. Lucy is buried in the Stanton lot in Union Cemetery in Steubenville, where a simple stone marker bears the worn and barely legible inscription on its underside: "Infant dau Lucy." The cemetery records do not indicate the date of burial or state whether a body or ashes were interred. Mr. P. Scott Dimit, manager of Union Cemetery, searched the records, found the marker under a layer of sod, and helped decipher the inscription.

any qualified banking group. Another law specified that all banks refusing to redeem their notes in specie should forfeit their charters, and that bank officers and stockholders should be jointly and severally liable for failure to comply. Meanwhile, the Whigs, undecided as to what banking system to endorse, denounced these Democratic measures as "dangerous" and assailed the Democrats as favoring a "social revolution."

Happy Democrats exulted. Stanton was visiting Tappan in Washington at the time of these events; on returning to Steubenville he wrote to an Ohio friend that "the way in which the Democratic legislature of Ohio was spoken of in Washington made me feel proud to be an Ohio Democrat . . . and it seems to me that if our folks continue to toe the mark the Whigs are bound to be badly licked next election." [8]

Stanton's zeal for the Democratic party did not overcome his sense of family responsibility. During the April 1842 election he went to Virginia and helped his brother Darwin obtain the Whig nomination for a seat in the House of Delegates; then he electioneered for Darwin in a campaign that resulted in his brother's election in a normally Democratic district. But not even Senator Tappan thought this strange political behavior; "I am very much pleased that Darwin is elected," he wrote to Edwin.

Back in Steubenville, Stanton helped arrange a large mass meeting which expelled the pro-bank secessionists from the county Democratic organization, thus providing precedent for similar actions throughout the state. On the Fourth of July, he addressed the Harrison County Democrats in what he described as one of the most enthusiastic meetings he had ever seen. He was renamed to the Jefferson County Central Committee and attended the county convention in September. In October the Democrats confirmed Stanton's predictions of success by sweeping Ohio, as they swept the nation, electing Shannon governor and regaining control over both houses of the legislature. And all the while, Stanton kept Tappan informed of Ohio developments: "I get more information from your letters as to Ohio matters," Tappan acknowledged, "than from all other sources." [9]

Tappan's information from Stanton often included gossip as well as politics. "The Devil is to pay among the new Methodists," he wrote on

[8] Stanton to ?, probably Tappan, Jan. 30, April 20, 1842, Stanton MSS; to Bela Latham, Feb. 26, 1842, owned by Ralph G. Newman; Holt, *op. cit.*, 89–95; Davis, "Economic Basis of Ohio Politics, 1820–1840," *loc. cit.*, 312–5.

[9] Flower, *Stanton*, 37; Stanton to Tappan, May 31, 1842, Stanton MSS; Tappan to Stanton, May 5, Stanton to Tappan, July 17, 1842, Wright Collection, LC; Steubenville *American Union*, Jan. 1, May 21, Sept. 17, 1842; Holt, *op. cit.*, 98.

The Stanton home, Cadiz, Ohio.

Stanton's first law office, over the home and cabinet shop of Joseph Hunter, Cadiz, Ohio.

Edwin McMasters Stanton. This photograph was probably taken in 1857.

one occasion. "They had quite a revival last fall among the young men and women, and *now* there is a prospect of considerable increase in the population by the birth of young members who are coming into the church without the preacher having been paid for the marriage ceremony." In another letter Stanton told how "Parson" Beatty of the Seminary connived with the Steubenville town council to augment a lot he owned by having High Street narrowed by twenty feet. Stanton wrote a newspaper article to expose the fraud, but the editor of the *American Union* found excuses for not printing it. Stanton was more successful in thwarting the efforts of a prominent farmer to buy lands foreclosed for taxes at much less than their value, and as the speculation involved only Whigs and "soft money" Democrats, Stanton was doubly delighted.

One of his favorite stories to Tappan concerned a tightfisted local physician, Dr. Mairs, who was sued by a Steubenville landlady for three dollars for board furnished his hired man. The doctor retaliated by suing her for five dollars, for alleged "attendance in abortion." For the outraged housekeeper, Stanton sued the doctor for slander and libel. In the slander suit, Mairs produced what Stanton described as "an Irishman that he had picked up in some gutter in Pittsburgh, brought him down here, washed and shaved him, . . . paid him wages, and brought him into court as a witness dressed up in the Doctor's own clothes." Stanton recognized the clothes and exposed the perjury. Mairs dropped his suit and paid $900 and costs. Stanton enjoyed playing the part of knight-errant against injustice, especially when the villains were Whigs or bolting Democrats.

Stanton's law cases were proving too commonplace to bring him legal prominence, financial security, or quick political advancement. To satisfy his intellectual wants, he started a literary society among his law students, which Mary and Pamphila joined, and in which each member wrote a weekly essay. Early in March 1842, he obtained the appointment as reporter of the Ohio Supreme Court. The salary was only $300 a year, but his duties kept him at Columbus, where more important law cases might be obtained and where he could widen his acquaintance with lawyers and politicians. He hurried back to Steubenville early in August 1842, in time to be on hand at the birth of a son, whom he and Mary named Edwin Lamson Stanton. The boy helped fill the void left by the death of Lucy, and the spirits of the Stanton family notably revived.[1]

[1] Wolcott MS, 75; Stanton to Tappan, April 22, 1842, Tappan Papers, May 31, 1842, Stanton MSS, and June 27, 1841, July 17, 1842, Wright Collection, LC.

By early December he was ready to set out again for Columbus. He had proved himself adept in maneuvering within the tangled world of county politics and in the practice of routine law cases. Stanton was ready now for wider horizons.

"Imagine yourself in a long dining room, with two lamps hanging from the ceiling, the walls trimmed with pine after the manner of Episcopal Churches on Christmas day. At one side are the fiddlers and on the floor any quantity of ladies in their best dresses, and gentlemen with their hair combed slick, and their pumps on. The fiddlers strike up and the men and women jump, and you have the Inaugural Ball in all its glories—at least all that I can remember of it." Stanton was describing Governor Shannon's inaugural celebration to his sister Pamphila. He had just arrived in Columbus and was finding the change of scene congenial.

Once again Stanton favorably impressed Columbus society. Journalist Donn Piatt described him as "young, ardent, and of a most joyous nature," with a ready sense of humor and a wonderfully hearty laugh. "He was not only a hard student in . . . his profession," Piatt continued, "but he had a taste for light literature that made his conversation extremely attractive." Stanton occasionally visited the Piatt homestead near West Liberty, where he once confided that he was writing a book on "The Poetry of the Bible." [2]

During that winter in Columbus, Stanton also became acquainted with Salmon Portland Chase, who sought to enlist him actively in the antislavery movement. Thus far the Jacksonians, fearful of a sectional schism within their party which would endanger their program of reform, had condemned agitation on the question of abolition or the extension of slavery. Tappan refused to present antislavery petitions to the United States Senate, and the opposition to fearless old John Quincy Adams's efforts to bring such petitions before the national House of Representatives came largely from Democrats. But it was inevitable that the reform impulse should direct itself against slavery, and make it a national issue. In Chase, a young Cincinnati lawyer who had formerly been a Whig, the newly formed Liberty party enlisted a zealous recruit.

Tall, massive, dignified, and handsome, Chase had flouted the displeasure of southward-looking Cincinnati by engaging in so many slave cases that he became known as "the attorney general for runaway

[2] Piatt, *Memories of Men Who Saved the Union* (New York, 1887), 50–1; Wolcott MS, 77–8.

slaves." Deeply religious but self-righteous and opinionated, he had determined to subordinate all other party interests to the central issue of slavery. Stanton tried to convince him that the Democratic party offered the best agency for his antislavery efforts and promised to support them if Chase would come over to it. But Chase thought opponents of slavery could work most effectively through a third party, which, after gaining the balance of power, could throw its strength to whichever major party would promise to take a forthright anti-slavery stand. Neither man was able to convince the other, but they became bosom friends.

Unlike Chase, Stanton wanted to hold back the slavery issue as much as possible. Issues of banking and currency remained paramount in Ohio politics, where most Democrats chose to treat the questions of slavery and its extension as dangerous and distracting matters.[3] Americans generally kept the dark cloud of slavery low on the horizon of the nation's conscience. Glorying in their country's strength, envisioning a magnificent "manifest destiny" in which the continent would be spanned, jingoes were demanding an end to the joint occupation of Oregon with Great Britain and the sole rulership over all the territory. The annexation of Texas, which had won its independence from Mexico, was becoming an urgent issue. But it was inextricably involved with the slavery extension question, and threatened such dire consequences to the unity of both major parties that Van Buren and Henry Clay, who seemed most likely to be the opposing presidential candidates in 1844, kept silent about Texas, though Van Buren was privately opposed to annexation.

Stanton supported Van Buren throughout the latter's political career and offered no objection to his policy of silence. Expediency rather than principle ruled the American political scene, and Stanton was no man to play Chase's quixotic role. His major concern at this time was to master his new responsibilities as court reporter, which proved more time-consuming than he had anticipated. Stanton gave due attention to this work, for it was greatly expanding his circle of acquaintances in the legal world. By April 1843 he felt enough in control of the situation to begin commuting between Steubenville and Columbus.

He continued to keep Senator Tappan in Washington informed of developments in Ohio politics. Soon after his arrival in Columbus, Stanton told Tappan of "a most glorious battle." Thirteen of the state's twenty-six banks were in collusion to refuse to reincorporate under the

[3] Chase to Jeremiah S. Black, April 14, 1870, Black Papers, LC, reprinted in part in New York *Tribune*, Nov. 11, 1870.

general banking law that the Democrats had passed earlier that year. Outgoing Whig governor Corwin in his farewell message to the legislature had urged some relaxation in the administration of the law, and a bill to extend the banks' existing charters had been introduced. Many persons feared that if the banks continued their opposition and allowed their charters to lapse, the state would not only suffer from inadequate banking facilities but would also be flooded with paper money issued by out-of-state banks. The "soft money" Democrats felt inclined toward lining up with the Whigs.

Stanton, operating subtly behind the scenes to keep wavering Democrats up to the mark, reported that "our men," especially one Caleb McNulty, kept the bill off the floor of the state legislature as long as possible, then tried to kill it with a filibuster. The lobbies were "thronged with bankers and their satellites, perfectly savage." The House got into an uproar, which lasted until midnight, when it adjourned without acting. "A more mortified, foiled and beaten set of fellows you never saw," wrote Stanton. "They had got so lost that they could not tell 'where they were or who was with them'; one of them wanted to whip the Speaker." Next morning the bank forces were still confused and the measure was voted down, in large part, Tappan learned, due to Stanton's tactical operations.[4]

Governor Shannon, Stanton found out, was backing Lewis Cass, of Michigan, a conservative Democrat on most issues, as the next presidential nominee. Shannon had tried to convince Stanton to abandon his advocacy of Van Buren, and now the young politician decided to take advantage of the governor's interest in having Ohio's Democrats come out early for Cass. "He having undertaken my conversion to that faith," Stanton confided to Tappan in February 1843, "I have become acquainted with some, and shall soon know all their calculations." Boring quietly into conservative Democratic ranks from within, Stanton, who remained secretly loyal to Van Buren, learned that the Cass backers expected John Calhoun, the South Carolinian, and Van Buren to kill off each other at the Democratic National Convention, whereupon "Cass will come in sweepstakes." Shannon's prime object was to enlist the support of Samuel Medary, fiery editor of the *Ohio Statesman,* hitherto a staunch hard-money man and an ally of Tappan and Stanton. Shannon told Stanton: "Sam

---

[4] Stanton to Samuel Medary, April 4, 1843, copy owned by the estate of Benjamin P. Thomas; same to Tappan, Dec. 27, 1842, Feb. 8, 1843, Stanton MSS; M. Birchard to Tappan, Jan. 3, 1843, Tappan Papers, LC; Stanton to E. Lane, Feb. 10, 1843, Lee-Kohn Memorial Collection, NYPL.

Medary has it in his power to make Cass President." Stanton agreed that Medary would be vastly influential; but a "truer [Van Buren] man never breathed," he wrote to Tappan—a description proved accurate by Medary's continued radicalism.

Throughout 1843 Stanton sought to consolidate Van Buren's strength in Jefferson and Carroll counties, to have Van Buren men chosen as delegates to the next Democratic state convention, and to see to it that loyal anti-bank candidates were nominated for the legislature and for Congress. "We both have enough to do," Mathew Birchard, a Democratic leader, wrote Tappan, referring to his and Stanton's schedules. In November, Stanton was named delegate to the Democratic state convention that was to convene soon after the new year; a month later, he arranged a testimonial supper in honor of Colonel Richard Johnson, which kept him in Columbus almost into the holiday season. Such application to party duty received recognition throughout Democratic circles in the state. Backers of a projected *Western Democratic Review* petitioned Tappan to "mention the subject to Mr. Stanton, and get his aid if possible, as a contributor." [5]

Back in Columbus after a happy Christmas time with his family in Steubenville, Stanton plunged into the work of the state convention as a prominent Van Buren man. The radical group he worked with gained control of the appointment of all delegates, and instructed them to support Van Buren. Stanton's able leadership was clearly recognized and was doubly applauded because the defeated faction accepted the result and another disastrous party split was avoided.

Tappan learned that Stanton had been "a tower of strength." Another Ohio party leader, who had attended every January convention since 1828, informed Tappan that he had never witnessed such good feeling as in the one just past. One Cass man had, it was true, threatened to wreck the carefully nurtured unity in favor of Van Buren which Stanton had helped create, but "Mr. Stanton of Steubenville *killed him dead on the spot!*—after which he was as harmless as he had been wicked, and peace was restored." [6]

[5] Stanton to Tappan, Feb. 18, 1843, Stanton MSS; B. B. Taylor to Tappan, Oct. 19, T. Umbstaetter to same, Dec. 22, and Birchard to same, Dec. 24, 1843, Tappan Papers, LC; Columbus *Ohio Statesman*, Dec. 13, and Steubenville *American Union*, May 27, July 8, Aug. 19, Oct. 21, and Nov. 18, 1843; Holt, *op. cit.*, 174–5.

[6] W. Medill to Tappan, Jan. 12, and W. Blacksom to same, Jan. 18, 1844, Tappan Papers, LC; Medill to William Allen, Jan. 11, 1844, Allen Papers, LC; Stanton to Tappan, Jan. 8, 1844, Stanton MSS (misdated 1833); Columbus *Ohio Statesman*, Jan. 8, 1844; Holt, *op. cit.*, 63–5.

Soon after the convention, David Tod, whom the Democrats had nominated for governor, publicly receded from his former hard-money position, thereby dampening the ardor of the radical Democrats. They also learned that the Ohio delegates to the forthcoming national convention were being pressured to support some candidate whose prospects of winning the election were better than Van Buren's. Stanton suspected that this movement originated in the South. He professed to believe that if the Southern bloc succeeded in defeating Van Buren at the national convention, or if they refused to support him after he had won the nomination, the Democrats of the free states should throw their united support to Birney, the Liberty party candidate, "and cut loose forever from Southern slavery and Southern dictation." He thought, however, that "if our friends remain firm and undaunted we are still safe. Their word should be Van Buren and *no other.*"

Van Buren came out publicly against the annexation of Texas on the ground that it would involve the United States in an unjust war with Mexico. The pronouncement cost him the support of warlike old Andrew Jackson. It pleased many Ohioans, however, and the Ohio delegation left for the national convention at Baltimore prepared to cast a unanimous vote for Van Buren, as Stanton had hoped they would.

Only heroic efforts by Medary prevented the delegation from switching to Cass, however, when it became evident that Van Buren could not be chosen under the new rule put through by the Southern delegates, which required a two-thirds vote to nominate. At last, with the convention deadlocked, the Ohioans reluctantly voted for a "dark horse," James K. Polk, and helped to nominate him.[7]

Things were going well for Stanton personally. His new baby boy was thriving after a series of illnesses; finances were in such good shape that Stanton had sold the Third Street house in Steubenville for $1,200 and leased a fine, larger place on the corner of Third and Logan, which he later purchased. Shade trees, shrubs, and flowers grew abundantly in the yard. Mary, under Edwin's guidance, had undertaken a varied reading program which filled her hours during his frequent absences. She was determined to have a hand in educating her child, and as an early feminist, she dreamed of playing a part in a future regeneration of world morality to be brought about by the

⁷ Stanton to Tappan, April 28, 1844, Stanton MSS; Wolcott MS, 158; Holt, *op. cit.,* 198–9.

education of women. She and Stanton remained warm and affectionate, full of hope for their life to come and pleasure in their past and present.

Tragedy, made more unbearable by its unexpectedness, shattered this happy relationship. Stanton was on his way to Steubenville from Columbus late in February 1844 when the frightening news came to him that Mary was desperately ill with "bilious fever." He hurried home. For a despairing fortnight he scarcely left her bedside. His brother and his brother-in-law, both doctors, were constantly in the house. But their medications and Edwin's prayers proved fruitless. Mary steadily weakened, and on March 13 she died.

Life grew dark for Stanton. He wrote a friend: "It has pleased God . . . to take from me my beloved wife, upon whom all my affections and happiness rested. . . . This calamity has overwhelmed me. I know not where to look or whither to turn. . . . We were both young and happy in each other, looking forward to a long life of joy and happiness. By incessant toil we were gathering around us all that we thought would promote our comfort and enjoyment and this spring had in our thought attained these. A few days ago I laid her in her grave, and to me they are now ashes, ashes."

His grief verged on insanity. Stanton ordered Mary's funeral dress altered and realtered. Moaning and weeping, he cried: "This is my bride and she shall be dressed and buried like a bride." At night he would leave his room, tears streaming from his eyes, and taking up a lamp, search the house, crying over and over: "Where is Mary?" He stealthily brought to her grave her wedding rings, jewels, and letters.

Gradually he returned to normality. But still he spent hours reading Mary's letters, which he later had printed in a brochure so that his son and a few close friends and relatives might remember her. "She was my guide, my counselor, and my familiar friend," he explained in a preface addressed to the boy; ". . . I have tried in vain by talking of her to you in familiar scenes and by her grave, to call up some thought of her in your mind. . . . It is better therefore to place some memorial of your mother beyond the vicissitudes [of memory], so that when you grow older you can . . . have her words, her example, her prayers, to counsel and direct you." [8]

For a long time the days remained bleak for Stanton. He was apathetic, barely rousing himself from his torpor to write Tappan in April of political happenings at Columbus. But his family required funds, and

[8] Stanton to Lewis Tappan, March 20, 1844, Lewis Tappan Papers, LC; Wolcott MS, 101–2, 108–10; Flower, *Stanton*, 39–40; Joseph P. Doyle, *In Memorium, Edwin Mc-Masters Stanton* (Steubenville, 1911), 26.

Stanton was back at law practice in midsummer 1844, and by August was deep in what obviously was for him the therapeutic jungle of politics.

When Polk won the Democratic nomination for President and the party platform declared for the "re-annexation of Texas," the enthusiasm of many Ohio Democrats of antislavery leanings measurably cooled. But Stanton, notwithstanding his earlier threat to join the Liberty party if Van Buren should lose the Democratic nomination, and perhaps to exhaust himself and so escape his grief at his wife's death, worked hard for Polk. In large part due to Stanton's efforts as chairman of the county Democratic committee, Polk carried both Steubenville and Jefferson County, though Clay carried Ohio. The Whigs gained control of the Ohio legislature and elected Mordecai Bartley governor.

With Whigs in control of the state patronage, Ohio Democrats looked to the Polk administration in Washington for jobs. It disgusted Stanton. "Every one is after some office," he wrote Tappan in December, "and every species of truckling to what is supposed to be an important influence in the coming administration is resorted to. I never expected to see anything of the kind out of the Whig party."

Control of federal patronage in Ohio would be decisive in the internal party struggles, and Stanton's anti-bank faction outmaneuvered the Cass clique and gained the inside track with Polk. Stanton was mentioned for a federal district attorney's office, but he wrote to Tappan: "I am not a candidate *and would not accept if appointed.*" He did, however, recommend suitable "hard money men" for various federal offices and became angry because some appointments were going to those he considered undeserving.[9]

Immediately upon his inauguration, Polk moved to realize the annexation of Texas. And now, for the first time, Stanton was disturbed by the prospect of annexation. The Ohio Democrats had been attempting to make a show of unity in support of Polk's policy, but Jacob Brinkerhoff, an Ohio Democratic congressman, finally broke the party traces with a speech denouncing annexation as designed for the benefit of the South, and demanding the exclusion of slavery from Texas as the price of Northern acquiescence in annexation.

Stanton sent Brinkerhoff congratulations. "There is too much inclination among northern men, to submit in silence to the insolent demands of the south," he wrote. ". . . You have set a manly and noble

---

[9] Stanton to Tappan, Jan. 14, 1845, Tappan Papers, LC; same to same, April 28, Dec. 26, 1844, Jan. 10, 27, March 26, 1845, Stanton MSS; Steubenville *American Union*, July 11, Aug. 15, Sept. 5, 19, Nov. 7, 1844.

example, in which many, besides myself, will to the uttermost sustain you." But Stanton kept his antislavery sentiments confined to private thoughts and communications. He was a party regular.

Expansionist sentiment proved too strong to resist. In the last days of 1845, when Texas was formally admitted to the Union, Stanton's stiff-necked Democratic loyalty wavered. Again he felt that his friend Chase might be following the wisest course in trying to keep the Liberty party dedicated to the single purpose of opposing slavery. Still, he remained within the regular Democratic ranks, so far as the world at large was concerned.[1]

The Whig-controlled Ohio legislature retired Tappan from the United States Senate, but before his term expired in 1845, both he and Stanton became indirectly involved in a scandal, when Caleb McNulty, who had been rewarded for his services to the Democratic party in Ohio with appointment as clerk of the House of Representatives in Washington, was charged with stealing $45,500 of House funds. The House dismissed him by unanimous vote, and in default of bail he was confined in the District of Columbia jail. McNulty, whom Stanton had once called "a glorious fellow," had made Stanton's brother, Darwin, his assistant, and Tappan was one of McNulty's sureties.

Stanton wrote to Tappan: "McNulty's blow up was not unexpected to either of us, but he has blown quicker, went higher, and is now fallen deeper than I anticipated. . . . Your Whig friends have been deeply sympathizing in what they fancied, or hoped was your loss. They deeply regretted that you should now, in your old age be broken up and ruined by McNulty. I advised them to spare their grief, and bottle their tears."

McNulty's guilt was taken for granted, and even the Democratic press demanded that he be punished and that his bondsmen make full restitution to the government in order to save the party from complete dishonor. It is a measure of Stanton's increasing competence as a lawyer that Tappan urged him to hasten to Washington and assist in McNulty's defense.

Stanton arrived in Washington at midnight; the case had been set for trial the next morning. Going directly to the jail, he consulted hurriedly with McNulty and then examined rules, statutes, and records until four o'clock in the morning. After two hours' sleep he put in more time examining the law. Stanton found that McNulty's other lawyers regarded the case as hopeless, but he persuaded them to allow him to

---

[1] Stanton to Chase, Aug. ?, 1846, Chase Papers, HSP; to Brinkerhoff, Jan. 19, 1845, in New York *Sun*, March 14, 1892.

draw up a motion to quash the indictment. The court was inclined to rule such a motion out of order at that stage of the proceedings, but Stanton bulled through all objections ("cavalierly" was Darwin's word for it) and gained permission to argue the motion the next day. Then, seizing upon every technicality, he convinced the judge that the indictment should be quashed and the prisoner discharged.

Stanton's performance was brilliant from a legal point of view and spectators in the crowded courtroom applauded him. Papers all over the country gave the case full coverage. When he left Washington on his thirty-first birthday, in December 1845, his name was widely known.[2]

More because of personal than professional reasons, he and Tappan dissolved their partnership in 1845, and Stanton formed a new association with George W. McCook, a native of Pennsylvania, now thirty-three years old, who had attended Franklin College, at Athens, Ohio, and studied law in Stanton's office. A large man, he was a lover of the classics, a staunch Democrat, and a member of a family that would later become known as "the Fighting McCooks." Stanton was also associated with S. G. Peppard at Cadiz, Theobald Umbstaetter and Jonathan H. Wallace at New Lisbon, and less closely with Daniel Peck at St. Clairsville, E. R. Eckley at Carrollton, and Joseph Sharon at Harrison. His relations with the Tappan family did not cease with the dissolution of his partnership with Tappan, but they became strained, for Oella's marriage to the senator's son, a somewhat erratic man, turned out unhappily. Oella left her husband for a time; and he seems to have held Edwin and Darwin responsible in some measure for his marital difficulties. "Since Oella returned home last fall we have lived together in harmony," the younger Tappan wrote to his father, "and she has already much improved in housekeeping as well as in other respects. As she is really trying to improve herself, and I do not intend to have her brother or brothers about the house, I have no doubt she will manage so as to give us both satisfaction." [3]

Nothing the divided Democrats could do managed to prevent the Ohio Whigs from passing a banking law which, in limiting the liability of stockholders and directors and the amount of notes a bank might issue, relaxed, without fully abandoning, the safeguards the Democrats had written into the banking code. The law caused new dissension in

[2] Stanton to Tappan, Jan. 27, 1845, Stanton MSS; Wolcott MS, 90–1; Flower, *Stanton*, 44; Gorham, *Stanton*, I, 31–3; Washington *Semi-Weekly Union*, Dec. 30, 1845.
[3] March 2, 1845, Benjamin Tappan Papers, LC.

both parties. Some Whigs wanted to return to a system of unrestricted banking. The "hard-money" radical Democrats of Stanton's faction accused the "softs," some of whom had voted for the new law, of surrendering to the bankers.

This banking law became the overriding issue in the state campaign of 1845, and the people sustained the Whigs. Undaunted, the "hard-money" Democratic faction planned to try to gain control of the party's next state convention at Columbus, in January 1846, and to renew the fight against the "money aristocrats." To lead them in this struggle, a strong candidate for governor was needed. A number of Democratic county organizations again endorsed David Tod for governor. But Ohioans who were worried that Tod might prove unreliable on the bank issue wanted Stanton in his place.[4]

By this time Stanton had completed his work as reporter for the Ohio Supreme Court, but he rebuffed all suggestions that he stand for elective office and made no effort to promote himself as a candidate for governor. He did, however, take a prominent part in the 1846 state convention, where Tod managed to satisfy Stanton and most of the other radical Democrats that he was sound on the money question. Stanton, thereupon, worked hard to secure the nomination for Tod, and when it was achieved he looked on it as a "triumph of principal [*sic*]," though he doubted that Tod could win the election. Later Stanton became joyous as Tod's prospects improved. But shortly before the election he was shocked when Democratic newspapers came out with a new watchword: "Vote for Tod and the Black Laws."

The Black Laws, which had been in force for many years, discriminated against the Negroes living in Ohio by denying them the right to testify against a white person in court, depriving them of a share of the school funds, and requiring them to furnish bond against becoming public charges, though the last provision had never been enforced. But as abolitionist agitation began to disturb the public conscience, a movement for the repeal of these unjust laws made headway throughout the state. The Liberty party came out strongly for repeal; Democrats and Whigs avoided the problem at first, but the new issue soon became crucial and threatened to split both major parties.

Tod said nothing until the Whigs discovered that as a candidate for the state senate in 1838 he had favored Negro participation in common school funds. Armed with this information, the Whigs branded Tod a "nigger lover." Queried on his position, he answered that he opposed

---

[4] H. C. Whitman to Tappan, Nov. 23, 1845, Tappan Papers, LC.

repeal of the Black Laws. His reply was widely printed, especially in southern Ohio; and as more and more Democratic newspapers stirred up race prejudice, Stanton felt sick at heart.

He confided to Chase his deep discouragement and his doubts that "just and true principles" could prevail unless they were pushed ahead by men of single-minded views who would eschew compromises. "Who would have thought," he asked, "that the battle between the Hards and Softs, in this State, would end, before the election, in a common shout for 'Tod and the Black Laws!' " [5]

Meanwhile, questions arising out of the annexation of Texas and Polk's efforts to acquire Upper California and other territory from Mexico had brought relations with that country to the verge of war. A border skirmish in disputed territory induced Polk to declare that Mexico had "shed American blood upon the American soil." On May 12, 1846, Congress resolved that a state of war existed. Excitement swept the country as men rushed to enlist.

The Whigs opposed the war from the beginning and accused Polk of taking wrongful measures against a feeble neighbor. The Democrats closed ranks to defend Polk. Stanton's skepticism about the annexation of Texas and his fears concerning Southern dominance in national affairs were submerged by the wave of patriotism that swept across the country. At a mass meeting in Steubenville he presented resolutions endorsing the administration's policies, declaring that the war was "necessary and just," and appealing for recruits.

A military company, the "Steubenville Greys," commanded by Stanton's partner, McCook, was speedily filled up. Stanton loaned his horse to the troop for their drill, and inspired the members of the Jefferson County Female Bible Society to donate Bibles and Testaments to the men, Stanton making the presentation speech and McCook responding for the company. In his enthusiasm for the war, Stanton tried to enlist, but Dr. Tappan advised him that the army surgeons would reject him because of his asthma. He was to sit out the Mexican War at home.[6]

Like his brother, Dr. Darwin Stanton tried to secure an appointment in the Army, but he was far more ill than Edwin. Darwin had resigned his post in Washington, and had returned to Hollidays Cove to resume the practice of medicine, when he was stricken with a fever that affected his brain. On September 23, 1846, he cut his throat, and in

[5] Nov. 30, 1846, Chase Papers, HSP; Holt, *op. cit.*, 136–40, 244–7.

[6] Steubenville *American Union*, May 28, June 11, 1846; Flower, *Stanton*, 44; Doyle, *op. cit.*, 27

gory surroundings—"The blood spouted up to the ceiling," recalled Dr. Alexander M. Reid—Darwin died.

Edwin was inconsolable. In the chill evening he ran, without hat or coat, into the dark woods. McCook joined others in a frantic hunt for the distraught man, fearing that he might also kill himself. They found Stanton and led him back to Hollidays Cove.

Responsibility returned Edwin to his senses. Darwin's wife was almost destitute, for her husband had left her only a small amount of insurance. Edwin brought her and her three children into his home and assumed their support. Three months later he wrote to his friend Chase: "Events of the past summer have broken my spirits, crushed my hopes, and without energy or purpose in life, I feel indifferent to the present, careless of the future—in a state of bewilderment the end of which is hidden." [7]

The tragedies of his brother's suicide and the death of his wife and their daughter in so short a time oppressed Stanton grievously. Formerly a hearty, cheerful man in private life, he now became morose. Finding a measure of comfort only in religion, he shunned social gatherings and, for a time, further political embroilment. Too much alone in the long winter nights, he brooded on his troubles.

Heretofore he had been known as a hard man only in court. Now, to conceal his craving for affection and yearning for lost loved ones, he began to turn a stern face to the world.

[7] Ms notebook of Dr. Reid, owned by Miss Alexandra Sanford; Stanton to Lewis Tappan, Nov. 23, 1846, Lewis Tappan Papers, LC; to Chase, Nov. 30, 1846, Chase Papers, HSP.

CHAPTER III

ON THE WAY UP

$\mathbb{S}$TANTON remained in Steubenville throughout the winter of 1846, lonely, but so crushed in spirit that he seldom left his house. He kept up law practice out of necessity, and dabbled fitfully in politics as an antidote to grief. Mostly he busied himself with correspondence, writing especially to his partner, McCook, who was now in Mexico commanding a cavalry troop. Their friendship grew warmer during their exchange of letters.

To Chase, with whom his relationship was also becoming very close, Stanton bared his innermost thoughts. His letters to the antislavery leader increasingly took on a vocabulary of rapturous spiritualism. "Allow me my dear friend this evening to enter your study," Stanton wrote on one occasion, "let me take you by the hand, throw my arm around you, say I love you, & bid you farewell." The words came from the heart of a desperately lonely man who had found an understanding friend. Chase, like Stanton a Kenyon student, had been twice a widower and had seen a number of his children die. In November 1846 he married for a third time, and Stanton found vicarious solace in Chase's new happiness.

Chase seized the opportunity offered by Stanton's eagerness to correspond, to draw the man out of himself and to recruit him for the antislavery cause. He seemed to be succeeding. Stanton deplored to his friend the conservative influences which were gaining dominance in both the Whig and the Democratic parties. "Last summer," he admitted to Chase, "I did not fully understand you, when speaking of aristocracy in this country, you insisted that its stronghold was in the South." But it had become clear to him from reading Thomas Arnold's *History of Rome*, at Chase's suggestion, that an aristocracy like the one in the

South had all the advantages in a contest with a popular party. Therefore Stanton was in a mood to renounce his Democratic allegiance and to place principle above party. "I go by faith more than knowledge," Stanton wrote Chase, "and have faith in your principles, confidence in your judgment." [1]

Not realizing that Stanton's words reflected deep despair more than firm decision, Chase accepted the mood of rejection for the fact of conversion. He was sure, for example, that Stanton would join him in defending John Van Zandt.

Van Zandt was an Ohioan who had been sued for damages for aiding a group of fugitive slaves. The case had been appealed to the United States Supreme Court. Chase asked Stanton to help prepare the argument for the defense, but Stanton begged off, pleading that he was not yet equal to the effort. Stanton did criticize the brief at Chase's request, and complimented him on an argument in which the friends of human freedom could take pride. When the Supreme Court decided against Van Zandt, however, Stanton admitted no surprise, "for in the opinion that I have of that tribunal it could not have been otherwise." He noted that Justice Levi Woodbury, of New Hampshire, had written the opinion. "The dirty work of the South has always found Northern hands to perform it," Stanton wrote, "and I can well imagine the deep scorn & contempt swelling in the bosoms of the Southern judges, as they beheld Levi on his belly crawling through that opinion." [2]

But however he vilified apologists for the extension of slavery, Stanton had no sympathy with Whigs who condemned the "unjust war" with Mexico. He considered such sentiments to be disloyal. Of course, the war would bring the United States a vast increase in territory, he wrote Chase, but he no longer opposed this or even the annexation of Texas. The pressure for national expansion was irresistible, and it would be folly for any party to stand against it. Stanton, predisposed against the Whigs and now insinuating that it was a party of treason, hinted that he could not now break with the Democratic organization, for it was the only party that had the capacity to serve patriotic ends. Instead of Stanton joining Chase in an antislavery third party, Chase should come to Stanton, so that the Democracy might better resist the expansion of slavery into the newly acquired territory.

[1] Stanton to Chase, Nov. 30, 1846, Jan. 5, Nov. 11, Dec. 2, 1847, Chase Papers, HSP; Jan. 15, 16, Feb. 27, 1847, McCook ms diary, owned by Mrs. McCook Knox.
[2] Jan. 16, Feb. 28, April 24, 1847, and undated, *ca.* March 1847, Letterbooks, Chase Papers, LC; Stanton to Chase, March 3, May 1, 1847, Chase Papers, HSP. See also 5 Howard 215–32; Leo Alilunas, "Fugitive Slave Cases in Ohio Prior to 1850," *OSAHQ*, XLIX, 160–84.

To that end, antislavery congressmen were uniting in favor of a resolution introduced by David Wilmot, a Pennsylvania Democrat, which would prohibit slavery in any territory gained from Mexico. Ohio's representatives stood staunchly for the Proviso, and Stanton guessed that "the Western democracy seems to be fairly committed on that question; I think they will stick."

News came that General Zachary Taylor had won a crushing victory at Buena Vista and that Winfield Scott had taken Veracruz on the seacoast and was advancing on Mexico City. The Whigs clamored more fiercely for a cessation of hostilities. At the same time, remembering how they had marched to victory behind Harrison in 1840, they watched appreciatively the rising stars of Scott and Taylor, both of whom were Whigs. Friends of the Wilmot Proviso kept sectional passions at the boiling point by continuing to push it forward in Congress.

Gauging the swirling currents, Stanton saw the nation entering upon a new era in which principle rather than expediency would determine party alignments. He hoped that principled Democrats would assume the leadership of the party, and rationalized his persistent party regularity by asserting that the Whigs could never advance the liberal standard of "the welfare of their fellow men," for they lacked principles altogether. Bitterly irrational when partisan animosity got the better of him, Stanton asserted that if Santa Anna had won at Buena Vista, the Whigs would have made him "the God of their idolatry." [3]

Spring came and Stanton shook off the torpor of mind and spirit that had borne him down all winter. He again assumed the chairmanship of the Democratic county committee and took on the new office of city solicitor which Steubenville had created. Stanton became a director of the fire department and enjoyed marching in full regalia at the head of the annual fire-company parade. He served on the board of visitors of a boy's school, was active in Masonry, became a director of a company that planned to introduce the telegraph west of Pittsburgh, and played a primary role in efforts to get a railroad through Steubenville.

Summer 1847 was brightened by George McCook's return from the war. Their correspondence had meant a great deal to Stanton, and he busied himself arranging a public welcome under Democratic party auspices, including decorations for the town, a dinner for three hundred persons, and a parade. He had undertaken to look after McCook's fiancée during his absence, and she and Stanton had extensively dis-

[3] Nov. 30, 1946, March 11, May 1, 1847, Chase Papers, HSP.

cussed her love for McCook. "I have passed through much that you have yet to feel," he wrote her; ". . . by the love for George which you now feel, the fountains of your heart were first opened; . . . the heart is a fountain of bitterness as well as of joy." Bitterness had no place, however, when McCook arrived in Steubenville to end his long voyage.

The veteran came to Stanton's home to change clothes before calling on his fiancée, and the two men drove in his buggy to her home. During the next few days the three were seen together everywhere, and Stanton's evenings were gladdened with their frequent visits to his home. "You need have no uneasiness about me," McCook wrote to his mother, "I am at Stanton's and have everything that could be desired." McCook suffered briefly from intestinal infections which he had picked up in Mexico, but the careful nursing of Edwin and Pamphila soon brought him around. Once well, McCook left for Pittsburgh to make arrangements for his marriage. Stanton brought the bride there from Steubenville and was best man at the wedding. Then Stanton had to stay in Columbus for several weeks and McCook returned to Steubenville to take over their office. Like Stanton, he found it boring. "In the office. The want of constant business makes me dislike to stay here," McCook wrote in his diary. And next day: "Not much business to do. And time drags wearily down in the dusty streets." [4]

McCook and Stanton agreed that Steubenville was too dull between court terms, and for Stanton too full of unhappiness, to justify his remaining there. Stanton decided to practice in Pittsburgh as partner to Charles Shaler, a former judge with wealthy connections and an established business. He did not plan to change his legal residence, however, or to terminate his partnership with McCook, who after all decided to remain in Steubenville. Late October 1847 found Stanton established in Pittsburgh.

When Chase heard that Stanton intended to move to Pennsylvania, he offered to take the stump in his behalf if he would stay in Ohio and run for governor. To Stanton, this was "out of the question. My mission is elsewhere." But he could not forsake politics altogether, and he allowed himself again to be named a delegate to the Ohio Democratic convention at Columbus, where he hoped to see Chase in January.[5]

[4] Steubenville *American Union*, March 25, June 17, 24, July 8, 1847; Steubenville *Herald*, April 8, Dec. 8, 1847; Stanton to Margaret Dick Beatty, undated, McCook Family Papers, LC; McCook ms diary, July 11, 17, Aug. 2, 25, 26, and McCook to "My Dear Mother," July 22, 1847, owned by Mrs. McCook Knox.

[5] Chase letterbook notation, Nov. 27, 1847, Chase Papers, LC; Stanton to Chase, Dec. 2, 1847, Chase Papers, HSP; Pittsburgh *Daily Morning Post*, Oct. 29, 1847.

Chase felt gratified that Stanton did not intend to renounce politics, for a showdown on the slavery issue could not be much longer deferred. Peace negotiations for the vast Mexican lands under American military control had already begun, and the Wilmot Proviso gave the antislavery men a rallying point. Stanton, however, began to hint that he might not be able to attend the Columbus convention, "much as my heart desires to strike for truth and freedom." The need to build up a practice in his new home city and his own reluctance to re-enter political involvements kept him in Pittsburgh.

He arranged with his brother-in-law, Pamphila's husband, Christopher P. Wolcott, a devoted abolitionist, to keep him informed of developments at the Columbus assembly. Wolcott warned Stanton that "a strong effort will be made to smother the Wilmot Proviso. . . . It will need strong arms and stout hearts to bear up the Proviso against the forces that are rallying against it." He seconded Chase's pleas that Stanton hurry to Columbus "at the time of need."

In Pittsburgh, Stanton eagerly scanned the accounts of the Columbus meeting. Conservative Ohio Democrats, in the majority, endorsed Cass, a foe of the Proviso, for President and nominated a reputed friend of Southern interests for governor. The platform, though deploring slavery as an evil, evaded the question of its status in the territories and declared that it was a matter for each state to control as it saw fit.[6]

Stanton and Chase had each expected too much of the other. The former had hoped that Chase would be able to commit Ohio Democrats to the support of the Proviso. Chase had come to Columbus only because he thought Stanton would be there to back up the pro-Proviso forces. "Why—why are you not here?" Chase wrote despairingly. The vote on the resolution concerning the Proviso had been close; Stanton's presence might have helped redress the balance. "I regret that your voice is not to be heard . . . honorably for yourself and usefully for your country!" Chase admonished him. "You have great gifts of God, energy, talent, utterance. And now a great cause demands more."

Stanton's reply questioned his ability to have affected the outcome of the convention, but he asked Chase's pardon for "the greater duty" that had kept him in Pittsburgh. He wrote Wolcott less modestly: "The Democratic Convention seems to have 'fizzled' out for want of some one who had courage enough to make them toe the mark." Stanton admitted to deep dejection as the battle lines shaped up. Neither of the

---

[6] Wolcott MS, 116; letters by Pamphila in New York *Sun*, March 14, 1892.

major parties offered much comfort to those opposed to the extension of slavery. He saw Jacksonian democracy as moribund.[7]

But though Stanton felt discouraged, Chase and other Northern anti-slavery leaders were resolved to continue the fight. When the Democrats nominated Cass and proposed to resist all efforts to bring the slavery issue before Congress, and when the Whigs nominated Taylor and ignored the slavery question altogether, antislavery Democrats and "conscience" Whigs alike revolted. In August 1848 they coalesced with Chase's Liberty men to form the Free-Soil party. Adopting as their slogan "Free soil, free speech, free labor, free men," they endorsed the Wilmot Proviso and chose Van Buren, aging but still sprightly, to be their standard-bearer.

Throughout the North, Jacksonian reformers rallied once again behind their long-time favorite. Stanton seems to have taken no part in the campaign beyond supporting the Free-Soil candidate in private discussions with friends and business acquaintances. To have done more might have antagonized some prospective clients in Pittsburgh, where he had now cast his fortunes as a lawyer. For the businessmen of the town had large dealings with the South, and the commercial community, like America itself, was divided on the slavery extension issue.

Like many other Democrats and Whigs, Stanton felt himself to be a man without a party that had any chance for success in 1848. November came and Taylor won the election, largely owing to Free-Soil inroads on the Democrats in crucial areas. "The presidential election has resulted in the overthrow of Cass," Stanton wrote his sister, "which for one, I do not regret." The campaign proved to him that Chase's strategy was the correct one, for he added: "It is to be hoped that the friends of liberty will keep up an organization, and, by preserving an armed neutrality, hold as they may the balance of power in the Free States, until one or the other party, by falling in line, secure their principles." [8]

In February 1849, Stanton, hard at work in Pittsburgh, read that a combination of Free-Soilers and Democrats in the Ohio legislature had elected Chase to the United States Senate. "How shall I express my joy upon reading the above paragraph this morning?" Stanton wrote to

[7] Chase to Stanton, Jan. 9, 1848, Stanton MSS; Stanton to Chase, Feb. 16, 1848, Chase Papers, HSP; Wolcott MS, 161.

[8] Wolcott MS, 163. Flower, *Stanton*, 53–4, states that Stanton spoke enthusiastically for Van Buren at a Steubenville rally. However, this seems doubtful and lacks any supporting evidence. William G. Keener, of Columbus, carefully searched the Steubenville, Columbus, and New Lisbon newspapers for 1848 and found no reports of any speech. On the Free-Soil convention, see E. H. Price, "The Election of 1848 in Ohio," *OSAHQ*, XXXVI, 206–37, 247–311.

Chase. "Thank God the day of small things in Ohio is over!" The new era foreseen by Stanton, in which men of principle would unite politically, seemed to have arrived.

And yet Stanton, notwithstanding the high-mindedness he exhibited in letters to his family and to Chase, remained singularly inactive in politics. He always seemed to find a reason for avoiding any public statement that would too obviously mark him as an antislavery man; yet, grieving for lost loved ones and craving affection, he could not bear to lose his intimate association with Chase or the respect of Wolcott. "To love, and to be loved, is a necessary condition of my happiness," he once wrote. But he had decided that the achievement of material success was also necessary for his happiness, and he would not risk his professional advancement in support of the antislavery party organization which could not win.

In later years his caution seemed like cowardice and hypocrisy to his critics. "From that time he should not have been trusted by Democrats," stated a business acquaintance of his early months in Pittsburgh.[9] But this judgment demands the insight that only hindsight can afford. In 1848 Stanton was withdrawing, not turncoating. Whatever political ambitions he may once have harbored, he now put behind him. His career henceforth would be the law. Only in the courtroom or with his family would he reveal his capacity for total commitment in any cause he felt to be worthy. But these characteristics remained part of him and could be evoked by the right persons and by certain kinds of events. Otherwise he played both ends against the middle when he had to, and played the game to win. And he would hide that soft spot behind a stony front.

The discovery of gold in California had started a stampede to the West Coast. Effective civil government was desperately needed to maintain order in the roisterous mining camps, but with California ready to apply for admission to the Union as a free state, some Southerners opposed her admission altogether, while others demanded some offsetting gain for the South. Headstrong men in both the North and the South clamored for an immediate definition of the status of slavery in New Mexico. Petitions deluged skittish congressmen, those from the North still supporting the Wilmot Proviso, those from the South protesting against the exclusion of slavery from the new territories as an affront

[9] Stanton to Chase, Feb. 24, 1849, Chase Papers, LC; William H. Smith to Jeremiah S. Black, Jan. 20, 1870, Black Papers, LC.

to that section, and even threatening secession if Southern rights should be denied.

Other questions aggravated sectional ill will. The boundary between Texas and New Mexico was in dispute, and as New Mexico seemed likely to become a free state, Northerners wished to push the boundary eastward, whereas Southerners wanted the limits of Texas extended as far west as possible. Northerners wished to outlaw the slave trade in the District of Columbia, whereas Southerners, led by John C. Calhoun, irritated by the action of Northern legislatures in passing Personal Liberty Laws which hindered the recapture of fugitive slaves, demanded a more stringent fugitive slave law.

Stanton exulted to see his friend Chase in the forefront of the frenzied fight in Congress. "The snarling and growling of the curs at your heels . . . can neither obstruct your path nor hinder your progress," he wrote Chase. "For myself, I am willing to risk with you with my whole heart." Stanton vowed that "in the battle for a living democracy in Ohio, you will never find me far from your side." Yet when Chase, trying to put men of antislavery convictions in places of power, again urged Stanton to run for governor, Stanton replied that he felt unfitted for and disinclined toward high political office and suggested Brinkerhoff "or some other equally sound man against whom there would be less acrimony than against myself." And again when Chase implored him to attend a Free-Soil meeting at Cleveland, Stanton replied that court work would keep him in Pittsburgh.[1]

With the country torn by sectional animosity that threatened to result in civil war, the venerable Senator Henry Clay early in 1850 introduced a series of resolutions designed to restore calm. His plan called for the admission of California as a free state, the organization of Utah and New Mexico as territories without reference to slavery, federal assumption of debts incurred by Texas in return for her renouncing her claim to any part of New Mexico, prohibition of the slave trade in the District of Columbia, and a stricter fugitive slave law. Clay's proposals touched off a heated debate in the Senate; throughout the country people came together to voice support or resistance. Chase, who regarded Pennsylvania as a pivotal state in the contest, urged Stanton to organize a meeting in Pittsburgh. "Let them declare not only the right but the sacred duty of Congress to prohibit slavery in the territories," he beseeched Stanton, who promised to start immediate arrangements for a Pittsburgh meeting.

[1] Chase to Stanton, July 2, Stanton to Maj. J. Sanders, July 17, 1849, Stanton MSS; Stanton to Chase, May 27, July 10, 1849, Chase Papers, HSP.

The next week there appeared on the walls of Pittsburgh buildings large posters announcing a meeting to support the immediate admission of California as a free state. About fifty persons gathered at the courthouse at the appointed time. The man called upon to take the chair protested that he did not know the organizers of the meeting and hoped someone would take charge. "No one responded to the repeated solicitations of the chair," the Pittsburgh *Gazette* reported, "and it became evident that no one present was inclined to assume any responsibility in regard to the meeting." It was finally resolved to adjourn the meeting until the following week; but again the crowd was small, and after adopting a resolution that "the Union be considered safe," the meeting adjourned sine die. If Stanton had taken any part in the meeting, he never showed his hand, and he left Pittsburgh soon after for an extended business trip, ostensibly to avoid a cholera epidemic.[2]

As Clay's compromise measures gradually won acceptance from moderate people throughout the country, Northern and Southern intransigents both stiffened their resistance. "There is no occasion for dismay," Stanton encouraged Chase, "much less for compromise or surrender." Perhaps it was "God's Providence" that California should become an independent republic "unfettered to the dead carcass of Southern slavery." Better that the Union should not add a star to its flag, he wrote, than that the slave power should increase its strength.

Chase agreed with him, and both men believed that Clay's measures would not pass. But they misjudged the temper of Congress. Upon the death of President Taylor, an opponent of compromise, and the accession to the presidency of Millard Fillmore, a proponent of Clay's measures, Clay and young Senator Stephen A. Douglas succeeded in rallying the moderates in Congress behind a series of bills which embodied the essential features of Clay's plan. Most fiercely disputed was the new fugitive slave law, which denied to alleged fugitives the right to testify on their own behalf, and the right to trial by jury at the place of apprehension, and put their fates in the hands of federal commissioners. The commissioner's fee was fixed at ten dollars if he decided for the claimant, five dollars if he decided for the slave, a virtual bribe in the eyes of antislavery men. And the law made anyone aiding a fugitive to escape liable to fine and imprisonment. Convinced that the basic issues were still unsettled, Stanton deplored the rigorous features of this law

[2] *Gazette*, April 9, 15, 1850; Pittsburgh *Daily Commercial Journal*, March 8, April 1, 6, 1850; Chase to Stanton, March 13, and Stanton to R. H. Walworth, July 29, Aug. 21, 1850, Ac. 6204-A, Stanton MSS; Stanton to Chase, March 27, 1850, Chase Papers, LC.

and the alacrity with which some former Wilmot Proviso men, beguiled by compromise, were becoming reconciled to it.[3]

Unable to heal the internal festers brought on by the sectional struggle, the Whig party was mortally sick; the Free-Soil movement had also spent its strength. Southern influence was becoming ever stronger in the Democratic party. When Cass and James Buchanan, two faithful party wheel horses, came on to take the lead as presidential possibilities for 1852, Stanton became disheartened. Court work took him to Washington in May, when the Democratic National Convention met in nearby Baltimore, and he could easily have slipped off to the sessions. But he had no desire to do so. Deadlocked on Cass and Buchanan, the convention finally nominated another dark horse, Franklin Pierce, of New Hampshire, on a platform that accepted the compromise measures of 1850 as a final settlement of the slavery issues.

Stanton had been in Washington a great deal the previous winter, but had found the city boring. "Besides the Presidential question there is nothing of any interest in Washington," he wrote. "There is no one in either branch of Congress that a person wishes to hear speak; neither is there any question of importance under discussion. . . . The Compromise is worn out, so that every body is sick of it. The Library [of Congress] is burnt up so that there are no books to read. There are not many pretty faces on the avenue to look at—handsome women are very scarce here. Stupid lectures are delivered at the Smithsonian." Lola Montez, the actress, furnished almost the sole attraction. Gossip said that Sam Houston, the doughty Texan, had been twice turned away from her lodgings. "She declined to see visitors in private," Stanton commented, "but shows herself nightly at the theatre for $1.50 per head." [4]

General Scott, the Whig presidential candidate, waged an ineffectual campaign. The New York "Barnburners," discouraged and thirsting for the spoils of victory, made peace with their Democratic brethren. Southern Whigs, offended by the antislavery proclivities of their Northern confreres, switched their allegiance to the Democrats. Pierce won in a landslide. The fact that this election spelled doom for the Whig party caused Stanton slight concern. But he deplored the degree to which the Democratic party was becoming the servant of complacency and vested interests.

Stephen A. Douglas also believed that the Democratic party needed

[3] Stanton to Chase, June 28, Sept. 7, 1851, Chase Papers, HSP; Chase to Stanton, July 16, 1851, Stanton MSS.

[4] To Tappan, Feb. 9, 1852, Wright Collection, LC; Gorham, *Stanton*, I, 74.

reinvigoration. This dynamic "Little Giant" was a heavy speculator in Chicago real estate and other western lands, and he therefore wanted a projected transcontinental railroad to run through the Nebraska region, instead of taking a more southerly route. He also hoped to give the Democratic party a new rallying cry that would appeal to Northerners and Southerners alike and thus loft him to the presidency.

To promote his railroad project, on which his other plans depended, it was essential for Douglas to encourage settlers to move into the Nebraska region. Accordingly, in January 1854, taking advantage of his position as chairman of the Senate committee on territories, he reported out a bill for the organization of Nebraska Territory. It would need Southern support to pass. Douglas offered a boon. His bill enunciated a principle which he called "popular sovereignty," by which settlers, after establishing a territorial government, could admit or exclude slavery as they chose.

Douglas's principle, as finally stated, meant the annulment of that provision of the 1820 Missouri Compromise which prohibited slavery in all of the Louisiana Purchase lying north and west of Missouri. He divided the new territory into Kansas and Nebraska, thereby giving Southerners a better chance of extending slavery into the southern part. President Pierce gave the bill the administration's support.

The slavery issue tore the country apart again. Antislavery Northerners were shocked at Douglas's cool renunciation of a solemn compact of thirty years' standing, which, after all, was of great antiquity in a nation only seventy-five years old. The South had no burning desire to extend slavery into Kansas. But Northern opposition to Douglas's measure made it a matter of Southern honor to demand equal rights in the territories, which meant the right to own slaves there.

Wholly unconcerned with the moral aspects of slavery, Douglas failed to understand the depths of Northern resentment and stuck grimly to his purpose. For months the battle that raged in Congress kept the nation at white heat. Visiting Washington in 1854, Stanton described the depression which the year's events had cast on the capital: "It . . . will not be a gay season. . . . The Hotels are not thronged as usual. . . . The . . . breaking up of all the old political organizations and the general uncertainties of the future in trade, politics, and finance, have cast a gloom over public spirit very visible here."

Party discipline triumphed. The bill was enacted into law. Northerners retaliated with new attacks on the hated fugitive slave law, with Charles Sumner, the tall, pedantic senator from Massachusetts, offering scathing speeches against it, to which Southerners responded with equal bitterness.

Stanton gained admission to the Senate floor, listened to one of Sumner's tirades, and expressed admiration for him. Chase had previously introduced him to the embattled New Englander, and Stanton sometimes encountered the pompous Sumner at the home of Dr. Gameliel Bailey, editor of the abolitionist *National Era,* and commended him on his course. Soon after, Stanton was able to help Bailey secure a substantial loan on some Washington real estate, and through this connection expanded his circle of antislavery connections.[5]

The passage of the Kansas-Nebraska Act resulted in drastic new party alignments, especially in the North. Abolitionists, Free-Soilers, old-line Whigs of antislavery convictions, and antislavery Democrats now took steps to join forces, drawn ineluctably into a loosely knit but aggressive new party that soon took the name Republican and avowed as its major purpose resistance to the further spread of slavery. Chase hastened to join it and became one of its leaders.

In a sense, the Republican movement was a resurgence of Jacksonian idealism, and this fact, together with the party's antislavery purpose, might have been expected to exert a strong pull on Stanton. But, so far as his correspondence shows, he felt no attraction to it. Though taking no public part in politics of any sort, he remained nominally a Democrat. He still professed antislavery sentiments to members of his family and to friends of like sympathies. To other persons he was reticent. He was keeping his resolve to stick closely to business.

Shortly before Stanton began practicing in Pittsburgh, his sister Pamphila and her husband had set up housekeeping in Akron. Stanton's mother and his young son Eddie went there to live with them, but Stanton promised his mother that he would always keep the Steubenville home so that she might return to it if she wished. This she did before many months had passed, taking Eddie with her.

As he prospered, Stanton employed a gardener and a handyman to maintain the Steubenville residence. An abandoned factory obscured the view of the river from the house, and Stanton had it torn down. On

---

[5] Stanton to Ellen Hutchison, Dec. 6, 1854, owned by Mrs. Van Swearingen; Wilson, "Jeremiah S. Black and Edwin M. Stanton," *loc. cit.,* 466; J.A.S. No. 130, pp. 45–6, No. 169, pp. 183–4, Recorder of Deeds, District of Columbia, on the loan. See also David Donald, *Charles Sumner and the Coming of the Civil War* (New York, 1960).

the extensive acreage thus cleared, which became known as "Stanton's Patch," he had a greenhouse built, and he himself planted fruit trees, flowers, and a vegetable garden. He bought a few head of purebred dairy cows, and on weekend visits from Pittsburgh he enjoyed milking them. Once in the haying season Stanton broke a new white-oak fork trying to show how big a load he could lift.

"He loved his son passionately," a servant recalled. "Often have I seen them walking about the yard . . . clasped arm in arm like two school girls." The boy had lost an eye as a result of an accident, and Stanton continually warned him to be careful at play. Each interlude in Steubenville meant presents for all, including the servants, and a visit to Mary's grave.[6] But as he prospered in the practice of law the opportunities to enjoy his Steubenville haven became fewer.

Stanton's natural gifts—energy, talent, utterance—fitted him particularly well for the life of a lawyer in Pittsburgh. With a population numbering some 46,000, it was already established as the "Iron City," where great workshops produced everything from tacks to steam engines. Paved with cobblestones, the downtown streets resounded to the clatter of one-horse drays and two-wheeled carts and the curses and shouts of sweating stevedores. At the junction of the Monongahela and Allegheny rivers lay the city's business center, already famous as the "Golden Triangle." Railroads, canals, and overland routes connected the city with Philadelphia and Baltimore; the Ohio River carried commerce to and from the western and southern markets.

Stanton saw opportunity for himself in this boom town. Though people were beginning to move out from the city's center to new homes on the high, steep hills to the north, he lodged downtown at the Monongahela House and later at the St. Charles Hotel, amid the din and the bustle. Here the industrial smoke lay so thick that one wag suggested that when the telegraph came to Pittsburgh, hams could be hung on the wires to cure. On the other hand, boosters claimed that sufferers from asthma benefited from the polluted atmosphere, which may have explained Stanton's choice of a downtown residence.[7]

He soon became a familiar figure. "It was here in his early prime that I, as a telegraph messenger boy, had the pleasure of seeing him frequently," recalled Andrew Carnegie, who rememberd Stanton as a "vigorous, energetic, and concentrated man, always intent upon the

[6] Wolcott MS, 130–1; Flower, *Stanton*, 49–51.

[7] Catherine E. Reiser, "Pittsburgh, the Hub of Western Commerce," *WPhM*, XXV, 121–34; Neville B. Craig, *The History of Pittsburgh* (Pittsburgh, 1851), 299–312.

subject in hand . . . ever deeply serious." Stanton's self-description
bears out Carnegie's impression. "The practice of law here and in
Ohio furnishes employment for all my time and facilities," he later
wrote Chase; ". . . my habits are gradually conforming to the daily
round of mere business and like a stage horse I am growing accustomed to the crib & the stall of a tavern." [8]

This peripatetic life was of his own choosing. Determined to raise
his professional reputation and income as quickly as possible, Stanton
was unable to sit back and wait for a rich practice to develop in Pittsburgh. Instead he busied himself with maintaining his Ohio clientele
and with extending his connections to Harrisburg, Philadelphia, and
Washington. Although he particularly welcomed corporate business and
became skilled in mercantile affairs, he took clients as they came.
Whether the case at hand was large or small, he was always out to
win. In the higher courts, as in the lower ones, he relied chiefly on
hard work. Stanton seemed to sense what correct legal behavior was.
He spoke vehemently when arguing before a jury in a lower court, and
was headstrong and impetuous in his manner. But he became calm,
deliberate, and dignified before a higher court, where reason rather
than emotion would be likely to govern the decision. In important cases
he composed his arguments in advance, then committed them to
memory, so that his audiences were impressed by the vigor of a seemingly extempore production which was as complete as a written speech.

Stanton's cold, clear logic more than compensated for his lack of
oratorical graces. Though he often spoke too rapidly for pleasant listening, his deep voice gave an impression of strength, and he sometimes achieved striking effects in his choice of words.[9]

His words could also sting. Earnest and combative, he hung on tena-
ciously, browbeating and ridiculing witnesses and often antagonizing
spectators. Emulating his superiors in their status-conscious snobbery,
Stanton practiced a haughty rudeness to those he considered to be in-
feriors in his profession. His cousin, young William Stanton, observed
him arguing an important case in the United States Court at Pittsburgh.
"The lawyers opposing him were country lawyers—from Kittatinny,
Pa.— It was hard to tell which were the most 'haughty, severe, domineering, and rude' in his treatment of those lawyers, Stanton, or the
Judge of the Court, Grier. I thought if anybody should treat me so I

[8] Carnegie, "Stanton, the Patriot," *OSAHQ*, XV, 293–4; to Chase, May 27, 1849,
Chase Papers, HSP.
[9] Supreme Court, *Eulogies*, 7; Gorham, *Stanton*, I, 45; Pratt, *Stanton*, 54–5.

would want very much to shoot him—and both Judge Grier and [Edwin] Stanton deserved it." [1]

Sometimes his victims did threaten him with physical violence in retaliation. Once he had the sheriff of Cadiz escort him to his office from the courthouse, less from cowardice, his colleagues believed, than from a wish to avoid fruitless controversy. On another occasion he was so rude to a witness in a Steubenville case that Roderick S. Moody, the opposition attorney, protested. Stanton lost patience. "Moody," he snapped, "you always whine when I question your witnesses." Moody, a capable lawyer four years Stanton's junior, retorted: "I don't know that a whine is worse than a bark." Stanton had the last word, saying out of the corner of his mouth: "Puppies whine."

Moody was furious. While the court recessed he waited for Stanton to emerge from the office of Stanton & McCook, up Third Street. Soon Stanton appeared, carrying a stout cane, for an injured knee still pained him. He had a big bundle of papers under one arm, his spectacles were on, and he was accompanied by McCook. As the two men reached the courthouse yard Moody rushed out of the building and flung himself on Stanton. Taken by surprise, Stanton went down hard, cane, spectacles, and papers flying in all directions. McCook pulled Moody off. Stanton, groping for his cane and pushing himself up with it, rushed at Moody, crying: "Damn him! I will punish him for this!" Spectators intervened, and McCook chided Moody for attacking Stanton without warning, whereupon the irate Moody squared off against McCook, whose service in the Mexican War had enhanced his reputation for fearless physical prowess. "Damn your impudence," cried the colonel, "would you dare fight me?" Quiet was restored at last, and court resumed; and over the years Stanton and Moody became good friends. [2]

Part of Stanton's brusqueness was an act designed to ward off intimacies and to preserve himself against new personal hurts. A fellow

[1] William Stanton to Mrs. O. S. Picher, Oct. 12, 1907, owned by William Stanton Picher.

[2] In fact, when Stanton's sister Oella had another falling out with her husband, Dr. Tappan, and decided to sue him for divorce, Stanton employed Moody as her attorney, serving as associate counsel himself. Moody won a divorce decree, with generous alimony, for Oella, but Dr. Tappan had previously disposed of most of his property and evaded the judgment. Stanton was obliged to provide a home for Oella and her five children, and his relations with the Tappans, which had been worsening for years, in 1853 reached the breaking point. Wolcott MS, 131; Flower, *Stanton*, 61–2; Stanton to E. L. Tappan, March 25, 1856, copy owned by the estate of Benjamin P. Thomas; Jefferson County Appearance Record K, 449, and Common Pleas Journal, XVI, 379–80.

lawyer asked him for a personal loan and was rudely repulsed. But that night the man found the needed sum in his room with a note from Stanton telling him to ask for more if and when necessary. Young William Stanton remembered how the older man was full of hospitality and help the moment the day's work was done. Edwin Stanton's instinct was to hide his need for friendship behind a stern mask, and to concentrate completely on the case at hand and win it. The law and the courtroom were serious matters to him, and he had no place for levity in his mind or manner. William Stanton recalled how Edwin became impatient at the humorous opening address of an opposition attorney. When the man finished, Stanton rose and said in a stern tone: "Now that this extraordinary flow of wit has ceased I will begin." The other lawyer retorted: "Wit always ceases when you begin." Ignoring the laughter that came from the judge and spectators, Stanton went ahead with his sober but convincing presentation, and won the case.[3]

Winning was what mattered to him, and he was willing to take risks in search of victory. When reprimanded by a judge for excessive behavior, and ordered to sit down, he obeyed, but he would be back on his feet immediately, and would gain his point. He established a reputation for obtaining verdicts and judgments for his clients and his business increased. Stanton's willingness to resort to any needed technique in order to impress judges and juries made him popular in this semi-frontier region where the law was nothing sacred and where a premium was placed on success. When seeking to establish a young man's paternity of an illegitimate baby, Stanton carried the child to the courtroom, held her on his lap during the preliminaries, and when he rose to speak, gently placed the baby in her mother's arms and in quiet, gentle terms established the facts of parentage. Defending a prisoner on a charge of first-degree murder, he deliberately swallowed some of the poison which had allegedly killed the victim in order to prove that because it could not be retained, the liquid could not kill. Horribly sick, he vomited it up, and saved his client's neck.[4]

A man accused of theft was brought to trial and the presiding judge asked him if he had an attorney to represent him. The defendant mumbled that he had not. Asked to look around the courtroom and choose as counsel anyone he saw, the man pointed to Stanton. Then the judge

[3] William Stanton to Mrs. O. S. Picher, Oct. 12, 1907, and Edwin to William Stanton, Oct. 20, 1854, owned by William Stanton Picher; John P. Usher, *President Lincoln's Cabinet* (Omaha, 1925), 23.

[4] Wolcott MS, 55; Howe, *op. cit.,* I, 896, 976, II, 177; Shotwell, *op. cit.,* 72-7; Hunter, "Pathfinders of Jefferson County," *loc. cit.,* 219.

read the indictment and asked the defendant to plead guilty or not guilty. Instead of replying, the fellow gazed vacantly this way and that, mumbling incoherently as he did so, and then laughed aloud. Stanton arose and asserted that his client was obviously insane, moved that the court discharge the prisoner, and when the judge agreed, led the man tenderly out of the building. Weeks later it leaked out that Stanton had coached the defendant in his cell before the trial. Stanton's fellow lawyers, the judge concerned, and many of the townspeople applauded this shrewd maneuvering.

Even in cold weather, the end of a day in court found this intense lawyer with wilted collar and clothes soaked in sweat. All of Stanton's associates were impressed by his combativeness in pleading. "Though the heavens fell," one recalled, "he would never let up; it was push through or die."

He enjoyed finding loopholes in the law. For example, Lisbon, Ohio, had an ordinance setting a ten-dollar fine for wagon drivers who rutted the hilly main street by driving down its sloping length with locked brakes. An old Quaker, refusing to be bound by restrictions, added deep trenches to the street's already lunar surface. Stanton got him off without penalty by making the point that the law prescribed punishment only for driving *down* the street; his client had perversely added yokes of oxen to his horse teams and strained *up* the grade with the brakes engaged.

Another case early in his career was of particular importance. It involved a client's suit against monopolists of grain and pork distribution in Ohio. "Stanton had about staked his life on winning," another Steubenbenville lawyer recalled. "He argued part of one day and all the next. Before noon he had torn off his cravat and opened the collar of his shirt, for he always feared apoplexy. As night drew on I thought he would drop dead. He was black in the face. In the evening the case went to the jury. Stanton left the chamber and all night he and I walked up and down in front of the courthouse, discussing the trial and waiting for the verdict. Finally, at sunrise, the jury brought in a verdict for Stanton, and his rejoicing was ten times greater than that of the client he had saved from ruin." [5]

Each time he returned to Pittsburgh after a round of such cases, Stanton retired to self-imposed obscurity. An occasional cigar, light wines, and books provided companionship for him during the solitary

[5] Flower, *Stanton*, 42–4; Howe, *op. cit.*, I, 972; Charles W. Batchelor, *Incidents in My Life* (Pittsburgh, 1887), 252–3; undated memo, *ca.* 1855, on cases described, in Stanton's hand, owned by the estate of Benjamin P. Thomas.

evenings. He reread Plutarch's life of Caesar, finding in it confirmation of his distrust of all aristocracies, enjoyed Charlotte Brontë's *Jane Eyre* and Madame de Staël's *Thoughts on the French Revolution*, and became a devotee of Dickens. Stanton found a new interest in studying the lives of great men, and, invited out one evening, he showed off his knowledge of Napoleon.

Finding this hermitic existence too bare to endure, Stanton reached out for friendship. To Daniel Sickles, a young lawyer thrilled at associating with Stanton, already prominent in the law, the older man was a kind, amusing colleague. They walked together along the Golden Triangle while Stanton "boosted" the future of the West. Once when Sickles was Stanton's house guest, he found that his host disapproved of his addiction to reading light novels. Before he left, Sickles deliberately put a few popular romances where Stanton could find them. Years later Stanton confessed to him that he had read and enjoyed them, and always after took pleasure in all kinds of fiction.[6]

But most of the people who did not know him so well found Stanton an unpleasantly intense person. Impressed by the beauty of some stories from *Godey's Lady's Book* which Pamphila sent him, Stanton learned that the author, Sarah Jane Clarke, lived near Pittsburgh, and quickly managed to meet her. "He was awfully earnest," she recalled. "A pun nearly cost me his friendship, and it was a good pun, too."

Stanton continued to find comfort in the Bible, and he became active in a Sunday-evening Bible class formed and directed by his Kenyon mentor, Heman Dyer. Heretofore the Acts of the Apostles and the Epistles of Paul had provided his favorite passages, but now Stanton discovered, as he wrote to Chase, that he had been "overlooking the merits of the great teacher, Christ, and dwelling on those below him."[7]

Business cares were a blessing to Stanton during this lonely period in his life. His office with Shaler was on Fourth Street, between Wood and Market, in the heart of the Golden Triangle. With Pittsburgh creating wealth at an astounding rate, fees began to come in so rapidly that the partners were impelled to call in Stanton's New Lisbon associate to handle the firm's finances.

Two cases were largely responsible for this quick rise to legal emi-

[6] Sickles, "Address on the Centennial of Jefferson County," OAHS *Publications*, VI, 330; Hunter, "Pathfinders of Jefferson County," *loc. cit.*, 219–21; Wolcott MS, 115, 127–30, 148.

[7] Agnes L. Starrett, *Through One Hundred and Fifty Years* (Pittsburgh, 1937), 113; *Abraham Lincoln: Tributes from His Associates* (New York, 1895), 110; to Chase, May 27, 1849, Chase Papers, HSP; Hiram Schock, "Edwin M. Stanton, Pittsburgh Lawyer," *Pittsburgh Legal Journal*, LXX, 3.

nence. Pittsburgh's burgeoning factories had given rise to miserable job and housing conditions. Workers, especially in the textile mills, demanded a reduction of the working day to ten hours. Their employers bitterly opposed this demand. To coerce the stubborn millworkers into submission, the owners closed the mills. Serious riots broke out. Imported scabs and strikers clashed in bitter fights, and a boycott of the struck plants cut sharply into the owners' local market.

Stanton, representing the owners, initiated a series of damage suits against the strikers, thirteen of whom, some of them women, received jail sentences. At the same time he achieved mutual acceptance of the ten-hour day, but the workers took with it a decrease in wages. When the struck mills reopened peaceably, Stanton had a profitable addition to his firm's clientele, and it soon brought in even richer business.[8]

The other case responsible for Stanton's success in Pittsburgh involved the very destiny of the city. Downriver at Wheeling, a Virginia corporation, with the consent of the state of Ohio, was throwing the longest suspension bridge in the world across the Ohio River. By facilitating travel along the National Road, it promised to make Wheeling the gateway to the West. The bridge's central span, though ninety feet above low-water level, did not allow sufficient clearance for the soaring smokestacks of the larger river packets. If the structure should prevent them from ascending the river beyond Wheeling, that city, as the head of navigation, would draw highway, railroad, and river traffic to it, leaving Pittsburgh sequestered.

On August 16, 1849, Stanton appeared before U. S. Supreme Court Justice R. C. Grier in the federal circuit court in Philadelphia to seek an injunction against the bridge company on behalf of the state of Pennsylvania at the instance of her attorney general. He claimed that the Ohio River was a navigable stream, free to the citizens of Pennsylvania as well as those of other states; that the bridge under construction would hinder those citizens in the use of the river and thus work irreparable injury to their trade, commerce, and business; and that the bridge would also diminish the revenues derived by the state of Pennsylvania from its system of canals and railroads to the point of rendering that system useless.

Grier declared that the private citizens who alleged injury must seek redress in a lower court. But the U. S. Supreme Court did have original

[8] To Walworth, Jan. 5, 1851, Ac. 6204-A, Stanton MSS; Henry K. Seibeneck, "Pittsburgh's Civil War Fortification Claims," *WPHM*, XXVII, 5–6; "The Factory Riots in Allegheny City, *ibid.*, V, 203–11; Leland Baldwin, *Pittsburgh, the Story of a City* (Pittsburgh, 1938), 227.

jurisdiction insofar as Pennsylvania itself was concerned, and he gave Stanton leave to file therein for an injunction on its behalf.

Stanton was delighted. He had feared that Grier would dismiss his motion entirely, for lack of jurisdiction. Now he was worried that the company would raise the height of the bridge without further proceedings. "But this I do not desire," he confessed to a friend. "Having my hand in I am disposed to push it to the girth."

An accident on Pittsburgh's icy streets resulted in a broken leg for Stanton. But he was able to travel painfully to Washington, where on February 25, 1850, he was admitted to practice in the U. S. Supreme Court and made his first argument. The Court met in a small room in the basement of the Capitol immediately below the Senate Chamber. Heavily carpeted and richly furnished, it had an atmosphere of awesome dignity. Reverdy Johnson, of Maryland, an acknowledged leader of the American bar, appeared for the bridge company and contended that the Court lacked jurisdiction. But the justices sustained Stanton on this all-important point, and appointed a commissioner to take testimony from the respective parties concerning whether the bridge was or was not an obstruction to navigation by steam or sail, and if so, what alterations in it would be necessary to make the river fully navigable.

To gather these facts, Stanton journeyed up and down the Ohio River obtaining data on how various smokestack heights affected vessels' fuel consumption and efficiency of operation, and stopping off at the larger towns to amass statistics bearing on the nature, volume, and value of commerce on the river and the relative costs and advantages of railroad and water transportation. While interviewing a pilot he fell into the hold of the steamer *Isaac Newton* and suffered a compound fracture of the kneecap on his already injured leg. Taken to Steubenville by steamer and carried to his home on a stretcher, he was obliged to lie flat on his back for several weeks.[9] For a time he feared that he would never walk again; when he did, it was with a severe limp, which improved but never entirely left him.

The Court's commissioner fully accepted Stanton's argument that the bridge unlawfully obstructed navigation and that it should be raised higher above the channel or removed altogether. At the next court

---

[9] Wolcott MS, 140–2; Office of the Clerk, U. S. Supreme Court, Attorneys Roll (1850) ; Stanton to Robert Walker, Nov. 20, 1849, HL; James M. Callahan, "The Pittsburgh-Wheeling Rivalry for Commercial Headship on the Ohio," *OAHSQ*, XXII, 40–6; Chase to Stanton, Dec. 14, 1849, and Stanton to Maj. John Sanders, undated, Stanton MSS. The case is in 9 Howard 647–59.

term, in December 1851, the Court upheld these findings, whereupon the bridge company asked permission to make a draw in the bridge, instead of raising it. Stanton then argued that the size of the vessels that would be using the draw, the strong current, and the winds would make passage through such a contracted space both dangerous and impracticable. The Court agreed, but granted the bridge company permission to obtain the opinion of an independent engineer. The engineer that the company consulted also thought that a draw in the suspension bridge would be impracticable, but said that one could be constructed in the wooden portion of the span over the western channel of the river, which flowed between Zane's Island and the Ohio shore, though this would also involve the opening of a new channel there.

This report became the subject of another argument before the Court when Stanton filed objections to it. At last, the Court gave the defendants the option of complying with its original decree by raising the bridge, or constructing a draw in the wooden bridge and clearing the obstructions from the western channel on their own responsibility, with leave to the plaintiff to reinstitute the suit if the latter procedure did not make the river fully navigable.

It was a signal triumph for Stanton. His dramatic maneuver in 1850 of chartering the steamer *Hibernia* and running it full-tilt under the bridge—delightedly watching its eighty-five-foot-tall smokestacks rip away and its superstructure collapse—in order to demonstrate the inadequate height of the bridge, received wide publicity. The minute, detailed researches he had conducted into navigation and commerce made his arguments overwhelmingly impressive and increased his stature as an inventive, able attorney. Stanton's work in the Bridge case brought him appeals from prominent persons that he take on the tutelage of their sons. It also gave him the entrance he craved into the higher levels of the law. The Erie Railroad became his client. Stanton successfully argued the right of David Levy Yulee, of Florida, to a seat in the United States Senate, asserting that each house of Congress had plenary powers to judge the qualifications of its members, independent of the executive and judicial branches of the government. He never forgot this conclusion concerning legislative autonomy.[1]

[1] Stanton's part in the Bridge case is best derived from ACS. 6204 and 6204-A, Stanton MSS, and the Simon Gratz Collection, HSP, and 11 Howard 528–9; 13 Howard 518–628. Congress bypassed the Court's decision by declaring the bridge part of a post road, but this did no harm to Stanton's reputation. See also Mary I. Ellet, "Memoirs," *Bucks County Historical Society Papers*, VIII, 319–20n.; Stanton to William Johnston, July 18, 1855, *WPHM*, XII, 266; Stanton, *Argument . . . in Florida Contested Election Case* (Washington, 1852).

Among the fruits Stanton enjoyed as a result of his handling of the Bridge case was an invitation to join with the country's ablest patent attorneys, George Harding, of Philadelphia, and Peter H. Watson, of Washington, in arguing a case of national significance. Back in 1831, in Lexington, Virginia, young Cyrus H. McCormick had put together a mechanical reaping machine that was immediately successful. A few years later he and his brother opened a plant for the manufacture of reapers in Chicago. McCormick made improvements and took out patents from time to time, but reapers came into such demand that other companies began to manufacture very similar machines. One of the most aggressive of these competitors was the John H. Manny Company, of Rockford, Illinois.

In 1854 McCormick brought suit for patent infringement against Manny and his associates in the federal district court at Chicago. With the demand for reapers swelling year by year, it would be a battle for high stakes. Both sides were prepared to spend money without stint, and they employed the best lawyers obtainable. That Stanton was chosen to assist Harding and Watson is the measure of his increasing prominence.

The chief problem confronting the defense attorneys as the case came on to trial in September 1855 was to disprove McCormick's right to the exclusive use of a divider device at the outer end of the cutter bar which separated the falling from the standing grain and kept the machine from choking up. To that end, Watson, who planned the strategy for the Manny side, used gross chicanery. He employed William P. Wood, a Washington modelmaker, to search the Virginia countryside for old reapers. Wood found one built in 1844, the year before McCormick obtained his patent. To make sure that it would appear to antedate McCormick's patent, Wood took the divider to a blacksmith and had him alter it to resemble Manny's, then "rusted over" the fresh marks by applying salt and vinegar, and even found witnesses who were willing to tell the court that this machine had been used as early as 1842 or 1843. But the witnesses broke down under cross-examination, whereupon Stanton's colleagues tried to show that McCormick had failed to patent his divider for so long that it had passed into public use. But again McCormick's lawyers refuted the adverse testimony.

Years afterward, Wood and Albert E. H. Johnson, a clerk in Watson's office at the time of the trial and later in Stanton's employ, told of their part in these subterfuges. They stated that Watson alone, of Manny's counsel, knew about the fraud. It is unlikely that Watson would or could have kept the secret from Harding, the senior man on Manny's staff. But it is quite possible that Stanton, much the junior of the trio, and assigned only to a particular phase of legal research in the case, knew nothing of what Watson was up to.

Most puzzling of all is why such deception was resorted to, when there would seem to have been no need of it. For Manny's lawyers amassed facts as well as fictions on his side, and the verdict supported him in every particular. It seems most probable from the evidence that Wood, aged and penniless, sold Watson a bill of goods by alleging that McCormick's patent rights were stronger than the facts warranted.[2]

Whatever Stanton's involvement in the assembling of untrue evidence, his role in the trial has been vastly overblown and distorted because of Abraham Lincoln's connection with it. Supposing the case would be tried in Chicago, Harding, in keeping with common practice, had sent Watson there to employ some lawyer who was well known in local court circles and who enjoyed the confidence of the judge. Watson heard of "Abe" Lincoln, of Springfield, Illinois, and though wholly unimpressed by the gawky, drawling fellow, employed him with a retainer of $400. Before the case came to trial, however, it was transferred to Cincinnati, and none of Manny's lawyers gave further thought to Lincoln.

One day as Harding and Stanton were leaving their hotel in Cincinnati to go to court, they saw a man standing on the steps. Harding realized from Watson's previous unflattering description that this was their now unwanted colleague, Lincoln. After an exchange of civilities, Lincoln proposed that they all go to the courthouse "in a gang." Stanton and Harding thereupon snubbed the interloper and went on without him.

Without question Stanton was rude, snobbish, and supercilious toward the unknown Lincoln. But so was everyone else connected with the case. Harding, for example, never opened the lengthy manuscript which Lincoln had prepared as his contribution. When one of the presiding jurists entertained the counsel on both sides, Lincoln was not invited. Although all the lawyers were staying at the same hotel, none asked Lincoln to share their table, to visit them in their rooms, or to join them on the daily walks to and from the court. Stanton never

---

[2] Wood's and Johnson's affidavits in Frank A. Flower's ms, "McCormick vs. Manny, History of Discovering the Trick by Which the U. S. Supreme Court Was Defeated and Defrauded (with Sworn Affidavits)," McCormick Collection, WSHS; Flower, *Stanton*, 64; William T. Hutchison, *Cyrus Hall McCormick* (New York, 1931), I, 431–52; 6 *McLean's Reports* 539–57.

mentioned him in his letters to family and friends, though he carefully described other persons connected with this important case. Everyone assumed, it appears, that Lincoln was an intruder because the case was now in Ohio rather than in Illinois. His presence in Cincinnati was entirely his own business, although Watson later paid him the agreed upon retainer, which Lincoln accepted. Stanton was merely one among those who made Lincoln's inferior position clear to him. Charles F. Benjamin, later a clerk in Stanton's employ, in describing this combination of personalities, "including Stanton's hauteur and Lincoln's gaucherie," correctly asserted that the Stanton-Lincoln relationship was but one among the many involved.

Stanton's role in the case itself has been greatly overstated. The major source of information has been a letter from one of Manny's partners to Stanton's biographer Flower, in which almost charismatic qualities are attributed to Stanton's legal and oratorical abilities. A far more accurate description of Stanton's modest role emerges from his own letters, only now available.

"Last evening I was very anxious," Stanton wrote the day after the case opened, "for Mr. Harding had been unwell several days, and I was apprehensive that he would not be able to be in the Court." Stanton feared that certain technical aspects of the case, which by agreement with Harding he had ignored, would become his responsibility. Characteristically, he stayed awake all night to inform himself on the technicalities of machine functions. Morning brought improvement to Harding, and Stanton was vastly relieved. "The case is the most important Patent cause that has ever been tried," he wrote, "and more money and brains have been expended in getting it ready for argument, than any other . . . ever has had bestowed upon it." Stanton confessed that Harding was a far abler lawyer than he at arguing intricate points of patent law: "His manner and style is admirably well adapted for scientific discussion and illustration, and that is precisely the duty required on the present occasion."

As the junior of the lawyers on Manny's side, Stanton performed ably as the diligent researcher in points of general law and in summing up the case for the court. Lincoln, who stayed on despite the rebuffs, and who admired the professional techniques of the counsel, learned important lessons in legal practice. But the rapturous reaction of judges and onlookers to Stanton's skill which Flower accepted is at least questionable.

Equally dubious is the account that Piatt, Stanton's journalist friend, gave of Stanton's reaction to Lincoln. Piatt has Stanton describing

Lincoln as "the long, lank creature from Illinois, wearing a dirty linen duster coat, on the back of which the perspiration had splotched two wide stains that . . . resembled the dirty map of the continent." According to Piatt, Stanton had declared: "If that giraffe appeared in the case I would throw up my brief and leave."

Stanton's acidulous description of Lincoln is believable, even though the precise language may not be accurate. But a decision to abandon the case if Lincoln participated is completely out of character. Lincoln was never in the case once it was moved from Chicago. There was no need for Stanton to make such a dire professional choice. And it should be remembered that Piatt, according to a contemporary, was widely known in Washington as two of the three greatest liars in the town.[3]

The strains of his demanding professional schedule, the effects of his injuries and his family tragedies, and the unnervement caused by a series of illnesses his son suffered, had combined to change Stanton. Piatt, who had known him in Columbus as a hearty, cheerful young man, encountered him in Washington and was amazed at his appearance, and Piatt's description in this instance is verified by other evidence. A beard now covered Stanton's once smooth chin and cheeks. "For a second," Piatt recalled, "the old, well-loved gleam of pleasure lit his face, and then faded out and a gloomy, sad expression took its place. . . . His manner, so cold, reserved, and formal, embarrassed me." Piatt later had occasion to call on Stanton in his hotel room. Leaving and then returning unexpectedly for a final word, he found Stanton sobbing.

Clearly, the substantial successes Stanton had achieved in the law and the comfortable income this was bringing him, failed to lift his spirits. He began to question his decision to dedicate all his effort to self-advancement, and even the desirability of life as a lawyer. Success as an attorney, he warned William Stanton, whose education he was overseeing, "depends upon many contingencies that cannot be foreseen, and even successful practice brings much smaller remuneration than is generally supposed by outsiders. . . . I would not advise

[3] On Stanton's role, new evidence in his letter to Ellen Hutchison, Sept. 25, 1855, owned by Mrs. Van Swearingen. See also Flower, *Stanton,* 62-3; Emerson Hinschliff, "Lincoln and the 'Patent Case,' " ISHS *Journal,* XXXIII, 361-5; Donn Piatt, *op. cit.,* 56; S. P. Pillsbury to Horace White, Oct. 14, 1913, and Charles F. Benjamin to same, June 1, 1914, White Papers, ISHL. An analysis of the evidence is available in Hyman, "A Man Out of Manuscripts: Edwin M. Stanton at the McCormick Reaper Trial," *Manuscripts,* XII, 35-9.

a son or friend of mine to choose the law; indeed I would rather my son did not. But on the other hand I would not dissuade any one who feels a clear call to the profession. . . . This only I can assure you; that you will have any aid and direction in the study that I may be able to give you."

Stanton came to realize that part of his need was for female companionship. In a rare moment of frankness, he admitted to Reuben Walworth, the Supreme Court's commissioner in the Bridge case, with whom he had established a close friendship, that "for myself I have been too much occupied with other engagements to think of what would probably much more contribute to my happiness."

He would never forget Mary. But his nature required someone to love as he had loved her. Without this, success lacked meaning.[4]

[4] Donn Piatt, *op. cit.*, 54–5; to Walworth, Jan. 5, 1851, Ac. 6204-A, Stanton MSS; to William Stanton, Oct. 24, 1854, owned by William Stanton Picher.

CHAPTER IV

AT THE HEIGHTS OF THE LAW

Time and professional preoccupation dulled the ache in Stanton's heart caused by Mary's death, and by the mid-1850's he was mingling more often in society. His renewed interest in social life had gained impetus from his acquaintance with Ellen Hutchison, a tall, well-poised girl, sixteen years his junior, with deep blue eyes and luxurious blond hair. Her father, Lewis Hutchison, was a descendant of the explorer Meriwether Lewis and had accumulated substantial wealth as a shipper, warehouseman, and wholesale foodseller. His family was socially prominent in Pittsburgh and owned the church pew directly in front of Stanton's. It was here, as the minister of the church later recalled to Ellen, "he experienced his first feeling of interest in you."

When Stanton met Ellen she was recovering from an unhappy love affair, and he afforded the young woman gentle sympathy. "The trouble of early love fell like a killing frost," he wrote, but assured her that happiness could again return. He sent her long letters from the varied places to which his cases took him, and warned Ellen that if he were to write her each time she was in his thoughts, his letters would become burdens.

They exchanged lengthy literary and philosophical observations, and Stanton delighted in her breadth of reading experience and variety of interests. He was troubled that she had no liking for poetry; "How can that be when you love Shakespeare and Milton and are so fond of music?" On a visit to Washington in 1854, he wrote her of the impressive ceremonies attending the opening of the Supreme Court session, adding: "You would laugh to see Judge Grier striding in with the tail of his gown flying in the wind."

He told Ellen of his daily routine in Washington: breakfast at nine, work in the Supreme Court from eleven till three, and dinner at four, followed by study in the law library or infrequently by social diversions until bedtime. The Bridge case occupied his thoughts by day and Ellen by night. By the end of 1854 he had confessed his love to her; in early February 1855 he proposed marriage. She withheld a definite reply. "Allow me then after the fashion of old to offer myself as your Valentine," he wrote two weeks later. "Be thou mine as I am thine." [1]

In their growing intimacy, Stanton revealed himself to Ellen. "There is so much of the hard and repulsive in my—(I will not say nature, for that I think is soft and tender) but in the temper and habits of life generated by adverse circumstances, that great love only can bear with and overlook." He dwelt on his first wife and their son, and described a Fourth of July outing with his mother, Eddie, and Darwin's widow and children in a wild glen near Steubenville, where he and Eddie, sprawling on a warm, moss-covered rock, had rested, talked, and recited poetry while the others fished or strolled in the woods.

But Stanton's courtship did not follow a smooth path. His temper, always ready to lash out, met Ellen's stubborn resistance. When Ellen's mother protested against her twenty-six-year-old daughter's contemplating marriage to a man of forty-one, Stanton wisely let Ellen handle Mrs. Hutchison in her own way. She eventually consented, but insisted that they live in the Hutchison home. Stanton refused, and was ready to suggest that he and Ellen make their home in Steubenville, which would have meant abandoning the rich practice he was building from his Pittsburgh office, when Mrs. Hutchison acquiesced in a separate Stanton household.

On March 16, 1856, he placed an engagement ring on Ellen's finger; they solemnized the event by exchanging a lawyerlike vow he had written: "To bind our hearts in a band of perpetual love, we do solemnly promise each other never to part without a kiss of love to each other—and if any difference or misunderstanding should hereafter occur between us . . . we will not separate without a kiss of forgiveness and reconciliation." Called again to Washington, he wrote of his attendance at a wedding party there and described the elegance of the

---

[1] Stanton to Ellen, Dec. 6, 1854, and ms memorandum by Lewis Hutchison Stanton, owned by Gideon Townsend Stanton; Oct. 10, 28, Dec. 3, 11, 1854, Feb. 14, 15, 1855, owned by Mrs. Van Swearingen; Rev. E. M. Van Deusen to Ellen, Jan. 4, 1870 (misdated 1869), Ac. 1039, Stanton MSS; Flower, *Stanton*, 66.

capital's social leaders—carefully adding that in nobility of features, sweetness of expression, and charm of manners, she ranked higher than the flashing beauties around him.[2]

June 25, 1856, their wedding day, dawned clear and mild. Stanton woke and wrote to his bride: "On this morning . . . I salute you with assurances of deep and devoted love, that this evening will be attested by solemn vow[s] before the world and in the presence of God. . . . May our Heavenly Father bestow his blessing upon the union." He had found again what he had thought lost forever with Mary's death— love of the abiding sort—and approached his second marriage "with calm and joyful hope, disturbed by no conflicting feeling, quiet and peaceful."

It was a small wedding, held in Ellen's home, with forty persons present and without ushers or bridesmaids. Ellen's dress was a white satin so heavy that her brother thought it would stand alone. George Harding, Stanton's associate in the Reaper case, sent Ellen a beautiful cross of heavy gold set with pearls and diamonds, which she wore on a chain. Dr. Theodore Lyman, rector of Trinity Episcopal Church, conducted the service, and the couple left on a honeymoon which took them to Niagara Falls, Montreal, Quebec, the White Mountains, and Nahant, Massachusetts.

Stanton had learned during their courtship that Ellen had a will of her own, but as a wife she brought cheer, social charm, and an element of common sense that had been lacking in Stanton's life. Her steadiness counterbalanced his excitability. She became a mother to young Eddie and was welcomed into the family by Stanton's mother and sisters, although this initial accord among the Stanton women later soured.

Uncertain at first whether to live in Pittsburgh, Philadelphia, or Washington, the Stantons finally decided on Washington, in part because he had assurances stemming from his associations in the Reaper case that he would secure a substantial practice before the Supreme Court. They took rooms in the National Hotel while looking for a house, and Ellen immediately became a victim of the mystifying "National Hotel disease," known now to have been amoebic dysentery, which

---

[2] Stanton to Ellen, May 21, 1855, undated (*ca.* Jan. 1856), Jan. 4, March 16, 1856, owned by Mrs. Van Swearingen; July 4, 1855, Jan. 31, April 11, 1856, owned by Gideon Townsend Stanton. Flower, *Stanton*, 66, accepts the recollection of Stanton's gardener in Steubenville that Edwin burned all of his and Mary's letters at about this time. This is incorrect, as Stanton later printed some of these in a brochure in order that his son might have them.

prostrated many of its guests. Soon they leased a house at 365 C Street, N.W., where Stanton had his office in the basement. But he maintained his Pittsburgh association with Shaler and, waiting proof that the Washington move would be permanent, he left his law library in Shaler's care.

For Stanton, life held new promise.[3] Sustained study and hard toil had won him an ample income and high rank in his profession. The agony of a lost love had become a tender memory, and his second marriage had again brought him the affection that he craved. Engrossed in business, he no longer took any public part in politics. While he concentrated on his own career, the nation moved along a fateful path toward disruption.

When Douglas's principle of popular sovereignty was applied in Kansas, a virtual civil war erupted there. President Pierce threw his support to the proslavery faction, which had forcibly gained control of the territorial legislature. With newspapers headlining these events, the presidential election of 1856 approached. The Democratic National Convention nominated Buchanan for President, with John C. Breckinridge, of Kentucky, as his running mate, and endorsed Douglas's popular sovereignty doctrine "as the only sound and safe solution of the slavery issue."

The vigorous young Republican party nominated John C. Frémont, the California "Pathfinder," and William L. Dayton, of New Jersey. An ephemeral third party—the Americans, or "Know-Nothings"—nominated former President Millard Fillmore and took enough votes away from Frémont in crucial areas to give Buchanan and the Democrats the victory.

As a resident of the District of Columbia, Stanton could not vote. The Republican platform embodied a great many of his beliefs, but even during his brief dalliance with the Free-Soilers in 1848, he had never broken with the Democratic party. He did not do so now, and this surface loyalty brought him professional dividends.

Years earlier Stanton had struck up a friendship with Jeremiah S. Black, chief justice of the Supreme Court of Pennsylvania, and it was an intimacy that he did not fail to cultivate when Black resigned from the bench to become Buchanan's Attorney General. Stanton wrote to

[3] Stanton to Ellen, June 25, 1856, owned by Mrs. Van Swearingen, who also owns the wedding jewelry. The ceremony and honeymoon plans are described in James A. Hutchison to Ellen, June 27, 1856, owned by Gideon Townsend Stanton. Other data in Wolcott MS, 132; Stanton to William Stanton, Jan. 26, 1858, owned by William Stanton Picher.

Black, offering congratulations, and adding: "Mrs. Stanton also desires me to say that as Edmund Sparkler told little Dorrit you will always find 'a knife a spoon and an apartment at your service' in her house." [4]

Tall, loose-jointed, and slouching, wearing dowdy clothes and a black wig that was often awry, Black, like Stanton, had a retentive memory, a sharp tongue, and an agile legal mind. Stanton's senior in age by four years, Black had the mental outlook of the lawyer. Legal principles and legal remedies, rather than moral precepts or political exigencies, determined the bent of his mind. He revered the Constitution with its safeguards to property, including property in slaves. Black regarded abolitionism as a manifestation of that holy zeal which so often in history, he felt, had led men to defy the law. In Buchanan, whom Black had supported politically for the past twenty years, he was sure the nation had a President capable of ending the vexed slavery question.

Two days after Buchanan's inauguration, to which Stanton invited his son and nephews, the Supreme Court handed down its historic decision in the case of Dred Scott, a slave who had sued for his freedom on the ground that he had been taken to and kept in territory where slavery was prohibited by the Missouri Compromise. The Court declared that a Negro was not a citizen and could not sue in a federal court. Going further, it held that neither Congress nor a territorial legislature, created by act of Congress, could deprive citizens of their property without due process of law. Hence, the already repealed Missouri Compromise, which denied slaveowners the right to their human property in federal territory, was unconstitutional and void.

The decision gave force to the contention of Southern Democrats that Congress, far from possessing the power to exclude slavery from federal territories, had a constitutional obligation to give it positive protection there. It cut from under the Republicans their contention

[4] Stanton to John W. Forney, Jan. 15, 1857, owned by Ralph G. Newman; same to Black, March 12, 1857, Black Papers, LC; same to Ellen Hutchison, Oct. 10, 1854, owned by Mrs. Van Swearingen. Stanton's former Steubenville law partner, McCook, had nominated Buchanan at the Democratic National Convention and had worked zealously for his election. According to Jared Dunbar, of Steubenville, McCook recommended Stanton for a cabinet post and arranged for Stanton to visit the President-elect at his Wheatland home. Buchanan asked Stanton to hold himself in readiness to enter the cabinet as Attorney General, but finally decided to give the post to Black. Dunbar claimed to have obtained this information from McCook; Steubenville *Daily Gazette*, Aug. 30, 1906. No further verification exists, and this reminiscence is of doubtful validity.

that Congress should prohibit slavery in the national domain. But it also cut the props from under Douglas's concept of popular sovereignty, now that the people had no legal means of excluding slavery from a territory. Douglas did some quick mental gymnastics. Regardless of the Scott decision, the people of a territory could still exclude slavery, if they chose to, he declared, by refusing to grant it the protection of local police regulations, without which it must perish.

This rationalization enabled Douglas to hold the support of his Illinois constituents and to regain favor in the North. But it cost him dearly in the South. Determined to reap the full benefit of the Court's decision, the Southern fire-eaters assailed the "Little Giant" for providing a way to circumvent it.

In Kansas, the proslavery territorial legislature called an election to choose delegates to a constitutional convention at Lecompton. Free-Soil men could have won in a fair vote, but, afraid of being defrauded, they stayed away from the polls. The proslavery party, in full control, framed a constitution that permitted votes only for the constitution with slavery or for the constitution without slavery. Either way, the right to property in slaves already in the territory would be guaranteed. Buchanan, favoring the proslavery interests but anxious to bring Kansas into the Union, slave or free, as speedily as possible in order to quell the sectional agitation, condoned this subterfuge.

Douglas, accusing the administration of bad faith, denounced Buchanan for obstructing the free operation of the popular sovereignty principle. Buchanan virtually read Douglas out of the party and swung the patronage whip on his adherents. A death struggle developed for control of the Democratic party. Black stood loyally with Buchanan, and Stanton stood with Black. "He was always sound on the Kansas question," Black wrote in later years, "and faithful among the faithless on the Lecompton Constitution."

This is not surprising. Stanton no longer had political ambitions, and he was moving up into the front rank of the nation's legal lights. He had accounts throughout the Ohio Valley as far south as Louisville and along the Atlantic coastline from Boston to Charleston. His friend Black was in a position to favor him with important government business, and Stanton had no intention of losing political step with him. Inwardly, however, he abominated the Buchanan administration's truckling to proslavery interests. Stanton had undergone no change of heart on the slavery question. But to the world at large he remained neutral regarding the extension of slavery. Stanton was effacing his real feelings in order to gain government favor. His obsequiousness would soon pay off.[5]

At the time California was ceded to the United States, the Treaty of Guadalupe Hidalgo stipulated that all valid Mexican land grants should be honored by the conqueror. Congress in 1851 created a board of commissioners to which all land claims were to be submitted for examination. Claims sprouted everywhere, involving titles to vast tracts of agricultural and mineral lands, extensive urban areas, strategically located islands and coastal points, and even the sites of government installations such as forts, lighthouses, customhouses, post offices, and hospitals. The fate of hundreds of millions of dollars was at stake.

Among the largest and most enterprising of the claimants was José Y. Limantour, a Frenchman, formerly a merchant at Monterey. Embraced in two of his claims that the commissioners had upheld were large portions of the city and county of San Francisco, and other valuable areas. The United States had appealed the findings of the commissioners with respect to these two claims, and the cases were pending in the district court when Black became Attorney General.

Black began receiving letters from a certain Auguste Jouan insinuating that Limantour's claims were fraudulent, that Jouan himself, as an employee of Limantour, had altered the date of one of the grants that had been upheld by the land commissioners. Now convinced that Limantour had attempted "the most stupendous fraud ever perpetrated in the history of the world," Black determined to oppose both claims in the courts.

More than the casual talents of run-of-the-mine government lawyers were needed for such a work as this. Besides outstanding legal ability, the task demanded a special counsel with unquestionable honesty, untiring energy, and tact combined with the initiative to act under the most general sort of instructions three thousand miles from the guidance of superior authority. Black had seen Stanton in action and knew the high standing he had gained. He was loyal to the Buchanan administration so far as actions were concerned and the President was acquainted with him personally and favorably. Black offered him the job.[6]

[5] Stanton to Black, March 16, 30, 31, April 13, May 14, Aug. 25, 1857, Black Papers LC; Black, "Mr. Black to Mr. Wilson," *Galaxy*, XI, 257–76; Wilson, "Edwin M. Stanton," *AM*, XXV, 16.

[6] Black to Stanton, Oct. 26, 1857, Black Papers, LC; Buchanan to Ogden Hoffman, Feb. 17, 1858, owned by Mrs. Van Swearingen; William N. Brigance, *Jeremiah Sul-*

Ellen was against her husband's taking on this task. It meant a lengthy separation. She and Edwin had been apart a great deal since their marriage, as he made the rounds of courthouses and clients in a dozen states while she remained lonely in Washington, unable to gain acceptance among the social leaders of the town. His health was not good, and Ellen, preparing for the birth of their first child, had not been as well as her worried husband wished. On May 9, 1857, she gave birth to a daughter, and they named her Eleanor Adams Stanton. But the mother suffered "a very dangerous fever following her confinement," Stanton wrote, and not until the end of that month were his fears for her recovery somewhat lessened. He secured for her the best nursing care, which proved so annoying to Ellen that she wrote him in June, as he was again traveling, that "much to my surprise I am *allowed* to write you a few lines." The couple had to discuss the projected California assignment, and Ellen told her husband: "Parting does not become easier."

With the California question uppermost in their minds, Ellen, Edwin, young Eddie, and little "Ellie" journeyed to Pittsburgh early in October to visit Ellen's parents. There Stanton made the decision to take on the work, with Ellen agreeing to remain in Washington. Stanton notified Black that he accepted the post and would be ready to go to California as soon as he could clear up pending cases. His fee was fixed at $25,000 with liberal allowances for expenses and the employment of a staff. On February 19, 1858, Stanton reached New York, accompanied by Eddie, Lieutenant H. N. Harrison, detailed to him by the Navy, and James Buchanan, Jr., a nephew of the President, to embark on the side-wheel steamer *Star of the West*. Out on the Atlantic the weather became cold, rough, and disagreeable, and most of the passengers on the crowded ship fell sick. Eddie and Harrison stayed well, but Buchanan kept to his berth. Stanton too had adequate sea legs. He wrote to Ellen every day, sitting on a stool and using a make-shift desk composed of his and Eddie's valises, and posting his accumulation of letters whenever the ship made port.[7]

---

livan Black (Philadelphia, 1934), 51–2. On background see John W. Caughey, *California* (New York, 1953), 309–10; U.S. Attorney General, *Land Claim Report to the House of Representatives, May 22, 1860,* House Exec. Doc. 84, 36th Cong., 1st sess., 1–5 (hereafter cited as *Land Claim Report*).

[7] Ellen to Edwin, June 10, July 1, 1857, and Stanton to Ellen, Feb. 21–6, 1858, owned by Gideon Townsend Stanton; Stanton to Alfred Taylor, Feb. 15, May 26, 1857, Ac. 5769-A, Stanton MSS; undated memoranda, *ca.* July and Aug. 1857, and Lewis to Mary Hutchison, Oct. 7, 1857, owned by Mrs. Van Swearingen; Stanton to Black, Feb. 17, 19, and March 28, 1858, Black Papers, LC.

When the ship docked at Kingston in Jamaica, one of the British possessions where Parliament had recently abolished slavery, Stanton went ashore and attended church. He was struck by the gentility of the colored members of the congregation and by the fact that whites and Negroes sat together. Stanton concluded from his observations that the economy of the island had suffered from emancipation and that some of the great estates were falling into ruin, though the condition of the blacks had improved. The tropics delighted him; hot days and "surpassingly lovely" nights succeeded each other as the ship steamed on across the Gulf of Mexico. At Aspinwall (Colon), Stanton and his party took the railroad to the Pacific side of the Isthmus. In the hot, crowded cars, white and colored travelers amazed him by their endless eating and drinking. He forgot discomfort as the tropical jungle flashed by, abounding in brilliant flowers. Arriving at Panama, Stanton felt the charm of the ancient Spanish town though he deplored its general dilapidation and the degradation of the people.

The party left Panama for San Francisco on the *Sonora*, a ship three times as large as the *Star of the West*. His asthma left him. The time passed pleasantly in reading, studying Spanish, completing for publication the text of his argument in the Reaper case, which had been appealed to the Supreme Court, and writing daily to Ellen. On the first Sunday out of Panama a minister held services in the ship's saloon, and Stanton and Eddie attended. But he wrote to Ellen that "it did not suit my notion of a preacher to lay off his gown and go to drinking wine and telling stories . . . within ten minutes after he had done preaching." The following Sunday, Stanton and Eddie read the morning service in their stateroom.[8]

Gales drove them off course as they moved up the coast; but Stanton had never felt better. Then engine trouble developed, and a fierce storm blew up. He and other passengers became badly frightened as giant seas swept the hurricane deck, knocked in ports, and poured through staterooms. But on March 19 the *Sonora* passed safely through the Golden Gate, and Stanton took quarters at the International Hotel.

Immediately he plunged into his task, and he soon discovered that it would involve the virtual restoration of the widely scattered archives of California for the period of Mexican rule, for only from reasonably complete records, systematically arranged, could the history of all

---

[8] To Watson, March 2, 10, 14, 1858, owned by Edward S. Corwin; Flower, "McCormick vs. Manny," 25, and 20 Howard, 402–12, on the Reaper appeal. To Ellen, Feb. 28, March 4, 6, 16, 1858, owned by Gideon Townsend Stanton.

claims be traced and their validity determined. Two weeks after his arrival he wrote Watson: "I spend about ten hours every day in examining and arranging Spanish documents, letters, records, etc., in the Archives office, and as I often have to resort to an interpreter, the work is slow." Within a month he not only was reading Spanish easily but had covered the years 1838 to 1844, "having with my own eyes examined every book and paper in the Archives," he informed Black. "I have six book binders at work," he added, "two clerks & Mr. Harrison, Mr. Buchanan, Eddie & myself from eight in the morning to six in the evening." Still he needed additional assistants to carry the work forward.

To facilitate his labors Stanton drew up two bills and sent them to Black for submission to Congress. One provided for the compulsory return to the archives of Mexican official papers, wherever they might be found, and the other prescribed severe penalties for making false claim to land or removing records from the archives. Both bills were immediately passed, and Stanton put emissaries on the trail of vanished records. Documents were turned up from Sacramento to San Diego.[9]

Coming upon the famous "Jemino Index," Stanton had a key to the location of all land titles in the official records up to 1844, and a second index was discovered for the remaining years of Mexican rule. For three months he examined and sorted records with the aid of clerks and translators. The most important documents were translated and printed. Others were photographed for presentation in court or for Black's files in Washington, to be used for comparison with those discovered in the archives. Finally Stanton obtained the names of all witnesses who had testified in support of suspicious claims and had them investigated. "The archives thus collected," declared Black, "furnish irresistible proof that there had been an organized system of fabricating land titles carried on for a long time by Mexican officials." He was sure that in Stanton he had chosen the right man for this imposing task.[1]

Stanton's staff sustained Black's opinion. "Mr. Stanton has had the stables of Augeas to clean," Lieutenant Harrison wrote to Black after working with Stanton for about two weeks, "but he brought to the task the powers of a Hercules. I have never seen a man of such un-

---

[9] Stanton to Black, April 16, 1858, Black Papers, LC; to Watson, April 2, and to Ellen, March 11, 12, 1858, owned by Gideon Townsend Stanton; Gorham, *Stanton*, I, 52, refers to a diary kept by Stanton in California, but it can no longer be found.

[1] *Land Claim Report*, 31; Gorham, *Stanton*, I, 55–6; Stanton to Watson, Aug. 4, 1858, CHS; H. W. Shutes, "Henry Wager Halleck," CalHS *Quarterly*, XVI, 197.

tiring industry, indomitable perseverance and well directed energy, and if he does not thro' Monsieur [Limantour] so high in the air, that he will be forced to commit his claim to the gods of the winds, then I am no prophet, and you shall be my Judge. You have selected *the* man, and I only wish my ability was equal to my zeal that I might give him more effectual aid, for I am very much attached to him. 'Behold a man indeed in whom is no guile,' can truly be said of him, and I thank you that such a man is my friend."

As Stanton got his task in hand he began to take trips around the bay and to visit nearby mines and other points of interest. Men loosed from family influences still made up the bulk of the population. For more moderate souls, two gentlemen's clubs provided cheer for home-sick men of means, and Stanton found club life pleasant. Several theaters stayed open seven days a week. "Occasionally a fancy danseuse makes her appearance," Stanton wrote Ellen. The churches were thronged every Sunday, and a revival meeting drew large crowds; markets displayed an abundance of delicious fresh fruits and vegetables, the meat and fish were excellent, and Stanton ate frogs for the first time.

Excitement swept the city whenever a steamer approached. Storekeepers locked their doors, lawyers closed their offices, and everyone rushed for the dock. Men cheered when the heavy mail sacks thudded on the wharf, and that night a long line would form at the post office and move slowly past the windows hour after hour.[2]

"This is a wonderful climate," Stanton wrote to Black; ". . . Eddie is sprouting like Jack the Giant Killer's bean—I can work from fourteen to eighteen hours a day the month round without flagging." Back home, however, Ellen became lonely and anxious, and chided her husband for neglecting her and their small daughter to further his ambition. In reply, Stanton insisted that his family and its welfare always came first, and that "like other mortals I may yield to the necessities of life, must bear its burthens . . . and perform its duties, but for all this the love of my wife and child will be the only and sweetest reward."

Ellen's criticisms came at a bad time for Stanton. From the moment he arrived in California he had been the target of local hostility

---

[2] Harrison to Black, June 4, 1858, Black Papers, LC; Stanton to Watson, May 7, 1858, in possession of Ralph G. Newman; to Ellen, undated, and to Umbstaetter, April 19, 1858, owned by Edward S. Corwin; and to Ellen, March 21, April 11, 1858, owned by Gideon Townsend Stanton.

inspired by parties whose holdings would be endangered by the successful completion of his mission. Now he was stalked by political hatchet men; the struggle between Buchanan and Douglas for control of the Democratic party in California resulted in a smear campaign against Stanton, who seemed to represent the administration. Douglas men spread rumors that Stanton, who before undertaking the California mission had been counsel for a company which held dubious title to lands he was now examining, had profited from this connection. Actually, Stanton had severed this affiliation before leaving the East. But he now grew discouraged, and only Black's entreaties kept him on the job.

In Washington, Buchanan and Black assured inquirers that the charges against Stanton were infamous and evanescent, and so it proved. The attempt of Douglas Democrats to impugn Stanton's honesty cemented his ties with the Buchanan wing of the party. He closely observed the California state elections of 1858, in which Douglas Democrats and the Republicans both sought to wrest control of the legislature from the Buchananites in a campaign unmatched for viciousness. As soon as the result became certain, Stanton wrote exultantly to Black: "It has been a most triumphant and glorious victory. . . . You say to the President that his own great name achieved the triumph. . . . The election is but an emphatic overwhelming endorsement of the President and his administration." [3]

Politics did not distract Stanton long from the land claims inquiry. Limantour was an adroit opponent. The Frenchman offered full and seemingly unimpeachable evidence and convincing witnesses in support of his claims, and the signature of Micheltorana, last but one of the Mexican governors of California, who signed Limantour's grants, supposedly in 1843, was genuine beyond a doubt. The petitions for lands and the grants themselves had apparently been written on the specially stamped paper provided by the Mexican government, and President Arista of the Republic of Mexico had commended the claims to the favorable consideration of the U.S. land commissioners.

But Jouan's assertions proved devastating in overthrowing Limantour. Four years after California had been ceded to the United States, Jouan avowed, Limantour had obtained eighty blank petitions and titles from Micheltorana, all of them signed, to fill in as he wished. In pre-

---

[3] Stanton to Ellen, July 5, Aug. 17, 1858, owned by Gideon Townsend Stanton; to Black, Aug. 1, and R. B. Taney to Black, Sept. 10, 1858, Black Papers, LC; Gorham, *Stanton*, I, 55–6, 77–8.

paring a spurious claim for Limantour, Jouan had made an erasure which left a hole in the paper. That document, with the telltale hole and erasure, Stanton now produced in court. And Jouan also provided one of the blank titles signed by Micheltorana.

Letters found by Stanton provided clinching proof of Limantour's fraud, for they made it clearly evident that the special stamped paper on which Limantour's grants were written had been manufactured at a later date. Stanton found two seals in the archives of the customhouse at Monterey, one the genuine seal used by customs administrators, the other a counterfeit of which only eleven impressions could be found—all on grants to Limantour or witnesses who appeared for him. Extending his search, through agents, to the archives of Mexico City itself, Stanton was able to certify that no confirmation of the Limantour grants by the Mexican Minister of the Exterior could be found in the Mexican archives, though alleged confirmations appeared on the margin of the grants. Some of Limantour's witnesses were caught in perjury; others were shown to have been readily available whenever testimony was needed in support of other suspicious claims.

As evidence of fraud piled up, all but one of Limantour's lawyers withdrew from the case after having labored on it for five years. On October 16, 1858, Stanton wrote that the remaining lawyer "had fled two days before." No rebuttal to the government's proofs was offered. The claims were rejected by the district court on the conclusive strength of Stanton's evidence, and Limantour, indicted for perjury, jumped his $35,000 bail and fled the country.

Stanton was now ready to leave for home, when Eddie fell ill. Then another fraud against the United States came to his attention, and Stanton again canceled his return passage, determined "to throw a brick" at the promoters of the New Almaden quicksilver mine, and to "stay to see where it hits," as he wrote to Watson.

The original mining grant, now worth an estimated $15,000,000, had been confirmed by the land commissioners, but Stanton obtained an injunction in the federal district court against the further working of the mine until ownership could be proved. During these proceedings Stanton encountered Henry W. Halleck, a man with whom he was destined to come into close contact in years to come. A retired army officer, Halleck had become a leading California lawyer and worked as an engineer for the New Almaden company. He offered testimony on the company's behalf, but the court found it unconvincing, and in some respects contradictory, and disallowed the documents he had brought forth. Stanton, seldom lenient toward an opponent in a lawsuit, unjustly suspected Halleck of perjury.[4]

Through his labors, Stanton's thoughts were with Ellen. He worried over the arrangements he had made for her support during his absence, and he repeatedly requested Black and Watson to look after her needs and his private and professional affairs. To Ellen he wrote of his anticipations of home-coming, and of his longing for her and their little girl. His cares increased as young Eddie's health failed to improve in the last months of 1858, although the plucky youngster summoned enough energy to write his infant half sister as her first birthday approached: "I am sorry that you can't say 'Eddie' but will try to come home soon and teach you."

Each time Stanton made plans to sail for home, his son's health worsened. His condition seemed critical for a time, but by late November he had improved to the point where he could be moved, though he was still unable to stand. Stanton prepared to start home on December 5: "Judgment has been entered in favor of the U[nited] States in all my cases," he wrote Watson, "—and my work is done." But Eddie was still sick at Christmas and it was early January 1859 before the Stantons boarded ship for home. "I write to tell you that we are coming, to tell Ellie we are coming, coming, coming at last!" Edwin exulted to Ellen. "My heart leaps for joy at the thought . . . we talk every day of you and are counting the hours."

Stanton rendered a great service in restoring the California archives and in defeating numerous fraudulent claims. If the procedures adopted by the American Government for the validation of claims placed an unreasonable burden of proof on claimants, involved both the innocent and the guilty in expensive court actions lasting in some cases a decade or even longer, and left California land titles in a state of uncertainty for an inordinately long time, the fault was not with him. He had a job to do and he did it with his usual single-minded earnestness. Moreover, not a little of the niggling and pettishness resorted to by the government lawyers had resulted from the necessity of combating suspicious claims with legal technicalities because of lack of

---

[4] In 1863, Stanton had the satisfaction of learning that the Supreme Court, employing his evidence, voided both the company's land claim and its mining grant. Halleck to E. A. Hitchcock, March 31, 1862, Hitchcock Papers, LC; Shutes, "Henry Wager Halleck," *loc. cit.*, 195–208; *Land Titles in California*, House Exec. Doc. 17, 31st Cong., 1st sess., 118–82; 67 *U.S. Reports*, 17–371; Stanton to Watson, Aug. 4, 1858, CHS; same, April 3, June 19, Sept. 3, Oct. 16, 1858, owned by Edward S. Corwin; Gorham, *Stanton*, I, 64–5.

evidence. Now, through Stanton's restoration of the archives, claimants as well as the government could support their cases with facts.[5]

To be sure, Stanton incurred resentment and suspicion from those who assisted him in California when promises of additional payment for services, which he had made to them, were not fulfilled. He filed their claims, but owing to Congress's indifference or its preoccupation with more vital matters that soon confronted it, funds for the payment of these obligations were not appropriated, and more than a decade passed in some instances before justice was done.

The government's inefficiency in meeting its obligations also affected Stanton's reputation in California. Late in 1860, James F. Shunk, Black's son-in-law, was there serving as a special federal agent. "Few people here," he wrote Black from San Francisco, "feel kindly to Stanton." Denying that he gave "ear to every bit of scandal that has reached me or the grumblings of every disappointed man who thinks he has not been paid enough for his work," Shunk nevertheless described the "general feeling" that Stanton was too lavish in his promises, and had put the blame on Black. "You may depend upon it," he wrote to Black, "that Stanton is not *a perfectly fair man. Don't start.* — I have made up my mind on that point . . . upon sufficient evidence. He has suffered you to bear all the odium of any disagreeable things you may have done, even at his suggestion, by representing that he was not on terms of intimacy with you. . . . When I remember how often I have seen Mr. S[tanton] puff his cigar upon your sofa for an hour at a time without alluding to business, I am compelled to think, that this statement was rather disingenuous." Shunk, knowing his father-in-law's regard for Stanton, acknowledged that his accusations must seem like "flat blasphemy," but he felt he had to report what he had learned.[6]

But Black's confidence in Stanton, far from being shaken by these

---

[5] Stanton to Watson, Nov. 25, 1858, owned by the estate of Foreman M. Lebold; Eddie to "Ellie," Sept. 19, 1858, owned by Mrs. Van Swearingen; Stanton to Ellen, Sept. ?, 19, 1858, Jan. 14, 1859, owned by Gideon Townsend Stanton; to Black, April 19, 1858, Black Papers, LC; and to Watson, April 18, Aug. 19, 1858, owned by Edward S. Corwin. On the significance of Stanton's work, see Caughey, *op. cit.*, 306–15; Alston G. Field, "Attorney-General Black and the California Land Claims," *PHR,* IV, 235–45.

[6] Shunk to Black, Oct. 12, Nov. 10, 14, 23, 1860, Black Papers, LC. Mary Della Torre to same, April 26, June 19, 1870, Stanton to same, July 24, 1860, and James Buchanan, Jr., to same, Nov. 13, 1860, *ibid.,* cover Stanton's efforts to get these and other persons paid; and see his letter to Treasury official George Harrington, Sept. 10, 1862, William K. Bixby Collection, MoHS; same to Eben Faxon, June 20, 1859, Simon Gratz Papers, HSP; same to same, May 14, 1860, MHS.

charges, became stronger than ever when the two men were thrown closer together by the march of events.

Arriving home in early February 1859, Stanton looked forward to a long vacation trip with his family. He first had to clear his desk of the accumulation of business matters, and this delayed their departure. Then he became involved in assisting Black in writing a series of opinions in government cases—many Washingtonians believed that Stanton was an official Assistant Attorney General—and advising President Buchanan on patronage matters, especially where California offices were concerned. "Every California crumb is closely watched and claimed by many," he wrote to one eager aspirant for a Treasury position there.

Despite his increased professional prestige and enhanced income, Stanton was suffering from a severe letdown after his exertions on the West Coast. "Everything . . . is duller on this side than on the Pacific slope," he commented.[7] His lassitude vanished, however, when he was asked to take part in a sensational trial.

His friend Daniel Sickles, after a turbulent career in New York politics, had overcome the dissolute habits of his youth since his marriage and was now a congressman. But socialite Philip Barton Key, a son of the author of "The Star-Spangled Banner," and United States Attorney for the District of Columbia, had started a love affair with Mrs. Sickles. Sickles eventually learned of it. On the peaceful Sunday morning of February 27, 1859, he shot Key to death on a Washington street, walked to Black's home, and surrendered himself into custody.

The prominence of the principals, the very thought of the illicit affair and the murder taking place within sight of the White House, put the nation in a flutter. Sordid gossip went the rounds, even to the point of insinuations that Mrs. Sickles had granted her favors to many men in addition to Key, and that her husband had risen in President Buchanan's esteem as she had been pleasant to "Old Buck."

One of the country's most celebrated criminal lawyers, James T. Brady, and his partner, John Graham, hastened down from New York City to conduct Sickles's defense, and immediately enlisted Stanton, as well as other Washington attorneys, as associate counsel. Humorless, thickset Robert Ould and wiry, fidgety J. M. Carlisle were attorneys for the people. The trial commenced on April 4 in the insufferably overheated Washington criminal courtroom.

[7] D. H. Hamilton to Black, July 6, 1867, Black Papers, LC; Stanton to Ogden Hoffman, April 27, 1859, and to G. Upton, March 7, 1859, HL.

Brady and Stanton complemented each other in courtroom tactics. The former was noticeably proper to the prosecuting attorneys, judge, jury, and witnesses; Stanton, however, hit at everyone with a sledge-hammer earnestness which stood out in contrast to his colleague's extreme politeness. Stanton's vigor excited general comment, and his obvious affection for the defendant added a sense of personal involvement to his conduct of the case.

The defense tried to prove that an adulterer may be slain with impunity by the injured husband, and that Sickles was so disturbed in mind at the time of the homicide as to be unaccountable for his acts. It was the first time in American jurisprudence that a plea of temporary insanity had been advanced in a murder trial. The prosecution was prepared to combat the plea by contending that Sickles cared nothing for his wife's affections, for he, too, had been living in adultery; but this line of testimony was excluded by the judge.[8] Whereupon the prosecution shifted its strategy to stress the deliberate, cold-blooded nature of the attack, and to pay as little heed as possible to Sickles's provocation.

A great deal of melodrama animated the proceedings. Stanton once called for a recess so that Sickles could regain his composure after the testimony of a friendly witness reduced him to tears, and counsel sometimes wept from the pathos of the case. Summing up for the defense, Stanton held forth on the sanctity of the marriage vows and a husband's right and duty to keep his home inviolate against seducers. The jurors sat spellbound. Cheers broke from the spectators, drowning out the judge's repeated warnings. A modern student of trial procedure describes Stanton's performance as "a typical piece of Victorian rhetoric, an ingenious thesaurus of aphorisms on the sanctity of the family." But its effect on the jury was profound, and an onlooker, Mrs. Olive Cole, recalled a decade later that "Brady did not half the service for Sickles that Stanton did."

From the first, however, there had been little doubt that Sickles would be acquitted. But there could always be a slip, and the defense also relied heavily on the plea of temporary insanity. Wild cheers rocked the courtroom when the jury, after deliberating only seventy minutes, brought in a verdict of "not guilty." The crowd, waving hats and handkerchiefs, made a rush for Sickles in the dock. Stanton's voice boomed out above the uproar: "I move that Mr. Sickles be discharged

---

[8] *Trial of the Hon. Daniel E. Sickles for Shooting Philip Barton Key, Esq., Reported by Felix G. Fontaine* (New York, 1859), 35–40; *Harper's Weekly*, III, covered the trial in its issues of March 12 to May 14, 1859.

from custody." The judge so ordered, and as Sickles pushed his way out of the dock, Stanton murmured in his ear: "Now go it!" An eyewitness reported that "Mr. Stanton, unable to repress the emotions of his big heart, . . . almost rivaled David when he danced before the ark of the Tabernacle." Brady, Stanton, and Graham were serenaded that night, and Stanton's name was now known far beyond the professional circles of the law.[9]

As the trial approached its close, Stanton's boredom had returned. "Everthing is in a dead calm," he wrote a California friend, and announced his plans to begin his long-deferred vacation. Early in May 1859, he, Ellen, Eddie, and little Eleanor set off for Akron to visit Pamphila, and his mother and Oella met them there. It was the first time that the entire family had been together in ten years. Only Pamphila's husband, Wolcott, was missing. As attorney general of Ohio, and an ardent Republican, he was defending a number of citizens who were facing federal prosecution, under the 1850 fugitive slave law, for aiding a slave to escape. Stanton and Chase helped Wolcott with his argument, and according to Pamphila, Stanton felt that their combined product was "the best on that side of the question he had ever seen."

The Stantons began their return to Washington by way of Pittsburgh, which was, Stanton noted, "as black and smoky as ever." After an absence of seven weeks, they were back in Washington. In the autumn they purchased a large lot on K Street, opposite the present Franklin Square, and began construction of a capacious brick-and-stone house. Ellen was soon immersed in blueprints, for, socially ambitious, she was determined that this house would fit her ideas of a home, even if its cost proved too large for their present means. These were busy, happy days for Stanton and his family. They were in good health, with even Stanton's asthmatic affliction at a low ebb, there were few financial problems, and his professional hopes were high.

In October the startling news came that John Brown, an abolitionist veteran of the Kansas troubles, had seized the federal arsenal at Harpers Ferry in an effort to instigate a slave revolt. Beleaguered by state and federal military forces, he and the other survivors were captured, put on trial for treason, and eventually hanged. Stanton, stopping off again at Pamphila's in the course of a business trip, showed

[9] Olive to Cornelius Cole, April 22, 1868, UCLA; Allan Nevins and Milton Halsey Thomas (eds.), *The Diary of George Templeton Strong* (New York, 1952), II, 440–1, 448 (hereafter cited as Strong, *Diary*); Richard B. Morris, *Fair Trial* (New York, 1952), 225, 253.

keen interest in the trial, and told her that he "would gladly have appeared in the defense had he been called upon by those having the matter in charge." [1]

Excitement mounted to fever heat in both the North and the South. Abolitionist spokesmen glorified Brown as a martyr, while Southerners saw his rash act as the fearful and inevitable result of antislavery agitation. As the presidential year of 1860 opened, an undertow of hate and suspicion pulled the country toward an awful abyss.

Most ominous was the fact that slavery had become an urgent moral issue. While Republicans demanded that it be treated as an evil, extremist Southerners insisted that it be recognized as a positive good. Determined to gain full protection for slavery in the territories under the Dred Scott decision, these hotspurs repudiated Douglas and his popular sovereignty doctrine. That doctrine, now that Douglas had attached his "police power" corollary to it, had become more hateful to Southerners than the Republican policy of delimiting slavery by congressional enactment. The Douglas doctrine threatened the unity of the Democratic party and the Southerners' control of it. Their last hope was to make that party the instrument of their will. If they failed, they would take the Southern states out of the Union.

The Democratic National Convention met in April 1860, in Charleston, South Carolina, where secessionist tinder needed only a spark to touch it off. From the beginning it was evident that the Douglas men would stand pat on popular sovereignty as the keystone of party policy, and that the fire-eaters from the cotton states not only would reject that doctrine but were prepared to go to any lengths to vanquish the "Little Giant." When the convention adopted the Douglas platform, the delegates of seven cotton states, along with a scattering of Northern sympathizers, stomped out of the hall. Unable to nominate Douglas under the party's two-thirds rule, the remaining delegates at last agreed to adjourn and meet again in Baltimore.

Stanton was dispirited by the course of events. "Everything is dark and obscure," he wrote to his friend Medary. "The friends of Douglas are confident and uncompromising. The Southern men seem equally decided against him. No solution of the problem has been suggested.

[1] Wolcott MS, 133, 165; Stanton to William Stanton, March 13, May 18, 26, 1859, owned by William Stanton Picher; to son Eddie, Oct. 31, 1859, owned by Gideon Townsend Stanton; to Lewis Hutchison, Oct. 27, 1859, Lee-Kohn Memorial Collection, NYPL; to Ogden Hoffman, April 27, 1859, HL; to Black, May 1, 1859, Black Papers, LC. See also Jacob R. Shipard, *History of the Oberlin-Wellington Rescue* (Cleveland, 1859), 195–225; and on the new house, Recorder of Deeds, District of Columbia, J.A.S. Vol. 185, pp. 136–7.

Disaster and overthrow impends upon the Democracy and no power seems able to avert a danger that can only be overcome by union and confidence." But confidence was lacking. When the Democrats reassembled on June 18, they split apart again. Then, meeting separately, one faction nominated Douglas, while the other, upholding the radical Southern point of view, nominated Breckinridge, Vice-President under Buchanan, who announced that he would support Breckinridge.

Meanwhile, the Republicans met in Chicago, and surprised Stanton and the country by passing over their front runners and nominating the almost unknown Abraham Lincoln. Stanton at least had met Lincoln during the Reaper trial. His low opinion of the Republican nominee remained unchanged.[2]

Adding to the confusion, remnants of the Whigs and Know-Nothings, alarmed at the possibility of civil war, came together in Baltimore to form the Constitutional Union party. They nominated John Bell, of Tennessee, and Edward Everett, of Massachusetts, on a platform acclaiming "the Constitution of the country, the Union of the States, and the enforcement of the laws."

Stanton aligned himself publicly with the Buchanan-Breckinridge forces. According to Black, neither abolitionists, Republicans, nor Douglas Democrats found favor in his eyes. "Mr. Stanton wholly denied Mr. Douglas' notions," he declared, "and blamed him severely for the unreasonable and mischievous schism which he had created in the party. . . . In the canvass of 1860 he regarded the salvation of the country as hanging upon the forlorn hope of Mr. Breckinridge's election. We knew the Abolitionists to be the avowed enemies of the Constitution and the Union, and thought the Republicans would necessarily be corrupted by their alliance with them. . . . Mr. Stanton shared these apprehensions fully. He more than shared them. To some extent he inspired them, for he knew Mr. Lincoln personally and the account he gave of him was anything but favorable."

It should be said in Stanton's behalf that while few outright antislavery men supported Breckinridge, thousands of Unionists in the North and the border states, regarding Bell as a hopeless long shot, looked upon Breckinridge as the only candidate whose election would prevent the severance of the nation. Though Breckinridge was the secessionists' candidate, he himself avowed his lifelong attachment to the Union, and Stanton, taking Breckinridge at his word, was sincere in his repetition of antislavery convictions to Pamphila.

[2] To Medary, June 4, 1860, BU.

Whatever Stanton's inner sentiments may have been, it behooved him to stay on good terms with Black. A good many California land cases were now coming to the Supreme Court on appeal, and Black was retaining Stanton to represent the government in the greater number of them. On the death of Postmaster General Aaron V. Brown, Black had suggested that Stanton replace him in the cabinet, but Buchanan decided in favor of Joseph Holt, of Kentucky, perhaps at Stanton's own request.

Stanton confessed to Ellen, vacationing in Pittsburgh, his disgust at the course of events. "I am weary and harassed and want to get away from here speedily as possible," he wrote from Washington in May 1860. "There is nothing but political confusion, turmoils, and anxiety. Public anxiety about the future, intrigues, and passions are manifest on all sides. I want to be with you." But the political confusion compounded the traditional slowness of governmental administrative and judicial procedures, and "nothing can be done."

To suitors for his intercession with the administration, Stanton stated that "I have no political power. . . . My relations with [Buchanan] . . . are simply professional." Despite his modest disclaimers, Stanton kept in close touch with events, especially through Black. He was convinced that schism in the Democratic party must result in the election of Lincoln. Giving no clue to his real feelings on the issues facing the country, he urged his brother-in-law to take advantage of his consistent Republicanism and come to Washington in search of official preferment. "The election of Lincoln," Stanton wrote Wolcott, "is as certain as any future event can be." In the last part of September, Stanton brought his family to Steubenville to attend Oella's second marriage. This was to be Stanton's last real vacation for five years, and the last moment of peace, repose, and calm in his life.[3]

State elections in October showed that the Democratic split had become irreparable and confirmed Stanton's prediction that Lincoln would be the next President. The ruffling drums of secession beat louder in the South. Stanton was in Steubenville when the news of Lincoln's election flashed over the wires. Arriving back in Washington, he was sought out by Black. Buchanan was preparing his annual message to Congress, which would assemble in December, and he had asked Black to comment on the legal aspects of secession and the gov-

[3] Wolcott MS, 165–6; Stanton to Eben Faxon, Dec. 7, 1859, YU; same to same, May 14, 1860, Norcross Papers, MHS; to Ellen, May 9, 1860, owned by Gideon Townsend Stanton; undated memo, "To the Public," in Black's handwriting, Black Papers, Vol. 51, No. 59812–23, LC.

ernment's means of combating it. Black wanted Stanton's opinion of the paper he had drawn up.

It was a limp argument insofar as the President's powers were concerned. Buchanan could use military force to repel "a direct and positive aggression" upon the government or government property, Black asserted. But for ordinary law enforcement he must rely on federal judges and other local federal officials. If feeling against the national government became so widespread in any state that these officials refused to act, the President, Black thought, could do no more than refer the matter to Congress.

According to Black, Stanton suggested only one slight change in this paper—which Black accepted—and then "not only approved but applauded enthusiastically" the final draft. Long deliberations over this message took place in the cabinet. Black learned that Buchanan intended to quote from his paper to the effect that the United States could not "coerce a State by force of arms to remain in the Union." Protesting that such phraseology, taken out of context, would misrepresent his views, Black prepared a second paper, bolder in tone, which accorded more closely with Stanton's views on the illegality of secession and the government's powers to suppress it than did Black's original opinion. It may have been this second paper, rather than Black's previous and weaker argument, that Stanton read and endorsed, for as his biographer Gorham asserted in a scathing indictment of Black's original opinion, it is most unlikely that Stanton would have approved that first document. Whatever Stanton's views on slavery may have been by now, there was no dissimulation in his staunch unionism.

On December 3, Buchanan delivered his message to Congress, and Stanton, like most Union-loving Northerners, felt that it conceded far too much to the South.[4] Declaring that the national crisis had been

[4] Gorham, *Stanton*, I, 94–110; "To the Public," Black Papers, LC; Black's reminiscence in Philadelphia *Weekly Press*, Aug. 11, 1881. In 1869, Stanton recollected that Buchanan had asked him to draw up a brief against nullification and secession and that he had complied; it appears he confused his work on the Black draft with the one he thought he had written for the President. See memo of John C. Ropes, Feb. 8, 1870, of a conversation with Stanton in Sept. 1869, Horatio Woodman Papers, MHS, and Philip G. Auchampaugh, *James Buchanan and His Cabinet on the Eve of Secession* (Lancaster, 1926), 75. Montgomery Blair, repeating an anonymous recollection he probably inspired in the New York *World*, June 3, 1865, asserted in his *The Rebellion—Where the Guilt Lies: Speech* . . . *Aug. 25, 1865* (n.p., n.d.), 15, and in the 1868 election campaign (*Harper's Monthly Magazine*, XXXVIII, 155) that Stanton applauded Jefferson Davis's secessionist speeches in the Senate in 1860. The weight of evidence, however, supports Stanton's unionism. However he felt, he would scarcely have publicly advocated secession.

caused by "the long continued and intemperate interference of the Northern people with the question of slavery in the Southern states," the President expressed sympathy for Southern fears that further agitation would bring on a slave revolt, and though denying that adequate cause yet existed, he admitted that, should it arise, "the injured States, after having first used all peaceful and constitutional means to obtain redress, would be justified in revolutionary resistance to the government of the Union."

But while admitting the revolutionary right of secession, Buchanan denied its legality. If South Carolina seceded, Buchanan could not recognize her as an independent nation. But he would present her case to Congress. Even Congress had "no power to coerce a state," he said, using the language that Black had advised him to avoid; and even if such a power existed, it would be unwise to exercise it, for the resulting loss of life and treasure would end all hope of reconciliation.

Having placed the responsibility for future action upon Congress, Buchanan then proceeded to advise Congress on what to do. It should pass and submit to the states a constitutional amendment sustaining slavery in the states that recognized it, guaranteeing protection to slave property in all territories until they were admitted to statehood, reaffirming the master's right to the recovery of fugitive slaves, and nullifying all state laws interfering with that right.

As the crux of Buchanan's proposal, positive protection of slavery in the territories, had already been renounced by the Douglas Democrats and was looked upon with abhorrence by the victorious Republicans, the President's program was sure to be rejected by a majority in the North. Nor was his message satisfactory to fire-eating Southerners. Two days after Buchanan delivered it, Howell Cobb, Secretary of the Treasury, the most outspoken secessionist in the cabinet, resigned from "a sense of duty to Georgia"; and four days later, Cass, the old and enfeebled Secretary of State, though himself a long-time dissembler on the slavery issue, also submitted his resignation on the ground that Buchanan had spoken too softly to the secessionists.

Then in Cincinnati arguing a case, Stanton received a telegram from Black urging him to drop everything and hurry to Washington. He guessed that it meant an invitation to join Buchanan's cabinet.[5]

Arriving in Washington on December 20, Stanton read in the morn-

[5] Memo of H. H. Leavitt, Oct. 1865, Stanton MSS; A. R. Newsome (ed.), "Letters of Lawrence O'Bryan Branch," *NCHR*, X, 79; James D. Richardson (comp.), *A Compilation of the Messages and Papers of the Presidents, 1789–1902* (Washington, 1907), V, 626–53 (cited hereafter as Richardson, *Messages and Papers*).

ing paper that he had been appointed Attorney General. Buchanan had appointed Black to succeed Cass as Secretary of State, and Black had prevailed upon the President to give Stanton the law portfolio, insisting that he was unwilling to leave the pending California land cases to anyone else. "Of course," Black insisted, "you will take it." Stanton replied that he was not sure; it depended on what course the President planned to take. Black assured him that Buchanan intended to uphold the Union. The two men left for the White House. There Buchanan confirmed Black's assurance. Stanton reluctantly accepted the position.

Black's reminiscent statement that Stanton was eager for the post and expressed his gratitude "in most exaggerated language," is quite questionable. Stanton was clearly materialistic. His many private cases had brought him an income of $40,000 in 1859 in addition to expenses and bonuses, and promised to increase substantially. Accepting the cabinet office even with the idea that it was only to finish out Buchanan's lame-duck term and with the probability of maintaining some private practice, meant a considerable financial sacrifice. It seems clear that patriotism and the hope of altering Buchanan's policies, mixed with desires to round out the California land cases satisfactorily and to gild his reputation with a brief tenure as the country's highest legal officer, inspired Stanton to accept the office. But in his own thinking, the patriotic impulse came first. He wrote his brother-in-law, a man unlikely to be deceived, that "I hold my present position only to defend the Government from its enemies—when it becomes apparent that defence will be unavailing I shall . . . spike my guns and retire to a stronger position and keep the flag of my country still flying."

On the same day Stanton accepted the commission, that flag descended in South Carolina, where an ordinance of secession passed without a single dissenting vote. An election of delegates to a Mississippi convention resulted in a top-heavy secessionist majority. Florida, Alabama, Georgia, Louisiana, and Texas prepared to renounce the Union.

Stanton did not enter upon his duties until December 27, although the Senate acted favorably on his nomination and with unwonted unanimity for the time. Wolcott, who was staying with Stanton in Washington, wrote to Pamphila: "This has been the dullest, dreariest Christmas within my recollection. . . . Everyone here talks and thinks of nothing but the threatened secession. Edwin, as you well knew he would be, is thoroughly right upon the question, but I doubt his ability to do anything with the head of the Government."

The new Attorney General, fully aware of the magnitude of the crisis facing the nation, put on a confident air. "Nothing in my power will be left undone to uphold the integrity of the Government," he wrote soon after taking office. "I do not believe this Government can be over-thrown—it may be overrun for a brief period but cannot be destroyed." Although Buchanan thought that Stanton "has not a superior as a lawyer in the United States," and newspapers across the North applauded the appointment, the question remained whether it could make any difference.[6]

[6] The major narrative is from Stanton's own account in Wolcott MS, 168–71; Ropes's memo of conversation with Stanton in Sept. 1869, Horatio Woodman Papers, MHS; letters of Pamphila in New York *Sun*, March 14, 1892; and Flower, *Stanton*, 85. Other data in Black, "Mr. Black to Mr. Wilson," *loc. cit.*, 260–1; Stanton to Jacob Brinkerhoff, Jan. 20, 1861, Personal-Miscellaneous Papers, LC; Buchanan to Harriet Lane, Nov. 4, 1860, Buchanan-Johnston Papers, LC.

CHAPTER V

FIRST BLOW FOR THE UNION

Stanton found little to encourage him in what he knew of the President and his suspicious and rancorous cabinet colleagues. Buchanan, nearing seventy, tired, infirm, and nervous, though wise in his resolve to avoid provocative action so long as compromise or sober second thought might reconcile the sections, lacked the courage, initiative, and will power to implement such a policy. A long career in politics had made him cynical and coldly calculating; his habit of taking the indirect approach degenerated at times into craftiness. Though anxious to preserve the Union, he felt in his heart that the South's grievances were just. He interpreted the Republican triumph of 1860 as a personal defeat; in resisting it, the Southern states were vindicating him.

Cobb's resignation had removed a blatant secessionist influence from the cabinet, but still vying with Black for Buchanan's ear were Jacob Thompson, of Mississippi, Secretary of the Interior, Philip F. Thomas, of Maryland, Cobb's successor at the Treasury, and John B. Floyd, of Virginia, Secretary of War. Thompson, a genial, able man, though moved by real loyalty to Buchanan, felt a higher loyalty to his state, and went no further in opposing secession than to suggest that overt action be postponed until the Republicans took office on March 4. Thomas was wholeheartedly sympathetic toward the South; and though Floyd, like most Virginians, had opposed secession thus far, he had been under the critical scrutiny of Republican congressmen because of his partisan, loose, and inefficient conduct of his office. Buchanan had asked for his resignation, which Floyd was reluctant to submit. Now, opposition to a firm policy on the part of Buchanan might afford Floyd a means of saving face.[1]

The fourth Southerner in the cabinet was Postmaster General Joseph Holt, from the border state of Kentucky, a champion of Buchanan's anti-abolitionist stand. Holt renounced secession as the South's rightful remedy, however, and Black and Stanton would find in him a staunch if unexpected ally.

Besides Black and Stanton, Isaac Toucey, of Connecticut, Secretary of the Navy, was the only other Northerner in the cabinet. But they could count on little help from him. Sympathizing, much as Buchanan did, with the position of the South, he usually waited for the President to speak, then echoed his opinions.

The very morning that Stanton entered upon his duties, news came that Major Robert Anderson, commanding the defenses of Charleston Harbor, had moved his scanty garrison from its exposed position at Fort Moultrie to Fort Sumter, a newly finished brick-and-mortar stronghold on a sand bar near the middle of the harbor. The "independent" state of South Carolina chose to interpret Anderson's move not only as a hostile act but as a breach of faith as well. For on December 9, in equivocal words that had been interpreted as a pledge, Buchanan had told a delegation of South Carolina congressmen that he had no intention of reinforcing the forts or altering the disposition of the troops unless South Carolina moved to take possession of government property.

About the same time that Buchanan's interview with the South Carolinians took place, Captain Don Carlos Buell, whom Floyd had sent to Charleston to appraise the situation, told Anderson to dispose his force in the safest manner, either at Moultrie or Sumter, whenever he had "tangible evidence of a design to proceed to a hostile act." Buell, returning to Washington, had Floyd endorse a memorandum approving the instructions he had given to Anderson. The secession of South Carolina made Anderson's position both crucial and perilous; and on December 21, Buchanan had allowed Black to draw up new instructions for the commander, which Floyd signed. Anderson was to "exercise a sound military discretion" but not to incur a "useless waste of life." If attacked by overwhelming force, he should yield on the best terms obtainable.

[1] Stanton to Wolcott, *ca.* Dec. 27, 1860, owned by Edward S. Corwin; Russell F. Weigley, *Quartermaster General of the Union Army; A Biography of M. C. Meigs* (New York, 1959), 104–12 (hereafter cited as Weigley, *Meigs*); Kenneth P. Stampp, *And the War Came* (Baton Rouge, 1950), 75–7.

On December 26, three South Carolina commissioners had arrived in Washington from Charleston to negotiate a treaty of friendship between the new "republic" and the United States. William H. Trescott, also a South Carolinian, who had resigned as Assistant Secretary of State when his state seceded, asked Buchanan to receive them. To do so officially would be to recognize South Carolina as an independent nation. Buchanan hesitated but finally agreed to consult with them the next day, but merely as private gentlemen, and to communicate to Congress any proposals they chose to offer.

But then came news of Anderson's surprising move. Trescott, along with two Southern senators, Jefferson Davis and R. M. T. Hunter, hastened to the White House and reported the developments to the President. Buchanan swore to God that Anderson's change of position had been against his orders and policy. The Southerners urged him to order Anderson back to Moultrie, reminding him that to do otherwise might mean war. But Buchanan, though fearful and excited, was also extremely stubborn. He refused to be rushed into action, and after postponing his meeting with the commissioners until the next day, called a cabinet meeting.

Stanton was arguing a case in the Supreme Court when he received news of Anderson's action. Excusing himself, he started for his office. On the steps of the Capitol he met Wolcott, who urged him to support Anderson. Stanton vowed that he would, though he "could not guess what aspect the treason might now assume."

Arriving at his office, Stanton found a summons to the cabinet meeting, the first that he would attend. When he walked in, somewhat late, Floyd was denouncing Anderson for acting without orders. A messenger, dispatched to the War Department, brought back Buell's memorandum, endorsed by Floyd. But, declared Floyd, Anderson had no "tangible evidence of a design to proceed to a hostile act." Black, Stanton, and Holt came to Anderson's support. Arrayed against them were Floyd, Thompson, Toucey, and Thomas.

Black wanted to know about Buchanan's alleged pledge to South Carolina. When and where had the pledge been made? Floyd and Thompson insisted to Buchanan's face, without his contradicting them, that he had promised to maintain the status quo in Charleston Harbor unless the forts were attacked. The meeting became a wrangle.

Floyd wrote out a demand that the federal troops be withdrawn from Charleston Harbor altogether. Black snapped out that if any English minister had ever advocated the apathetic surrender of a defensible fortress to the enemy, as Floyd was doing, he would have lost his head on the block. Stanton added that to give up Sumter would be a crime equal to Benedict Arnold's and that anyone participating in it would deserve to be hanged like Major André. Floyd and Thompson started angrily from their seats, but Buchanan, raising his hands deprecatingly, said: "Oh, no! Not so bad as that, my friend—not so bad as that!" [2]

The meeting lasted until after dark and was resumed that evening. When the tired and angry cabinet members at last trooped off to bed, Buchanan had reached no decision. Next morning, December 28, brought news that Governor Pickens had seized the abandoned Fort Moultrie and the defenseless Castle Pinckney, the third fort in Charleston Harbor, along with the arsenal, the post office, and the customhouse. Decrepit old Winfield Scott, commander in chief of the armies, after a sleepless night, urged that not only Sumter but all other key forts in the South be immediately reinforced lest they be taken by surprise.

When Buchanan met the South Carolina commissioners that afternoon, they accused him of breaking his word to the South Carolina congressmen. Buchanan denied that he had made a pledge. The emissaries only redoubled their efforts, urging Buchanan not merely to send Anderson back to Moultrie but to withdraw the federal force from Charleston Harbor altogether. Otherwise they would break off negotiations and bloodshed might follow. Buchanan, petulant, insisted that he must have more time for thought and prayer.

Stanton, encountering Trescott, lashed out at him: "You say the President has pledged himself. I don't know it, I have not heard his account, but I know you believe it." In any case, it made no difference now, said Stanton, for South Carolina in breaking her part of the bargain—if there had been a bargain—by taking possession of government property, had freed Buchanan's hands. "The President's pledge may be broken or not," added Stanton; "that now concerns him individually. As to the Government, you have passed by the pledge and

[2] Wolcott MS, 169; Gaillard Hunt (ed.), "Narrative and Letter of William Henry Trescott," *AHR*, XIII, 531–4; Auchampaugh, *op. cit.*, 160. Gorham, *Stanton*, I, 158–9; Ropes's memo of a conversation with Stanton in Sept. 1869, Horatio Woodman Papers, MHS; and Morse, *Welles Diary*, II, 273–4, offer three instances in which Stanton described this scene in these terms; and see the analysis of the conflicting evidence as to what took place at this and subsequent cabinet sessions in Pratt, *op. cit.*, 461–6. Thompson, on the other hand, recalled ten years later that he did not remember Stanton's doing anything at all, and that no remarks reflecting on individuals were passed; to Black, Oct. 10, 1870, Black Papers, LC.

assumed in vindication a position of hostility—with that alone I have to deal."

That night the demands of the commissioners, reduced to writing, were considered in cabinet meeting. Thompson immediately launched into a demand for the evacuation of Sumter. Buchanan, wrapped in an old dressing gown, sat in a corner near the fire. Floyd was lying on a sofa between the windows. "We had high words," Stanton recalled, "and had almost come to blows. . . . Thompson was a plausible talker—and as a last resort, having been driven from every other argument, advocated the evacuation of the fort on the plea of generosity. South Carolina, he said, was but a small State with a sparse white population—we were a great and powerful people, and a strong vigorous government. We could afford to say to South Carolina, 'See, we will withdraw our garrison as an evidence that we mean you no harm.' "

Thompson's argument was well calculated to appeal to Buchanan, who still favored conciliation rather than coercion; but Stanton broke in: "Mr. President, the proposal to be generous implies that the government is strong, and that we, as the public servants, have the confidence of the people. I think that is a mistake. No administration has ever suffered the loss of public confidence and support that this has done. Only the other day it was announced that a million of dollars has been stolen from Mr. Thompson's department. . . . Now it is proposed to give up Sumter. All I have to say is, that no administration, much less this one, can afford to lose a million of money and a fort in the same week." [3] Floyd offered no reply.

Next morning, Saturday the twenty-ninth, found the cabinet again in session, but there was one vacant place. Floyd had at last resigned. Cloaking his own incompetence in haughty insolence, he wrote that he could no longer remain associated with an administration that violated solemn pledges and plighted faith.

The demands of the South Carolina commissioners were again the chief subject before the cabinet meeting. Buchanan finally decided to draft a reply himself and read it to the cabinet that evening. Only Toucey was satisfied with it. Thompson and Thomas protested that it

[3] Hunt, "Narrative . . . of Trescott," *loc. cit.*, 552–3; John G. Nicolay and John Hay, *Abraham Lincoln, A History* (New York, 1890), III, 73–4 (cited henceforth as Nicolay and Hay, *Lincoln*); Helen Nicolay, *Lincoln's Secretary, A Biography of John G. Nicolay* (New York, 1949), 129–30 (hereafter cited as Nicolay, *Lincoln's Secretary*). See also W. A. Swanberg, *First Blood, the Story of Fort Sumter* (New York, 1957), 102–15; Stampp, *op. cit.*, 75.

was hostile to South Carolina, whereas Black, Holt, and Stanton thought it was too conciliatory.

Black and Stanton became highly excited when Buchanan, displaying the stubborn streak that alternated with his periods of irresolution, seemed determined to transmit the reply to the commissioners as he had written it. "These gentlemen," Stanton protested, "claim to be ambassadors. It is preposterous! They cannot be ambassadors; they are lawbreakers, traitors. They should be arrested. You cannot negotiate with them; and yet it seems by this paper that you have been led into doing that very thing. With all respects to you, Mr. President, I must say that the Attorney-General, under his oath of office, dares not be cognizant of the pending proceedings. Your reply to these so-called ambassadors must not be transmitted as the reply of the President. It is wholly unlawful and improper; its language is unguarded and to send it as an official document will bring the President to the verge of usurpation." [4] Black spoke equally plainly; but when the meeting broke up, late that night, Buchanan gave no indication that he had changed his mind.

Buchanan's seeming willingness to give in to the South Carolina commissioners brought Stanton to despair. Unable to sleep, barely taking time for meals, he visited his friend Sickles's apartment, and in an unquiet mood walked back and forth, saying: "Something must be done."

He came to a momentous decision: he decided to throw party fealty and cabinet secrecy to the winds and to work behind the President's back. To be sure, he had alternative courses of action. Stanton could have resigned his office, openly signaling his individual protest against Buchanan's course, and resigning now would have added to his already large reputation, returned him to a lucrative private practice, and relieved him of all the heavy responsibility involved in the crisis at hand.

But he feared that Buchanan might replace him with someone susceptible to Southern arguments, who might in turn persuade the pliant President to abandon all firmness concerning secession. Unless Stanton's resignation was accompanied by Black's and Holt's, it might be construed as a merely individual difference of policy with Buchanan. And he was egotist enough to feel, with much justice, that his departure from the cabinet would delight Southern extremists and add

---

[4] Flower, *Stanton*, 88; Morse, *Welles Diary*, II, 273–4. For an opposite view of Floyd, see Robert M. Hughes, "John B. Floyd and his Traducers," *VMHB*, XLIII, 316–29. The text of Buchanan's Dec. 29 reply has disappeared from the records.

weight to that segment of Northern opinion which agreed with Buchanan that no way existed to keep the states united.

Stanton could not shut his eyes and let matters slide. As ever with this stubborn, combative man, results were what counted. He had never surrendered a case in court and he would not do so now. As a lawyer he had not displayed great respect for abstract constitutionalism. All about him were evidences that legalistic interpretations concerning the nature of the Union and limitations upon the power of the national government were sustaining mainly those persons who sought to kill the Republic. This was, in his mind, no time to worry over proprieties or to be concerned with theories of the separation of powers. Defections, conspiracies, and treasons were everywhere. Stanton was worried that his own life was in danger. Far from becoming hysterical, however, he chose a deliberate course of quiet action.

The path he selected to travel led to Capitol Hill. Ever respecting power, Stanton realized that the White House was moribund, the Supreme Court irrelevant and discredited, and the Democratic party hopelessly divided. Congress and its Republican leaders were the last hope for a strong policy, the last place for him to turn. He barely stopped to consider the fact that as a cabinet officer he was the President's servant, and that in dealing secretly with congressmen he was violating his oath of office. In later years he responded to this criticism of his decision with the assertion that by the oath he had sworn he was also the nation's servant.

His decision to inform opposition congressmen concerning cabinet developments was an ultimately successful effort to bypass the partisan and institutional obstructions to communication which now blocked Pennsylvania Avenue and which were bringing the nation to an attitude of helpless weakness. During his stay in Washington, and especially in his brief cabinet tenure, Stanton had come to realize that the peculiarly rigid triangular structure of American national government had become even more inflexible because of the political and sectional divisions that were rending the land. Partisanship was preventing the exercise of national power. Stanton would cast party aside in favor of power, for only by some show of strength might the nation survive until the President-elect took office.

Stanton's actions brought him to a thin line separating patriotism in the nation's cause from betrayal of his official trust as a cabinet officer. The sincerity of his patriotic impulse is the only justification for Stanton's becoming a devious informant. Holt and General Scott were soon to decide upon similar courses; few Americans would be able to escape choices of allegiance in the weeks and years to come.

Once decided, Stanton shrewdly chose such former Whigs as Thomas Ewing and such Republicans as Seward as his channels to Congress. On the same day as the explosive cabinet meeting—December 29— Seward wrote to Lincoln: "At last I have gotten a position in which I can see what is going on in the councils of the President. It pains me to learn that things are even worse than understood." Buchanan, according to Seward's informant, might still recall Anderson, surrender Sumter, and continue to permit arming of the South. A plot was forming to seize the capital before or on Lincoln's inauguration day, and high officials were involved. More he would not commit to paper, Seward warned, "but you must not imagine that I am giving you suspicion and rumors. Believe me I know what I write." Stanton also met with Ewing "nightly for ten or twelve nights," and, as Ewing later recalled, "reported the condition of things and consulted as to future measures." But Stanton thought that it was more circumspect to keep his meetings with Seward as secret as possible.

Watson, Stanton's associate in the Reaper case, served as their intermediary. Scarcely a day passed that Watson did not convey a message to Seward, sometimes in writing but usually by word of mouth. In some cases "particularly perplexing," Seward declared, he had Stanton's permission to identify him as the source of confidential cabinet information, especially to Lincoln and other high-ranking Republicans.

Every day, when Seward returned home, he would ask: "Has anyone called while I was at the Senate?" And often the reply would be: "Yes, Mr. Watson was here to talk about a patent case." Only twice from the end of December to March 4 of the next year did Stanton and Seward talk together personally, but the channel existed through Watson and it achieved Stanton's purposes.[5]

As Washington's church bells sounded the call to Sunday worship on December 30, Black, who remained ignorant of Stanton's dealings with the Republicans, went to Stanton's house and told him that if

[5] Wilson, "Jeremiah S. Black and Edwin M. Stanton," *loc. cit.*, 465–8; Frederick W. Seward, *Seward at Washington, 1846–1861* (New York, 1891), 492 (cited hereafter as Seward, *Seward*) ; Ewing's reminiscence in Cincinnati *Commercial*, Nov. 3, 1864; Muriel Burnit (ed.), "Two MSS of Gideon Welles," *NEQ*, XI, 589; Sickles, "Address . . . ," *loc. cit.*, 331. See also Burton J. Hendrick, *Lincoln's War Cabinet* (Boston, 1946), 254. On the ethicality of Stanton's action, see Richard F. Fenno, Jr., *The President's Cabinet* (Cambridge, 1959), 139.

Buchanan insisted on sending the commissioners the letter he had read to the cabinet, he would resign. Stanton, equally agitated, stated that he and Holt would follow Black in the same course. As he had advised Wolcott, such an action by several of the Northern cabinet officers would be like Anderson's move to Sumter—the spiking of guns in order to move to a stronger position and thus keep the country's flag flying.

Still, Black hesitated to approach Buchanan, perhaps because of the hard words he had spoken to him the night before; so he found Toucey and asked him to tell the President what he intended to do. Buchanan was confounded by the news, and sent for Black. With the North in a fever of anxiety over Sumter and with newspapers denouncing the administration for impotence and cowardice, these resignations, following so soon after that of Cass, would leave the administration bereft of Northern support.

When Black walked into the White House, Buchanan said that he had thought that Black, of all persons, would not desert him in this bitter hour, the darkest he had known. Black responded that he longed to stand by, "but your answer to the commissioners . . . sweeps the ground from under your feet; it places you where no man can stand with you, and where you cannot stand alone." After refusing his request that Fort Sumter be reinforced, Buchanan turned over to Black the reply he had written to the commissioners, and promised to revise it if Black would put his objections in writing and have them in the President's hands by six o'clock that afternoon.[6]

Black hurried to Stanton's office. Stanton thought Buchanan should not answer the commissioners at all, but as he seemed determined to do so, Stanton joined Black in studying Buchanan's paper point by point. Black wrote out his objections, Stanton incorporated them with his own, and then he copied the written sheets as rapidly as he could, both men laboring under high excitement. They deprecated even an implied acknowledgment of South Carolina's right to send diplomatic representatives to treat with the United States; the Charleston forts belonged to the government, and the power to retain the public property even against state forces must not be frittered away. That power, the Black-Stanton argument ran, might legitimately involve coercion of a state. Buchanan must contradict the Carolinians' claim that he had made a pledge concerning the forts, for if undenied "it . . . ties his hands so that he cannot, without breaking his word, 'preserve, protect,

[6] Undated memo No. 56426, Black Papers, LC; Wolcott MS, 169; No. 3761, undated, Holt Papers, LC; Black's reminiscence in Philadelphia *Press*, Sept. 10, 1883.

and defend the Constitution and see the laws faithfully executed.' "

While Black took the document to the President, Stanton relieved his excited feelings by penning a letter to a Pittsburgh friend, explaining the current situation: "Judge Black is closer to the President than myself and exercises a great deal of influence over him. He will present the written objections, which I have just prepared, and stand by for the purpose of extricating the President from his present peril. If he shall refuse to recede from it, it seems to me there is no escape for Black, Holt, and myself except resignation." For Stanton believed that if Buchanan bowed to the Carolinians, "there will not be a semblance of a Union left by March 4, next."

Stanton's reference to "the written objection, which I have just prepared," might be taken as proof that he composed most of the objections, and he told Holt a similar tale that day. On the other hand, Black stated to Holt that the President had authorized him to suggest such changes as he desired in Buchanan's intended reply, and that "I shall propose a radical alteration of the whole document." So far as authorship is concerned, however, the "Observations" Black had taken to the White House embodied the thinking of both men on points wherein they agreed fully. It is of little significance to decide, even were it possible, who fathered any specific phrase.

In later years Black claimed to be the sole author, and more than that, having had a falling out with Stanton, he depicted Stanton as following his lead—in effect giving Black two votes in the cabinet. "He did not furnish one atom of the influence which brought the President round on the answer to South Carolina," Black asserted.[7]

The important point is, of course, that Buchanan did come around, and for this stiffening in policy both Stanton and Black were responsible. To his credit, Stanton never denied Black's influence with Buchanan. All Stanton ever claimed was that he had played a part in these proceedings.

There seems no doubt that Stanton was steadfast enough to influence Buchanan directly as well as through Black. For example, Thompson wrote to Cobb: "Old Buck, at heart, is right with us, but after Stanton came in, I have seen him gradually giving way." Talking with Wolcott during the hectic December 27–30 period, Stanton had confided that

[7] Undated memo, "To the Public," Black Papers, LC; Black's reminiscence in Philadelphia *Press*, Sept. 10, 1883; Flower, *Stanton*, 90–3; Stampp, *op. cit.*, 77–8; Roy Franklin Nichols, *The Disruption of the American Democracy* (New York, 1948), 432.

"he [Stanton] will insist that Anderson shall be backed up with the whole power of the Government."

The news of Floyd's resignation had made Wolcott (and Stanton, from whom he derived his views) hopeful that Buchanan would deal sternly with South Carolina. There were rumors that the President intended to put Stanton in as Secretary of War in Floyd's place, and if that should happen, Wolcott wrote, "you 'may look for thunder about these days.' " But Stanton was not to get the war office.

Buchanan had been outraged by the insulting tone of Floyd's letter of resignation. When Floyd learned of the President's resentment he wrote an apology to Buchanan and offered to modify his words. Rumors flew around Washington that Southern emissaries had got to Buchanan and persuaded him to order Anderson back to Moultrie from Sumter, whereupon South Carolina would evacuate Moultrie and respect the status quo in Charleston Harbor until the end of Buchanan's term in office. Another rumor had it that Buchanan intended to take Floyd back into the cabinet.

The South Carolinians had indeed suggested the compromise; but Buchanan had rejected it. And he was through with Floyd. On Monday morning he accepted Floyd's resignation with a brief note, and that afternoon asked Holt to take over the war portfolio. Holt accepted, and Assistant Postmaster General Horatio King, of Maine, a firm Unionist, was put in charge of the Post Office Department.[8]

Although these evidences of a stiffening of attitude on Buchanan's part were encouraging to Stanton, he could not feel sure that the President would continue on this desirable track. Stanton therefore remained alert to combat any regression into the old weakness and, in addition to slipping news to Seward, busied himself in a dozen activities calculated to sustain national feeling and security.

He learned that, before resigning, Floyd had ordered 124 cannons shipped from the Allegheny Arsenal to Southern destinations. Part of this armament had been hauled to the Pittsburgh wharf and was being loaded on shipboard when a crowd gathered in front of the courthouse

[8] Wolcott MS, 170-1; U. B. Phillips (ed.), "Correspondence of Robert Toombs, Alexander H. Stephens, and Howell Cobb," AHA *Annual Report* (1911), II, 352; Gorham, *Stanton*, I, 151-8; and Morse, *Welles Diary*, I, 60. Other data in Nichols, *op. cit.*, 432-3; George Ticknor Curtis, *Life of James Buchanan* (New York, 1883), II, 52-3 (hereafter cited as Curtis, *Buchanan*); August Schell to Black, July 28, Black to Schell, Aug. 6, Buchanan to Black, Sept. 25, 1863, Black Papers, LC; David Davis to William W. Orme, Jan. 19, 1862, copy owned by Willard L. King.

to voice a public protest. Ellen's brother, James Hutchison, helped
to organize the meeting, and Shaler, Stanton's law partner, delivered a
rousing speech. Advised by telegraph of what was happening, Stanton
hurried to the War Department, where no one seemed to know about
Floyd's order. Stanton took the information to the President, who
showed neither surprise nor concern, although he asked Black to find
out about it. Black discovered that the order had been given orally to
the commander of the arsenal, and advised Buchanan to rescind it at
once.

A committee from Pittsburgh arrived in Washington, and Stanton
accompanied them to the White House. Buchanan consulted Holt and
as a result the order was canceled. Pittsburgh's city council sent a vote
of thanks to Buchanan, Stanton, and Holt.

Meanwhile, Buchanan, with the memorandum written by Black and
Stanton before him, revised his reply to the South Carolina commissioners. He restated his desire that Congress should deal with the
situation in a manner that would avoid war and denied that he had
made a pledge respecting the forts. Now, under threat of bloodshed, he
was being asked to remove the government forces entirely from
Charleston Harbor. "This I cannot do; this I will not do," he said
in the clarion language that Black and Stanton had hoped he would
use.

The South Carolina commissioners received the President's answer
on New Year's Eve. Next day at Buchanan's reception, grim-faced
Southerners, marching through the receiving line wearing blue secessionist cockades, rudely spurned the President's hand. Stanton, fearing
that indecision might again sway Buchanan, called his friend Sickles
to his office and arranged to send the tidings of the President's decision
to support Anderson to the principal Northern cities. "Fire some
powder," Stanton urged, ". . . go and fire some cannon and let the
echoes come to the White House." Sickles arranged mass meetings in
several Northern cities in order to bring pressure to bear on the
wavering Buchanan.

Stanton wrote to Harding, his colleague in the Reaper case, urging
him to promote a Union mass meeting in Philadelphia; on January 5
a gathering of 7,000 citizens adopted resolutions lauding Anderson
and calling on the President to provide him with all the forces he
required. At Stanton's instigation, Henry Winter Davis, a former
Kenyon acquaintance, now a congressman, wrote a public letter to his
constituents asserting that Maryland's interests demanded that the

Union be preserved and that she must not countenance revolutionary violence to redress imaginary wrongs.[9]

Smarting from failure and convinced that they were victims of executive deceit, the South Carolina commissioners sent an insulting rejoinder to Buchanan, accusing him of falsehood and warning that his course had "probably rendered civil war inevitable." Buchanan read the message with mounting anger, and on the advice of the Union members of his cabinet, wrote across the paper that its nature was such that "the President . . . declines to receive it." A messenger returned it to the disgruntled South Carolinians, who soon afterward left for home.

Convinced at last that the menace to Anderson was sufficiently acute to warrant his being reinforced, Buchanan instructed General Scott to put the warship *Brooklyn,* at Fort Monroe, in readiness to proceed to Charleston. Scott, fearing that the *Brooklyn* could not cross the bar at Charleston and wishing to act with all possible speed and secrecy, asked Buchanan to allow him to charter the fast unarmed merchant ship *Star of the West,* then lying at New York, and send it in place of the powerful *Brooklyn.* Buchanan yielded against his better judgment, and at 9 p.m. on January 5 the side-wheel steamer that had taken Stanton on the first leg of his journey to California churned across the bar at Sandy Hook, carrying 200 troops, 4 officers, supplies, arms, and ammunition. At the last minute word came from Anderson that he was fully able to hold out. Buchanan tried to countermand Scott's orders. But the ship had put to sea.

Somehow, Interior Secretary Thompson remained strangely unaware of the *Star of the West's* departure, and wired southward that no troops had been sent South, "nor will be" while he remained in the cabinet. But news of the expedition leaked out, and Thompson, seeking confirmation from Buchanan, became enraged at the President's deceit, as he defined it. He and others rushed off telegrams of warning. When the *Star of the West* steamed in toward Sumter on January 9, she was greeted by shells from South Carolina batteries. Helpless to return the fire, she put about and returned to New York.

Disgruntled, Thompson resigned from the cabinet, and Secretary of the Treasury Thomas followed him. "One by one the Secessionists

[9] Gorham, *Stanton,* I, 148–64; Bernard C. Steiner, *Life of Henry Winter Davis* (Baltimore, 1916), 171–7; Sickles in New York *Times,* Sept. 13, 1865; Clarence E. Macartney, "Some Prominent Pittsburghers of 1840–1850," *WPHM,* XXVIII, 44; Auchampaugh, *op. cit.,* 91–2; Curtis, *op. cit.,* II, 416–17.

have been worked out," Stanton wrote to Wolcott. "We are now a unit. Who will come to the present vacancies is uncertain. I think no retrograde step will be made. How far we can advance is uncertain.[1]

Buchanan, seeking a successor to Thomas for the Treasury portfolio, settled on John A. Dix, of New York. Stanton was delighted, for Dix, formerly a United States senator, had supported the Wilmot Proviso, favored the nomination of Van Buren by the free-soil Democrats in 1848, and opposed the organization of New Mexico or the admission of California unless slavery was excluded from them. Courageous, decisive, fluent, and possessed of proven executive ability, he would vastly strengthen the Unionists in the cabinet.

At first Buchanan had proposed to make Dix Secretary of War, moving Holt back to the Post Office Department in place of King and choosing someone else, probably a Southerner, for the Treasury. Stanton wanted no more Southerners in the cabinet and preferred that Holt stay where he was; so he enlisted the help of King to get a quick acceptance of the Treasury post from Dix before Buchanan could change his mind again.

Dix was already on his way to Washington. King met him at the depot, and on the way to Willard's Hotel obtained his acceptance of the Treasury headship. "Taking leave of him for the night," wrote King, ". . . I was driven at once to Mr. Stanton's residence. . . . Having company in the parlor, he met me in the hall, and when I informed him that all was as he desired, he was so filled with delight that he seized and embraced me in true German style."

When Dix's nomination was sent to the Senate, Stanton urged Seward to help bring about a speedy confirmation. At Buchanan's request, Dix took a room in the White House, where, almost every night for the next six weeks, he discussed affairs with the President and helped stiffen his will.

Soon after taking office, Dix sent a Treasury officer to New Orleans to take charge of a number of revenue cutters which had been tied up there and to dispatch them to New York. A Southern captain refused to surrender his vessel. Dix wired immediately to put him under arrest, and added: "If anyone attempts to haul down the Union flag, shoot him on the spot." General Scott and Stanton were the only officials who saw the order before it was sent, and Stanton commended Dix on its resolute tone. Stanton supported Scott in his quiet transferring of small detachments of regular soldiery to the Washington area,

---

[1] Wolcott, MS, 170; Brigance, *op. cit.*, 105–6.

which was made possible only by the fact that the cabinet was now clear of secessionist sympathizers.[2]

Though still obsessed with the idea of avoiding bloodshed, the President was aware that he had been ill rewarded for his friendliness toward the South. Alabama, Florida, and Georgia were taking over federal fortifications in emulation of South Carolina. Though still timid, Buchanan was surrounded now by firm Unionists—Black, Stanton, Holt, Dix, and King. He still believed, as did some of them, that compromise could be achieved. But come what might, he was now determined not to condone secession or surrender more government property.

Loyal Northerners entered upon the new year with rising spirits born of revived faith in the government. Holt drew warm praise for co-operating with Scott in raising the efficiency of the War Department. Black was commended for his consistently firm role. Dix had won immediate acclaim. And Stanton, according to Henry J. Raymond, of the New York *Times,* and Horace White, of the Chicago *Tribune,* was the backbone of the administration, responsible in large part for the change in Buchanan's attitude. Thurlow Weed confided to Lincoln that "Secretaries Stanton and Holt are doing their duty nobly."

Stanton does deserve a large measure of credit for whatever gains the Union cause had made. But he could not share in the growing confidence that the South would alter its disruptive course. "Public affairs are just now in . . . a dark and gloomy state," he confided to William Stanton. "How long we shall have any Government at Washington is doubtful." Stanton was tiring, his almost limitless energy draining away in unceasing activities, but more through fear that Buchanan would again reverse course and knuckle under to the South. And Stanton lacked confidence in Lincoln to improve the situation, even if the nation held together until he took office.[3] But he hid his doubts and, shrugging away fatigue, went on.

[2] King, *Turning on the Light* (Philadelphia, 1895), 189; Seward, *Seward,* 492; Frederick W. Seward, *Reminiscences of a War-Time Statesman and Diplomat, 1830–1915* (New York, 1916), 166 (hereafter cited as Seward, *Reminiscences*). See also Morgan Dix (ed.), *Memoirs of John A. Dix* (New York, 1883), I, 372; Martha J. Lamb, "Major-General John A. Dix," *MAH,* XIV, 167. Black later claimed that there had never been any thought of making Dix War Secretary or any possibility that King would lose his position; Stanton had deceived them all. See undated memo, box labeled "Legal Briefs," Black Papers, LC. Black's charge is controverted by all other evidence.

[3] Stanton to William Stanton, Feb. 26, 1861, owned by William Stanton Picher; undated clippings in Montgomery Meigs scrapbook, LC; Weed's letter in David C. Mearns (ed.), *The Lincoln Papers* (New York, 1948), II, 399.

On January 8, Buchanan submitted a special message to Congress, which, while demonstrating the augmented influence of his Unionist advisers, also revealed his continuing reluctance to take decisive action. Declaring his intention to "collect the public revenues and protect the public property," the President, in the next breath, commended the existing "revolution" to the attention of Congress and asserted that all responsibility rested on the intransigent Southerners. He backed off from his position of the preceding December; now he recommended that something akin to the 36° 30' dividing line of the Missouri Compromise extend to the Pacific, with slavery protected below it and forbidden elsewhere. Without comment, he submitted his correspondence with the South Carolina commissioners to Congress.

No sooner had the message been read than William A. Howard, representative from Michigan, secured passage of a resolution that the House appoint a special committee to inquire, among other matters, "whether any executive officer of the United States has been or is now treating or holding communication with any person or persons concerning the surrender of any forts, fortresses, or public property of the United States . . . [or] has at any time entered into any pledge, agreement, or understanding with any person or persons not to send any reinforcements to the forts of the United States in the harbor of Charleston."

Howard later wrote that the resolution was inspired by "loyal members of the Cabinet," who had prodded him to introduce it and to take its chairmanship. "I do not know that Mr. Stanton wrote the resolutions creating the Committee," he recalled. "I did not see him write them. I never heard him say he wrote them. It would be easier, however, to persuade me that Mr. Jefferson did not write the Declaration of Independence than that Mr. Stanton did not write these resolutions."

After weeks of investigation, a majority of the Howard committee recommended a bill specifically empowering the President to call out the militia to defend and recover forts and other government property, and another authorizing him to use the Navy to close insurrectionary ports. It presented a resolution declaring that suppressing treason was not the same as coercion of a state, and that the President had no authority to negotiate with persons who were dishonoring the flag.

In some of the actions of the committee, Stanton unquestionably had a hand. Committeeman Henry L. Dawes, of Massachusetts, recalled that memoranda, sent secretly by Stanton through Seward or directly to Howard, frequently gave the committee the lead to the next day's cross-examination. Chairman Howard remembered that he and Stanton did not meet "at any time between the 1st of January and the 4th of March, 1861, but I think I heard from him more times than there were days in those two months. The clearest statements . . . defining the boundaries of treason, the most startling facts, when the evidence of treachery could be found, were furnished."

There was treachery enough. The committee was tipped off that the officer who had surrendered the Pensacola navy yard to the secessionists was arranging to back-date his resignation to avoid a charge of treason. "We were put upon the inquiry," Howard remarked, "by a 'bird' which flew directly from some Cabinet minister to the committee room." In another instance, the Navy sent warships to Pensacola Harbor with reinforcements for Fort Pickens, but Senators Mason, of Virginia; Mallory, of Florida; and Slidell, of Louisiana interceded with Buchanan, urging him to avoid a hostile gesture by keeping the troops on shipboard unless the fort was threatened with attack. Buchanan put the proposal before the cabinet. Black, Stanton, and Dix were most earnestly opposed. Toucey favored acquiescence, and Buchanan authorized an order to that effect. Stanton, who detested Toucey for his tenderness toward the South, warned the committee that it should be prepared to arrest him on short notice.[4]

Since the convening of Congress in early December 1860, both houses had been trying to devise some formula of compromise. The House committee of thirty-three, one member from each state, had bogged down in futility; but the Senate committee of thirteen, composed of able men, suggested a number of plans. The only one that appeared to have a chance of adoption, however, was the handiwork of Crittenden, of Kentucky. He proposed a series of permanent amendments to the Constitution whereby, among other provisions, the territorial problem would be settled by extending the Missouri Compromise line of 36° 30′ to the Pacific; in effect, slavery was to be forever excluded north of it and guaranteed in all territory to the south then owned or thereafter acquired by the United States.

A considerable number of congressmen looked with favor on this plan. But Lincoln advised the Republican leaders that it might impel Southern expansionists to try to annex Cuba or to grab more land from Mexico. Urging them confidentially to hold firm on the Republican

---

[4] Wilson, "Jeremiah S. Black and Edwin M. Stanton," *loc. cit.,* 467, for Howard's letter, and see Hendrick, *op. cit.,* 255–6. Richardson, *Messages and Papers,* V, 655–9, has Buchanan's message.

platform of uncompromising opposition to the expansion of slavery on any terms, he blocked the adoption.

While Congress worked itself into stalemate, Mississippi, Florida, Alabama, Georgia, Louisiana, and Texas passed secession ordinances. The four states of the upper South—Virginia, Arkansas, Tennessee, and North Carolina—though taking no overt action at this time, made it clearly evident that they would resist any effort of the government to coerce their sister slave states, and Virginia proposed that the states send delegates to a Peace Conference at Washington on February 4, to work out a formula of compromise on the basis of Crittenden's proposal. But none of the states that had seceded manifested any interest in the conference.

Senators and representatives from those states had begun to resign from Congress, though several of them stayed on in Washington as potential troublemakers. Government workers gave up their jobs and started South. Others were suspected of keeping their positions only to spy. The capital seethed with rumors of plots and dark designs. Holt, Stanton, and General Scott joined Black in pleading for the immediate reinforcement of the city. The Howard committee, at Stanton's instigation, began to investigate subversion in the capital and among federal employees.

Stanton confidentially advised Chase that he believed an effort to set up a provisional Confederate government in Washington would be made before March 4, and that it might very well be successful. Holt would resist it with every weapon at his command, but the available force was wholly inadequate. Buchanan had no power to accept offers of volunteer troops from the loyal states without authorization from Congress and would not ask for permission. The Union men in Congress should go ahead and pass such a law on their own initiative, said Stanton. In fact, they should have done it before this.

Armed men were drilling in companies and battalions in Washington every night, Stanton informed Chase. But Buchanan could not be persuaded that the country faced an emergency. Stanton believed that the crux of the situation lay in the retention of the capital, "keeping the forms, archives, and symbols of established government out of the hands of the revolutionists. If they do not get possession of these, all the seceding ordinances, laws, etc.. are nothing more than paper filibustering, which must soon be exhausted and give place to the reestablishment of law & order—even in the seceding states."

An attempt to seize Washington was imminent, he warned, and those "who mean to maintain the Government & enjoy their constitutional right to administer it for the next four years, should be diligently preparing & making ready for the emergency that will surely soon be upon them, and may come at any hour." Having obtained the capital, the revolutionists would seek recognition from foreign governments. That gained, their power would be unshakable.[5]

On January 24, while Chase read this, doddering former President Tyler, head of the Virginia delegation to the Peace Conference, arrived in Washington and received Buchanan's promise to support the efforts of the conference. Next day, Stanton had an interview with Sumner, who, like Chase, would command great influence when the Republicans came to power.

Stanton drew Sumner into his office. Then, glancing around at the clerks, he took him through six different rooms and, finding them all occupied, finally led him into the entry. "He told me," Sumner reported to Republican Governor John A. Andrew, of Massachusetts, "that he was 'surrounded by secessionists'—who would report in an hour to the newspapers any interview between us—that he must see me at some other time & place—that everything was bad as could be." Stanton warned Sumner that the Virginia peace effort was merely a smoke screen and would come to nothing, "that Virginia would most certainly secede—that the conspiracy there was the most wide-spread & perfect." Kentucky would follow Virginia, and Maryland would go too. Virginia's real purpose was not to bring peace, but "to constitute a Provisional Govt. which was to take possession of the Capital & declare itself a nation." Recounting this conversation to Governor Andrew, Sumner urged him to "keep Massachusetts out of all these schemes," and agreed with Stanton that "we are in the midst of a revolution."

Three nights later Stanton had another conference with Sumner. "I know from him what I cannot communicate," Sumner wrote to Andrew. "Suffice it to say, *he does not think it probable, hardly possible* that we shall be here on the 4th March. The Presdt has been trimming again; . . . Genl. Scott is very anxious." [6]

On February 2, five days after talking with Stanton, Sumner met with Buchanan. The President insisted that the best thing Massachu-

[5] Stanton to Chase, Jan. 23, 1861, Chase Papers, HSP; Black to Buchanan, Jan. 22, 1861, Black Papers, LC.

[6] Jan. 26, 28, 1861, Andrew Papers, MHS; Wilson, "Jeremiah S. Black and Edwin M. Stanton," *loc. cit.*, 466. The latest scholarship on this meeting is in Robert G. Gunderson, *Old Gentlemen's Convention: The Washington Peace Conference of 1861* (Madison, 1961).

setts could do for the country was to approve the Crittenden proposition. Sumner vehemently expressed his disbelief in the wisdom or desirability of such a course. Stanton had steeled the senator to stand fast. Sumner would have been surprised to learn that Stanton, shortly before warning him to shun the Peace Conference which hoped to bring about the adoption of the Crittenden plan, had advised some Steubenville residents that if the Republicans in Congress would endorse the compromise proposal, "I think the troubles that now disturb and endanger the country would be speedily removed."

Here again Stanton was playing both sides, for he had to retain Buchanan's confidence or else lose all influence with the uncertain President. Stanton's liaison role with the Republicans was the secret one, although his Unionist position in cabinet proceedings was frank enough. So far as the rest of the world was concerned, however, he took the official Buchanan posture of conciliation for the South.[7]

Former Governor John H. Clifford and Stephen Philips, of Massachusetts, were in Washington at this time, and on January 30, Stanton gave them the same sort of warning he had given to Chase and Sumner about an attempt to seize Washington, and asked them to convey it to Governor Andrew. Stanton had told them of the development of "a terrible and treasonable conspiracy," conceived at the 1860 Charleston convention, to take over the North, not merely to remove the South from the union of states. Thus, the "symbols of government," the public buildings and records of Washington, were in danger of seizure. Stanton, Scott, and Holt were "pressing the President every way with poor success." The issue must become military, not political, Stanton had insisted, but in view of Buchanan's refusal to assemble troops, all he can do "is to pass the word along & beg true men to see that all is done which can be done."

Stanton did not suffer from "a nervous trepidation; I am sure I only state what Stanton evidently believes," Philips wrote Andrew. He was impressed by Stanton's logic, by his concern for the safety of the capital and the necessity to keep the border states for the Union, which foreshadowed Lincoln's policy a year later. Buchanan only that morning had refused the army commander his request for a substantial increase in the military forces near Washington.[8]

---

[7] Doyle, *op. cit.*, 67–9; Nevins, *The Emergence of Lincoln* (New York, 1950), II, 431.

[8] Philips to Horace Gray, Jan. 31, 1861, Gray Papers (photostat), LC; Clifford to Andrew, Jan. 30, 1861, NYHS; Charles Francis Adams to Andrew, Jan. 4, 1861, Andrew Papers, MHS.

Andrew conveyed the substance of Stanton's warning to the Massachusetts legislature, which on February 3 voted an emergency fund of $100,000 to be placed in the hands of the governor. The governor sent a state official to Washington to confer with General Scott, and, fearful that the land route to Washington would be blocked if Maryland seceded, as Stanton had warned, he authorized an investigation of a possible water route to the capital.

Scott, responsible for the military safety of the capital, and sharing Stanton's fears and uncertainty over the degree of Buchanan's support, mustered what weak strength the regular army offered for the defense of Washington. But on the day the Peace Conference assembled, Stanton wrote to his former Steubenville partner, McCook, that these forces would easily be overcome if Maryland and Virginia should secede. South Carolina had made another demand for Fort Sumter, but it had been pitched in a lower key, and Stanton did not believe that Anderson would be attacked. The presence of the *Brooklyn* and the *Macedonia* had made the insurgents more cautious at Pensacola. "It was very plain," wrote Stanton, "that as long as the United States continued to run away there would be no 'bloodshed' and now that the Government has determined to stand its ground there will still be 'no bloodshed.' " [9] The new policy of firmness was paying off, he felt. Within a week, however, delegates from the seceding states met in Montgomery, Alabama, proclaimed the Confederate States of America, and elected Jefferson Davis President.

Excitement in Washington mounted as February 13, the day for counting the electoral votes, approached; Stanton, along with many others, feared that secessionist conspirators might choose this time to attempt their *coup d'état*. Additional companies of regulars were stationed at strategic points throughout the city. Militia guarded the Potomac bridges. Officers were ordered to be ready for instant action, day or night.

But no hostile demonstrations took place. The day passed quietly. Five days later Jefferson Davis took the oath of office as President of the Confederacy, and Lincoln started for Washington by a winding route that would take him through many Northern cities.

Stanton, Holt, and Scott, fearing that the attempt to take the capital had merely been deferred and that Lincoln's inauguration would be the signal for an outbreak of revolt, again urged Buchanan to ask

[9] To McCook, Feb. 4, 1861, McCook Family Papers, LC; Harrison Ritchie to Andrew, Feb. 6, 1861, Andrew Papers, MHS; Henry G. Pearson, *Life of John A. Andrew* (Boston, 1904), I, 159–60 (hereafter cited as Pearson, *Andrew*).

Congress to increase the strength of the Army so that it could meet any emergency. When their efforts were unavailing, Stanton went to his cousin, Benjamin Stanton, of Ohio, chairman of the House Committee on Military Affairs, and urged him to initiate action. Congressman Stanton's committee reported out a bill authorizing the President to call out the militia in case of a general insurrection. But conservative congressmen feared that the bill would antagonize the recently convened Virginia state convention, where loyal delegates were holding out against impatient secessionists. Lincoln, arriving in Washington on the twenty-third, also threw his influence against the measure, and it failed to pass.

During all this time, Black and Buchanan had no inkling of Stanton's secret dealings with the Republicans. A decade later, when former Senator Henry Wilson, of Massachusetts, revealed part of Stanton's clandestine activities, Black declared in amazement: "Surely, if these things are true, he was the most marvellous impostor who ever lived or died." [1]

As a matter of fact, Holt and General Scott as well as Stanton were working closely with Benjamin Stanton, who in 1865 denied a claim made by Montgomery Blair that Edwin Stanton in 1860 and 1861 had been in full sympathy with the Southern leaders in Congress who were dragging the South into secession. Blair had learned from Albert G. Brown, senator from Mississippi, that in early January 1861 Brown had met Stanton just after Mississippi had seceded and Brown had resigned from the Senate. According to Brown, Stanton had approved his actions and stated: "You have only to secede to secure your rights. . . . It was the only course to save the South."

Such a statement of Brown's, if unsupported, might be dismissed as sheer vindictiveness which Blair, who hated Stanton, was uncritically willing to accept. But if supported, Brown's recollection indicates that Stanton may sometimes have advocated the extremist Southern view in order to conceal his secret arrangement with Unionist leaders and to gain information, all the while publicly supporting the Buchanan position of favoring the Crittenden proposal. If this is true, Stanton was indeed a master of duplicity, however lofty his purpose.

[1] Benjamin Stanton to Holt, Sept. 19, 1865, Holt Papers, LC; Wilson, "Jeremiah S. Black and Edwin M. Stanton," *loc. cit.*, 463–75; Black, "Senator Wilson and Edwin M. Stanton," *Galaxy*, IX, 817–31; same, "Mr. Black and Mr. Wilson," *loc. cit.*, 257–76. Thompson (to Black, June 7, 1870, Black Papers, LC) wrote that he would have believed Holt rather than Stanton capable of such duplicity.

The only evidence in support of the Blair-Brown argument, however, is fragmentary and does not convince that Stanton ever supported secession. To be sure, his friend, the Washington lawyer of Southern birth, Philip Phillips, years later recalled that in 1861 Stanton was "a stronger sympathizer with the South than I was." Stanton's conduct during the secession winter became the subject of reminiscences at a dinner party ten years later, and Caleb Cushing, prominent Massachusetts Democrat and former trusted Buchanan lieutenant, stated that he, Stanton, and others had met frequently in early 1861 to talk over events, and that Stanton had been so outspoken in defense of Southern rights that listeners thought him a "rebel."

According to Cushing, Stanton was "a duplex character." And perhaps he was. But James E. Harvey, who recorded Cushing's allegations, noted that "*I* think he [Cushing] is even a triplex," and that everyone knew of the long-standing personal, professional, and political enmities which had marred Stanton's relationship with Cushing.[2]

But neither Blair nor Cushing ever advanced more than their own recollections or assertions concerning Stanton as an advocate of secession. Indeed, when Blair in 1865 searched for proof that Stanton had pressured Robert Tyler toward secession, knowing that evidence from Tyler would be believed above other accusers of Stanton, he had to admit that his quest was unsuccessful. Stanton may have been all that Black, Blair, Cushing, and others claimed. The fact remains that they did not prove it, and Stanton's actions as a Unionist give the lie to the claims.

Assuming, however, that any or all of these accusations of two-faced action are true, the question arises: Was he looking out for himself, as Blair claimed and Gideon Welles believed, so that he would benefit no matter which way the cards might fall, or was he acting deceitfully and unselfishly to promote the Union cause? In the law as well as in politics he had resorted to trickery to gain his ends. Playing now for the survival of the Union, Stanton would not have scrupled to employ deceit. He shared with many other men during the last, wearying months of Buchanan's incumbency, a genuine fear and conviction that secessionists were plotting to gain control of Washington. To learn the

---

[2] Blair, *op. cit.*, 15, and Brown in New York *Herald*, Feb. 4, 1865; Harvey to Black, Oct. 2, 1870, Black Papers, LC; Phillips, ms, "Summary of the Principal Events of My Life," UNC; Albert E. H. Johnson, "Reminiscences of the Hon. Edwin M. Stanton, Secretary of War," ColHS *Records*, XIII, 69.

details of such a plot, Edwin Stanton would have posed as the devil himself.[3]

To most of Stanton's contemporaries of 1861, he was clearly a nationalist "of the same school of politics with Judge Black," as Benjamin Butler later recalled. Though Black was shocked when he learned years later of Stanton's liaison with the Republicans, the members of that party who knew about Stanton's actions regarded him as a man who put patriotism above party, and Lincoln even considered a suggestion that he take Stanton, as well as Holt and Dix, into his cabinet, notwithstanding Stanton's rudeness to him in the Reaper case.

News that Lincoln was toying with the idea of keeping some of Buchanan's cabinet in his own administration soon spread over Washington. Stanton must have gloried that his exertions of recent weeks would receive public approbation.

But Lincoln, although willing to forget the rudeness he had formerly suffered at Stanton's hands, had to choose other men than these for his official family. In addition to his continuing contempt for the gawky Illinoisan, Stanton now added anger born of disappointment at the cessation of his chances for continued official recognition and, in his own mind, for further opportunities to forward policies he felt were desirable for the country.

On February 25, two days after Lincoln entered Washington in partial disguise because of a rumored plot to assassinate him, the "Public Man," an anonymous writer whose identity has never been discovered, recorded in his diary that Stanton had stopped him to ask if he had seen the President-elect since he had "crept" into Washington. "It is impossible to be more bitter and malignant than he is," wrote the diarist; "every word was a suppressed and a very ill-suppressed sneer, and it cost me something to keep my temper in talking with him even for a few moments. When he found that I had only met Mr. Lincoln once, to my recollection, he launched out into a downright tirade about him, saying he 'had met him at the bar, and found him a low, cunning clown.' " [4] The new President would have to accomplish great things to gain Stanton's respect.

[3] Blair to Tyler, undated, *ca.* Aug. 1865, in "Original Letters," *WMQ*, 1st ser., XX, 123; Buchanan to Horatio King, April 21, 1866, King Papers, LC; Morse, *Welles Diary*, I, 355–60; Samuel Sullivan Cox, *Three Decades of Federal Legislation, 1855 to 1885* (Providence, 1885), 200.

[4] T. J. Coffey and others to Cameron, Feb. 22, 23, 1861, Cameron Papers, LC; Butler to Dwight Roberts, Butler Letterbook, LC; F. Lauriston Bullard (ed.), *The Diary of a Public Man* (New Brunswick, 1946), 55–6; and see F. M. Anderson, *The Mystery of 'A Public Man'* (Minneapolis, 1948).

Stanton was now too busy to pay more than passing attention to political surmise. He was simultaneously working with Holt, Black, and Dix to sustain Anderson at Sumter, to maintain the uneasy "truce" which existed at Fort Pickens in Florida, and almost incidentally to keep up the schedule of his own department. In this last, he failed. On March 2, he had to assemble a list of "references which could not be considered by Attorney General Stanton in consequence of the want of time and the pressure of business, and which were therefore returned without opinions."

March 4 came, and while crowds gathered in the streets, waiting for the inaugural procession, Buchanan and his cabinet assembled in the President's room at the Capitol for the consideration of any last-minute bills that Congress might send to the President. Stanton had hoped that one bill that he had drawn to expedite the operations of the federal courts, and which Seward had forwarded in Congress, might come in time, but it failed to pass in the closing rush of legislation.[5]

Outside an artillery battery wheeled into place on Capitol Hill. The city was well guarded, owing to the alertness of Stanton and his cabinet colleagues and the loyalty of General Scott. Shortly before noon, Buchanan left to accompany Lincoln to the inaugural ceremonies, and the group broke up.

Stanton listened with gratification not unmixed with personal disdain as Lincoln, standing on a platform erected in front of the Capitol and speaking in a high-pitched voice with a Kentucky accent that sounded inelegant to Easterners, enunciated the same sort of policy that Stanton, Black, and Holt had been instrumental in persuading Buchanan to adopt. He had no intention of interfering with slavery where it existed, the new President declared. He would enforce the fugitive slave law and even support a proposed constitutional amendment guaranteeing slavery in the states against federal interference. But he denied the right of secession, and expressed a determination to enforce the laws in all the states, "unless my rightful masters, the American people, shall withhold the requisite means, or, in some authoritative manner, direct the contrary." Like Buchanan, he deplored the use of force. And yet, unlike Buchanan, Lincoln asserted that he would meet force with force.

Stanton left the inauguration scene buoyed up in his hope, but re-

[5] Stanton to Seward, Feb. 23, 1861, Seward Papers, UR; Stanton's report is in Miscellaneous Collection No. 2133, LC; Holt's report, in Robert Anderson Papers, LC, surveys the Sumter crisis and the roles of Buchanan's cabinet personnel in preventing the abandonment of the fort.

luctant to place his trust in the hands of the new President. "The inauguration is over and whether for good or evil Abraham Lincoln is President of the United States," Stanton wrote that afternoon. "Who will form the Cabinet is yet uncertain in respect to some officers—others are known."

He grew pessimistic even as he wrote—"The inaugural will do no good towards settling difficulties—probably aggravate them." But he would keep alert and for at least two days more would stay on in his office to introduce whoever would succeed him.

That evening Buchanan and the members of his cabinet gathered at a private residence to say farewell to one another. A few days later Stanton dined with Seward, now Lincoln's Secretary of State, at Seward's home. Thurlow Weed, Seward's inseparable political confidant, recorded that "it was then and there that I learned how large a debt we owed him [Stanton] before the Rebellion began."

Indeed, Stanton had done his full share to keep the national government in existence. He returned to private life still certain that Buchanan had never fully wakened to the implications of the crisis with which Lincoln now must deal.[6]

[6] Stanton to P. D. Lowe, March 4, 1861, BU; Thurlow Weed Barnes, *Memoir of Thurlow Weed* (Boston, 1884), 331–2; Weed in New York *Times*, Sept. 7, 1865; Stanton's comments to Weed on Buchanan in Steubenville *Herald*, May 10, 1867; Brigance, *op. cit.*, 116. The inaugural speech is in Richardson, *Messages and Papers*, VI, 5–12.

CHAPTER VI

FROM CRITIC TO COLLEAGUE

$\mathbb{A}$LONE of Buchanan's former cabinet, Stanton remained in Washington. Little Eleanor had fallen dangerously ill, and so he kept close to the center of events, although he and his family mingled little in the crisis-torn society of the capital.

On March 5, Lincoln submitted his cabinet choices to the Senate, and all of them were speedily confirmed: Stanton's friend Seward, Secretary of State; his old Ohio confidant, Chase, Secretary of the Treasury; Simon Cameron, Secretary of War; Gideon Welles, Secretary of the Navy; Caleb B. Smith, a supposedly influential Indiana politician, Secretary of the Interior; Edward Bates, a prominent Missouri lawyer, Attorney General; and Montgomery Blair, of Maryland, scion of a family whose power in politics dated back to Jackson's time, Postmaster General.

Stanton watched the beginnings of the new administration with a suspicious and critical eye, for like Buchanan he anticipated a spate of Republican investigations into their official conduct and had no confidence whatever in Lincoln. The progress of events during the first weeks of his administration confirmed the worst forebodings. It appeared that some members of Lincoln's cabinet intended to abandon the Southern forts that Stanton and his colleagues in Buchanan's council had striven so desperately to hold. Having presumed that Lincoln, with no Southern entanglements, would act decisively for the Union, he was angrier with the new President than he had ever been with Buchanan or Buchanan's secession advisers.

A horde of office seekers had descended on Washington, paralyzing government business. "Every department is overrun," he informed Buchanan, "and by the time that all the patronage is distributed the

Republican party will be dissolved." Stanton advised Seward to "fill all the places as soon as possible so as to get at the real work before you." But Stanton, too, sought office for some of his friends, and he himself was pushed forward so insistently by Seward and Chase that he could scarcely have been ignorant of their efforts in his behalf.[1]

In cabinet, Seward and Chase several times proposed Stanton for federal attorney of the District of Columbia. Lincoln, from no love for Stanton but out of his desire to gain Northern Democratic support, was willing to try him, but decided that the disposition of this office properly belonged to Attorney General Bates. Stanton, meanwhile, busy with private affairs, told Chase that he wanted no official post, and thus the matter was decided.

Seward and Chase still felt that Stanton deserved to be rewarded, and Weed, who watched closely over patronage, suggested that Stanton get the diplomatic post at Constantinople. Nothing came of this proposal, however, and if Stanton prompted these efforts in his behalf, resentment and disappointment may have inspired the criticisms he was leveling at the Lincoln administration as it fumbled for a policy regarding Sumter. The critical situation had worsened in Charleston Harbor. Word had come from Anderson that his supplies would be exhausted in four or five weeks.[2]

Dispirited, Stanton asked Dix, in New York City, to sell his government bonds for him on the market. "My reason for selling so soon is, that every sign here is discouraging," he explained. "There is no settled principle or line of action—no token of any intelligent understanding by Lincoln, or the crew that govern him, of the state of the country, or the exigencies of the times. Bluster & bravado alternates with timosity & despair—recklessness and helplessness by turns rule the hour. What but disgrace and disaster can happen?"

However, Stanton did not believe that the war, if it came, would last long. "Nor indeed do I think hostilities will be so great an evil as many apprehend," he confided to Dix. "A round or two often serves to restore harmony; and the vast consumption required by a state of hostilities, will enrich rather than impoverish the North."[3]

[1] Curtis, *Buchanan*, II, 529, 533–4; Seward, *Seward*, 525; Stanton to Horatio King, March 15, 1861, King Papers, LC; Caleb Smith to R. W. Thompson, April 16, 1861, LNLF; Flower, *Stanton*, 108.

[2] Curtis, *Buchanan*, II, 528–30; Morse, *Welles Diary*, I, 54–7; Hendrick, *op. cit.*, 259–60; Weed to Seward, May 13, 1861, Seward Papers, UR.

[3] Quoted in Martin Lichterman, *John Adams Dix, 1798–1879* (Ph.D. thesis, Columbia University, 1952), 413–16.

On April 10, Stanton heard that the District militia had been called to arms and soldiers were guarding the departments. A midnight rumor said that Sumter had already been fired on. Washington woke to a tense dawn, and Stanton again relieved his feelings in a letter to Buchanan. No one knew what to believe about Sumter, he declared, but it seemed likely that an expedition had been sent. Virginia was expected momentarily to secede, and disloyalists in Washington had become extremely bold. Few persons respected Lincoln or the administration. Of the cabinet members, only Seward had rented a house in Washington; none of them had brought his family to the city, and Stanton thought that all of them were ready to "cut and run."

Activity at army posts and at the Brooklyn Navy Yard confirmed the rumor that supplies and perhaps troops were on their way to Anderson. People waited anxiously for news. On April 12 it came: guns were flashing in Charleston Harbor! Stanton wrote hastily to Buchanan: "We have the war upon us! . . . The impression is held by many: 1st, that the effort to reinforce will be a failure; 2nd, that in less than twenty-four hours from this time Anderson will have surrendered; 3rd, that in less than thirty days Davis will be in possession of Washington."

Actually, there had been no attempt to reinforce the fort. But to the Confederates the announcement of Lincoln's intention to send supplies to Anderson had meant the continued presence of a "hostile" force in one of their principal harbors. Unwilling to tolerate such a situation any longer, they had opened a destructive fire on Sumter. After holding on for thirty hours, Anderson surrendered.

The news from Sumter sent a wave of patriotism surging through the North. Even persons who had been sympathetic toward the South now cursed the Confederates for beginning a brothers' war. Lincoln issued a proclamation convening a special session of Congress on July 4 and calling on the states for 75,000 militia to serve for thirty days. Volunteers responded so eagerly that state authorities were swamped. In cities, towns, the villages, men joined up and drilled to the cheers of onlookers. Drums rolled, fifes trilled, flags rippled everywhere.

But disaster already threatened; for Lincoln's proclamation, while inspiring the North, also moved the slave states to band together in defense of Southern rights. Within two days the Virginia state convention had passed an ordinance of secession. Arkansas and Tennessee quickly followed Virginia's lead. North Carolina made it evident that

she would join her sister slave states. The border slave states—
Delaware, Maryland, Kentucky, and Missouri—teetered uncertainly.

On April 19, the 6th Massachusetts Infantry, en route to Washington, was mobbed as it passed through Baltimore. Secessionists tore up
railroad tracks and telegraph wires leading north and west from
Washington. Virtually defenseless, the city was cut off from the North.
Across the river hostile campfires flickered in the night. Stanton wrote
to Dix, who was striving mightily to rally Union spirit in New York
City, that the state of affairs in Washington was desperate beyond
conception. "If there be any remedy—any shadow of hope to preserve
this government from utter and absolute extinction—it must come from
New York without delay." [4]

Silence settled over Washington as stores were closed and boarded
up. Barricades protected public buildings. Army and navy officers
resigned by the score, civil workers by the hundred, most of them
starting south, but some of them prowling the city, for what dread
purpose no one could be sure. "For ten days our mail has been cut
off," Stanton wrote to his son Eddie, after communication with the
North had been restored and troops had begun arriving. ". . . Last
week there was a great panic here. The Virginia and Maryland
people stopped everything from coming to market and there seemed to
be danger of a famine. . . . Almost every family that could leave
town did so by waggon carts, boats or any vehicle they could obtain
while some of them went on foot at night. . . . There are now about
twenty thousand troops here."

Eddie, now at Kenyon, had asked his father's advice about enlisting
in a drill company. Stanton had no objections, he said, but he hoped
Eddie would not volunteer for active service; there were men enough.
He had been glad to learn that most Kenyon students were sticking to
their studies, for "they are remote & secure from all danger and while
passions are arming & raging elsewhere their time & thoughts should
be diligently devoted to their studies so that when the hour comes for
them to enter the busy scenes of life they may be well prepared."
Concealing from Eddie the alarm he had expressed to Dix, Stanton
assured him that neither he nor Ellen felt disturbed concerning the
safety of Washington. "We shall remain here feeling perfectly secure."

As troops continued to arrive, Franklin Square, across from the
Stanton home, became a camp. The din and bustle bothered him and
especially Ellen, who had been ill, so he moved his family temporarily

---

[4] Gorham, *Stanton*, II, 213; Curtis, *Buchanan*, II, 538–42.

to a rented house on H Street. He still felt anxious for the safety of the city, despite the evidence of martial preparations and his knowledge that Scott was sure he could hold out until aid arrived.

Stanton, like most Washingtonians, was far less sure, and he believed that Confederate forces at Harpers Ferry and Manassas Gap far outnumbered the untrained volunteers parading the streets of the city. He would have liked to visit Buchanan at Wheatland and help the former President prepare a defense of the crucial last months of his administration. Stanton also wanted to attend to long-neglected business and family matters in Pittsburgh and Steubenville; but he dared not leave his home and family with the enemy so close at hand.

Scott and the cabinet were squabbling over strategy, Stanton reported to Buchanan. Judge John A. Campbell, of Alabama, who had acted as an intermediary between Seward and commissioners sent by the Confederacy to arrange for the peaceable surrender of Sumter, had recently told Stanton that Seward had assured him some time previously that the fort would be given up, provided the commissioners exercised patience, whereas it now appeared that the administration had always meant to hold it. The story broke in the papers and put Seward in a bad light. "Mr. Seward's silence will not relieve him from the imputation of double-dealing in the minds of many," Stanton wrote to Buchanan, "although I do not believe it can justly be imputed to him. I have no doubt he believed that Sumter would be evacuated as he stated it would be. But the war party overruled him with Lincoln, and he was forced to give up, but could not give up his office. That is a sacrifice no Republican will be apt to make." [5]

Shortly after the attack on Sumter, Lincoln proclaimed a blockade of Southern ports, knowing that the Navy, though rapidly augmenting, was still far too small for this task. It was questionable whether the blockade had been made sufficiently effective to be legal under international law, and whether, in any event, a nation had the right to blockade its own ports. A test case came up when the Treasury Department instituted proceedings in the United States District Court in Washington for the condemnation of ships taken as prize.

Stanton felt disturbed to learn that the U. S. District Attorney had consented to the release of some of these ships, because, through ignorance, or otherwise, they had broken the blockade unintentionally.

[5] To son Edwin, May 1, 1861, owned by Gideon Townsend Stanton; to Buchanan in Curtis, *Buchanan*, II, 547–50; to Capt. John F. Oliver, June 29, 1861, Stanton MSS; Col. Charles P. Stone, "A Dinner with General Scott in 1861," *MAH*, XI, 531–2.

Furthermore, in the cases that were argued, the government's lawyers performed poorly, citing not a single authority, and confining themselves, so it seemed to Stanton, to "prophetic declarations of the policy and intent of the present administration, & vituperation of the last one."

Greatly concerned lest the court decide against the government, he decided to seek an interview with Chase and to offer his services as a lawyer. But he met with such an uncivil reception from one of Chase's assistants that he gave up the idea of seeing him and went home and wrote him a hurt letter instead. Stanton also protested to Chase about Cameron's treatment of Dix, whose brief tenure as Secretary of the Treasury under Buchanan had enabled the new administration to take over the government with a comfortable working balance, and who had since spurred Union sentiment in New York City. Governor E. D. Morgan, of New York, had appointed Dix a major general of volunteers, but the War Department had delayed so long in confirming the appointment that he had been left with no command. Dix, on the point of resigning, asked Stanton to learn from the Secretary of War why he "had been side-tracked in such a humiliating manner." After trying for a week to get an interview at the War Department, Stanton obtained Cameron's assurance that he would refer the matter to General Scott.

Vexed at the lack of warmth he had encounterd at both the Treasury and the War departments, Stanton vented his rancor to Dix. "No one can imagine the deplorable condition of this city and the hazard of the Government," he wrote, "who did not witness the panic of the Administration, and the painful imbecility of Lincoln. The uprising of the people of the United States to maintain their government and crush the rebellion has been grand, so mighty in every element, that I feel it a blessing to be alive and witness it. . . . But when we witness venality and corruption growing in power every day, and controlling the millions of money that should be a patriotic sacrifice for national deliverance, and treating the treasure of the nation as a booty to be divided among thieves, hope dies away . . . and between the corruption of some of the Republican leaders and the self-seeking ambition of others some great disaster may soon befall the nation." [6] A disaster came sooner than even the pessimistic Stanton had anticipated.

[6] Stanton to Chase, June 9, 1861, Chase Papers, HSP; Dix, *op. cit.*, II, 17–20; Gorham, *Stanton*, I, 217–18.

Ellen Hutchison Stanton, around 1865.

Edwin Lamson Stanton as his father's assistant in the War Department, 1865.

Stanton in 1865.

So far, except for the attack on Sumter and a few unimportant skirmishes, it had been a war of nerves, with both sides mustering their resources and maneuvering for position. But now, in the warm, bright summer days, "On to Richmond" became the cry. Northern troops were still ill-organized and raw, but so were those of the enemy. Lincoln yielded to the public clamor, against the advice of General Scott. A Union army, under General Irvin McDowell, made ready to attack the Confederates at Manassas Junction.

On Sunday, July 21, hundreds of civilians, believing that the impending battle would put a quick end to the war, wished to take advantage of what promised to be their sole chance to see a fight. Stanton's brother-in-law, Wolcott, obtained a pass to go "to the front," but Stanton persuaded him to stay behind. So Wolcott was not in the soaked and terror-stricken throng that rushed frantically back to Washington in pelting rain through the late hours of the night and far into the dismal morning. For at Bull Run the Union army, after fighting gallantly for several hours, had given way to panic and fled ingloriously.

Stanton had predicted that the administration's blundering would bring catastrophe. Now, he wrote to Buchanan, an irretrievable misfortune and a disgrace never to be forgotten had been added to business ruin and national bankruptcy "as a result of Lincoln's 'running the machine' for five months." He thought it likely that the disaster would bring changes in the War and Navy departments—"until Jefferson Davis turns out the whole concern." That might happen any day, he warned, for the city remained unguarded, while "Lincoln, Scott, and the cabinet are disputing who is to blame." He saw little hope of saving the nation until those now sporting epaulets and those in high civil office were replaced by earnest, capable men. Yet, "with all the calamity that is upon us I still do not . . . despair of the Republic," Stanton declared to Wolcott; "if our people can bear with this Cabinet they will prove able to supprt a great many disasters." [7]

Bull Run brought the realization to the Northern people that they faced stern and bloody days and a long, hard war. Lincoln resolutely planned to see it through, and ordered a new outpouring of troops. Soon more than a quarter of a million men had been enrolled, and the War Department, unable to supply and equip them, authorized the state governors to buy whatever was needed and present their bills.

[7] Wolcott MS, 173–5; Curtis, *Buchanan*, II, 559.

This system, which was sanctioned by Congress in subsequent legislation providing for reimbursement of the states, resulted in wild extravagance and monstrous graft. With a score of states competing not only against one another but against the federal government as well, profiteers cornered the scanty stores and demanded exorbitant prices for commodities which, more often than not, were defective, useless, or spoiled. Through haste, negligence, and criminal collusion, state and federal officials accepted almost anything, regardless of price or quality.

A concerted movement developed for the dismissal of War Secretary Cameron, and his friends warned him that Democratic partisans wanted him replaced by Holt. But Cameron's supporters were active too, defending his honesty and pointing out, accurately enough, that in the gigantic and unprecedented task that had devolved upon him, errors of judgment and misplaced confidence could scarcely have been avoided.

Whether or not Stanton was active in this movement to displace Cameron can only be conjectured. Wolcott advised certain New York bankers to loan no more money to the government unless Cameron was dismissed, although there is no evidence, beyond the unsupported statements of Gideon Welles, that Wolcott acted at Stanton's instigation. So far as Stanton's relations with Holt at this time are concerned, they were friendly but far from intimate, and were hardly of the quality to cause Stanton to become Holt's champion as a replacement for Cameron.[8]

Stanton meanwhile had achieved cordial relations with Cameron; his recommendations for commissions and patronage now received generally good reception. Cameron turned to him for legal arguments justifying War Department purchasing policies, and he successfully defended the government's right to keep militiamen under arms for the period specified in Lincoln's call for troops. While at work on these special assignments for the war office, Stanton heard that Lincoln had summoned General George Brinton McClellan from western Virginia to command the Army in the field. At first Stanton doubted his ability to change things: "But if he had the ability of Caesar, Alexander, or

---

[8] Stanton to Dix, Sept. 8, 1861, owned by Ralph G. Newman; Morse, *Welles Diary,* I, 57; Wolcott MS, 175–7; William P. Fessenden to Cameron, Aug. 28, J. D. Hoover to same, Aug. 29, and R. M. Blatchford to same, Sept. 6, 1861, Cameron Papers, LC. See also Weigley, *Meigs,* 163–8, 182–4; Fred A. Shannon, *The Organization and Administration of the Union Armies* (Cleveland, 1928), II, 53–69.

Napoleon, what can be accomplished?" Stanton asked Buchanan. "Will not Scott's jealousy, cabinet intrigues, and Republican interference thwart him at every step?" Almost at once, however, a new spirit of optimism began to infuse the Army and the nation, for McClellan gave the impression of a man born to command.

Stanton and McClellan soon met through their mutual acquaintances in Democratic party circles. The general had cause to thank him. Soon after the attack on Sumter, a group of men from western Virginia had hurried to Washington to plead with Lincoln and Cameron for arms with which to hold off secessionist control of their portion of that state. Neither saw a legal way open to them to dispose of available guns to private persons. The Virginians then went to Stanton, whose opinion that "Lincoln was Chief Magistrate of the *whole* people, not of the *States*," convinced Cameron that authority existed. Stanton then offered his total personal wealth as bond for the proper use of these guns, and prepared a formal legal justification for a transfer of arms at the discretion of the Secretary of War. Cameron hastened the business through the cumbersome departmental machinery, and the Virginia Unionists, triumphant, carried enough weapons home to hold key points until McClellan received orders to secure their region.[9]

The short, broad-shouldered, powerfully knit young general immediately set to work, superintending the erection of defense works around Washington, emptying its streets of the ragged, drunken mobs of soldiers that had become a plague, and indefatigably making the rounds of far-flung camps to watch raw recruits learn discipline and precision. McClellan felt vast pride in "his" hard, efficient army that was taking on shape and spirit under his directing eye, and the troops, responding to the pull of his magnetic personality, called him "Little Mac" and "the Young Napoleon."

Born in Philadelphia of a wealthy family, McClellan had attended the best preparatory schools before entering West Point, where he graduated second in his class. As an engineer officer on Scott's staff during the Mexican War, he won praise from his superiors. The War Department then sent him to the Crimea to study the organization and

[9] George P. Smith, a member of the 1861 Virginia committee, to Stanton, Oct. 14, 1865, Stanton MSS, offering to certify to the accuracy of a description of these events in the New York *Times*, Aug. 29, 1865, which in turn was inspired by a speech of Blair's attacking Stanton's prewar Unionism. Stanton's statement on the Secretary of War's powers, dated only 1861, is in Cameron Papers, LC. Other data in Stanton to Cameron, May 29, 1861, LMU; Curtis, *Buchanan*, II, 559; Seward, *Seward*, 604–5.

techniques of contending armies. But he could not stand the boredom of peacetime army life, and resigning his captain's commission, he became a railroad executive in Cincinnati.

In the scramble for retired West Pointers during the early days of the war, Governor William Dennison had persuaded McClellan to take command of all the Ohio volunteer regiments, with the rank of major general. Then came an appointment as major general in the national army, commanding the Department of the Ohio, with seniority next to Scott. This department included the loyal counties of western Virignia, and McClellan, dispatching troops into that area, saved it for the Union. The Confederate force that he defeated was small, untrained, and ill equipped, but the flamboyant proclamations with which he heralded his victories gave him a military stature far beyond what he had earned. And so he came to Washington, a hero in the eyes of the nation, but actually untested and unready for high command.

Unused to the adulation that now came to him, McClellan allowed it to go to his head. "The people call on me to save the country," he wrote to his wife in August 1861; "I must save it, and cannot respect anything that is in my way." His disposition to vanity, despite occasional self-doubts, became a Messianic complex. Untempered by experience and afraid to seem unsure, he became jealous of superior authority and resentful of advice.

McClellan was proud to have been a lifelong Democrat and found it intolerably irksome to defer to upstart Republicans. "I can't tell you how disgusted I am becoming with these wretched politicians," he confided to his wife; "they are the most despicable set of men & I think Seward is the meanest of them all—a meddling, officious, incompetent little puppy . . . The Presdt is nothing more than a well meaning baboon. Welles is weaker than the most garrulous old woman you were ever annoyed by. Bates is a good inoffensive old man—so it goes only keep these complimentary opinions to yourself, or you may get me into premature trouble."

During the course of the summer Stanton and McClellan became intimate. They held the same low estimate of the Lincoln administration. Like most loyal Democrats, they believed that the maintenance of the Union should be the sole purpose of the war. If it became a crusade against slavery, popular support would crumble and the volunteer forces would melt away. The rebel armies, not the Southern people, should be the object of attack. Injury to the property of noncombatants should be avoided whenever possible; masters should not be disturbed in the possession of their slaves. Reconciliation, not subjugation, should be the Northern aim. These, in any event, were McClellan's views, and he believed from their frequent conversations that summer that Stanton shared them.[1]

If so, neither man had reason to complain of Lincoln's attitude toward slavery during the early months of the war. For he scrupulously observed his pledge not to molest slavery in the states, not only as a matter of honor but also because his chief concern at the moment was to avoid taking any action that might cause the loyal border states to join the Confederacy. Congress was not so circumspect, however, and when it showed a disposition to pass legislation hostile to slavery, Stanton predicted to Dix that such action would incur the ill will of Northern Democrats and might even cause them to oppose the further prosecution of the war.

Some Union commanders, notably General Frémont at St. Louis, were also disposed to act precipitately. Unable to crush the elusive Confederate guerrilla bands that ceaselessly harassed Missouri, Frémont prepared to confiscate the property of persons who were in arms against the government, and declared their slaves emancipated. The Republican antislavery radicals acclaimed Frémont a hero. But an outburst of resentment in Kentucky ensued that threatened to take the state out of the Union. Unable to persuade the headstrong general to recall his edict, the President repealed it himself. Corruption, favoritism, and mismanagement had flourished in the Department of Missouri, and this was the last straw. Lincoln removed Frémont from command.

The resulting outburst of indignation against Lincoln from the Republican radicals surprised Stanton. Sentiment against slavery was stronger than he had thought, and it was clearly growing stronger. Gradually, and in large measure inscrutably, he now began to shift back to the antislavery side, about which he had been mute or evasive for the past ten or twelve years. He was still determined to be cautious, however, and was willing to sit astride the rising fence which the question of the Negro was building in the midst of war.

A great army took form as recruits poured into McClellan's camps all through the summer and autumn. But he showed no disposition to order an advance, although Confederate artillery batteries dominated

---

[1] McClellan, *McClellan's Own Story* (New York, 1885), 85, 478 (hereafter cited as McClellan, *Own Story*); Oct. 1861, ms "Extracts from Letters to Wife," McClellan Papers, LC.

the Potomac River, practically closing Washington's outlet to the sea, and at Harpers Ferry rebel raiders had cut the Baltimore & Ohio Railroad line, the capital's main line of communication to the west. Imperturbably McClellan continued to drill and review his troops. When criticized for inactivity he protested that his army was not ready, or put the blame on General Scott.

Put under terrific pressure by Republican congressmen, who resented McClellan's appointment and had shown suspicion of him from the first, Lincoln asked the general to prepare a report showing his own strength and that of the Confederates and estimating the number of troops he required for an advance. McClellan hurried to Stanton's residence. "I have not been at home for three hours," McClellan wrote to his wife, "but am concealed at Stanton's to dodge all enemies in the shape of browsing Presidents, etc.," assembling proof "that I have left nothing undone to make this army what it ought to be and that the necessity for delay has not been my fault."

McClellan's report, the significant portions of the first draft all in Stanton's handwriting, put his own strength at 168,318, and the enemy's force at 150,000, "well drilled & equipped, ably commanded & strongly entrenched," a rank exaggeration in every respect except that Confederate General Joseph E. Johnston was indeed able. McClellan estimated that he would need 208,000 troops for an advance and recommended that all recruits be assigned to him, leaving only defensive garrisons elsewhere. He was anxious to advance, he assured Lincoln, but it was folly to underestimate the rebel strength or to hazard the safety of the capital by a premature attack.

There is no doubt that Stanton, in addition to writing a fair share of this report, accepted its premises and supported the general's conclusions, which were based upon misleading and exaggerated intelligence concerning the enemy's strength. But there is more to it than this, so far as Stanton is concerned. He always had a capacity for total identification with a cause, an institution, or a person. As a lawyer, Stanton had exhibited devotion to his clients transcending the normal obligation of an attorney. In Buchanan's cabinet he had found a new symbol—the Union—and secretly sacrificed his lifelong party regularity in its cause.

He kept this burning devotion after leaving the cabinet. In McClellan, Stanton now had a champion who he thought could help bring military victory closer. So he was proud of his intimacy with the spectacular young general. Ellen wrote boastfully to young Eddie of newspaper accounts which described his father as "General McClellan's confidential adviser," and Stanton confided to his friend Dr. Reid: "I believe the life of the Republic depends on that man." [2]

Success was always Stanton's touchstone, and McClellan's star seemed to be rising irresistibly. Stanton was impressed when General Scott, worn, ill, resentful, and unable to endure the way McClellan contemptuously bypassed him and assumed the right to control all military operations, requested relief from duty. On November 1, Lincoln placed McClellan in charge of all Union armies, while also maintaining him in immediate command of the Army of the Potomac.

What was not yet clear was that the Union lacked a formula of command. The army structure, built for peace, was groaning under the strains of a great war. Under Cameron's deficient administration, the civilian War Secretary disbursed funds but commanded nothing. Now the nation was entrusting its fate to a military officer, with only Lincoln, still an uncertain quantity as President and commander in chief, as a check on McClellan, who considered him a cowardly buffoon. Considering the manifold problems of policy requiring decisions and the temperaments of the two men, trouble was almost certain to come.

Informed gossipers expected Cameron to quit the cabinet at the same time Scott left. Stanton heard that Lincoln was thinking of him as a possible replacement for Cameron, and canceled a planned partnership with S. L. M. Barlow, a wealthy lawyer and Democratic leader of New York City. As weeks passed and no word came from the White House, Stanton became increasingly perturbed and his critical views of the Lincoln administration were more freely expressed, although he continued to serve Cameron as special War Department counsel. But in his connection with McClellan, Stanton remained close to the center of events, and early in November he again proved his influence with the general.[3]

About a week after McClellan became commander in chief, Captain Charles Wilkes, commander of the warship *San Jacinto*, cruising

[2] McClellan, *Own Story*, 176; ms "Extracts from Letters to his Wife," Nov. 1, 1861, McClellan Papers, LC; Lichterman, *op. cit.*, 445, 464. Ellen's letter is in Gorham, *Stanton*, I, 232; Dr. Reid's ms reminiscence is owned by Alexandra Sanford. McClellan's report, attributed to Oct. 30, 1861, but actually completed in late November, is in U. S. War Department, *Official Records of the Union and Confederate Armies* (Washington, 1880–1901), ser. 1, V, 9–11 (cited hereafter as *O.R.*; ser. 1 unless otherwise noted).

[3] Maunsell B. Field, *Memories of Many Men and Some Women* (New York, 1874), 269–70 (cited henceforth as Field, *Memories*); Gen. John MacAuley Palmer, "Abraham Lincoln, Commander-in-Chief," ALA *Papers* (1938), 25–48; Stanton to Scott, Oct. 3, 1861, HL.

in the Bahama Channel, stopped the British mail packet *Trent* and, over the protests of her captain, took into custody James M. Mason and John Slidell, Confederate diplomats, who were on their way to London. The Northern people acclaimed Wilkes as a hero; but in England his highhanded action caused a wrathful outcry and the British Government prepared for war. The Lincoln administration found itself holding a raging British lion by the tail. To let go meant a serious loss of face in the eyes of Northern patriots; to hold on might embroil the dissevered nation in still another war.

As the dispute posed this possibility, Lincoln asked McClellan to sit in on a cabinet session. McClellan wrote to his wife: "I shall be obliged to devote the day to endeavoring to get our Govt to take the only prompt & honorable course of avoiding a war with England & France. Our Govt has done wrong in seizing these men on a neutral ship:—the only manly way of getting out of the scrape is a prompt release with a frank disavowal of the wrong—before a demand for reparation is made. . . . I will try again to write a few lines before I go to Staunton's [*sic*] to ascertain what the law of nations is on the Slidell & Mason seizure."

Stanton completely changed McClellan's mind. "I have just returned from Staunton's [*sic*]," the general wrote, "where I have had a long discussion on the law points of the M & S capture. I am rejoiced to find that our Govt is fully justified by all the rules of International Law & all the decisions in the highest courts which bear upon the case —so it matters but little whether the English Govt & people make a fuss about it or not, for as we are manifestly & undeniably in the right it makes little difference to us, as we can afford to fight in a just cause." Still abominating the supposed weakness of the Lincoln administration, Stanton had held forth on the desirability of taking a firm stand. But Stanton's opinions were at odds with American precedent and with the policy Lincoln chose to follow.[4]

The drift of public opinion continued to favor the antislavery Republicans. Even some members of Lincoln's cabinet, notably Cameron, were ready to disavow the President's cautious "border state policy." So far, the administration, while employing more and more Negroes as laborers in the Army, had refused to permit their enlistment as soldiers; not even free Negroes living in the Northern states had been allowed to bear arms. The President regarded all matters affecting the

[4] Nov. 17, 1861, McClellan Papers, LC. The general had Barlow check on Stanton's argument: Barlow to Stanton, Nov. 18, 1861, Barlow Papers, HL.

Negro's status as political questions of paramount importance, which were to be decided, not by generals or department heads, but at the top level, by himself or Congress.

On November 13, Colonel John Cochrane, near Washington, made an inflammatory speech, and brought the question of arming Negroes into the open. "Take the slave by the hand," he said, "place a musket in it, and in God's name bid him strike for the human race." Cameron warmly endorsed Cochrane's remarks, and immediately gained stature in the eyes of the radical Republicans. He was probably not unmindful of the possibility of re-establishing himself politically by means of their support.

Stanton, according to a reminiscence of a decade later, was so indignant that he begged McClellan to cashier Cochrane and declared that if he commanded the Army he would never permit Cameron to enter its camps. Cameron soon afterward repeated these sentiments, whereupon Secretary of the Interior Smith publicly rebuked him for advocating a policy of which the President, like Stanton, disapproved.

Republican dissension was sweet to the taste of Democratic politicians. Barlow, prominent in a Democratic clique that hoped to make McClellan President, wrote Stanton of the satisfaction he derived from reports of the two members of the Republican cabinet at loggerheads. "Such quarrels should be fostered in every proper way," he advised Stanton, "though the General must, if possible, keep entirely free of them." If Stanton was a party to this Democratic scheming, he for once used the utmost candor in answering Barlow's letter: "I think the General's true course is to mind his own Department and win a victory. After that all other things will be of easy settlement." [5]

One night not long after this, Cameron and Smith renewed their altercation over the use of Negro troops in the private suite of John W. Forney, who recalled that "the controversy became exceedingly animated, enlisting all the company, silencing the music, and creating a deal of consternation . . . while Edwin M. Stanton, then a quiet practitioner of the law, stood by, a silent figure in the scene." He was still determined to keep his views to himself on this divisive issue.

The time came for Cameron to prepare his annual report, which would accompany the President's message to Congress. Anxious to re-

[5] Flower, *Stanton*, 122; on Cameron, see New York *World*, Oct. 20, 1870; Benjamin Quarles, *The Negro in the Civil War* (Boston, 1953), 108; Barlow to Stanton, Nov. 21, Caleb B. Smith to Barlow, Nov. 22, and H. D. Bacon to same, Nov. 24, 1861, Barlow Papers, HL.

affirm his sentiments with regard to arming Negroes, but realizing the delicate nature of the question, Cameron invited a number of persons, chiefly fellow Pennsylvanians, to his home for consultation. Among those present were Forney and David Wilmot. Someone read a portion of Cameron's report in which he recommended the use of Negro troops. Nearly all the men except Wilmot pleaded that Cameron's proposed statement would be impolitic.[6]

Cameron recalled years later: "I sought out another counsellor— one of broad views, great courage, and of tremendous earnestness. It was Edwin M. Stanton. He read the report carefully, and after suggesting a few alterations, calculated to make it stronger, he gave it his unequivocal and hearty support." Indeed, Stanton's "alterations" had pushed Cameron into an extreme position.

Without consulting Lincoln, Cameron had his report printed and readied for release at the same time as Lincoln's message. Too late, Lincoln discovered what had happened. He immediately telegraphed an order recalling all copies of the report and instructed Cameron to delete the unauthorized passage before presenting it to Congress. But the unexpurgated version had already reached the press. Again the radicals denounced Lincoln for being too soft toward slavery, and for repudiating Cameron.[7]

Lincoln endured the criticism and said nothing further to Cameron about the trouble he had caused. But he decided to get rid of the Secretary whenever he could do so gracefully. Wittingly or unwittingly, Stanton had prepared the way for Cameron's downfall. A change in the War Department, which Stanton had long been advocating, would not be much longer deferred.

What moved Stanton to advise Cameron as he did? Was he express-

---

[6] [W. H.?] Cobb, ms memo, "Reminiscences of Washington in 1861," no date or place, Cameron Papers, LC; Forney, *Anecdotes of Public Men* (New York, 1873–81), I, 76 (cited hereafter as Forney, *Anecdotes*).

[7] Actually, Cameron's report contained a whole paragraph written by Stanton, which stated: "Those who make war against the Government justly forfeit all rights of property, privilege, and security derived from the constitution and the laws against which they are in armed rebellion; and, as the labor and service of their slaves constitute the chief property of the rebels, such property should share the common fate of war to which they have devoted the property of loyal citizens. . . . If it shall be found that the men who have been held by the rebels as slaves are capable of bearing arms and performing efficient military service, it is the right, and may become the duty of the Government to arm and equip them, and employ their services against the rebels, under proper military regulation, discipline, and command." Flower, *Stanton*, 116; Nicolay and Hay, *Lincoln*, V, 125–6. Cameron's statement is in Wilson, "Jeremiah S. Black and Edwin M. Stanton," *loc. cit.*, 470, and "Edwin M. Stanton," *AM*, XXV, 238.

ing his true opinion in advocating the use of Negro troops, or was he fomenting a quarrel within the Lincoln administration, as Barlow had urged him to do? He may have been doing both, but this much is certain: If the opinion he set forth for Cameron reflected his true views, they were strikingly at odds with the opinions he was expressing to McClellan and his other Democratic friends, who did not learn until years later that he was the real author of this part of Cameron's report.

Congressman Henry Dawes, returning to Washington after the Christmas holidays, found everything dark and gloomy. "Confidence in everybody is shaken to the very foundation," he wrote to his wife. "The credit of the country is ruined—its army impotent, its Cabinet incompetent, its servants rotten, its ruin inevitable." And worst of all was the War Department, which was still being mismanaged by Cameron.[8]

The War Secretary's shortcomings, evident from the first, had now become intolerable. Cameron realized that he had not measured up to the demands of his job and was willing to step out, provided he could do so without losing face. Learning that the ministry at St. Petersburg was about to be vacated, he told the President that the position might be acceptable to him.

No sooner had Chase learned of Cameron's willingness to resign than he began to boost Stanton as the best man to succeed him. Chase, besides managing the Treasury Department, had kept watch on the War Department. He regarded himself as the most competent man in the government and was incurably meddlesome; but he acted in this instance in accordance with Lincoln's wishes.

Cameron, either of his own accord or owing to Chase's persuasiveness, also favored Stanton as his successor. He regarded him as a fellow Pennsylvanian whose appointment to the cabinet would preserve Pennsylvania's influence in the government and might be taken, however remotely, as an endorsement of his conduct of the war office. Lincoln must have been impressed when Chase and Cameron, the two cabinet members who were most familiar with the operations of the War Department, both recommended Stanton to head it if a change was to be made.[9] Moreover, Lincoln had thought for a long time that

[8] Dawes to wife, Jan. 6 and 7, 1862, Dawes Papers, LC; Montgomery Blair to James E. Harvey, undated (*ca*. Jan. 1870), Blair Family Papers, LC.

[9] Chase to Black, July 4, 1870, Black Papers, LC; David Donald (ed.), *Inside Lincoln's Cabinet: The Civil War Diaries of Salmon P. Chase* (New York, 1954), 12–13 (hereafter cited as Chase, *Diary*) ; Field, *Memories*, 266–9.

the loyal Democrats would support the war more ardently if they were represented in the cabinet, and Stanton was a Democratic regular and a tested Unionist. But Holt still had his supporters, Montgomery Blair was urging Lincoln to appoint Ben Wade, and Lincoln wondered if Blair himself, with his West Point training, might be the best man for the post.

Early in January, John A. Bingham, now a Republican senator from Ohio and an old political opponent of Stanton's in their Cadiz days, had an interview with Lincoln. The President adroitly led Bingham to reveal his high estimate of Stanton as a possible replacement for Cameron. Stanton pulled further ahead in this sweepstakes when Lincoln learned, upon inquiry, that Seward also favored him. To find Chase and Seward in agreement was unusual and gratifying. Perhaps Lincoln saw Stanton as a makeweight between the discordant factions of the cabinet. Chase, having known Stanton best in the Ohio years, regarded him as an antislavery man and hence as a potential ally; whereas Seward, having known him as a Buchanan Democrat devoted to the Union, thought that he would align himself with the moderates. Stanton's dexterity in enlisting the backing of these cabinet rivals offers another striking instance of his wily versatility in ingratiating himself simultaneously with men of widely divergent views.[1]

Lincoln invited Stanton to call on him at the White House, accompanied by George Harding, who feared that the memories of that last meeting at the Reaper trial would make for an unpleasant scene. But, according to Charles F. Benjamin, to whom Harding later described the meeting, when Harding "reintroduced the two men to each other, to the[ir] credit . . . he was the most embarrassed of the three. The meeting was brief but friendly and Lincoln and Stanton shook hands cordially at parting, both thanking him for the trouble he had taken in bringing them together."

On Sunday, January 12, Cameron called on Chase at his home. The Russian post had become vacant, and Cameron suggested that Chase should again see Lincoln on behalf of Stanton. Chase thought it would be better to enlist Seward's support first, and drove to Willard's Hotel to see him. He did not know that Seward had already spoken favorably

---

[1] Blair to Andrew, Jan. 14, 1862, Andrew Papers, MHS; A. H. Meneely (ed.), "Three Manuscripts of Gideon Welles," *AHR*, XXXI, 491; Field, *Memories*, 266–7; undated memo, *ca.* Aug. 1870, J. W. Schuckers Papers, LC; Speed to Holt, Dec. 8, 1861, Holt Papers, LC; Bingham, ms "Recollections of Lincoln and Stanton," owned by Milton Ronsheim; Edwards Pierrepont to Seward, Feb. 9, 1862, Seward Papers, UR.

of Stanton to Lincoln, and Seward let Chase imagine himself the chief architect of Stanton's appointment.

At that point Cameron came in. He had just received a curt letter, from Lincoln stating that the President was now prepared to accept his resignation and proposed to nominate him as minister to Russia the next morning. Cameron felt deeply offended. Chase and Seward assured him that Lincoln could not have been intentionally discourteous, and prevailed on him to discuss the matter with the President the next day. Chase suggested that Cameron should also state frankly that another Pennsylvanian should be appointed to the war office and that Stanton was the man. Then Chase and Seward would see Lincoln and second the suggestion. Cameron agreed to this procedure.[2]

On the day after Seward, Chase, and Cameron decided on their line of attack, Cameron resigned, and Lincoln on January 14 appointed Stanton in his place. Lincoln had soothed Cameron's wounded feelings by subscribing an antedated letter expressing his "undiminished confidence" in Cameron and his "affectionate esteem."

Stanton, as he wrote to both his sisters, had little opportunity for deliberation when he was offered the cabinet post. He discussed it with his wife, who urged him to decline, and with his friend and former associate in the law Peter H. Watson, who insisted that he accept as a patriotic duty, though to do so meant giving up again an annual income now of more than $50,000, which he might greatly and quickly expand, for the inelastic $8,000 salary of a cabinet officer. Stanton also talked with Jeremiah Black, who, in seeming jest, threatened a "disclaimer of this administration if I go in it." He then conferred with Supreme Court Justice Grier, a fellow Pennsylvania Democrat, who discussed the matter in turn with his judicial brethren Nelson, Clifford, and Catron. All agreed that Stanton should accept in order to resurrect national confidence.

Last, Stanton went to see McClellan. According to the general's account, Stanton burst into his house while he was dressing for dinner, and said he would accept if McClellan thought that this would aid the army commander in suppressing the rebellion. McClellan hoped that Stanton would accept.

Admiral David Porter presents a significantly different recollection. Porter and the Prince de Joinville were dining with McClellan at

[2] Benjamin to Horace White, June 1, 1914, ISHL; Cameron to Frank A. Flower, March 6, 1887, Cameron Papers, LC; Flower, *Stanton*, 117.

his home either on the evening of Cameron's resignation or during one of the two days immediately preceding it. Stanton came to the open door of the dining room, and although McClellan saw him, he rudely kept him waiting there, finally admitting him only to keep him standing by the table for five minutes. Stanton kept his poise, Porter remembered, and McClellan finally invited him to join the trio at dinner; Stanton sat down and ate "with remarkably good appetite, but the general never introduced him to either of us at the table." Stanton was not a man to forget such arrogance.³

Next day, according to McClellan, Lincoln called to apologize for not having consulted him about Stanton's appointment. He had assumed that McClellan would be glad to have a friend at the head of the War Department, he said, and he had feared, if he consulted McClellan beforehand, McClellan's critics would say that the general had "dragooned" him into appointing Stanton. If McClellan had chosen to oppose him, Stanton probably would not have received the position, but the evidence is conclusive that Stanton was not, as Barlow asserted, "appointed at the request of General McClellan."

Few informed observers believed that Cameron's departure from the cabinet was either voluntary or unfortunate. "There appears to be much exultation over the forced resignation of Cameron," canny, inquisitive General Marsena Patrick noted, "by almost all I hear speak of it." Journalist Horace White, who was also the clerk of the Senate Military Affairs Committee, reported to the Chicago *Tribune* that the excuse which Cameron's friends offered for his resignation—his antislavery views—is "all bosh." White insisted that congressional exposures of Cameron's incapacity made his remaining in the cabinet impossible—"Every Republican Senator but one or two were determinedly hostile." Among Cameron's critics was Lyman Trumbull, who commented: "The slavery question, I presume, had nothing to do with Cameron's removal. There were probably enough causes for it, without supposing that to be the one." ⁴

³ Wolcott MS, 177, 179–80; Chase, *Diary*, 62; Stanton to Black, undated, *ca.* Jan. 1862, incorrectly filed in 1858, Black Papers, LC; Chase to Black, July 4, 1870, in New York *Evening Post*, Nov. 11, 1870; Grier to Stanton, Jan. 13, 1862, Stanton MSS; McClellan, *Own Story*, 153; Porter, ms Private Journal #1, 174–5, Porter Papers, LC; Meneely, "Three Manuscripts of Gideon Welles," *loc. cit.*, 492; S. W. Crawford's ms notes on Cameron, July 1883, ISHL.

⁴ Jan. 14, 1862, Patrick ms diary, LC; transcript of *Tribune* article, Jan. 15, 1862, and White to F. J. Garrison, Nov. 8, 1914, White Papers, ISHL; "Trumbull Correspondence," *MVHR*, I, 103; McClellan, *Own Story*, 152, 161; Barlow to August Belmont, Jan. 17, 1862, Barlow Papers, HL.

For the rest of his life, however, Cameron insisted that he left Lincoln's cabinet as a result of his championing the use of Negro soldiers, and that it was due only to his recommendation and maneuvering that Stanton came in as his successor. His insistence convinced Henry Wilson and Frank A. Flower, among others, who used Cameron's version of these events as the basis for their later writings on Stanton. It appears, however, that Gideon Welles was correct when in 1870 he described Cameron's account as "preposterously absurd." Cameron, as L. E. Chittenden asserted in 1867, resigned "in obedience to the universal sentiment of the [Republican] party." Stanton succeeded him as the choice of the most influential cabinet officers and congressmen and especially Lincoln himself.[5]

Some Republicans feared that Lincoln's choice of a Democrat for the War Department foreshadowed a more conciliatory policy toward the South. When Stanton's nomination came before the Senate, William P. Fessenden, of Maine, interviewed him. "He is just the man we want," wrote Fessenden afterward. "We agree on every point: The duties of the Secretary of War, the conduct of the war, the negro question, and everything else."

The next morning Cameron arranged a breakfast at his home which Stanton, Wade, and Zachariah Chandler attended. This meeting, too, had good results. Trumbull reported that "our earnest men here who have conversed with him, say he is fully up to all they could ask . . . I feel very much encouraged by the change." Later that day the Senate speedily confirmed Stanton's nomination.[6]

A few private doubts were raised concerning the wisdom of Stanton's elevation to the war office. Henry Halleck, now a Union Army

---

[5] Cameron's versions are in New York *Times*, July 16, 1865, and New York *Tribune*, March 10, 1869. See also the anonymous "Edwin M. Stanton: Secret History of Lincoln's Cabinet," *Lippincott's*, V, 230–1; and the Cameron-Flower correspondence, Jan.–March 1887, in Cameron Papers, LC, and Flower Papers, WSHS. For other data, A. K. McClure to Welles, Sept. 22, 24, 1870, Welles Papers, LC; Beale, *Welles Diary*, I, 54–69; Chittenden, *Address on President Lincoln and His Administration at the Beginning of the War* (n.p., 1867); John Russell Young, *Men and Memories* (New York, 1901), I, 54 (hereafter cited as Young, *Men and Memories*).

[6] By agreement between Cameron and Stanton, the former retained the office until January 20 while Stanton settled pressing personal affairs; Cameron committed himself to making no new army appointments during those six days, leaving recommendations for Stanton to deal with. See Meneely, *The War Department, 1861* (New York, 1928), 370. Other data in Francis Fessenden, *Life and Public Services of William Pitt Fessenden* (Boston, 1907), I, 299–31; Cameron's endorsement on letter of Feb. 2, 1862, Lamon Collection, LC; "Trumbull Correspondence," *loc. cit.*, 103; A. G. Riddle, *Recollections of War Times* (New York, 1895), 350–1.

general, who nursed a feeling of injury dating from Stanton's California investigations, and who had hoped to see Holt get the place, confided to his wife that "Mr. Stanton does not like me, and of course will take the first opportunity he can to injure me. I shall take my precautions accordingly so as not to give him a chance." Holt, for his part, quickly subdued any resentment he may have felt and wrote for the press a rhapsodic eulogy on Stanton's virtues, which served to make the appointment acceptable to many moderates of both parties in the North, and this was a substantial assistance to the new Secretary.[7]

Sam Ward, a New York financier and lobbyist, who had lost a fortune in California, recognized that conservatives applauded the new War Department head, but he admitted to Seward that "to me, he is personally distasteful from the bitterness and injustice with which he persecuted some of my California friends." Ward was worried that the new appointee would be "likely to gain great ascendancy over the President . . . for *Stanton was a dangerous foe*—a sleuthhound sort of man who never lost his scent or slackened his purpose." Seward, Ward advised, had best make an ally of this unknown quantity.

Many Democrats were delighted that one of their party had gained such an important post, and looked for a statement from Buchanan to this effect. But the former President could find no charity for a former counselor who had joined the enemy camp.[8] And McClellan, who actually detested Cameron, privately let him know that he regretted the change in the War Department and that he was sure Cameron was leaving fully of his own accord, while at the same time the general exulted to Barlow over the shift. Years later, long after he and Stanton had become bitter enemies, McClellan insisted to Fitz-John Porter that he had "deprecated the tricks which were resorted to to secure . . . [Cameron's] resignation and the appointment of . . . [his] successor." As in other testimony McClellan asserted that he had known nothing of the impending change until Stanton asked his advice about accepting the office, it appears that McClellan's memory was playing him false.

There were few sour notes like these intruded or privately voiced,

[7] Halleck, Jan. 15, 1862, in *Collector*, XXI, 29; New York *Times*, Jan. 25, 1862, has Holt's speech, and its effects are described in T. S. Bell to Holt, May 16, 1862, Holt Papers, LC; Union League Club of New York, *Proceedings in Reference to the Death of Edwin M. Stanton* (New York, 1870), 12.

[8] Ward to Seward, Jan. 14, 1862, Seward Papers, UR; Curtis, *Buchanan*, II, 522–3; and see Buchanan to Horatio King, Jan. 28, 1862, King Papers, LC.

for the change at the War Department was as well received throughout the country as probably any change would have been. Congratulations showered on Stanton. William Stanton wrote that men of all parties in Stanton's home state were delighted. John G. Nicolay, Lincoln's secretary, thought the change "a very important and much needed one. I don't know Mr. Stanton personally but he is represented as being an able and efficient man. I shall certainly look for very great reforms in the War Department."

From Joseph Medill, editor of the Chicago *Tribune,* came a warning that Stanton would encounter rottenness and rascality at all levels of the War Department, and scores of lukewarm, half-secessionist army officers. "The country looks to you," Medill wrote, "to infuse vigor, system, honesty, and *fight* into the services. The army has lost more men in the past four months from inaction and ennui than it would have done from ten bloody battles." Barlow, congratulating Stanton, said that he realized the great sacrifices the new Secretary had made in taking on the post, and warned that "apart from the grand drama of politics, you will have your hands full, in stopping the terrible leaks, monstrous frauds, which have recently been perpetrated . . . by the . . . War Department." [9]

Most baffling is how Stanton was able to satisfy the radical Republicans concerning his views on the Negro without arousing the suspicions of moderate Republicans and without forfeiting the confidence of McClellan and other Democrats. Barlow, for example, described Stanton as "a firm, consistent Union man, but as firm a Democrat as I know. . . . I know he is all right & he is withal a man of strong mind & will—not afraid of anything or anybody—honest—not ambitious of political preferment & will have his own way."

But what was his way? Wade warned that "if the democrats think they have gained anything by the appointment of Stanton . . . they will find they have caught 'a tartar.' " Lincoln assured an inquirer that Stanton had not been "selling . . . his old friends out" by coming into his cabinet; but the burning question remained, voiced succinctly by the New York *Tribune* editor Charles A. Dana: "Can you tell me what Stanton's sentiments really are about slavery?" Here was the heart of the matter.

[9] Barlow to Stanton, Jan. 14, and McClellan to Barlow, Jan. 18, 1862, Barlow Papers, HL; Porter to Cameron, Dec. 19, 1886, Cameron Papers, LC; William Stanton to Stanton, Jan. 16, 1862, owned by William Stanton Picher; Nicolay to Therena Bates, Jan. 14, 1862, Nicolay Papers, LC; Medill in Bernard A. Weisberger, *Reporters for the Union* (Boston, 1953), 222–3.

For Stanton, summoned a second time to the cabinet of a President whose abilities he distrusted and whose policies he hoped to change, though in what direction only he knew, his appointment meant both personal sacrifice and patriotic opportunity. This man, to whom the acquisition of wealth, the sublimation of personal convictions in favor of self-advancement, the avoidance of involvement in public controversies, had been the guideposts of living, was again prepared to abandon these attitudes.

A month after he took office, Stanton poured out his heart to his friend Nahum Capen. "No public man in times like these can fail to have both his words and acts misunderstood," he wrote. "My official position was not sought for; it is held at great personal sacrifice, and aspiring to nothing beyond, having a heart single to the one great object of overcoming the rebellion and restoring the authority of the government in time to save the nation from the horrible gulf of bankruptcy—bankruptcy not to the Government only but to every citizen —I am content to bear admonition and reproof for any real or supposed errors with humble submission." [1] It was well that he was ready and willing to bear reproof, for it was not long in coming.

[1] To Capen, Feb. 24, 1862, owned by Justin G. Turner; Lincoln quoted in H. D. Bacon to Barlow, Jan. 20, and Barlow to August Belmont, Jan. 17, 1862, Barlow Papers, HL; Wade in Isaac Arnold, *The History of Abraham Lincoln and the Overthrow of Slavery* (Chicago, 1866), 250; Dana to Sumner, Feb. 21, 1862, Sumner Papers, HU. The question of bankruptcy is fruitfully examined in Bray Hammond, "The North's Empty Purse, 1861–1862," *AHR*, LXVII, 1–18.

SECRETARY OF A WAR

$\mathbf{F}$ROM HIS WORK as special counsel during Cameron's tenure as War Secretary, Stanton knew that the commission he accepted on January 20, 1862, had thus far represented a source of weakness more than of strength in the nation's military effort. In the development of the government's institutions before 1861, the war office had been either an insignificant clerical convenience for army officers to employ or else an annoying obstacle for them to circumvent or overcome. The few prewar Secretaries who had tried to improve on this pattern had been evaded or merely outwaited by the military galaxy. No one knew what the authority of that office was.

This ambiguity could mean opportunity to a Secretary who seized the chance and expanded his powers, but the corruption and confusion that developed in Cameron's lax regime had lessened the power and prestige of an office that had none to spare. Under him, the heads of the Army's bureaucracy plodded along in accustomed paths, binding up the growing regiments in rigid tentacles of bookkeepers' techniques, while spoilsmen fattened on the great profits available from the nation's emergency needs.

Far worse was the fact that the field commanders remained virtually independent of the civilian Secretary and the President. Generals such as Frémont and McClellan, enjoying strong political backing from their states and from congressional cliques, were taking matters of policy into their own hands. In default of action by Cameron, Lincoln interceded in the most outrageous cases. But this involvement forced Lincoln to defy some of the leaders of his own party, and thereby the chances of Confederate victory were improved.

For the South needed to win no battles in order to gain its goal of independence; it merely had to endure until the North abandoned the struggle. It was not only that the rebels enjoyed the traditional military advantages of waging defensive war. The North had to learn how to come to an offensive spirit, and to maintain it despite the cost. If Northerners failed to find and to keep that spirit, or became unwilling to sustain the prosecution of the war regardless of the courses it took, then the capacity of Yankeedom to continue its crusade for the Union would vanish.

Whatever its defects, the Republican party, together with war Democrats like Stanton, formed the only group in the North committed to the reunification of the states at any cost. The Republican organization was young, faction-ridden, straining its seams from the conflicts over patronage and policy being waged by the ambitious men who were its leaders. Too many collisions over military policy between the party's leaders and the President could crack the fragile structure beyond repair. If this occurred, then the South had won.

Like his party and the nation he served, Lincoln had no surpluses of power to dissipate in fruitless arguments between White House and Congress or between party leaders. Since the days of Andrew Jackson, Presidents of the United States had let slip the reins of leadership which that old warrior had held so firmly. Now in the midst of a shattering war Lincoln, like Stanton, had to repair the prestige of his office.

The War Department would inevitably be a source of strength to Lincoln in this essential need, or the cause of his failure, and with it the final collapse of the Union's cause. Military victories or defeats reflected directly upon the untried President and his inharmonious party, for the nation, hazarding its future on the men in uniform, focused unwavering attention on the rapidly growing armies. Never since the days of Valley Forge had the destiny of America been so dependent upon its military power. What the War Department did, or failed to accomplish, was now a matter of moment to millions of Americans.

Already in this war, unlike the brief, cheap, simple conflict against Mexico fifteen years earlier, men from every loyal state were coming under arms, grain and cattle from midwestern farms and metals from Appalachian mines were being turned into food and guns in eastern factories, tens of thousands of draft animals were being purchased and shipped. A knowledgeable central authority was needed to assemble the men and supplies and to train the one to use the other, and then to move them to where they were needed. The new communications technology of the railroad, steamship, and telegraph could, if understood and exploited from Washington, provide a novel kind of mobility for the conduct of war.

But if civilian authorities did not retain control over this vast out-pouring of a nation's resources, if men in Washington did not learn how to direct the growing military might—already there were more soldiers than any earlier Americans had ever commanded—then demo-cratic, civilian government in the North might collapse while seeking to crush the South. Great expenditures of money were necessarily involved. If army contracts were tainted with corruption, as had been occurring under Cameron, the soldiers would despair of the pur-poses for which Lincoln was asking them to die, and moral as well as fiscal bankruptcy could kill the Union forever.

For the same reasons, the President required of Stanton a better job in suppressing home-front subversion than anyone was presently performing. He had to have a subordinate in the war office who agreed with him that the question of the Negro required delicate balancing with the strategic problem of retaining the allegiance of the slavehold-ing border states and with the fact that most Northerners detested slavery in the abstract but bore no love for free blacks. Lincoln wanted a war minister who would keep in check army commanders who had a different opinion on this issue, so that any action on the Negro ques-tion could come from the White House when and if the President thought the time ripe.

Workable solutions to these problems had to be found quickly and applied with unrelenting strength yet with great sensitivity. Lincoln had simultaneously to infringe upon the civil liberties of a people un-accustomed to restraint and still retain enough popular support to win free elections. The mere wastage of time, the development of war-weariness in the North and of cynicism among Union troops, could give victory to the rebels, or degrade civilian authority in the North to a point where the war might as well be lost. In the last analysis the fate of the nation depended upon the ingenuity, skill, and determination of the President and his War Secretary in finding leaders, manpower, and materials for the battle fronts while maintaining unity on the home front. An adequate Secretary must lead the President yet obey him always; rule the Army while sustaining its commanders; and keep legislators and the public in support of Lincoln's decisions.

A man of mediocre talents like Cameron had clearly been inadequate for this demanding role. Lacking will and insight, he could not create an effective partnership between his office, the White House, army head-quarters, Capitol Hill, and state capitals. Ever the politician, he failed to do more than improvise where brave leaps were needed. Only if there had been no war might Cameron have been acceptable as Secretary of War.

Stanton realized that he was secretary of a war, and that the only way to victory was on the battlefield. "Instead of an army stuck in the mud of the Potomac," he wrote privately to Dana, with whom he had established close relations and who would later become his assistant, "we should have . . . one hundred thousand men thrusting upon Nashville and sweeping rebellion & treason out of Kentucky with fire & sword." The North had the human and productive resources needed to crush the rebels. What was lacking was the "military genius to command our armies." The nation must realize that the job had barely begun: "We have had no war," he told Dana two weeks after taking over; "we have not even been playing war." [1]

But brave words were cheap, and could not overcome the black mood that hung over the North when Stanton took office. Informed Washingtonians feared European recognition of the Confederacy and worried over the failing state of the nation's finances. Stanton was an unknown quantity, and although many persons were relieved that Cameron was at last gone from the war office, they could not see that his successor could improve things substantially or in time.

The new Secretary of War refused to admit despair, and immediately set to work. Before any efforts he exerted could count, Stanton had to learn the tangled routines of the War Department. He was soon so busy at the task that he wrote Pamphila: "Ellen and I have not seen each other for days at a time." [2] Yet despite this preoccupation, or perhaps because of it, during the first, hectic days in the war office Stanton favorably impressed those who saw him. "Standing at his desk in an ante-room I found a very pleasant gentleman, . . . scrupulously neat in appearance, with heavy frame and immense black beard, an intelligent eye and business manner, he looked for all the world like the photographs which represent him. At a glance you knew him to be the Secretary of War," wrote an admiring New York *Times* reporter. George Templeton Strong, treasurer of the United States

---

[1] To Dana, Feb. 2, 1862, YU. On the Secretary's office, see *Memoirs of General William T. Sherman* (2d ed., New York, 1887), II, 446–50 (hereafter cited as Sherman, *Memoirs*) ; Weigley, *Meigs*, 215–17; Louis Smith, *American Democracy and Military Power* (Chicago, 1951), 109; Emory Upton, *The Military Policy of the United States* (Washington, 1912), 74, 129, 280–1, 394; Nevins, *The War for the Union: The Improvised War, 1861–1862* (New York, 1959), 164–72; T. Harry Williams, *Americans at War*, 47–81.

[2] Wolcott MS, 179; Boston *Transcript*, Jan. 20, 1863.

Sanitary Commission, forerunner of the Red Cross, felt, after calling on Stanton, that at the lowest estimate he was worth "a wagon load of Camerons." He was not a handsome man, thought Strong; in fact, he was "rather pigfaced"—a robust, "Luther-oid" type of man. Prompt, intelligent, earnest, and warmhearted, he was "the reverse in all things of his cunning, cold-blooded, selfish old predecessor." At the moment Stanton was the most popular man in Washington. But, asked Strong, "will it last?" [3]

It did not last, for Stanton proved careless of his own popularity. But he was shrewd enough to exploit the indefinite boundaries of his position instead of being confused or restricted by them. His personal friendships among leading Democrats and prominent Republicans in Congress, and with McClellan, now paid dividends.

A few days before Stanton took office, he met with McClellan and trusted journalists at army headquarters. In an off-the-record interview Stanton promised to support him and Lincoln, carefully avoiding the question of policy differences between the two. Washingtonians remarked that the Secretary and the general were sometimes together from dawn to dusk. The relations between the two men were obviously cordial; and the New York *Evening Press* reported that "the one has unlimited confidence in the other." McClellan thought that Stanton was his willing assistant who could warn him of radical plots. "They are counting on your death," McClellan quoted Stanton as saying in this period, "and are already dividing up . . . your military goods and chattels." [4]

At the same time Stanton began a close and lasting co-operation with the chairmen and members of radical-dominated congressional committees and with important individual legislators. He suggested to William D. Kelley, a potent representative from Pennsylvania, that they henceforth meet each morning to discuss pending legislation and future policy. On his crowded first day in office, Stanton made a friend of Wisconsin's spectacular disloyalty hunter, John Fox Potter, whose House committee was claiming that the civil and military services were infested with secessionist sympathizers. Cameron had curtly refused even to receive Potter's wild accusations and patronage nominations. Stanton invited Potter to call, and after going over the legislator's bulging files, dismissed one officer and three clerks. Although Potter

[3] Strong, *Diary*, III, 203; *Times*, April 5; *Tribune*, Jan. 21, 1862.
[4] Malcolm Ives to James Gordon Bennett, Jan. 15, 1862, Bennett Papers, LC; *Evening Press*, Feb. 7, 1862; McClellan, *Own Story*, 155; same to Barlow, Jan. 18, 1862, Barlow Papers, HL.

had accused more than fifty of disloyalty, he was delighted. As a result, Stanton was able to swerve the Potter Committee from its vendetta against the War Department, and thus eased the fearful hysteria among the officers and clerks. But Stanton did not hesitate to appoint to a clerkship a former Librarian of Congress, Pontius D. Stelle, who after thirty years of service had been discharged on unsupported allegations of disloyalty. As a frequent borrower from that library, Stanton knew the man and trusted him. Potter, who would have risen in a pyrotechnic display of outraged patriotic wrath had Cameron done this, said nothing.[5]

Stanton found other, more significant congressional allies in the Joint Committee on the Conduct of the War. Its most influential members—"Bluff Ben" Wade, a profane, barrel-chested senator whom Stanton had known in Ohio, intemperate Senator Zachariah Chandler, of Michigan, resolute Andrew Johnson, of Tennessee, combative Brooklynite Moses Odell, the only Democrat besides Johnson on the committee, and fiery John Covode, of Pennsylvania—through their power of subpoena, could elicit information that he could not obtain himself, could scourge unfitness and cowardice, uncover fraud and waste, and probe the enigmatic workings of the military mind.

During Stanton's first day in office the whole committee met with him. "We must strike hands," he said to Chairman Wade, "and uniting our strength and thought, double the power of the government to suppress its enemies and restore its integrity." Finding an eager ally in the new Secretary, the committee began to hold long and frequent sessions. Its members were sworn to secrecy, and as many of its transactions were not put on paper, much of what happened at its meetings will never be revealed. Stanton was a welcome attendant at many of its sessions. "The utmost confidence was exchanged," Chandler wrote, ". . . and the files and records of the committee were constantly referred to and relied upon as sources of exceedingly useful knowledge at the White House and at the War Department." Committeeman Julian was "delighted" with Stanton, "and had perfect confidence in his integrity, sagacity, and strong will." [6]

---

[5] Hyman, *To Try Men's Souls: Loyalty Tests in American History* (Berkeley, 1959), 157–62; Flower, *Stanton*, 119; Maude B. Morris, "Life and Times of Pontius D. Stelle," ColHS *Records*, VII, 65; Kelley, *Lincoln and Stanton [Questions of the Day, No. 29]* (New York, 1885), 38–9; A. E. H. Johnson in Washington *Star*, Nov. 11, 1895.

[6] Julian, *Political Recollections, 1840 to 1872* (Chicago, 1884), 204; *Zachariah Chandler: An Outline of His Life and Public Service. By the Detroit Post and Tribune* (Detroit, 1880), 219 (hereafter cited as Detroit *Post, Chandler*).

Stanton's shrewd public relations work with congressmen paid immediate dividends to the executive arm. Legislative impediments to needed appropriations, appointments, and policies lessened noticeably.

Forced by the needs of his position to work closely with the radical Republicans who controlled these committees, a man of Stanton's impassioned nature could scarcely have remained uninfluenced by their determination to "get results" and their fiercely partisan attitude. Stanton soon actively aided Wade, who was uncertain of re-election by the Ohio legislature. The Secretary sent word back to Columbus that he and Lincoln would view Wade's defeat "as a great national calamity." Wade won, and Ohio political observers attributed a large part of his victory to Stanton's support from Washington.

Wade, convinced of this, wrote appreciatively to William Stanton, remarking how "the political horizon has brightened" since Edwin had taken the helm. "I have no doubt," Wade continued, "that his courage, and consummate statesmanship, will enable him to surmount all the difficulties of his position, crush out the rebellion, preserve the old Constitution, and defend the authority of the old flag throughout every State of the Union. This is something of a job, but of all the men I know he is the best calculated to perform it. He has the confidence of Congress and the whole country and he will never disappoint them." [7]

Stanton's success also depended, if to a lesser degree, upon the co-operation he could obtain from his cabinet colleagues, each of whom controlled blocks of political power and sought differing policies. He impressed Attorney General Edward Bates most favorably. Bates, the oldest member of the cabinet, slim of body but rugged of face, and a cautious logician, sized up the newcomer as "a man of mind and action." To Halleck, who feared Stanton's enmity, Bates wrote in praise of the new Secretary that he "will soon have matters moving with greater method & precision than heretofore, & moving with a rush."

While Chase courted Stanton openly, the canny and cryptic Seward resorted to subtler methods. He seldom called at the War Department, but the Stantons were regularly invited to his frequent dinner parties, where he expounded his moderate views to the new Secretary while

[7] William Stanton to Edwin, Feb. 15, Edwin to William Stanton, Feb. 18, and Wade to William Stanton, March 22, 1862, owned by William Stanton Picher; Joseph Geiger to Wade, Feb. 20, 1862, Wade Papers, LC; ms diary of William T. Coggeshall, Military Secretary to Governor Dennison, Feb. 23, 1862, owned by the estate of Foreman M. Lebold (this ms is now at OHS).

the two men lounged comfortably in his library, puffing on their after-dinner Havanas and sipping Seward's vintage wines.

This association deluded and outraged Postmaster General Montgomery Blair, six feet tall, erect, a West Pointer turned lawyer, with a contriving mind fixed on stubborn purposes. Blair immediately questioned Stanton's personal and political honesty, although he had so detested Cameron that he had vowed support to anyone who succeeded him. But Blair's father, Frank P. Blair, Sr., once a member of President Jackson's "kitchen cabinet," now enjoying the role of elder statesman, felt that when Cameron left the War Department he himself had been turned out.

The Blairs at first believed that Stanton was McClellan's puppet. They later changed their tune. But their relations with Stanton never improved, and the women of the Blair family maintained a social ostracism against Ellen. Montgomery Blair publicly announced early in 1863 that he "did not speak to Mr. Stanton on business." He accused Stanton of accepting bribes and said that he "would not be surprised to hear that he was in the pay of Jeff. Davis." In another instance, Montgomery and Frank Blair, Jr., told General Patrick that *"we will give it to Stanton someday"*; and that Stanton was Seward's tool.[8]

Stanton would have little personal or official connection with Caleb Smith, Secretary of the Interior. But he had to deal frequently with Navy Secretary Gideon Welles, a onetime Jacksonian Democrat and close friend of the Blair family, a former Connecticut editor, an honest, plain-spoken man, fearless, with the Puritan's penchant for more readily discerning men's faults than recognizing their virtues. Shy and unsocial, Welles toothsomely gossiped with himself during his leisure hours while recording his impressions of people and events in his voluminous and penetrating diary. Welles's Olympian visage—a wig of long hair and a magnificent gray beard, thick eyebrows, and a commanding nose—caused Lincoln, out of his hearing, to call him "Father Neptune," just as he would come to call Stanton "Mars."

When Stanton entered the cabinet, Welles, although respecting Stanton's ability, suspected that Stanton had been predisposed against

<hr>

[8] On Seward, see correspondence owned by Mrs. Van Swearingen. Morse, *Welles Diary*, I, 60–1, for Chase. For Bates, Howard K. Beale (ed.), *The Diary of Edward Bates, 1859–1866* (Washington, 1933), 228 (cited henceforth as Bates, *Diary*); and Bates to Halleck, Jan. 31, 1862, LNLF. On the Blairs, see F. Blair, Sr., to Cameron, Jan. 30, 1863, Cameron Papers, LC; M. Blair to Andrew, Jan. 7, 1863, Andrew Papers, MHS; C. Gibson to Gov. Gamble, Jan. 6, 1863, Gamble Collection, MoHS, quotes Montgomery Blair; and Dec. 30, 1864, Patrick ms diary, LC. On social ostracism, Elizabeth Blair Lee to "Phil," Jan. 9, 1867, Box 13, Blair-Lee Papers, PU.

him by political rivals and disgruntled contractors who had put Welles under fire from the press, and he grew to regard Stanton with as great personal aversion as did Blair. Stanton soon stirred Welles's bile by acting as though the Navy were merely an adjunct of the Army. After one or two incautious assaults that left him somewhat chopfallen, Stanton side-stepped the peppery old shellback whenever he could.

Welles sized up Stanton as a man who loved the exercise of power. Granting that he was vigilant, devoted, and a dynamo for work, Welles thought he lacked moral courage and self-reliance under stress. "He took pleasure in being ungracious and rough towards those who were under his control," Welles wrote, "and when he thought his bearish manner would terrify or humiliate those who were subject to him. To his superiors or those who were his equals in position he was complacent, sometimes obsequious." Welles believed, too, that Stanton toadied to the Committee on the Conduct of the War so that it would cover up the War Department's shortcomings.

The President, who found himself in the middle of all this scuffling, and who never really tried to run his cabinet in a single harness, revealed his attitude toward the vigorous new Secretary to Congressman Dawes. Lincoln agreed that Stanton was making a grand beginning, although he had been warned that he might "run away with the whole concern." Stanton reminded him, said Lincoln, of an old Methodist preacher who performed so energetically in the pulpit that some of his parishioners wanted to put bricks in his pockets to hold him down. "We may be obliged to serve Stanton the same way," Lincoln observed, "but I guess we'll just let him jump a while first."

For Lincoln was observing Stanton's work closely and was pleased with what he saw. The President, heartsick over the failures that had attended the Union cause thus far, and weary of the ineptitude and incapacity of many of those who served him, saw in Stanton the man he needed. Almost immediately a deep intimacy began to grow up between these two disparate personalities. Lincoln never referred to the abuse he had suffered at Stanton's hands in earlier years, or to the epithets Stanton had used against him more recently. Stanton had found a man to follow. As Chase foresaw, Stanton "would be master of his Department, and yield to no one save the President." [9]

[9] Morse, *Welles Diary*, I, 60, 67–9; Beale, *Welles Diary*, I, xix; Chase, *Diary*, 64–5; B. P. Thomas, *Abraham Lincoln* (New York, 1952), 295–7; William W. Pierson, Jr., "The Committee on the Conduct of the Civil War," *AHR*, XXIII, 574; Dana, *Lincoln and His Cabinet* (Cleveland, 1896), 9–20.

Stanton had immediately set himself to cleaning out the rats' nests in the dilapidated brick building at the corner of Pennsylvania Avenue and Seventeenth Street which had housed the War Department for more than forty years. It was literally falling apart, and was poorly illuminated and badly ventilated. He secured a special appropriation to double the existing two-story height; this expansion, and the destruction of long-useless partitions and corridors on the lower levels, far more than doubled the office and filing spaces available. This, in turn, let Stanton bring to the growing building scores of Department workers who for years had been housed in rooms scattered across the capital.

Far more vital were the problems involved in bringing the personnel, equipment, and procedures of the Department into line with vastly enlarged requirements of clothing, food, weapons, and innumerable items of equipment for an army that now numbered more than a half million men. Stanton's task would be to augment, reform, and systematize, to maintain unrelenting pressure on half a hundred different civilian and military officials, and to deal with the manifold political and economic intricacies that faced him daily.

He was able to build on what Cameron had begun. But the greater effort had to be his. The War Department was still seriously undermanned for such an all-out effort and burdened with old functionaries and obsolete procedures. Unopened mail accumulated on tables and desk tops. Letters were sent to the wrong persons. Some duties needlessly overlapped, while others remained unassigned. Officers seeking promotions, soldiers wanting leave, civilians on every imaginable sort of business, thronged the rooms and hallways. Noise, confusion, and lack of system made the place deserve its popular name—"the lunatic asylum."

Stanton quickly secured Lincoln's permission to reform the creaking bureau structure of the Department and persuaded Congress to authorize the appointment of two more assistant secretaries, forty-nine clerks, four messengers, and two laborers, and the further addition of ten noncommissioned officers to the Adjutant General's staff. New jobs brought a rush of eager applicants, most of whom were dismayed when Stanton gave preference to soldiers unfit for field service because of wounds or minor physical defects.

He appointed his trusted friend Peter Watson to one of the new assistant secretary posts; he had promised to take on this responsibility before Stanton had been willing to join Lincoln's cabinet, and Stanton now insisted that he redeem this pledge. Short, stout, with red hair and beard, a man of business acumen whose driving energy matched that of Stanton, Watson, like Stanton, sacrificed an income amounting to many times his government salary in accepting the post. The country's leading patent attorney, Watson had an expert knowledge of mechanical principles and devices. Stanton allowed him practically unlimited discretion with respect to ordnance, and entrusted him with confidential assignments such as organizing and supervising a secret police force called the "National Detectives," headed by Colonel Lafayette C. Baker, and with giving to selected newspapermen the information that the Department wanted to have printed.[1]

For his other new assistant secretary, Stanton chose John Tucker, a Pennsylvanian who had helped Cameron organize rail and water transportation in the East. As the holdover assistant secretary, Thomas A. Scott, formerly vice-president of the Pennsylvania Railroad, was, like Tucker, from the Keystone State, the appointment brought outcries from New York's political spoilsmen, who claimed that Tucker had profited personally from questionable contracts during Cameron's tenure of office. Stanton vouched for his honesty and the Senate confirmed him. As personal clerk, Stanton chose Albert E. H. Johnson, who had performed confidential service for him in the Reaper case.

Stanton's professional experiences had made him aware of the importance of railroads and the telegraph as instruments of war. He prepared a bill authorizing the President to assume control of them, although he believed that Lincoln, as commander in chief, had the constitutional power to seize these utilities in any case. The measure lagged in the Senate, and Stanton wrote urgently to Wade: "Please communicate confidentially with the loyal and honest members of both houses and have action—immediate action." Most Northern railroads, as events proved, would render satisfactory service under private management, and in their case the full powers granted to the government by the act Wade pushed through Congress would be invoked only in rare instances.

But Stanton kept the powers the law conferred on Lincoln—which

---

[1] Stanton to Lincoln, Jan. 24, 1862, Stanton MSS; William E. Doster, *Lincoln and Episodes of the Civil War* (New York, 1915), 126–7; IGO, Register of Reports, 1861–5, Feb. 5, 1865, RG 159, and statements of Stanton, Watson, and General G. D. Ramsay, Dyer Court of Inquiry, II, 399–400, 523, RG 153, NA; Meneely, *op. cit.*, 374–5; E. D. Townsend, *Anecdotes of the Civil War* (New York, 1884), 77–8 (cited hereafter as Townsend, *Anecdotes*).

Stanton : The Life and Times

the President delegated to him—as a club to push reluctant railroad managers into obedience. He, McClellan, and Quartermaster General Montgomery Meigs, who put his genius for organization fully at Stanton's disposal, met with a group of railroad operators at Willard's Hotel late in February, to achieve a rate formula that would prevent gouging overcharges against the government. Stanton ordered the roads to standardize track gauges, freight-car utilization procedures, and signaling systems. He told them that the government's needs must have priority over their private interests but that he "infinitely preferred" having the railroad companies regulate themselves to exercising himself the despotic powers Congress had granted. The officials took the hint.[2]

The telegraph was a different matter. Constant rather than intermittent control of the telegraph system was essential to military secrecy, and Stanton would keep close watch over it. He appointed Edward S. Sanford, president of the American Telegraph Company, to be military supervisor of telegrams, and clamped on a rigid censorship. Newspapermen had to work through Watson, who could screen out undesirable journalists. Any reporter soliciting information from anyone else in the Department was to be dealt with as a spy.

His order occasioned some disagreement, but support and commendation were far more common. For example, John Murray Forbes, a Massachusetts entrepreneur, wrote William Cullen Bryant that "the telegraph is a mighty *engine of war*," vital to direct battles and to co-ordinate transportation of goods and men. "Stanton's move to control it," Forbes insisted, "seems to me one of the best things he has done."[3]

News continued to seep out, however, and Stanton ordered Watson to investigate. Though unable to locate the leak, Watson reported that Captain Thomas T. Eckert, telegraphic supervisor of the Army of the Potomac at McClellan's headquarters, where the central telegraph office was located, was often absent from duty and was withholding information from the Secretary of War. Stanton made out an order for Eckert's dismissal and told Sanford to see that it was carried out,

---

[2] Stanton to William Stanton, March 4, 1862, owned by William Stanton Picher; same to Wade, Jan. 27, 1862, Stanton MSS; Meigs's circular on rates, May 1, 1862, QMG Letterbook LX, 33–5, RG 107, NA; Samuel R. Kamm, *The Civil War Career of Thomas A. Scott* (Philadelphia, 1940), 83–5; news clips in A. E. H. Johnson scrapbook, owned by Mrs. Lois Reeside Sherrerd.

[3] H. T. White to Stanton, May 19, 1866, Sec. War Correspondence File, Box 319, RG 107, NA; *O.R.*, ser. 3, I, 899; Sarah F. Hughes (ed.), *Letters and Recollections of John Murray Forbes* (Boston, 1899), I, 291.

but grudgingly consented to let the young supervisor tell his side of the story. Eckert came to Stanton's office and stood before his desk for several minutes before Stanton deigned to look up. Then, in a loud voice, Stanton accused Eckert of neglecting his duties and divulging news. Pointing to a large pile of telegrams, all in Eckert's handwriting, he demanded to know why they had not been delivered to him at the time they were received.

Eckert explained that an order of Cameron's, which had never been revoked, required that all telegrams be sent to the commanding general and no one else. Stanton grunted and asked why Eckert was so often absent from his office. There must be some mistake, Eckert replied; for three months he had scarcely taken off his clothes except to change his linen, and spent night after night at the office. He tendered his resignation.

An arm fell on Eckert's shoulder. The President had silently entered the room. "Mr. Secretary, I think you must be mistaken about this young man neglecting his duties," Lincoln said, "for I have been a daily caller at General McClellan's headquarters for the last three or four months, and I have always found Eckert at his post. I have been there often before breakfast, and in the evening as well, and frequently late at night, and several times before daylight to get the latest news from the army. Eckert was always there, and I never observed any reporters or outsiders in the office."

Soon afterward Stanton moved the telegraph office from McClellan's headquarters to the War Department, in what had been the library, next to his own office, with an adjoining door for the cipher operators. Eckert, detached from McClellan's staff and promoted to major, was given full charge of it. The change enabled Stanton to exercise closer control of army communications and news releases.

To co-ordinate the War Department and the armies in the field, Stanton set apart two rooms in the Department building as headquarters for the commanding general. But McClellan was piqued at the removal of the telegraph office and later asserted that Stanton was plotting to be commanding general as well as Secretary. He preferred to operate from Army of the Potomac headquarters in a fine residence on Jackson Square, away from Stanton's oversight, and seldom even entered the rooms that Stanton had provided for him.[4]

[4] David Homer Bates, *Lincoln in the Telegraph Office* (New York, 1907), 39–40; Meneely, *op. cit.*, 238, 251; McClellan to Grant, Dec. 26, 1866, McClellan Papers, LC; Roscoe Pound, "The Military Telegraph in the Civil War," MHS *Proceedings*, LXVI, 185–203, and G. R. Thompson, "Civil War Signals," *MA*, XVIII, 199.

Seeking closer control of purchases, Stanton revoked all authorizations to buy supplies abroad if similar articles of domestic manufacture could be obtained. This order, though reflecting Stanton's constant fear that the government might go bankrupt, may have been instigated by Chase. In any event, Chase was consulted about it, for the war was already costing more than a million dollars a day, and with specie draining off to Europe, the price of gold on the New York market had jumped alarmingly. Seward protested that the order would "complicate the foreign situation"—England still smarted over the *Trent* affair, and Louis Napoleon was waiting only for some pretext to recognize the Confederacy. "It will have to be issued," Stanton replied to Seward's protests, "for very soon there will be no situation to complicate."

Stanton required all firms and persons claiming to have contracts with the War Department to have them immediately validated and put in legal form on pain of cancellation. Despairing of the adequacy and trustworthiness of existing Department procedures and personnel, Stanton appointed a special investigating commission, headed by Holt and Robert Dale Owen, to audit and adjust all contracts, orders, and claims in the files of the Department relating to arms, ammunition, and ordnance. Other commissions were dispatched to various field depots to report on unsettled claims. Stanton ordered a large quantity of defective arms and clothing returned to the contractors without payment and threatened criminal action against a number of offenders.

With Stanton's approval, and perhaps at his instigation, Congress passed laws in June and July 1862 correcting the methods of letting contracts. These laws made open and competitive bidding mandatory, forbade subletting, and stipulated that all contracts must be in writing and with loyal suppliers. Contractors were made subject to martial law and liable to court-martial if indicted for fraud. Stanton, not waiting for legislative sanction to cleanse the corrupt purchasing and inspection procedures, authorized the arrest of harness makers, food suppliers, and plumbing contractors who failed to keep their products up to the standards specified in their commitments. Later, when supplies were more plentiful, Stanton barred from all dealings with the War Department any contractor who was suspected of disloyal sentiments, and he sometimes extended this definition to embrace Democratic party affiliation.[5]

[5] *Francis McGhan* v. *Lewis Clephane* (1866), in WD, Letters Received, CLXIII, 175, RG 107, NA, describes penalties imposed on fraudulent and disloyal contractors; see also Stanton to Dana, June 6, 1862, Dana Papers, LC; to Henry S. Sanford, Jan.

Among Stanton's responsibilities, internal security became second in importance only to military matters. Lincoln had divided cabinet responsibility for the suppression of disloyalty, with most of the burden going to Secretary of State Seward out of distrust of Bates and Cameron. Seward had created a sprawling, unsystematic, undisciplined, but ubiquitous security apparatus, staffed with a congeries of federal, state, and local officials both civil and military. Many hundreds of persons were jailed on suspicion of intention to commit subversive acts, and Lincoln's suspension of the privilege of the writ of habeas corpus made it possible to hold them indefinitely without charge.

A storm of protest had grown up in opposition to the arbitrary arrests. Democrats naturally delighted in highlighting the Lincoln administration's harsh policy. Critics gained a substantial assist when Chief Justice Taney rebuked the President for acting unconstitutionally. The jurist, speaking for himself, not the Supreme Court, although still voicing an official judicial opinion, insisted that only Congress could suspend the writ and only in areas where the civil courts had ceased to function. Lincoln replied that the Constitution gave him the first duty to preserve the Union, and it would be gravely imperiled if the government waited until the commission of an overt act before moving against possible traitors.

He had agreed with Stanton before the new war minister took office that internal security was an inseparable part of the military responsibility, and that, as much as possible, it should be centralized in the War Department rather than placed on lower army command levels or left in irresponsible local and vigilante hands. The two men, although deeply troubled by the human suffering the arbitrary arrests imposed, were anxious that the security apparatus should prevent and punish disloyalty without further disrupting unity. They were willing to suppress civil liberties when necessary but were determined to preserve political democracy; they wanted results rather than rituals.

Neither man, therefore, suggested softening the security system, for the dangers were too immediate and real. Both wanted to reform and to expand it, to make it more reasonable, responsible, and humane, and thereby increase its utility as an adjunct of the expanding armies. Stanton took on the job of jailer knowing that it would bring him criticism even from loyal Northerners and the calumny of

---

29, Feb. 28, 1862, Sanford Papers, HML; *U. S. Statutes-at-Large*, XII, 441–2, 596; *O. R.*, ser. 3, I, 927; Meneely, *op. cit.*, 262–4, 372–3; Weigley, *Meigs*, 200–3.

all others. With Lincoln's approval, he recommended that, before the War Department assumed the task, Seward release all except the most dangerous prisoners if they would swear to refrain from giving "aid and comfort" to the enemy; this was done. Stanton then appointed another special commission—this one composed of Dix and an old friend of the law courts, New York City Democratic leader Edwards Pierrepont—to tour Northern prisons as a loyalty review board, checking on civilian prisoners of the War Department who offered to swear loyalty in order to gain release, and to lodge no suits alleging false arrest against any officials. If the government had no real evidence against the individual, Stanton's reforms opened a way from prison for him.

To the Northern public generally, Stanton seemed like a merciful and gentle official as compared with Seward because of this policy of quickly releasing all but the most dangerous internal foes. "The favorite of the day is Mr. Stanton," wrote English journalist William H. Russell; "he has touched the hearts of his countrymen. . . . One of his boldest acts has been the liberation of the victims of the *lettres de cachet* of the State Department." Grateful former prisoners and relatives and friends of released persons filled Stanton's mail with thankful praises. One such tribute, "Called forth upon hearing the order of the Secretary of War for the release of the political prisoners," prayed on Stanton's behalf:

> *That happiness be yours that on such deeds attend*
> *Be yours those pleasures which have no alloy*
> *And may thy earthly cup o'erflow with joy*
> *Around thy home may guardian angels play*
> *And flowers immortal blossom on thy way . . .*
> *And when life fades those spirits hovering near*
> *May place upon thy brow the crown won here*
> *And lead thee to the home prepared above*
> *For those whose deeds were charity and love.*

But the grim pressures of civil war soon altered the public's picture of Stanton. In 1862 and 1863 especially, Northern prisons again filled with civilians, and although he released the majority of them after a few days or weeks at the most, Stanton lost his early reputation as a gentle reformer. He became depicted, instead, as the harsh, oppressive, vindictive taskmaster of the Union. Stanton accepted the popular verdict without attempting to defend himself. He was too busy to bother.[6]

[6] Poem owned by Mrs. Van Swearingen; Russell in Washington *Star*, March 31,

Stanton realized that he knew nothing of how war was organized and there was precious little time for him to learn. But he felt that he must prepare himself. Anticipating that Lincoln would soon call on him for policy consultations and that the early impression he made would go far in determining the degree of trust the President could extend to his new Secretary of War, Stanton plunged into research on the administration of armies as he had immersed himself in the Bridge, Reaper, and California cases.

The nation boasted almost no professional military literature, and its army officers maintained no permanent, critical journal of military thought. Stanton turned to the professional soldiers, and organized the Army's bureau chiefs into a primitive kind of general staff. Association with the career army officers on War Department duty quickly tempered his distrust of the soldier, though he continued to respect men in the ranks more than those sporting gold braid. Although Stanton became willing to proffer his personal esteem and trust to volunteer and regular officers who proved their competence, he never esteemed their profession. He saw a potential dictator in every general who vaunted his self-importance, was contemptuous of incompetent commanders who were too toplofty to learn the craft of war, and firmly believed that the civil arm must use the military and not be used by it. All these were typical attitudes of his generation and he shared them with millions of other Americans.

But to function effectively as secretary of a war, Stanton had to modify some of these preconceptions, though he never abandoned their fundamental spirit. Paradoxically, he came to love the citizens' army and to revere the men who in its service sacrificed their lives and health. From his war council, he grew to appreciate the endless complexities involved in building a war machine. Stanton also came to sense the soldier's conviction of mission, and he ultimately accepted the military man's identification of the Army's welfare with the nation's destiny. That Lincoln also intuitively grasped this equation became the first and strongest bond between the two men.

His war board improvisation at least afforded Stanton a degree of insight into army operations that Cameron had never even sought to achieve. The board consisted of Adjutant General Lorenzo Thomas, whom Stanton detested on sight; Meigs, the hard-working, combative

---

1862; Hyman, *op. cit.*, 139–97; Francis Lieber's memo on habeas corpus suspension, HL.

Quartermaster General; General James W. Ripley, Chief of Ordnance; General Joseph G. Totten, Chief Engineer; and Colonel Joseph P. Taylor, Commissary General—reinforced by any field officer who might be in Washington, and later by Stanton's "military aide," General E. R. S. Canby, a tough young combat veteran. Stanton met with the board several times each week, and the verbatim reports of its sessions give penetrating insight into his rough, effective method.

Meigs reported at one meeting that a quartermaster had asked for authority to buy artillery horses. Stanton answered: "Authorize him to buy, but tell him that . . . the present Secretary of War holds it as a principle of law that any Quartermaster or any agent of the government who gives more for an article than the market price, will be held liable for the difference." An officer had complained that a Cameron appointee serving under him was unfit for the service. Stanton asked why Meigs did not authorize the man's dismissal. "If you will take the responsibility and do your duty, I shall not haul you over the coals," he said.

A matter touching a close friend of the President arose when it was alleged that Colonel Edward D. Baker, killed at the battle of Ball's Bluff, had failed to account for money granted to him to raise a regiment. A Philadelphia firm had submitted a bill for $600, duly attested, which it had spent, on Baker's authorization, for newspaper advertisements soliciting recruits. Stanton told Thomas to advise the firm to make claim against Baker's estate. "I hear that Baker had an interest in contracts for clothing," Stanton said, "and I would tell these parties that he had no lawful authority to bind the United States. . . . I would just reject the account, and send the parties to the Court of Claims."

Stanton noticed that General "Jim" Lane, a Kansas senator, who had bivouacked a "Frontier Guard" in the East Room of the White House during the first trying days of the war, was an outstanding offender in the matter of illegally overblown staff rosters. Recently the President had offered him the command of an expedition into Arkansas. Now Lane was pirating officers from eastern commands, and Thomas did not know where he had gone.

"I would not hunt for him or his staff," said Stanton.

"But his staff are on duty," answered Thomas.

"I would stop their pay," said Stanton.

"But I want to discharge them," protested Thomas.

"Well, strike them from the rolls," said Stanton.

"One of the persons on the staff the President does not want discharged. If I discharge one I must discharge all."

"While I administer this office, I will not sanction an abuse of that kind. Discharge them all," rumbled Stanton. "If the President don't like it, let him so intimate, and I will retire." [7]

Stanton's energy quickly permeated the War Department. Heads of bureaus, accustomed to the leisurely, gentlemanly procedures of earlier Secretaries, were startled to find "Report Forthwith" scrawled across papers he referred to them, in the harsh, strong script they were to come to know so well. Applicants for interviews with the Secretary, even influential senators such as Wade, were amazed to receive appointments at 9 a.m., a previously unheard-of hour. On public days, Stanton held reception hours at 10 a.m. and at 3 p.m., and while crowds waited in his anteroom he met with one person at a time, standing at a chest-high writing desk for all the world like a hectoring minister. The desk was there at the suggestion of doctors, who, concerned that Stanton took no exercise, hoped that a peripatetic office regimen might be of some benefit.

Stanton's unresting efforts brought quick results. Joshua F. Speed, calling at the Department to obtain arms for use in Kentucky, wrote to Holt that he had "accomplished in a few days what heretofore would have taken as many weeks. . . . Instead of that loose shackling way of doing business in the War Office, with which I have been so disgusted & which I have had so good an opportunity of seeing— there is now—order, regularity and precision." He expected Stanton to "infuse into the whole army an energy & activity which we have not seen heretofore." [8]

But some old-timers in the Department were not so greatly impressed. K. Pritchett, a clerk, writing to let Cameron know how things were coming along without him, complained of "a general moan around the walls of the Department. It appears in truth as if daily confusion grows worse confounded. . . . We have orders upon orders, all seem-

---

[7] Proceedings of the War Board, March 14, 21, 26, 1862, Stanton MSS, and with fuller copies supplied by Gideon Townsend Stanton; Stanton to John H. Clifford, May 7, 1867, NYHS. On attitude toward officers, see Doster, *op. cit.*, 118; Theodore C. Smith (ed.), *Life and Letters of James A. Garfield* (New Haven, 1925), I, 238 (hereafter cited as Smith, *Garfield*).

[8] Speed to Holt, Feb. 4, 1862, Holt Papers, LC; Colonel L. C. Duncan, "The Strange Case of Surgeon-General Hammond," *Military Surgeon*, LXIV, 102–3; Watson to Wade, Feb. 11, 1862, Wade Papers, LC; New York *Times*, Jan. 25, 1862.

ing predicated upon the idea that every thing heretofore was disorder and fraud." Papers were now filed "under as many heads as the curiosities at Barnum's museum." To find anything was like "digging out a badger with the aid of a dozen ferrets and as many terriers." With legal-minded Assistant Secretary Watson every letter was a "Declaration," every order an "Indictment," Pritchett reported, and asserted that Meigs felt distressed at his inability to "penetrate the rubbish, and get at the new machinery to set his wheels a'going, which are all at a standstill for want of motion of the main shaft, the tinkering and oiling occupying all the time and nothing done." Clerks worked until midnight, sometimes until three in the morning. "Secretary Stanton is doubtless a great man, since you have endorsed him," conceded Pritchett; but it seemed to persons in the Department that he showed "but little sympathy and small appreciation for labors that are breaking many of us down."

Stanton asked no more of others than he was willing to do himself. Seldom quitting the Department before ten o'clock at night, he was the first to break down, confirming the fears of his friend Barlow that he was working too hard. Less than a month after taking over, he collapsed one day in his office, suffering, Lorenzo Thomas reported, "with a rush of blood to the head." An army ambulance took Stanton home, and Washington blossomed with rumors of a change in the cabinet. Congressman Dawes wrote: "My heart has never so failed me as when I heard it. It did seem to me as though God had turned his face away from us and we were left to utter wreck." But Stanton was suffering merely from exhaustion; he was back at work within four days, boasting of being able to exceed his former schedule. When, later in February, a rumor spread that he was again ill, he wrote to Dana: "I was at the Department or in Cabinet from 9 a.m. until 9 at night & never enjoyed more perfect health."

Watson, who like his superior officer kept working until he could scarcely stand, became ill and, as Stanton phrased it, broke down "flat." Stanton ordered him home and instructed the sentries at the door not to admit Watson to the building until Stanton told them to.[9]

Stanton's brief illness afforded the employees a chance to catch their breath. Cameron heard that General Thomas's legs were reduced to the thickness of pipe stems from standing at Stanton's elbow, "ready to be questioned in behalf of the service," and Thomas and another

[9] Pritchett to Cameron, Feb. 2, 1862, Cameron Papers, LC; Dawes to Mrs. Dawes, Feb. 11, 1862, Dawes Papers, LC; Stanton to Dana, Feb. 23, 1862, Ac. 2626, Dana Papers, LC; Wolcott MS, 180; Barlow to Stanton, Feb. 23, 1862, Barlow Papers, HL.

Department officer, reminiscing over the easier days, "yesterday compared the present with the past and we sighed for a good old gentleman [Cameron] . . . up in Pennsylvania," who had delightfully mingled social courtesies with the intelligent and prompt dispatch of business.

General Thomas had found himself in an unenviable position under Stanton. Suspecting him of disloyalty, the Secretary felt that Thomas was "only fit for presiding over a crypt of Egyptian mummies like himself." Unable to pin any specific charge on Thomas, Stanton sent him off on frequent field trips and assigned his duties to able, discreet, hard-working General E. D. Townsend.[1]

Business in the War Department began officially at nine o'clock. As Stanton's carriage turned off Pennsylvania Avenue around that time, the doorkeeper would stick his head inside and announce: "The Secretary." The word spread; stragglers and loungers scurried to their desks, and the place quivered with activity. Alighting from his carriage, Stanton was usually beset by favor seekers waiting on the sidewalk. He might stop for a word with an enlisted soldier or a needy-looking woman, but he would curtly tell the others to go to his reception room upstairs.

Proceeding to his private office on the second floor in a corner overlooking the White House, Stanton immediately began pulling on the tasseled cord that set a bell to jangling in the hallway and brought messengers on the run. All day that bell would jangle like a "moral tone," as one clerk put it, "filling the ears and minds of the working staff with lessons of duty and necessity."

Stanton considered it a duty to see as many business callers as he could, but it was impossible to give everyone a private audience, and even cabinet colleagues, senators, and representatives, sometimes finding it impossible to see him, took "potluck" with the crowd in his reception room. Colonel James A. Hardie, a handsome officer who spoke with a Scotch burr, presided in this room, ascertaining each caller's business and dispatching it if he could, or sending in the names of those individuals whom he thought the Secretary would wish to interview personally. Naturally, those not admitted were offended, and Attorney General Bates once protested, after being stopped at Stanton's door, that Stanton's clerks were actually empowered to "prevent the meeting and consultation of the heads of Departments."

[1] Townsend, *Anecdotes*, 79–80; Samuel Wilkeson to Cameron, Feb. 12, 1862, Cameron Papers, LC.

The reception room was always jammed. Stanton, emerging from his office, walked across the room with a somewhat awkward gait because of his stiff knee and took his place behind the high desk. Waving back those who approached him, he would make a slow, deliberate scrutiny of the crowd, confer briefly with Hardie to learn whether any cases merited special attention, then summon someone forward. Soldiers usually got first chance, then soldiers' wives or widows. If a soldier carried crutches or showed the marks of wounds, Stanton often left the desk and talked to him where he sat. Wounded officers were also granted solicitous attention; otherwise shoulder-straps were likely to meet a cool reception. Everyone was required to state his business quickly in the hearing of the others.

Stanton personified force and competence as he stood behind the tall desk, looking each visitor squarely, almost defiantly, in the eye, his own eyes glittering through his steel-rimmed spectacles, his broad nostrils tremulous when he became excited, his wide forehead flushed and often perspiring, his complexion dark and mottled as though from high living, his dark hair beginning to thin a bit, and his lips compressed above his immense black beard, which gave off a mixed odor of tobacco and cologne. Middle age had put a considerable amount of flesh on his short frame. His movements were deliberate, almost studied. He reminded Provost Marshal William E. Doster of a schoolmaster who had had a poor night's sleep.

At Stanton's entrance a hush fell on the room. People conversed under their breath, and the clerks and orderlies moved about with soft-footed deference. " 'Influential' people tried their influence only once," Doster declared, "acquaintances at the bar tried it and were rebuffed, corrupt people found themselves suspected before they drew near. Women in tears, venerable old men, approached slowly—but withdrew quickly as if they had touched hot iron. A few got what they wanted and earned it in the getting."

The Secretary's brusque rudeness, Doster acutely realized, was in part natural to his character, and sometimes he assumed it as a protection against influential favor seekers, especially congressmen.[2] Stanton decided to request the Senate, many of whose members were guilty of absorbing excessive amounts of War Department energy in seeking commissions and contracts for constituents, to suspend confirmation of military appointments and promotions until he could scan

---

[2] Doster, *op. cit.*, 114–17; William Stanton to Mrs. O. S. Picher, Oct. 12, 1907, owned by William Stanton Picher; Bates to Stanton, Letterbook C, 254, RG 60, NA.

the list of more than 1,400 names with a view to rewarding "merit or honors in the field." The existing system, he wrote General Don Carlos Buell, "has been against my judgment and wishes."

Stanton's efforts to take army appointments out of politics brought strident complaints from the spoilsmen. "The pressure of members of Congress for clerk & army appointments [increases] notwithstanding the most stringent rules," he complained to Dana; "and the persistent strain against all measures essential to obtain time for thought, combination, and conference is damaging in the extreme." Stanton grew momentarily discouraged—"It often tempts me to quit the helm in despair," he confessed—but his spirits bounced back with the need for action. He was able to arrange the Department schedule so that congressmen had Saturdays reserved for their patronage business. From Tuesday through Thursday of each week only matters directly relating to active military operations were permitted; the public could call only on Mondays, and Stanton would see no one at his home on business. Some congressmen complained, but Stanton maintained his stand, even against Mrs. Lincoln.

The day after he took office, a man Stanton recalled as "one of those indescribable half loafers, half gentlemen," came to him with a card from the President's wife, bearing the request that he be given a commissary's appointment. Stanton lost his temper, tore up the card, and excitedly told the man that "the fact that you bring me such a card would prevent me giving it to you."

The next day, "with a kind of small triumph in his eye," the persistent job seeker returned, this time with Mrs. Lincoln's formal request that he be placed. Stanton tore up this letter as he had the card, later that day called on Mary Lincoln, and lectured her on her duties to the nation and to her husband. She subdued her own temper, told the war minister that he had been correct, and promised never to bother him again with such requests. Stanton was proud that he almost never allowed personal relationships or official connections to swerve him from duty.[3]

For example, Ben Wade used the full force of his influence in an attempt to obtain a commission for William Stanton; reporting failure,

---

[3] Stanton to Dana, Feb. 1, 1862, Ac. 2626, Dana Papers, LC; to Buell, *O.R.*, X, pt. 2, 617; Meneely, *op. cit.*, 371–3. The incident involving Mrs. Lincoln is in Boston *Daily Evening Transcript*, Jan. 7, 1870, and was undoubtedly written by Stanton's friend Horatio Woodman; see Ruth Painter Randall, *Mary Lincoln: Biography of a Marriage* (Boston, 1953), 323–4; on relatives see William Stanton to Mrs. O. S. Picher, Oct. 12, 1907, owned by William Stanton Picher.

Wade informed the younger man: "He placed it entirely on the ground of relationship; I argued against him and told him it was a great hardship to place you on any worse ground on that account, but could not argue him out of the absurd position he had taken." When his nephew Benjamin Tappan, Jr., the son of Stanton's beloved sister Oella, applied for a commission in the regular army, Stanton rejected the application, maintaining that to accept it would violate his rule against such appointments except as a reward for meritorious service. Then Lincoln interceded, writing that if Stanton "knows no objection . . . except that he is a relative of his, let him be appointed on my responsibility." [4]

Stanton's sternness toward favor seekers so impressed everyone that John Hay, one of Lincoln's secretaries, felt it preferable to "make a tour of a smallpox hospital" rather than to ask special favors from Stanton; businessman Forbes asked a friend for "such a letter . . . as will convince him that I do not come to steal anything from 'Uncle Sam' "; and Stanton's onetime friend, political intimate, and professional associate, Barlow, learned from Governor William Sprague that "the Secretary of War will permit no interference in matters like that of which you request my influence."

Working like a man driven, Stanton expected the same dedicated performance from his subordinates. Once the gruff Secretary surprised hard-working Colonel Ramsay, of the Washington Arsenal, with an order to go on leave: "You have a right to relaxation & I pray you take it." But Stanton rarely felt that he had the same right himself.

Overwork did not sweeten Stanton's temper. A word taken amiss or a gesture subject to misconstruction caused him to explode, and with a quick snap he would dash his glasses from before his eyes as though they obstructed his vision, thrusting them far back on his flushed forehead, while the muscles of his face twitched spasmodically and his voice trembled with passion. "But the storm would pass away as quickly as it came," a clerk recalled, "and be succeeded by a calmness of demeanor almost as painful by reason of the sudden contrast." If the victim was a subordinate, Stanton at their next meeting would put his hand on the man's shoulder in a kindly and seemingly unconscious manner, or comment that he looked tired and must take a little rest, and perhaps invite him to share a simple luncheon. If the offended per-

---

[4] Wade to William Stanton, March 9, 1863, Feb. 5, 1864, owned by William Stanton Picher; on Tappan, photo of Stanton's and Lincoln's endorsements on the application, May 13, 23, 1862, Washington, D.C., *Evening Star*, Aug. 9, 1960 (document discovered by Mr. Joseph F. Thompson, Jr., and reproduced in University of Kentucky Library, *Lincoln Facsimile*, No. 9, Jan. 1961).

Writing on the back of an envelope, Lincoln approves a commission in the Army for Stanton's nephew, Benjamin Tappan, Jr., but the Secretary of War "declines to make the appointment."

son stood high in the Department, Stanton might tell him an important piece of news in confidence. He was reluctant to apologize directly and tried to find some other means of expiation, even if it amounted to no more than a word of appreciation for a new blotter on his desk.

William Stanton, observing this "brusque and busy man," wondered how he could keep the pace he set for himself and demanded of others. The Secretary allowed himself few regular indulgences. Three mornings a week, before going to the Department, he visited the city market, according to a practice he had begun before the war, to provide for his family table. He liked to exchange gossip and banter with the garrulous stallkeepers and in the sights and smells of a busy market to recall memories of pleasant country living. A manservant paid for his purchases—for Stanton never carried money on his person—and took the parcels home.

Like Lincoln, Stanton wore the formal frock coat and tall hat of the fashionable gentleman, but unlike the President, he was very particular about his clothes. Twice a week a soldier-clerk shaved his upper lip in his office. Sometimes when the burden of his work became unendurable, Stanton shut himself up in the office and, stretched out on the leather sofa for an hour or so, read English magazines and Dickens, being particularly fond of *Littell's Living Age* and of *Pickwick Papers*. Apart from spending time with his family, this was his only relaxation.[5]

Even those who distrusted Stanton in 1862 and hated him later, had to admit that his methods, personality, and energy were what the Union needed in those dark days, and that he did not spare himself. As Stanton took hold, Dana recalled, the armies "seemed to grow," and events quickened their pace.

Stanton's accession to the war office accompanied changes in the rhythm and intensity of the conflict. The early fumbling of the "improvised war" was ending. He was to help to alter the nature of the conflict until Americans across the land were affected by its course.[6]

[5] Nicolay, *Lincoln's Secretary,* 115; Hughes, *op. cit.,* I, 288; Benjamin, "Recollections of Secretary Stanton," *CM,* XXXIII, 75–86; Johnson, "Reminiscences of Hon. Edwin M. Stanton," *loc. cit.,* 79; William Stanton to Mrs. O. S. Picher, Oct. 12, 1907, owned by William Stanton Picher; Stanton to Ramsay, June 28, 1863, HL; Sprague to Barlow, Aug. 2, 1862, Barlow Papers, HL.

[6] Dana, *Lincoln and his Cabinet,* 20.

CHAPTER VIII

ORGANIZING VICTORY

O<small>N THE</small> huge map which he ordered placed near his desk during his first day as War Secretary, Stanton could see what the Union had achieved in nine months of civil war. Considering the unready state of the nation when Sumter fell, there had been great accomplishments. Scratch forces had taken important rebel fortifications off the Carolinas. Westward, improvised armies had saved Kentucky and Missouri from secession, were enlarging a Unionist center around Wheeling, and were poised to move toward Tennessee and Arkansas.

In the East, likewise, swift and brave action had thwarted Maryland's secessionists, and the safety of Washington was no longer a daily gamble. Since Bull Run blighted hopes of a swift victory, McClellan had wrought vast improvements in the spirit, discipline, and drill-field performance of the greatly augmented Army of the Potomac. But though the huge force McClellan commanded now maneuvered with impressive snap, it fought only a few indecisive skirmishes. Nothing he accomplished compared with the successes of Union commanders in the Mississippi Valley.

Throughout the last half of 1861, Stanton had shared in the Northern expectation that McClellan was readying a massive onslaught southward. He came to the war office convinced that the general's immobility had been a tragic error, permitting the South to improve its defenses. During his first days in the war office, Stanton gained information that sustained him in this conviction.

Consulting the members of the Joint Committee on the Conduct of the War, and examining their files, Stanton found ample evidence, partly from McClellan's own generals, that he had merely been toying with an army which had been fully prepared to advance against the enemy for many months, and even now had no plan for throwing it into action. Nor could Stanton have failed to note during the past months that McClellan possessed many of those qualities that he found obnoxious in the professional military man—swagger, ostentation, questionable professional competence, and contempt for the civil government. Viewing the general from a new vantage point, Stanton quickly adopted the low opinion of him that the committee entertained. Committeeman Julian was delighted that Stanton "agreed with us fully in our estimate of McClellan and as to the necessity of an early forward movement."

Stanton's ability to master great masses of complex data with extraordinary rapidity was exhibited as never before. After four days of this education, Stanton advised Dana confidentially that McClellan "has got to fight or run away; and while men are striving nobly in the West, the champagne and oysters on the Potomac must be stopped."

Probably on the same day he wrote to Dana, January 24, Stanton talked with Lincoln. The Secretary argued that McClellan should quickly bring war to the enemy. To his pleased surprise, Stanton learned that the President had also concluded that the North must mount concerted military offensives in order to crack the Confederacy. McClellan's inactivity had already strained Lincoln's patience. Stanton's estimation of Lincoln commenced an ascent that never slackened; his view of McClellan began a descent that he never found reason to alter.[1]

Three days after this meeting, Lincoln issued a general order, which Stanton helped to inspire, commanding all the Union armies to make a concerted advance by Washington's Birthday. Four days later a special order from the White House enjoined the Army of the Potomac to begin an overland advance toward Richmond within the time prescribed.

It brought an immediate protest from McClellan. He wanted to leave his position in front of Washington, transport his army by water to Urbana, on the Rappahannock River, and advance on Richmond from there. Neither Lincoln nor Stanton thought well of the plan. It meant further delay, and it would leave Washington uncovered. Stanton would have rejected it out of hand, but Lincoln decided to get the opinions

---

[1] Perhaps because he did not yet trust anyone at the War Department, Stanton made notes on these matters on some blank pages in a copy of Helper's *Impending Crisis.* He entitled these notes "Events; Ideas, Jan. 15–24, 1862." Mr. Thomas examined the Helper volume and copied Stanton's annotations, and this account is based on Mr. Thomas's record. To Dana, Ac. 2626, Dana Papers, LC; Julian, *op. cit.*, 204.

of McClellan's division commanders. Seven of them voted for Mc-Clellan's proposal unconditionally, and one more approved it provided that the Confederate batteries along the Potomac were first reduced. Four opposed McClellan's project, but only two of these supported the more direct offensive that Lincoln and Stanton had endorsed.

"We saw ten generals afraid to fight" was Stanton's comment. Lincoln, who two weeks earlier had felt so desperate about the immobility of the Union armies that he had thought of personally taking field command, agreed that Stanton's analysis was probably correct, but thought it unwise for two inexperienced civilians to place their judgment above the opinions of the generals. Though Lincoln did not revoke his order for a direct attack on Richmond, he tacitly assented to the council's verdict. On February 27, Stanton, albeit reluctantly, instructed Assistant Secretary Tucker to begin assembling transports to move the army down Chesapeake Bay.

Lincoln's curious military orders, and his contradictory willingness to defer to McClellan, reflect the indefiniteness of power relationships and allocations of functions at this time. As the war progressed, things changed, so that Lincoln's intercessions in military strategy became fewer. But the President, as he learned how to steer the ship of state, kept firm control of the policy wheel. A succession of generals and civil officials learned to their sorrow of his determination to be master in his White House. Stanton sensed this sooner than most, and bent his own impetuous will to the decisions of his superior.[2]

However, Lincoln was never fully able to co-ordinate the efforts of his cabinet officers; indeed, he never realized the need to do so. Since November 1861, the Navy Department had been preparing to attack New Orleans, and Welles had ordered that all news of the plan be withheld from the War Department for fear that details would leak to the enemy. He had, however, taken McClellan into the secret because troops would be needed to occupy the city once the Navy had won it.

But paunchy, prying General Benjamin F. Butler, Massachusetts Democratic politician turned soldier, was able somehow to sniff out Welles's plan, and he told Stanton of it. Stanton, as Welles recalled, "seized hold of the information [on the New Orleans expedition] with

[2] Fry, *Military Miscellanies* (New York, 1889), 285–7; Flower, *Stanton*, 138–40; Hay, *Diaries and Letters*, 36; T. C. Pease and J. G. Randall (eds.), *The Diary of Orville Hickman Browning* (Springfield, 1925, 1933), I, 523 (cited hereafter as Browning, *Diary*). See also Warren Hassler, Jr., *General George B. McClellan: Shield of the Union* (Baton Rouge, 1957), 52–62; McClellan, *Own Story*, 228–9, 237; Randall, *Lincoln the President* (New York, 1954), II, 74–9; Kelley, *op. cit.*, 33–4.

avidity and gave hearty support to the movement." As Stanton had learned of the secret, Welles did not rebuff him, perhaps because McClellan had been indifferent toward the project and had shilly-shallied about appointing anyone to command the troops. But soon after Stanton entered the war office, McClellan gave Butler the command.[3]

Now it was obvious to Stanton that McClellan's voice was to dominate strategy in the East; the New Orleans campaign was primarily a navy show. The vital midwestern region, controlling the complex of the Ohio and northern Mississippi rivers and the immensely important tier of slaveholding border states, clamored for the attention of the officials in Washington. Stanton was still distrustful of the bureau heads in the War Department, and sent Assistant Secretary Scott on a tour of the Midwest.

Lincoln had been disappointed in Buell, commanding the Army of the Ohio, because of his failure to move into eastern Tennessee, where Unionists were being harassed by the Confederates. But Scott reported that Buell had been immobilized by bad weather and poor roads; moreover, Buell had a better plan. With forty or fifty thousand troops from the inactive Army of the Potomac, Buell would break the Confederate defense line along the railroad from Bowling Green to Columbus, occupy both Nashville and Memphis, and then have a permanent base for future operations in the heart of the enemy's country.

Buell also pointed out to Scott the necessity of achieving better coordination between the Union armies in the West. General Ulysses S. Grant, one of Halleck's commanders, was operating within the area of Buell's command at that moment, but Halleck had made no effort to put him in rapport with Buell. Grant, in conjunction with a fleet of gunboats under Commodore Andrew H. Foote, had just captured Fort Henry, eighty miles up the Tennessee River from the Union base at Paducah; but Buell warned that at Fort Donelson, on the Cumberland, the Confederates were building up a strong force. Grant would be obliged to retire and might even be cut off unless quickly reinforced, and Buell could send him little help because of the miry roads.

---

[3] Jesse A. Marshal (ed.), *Private and Official Correspondence of General Benjamin F. Butler during the Period of the Civil War* (Norwich, 1917), I, 323, 331 (cited hereafter as Butler, *Correspondence*); Butler, *Butler's Book* (Boston, 1892), 335–6; Morse, *Welles Diary*, I, 60–1; Welles, "Admiral Farragut and New Orleans," *Galaxy*, XII, 817–32; Pearson, *Andrew*, I, 304–10; ms proceedings of the war board, March 18, 1862, Stanton MSS; *O.R.*, V, 40; VI, 677–8.

This advice from the scene of action impressed the civilians in Washington. Stanton wired Buell on February 9 that Lincoln wanted the western commanders to co-operate, and "says that your two heads together will succeed." But co-operation was not won so easily as this. Grant moved to invest Fort Donelson. Word came to the War Department that Foote's gunboats had taken a severe battering and been obliged to draw off. Grant was in a predicament. It began to appear that Buell had been right.

Stanton fretted and worried. "We have had a disaster, I think, at Fort Donaldson [*sic*]," he wrote Chase, "and I apprehend still worse results, unless movements are forced from the Potomac."

Then, on February 17, news came that after a bloody fight in bitter weather, Grant, assisted by General C. F. Smith, had won Donelson and had taken more than 14,000 prisoners. It was Monday, and Stanton's reception room was jammed when he read Grant's "unconditional surrender" dispatch to the crowd. Jumping with excitement, Stanton proposed three cheers in Grant's honor; the shouts, a clerk wrote Cameron, "shook the old walls, broke all the spiders' webs, and set the rats scampering."

Meanwhile, Scott had moved on to appraise the situation at St. Louis. Halleck, in command there, agreed with Buell that fifty thousand troops from the Army of the Potomac should be sent West. But he thought that he, not Buell, should have them. Halleck also suggested that Buell, Grant, and Pope be made major generals, "and give me command in the West. I ask this in return for Forts Henry and Donelson."

Lincoln and Stanton were a jump ahead of the immodest Halleck so far as Grant was concerned, for that night Stanton brought the President a nomination promoting him. The Secretary was exuberant, complaining only that John B. Floyd, his former colleague in Buchanan's cabinet and now a Confederate general, had escaped from Donelson.[4]

While Grant was moving on Fort Donelson, an amphibious force under General Ambrose E. Burnside and Commodore L. M. Goldsborough captured Roanoke Island, off the North Carolina coast. And now came word that Buell had seized Bowling Green and that General Samuel R. Curtis, another of Halleck's commanders, had virtually ended the threat to Missouri by routing a Confederate army at Pea Ridge,

[4] Nicolay, *Lincoln's Secretary*, 130–1; K. Pritchett to Cameron, Feb. 17, 1862, Cameron Papers, LC; Scott's reports, Feb. 5–21, 1862, Stanton MSS. See also Stanton to Buell, Feb. 9, 1862, BU; same to Chase, Feb. 16, 1862, Chase Papers, HSP; Kamm, *op. cit.*, 86–113; and *O.R.*, ser. 3, I, 889.

Arkansas. Five Union victories in a little more than a week! But elation turned a bit sour for Stanton when the Washington *Star* lauded the military genius of McClellan: utilizing the telegraph, he had brought about these remarkable achievements at points far distant from one another as though sitting face to face with his generals over a single table. Stanton, anxious for credit to be given where it was due, wrote disgustedly to Dana that, as a matter of fact, McClellan had cut a ridiculous figure in the telegraph office, making a great show of energy and "by sublime military combinations capturing Fort Donelson six hours after Grant & Smith had taken it sword in hand & had victorious possession. It would be a picture worthy of Punch."

Before receiving this note, Dana had published an editorial giving Stanton the chief credit for organizing the recent Union victories. Stanton immediately protested that no one could "organize victory." Battles are to be won "now and by us in the same and only manner that they were won by any people, or in any age, since the days of Joshua," he wrote Dana, "by boldly pursuing and striking the foe." Grant's message to rebel General Buckner—"I propose to move immediately upon your works"—seemed to Stanton to embody the needed spirit of victory, and he made it clear by inference that he wished McClellan would show some of that spirit, too.

Dana published Stanton's letter along with another editorial. The War Secretary's modest disclaimer, Dana wrote, did him honor. If Stanton had not organized victory, he had at least unbound it and set it in motion.[5]

Public reaction to this exchange was as partisan as the participants, for this was the first open test of Stanton's position on McClellan. Stanton's "admirable" letters excited George Templeton Strong to note in his diary: "No high official in my day has written a dozen lines half as weighty and telling. If he is not careful, he will be our next President."

McClellan's supporters were no less quick to take sides. Assistant Secretary of the Navy Fox, an intimate of the Blairs and McClellan, insisted that "no other man in the U. S. would have accomplished in 'organizing victory' . . . what McClellan has." And the Washington *Star*, which had started the inky tempest, editorialized that the whole affair represented an abolitionist attempt to pit Stanton against Mc-

[5] Flower, *Stanton*, 129–31; Stanton to Dana, Feb. 19, Stanton MSS; same, Feb. 23, Ac. 2626, Dana Papers, LC; Washington *Star*, Feb. 18, 1862. Hassler, *op. cit.*, 52, sees this as a slap at McClellan. Although this was part of Stanton's intention, it is still an honest statement of his beliefs.

Clellan, and declared that Stanton's declarations as published were fictions and that he and McClellan were fast friends.[6]

Events would again set Secretary and commanding general against each other. Meanwhile, the unceasing pressure continued at the War Department, as did the grinding mass of work and the endless, accumulating horror at the human cost of the war represented in the casualty lists that passed over Stanton's desk.

The West kept Stanton's attention. Commodore Foote took Clarksville. The Confederate commander, Albert Sidney Johnston, abandoned Nashville and fell back on Columbus, forty miles to the south. Halleck felt sure that the way into the interior of the Confederacy lay open before him. With those fifty thousand troops from the Army of the Potomac and over-all command, he wired McClellan, he could end the war in the West. When McClellan refused to act, Halleck went over his head and appealed to Stanton. The ambiguities of the army command structure were again creating trouble, and not for the last time.

Stanton could not act without consulting Lincoln, but the President's eleven-year-old son, Willie, was so critically ill, and the father "so much depressed by anxiety," Stanton informed Chase, that he could not obtain an appointment with him. And Stanton got nowhere with McClellan about sending troops to the West; or about another scheme he had conceived—having "Mac" go to the West himself, so that Lincoln could replace him with a more active man and still avoid a political explosion. In hopes that McClellan would agree to send a force to the West, Stanton nevertheless began to prepare the necessary transportation.

Willie Lincoln died in the last days of February, but Stanton thought the matter sufficiently urgent to break in on Lincoln with it. Lincoln gave it full consideration but decided against a change in the organization of the military departments at the moment. McClellan put the seal on Halleck's hopes with a terse telegram to Scott: "At present no troops will move from East. Ample occupation for them here. Rebels still hold at Manassas Junction." [7]

Stanton sympathized deeply with Lincoln in the loss of his son, for his own youngest child, James, was desperately ill at this time. He had

[6] Strong, *Diary*, III, 208; R. M. Thompson and R. Wainwright, "Confidential Correspondence of Gustavus Vasa Fox," *NHSP*, X (1918), II, 297–8 (cited hereafter as Fox, *Correspondence*); *Star*, Feb. 26, 1862.

[7] Stanton to Chase, Feb. 16, 1862, Chase Papers HSP; *O.R.*, VII, 642, 645, 652, 655; Halleck to his wife, March 5, 1862, in James Grant Wilson, "General Halleck—A Memoir," *JMSI*, XXXVI, 555; Barlow to McClellan, Feb. 8, 1862, Barlow Papers, HL, on the western scheme.

been a hearty, thriving baby until he was vaccinated. The vaccine had caused a hideous eruption, and he was not expected to survive. Ellen had almost worn herself out watching over the baby night and day, and Stanton had been able to spend but little time at home. "Every minute has its call," he wrote to Oella. Stanton's increasing brusqueness toward McClellan may be partially explained by his concern over his sick son.

The rift between Stanton and McClellan widened as a result of the supposedly secret railroad conference which the two men attended on February 20. According to the pro-McClellan Washington *Star,* Stanton expressed "the utmost confidence" in McClellan, "whose military schemes, gigantic and well-matured, were now exhibited to a rejoicing country." The account depicted Stanton as praying, with upraised hands, for God's aid to the general.

Dana, incredulous, asked Stanton to verify it. He replied that the item was "a ridiculous and impudent effort to puff the General." He would not dignify the false publication with a public retraction, but he kept digging until he learned that Barlow, the Associated Press, and the New York *World* were responsible for the fabrication.[8]

This incident, together with the impending movement of McClellan's army down Chesapeake Bay, pointed up the necessity for a stricter censorship. On February 25, Stanton ordered that any newspaper publishing military information "not expressly authorized by the War Department, the general commanding, or the generals commanding armies in the field in the several departments," should be deprived of the privilege of receiving news reports by telegraph and shipping copies of their publications by rail. The press protested so vigorously that Stanton immediately modified this order so as to permit the publication of "past facts," provided they did not reveal the strength or whereabouts of military forces.

A month later, Postmaster General Blair, at Stanton's instigation, issued an order barring offending newspapers from the mails. The order was most ambiguously worded, and journalist Horace White reported navy man Fox's jibe that "Stanton had taken possession of the Navy & Post Office Depts. & was playing H—l generally. . . . Stanton is a kind of Mephistopheles & the only good thing about him is that he hates McClellan profoundly."

The Secretary's growing antipathy to the general was becoming increasingly evident. Three days after Grant's victory at Fort Donelson,

[8] *Star,* Feb. 21, 1862; Stanton to Dana, Feb. 23, 1862, Ac. 2626, Dana Papers, LC. On James's illness, see Wolcott MS, 179–80. Other data in Barlow to Stanton, Feb. 22, and S. Deming to Barlow, Feb. 22, 1862, Barlow Papers, HL.

Senators Wade and Johnson, acting as a subcommittee of the Committee on the Conduct of the War, called on Stanton to see what could be done about driving off the Confederate batteries that still menaced the Potomac River and regaining possession of the Baltimore & Ohio Railroad at Harpers Ferry. Stanton said that he had been trying to persuade McClellan to do something ever since he took over the Department, but "he was not the head and could not control the matter."

McClellan, called into the conference, told the members of the subcommittee that he planned soon to clear the Baltimore & Ohio Railroad line by moving troops across the Potomac River at Harpers Ferry on a temporary bridge, and then advancing up the Shenandoah Valley to Winchester. But he could not do so until a possible retreat had been provided for.

Wade growled that with 150,000 good troops already on the other side of the river there was no need for a bridge, and if they had to recross the river, let them do it in their coffins. In reporting to the full committee, Johnson stated that Wade used "pretty strong and emphatic language" to McClellan and that Stanton "endorsed every sentiment he uttered. The Secretary feels as strongly upon this subject as this committee does." [9]

A few days later, McClellan left to direct the operation in person. Stanton went to the White House on the night of February 27 to read Lincoln two dispatches. The first one reported that McClellan had bridged the Potomac with pontoons and that some of his troops had crossed. Wagons, artillery, and other heavy equipment would be taken over on a bridge to be made of canalboats, which were being sent to Harpers Ferry through the Chesapeake and Ohio Canal. McClellan suggested that some of his officers be brevetted for their splendid achievement.

Stanton then closed the door to Lincoln's office and turned the key in the lock. "The next is not so good," he said. The operation had stalled when the canal locks proved to be too narrow for the passage of the boats. McClellan would try to protect his pontoon bridge, but he had abandoned his plan to move on Winchester.

"What does this mean?" Lincoln asked.

"It means," said Stanton, "that it is a damned fizzle. It means that he doesn't intend to do anything."

[9] *Report of the Joint Committee on the Conduct of the War*, Sen. Rept. 108, 37th Cong., 3d sess., I, 81–5 (hereafter cited as *CCW*); Detroit *Post, Chandler*, 227; White in J. Cutler Andrews, *The North Reports the Civil War* (Pittsburgh, 1955), 194; and see *O.R.*, ser. 3, I, 889.

Lincoln was utterly despondent. Stanton tried to cheer him up. But as he left he could not resist saying: "Mr. Lincoln, how about those brevets?" Lincoln swore under his breath. He abandoned his usual reticence and told Sumner that "Genl. M. should have ascertained this [the width of the boats] in advance, before he promised success." The President, according to General R. B. Marcy, McClellan's father-in-law and chief of staff, was "in a hell of a rage." Lincoln conspicuously failed to see McClellan after the general's return to Washington, and General Patrick heard that "McClellan's influence is good for nothing."

As McClellan viewed the situation, Stanton was behind his troubles. The commanding general confided to Patrick that he was prepared for a blow from the White House, for Stanton, having "sold out to the Tribune," was helping the radical Republicans gain control over Lincoln.[1]

On March 7, General Marcy was asked by Patrick "how much McClellan knows of the plots against him." Marcy's reply satisfied Patrick that McClellan "knows them all, evidently, and this very day has done something . . . to bring matters to a head." The commanding general had finally come to grips with the President and the Secretary of War on the question of reorganizing the Army of the Potomac into corps. Stanton, following the advice of his war council, insisted that an army of 150,000 men was too unwieldy when organized only by divisions and brigades. McClellan had, weeks before, agreed in principle, but had procrastinated, claiming that he wished to test his generals in battle before deciding which of them were competent to be corps commanders. Because, out of a jealous determination to keep all control in his own hands, he had delegated as little authority as possible, McClellan was easily able to deny his subordinates' capacities for independent commands.

Lincoln, after long conferences with the radical leaders of the Committee on the Conduct of the War, and with Stanton's firm concurrence, decided to force the change. On March 8 the President issued an order organizing the Army of the Potomac into corps and specified the officers to command them. McClellan was also enjoined to make no change of base without leaving a force in and around Washington which in his

[1] Feb. 28, March 6, 1862, Patrick ms diary, LC; Sumner to Andrew, March 2, 1862, Andrew Papers, MHS. Other data in John C. Ropes memo, Feb. 8, 1870, of a conversation with Stanton in Sept. 1869, H. Woodman Papers, MHS; Nicolay, *Lincoln's Secretary*, 143; McClellan, *Own Story*, 192–6; Marcy to McClellan, in Horace White to Joseph Medill, March 3, 1862, Ray Papers, HL; Sam Ward to Barlow, March 10, 16, 1862, Barlow Papers, HL.

opinion and that of the corps commanders would render the city "entirely secure." [2] And there was still worse to come for McClellan; but an intervening crisis delayed the moment of climax.

While Stanton was ill in February, he received reports concerning the construction by the rebels of an ironclad vessel, the *Merrimac*. The information was hazy, but Stanton advised Lincoln of the possible dread consequences if such a ship contested the Union naval blockade. Then, on Sunday, March 9, at about 10:30 a.m., Captain John A. Dahlgren, commander of the Washington Navy Yard, learned that the President was waiting to see him outside his door. Lincoln brought Senator Orville H. Browning, of Illinois, into the office with him. There was "frightful news," he said. The day before, at Hampton Roads, where the James River empties into Chesapeake Bay, the formidable *Merrimac* had nosed out from the Confederate navy yard at Norfolk, smashed the U. S. warships *Cumberland* and *Congress*, and driven the *Minnesota* aground. The government had nothing but wooden ships with which to meet this juggernaut, and they were helpless against it. Lincoln wanted Dahlgren to come to the White House with him.

Arriving there, they found Stanton, McClellan, Welles, Seward, Meigs, Watson, and Nicolay waiting in the President's office. Everyone started to talk at once, regardless of rank. Stanton was the most excited of them all, according to Welles, who described him as pacing back and forth, going to the window every few minutes to gaze down the Potomac, uttering warnings and imprecations, and casting baleful glances at the Navy Secretary as though he were to blame for it all. Hay, too, recorded that Stanton was "fearfully stampeded. He said they would capture our fleet, take Ft. Monroe, be in Washington before night." Lincoln also had been unnerved at first receipt of the dire news, "but blew less than Stanton." Like him, Stanton soon calmed down.

Dahlgren most accurately described the mood of this meeting. "We were too much interested here to be mortified or dejected at the loss of vessels . . . ," he wrote to his son, "for it behooved us to take care of the consequences." Welles offered a measure of hope. On the way to Hampton Roads was a new type of ship, the *Monitor*, which might be a match for the *Merrimac*. She, too, was an ironclad, Welles explained, her deck almost flush with the water and surmounted by a revolving turret housing two guns. Stanton, with the landlubber's ignorance of

[2] March 7, 1862, Patrick ms diary, LC; Hassler, *op. cit.*, 62–3; Randall, *Lincoln the President*, II, 82–3; McClellan, *Own Story*, 222; *CCW*, II, 86–7.

naval matters, snorted at the mention of only two guns, and, to second Stanton's pessimism, navy man Dahlgren suggested that a steamer be sent to scout near the mouth of the Potomac and that boats filled with rocks be sunk in the channel if the *Merrimac* approached.

The plan was accepted over Welles's objections. He thought it was absurd. The rebels had recently withdrawn the batteries which menaced the Potomac, and now Stanton and Dahlgren proposed to block the river on their own account, he said.

As the President approved the operation, Welles was powerless to stop it, but he insisted that it would have to be carried out by the War Department at its own expense. Stanton replied crisply that the War Department would bear both the expense and the responsibility. "The passages were sharp and pungent," Welles recorded.[3]

Early that same evening, Stanton, Seward, and Dahlgren put out on a steamer to find a likely place to sink the rock-laden boats. At 9 p.m., Dahlgren informed Lincoln that preparations had begun. Meanwhile, Stanton had been flashing messages to governors of seaboard states urging them to block their harbors. He took measures to organize a committee of marine engineers in New York City, urging them to devise some speedy means of capturing or destroying the Confederate leviathan.

Later that night the telegraph brought news that the *Monitor*, arriving at Hampton Roads ahead of schedule, had met the *Merrimac* when she came out a second time to finish off the remaining Union ships. Neither ship suffered serious damage, but the *Merrimac* finally drew off and returned to Norfolk.

Next morning the cabinet met again, with Meigs and Dahlgren also present. Wounded, bandaged Commander John L. Worden, of the *Monitor*, was ushered in, and gave a spirited account of the battle between the ironclads. Stanton and Meigs still wanted to block the Potomac channel, but Welles again argued against it. Lincoln, belatedly convinced that the *Monitor* could immobilize the *Merrimac*, ordered Stanton to wait.

A few weeks later, when Lincoln, Stanton, and other officials went down the river in a steamer, they passed a long line of rock-filled boats

[3] Le Grand B. Cannon, *Personal Reminiscences of the Rebellion, 1861–1866* (New York, 1895), 78–9; Madeline Vinton Dahlgren, *Memoirs of John A. Dahlgren* (New York, 1891), 358–9; Dahlgren to Ulrich Dahlgren, March 11, 1862, Dahlgren Papers, LC; Hay, *Diaries and Letters*, 36; Browning, *Diary*, I, 533; Morse, *Welles Diary*, I, 61–7.

drawn up along the shore. "That is Stanton's navy," Lincoln said, according to Welles. "That is the fleet concerning which he and Mr. Welles became so excited in my room. . . . Stanton's navy is as useless as the paps of a man to a suckling child. They may be some show to amuse the child, but they are good for nothing for service."

If Welles's account is correct, then Lincoln had uncharitably forgotten his own uneasiness over the *Merrimac*. To be sure, everyone, including Stanton, was nervous, but not so much so that the War Secretary neglected his primary responsibility to seek measures to counter the threat. This was not a situation calling for physical courage on the part of anyone in the cabinet. Stanton, as well as Dahlgren, McClellan, and Meigs, in underestimating the *Monitor*, guessed wrong. And it should be noted that with McClellan preparing to move his army down Chesapeake Bay, the possibility of new forays by the *Merrimac* was still a legitimate cause of worry to the Army's bureau chiefs, upon whose advice Stanton had to lean.

He offered Welles, at their suggestion, a number of hulks to be sunk in the Norfolk channel so the *Merrimac* could not come out again. The Navy now seemed unconcerned, though Lincoln was worried enough to have Fox and Stanton in to discuss the matter. Reporting this to his war board, Stanton was obviously stung by the Navy's scornful attitude toward his defensive activities.

"Is Mr. Welles to remain in the Cabinet?" Meigs asked. That was up to Lincoln, Stanton replied. "He leans to the judgment of Mr. Fox, who he seems to think is in possession of the entire amount of knowledge in the naval world. Not being a sailor myself, I do not pretend to know anything about such matters."

Stanton called Charles Ellet to another meeting of the war board. Builder of the Wheeling Bridge and a railroad expert, he had been summoned into council by both sides during the Crimean War. Ellet offered the opinion that the *Monitor* could not be relied on. General Totten said he had received a letter suggesting the use of a sort of raft alongside a vessel to ward off the attack of rebel steam rams, and wondered whether he should refer it to the Navy Department. "It might as well be put in the fire," Stanton commented sourly.

Rebuffed by the Navy, Stanton asked bumptious old Cornelius Vanderbilt, the New York steamboat magnate, on what terms he would contract to sink or bottle up the *Merrimac*. Vanderbilt agreed to convert his $3,000,000 yacht *Vanderbilt* into a warship and turn her over to the government. Lightning-fast, she could outmaneuver the ponderous

Merrimac, and ram and sink her. When the *Vanderbilt* arrived in Hampton Roads, the Navy at once took her in charge over Stanton's bitter protests.[4]

Close behind the frightening news on March 9 of the *Merrimac's* foray came intelligence that the Confederates had fallen back from Manassas Junction. McClellan hurried off to the army to verify the news. His staff was jubilant at the unexpected windfall, but soon let it be known that McClellan had been anticipating it and had never intended to attack Manassas at all.

That night he telegraphed to Stanton that he was so busy preparing to put the troops in motion that he had no time to carry out Lincoln's order about organizing the army into corps. Would Stanton suspend the order? McClellan asserted that unless the suspension was granted he must call off his advance. Not wishing to delay the long-awaited movement of the army, Stanton yielded.

McClellan marched the Army of the Potomac in all its impressive might to the abandoned Confederate position. But at the Confederate entrenchments he met a surprising sight—many of the cannon whose menacing appearance had held him back for months were nothing but logs painted black.

The cabinet met that afternoon. Stanton complained that army matters were in a wretched state. Ignorance, negligence, disorder, insubordination, and reckless extravagance characterized the whole concern, he said. McClellan doctored all reports and told Stanton only what he chose to. If he had any plans for an attack, he kept them to himself. Stanton refused to bear any further responsibility if his hands remained tied. He demanded that the armies and the country be relieved of "the Potomac incubus." Supporting him, Bates urged the President to assume the power the Constitution granted him and "command the commanders."[5]

[4] As a result of the *Merrimac* scare, Stanton commissioned Ellet to build a fleet of Union rams. Ellet converted steamboats into rams, which were finished in an amazingly short time and did valuable service on the Mississippi and its tributaries throughout the remaining years of the war. Much of the time they operated under Navy orders, but Stanton saw to it that the Army retained at least the nominal control of them. Warren D. Crandall and Isaac D. Newell, *History of the Ram Fleet and the Mississippi Marine Brigade in the War for the Union on the Mississippi and Its Tributaries* (St. Louis, 1907); *O.R.*, IX, 18–22, 28–9, 31–2; X, pt. 3, 26; Morse, *Welles Diary*, I, 66–7, III, 473–4; Browning, *Diary*, I, 535–6; ms proceedings of the war board, March 13, 14, 20, 1862, and Stanton-McClellan exchange, March 9–12, 1862, Stanton MSS; Dahlgren, *op. cit.*, 360.

[5] McClellan, *Own Story*, 223–4; March 9, 1862, Patrick ms diary, LC; Bates, *Diary*, 239; Flower, *Stanton*, 140; Kamm, *op. cit.*, 119.

That night Lincoln called Stanton, Seward, and Chase to his office. Seward arrived first. Lincoln read him a War Order No. Three. It stated that as McClellan had personally taken the field, he would now be relieved as general in chief and would command only what was to be known as the Department of the Potomac. Halleck would have a new Department of the Mississippi with Buell as a subordinate. A Mountain Department, between the others, was assigned to Frémont. All department commanders would be ordered to report "severally and directly" to the Secretary of War.

Seward commended Lincoln for the decision and suggested that the order of removal go out in Stanton's name in order to strengthen the War Secretary's position. Stanton arrived just at that time and protested that "a row had grown up" between him and McClellan's friends, and he feared that the order would be ascribed to "personal feelings" if his name appeared on it. Lincoln agreed, and the order went out in his name.

The first year of war had now produced another experiment in the command structure of the Union armies, and in the relationships between the civilian President and Secretary of War and the military commanders. Lincoln's order explicitly made Washington the center of policy, of supply, and of communications; he and Stanton were now the commanding general of the Army.

To be sure, political pressures against McClellan had helped to create this demotion for him. But a change of this nature was overdue. Quite apart from the question of efficiency, McClellan had opposed Lincoln's policies; worse, he had failed to take the war to the enemy, as Lincoln and Stanton had insisted that he do. Only time could tell if this reform would work better than the chaotic triangle of authority that had preceded it.[6]

Meanwhile Stanton was working out relationships with the other army commanders, who may have had some advantage over McClellan in working at some remove from the immediate neighborhood of the busy, prying Secretary. If Stanton disliked Halleck, as that officer suspected, he did not permit his personal feelings to stand in the way of Halleck's advancement. On the other hand, Stanton apparently had nothing to do with elevating Frémont, who, ever since the issuance of his abortive emancipation edict, had been the knight-errant of the radical Republicans.

Soon after Stanton became Secretary of War, Wade had approached

[6] Hay, *Diaries and Letters*, 37–8; McClellan, *Own Story*, 218; *O.R.*, V, 54; X, pt. 2, 28–9; XI, pt. 1, 224; Hassler, *op. cit.*, 66–9.

him in Frémont's behalf. It behooved Stanton to keep on good terms with the chairman of the powerful Committee on the Conduct of the War, and he had commented to Dana, who also interceded for Frémont: "If Gen. Frémont has any fight in him he shall (so far as I am concerned) have a chance to show it, and I have told *him* so . . . having neither partialities nor grudges to indulge, it will be my aim to practice the maxim 'the tools to him that can use them.' " But it was Lincoln, not Stanton, whom the radicals prevailed on to give Frémont another chance.[7] Stanton would soon find himself hampered by Lincoln's determination to keep faith with the radicals in this matter.

Stanton, as a matter of fact, dealt sternly with Frémont. When the general sent a list of proposed staff appointments to the War Department from New York City, the Secretary told General Thomas: "I will not allow Generals to carry on the war . . . holding court in New York, taking proposals for appointments on their staffs. I see that they are organizing just such a gang as they had at St. Louis, and I intend to prevent it."

When Frémont joined his command and began to employ the same loose methods that had contributed to his undoing in Missouri, Stanton brought him up short and ordered him to follow standard procedures. Later Frémont advised Sumner that Stanton "has been an insidious enemy of mine since his advent to his office." [8] Frémont was likely to see a personal enemy in anyone who opposed his whims and, like McClellan, he became convinced that Stanton had helped ruin him, but the nature of the relationship between him and Stanton goes counter to the contention of some historians that Stanton was a catspaw of the radical Republicans.

McClellan accepted his demotion with surprisingly good grace, perhaps because he believed that he would soon again dominate Lincoln and Stanton. A McClellan supporter quoted Lincoln on March 18 as promising "that he should sustain the General in spite of opposition," which may have meant no more than it said—that McClellan would be supplied, his units manned, and his troops armed, as well as any other command. But to McClellan, such reports augured differently. "The President is all right," he wrote to Barlow, "he is my strongest friend."

---

[7] *O.R.*, VIII, 596, 602, 831–2; Stanton to Dana, Feb. 1, and Wade to Dana, Feb. 3, 1862, Dana Papers, LC; Frémont to Stanton, Feb. 10, 1862, Stanton MSS; Ethan Allen Hitchcock to Henry Hitchcock, May 30, 1862, Hitchcock Papers, MoHS.

[8] Frémont to Sumner, Dec. 14, 1863, HU; *O.R.*, XII, pt. 3, 40; proceedings of the war board, March 21, 25, 1862, Stanton MSS; Ward to Barlow, March 22, 1862, Barlow Papers, HL.

And McClellan did not hesitate to resume his former role of mentor to the man he thought of as the inexperienced, incompetent, and perhaps untrustworthy head of the War Department. Obviously, he had learned nothing from his humiliation of what was expected of a Union general.[9]

On the whole, this reshuffling increased Stanton's popularity. Frémont's restoration to command pleased the radicals, who forgave Stanton his opposition to the promotion, and they congratulated the Secretary, as Wade expressed it, on "the signal victories which have been achieved under the administration of your department." Professional soldiers voiced their approval of Halleck's elevation. General William T. Sherman wrote to his brother John, Wade's Ohio colleague in the Senate, of his "unlimited confidence in Halleck," and Ulysses S. Grant told his wife that with Halleck in command in the West the Committee on the Conduct of the War would find little to criticize there.

Stanton lost some reputation for his already legendary panic at the *Merrimac*'s appearance; McClellan's supporters derided all of his accomplishments. But the fact was that in a very short time in office, Stanton, though unable yet to force co-operation among the several army chieftains, had secured effective civilian control of the armies in the field and was forcing reforms on army headquarters in Washington. It is in part to Stanton's credit that the government was waking up to a consciousness of the nature, scope, and cost of the war it was waging.[1]

Now that the civilians held the reins, Stanton knew that he and Lincoln required professional military counsel more than ever before. Although both men distrusted most regular army officers, Stanton turned to a general, Ethan Allen Hitchcock, living in retirement in St. Louis, and asked him to come to the War Department. A West Point graduate and a former commandant of the Military Academy, a veteran with forty years service including a distinguished record in the Mexican War, Hitchcock was highly regarded by his brother officers. But he was almost sixty-four years old, in poor health, and recently had shown more interest in philosophy, spiritualism, and mysticism than in the practice of war.

[9] *O.R.*, LI, pt. 1, 551; McClellan to Stanton, Feb. 18, 1862, Simon Gratz Collection, HSP; to Barlow, March 16, and J. G. Barnard to McClellan, March 19, 1862, McClellan Papers, LC; Benjamin Stark to Barlow, March 18, 1862, Barlow Papers, HL.

[1] Wade to Stanton, Feb. 19, Stanton MSS; W. T. to John Sherman, Feb. 23, W. T. Sherman Papers, LC; Grant to Julia Grant, Feb. 24, 1862, owned by the estate of Foreman M. Lebold.

Although he did not want to stay in Washington, fearing that he would become an anti-Frémont counter, Hitchcock finally succumbed to Stanton's earnest pleas. After refusing in turn the Secretary's offers of command of the Army of the Potomac in place of McClellan, the adjutant-generalship, and charge of the Ordnance Bureau, Hitchcock agreed to serve as Stanton's adviser, without rank. His decision was wiser than Stanton's tenders. Hitchcock was a ridiculous choice for any active command, and to contemplate entrusting him with the Army of the Potomac, upon whose successes the life of the Republic hinged, was a gesture of folly on Stanton's part. It is also a measure of how desperately the Secretary felt the nation required a capable, venturesome, obedient top commander.

As an adviser, Hitchcock warned the Secretary that some War Department reforms were progressing too rapidly: "The Army is something like an organic (living) body; a whole within itself, and yet containing many subordinate organisms. . . . The whole may need improvement; and so may the parts; I do not deny it. But, it is exceedingly dangerous to make changes, unless called for by urgent necessity—a necessity so apparent that the subordinates themselves shall appreciate it." Hitchcock pointed to the dangers which he saw in Stanton's rough handling of the Adjutant General's operations. "Touch the head of the Department and you shake the whole system," he warned, and Stanton heeded this advice.

It amazed Hitchcock that the tempestuous Stanton accepted suggestions with perfect calm. "His earnestness in behalf of the country and the government," Hitchcock noted, "had such complete possession of his faculties, that he had no place for any feeling that . . . could stand in the way of success." Each morning, when Stanton assembled the War Department bureau chiefs in his office, Hitchcock witnessed Stanton's "dedicated purpose to put down the rebellion by every effort that human wisdom would suggest." [2]

Hitchcock was witnessing a spiritual transformation in Stanton, who now identified the Union with morality. Stanton had recommended regular church attendance, and in late March he wrote a minister friend of "how deeply—intensely—I feel the need of acknowledging Divine power and imploring Divine aid in this hour of national trial. And how

---

[2] Hitchcock's memos to Stanton, March 17, 19, and Stanton to Hitchcock, March 18, 1862, Hitchcock Papers, LC; Hitchcock to Henry Hitchcock, March 10, 17, 1862, Hitchcock Collection, MoHS; March 21, 1862, Hitchcock ms journal, GI; W. A. Croffut (ed.), *Fifty Years in Camp and Field, Diary of Major-General Ethan Allen Hitchcock, U.S.A.* (New York, 1909), 437–40.

weak and helpless I feel my own efforts to be in the part I have been called upon to fill!" He asked for prayers "in this hour of apparent victory" for the guidance of public officers, "lest calamity come upon us."

Disaster could come only from delay in carrying war to the enemy, and his impatience with McClellan increased. The withdrawal of the Confederate forces to a position behind the Rappahannock River rendered it impossible for McClellan to use Urbana as a base; so he now proposed to advance on Richmond by way of the Yorktown Peninsula. After approving the plan, a council of his corps commanders estimated that from 40,000 to 50,000 troops would be required to assure the safety of Washington under Lincoln's March 8 directive. Stanton informed McClellan that Lincoln "makes no objection" to the plan, provided Washington and Manassas were secure from attack. The note of impatience—"Move the remainder of the force down the Potomac, choosing a new base at Fortress Monroe, or anywhere between here and there; or at all events, move the remainder of the army at once in pursuit of the enemy by some route"—was probably lost on McClellan.

The War Department provided McClellan with a fleet of transports; troops began embarking on March 17.[3] McClellan left for the Peninsula on April 1, rejoicing at the coming isolation from Washington, "that sink of iniquity." Lincoln had further displeased him just before he sailed by apologetically informing him that he had been obliged for political reasons to withhold General Louis Blenker's division from him and send it to Frémont. Although Lincoln wished primarily to placate the radicals, he also hoped that reinforcements might enable Frémont to take Knoxville and aid the loyalists in eastern Tennessee.

McClellan waited until he was on shipboard to report on the number of troops he had left to defend Washington. Then, by some legerdemain with figures that brought forces in the Shenandoah Valley and elsewhere into his count, he calculated that the city was guarded by 77,000 soldiers. A more realistic count by General James S. Wadsworth, commanding the Washington defenses, showed that McClellan had left him only 19,000 men in the forts around the city and at Manassas in front of it, and that his force was insufficient for the important work assigned to it. Stanton instructed Generals Hitchcock and Lorenzo Thomas to verify Wadsworth's figures. They found them to be correct.

[3] Stanton to Rev. I. Prince, March 26, 1862, Simon Gratz Collection, HSP; *O.R.*, XI, pt. 1, 224; LI, pt. 1, 551; Kenneth P. Williams, *Lincoln Finds a General* (New York, 1949–59), I, 159 (hereafter cited as Williams, *Lincoln Finds a General*); Dahlgren, *op. cit.*, 361.

Stanton went with Hitchcock and Meigs to take the dire news to Lincoln.

Like Stanton, Lincoln felt that the symbolic importance of Washington was inestimable. Its capture would plunge the North into dejection and reanimate the South, and by winning recognition of Southern independence from European nations might well determine the outcome of the war. The President, having withheld Blenker's division from McClellan, disliked interfering with him again, but something had to be done. Two of McClellan's corps were still waiting to embark at Alexandria. After consultations with Stanton and his bureau chiefs, Lincoln decided that one of these corps must be retained in front of Washington. Stanton selected the First Corps, commanded by McDowell.[4]

Meanwhile, McClellan, arriving at Fort Monroe on April 2, had pushed his army forward. The Confederates, under General J. B. Magruder, vastly outnumbered, rapidly gave ground, preparing to fight a delaying action from behind the Yorktown redoubts and the boggy Warwick River. But cautious probing convinced McClellan that the Warwick River line could not be taken by assault. He began to bring up heavy guns to put Yorktown under seige.

McClellan was sitting quietly on the ground listening to his artillery firing practice salvos when he received a telegram informing him that the President had decided to keep McDowell's corps in front of Washington. He wired a hope that Lincoln would reconsider.

Later that same day, Stanton sent McClellan more displeasing news. The President had established two new military departments—the Department of the Shenandoah, to be commanded by General Nathaniel P. Banks, and the Department of the Rappahannock, to be under McDowell. McClellan protested that such an arrangement would deprive him of the power of ordering up supplies and ammunition. Stanton assured him that "the whole force and material of the government will be as fully and speedily under your command as heretofore, or as if the new departments had not been created." Lincoln urged McClellan to attack at once. The enemy would profit more by delay than McClellan could, he wrote. But McClellan, magnifying the numbers of the enemy, continued to dally and complain.

[4] *O.R.*, V, 58–9; XI, pt. 1, 230–1, pt. 3, 52, 57, 60–2; *CCW*, I, 305; Hitchcock to Mrs. Horace Mann, July 14, 1864, Hitchcock-Mann Letters, LC; Roy P. Basler (ed.), *The Collected Works of Abraham Lincoln* (New Brunswick, 1953), VI, 175–6 (hereafter cited as Lincoln, *Works*); John C. Ropes, "General McClellan's Plans for the Campaign of 1862 and the Alleged Interferences of the Government with Them," *MHSM* (1895), I, 61–87; McClellan, *Own Story*, 306.

Despairing, Stanton admitted to Lincoln's friend Orville Browning that in his opinion McClellan should have been removed from command long before, that he was not in earnest, could not emancipate himself from Southern influences—but was not disloyal, as was rumored—and was unwilling to do anything calculated seriously to damage the South. Ready to grasp at any straw, Stanton wanted Browning to suggest to Lincoln that Colonel N. B. Buford be made a major general and given command of the Army of the Potomac.[5] Buford would eventually prove himself to be a competent cavalry commander, but at this point in his career it would have been the wildest sort of gamble to entrust him with the command of the nation's largest army.

Republican politicians and editors renewed their criticism of McClellan, and Lincoln again warned him of the critical position in which he was placing himself by his failure to attack. "And, once more let me tell you, it is indispensable to *you* that you strike a blow," he wrote on April 9; "*I* am powerless to help this. You will do me the justice to remember I always insisted that going down the Bay in search of a field, instead of fighting at or near Manassas, was merely shifting, and not surmounting a difficulty—that we would find the same enemy, and the same, or equal, intrenchments, at either place. The country will not fail to note—is now noting—that the present hesitation to move upon an intrenched enemy, is but the story of Manassas repeated." The President declared that he had never spoken in greater kindness, nor with a fuller purpose to sustain the general. "*But you must act,*" he concluded.

McClellan seemed to miss the point. He sent a plea for Franklin's division, which was part of McDowell's command. Stanton argued that McDowell's corps should be kept together and sent forward by land on the shortest route to Richmond, thus aiding McClellan but at the same time covering Washington.[6] Hitchcock, Meigs, and Thomas agreed with him, but McClellan kept insisting that all reinforcements be sent to him by water. Lincoln, anxious for McClellan to have no further cause for complaint, decided to send Franklin's 11,000 men on transports, and Stanton reluctantly acquiesced. When Franklin's troops reached Fort Monroe, McClellan kept them on shipboard for more than two weeks.

[5] Stanton's information on McClellan's pro-Southern attitudes probably came from Senator John Sherman; see Mrs. W. T. Sherman to John Sherman, March 24, 1862, W. T. Sherman Papers, LC; Browning *Diary*, I, 538–9. See also *O.R.*, XI, pt. 3, 67–8, 71, 73–4; Hassler, *op. cit.*, 74–87.

[6] *O.R.*, XI, pt. 1, 14; XIX, pt. 2, 725–8; Lincoln, *Works*, V, 185.

Then the telegraph brought news of a bloody battle in the West— a near disaster for Grant. After the capture of Fort Donelson, Halleck had ordered General C. F. Smith with 30,000 troops to Pittsburgh Landing, on the Tennessee, where Buell was to join him with 25,000 men by an overland march from Nashville. Then the combined Union armies would push southward to complete the conquest of the Mississippi Valley.

Grant had been removed from command for being absent without leave and for failing to report regularly to Halleck. Actually, he had gone to Nashville to consult with Buell, and his dispatches had failed to get through to Halleck because communications had broken down. When Halleck learned the truth, he restored Grant to command. The stubby general rejoined his troops at Pittsburgh Landing.[7]

But the Confederates, under Albert Sidney Johnston, had a surprise in store for Grant. Johnston and P. G. T. Beauregard, his second in command, had reorganized their shaken troops more quickly than Grant had expected them to, and they started north with 50,000 men to strike Grant before Buell joined him.

Sunday, April 6, dawned quietly. The Union troops were at breakfast when a burst of rifle fire sounded from the direction of Shiloh Church. When Grant arrived on a dispatch boat from his headquarters, nine miles downstream, he found his army fighting a battle for survival. But the troops held on until nightfall, when Buell's divisions began arriving. Grant counterattacked the next morning. The Confederates gave ground grudgingly, then broke in full retreat.

Reports of more than 13,000 Union casualties and ugly rumors about Grant sullied the tidings of victory. Soon after Stanton became Secretary of War, charges of drunkenness had been filed against Grant by a disgruntled quartermaster, but Assistant Secretary Scott had reported to Stanton that the accusations were unfounded. Now Stanton rushed off a telegram to Halleck, demanding to know if Grant was to blame for "the sad casualties that befell our forces on Sunday."

Replying, Halleck mentioned no shortcomings on the part of Grant, like himself a West Pointer. In a private letter to Hitchcock, however, Halleck was sharply critical of Grant. "Brave & able on the field," he wrote, "he has no idea of how to regulate & organize his forces before a battle or how to conduct the operations of a campaign."[8] Stanton

---

[7] Grant to his wife, March 29, 1862, owned by the estate of Foreman M. Lebold; and see Wilson, "General Halleck—A Memoir," *loc. cit.*, 555.

[8] Scott to Stanton, Jan. 26, 1862, Stanton MSS; *O.R.*, X, pt. 1, 98–99; T. Harry Williams, *Lincoln and His Generals* (New York, 1952), 85–6, and see Buell's version of events in *Columbia University Forum*, IV, 54.

probably saw this letter; for Hitchcock, one of the major molders of Stanton's ideas at this time, wrote from Washington that there "is but one opinion here. General Grant is absolutely disgraced and dishonored." Hitchcock felt that Grant's errors were too gross for forgiveness. "He has been little better than a common gambler and drunkard for many years." To Stanton, such assertions were another indication that his own responsibility to oversee the conduct of the army commanders must never be ignored, and that the West Pointer's proclivity to protect fellow alumni from civilian overseership must be thwarted.

As though to balance events, the second day of Shiloh brought news of a real Union victory, when General John Pope, supported by Foote's gunboats, took Island Number 10 in the Mississippi River and opened the way to Memphis. Scott reported to Stanton that Pope had performed brilliantly. And still more good tidings would be coming from the West.

Since overriding McClellan to make sure that the Army would cooperate in the Navy's New Orleans expedition, Stanton had kept hands off and let the Navy run that show, as well as most river operations. "Our naval friends," Scott wrote, "are very sensitive on all such points." [9] For weeks not even the Navy Department knew much about what was happening. But three weeks after Shiloh, a barrage of news arrived. Farragut had steamed into the lower reaches of the Mississippi River, opened a destructive bombardment on Forts Jackson and St. Philip, swept past them under cover of night, and moved upstream through Confederate rams and fireboats to land Butler's troops at New Orleans. Stanton could take satisfaction in having seen to it that the Army played its proper part in the action. But though the North celebrated the news of these triumphs in the West, Stanton more than any other man was soon to know how far the war was from being won. Until he learned this, he made serious errors in setting policy. Like all Americans, Stanton had to be educated in how to fight this war.

[9] Scott to Stanton, April 16, 1862, Stanton MSS; unsigned, undated fragment in Hitchcock's writing, addressed to "Dear Cox," Hitchcock Papers, LC.

CHAPTER IX

FAILURE AND FRUSTRATION

WHILE western forces were on the move and fighting, down on the Yorktown Peninsula there was no sound of battle—just the dreary drip of rain. Mist enshrouded the low, flat countryside, blurring the outlines of buildings on the scattered farms and gloomy woods along the swelling Warwick River. The roads became clutching quagmires, and in the army encampments the sick lists began to lengthen. General Joseph E. Johnston, arriving to take over the Confederate command, found that he had only 53,000 troops, and prepared to pull back whenever McClellan started an assault or a bombardment.

Fair weather finally came, and McClellan advised Lincoln not to misunderstand "the apparent inaction here." Though Lincoln kept his impatience in check, an increasingly strident public outcry arose against McClellan. Democratic spokesmen countered with a vicious onslaught on Stanton, stressing the implication that, by reappointing Frémont, the supposedly conservative War Secretary had allied himself with the Republican abolitionists and was trying to cripple McClellan by denying him men and supplies, as he would "tomahawk anyone he disliked," in Sam Ward's words. "If we are disappointed in Mr. Stanton," wrote David Davis to Holt, "the confidence of conservative men will receive a terrible shock."

It was true that Stanton would have liked to remove "Little Mac" from command, but his own and Lincoln's caution held back this decision. But at the same time Stanton supplied McClellan with all that he requested. Assistant Secretary Tucker, sent to the Peninsula by Stanton to help solve McClellan's transportation problems, although recognizing the general's difficulties, reported the roads literally covered with wagons. Hitchcock visited McClellan to see if anything was lacking, and decided that the War Department could have done nothing more to contribute to the success of the movement against Yorktown. And none of McClellan's supporters in the press then asserted that their champion was lacking in men or supplies. "The Secretary had determined to give McClellan everything he wants, no matter what," confided ordnance officer George T. Balch.[1]

At last, on May 3, everything seemed ready for opening the bombardment. But Johnston, having delayed McClellan for a month, saw nothing to be gained by tarrying longer. He quietly abandoned Yorktown and pulled back from his defenses along the Warwick River. McClellan wired Stanton triumphantly: "Yorktown is in our possession." Stanton sent him congratulations and expressed the hope that he would soon hear of his arrival in Richmond. But Stanton shared a wish expressed by Dix that the enemy "could have been thrashed instead of being frightened off."

Surprised by Johnston's withdrawal, McClellan sent his army forward in an ill-organized pursuit. Johnston made a stand at Williamsburg, then dug in before Richmond. McClellan inched forward until his troops could see the city's steeples—and stopped.

Meanwhile, on April 22, Tucker informed Stanton that two hundred Norfolk workmen, swarming over the *Merrimac* day and night for the past three weeks, had repaired and strengthened her to the point where she would soon be ready to venture forth again. The ability of the *Monitor* and the *Vanderbilt* to cope with her was still conjectural; if they failed, she could bring disaster to McClellan by destroying his transports and supply ships. Stanton proposed to Lincoln and Chase, in whom Lincoln still reposed great confidence and who was continuing to dabble in War Department matters, that the three of them try personally to dispose of the Confederate terror about which the Navy Department seemed so unconcerned.[2]

On May 6, Lincoln joined Chase and Stanton on board the *Miami*, a Treasury revenue cutter. While the ship was anchored off Fort Monroe next night, plans were completed for an attack on Norfolk, and the three civilians were watching from a tug when the big naval guns commenced firing next morning. Stanton then busied himself reading telegrams from McClellan, and sent off a wire to Ellen that he wished she

---

[1] Tucker to Stanton, April 16, and Hitchcock to same, April 19, 1862, Stanton MSS; Davis to Holt, April 28, 1862, Holt Papers, LC; Holt to Davis, May 3, 1862, owned by Willard L. King. Other data in Lincoln, *Works*, V, 203–4; Balch to wife, July 16, 1862, UCB; Ward to Seward, April 9, 1862, Barlow Papers, HL.

[2] Flower, *Stanton*, 156; Dix to Stanton, May 5, 1862, Stanton MSS; *O.R.*, IX, 392.

and their sick baby could be with him to enjoy the perfect weather.

When night fell, Lincoln, Stanton, and Chase went scouting on the rebel shore to find a place suitable for landing troops, and in the bright moonlight, which made the party clearly visible to any sniper lurking in the dunes, a spot selected by Chase was chosen. Stanton went back to Fort Monroe with Lincoln in order to keep him out of further danger, and in the middle of the following night Chase rejoined them with news that Norfolk had fallen. Lincoln beamed with joy, and "Stanton . . . was equally delighted," Chase reported to his daughter. And later that night they heard a dull boom across the water; the Confederates had destroyed the *Merrimac*. McClellan wired Stanton congratulations "from the bottom of my heart" on the destruction of the *Merrimac*, and on the access to the James River that was now afforded. Congratulations were deserved, for the amateur strategists had waged a brilliant campaign. McClellan's supply lines and flank were secure and the James was open to Union naval penetration. Chase gave the chief credit for the accomplishment to Lincoln, but the expedition had been Stanton's idea.

Although he disparaged his own role in these events, Stanton was not one to minimize the Army in public accounts, and this made naval officers bristle. In a confidential letter, Goldsborough termed Stanton a "little man" who "indulges spasmodically in the belief that he is a military genius, but to my mind, bungles every thing he undertakes to direct on his own accord." Lawyers cannot command armies, Goldsborough wrote, merely because they know how to impress a courtroom. "They are playing the wild with our country, & Mr. Stanton is among the worst of them, because he is in power, & has a very arbitrary & conceited disposition."

But the country generally applauded the civilian strategists. And Stanton became a casualty. He contracted a severe case of ophthalmia during his stay in the Peninsula and after returning to Washington was almost blind for several days.[3]

On May 14, McClellan telegraphed Lincoln that the Confederates were concentrating their forces and that he would be compelled to fight "perhaps double my numbers" in order to take Richmond. He pleaded that every man that could be mustered be sent to him "by water."

[3] Gen. E. L. Viele, "A Trip with Lincoln, Chase, and Stanton," *Scribners Monthly*, XVI, 814–22; W. E. Baringer, "On Enemy Soil," *ALQ*, VII, 4–26; Cannon, *op. cit.*, 153–66. See also Stanton to Ellen, May 8, 1862, Stanton MSS; Chase, *Diary*, 84–5; *O.R.*, XI, pt. 3, 153, 164, 176; Fox, *Correspondence*, I, 273–4; Goldsborough to wife, June 13, 1862, Goldsborough Papers, DU.

The only troops readily available were those commanded by Mc-Dowell, who had advanced from Manassas to Fredericksburg and pushed one of his divisions, under General James Shields, into the Shenandoah Valley to support Banks. Lincoln, in consultation with Stanton and the War Department bureau chiefs, now decided to bring Shields back to Fredericksburg and then move McDowell's entire force to the Peninsula, not by water, as McClellan had requested, but directly against Richmond by the shortest overland route, the approach that Stanton had always favored.

McClellan protested immediately that unless he could exercise complete control over McDowell's troops, they would be of little use to him, and insisted that the troops be sent by water to save time. Later, in an afterthought of self-justification, he claimed that the President's order made it impossible for him to use the James River as a base—although he had already selected the Pamunkey River for that purpose—and that in extending his lines northward to link up with McDowell, he left his right wing fatally exposed. "Herein," he said of Lincoln's order, "lay the failure of the campaign."

Lincoln and Stanton decided to stick to their decision. Mindful of what they had accomplished on their trip to the Peninsula, the two men, on the night of May 22, again quietly left Washington by boat, for Aquia Creek, to visit McDowell's headquarters and speed up his movement, taking Dahlgren along.

Arriving at Aquia next morning, they transferred to the military railroad and traveled in a common baggage car equipped with camp-stools. McDowell met them at Potomac Creek and insisted on their examining the new railroad bridge, 400 feet long and almost 100 feet high, with which his chief of railroad transportation, General Herman Haupt, had spanned the ravine, and which Lincoln described afterward as having "nothing in it but beanpoles and cornstalks." Stanton took satisfaction in the fact that it was he who had enlisted Haupt's services for the Army.

The footway of the bridge consisted of a line of single planks, but Lincoln said: "Let's walk across," and started out, McDowell, Stanton, and Dahlgren picking their way after him. Halfway across, Stanton, peering down into the forbidding chasm, said he felt dizzy and feared he would fall. Dahlgren stepped past him, took his hand, and led him the rest of the way, not admitting that he, too, felt somewhat giddy.

At McDowell's headquarters horses were provided so that the party could review the troops. Stanton could not mount because of his stiff knee, and Dahlgren kept him company in an army ambulance, which jounced horribly. The soldiers cheered wildly when the President went down the lines, and Stanton became irritated when the horsemen left his vehicle behind.

McDowell told Lincoln that Shields's division had arrived from the Valley but the men needed shoes, uniforms, and ammunition. He could have them refitted by Sunday, the twenty-fifth, but knowing Lincoln's dislike of Sunday operations, wondered if he should put off their departure toward Richmond till Monday. Lincoln asked him to make "a good ready" on Sunday and start them early Monday morning.[4]

Reaching Washington on May 24, Lincoln and Stanton found confusion rampant, and decision necessary. With Shields's force withdrawn from the Shenandoah Valley, Thomas Jonathan Jackson, a Bible-reading Confederate general who had earned the name "Stonewall" at Bull Run, had surprised the small Union garrison at Front Royal, come in on Banks's flank, and forced him to take off posthaste from Strasburg in the direction of Winchester to avoid destruction or capture.

Reports put Jackson's force at anywhere from ten to twenty thousand men. Was he merely creating a diversion to ease the pressure on Richmond or was he cutting through the scattered Union forces toward Washington? The crux of the problem was McDowell. Should all or part of his force go to the Valley, from which Shields had so recently been withdrawn, or should he be thrown forward against Richmond as planned? A powerful thrust at Richmond would be an effective counterpoise to Jackson, but would McClellan make the most of his chance?

His record made it doubtful. At 4 p.m. Lincoln wired McClellan: "In consequence of General Banks's critical position I have been compelled to suspend General McDowell's movement to join you. The enemy are making a desperate push upon Harpers Ferry, and we are trying to throw Frémont's force & part of General McDowell's in their rear." Danger faced the Union with its martial resources far away with McClellan.

Stanton urged the governors of the Northern states to send forward immediately all the militia at their disposal and all the three-month volunteers they could enlist. The War Department took temporary control of the railroads to facilitate troop movements. News came that Banks, though severely cut up near Winchester, had avoided capture and was in full retreat toward the Potomac. Stanton ordered General Rufus Saxton to take command at Harpers Ferry.

[4] Dahlgren, *op. cit.*, 368–70; *CCW*, III, 428; *O.R.*, XI, pt. 1, 28, 97–8; McClellan, *Own Story*, 345–6.

Having caused pandemonium in Washington, Jackson feinted at Harpers Ferry, then prepared to retreat; time was running out on him as the dispersed Union forces began closing in. Shields's division, having been turned around when it reached Fredericksburg and headed back toward the Valley, was not approaching Front Royal. The rejuvenated Banks was pressing Jackson from the rear. But one detail had gone awry. Frémont, instead of marching to Harrisonburg, where he would have blocked Jackson's escape route, misunderstood his orders and turned up far to the north. Lincoln ordered him to go at once to Strasburg, where he might still intercept Jackson. He promised to be there the next day. But that night, May 30, a terrific rainstorm swelled the mountain streams to torrents and gullied the tortuous roads. Frémont's advance units moved into Strasburg just in time to see Jackson's rear guard hurrying southward out of town.

Union forces began a rapid pursuit of Jackson's footsore men. On June 8, Jackson turned on Frémont and fought a sharp engagement at Cross Keys. Disappearing in the night, he whipped Shields's small detachment at Fort Republic the next day. Then he slipped away. Lincoln and Stanton, recognizing that further pursuit was useless, ordered Shields back to Fredericksburg, commanded Frémont to halt at Harrisonburg, and assigned Banks to guard Front Royal.

The amateurs in Washington had shown considerable military competence in countering the crafty and swift-footed Jackson. Successful execution of Lincoln's orders would have brought Jackson to bay at Strasburg against a Union force three times his own, and Stanton had performed splendidly in implementing Lincoln's strategy, co-ordinating the water, rail, and road transport by which McDowell's troops were sent forward and maintaining swift communication between Washington and the various Union columns. But Jackson accomplished his purpose of reducing the pressure on Richmond, and an important factor in his success was the divided Union command.[5]

Such a situation was deplorable from a military point of view, and, as will be seen, both Lincoln and Stanton were responsible—Lincoln for allowing political considerations to determine military policy and Stanton through distrust of McClellan that had helped deprive the Union armies of a commander in chief. But that McClellan, had he still commanded all the Union forces, could have captured Jackson seems highly improbable.

[5] Upton, *op. cit.*, 293–5; Williams, *Lincoln Finds a General*, I, 210–3; *O.R.*, XII, pt. 1, 629; pt. 3, 219, 226, 228, 241.

Banks, the former Massachusetts politician, had fared badly during the campaign, and the Boston *Advertiser* lashed out viciously at Stanton for leaving Banks alone in the Valley to withstand the full force of Jackson's drive. Stanton's enemies exulted in his discomfiture. Even Henry L. Dawes, normally friendly to Stanton, felt that the alarm in Washington caused by Jackson's raid was "but the flurry of a girl who meets a cow in the street."

But Stanton also had defenders. Horatio Woodman, a Boston journalist, took Stanton's part in long articles in the Boston *Transcript* and the New York *Herald*. Stanton made no effort to speak out in his own behalf, although Woodman and others felt they could prove that the debatable decisions were the products of Lincoln and the war council rather than of Stanton alone. But the journalistic defenses comforted Stanton and served to convince others on his behalf. George William Curtis congratulated Woodman for the corrections the journalist had put in the record, and commented that "the petulant criticism which dogs Stanton is as unreasonable as the *evoe!* which hailed his bulletin of congratulations at Mill Spring as if it had been a victory." Curtis felt that Stanton had done well: "He understands that the conditions of war are not those of peace." [6]

The harassed Secretary found his greatest comfort in the fact that Lincoln admitted confidentially to Sumner that he had conceived the controversial orders. But only a few persons ever came to know this. One of these intimates was Hitchcock, who wrote privately of the "flippant charges" levied against Stanton, and who confirmed that it was the President who had blundered in leaving Banks unsupported and that Jackson would never have dared to attempt his movement down the Valley if Stanton had been allowed to have his way. "Be very careful that it does not get out," warned Hitchcock. This is the story Hitchcock told, and which Stanton never revealed.

When Hitchcock had assumed his duties at the War Department, Blenker's division of 11,000 men, which Lincoln had ordered to join Frémont in the newly created Mountain Department, had moved only as far as Winchester. Banks, who was then at Staunton, and Shields, near Front Royal, constituted the right wing of the Union forces in

---

[6] Samuel Hooper to Woodman, June 5, and Curtis to same, June 6, 1862, Woodman Papers, MHS; and see "From the Papers of Horatio Woodman," MHS *Proceedings*, LVI, 232–5; Dawes to wife, May 29, 1862, Dawes Papers, LC; *Advertiser*, May 28, *Transcript*, June 2, and *Herald*, June 10, 1862.

Virginia. As an obvious move by the Confederates to relieve the pressure from the Union left at Richmond would be to strike down the Valley at the Union right, Hitchcock had deemed it of vital importance to keep Blenker's troops in the Valley, where they could support Banks or Shields.

Hitchcock had explained the situation to Stanton and won his full agreement, and the two of them had so advised the President. But Lincoln was determined to send Blenker to Frémont, explaining that he had promised that general and his radical supporters that he would command an impressive force. Hitchcock had been so fearful of leaving the Shenandoah corridor inadequately defended that he returned to the War Department and put his arguments in writing, pleading that if all of Blenker's force could not be left in the Valley, at least part of it should be. Stanton again agreed with him. But Lincoln refused to budge.

When Shields had been moved eastward from the Valley to rejoin McDowell, Blenker's troops had still been immobilized at Winchester. Hitchcock had pointed out to Stanton that when they moved to join Frémont, Banks would be left with no support whatever, except for the 6,000 Union troops at Harpers Ferry. There was more reason than ever for keeping Blenker where he was. Stanton had been so impressed by Hitchcock's reasoning that he prepared an order holding Blenker at Winchester. Soon afterward, however, Blenker's troops departed to join Frémont. Hitchcock observed: "I presume that the order of the Sec'y was never received." [7] More likely, Stanton never sent it. To do so would have been to flout the President. But now that Banks had suffered the consequences of Lincoln's decision, Stanton was taking the blame.

Not only was he denounced for Banks's embarrassments but his call for troops on May 25 also brought him a lambasting. As soon as Governor Andrew received Stanton's telegram asking for troops, he had ordered the Massachusetts militia to report on Boston Common. Then Stanton had learned that Banks had made good his retreat. With Union detachments moving to intercept Jackson, Washington was safe and short-term militia would be of little use. But the upsurge of patriotism might be used to bring about an outpouring of new troops that would put an end to the war. So Stanton telegraphed the loyal governors:

[7] Sumner to Andrew, May 28, Aug. 14, 1862, Andrew Papers, MHS; Hitchcock to Henry Hitchcock, May 30, 1862, Hitchcock Papers, MoHS; to Winfield Scott, May 28, 1862, Hitchcock Papers, LC.

"The President directs that the militia be released and the enlistments made for three years or during the war. This I think will practically be no longer than for a year."

By that time the number of militia on Boston Common had increased to 4,000. But there had been a feeling of utter revulsion when Governor Andrew was obliged to tell them that in order to serve they must leave their militia organizations and enlist for three years or the duration of the war. Andrew telegraphed Massachusetts congressman Samuel Hooper: "Hunker press of Boston now assumes that Sunday's telegram ordering militia was Stanton's personal panic, that President did not approve, that no justifiable occasion existed. It is infamous abuse. Do telegraph immediately the facts."

Hooper conferred with Lincoln, Stanton, and Seward. "I am authorized by the presdt," he wired Andrew, "to say . . . the order for the militia and three months men was made by the president himself upon deliberate consultation with the Secretary of War & other members of the cabinet and his military advisers. You are requested not to make any public use of this." Again the backstage happenings at the War Department were kept secret and Stanton took the blame for the confusion.

Other governors seconded Andrew's protests about the rejection of three-month men. Stanton would have ignored their complaints, but Lincoln, more sensitive to political pressures, thought the governors should be mollified. After considerable argument, Stanton gave in part way and agreed to accept those three-month regiments that had already been armed and equipped and were ready for immediate service. This second reversal of policy led to still further confusion, and Stanton explained to the disgruntled governors that the vacillation of the government resulted from "a conflict of opinion here" that had been resolved by compromise.[8]

One basic manpower difficulty, however, could not be compromised, and its complications tripped him badly. The War Department was actually administering two armies: a volunteer force authorized by act of Congress of July 22, 1861, and now totaling almost 700,000 men, and a regular army with an authorized strength of 42,000 men, with no more than half that number enrolled. In raising the volunteer army the federal government had made the calls and assigned quotas to state authorities, which had recruited the men, appointed the officers up

[8] *O.R.*, ser. 3, II, 68–70, 85–114, 206–7; Hooper to Andrew, May 28, 1862, Andrew Papers, MHS; Pearson *op. cit.*, II, 17–22.

through the rank of colonel, and turned over to the government fully organized units.

A recruiting service almost wholly under state control left something to be desired, and McClellan, by an order of December 3, 1861, had attempted to center it more directly in the War Department. After the units then in process of organization in the various states had been mustered into federal service, no more troops were to be enlisted except on requisition from the War Department, which was also to appoint superintendents of recruiting to take charge of central depots in each state, where volunteers would be concentrated, outfitted, and drilled. This, like the old system, provided only for recruiting new units, not for keeping old ones at full strength. To remedy that deficiency, two officers and four privates from each regiment already in the field were detailed to act as recruiting squads to tour the country and send volunteers to a replacement depot for old regiments.

The government had also been accepting regiments recruited by individuals, who naturally expected to command them. This practice had led to some deplorable results, and soon after taking office Stanton stopped it.

Just when the new machinery was beginning to function, Stanton, sharing with his bureau chiefs the erroneous and widespread belief that victory must come very soon, and intending to reform the recruiting maze, committed what has properly been called one of the colossal blunders of the war. On April 3, 1862, just before the need for more men began to soar, he closed the government recruiting offices in every state and instructed the officers and men who had been detailed to that service to report back to their regiments. An order of May 1 stated that on the request of the various field commanders, the War Department would authorize the respective governors to recruit undermanned regiments to full strength.

Stanton properly evaluated the need for revitalizing the skeletonized regiments instead of continuing to create new ones. He explained to the Senate Military Committee, before issuing these orders, what he was about, and declared that the suspension of recruiting would be for one or two months at most.

The suspension of the recruiting service did accomplish some good. Officers and men on soft recruiting assignments were returned to duty, and some needed economies resulted from consolidations of undermanned units. On June 6, 1862, exactly as he had estimated, Stanton re-established the recruiting service. But valuable time had been lost, and the public, unaware that Stanton had planned from the first to resume recruiting, blamed him for the confusion and for the frustrating immobilization of McClellan so close to Richmond.[9]

Editorials hammered on the theme that McClellan would have bagged the rebels by this time if Stanton had not interfered with him. Stanton was accused of aspiring to the presidency and of wishing to ruin Mc-Clellan, who would be his most dangerous rival, and of currying favor with the abolitionists by devising McClellan's downfall. The press assailed him all the more zealously because of resentment against the strict censorship he had imposed and his rough treatment of many journalists.

Stanton, though he thought for a little while of resigning under this fire, abandoned this recourse at Lincoln's behest. He put on a brave front, wiring Governor Andrew that "I am not disturbed by the howling of those who are at your heels and mine." But he was actually deeply hurt by the nature and venom of the accusations made against him. Meanwhile, he continued to see to it that McClellan was fully sustained by all the resources of the War Department.[1]

McClellan's lines drew ever closer to Richmond. On May 31, the Confederates attempted a quick but massive sortie at Seven Pines; it was repulsed, and "Joe" Johnston, critically wounded during the action, was sent to the hospital. Courtly, competent Robert E. Lee took command of the rebel Army of Northern Virginia, called up reinforcements from Georgia and the Carolinas, and ordered Jackson to return from the Shenandoah Valley.

Utterly failing to appreciate the resourcefulness of the man who now opposed him, McClellan welcomed the change in Confederate command. Still, he never ceased to ask for more troops, and Lincoln and Stanton now had some they could spare. They sent McCall's division of McDowell's corps and seven new regiments to McClellan by water, and prepared to move the remainder of McDowell's force overland toward Richmond according to the plan that had been put in abeyance when Jackson began his foray. But Shields's troops returned from the Valley so footsore and ragged that the execution of the movement again had to be suspended.

Halleck's glacierlike victory at Corinth, Mississippi, inspired McClellan again to suggest that large numbers of men from the West be

---

[9] *O.R.,* ser. 3, II, 28–9, 109; and see Wilson, "Edwin M. Stanton," *loc. cit.,* 239; Shannon, *op. cit.,* 261, 265.

[1] To Andrew, May 28, and Sumner to same, April 22, 1862, Andrew Papers, MHS; and see Gorham, *Stanton,* I, 426–32.

sent to him. As bad weather threatened to delay his advance, McClellan felt that these troops would arrive in time to take part in the attack on Richmond. Even if they did not, "the moral effect would be great, and they would furnish valuable assistance in ulterior movements."

Just what additional moral effect was needed beyond the capture of Richmond can scarcely be imagined. Stanton must have summoned all his self-control to answer temperately. He ignored McClellan's request for western troops, sympathized with the difficulties imposed by the weather, insisted that he was rendering the general every aid in his power, and added that whatever some persons might be saying, "you have never had, and never can have, any one more truly your friend, or more anxious to support you, or more joyful than I shall be at the success which I have no doubt will soon be achieved by your arms."

Perhaps Stanton hoped to boost the general's morale by professing still to be his friend. Or perhaps, as Stanton's enemies later alleged, the devious Secretary thought that the tide was turning in McClellan's favor and that it behooved him to remain on good terms with the general. Although McClellan later came to disbelieve Stanton's veracity in all things, he now was impressed by his assertions of support. "The Secretary and President are becoming quite amiable of late," he wrote to his wife. "I am afraid I am a little cross to them, and that I do not quite appreciate their sincerity and good feeling." But he warned her to guard her speech concerning "Stanton, McDowell, or any of that tribe" when around certain War Department personnel, who were, the general thought, Stanton's spies. Good faith no longer existed between the general and the Secretary, but the President was still determined to keep McClellan in command.[2]

Throughout Jackson's Valley campaign McClellan was optimistic about capturing Richmond, though he failed to seize the opportunity that the diversion of rebel troops to Jackson offered him. New rumors of a Confederate build-up plunged him into uncertainty and dejection. Estimating Lee's strength at 200,000 when it was really 85,000, he wrote to Stanton on June 25 that if the forthcoming battle resulted in disaster, "the responsibility cannot be thrown on my shoulders; it must rest where it belongs." Stanton showed this dispatch to Lincoln, who answered it himself. McClellan's tone pained him very much, he said. "I give you all I can, and act on the presumption that you will do the best you can with what you have." It was ungenerous of McClellan to

[2] June 12, 1862, ms "Extracts from Letters to Wife," McClellan Papers, LC, is far fuller than the printed portion in *Own Story*, 402, and see *ibid.*, 387-9, 399-400; *O.R.*, XI, pt. 3, 216, 219.

presume that Lincoln had more men to send; "I have omitted and shall omit no opportunity to send you reinforcements whenever I possibly can."

Lincoln was convinced by the ineffectual effort to trap Jackson in the Shenandoah Valley that he had committed a grave error in dividing Virginia into so many different commands. He and Stanton visited McDowell at Manassas on June 19 and 20, to seek his advice and to comfort him, for he had been badly injured and his spirit had been crushed by McClellan's public contumely. They returned to Washington agreed that McDowell was not the man for a top command. Still determined to achieve greater unity of organization for the Union's forces in northern Virginia, Lincoln instructed Stanton to summon General John Pope to Washington. Then, belatedly recognizing the desirability of seeking disinterested professional advice, Lincoln at Stanton's suggestion slipped off to see Winfield Scott at West Point. Hitchcock was not now available; that veteran had put himself under a doctor's care in New York.

News of the President's trip leaked out and gave rise to new rumors that Stanton was on his way out of the cabinet. McClellan's supporters were jubilant. General Patrick confided to his diary the fervent hope that "Stanton is doomed!" Barlow, a bitter enemy of the Secretary since falling afoul of Stanton's security apparatus, spread the word that he was insane.

Stanton's friends hurried to press him to stay. In a speech in Jersey City on his way back to Washington, Lincoln assured the country that Stanton would stay on and that he was not "making or unmaking any General." He added jokingly that Stanton held a tight rein on the press, "and I am afraid if I blab too much he might draw a tight rein on me." [3]

Pope arrived in Washington while Lincoln was visiting Scott. The dark, handsome, bearded general had performed creditably under Halleck. He knew Lincoln personally; his Illinois friends had been pulling wires to get him an important command. Reporting to Stanton, Pope found a short, stout, disheveled man, whose long beard was turning gray and who "had the appearance of a man who had lost much sleep and was tired both in body and in mind." The Secretay informed him that the government planned to combine the forces of McDowell, Banks, and Frémont into a new army with Pope in command. It would

[3] Lincoln, *Works*, V, 284, 286; July 5, 1862, Patrick ms diary, LC; "Woodman Letters," MHS *Proceedings*, LVIII, 322–3; Woodman to E. L. Stanton, Jan. 9, 1870, Stanton MSS; *O.R.*, LI, pt. 1, 79; McClellan, *Own Story*, 392–3; Barlow to J. T. Doyle, Letterbook VII, 955, Barlow Papers, HL.

demonstrate in the direction of Charlottesville and Gordonsville, thereby drawing off part of the force that was opposing McClellan at Richmond.

Either Stanton had misunderstood Lincoln's purposes or the President had decided to give Pope a greater opportunity than merely defending Washington. For the June 26 order creating the Army of Virginia with Pope at the head stated that he was to help capture Richmond, while screening the capital. Lincoln and Stanton evidently contemplated a pincers movement; McClellan coming at Richmond from the east and Pope from the west.

Stanton quickly discerned some striking differences between Pope and McClellan. If "Little Mac" overestimated dangers, Pope disregarded real threats. McClellan sheathed his thunderbolts in flannel; Pope proposed to unleash them raw. Boasting that in his western command he had been accustomed to seeing the backs of the enemy, Pope wanted his new soldiers to forget all about lines of retreat and to prepare to attack. His brave words were soon to be tested.

On the same day Lincoln's order set up Pope's new command, Lee made his first stab at McClellan. The Army of the Potomac was split astride the rain-swollen Chickahominy River, Fitz-John Porter's command on the north bank and the other corps south of the stream. Porter's flaming batteries repulsed Lee's thrust near Mechanicsville, and McClellan claimed a great and complete victory.

But Lee was only beginning his main drive. He unleashed it the next day, aimed at McClellan's base at White House Landing, throwing 55,000 troops in a vicious attack against the 35,000 of Porter's corps. Only fragmentary information reached Washington throughout the long, tense day.[4]

The Army of the Potomac had fought well and had suffered no loss of morale on this first day of decision. A determined drive south of the river, where the rebel forces were weak, might have taken the troops straight into Richmond. But McClellan, severely shaken by the reverses of the day, lacked the nerve to launch a counterattack. Shortly after midnight, he wired hysterically to Stanton: "I feel too earnestly tonight. I have seen too many dead and wounded comrades to feel otherwise than that the government has not sustained this army. If you do not do so now the game is lost.

"If I save this army now, I tell you plainly that I owe no thanks to you

[4] *O.R.*, XI, pt. 3, 266, 435; Robert U. Johnson and Clarence C. Buel (eds.), *Battles and Leaders of the Civil War* (New York, 1884–7), II, 449–50 (hereafter cited as *Battles and Leaders*).

or to any other persons in Washington. You have done your best to sacrifice this army."

The telegrapher on duty at the war office stiffened with shock at the words and summoned Sanford, military supervisor of telegrams, to read the message. Sanford's eyes widened in amazement. Before taking the dispatch to Stanton, he ordered it recopied with the last two sentences deleted. But even without its censored passages, the telegram contained a nasty charge and an insubordinate spirit. Stanton, not knowing of the change in its text, showed the message to Lincoln, and remarked: "You know, Mr. President, that all I have done was by your authority." Lincoln nodded in agreement. Notwithstanding, they set to work to aid the embattled commander. Stanton ordered Burnside at Roanoke Island, Hunter at Hilton Head, and Halleck to detach troops from their commands and rush them to McClellan. Lincoln instructed McClellan: "Save your army at all events. We send reinforcements as fast as we can."

Holding off the enemy by day, McClellan retreated by night. At sundown on June 30, after a series of sharp engagements, his weary, battered regiments were forming at Malvern Hill, a strong position near the James River, where gunboats could support them. Stanton's quartermaster and ordnance bureaus had already provided an enormous amount of stores at Harrisons Landing, where McClellan had established a new base, to replace the matériel burned in the retreat. The general's mood was still bitter. "If none of us escape," he wired Stanton, "we shall at least have done honor to our country." And he asked for more gunboats.[5]

McClellan's predicament again pointed up the magnitude of Stanton's error in stopping recruiting back in April. The Confederacy had faced up to the need for new troops and was getting them by conscription. Stanton's appeal to the loyal governors during Jackson's campaign in the Valley and the subsequent reopening of the recruiting offices had brought only a trickle of enlistments. Now more troops were urgently needed. But to call for them by presidential proclamation might cause the people to fly into panic, fearing that the situation was more desperate than it actually was. Lincoln, Stanton, and Seward decided to have Seward go secretly to New York City to consult with Governor Morgan, of New York, Governor Andrew Curtin, of Pennsylvania, Thurlow Weed, and members of the Union Defense Committee.

[5] *O.R.*, IX, 404–7; pt. 3, 271, 280, 290–1; XV, pt. 2, 74–5; Lincoln, *Works*, V, 289; Halleck to wife, July 5, 1862, in *Collector*, XXI, 39; Bates, *op. cit.*, 109–11; Browning, *Diary*, I, 558; McClellan, *Own Story*, 424–5.

Seward worked out a scheme whereby the governors petitioned Lincoln to call for more troops—the number finally agreed on was 300,000—and Stanton helped to smooth out the complex problem of the federal government's contribution to each state's bounty payment. The War Department fixed the state quotas and issued formal orders for raising the troops, but the recruiting and management of the new contingents until they were mustered into service were left to the governors, as had been the case under previous calls.[6]

This intense backstage maneuvering succeeded in securing reinforcements without seriously dampening the public spirit of the North. Meanwhile, news came that McClellan's artillery, lined up hub to hub on Malvern Hill, had blasted Lee's attack to bits. McClellan wired that 50,000 fresh troops would enable him to regain the offensive, and that the arrival of even a few thousand men immediately would revive the morale of his weary troops. Stanton replied that 5,000 soldiers from McDowell's corps were already on their way and that 25,000 from Halleck's army should arrive within two weeks. Lincoln wired the state governors that he would need only half the troops he had called for, if he could have them at once, and that with them he could substantially end the war within two weeks. "But *time is everything. . . .* The quicker you send, the fewer you will have to send. *Time is everything.*"

One governor after another responded that recruiting was terribly difficult, chiefly because of the length of time the men would be required to serve. To meet this emergency, Congress, at Stanton's instigation, empowered the President to call out the militia for nine months' service and to apportion quotas to the states, making all men from eighteen to forty-five liable to militia duty and providing that if the enforcement machinery in any state proved inadequate or broke down, the President might do whatever might be necessary to make the act effective. It became law on July 17. At the same time, Stanton authorized four northwestern governors to draw on the War Department for funds for encouraging enlistments by using speakers or any other means the state officials felt useful; he had earlier stopped all requests for leaves of absence from officers.

Under the pressure of unceasing work and strain, Stanton's health again grew uncertain and his temper became shorter. He could find no time to relax; he had been looking forward to spending the Fourth of July boating on the Potomac with Meigs and their families, but he

---

[6] William B. Hesseltine, *Lincoln and the War Governors* (New York, 1948), 198–200 (hereafter cited as Hesseltine, *War Governors*); Lincoln, *Works*, V, 302; telegrams, June 30, July 1, 1862, Seward Papers, UR; *O.R.*, XI, pt. 3, 276–7.

spent the national anniversary instead with McClellan's chief of staff, General Marcy, who told him that unless McClellan was generously reinforced, he might be obliged to capitulate if Lee should launch a new assault. Stanton, alarmed, told Lincoln what Marcy had said. Lincoln sent for Marcy and put him on the carpet. The word "capitulate" must never be used in connection with the Army of the Potomac, he declared. Marcy stuttered a retraction; Stanton must have misunderstood him— which was untrue, for Marcy had said the same things to others as well. After his interview with Lincoln and Stanton, Marcy wrote to McClellan: "The President and Secretary speak very kindly of you and find no fault."

But whatever Stanton may have told Marcy, he was finding plenty of fault. In his first and last recourse to nepotism, Stanton had recently brought his brother-in-law, Wolcott, into the War Department as an assistant secretary to replace Scott, who had returned to the Pennsylvania Railroad, and Wolcott wrote to Pamphila that everyone except Lincoln thought McClellan should be removed. "Edwin urges his dismissal," Wolcott stated, "but does not insist upon it and so nothing is done." Stanton told his friend Israel D. Andrews that it was only Lincoln's insistence on pacifying the conservatives that kept McClellan in the Army.[7]

Stanton planned to have another talk with Marcy before the officer returned to the Army of the Potomac. Summoning Marcy, Stanton entrusted him with a letter to McClellan telling of the mortal illness of his child. In this letter Stanton swore to McClellan that "there is no cause in my heart or conduct for the cloud that wicked men have raised between us for their own base and selfish purposes. No man had ever a truer friend than I have been to you and shall continue to be." Stanton assured McClellan of his continuing official support and personal friendship.

Could Stanton have deliberately played the hypocrite at such a solemn moment, when he was moved by the loftiest feelings with the hand of death on his child? The presence of death always upset him, and often caused him to act impulsively. Now, in a highly emotional state, perhaps he regretted the hard things he had said against McClellan, and took this means of making atonement.

Acknowledging Stanton's letter, McClellan expressed sympathy in the illness of his child and then reviewed their past relations. When Stanton

[7] Lincoln, *Works*, V, 304; Wolcott MS, 181, 184–5; Browning, *Diary*, I, 558–60; Andrews to Andrew, July 3, 4, 1862, Andrew Papers, MHS; Stanton to Meigs, July 4, 1862, Meigs Papers, LC; *O.R.*, II, 213; XI, pt. 3, 281, 294.

took over the War Department, McClellan had regarded him as his friend and counselor, he wrote. But soon thereafter Stanton had acted in a manner "deeply offensive to my feelings and calculated to affect me injuriously in public estimation." Stanton's supposed part in withholding reinforcements had induced the general to believe that "your mind was warped by a bitter personal prejudice against me." Now Stanton's kind letter caused him to think he had been wrong, he wrote, and that he had misconstrued Stanton's motives. With a feeling of relief, he now stood ready to act with the same cordial confidence that had once marked their relationship.

If Stanton was playing the hypocrite, however, McClellan was matching him card for card. On the day he wrote to Stanton, McClellan advised his wife that his reply to Stanton had been diplomatic; but "if you read it carefully you will see that it is bitter enough—politely expressed, but containing more than is on the surface." Actually, McClellan wrote, Stanton "is the most unmitigated scoundrel I ever knew, heard or read of"; if Stanton had lived during Jesus' lifetime, Judas Iscariot would have "remained a respected member of the fraternity of the Apostles" and would have been shocked at Stanton. "I *may* do the man injustice," McClellan mused in a rare moment of self-doubt; "God grant that I may be wrong—for I hate to think that humanity *can* sink so low—but my opinion is just as I have told you." [8] The Union high command was in a perilous state with two such suspicious, sensitive individuals obliged to work with each other.

[8] July 13, 18, 1862, ms "Extracts from Letters to Wife," McClellan Papers, LC; Gen. Henry M. Naglee, *Testimony: McClellan vs. Lincoln* (n.p., 1864) ; McClellan, *Own Story,* 475–8; *O.R.,* XI, pt. 3, 298; and see McClellan to Barlow, July 15, 1862, Barlow Papers, HL.

CHAPTER X

RELENTLESSLY AND WITHOUT REMORSE

U NSURE of what to do and whom to trust, Lincoln left for Harrisons Landing to appraise the condition of McClellan's army for himself. The general brashly handed him a letter of advice on political matters. Admitting that he was transcending the scope of his official duties, he asserted that his views amounted to convictions and he felt obliged to speak out. First of all, the war should be conducted on the highest Christian principles. Lincoln must adopt a conservative policy and assure the people of the South that they would not be subjugated. "A declaration of radical views, especially upon slavery," the general warned, "will rapidly disintegrate our present armies." McClellan suggested that a general in chief be appointed to command the armies on all fronts. "I am willing to serve in such position as you may assign me," he added.

McClellan informed Stanton that he had given Lincoln his views on general policy. "You and I during the last summer so often talked over the whole subject," he wrote the Secretary, "that I have only expressed the opinions then agreed upon between us."

Whatever opinions on these matters Stanton may once have expressed to McClellan, he no longer agreed with him on the advisability of waging a "soft" war. From the time he became Secretary of War his purpose had been to put new drive into the war effort, to smash the enemy decisively and as quickly as possible. To that end Stanton had come to favor the use of any and every instrument and resource available to the government—and the amazing thing about it was that McClellan was ignorant of any change in Stanton's views and never realized that war can alter purposes and goals, that this war was assuming a revolutionary character.

It may be another instance of Stanton's trying to be all things to all men. But it seems more likely, as the two men had not discussed matters with each other for a year, that McClellan, righteous in his own conceits, had been too obtuse to perceive Stanton's sensitivity to the changing nature of the war, and the fact that his own military failures made a mockery of his propensity to direct political policies. McClellan's relationship with Stanton had long since reached that point of no return where the two men distrusted each other's motives as well as conclusions.

For Stanton, personal tragedy wiped from his mind for the moment the developing impasse with McClellan. Little James Hutchison Stanton died, not quite nine months old. Lincoln returned to Washington in time to attend the funeral along with most of the cabinet.[1] The child's death came just as Stanton, sick with grief and fatigue, became the target for the most powerful attack he had yet known, unleashed by the stunning news of McClellan's retreat from Richmond. The public denounced Stanton and praised McClellan for the latter's defeats; the Secretary was condemned publicly as being worthy of death, and ordnance man Balch commented that if Stanton should "venture" where McClellan's men could lay hands on him, he "would be badly abused."

Much of the antipathy toward Stanton was spontaneous and genuine. But some substantial part of the growing anti-Stanton sentiment that marked the spring and summer months of 1862 was manufactured to increase newspaper circulation and—the goal of the Blair tribe—to divide conservative Republicans from their radical party brethren and thus expand Blairite influence.

The New York *World* was the mainspring of the attack on Stanton. Its able publisher, Manton Marble, was a partisan Democrat, heartily Unionist, and wholly dedicated to increasing the circulation of his newspaper. An anti-Stanton stand, he and his associate Barlow had decided, was good for the country and for the *World*. His correspondents on the Peninsula, favored by McClellan and angry at Stanton's press restrictions, sent Marble the kind of dispatches he wanted.[2]

Stanton could not win a popularity contest against the dashing and idolized McClellan. But what he most worried about was that Lincoln

---

[1] Morse, *Welles Diary*, I, 70; McClellan, *Own Story*, 478, 487-9.

[2] Blair, Jr., to Andrew, July 7, 1862, Andrew Papers, MHS; J. M. Bloch, *The Rise of the New York World during the Civil War Decade* (Ph.D. thesis, Harvard University, 1941), 121-30; Balch to wife, July 13, 1862, Balch Papers, UCB.

might succumb to the pressure and bring McClellan into the cabinet in his place, as a uniformed Secretary of War. Actually, McClellan, believing that it was his destiny to save the Union, had this in mind.

To Stanton, he was a wrecker instead of a savior, unless kept in check. So the Secretary fought back. Wolcott temporarily blunted the *World*'s thrusts by warning Barlow that if they continued, Congress might turn the local customhouse "inside out." Stanton, Wolcott wrote, "cared not much for the pounding you gave him. He is a lawyer and a hard-hitter too . . . the *World*'s abuse of Stanton has been a frightful error—a dreadful waste of opportunity and material. As to the man himself, he is as honorable & honest as you or I." It meant the final severance of Stanton's friendship with Barlow and his conservative associates.

But newer friends proved their worth. Chandler came to his defense in the Senate, and in a terrific blast denounced McClellan's Democratic supporters as disloyal partisans. Although Stanton had restrained Chandler from attacking McClellan a few weeks earlier, he now endorsed his remarks, and repeated their theme in articles, sent out under pseudonyms, which Woodman planted in New England and Ohio Valley newspapers. Stanton was ready to bring his covert opposition to McClellan out into the light of day.[3]

By the end of July, the counterattack was succeeding. Many men found in Lincoln's support of Stanton adequate reason to sustain the Secretary. "Public opinion is fast turning," George Bancroft estimated, adding that the whole Yorktown campaign exhibited McClellan's incapacity and Lincoln's "successive, hasty, & contradictory acts of interference." Interior Secretary Smith wrote to Stanton that at last the attacks on him were beginning to recoil upon their authors, the friends of McClellan.

It was sweet news to Stanton. He replied to Smith that "the dogs that have been yelping at my heels, finding how useless it is, appear to be giving up the hunt and contenting themselves with an occasional snarl." [4] But the yelping and snarling never entirely ceased.

A major item of controversy, even to this day, was what Lincoln called "the curious mystery" of the number of troops that had been sent to McClellan. He had planned to operate with about 150,000 men. The

[3] Wolcott to Barlow, *ca.* July 1862, undated file, Barlow Papers, HL; July 13, 1862, ms "Extracts from Letters to Wife," McClellan Papers, LC; Detroit *Post, Chandler,* 228–9; *Congressional Globe,* 37th Cong., 2d sess., 3148–50, 3386–92.

[4] Bancroft to son, July 28, 1862, Bancroft-Bliss Papers, LC; Smith to Stanton, July 29, 1862, Stanton MSS; Stanton to Smith, July 30, 1862, copy owned by Gideon Townsend Stanton.

diversion of Blenker's division and the withholding of McDowell's contingent left him with only 93,000, he said. Deducting men on leave and unfit for field duty left him, McClellan claimed, with only 70,000 effectives at the beginning of the campaign.

On the other hand, McClellan's own returns showed 158,419 troops under his command on April 1, including those of Blenker and McDowell, and 156,838 under his command on June 20, just before the Seven Days' battle, so that all but 1,581 of the troops withheld from him, as well as his losses up to the latter date, had been made up. Probably the largest number of effectives that he could send into battle was around 100,000. The Confederates at the peak of their strength could muster 85,000.

In the beginning McClellan had overwhelming superiority of numbers. But he failed to utilize that superiority when, instead of attacking, he put Yorktown under siege. Later, according to accepted military theory, he lacked the numerical superiority necessary for successful offensive operations. So did Lee. But Lee took the offensive anyway—with a large measure of success. McClellan's trouble was not lack of troops; it was overcaution, and lack of any real will to fight.

Lincoln went into this matter of numbers when on August 6 he finally chose to speak out in Stanton's defense. The President said he never liked to say anything in public unless he could produce some good by it. "The only thing I think of just now not likely to be better said by someone else, is a matter in which we have heard some other persons blamed for what I did myself." There were cries of "What is it?" and Lincoln explained that there had been a widespread attempt to involve Stanton and McClellan in a quarrel. From his own observation, "these gentlemen are not nearly so deep in the quarrel as some pretending to be their friends." McClellan naturally wanted to be successful, Lincoln said. So did the Secretary of War. But both the Secretary and the President must fail if their generals failed. They both wanted McClellan to succeed.

"Sometimes we have a dispute about how many men Gen. McClellan has had," Lincoln added, "and those who would disparage him say that he has had a very large number, and those who would disparage the Secretary of War insist that Gen. McClellan has had a very small number. The basis for this is, there is always a wide difference, and on this occasion, perhaps, a wider one between the grand total on McClellan's rolls and the men actually fit for duty; and those who would disparage him talk of the grand total on paper, and those who would disparage the Secretary of War talk of those present fit for duty. . . .

And I say here, as far as I know, the Secretary of War has withheld no one thing at any time in my power to give him . . . and I stand here, as justice requires me to do, to take upon myself what has been charged on the Secretary of War, as withholding from him." [5]

The failures and frustrations of the Valley and Peninsular campaigns convinced Lincoln that he must shake up the Union high command. Running the show himself had proved too much of a weight and exposed him to criticisms almost beyond enduring. A military expert was needed in Washington who would command as well as counsel, obey as well as fight. Lincoln required a top general who had the respect of the Army's bestarred echelon and who would be willing to serve as a buffer for the President by accepting the onus of unpopular decisions.

Hitchcock had rarely been available even to offer advice recently, much less to provide for the other needs Lincoln felt. The old officer was physically ill and disgusted at the inside workings of government, and he decided to resign. He had come to detest Stanton, even though the Secretary had never been offensive to him and despite the fact that Stanton and he had always agreed on strategy. Hitchcock and Stanton were two of the very few persons in the government who knew that Lincoln had been the final arbiter in policy disputes.

Stanton pressed him to stay, or at most to take a leave of absence. The Secretary correctly anticipated that the military man whom Lincoln chose to replace Hitchcock would stand close to the President, where Stanton had made a place for himself up to this time. Stanton never interfered, however, as Lincoln searched for the right man.

First the President offered Burnside the command of the Army of the Potomac, but he refused to supersede McClellan. Then, on July 11, Lincoln summoned Halleck to Washington. He ordered him to take command of the land forces of the United States with the title of General in Chief. Stanton felt about Halleck the same lack of enthusiasm that Wolcott manifested. Writing to Pamphila, Wolcott stated that Halleck "isn't by any means my pattern of a man," but it was a forward step in securing unity of military command and action, "substantially degrades McClellan into a mere subordinate," and might keep Lincoln from future interferences in policy.[6]

[5] *Works*, V, 358–9; Williams, *Lincoln Finds a General*, I, 216.

[6] Croffutt, *op. cit.*, 443; *CCW*, I, 650; Lincoln, *Works*, V, 312–3; Wolcott MS, 186. Years later, McClellan asserted that Stanton at this time warned him that Halleck was a "scoundrel" and "bare faced villain," and when Halleck arrived, the new supreme commander came to McClellan to warn him, in much the same terms, against Stanton;

Halleck arrived on July 22, and high government officials and fellow officers scrutinized him closely. His uniform fit tightly across an ample paunch. A crescent of thin gray whiskers fringed his flabby cheeks and dimpled chin. His eyes bulged out beneath a high, wide brow that made his sobriquet, "Old Brains," deriving from his authorship of books on law and war, seem strikingly appropriate.

Forty-seven years old when he assumed the Union high command, Halleck had won a Phi Beta Kappa key at Union College before enrolling at West Point. His military service in the Mexican War had been limited to minor operations in California. Resigning from the Army in 1854, he had become director and superintendent of the New Almaden quicksilver mine, in which capacity he had run afoul of Stanton.

Coming back into the Army in 1861, Halleck had done an efficient job of military administration while commanding in the West. But he lacked dash and magnetism. The important victories in his department had been won by his subordinates; when he took the field in person, he had been painfully overcautious. A planner and co-ordinator rather than a field commander, he shared Hitchcock's opinion that the Union armies were operating on too many fronts. And yet, after taking Corinth, he had dispersed his troops throughout the Southwest, instead of finishing the all-important work of clearing the Mississippi River. But whatever Halleck's deficiencies, no general had shown to better advantage for the job of supreme command behind the lines.

And so men who had been disappointed in the Union's failures thus far looked hopefully to Halleck to alter things. If he or Stanton was nervous about encountering the other in person once again—Sam Ward gossiped to Seward that "it must be delightful for him [Halleck] to meet Mr. Stanton on an intimate footing after the latter's published report . . . that Halleck the lawyer had perjured himself in the New Almaden case!"—neither man exhibited it on the day after Halleck's arrival, when Lincoln, Stanton, Halleck, Pope, and Burnside held a long consultation. Lincoln told Halleck his opinion of McClellan. As a result, the command of the Army of the Potomac was again offered to Burnside. When he declined it a second time, Lincoln and some members of the cabinet, including Stanton, urged Halleck to remove McClel-

---

see McClellan, *Own Story*, 137. The whole story seems improbable, is totally unsupported by other data, and is contradicted by Halleck's testimony in Wilson, "General Halleck—A Memoir," *loc. cit.*, 557. Welles's contention that Stanton plotted Pope's and Halleck's ascents, solely to diminish McClellan, is a misreading of the events; Beale, *Welles Diary*, I, 108–9.

lan anyway. He shied away from this step. "They want me to do what they are afraid to attempt," Halleck wrote to his wife. But he was more afraid than they.

Detested by the antislavery radicals, McClellan had become the idol of the Northern Democrats, and his soldiers worshipped him in spite of his recent defeats. True, Lincoln and most of his cabinet members considered McClellan a failure and thought the time had come to remove him. But for Lincoln or Stanton to initiate such action would give rise to a charge of partisan prejudice which might turn the Union Democrats against the war and arouse the ire of the Army. If Halleck shouldered that responsibility, McClellan's removal could be defended as a nonpartisan act of military necessity.

Though Halleck soon found that McClellan, furious at Halleck's ascent over him, was uncontrollable, he also suspected that radical pressure on the administration was the reason behind the desire to dismiss McClellan. Abhorring abolitionism himself, he hoped it would never be necessary to yield to the radicals and put McClellan on the shelf, and he persisted in the hope that "Mac" under his direction would improve in obedience and effectiveness. Yet when this hope proved illusory, Halleck failed Lincoln's need by evading the right decision to remove the cocky young commander.[7]

After a number of consultations, Halleck offered McClellan a choice of renewing his campaign against Richmond with 20,000 new troops or calling it off once and for all. McClellan said he wanted to attack but would need more men. No one was satisfied. McClellan complained to his wife that Halleck "has done me *no good yet*," and repeated gossip that the new general in chief praised him to friends but told enemies that he was too dilatory.

After returning to the capital from these consultations at McClellan's headquarters, Halleck was still reluctant to displease McClellan, but that general's own report had given him an exaggerated notion of Lee's strength. As he now considered it hazardous to keep the Union armies separated, Halleck, on August 3, ordered McClellan to move his army to Aquia Creek within supporting distance of Pope, whose troops were now at Culpeper. McClellan insisted that the fate of the Union must be decided on the James and found one excuse after

[7] Halleck to wife, July 13, Aug. 9, 1862, in *Collector*, XXI, 40, 52; to McClellan, March 8, 1862, McClellan Papers, LC; Ben Perley Poore, *The Life and Public Service of Ambrose E. Burnside* (Providence, 1882), 154; Ward to Seward, July 23, 1862, Seward Papers, UR; *O.R.*, XI, pt. 3, 325.

another for delaying the embarkation. Halleck began to suffer from the heat and the labor, and more responsibility than he cared to assume. "I am almost broken down," he wrote to his wife, ". . . I can't get General McClellan to do what I wish."

Still avoiding decision, Halleck sent Burnside to the Peninsula to hurry the troop movement to the north, but Stanton guessed that the real purpose of Burnside's assignment was to keep McClellan under control. Stanton revealed his own diminished role in affairs, which Halleck's arrival had initiated. He now had to ask Chase, whom he had criticized before for trying to meddle in War Department matters, to find out from Halleck what Burnside's orders were—a humiliating request for this Secretary of War to make, who had boasted that he would suffer no interference in the conduct of his office from President, generals, or other cabinet officers.

This isolation from intimate participation in command decisions was a foretaste of what Stanton was to suffer in the next few weeks. From being Lincoln's close adviser during the period of amateur control of the armies, he now found himself demoted to virtual exclusion from the inner councils. Now top-level military matters were in Halleck's hands, and ordnance officer Balch, a confidant of the Secretary, wrote that Stanton "has at last found out that he can't *quite* manage the war."

But Stanton was not the sort of man to be pushed aside for long. Questions of strategy and slavery soon combined to return him to the control center around Lincoln, but for a time Halleck was to be the more vital partner in that ring.[8]

Prompted by Stanton, and evidently with Lincoln's acquiescence, Pope had issued a series of orders renouncing McClellan's policy of "gentlemanly war." His commanders were instructed to arrest all disloyal persons both male and female found within their lines and have them swear allegiance to the government or betake themselves South on penalty of being treated as spies. Bushwackers were to be shot without civil process, and his army was to live off the country, "not wasting force and energy" in protecting the private property of persons hostile to the government. Pope later claimed that Stanton wrote this

[8] Williams, *Lincoln Finds a General*, V, 271–82; Stephen E. Ambrose, "Lincoln and Halleck: A Study in Personal Relations," ISHS *Journal*, LII, 208–24; Halleck to wife, August 9, 13, 1862, in *Collector*, XXI, 52; July 30, 1862, ms "Extracts from Letters to Wife," McClellan Papers, LC; Chase, *Diary*, 112–13; *O.R.*, XI, pt. 3, 337–8; Balch to wife, July 16, 1862, UCB.

pronouncement; and indeed it was in the spirit of the Secretary's answer to a journalist's query concerning the disposition of captured rebel guerrillas: *"Let them swing."*

There can be no doubt that Pope's proclamation was an invitation for some Union soldiers to make free with the property, and in some instances with the persons, of Southern civilians. McClellan, accustomed to more traditional and restrained policies, complained that the order aggravated the problem of maintaining discipline and invited countermeasures by the outraged South. But it must also be said that, even before this, many individual soldiers and whole units of the eastern commands had behaved toward enemy civilians as Pope now permitted officially. On the other hand, Pope's order was rarely if ever carried out to the permissible limits of conduct. And across the mountains, where West Point's concepts of restrained war never rooted as strongly as they did along the Atlantic seaboard, the assumptions underlying Pope's order were in far more general practice than they were in the Army of the Potomac.

Harshness and cruelty could not be kept out of this war. To be sure, the Union government should never have approved any excesses that its soldiers committed, and Stanton and Pope erred seriously by weakening the moral position of the government. But neither man created the hatreds that were growing between the Yankee soldier and the white man of the South. The Union trooper distrusted all white residents in occupied territory. He thought of them as the source of the guerrillas, the snipers, and the informers for the Confederate Army which made his life wretched and unsure. To him, Pope's order made sense.[9]

As Pope began to feel the heavier weight of troops that Lee sent against him, he posted his army behind the Rappahannock River and tried to hold the crossing until reinforcements arrived from McClellan. At last the armada bearing the Army of the Potomac came wallowing up Chesapeake Bay.

Balked at the river crossings but determined to smash Pope before McClellan's troops arrived in force, Lee hurried Jackson off on a bold sweep around Pope's right flank. Taking Pope by surprise, Jackson crashed in on the Union rear. On August 26 word flashed to the War

[9] On Stanton's authorship, see James Ford Rhodes, *History of the United States* (New York, 1907), IV, 101, and Jacob D. Cox, *Military Reminiscences* (New York, 1900), II, 221–3. Washington *Star*, June 13, 1862, on guerrillas; Aug. 10, 1862, ms "Extracts from Letters to Wife," McClellan Papers, LC.

Department that Pope's communications had been cut and that the Confederates were moving up the railroad toward Manassas Junction, his advance supply depot. Then the telegraph went dead. The elusive Jackson slipped away to the northwest, stalling and stabbing to keep Pope off balance until Lee had time to join him with the remainder of the Confederate army.

On August 30 news came that the two armies had begun to slug it out on the old field of Bull Run. Halleck urged McClellan, who had now arrived at Alexandria in person, to get his troops into the fight. McClellan responded with objections of one sort or another, insisted upon a clarification of his status, and accomplished virtually nothing.

Heavy connonading on the second day of the battle could be clearly heard in Washington. The acrid smell of gunpowder came in on the west wind. Stanton commandeered hacks and private carriages to take convalescent soldiers to the railroad station for removal to Philadelphia and New York, for all available cots in Washington would be needed when Pope's casualties began to arrive. He recruited male nurses to go to the battlefield, and closed Washington's saloons, but not soon enough; many of his nurses were already weaving drunk. Haupt protested against using badly needed railroad cars to take this sodden crew to the front, and soon brought them back to the city, hungry and with hangovers, to get them out of the way.

Excitement in Washington mounted as wild rumors floated in from the front. McClellan wrote to his wife that if he could slip away to the city, he would send their silver off. Stanton, who early in the day believed that Pope had won a victory, nevertheless had the more important papers in the War Department gathered into bundles, ready to be carted to safety. He ordered the arms and ammunition in the Washington arsenal shipped to New York forthwith, but Colonel Ramsay, commander of the arsenal, chose to disregard the order, thereby incurring a black mark in Stanton's book.

Halleck urged McClellan to hurry the movement of troops to Pope. McClellan, considering Pope's situation hopeless, advised Lincoln to look to the defense of Washington and let Pope get out of his fix as best he could. Halleck, distraught and weary, virtually abdicated his authority and allowed McClellan to do as he pleased. No more troops reached Pope.

Stanton had refrained from interfering with field operations since Halleck assumed command, but now he could restrain himself no longer, and by his forthrightness soon returned to the highest level of influence around Lincoln. He directed Halleck to report whether, in his opinion, McClellan had acted with the promptness and energy required by the national safety. Halleck's reply blamed McClellan for slowness and ineptitude. Stanton then obtained Chase's assurance of support and drew up a remonstrance to the President. It accused McClellan of incompetence, charged him with imperiling Pope's army through disobedience of orders and inactivity, and declared that the signers felt unwilling to be accessories to "the destruction of our armies, the protraction of the war, the waste of our national resources, and the overthrow of the government, which we believe must be the inevitable consequence of George B. McClellan being continued in command."

After signing the protest themselves, Stanton and Chase set out to obtain the signatures of other cabinet members. The document was a virtual ultimatum to the President that he must choose between retaining McClellan in command and forming a new cabinet.

Attorney General Bates, reading the remonstrance, suggested that it be toned down by withholding the bill of particulars against McClellan until Lincoln asked for one. Stanton allowed Bates to rewrite the document, whereupon he, Chase, Smith, and Bates signed it. Welles agreed that McClellan should be removed and promised to back up the remonstrants orally, but he refused to sign the protest because he thought it discourteous to the President. Stanton responded with some degree of heat that he knew of no particular obligation he was under to the President. Lincoln had called him to a position involving labors and responsibilities which one man could scarcely carry at best, and had then made his task intolerable by trammeling him with a commander who did nothing but embarrass him, and he did not propose to submit to a continuance of this state of affairs. Welles admitted that Stanton had good cause for complaint.

As Chase and Stanton knew that Blair still had faith in McClellan, they did not present the remonstrance to him; and Seward had left Washington for a brief vacation, perhaps, as Welles suspected, to avoid committing himself. Meanwhile, by Sunday, August 31, little doubt remained that Pope had been defeated with heavy losses.

The cabinet met next day to learn that McClellan had arrived in Washington in response to a summons from Halleck. Anxious to find out what was going on, for Lincoln was revealing his intentions to no one, Stanton invited Halleck and John Hay to his home. But all his undelicate "digging" failed to reveal what McClellan's role was to be, for only Lincoln knew.

Next day the cabinet finally learned from Lincoln that he had in-

The War Department Building, Seventeenth Street and Pennsylvania Avenue in Washington. Stanton's office was on the third floor.

"Council of War," by John Rogers. A depiction of a session which never occurred but which reflects the sculptor's insight into the Lincoln-Stanton relationship.

A more common view of Lincoln and Stanton. The officer is Halleck. From Vanity Fair, *May 31, 1862.*

"NORFOLK IS OURS!"

FRISKY MANNER IN WHICH THE NEWS WAS RECEIVED BY THE PRESIDENT AND SECRETARY OF WAR.

SALMON P. CHASE

WILLIAM H. SEWARD

MONTGOMERY BLAIR

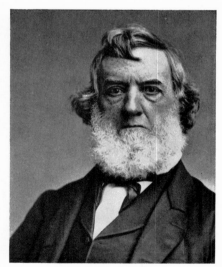

GIDEON WELLES

Friends, Enemies, and Colleagues, I.

GENERAL HENRY W. HALLECK

GENERAL E. A. HITCHCOCK

GENERAL MONTGOMERY MEIGS

GENERAL LORENZO THOMAS

Friends, Enemies, and Colleagues, II.

structed McClellan to take command of all incoming troops in order
to safeguard the capital. The news fell like a bombshell on the meeting.
His voice trembling with excitement, Stanton joined with Chase in
leading a chorus of complaint. Lincoln, clearly distressed to find himself at odds with most of the cabinet, explained that he had acted on
his own responsibility for what he considered the country's best interest.
He held no brief for McClellan; he admitted the general had the
"slows." But he also knew the ground around Washington and was
qualified beyond anyone else to whip the army back into shape.

The remonstrance against McClellan remained in Stanton's pocket.
Lincoln had made up his mind, and experience had taught Stanton that
argument in such circumstances was fruitless. He plodded back to the
War Department "in the condition of a drooping leaf," his secretary
recalled, and he was morose and silent all day. Lincoln never saw the
remonstrance.[1]

Stanton took a petty revenge. He saw to it that the order assigning
McClellan to command went out under Halleck's name rather than his
own, and enjoyed receiving protests against McClellan's appointment.
When Chandler wrote in this vein, Stanton answered: "I understand
and appreciate all you say . . . but am powerless to help it."

None too happy himself, Lincoln confided to Hay and to Welles that
McClellan had behaved despicably toward Pope and "wanted him to
fail. That is unpardonable, but he is too useful now to sacrifice."
McClellan and Pope could no longer be kept in the same theater, how-
ever; so Lincoln assigned Pope to an unimportant command in the
West.

Feeling himself justified by his reappointment, McClellan wrote to
his wife that Halleck had begged him "to help him out of the scrape,"
and of how he had gone to Washington "mad as a march hare, & had
a pretty plain talk with him & Abe." Only after this conversation,
McClellan added, did he "reluctantly" agree "to take command here
& try to save the Capital." Unless Lincoln put the whole Army under
his command, he would resign.

Stanton's discomfiture was obvious. Lincoln had not shared his
decision concerning McClellan with him. McClellan, in whom Stanton
had no confidence, had somehow proved to the President that the Army

---

[1] Gorham, *Stanton*, II, 29–41; Chase, *Diary*, 116–20; Morse, *Welles Diary*, I, 93–108;
Hay, *Diaries and Letters*, 45–6; McClellan, *Own Story*, 520; *O.R.*, XII, pt. 3,
706, 766, 793–4, 807; ser. 3, II, 496; A. E. H. Johnson in New York *Evening Post*,
July 13, 1891. Flower, *Stanton*, 177, incorrectly states that Lincoln not only saw the
remonstrance but in Stanton's office wrote an answer to it, which they kept secret.

of the Potomac would follow only him. Halleck was now proved to be too timid to assume the role of over-all military co-ordinator and courageous adviser as Lincoln and Stanton had expected and hoped.[2]

Now it seemed to Stanton that Lee, having defeated Pope, could take Washington if he chose to. Halleck confided to his wife that "Generals Collum, Meigs, and the Secretary of War and a few members of my staff, were the only persons to whom I told what I considered the real danger—the capture of Washington."

Lee, however, turned his gaze toward Maryland. An invasion of that slaveholding state might induce it to join the Confederacy, in which case Washington would fall anyway. He could replenish his supplies from Maryland's ripening fields and give the North a taste of war. And a Confederate victory on Northern soil might induce hesitant European governments to recognize the Confederacy.

On September 4, Lee with 55,000 men crossed the Potomac and moved toward Frederick. Foreboding gripped the North.

Lincoln merged all units of the Army of Virginia into the army of the Potomac and put McClellan in command of it. Knowing that Stanton would object to giving McClellan over-all field command, Lincoln did not consult him. The lift in morale that McClellan imparted to the soldiers affirmed Lincoln's judgment in restoring him to command. Governor Curtin asked Stanton for troops to defend Harrisburg. The Secretary, accepting McClellan's reappointment with what grace he could muster, answered that "the best defense . . . is to strengthen the force now moving against the enemy under General McClellan." [3]

Swinging westward toward Boonsboro, Lee sent three separate detachments from his army to capture Harpers Ferry and thus open a line of communication through the Shenandoah Valley. McClellan, following him cautiously, entered Frederick, where good fortune greeted him. An Indiana private, picking up a bunch of cigars at an abandoned Confederate camp site, found that they were wrapped in a copy of Lee's orders, disclosing the fact that Lee's army was divided and might be destroyed in detail.

McClellan's force amounted to 90,000 men. He decided to strike. But overestimating the number of Lee's troops as usual, he still moved warily. Holding him off at the mountain passes, Lee tried desperately

[2] Townsend, *Anecdotes*, 68–70; *O.R.*, XII, pt. 3, 807; Stanton to Chandler, Sept. 18, 1862, Chandler Papers, LC; Hay, *Diaries and Letters*, 46; Morse, *Welles Diary*, I, 109, 112–13; Sept. 2, 1862, ms "Extracts from Letters to Wife," McClellan Papers, LC.
[3] *O.R.*, XIX, pt. 2, 204, 217, 247; Halleck, Sept. 5, 1862, *Collector*, XXI, 53; S. Bettersworth to Barlow, Sept. 23, 1862, Barlow Papers, HL.

to bring his forces together again near Sharpsburg, behind Antietam Creek. By the time McClellan threw his army into action on September 17, all the scattered Confederate divisions had come up.

The hours dragged that day while Lincoln, Stanton, and Halleck, at the War Department, waited anxiously for news. At 5 p.m. came an uninformative wire from McClellan. Silence followed. Communication was broken. But at ten o'clock a message, coming through by way of Hagerstown, asked that ammunition be sent by rail at once. Stanton ordered the B & O tracks cleared, and a laden train left Washington a little after two o'clock in the morning. It went through so fast that the journal boxes of the cars were on fire a good part of the way. Stanton sent another ammunition train; and a division of fresh troops and two batteries of artillery under General Andrew A. Humphreys marched all night from Frederick under Stanton's orders and joined McClellan the next morning.

Reports from Hagerstown and Harrisburg on the eighteenth said that McClellan had pinned Lee against the Potomac. Next day McClellan wired: "Our victory is complete. The enemy is driven back into Virginia. Maryland & Pennsylvania are safe."

More information trickling into Washington made it evident, however, that what might have been an annihilating defeat for Lee was only a severe repulse. McClellan had wasted his superior strength in a series of un-co-ordinated attacks, all of them partially successful but none of them pressed home. He had never used his reserves, but had allowed Lee's crippled army to recross the Potomac unmolested.[4]

Lincoln, Stanton, and Halleck tried frantically to induce McClellan to follow up his victory by throwing a knockout punch at Lee. Finally, on October 6, Lincoln directed him to cross the river at once and give battle to the enemy and drive him south. Telegraphing this order to McClellan, Halleck added that he and Stanton "fully concur" with Lincoln in this directive.

But success had put McClellan in an overweening mood. He was ready to demand a guarantee from Lincoln that he would no longer be interferred with, and contemplated tendering his resignation unless Lincoln dismissed Halleck and Stanton and made him general in chief. In turn, Stanton wanted to remove McClellan on the spot, but Lincoln restrained him. Again rebuffed, Stanton told Chase that he was almost ready to quit, feeling that his usefulness was ended. What galled him

[4] Morse, *Welles Diary*, I, 142; McClellan, *Own Story*, 536, 614; McClellan to Halleck, Sept. 19, 1862, R. T. Lincoln Papers, LC; Williams, *Lincoln Finds a General*, II, 458–60.

most were the attempts of McClellan and his "creatures" to blame him for the army's inactivity.[5]

McClellan first complained that he could not move for lack of horses; those he had were ill, sore-tongued, and tired, he said. Lincoln asked sarcastically what they had done since Antietam that would fatigue anything, and Stanton demanded immediate reports on the army's horse supply. Meigs responded that large numbers of horses had been going to McClellan every week. General Rufus Ingalls, McClellan's own quartermaster, reported that on October 1 he had a total of 32,885 animals, one to every four men. Halleck commented in a letter to McClellan: "It is believed that your present proportion of cavalry and of animals is much larger than that of any other of our armies."

Next, McClellan argued that his requisitions for shoes and clothes had not been filled. Again Stanton demanded reports. Meigs responded that 48,000 pairs of boots and shoes were receipted for by McClellan's quartermasters; Ingalls reported: "The suffering for want of clothing is exaggerated, I think, and certainly might have been avoided by timely requisitions of regimental and brigade commanders." Halleck assured Stanton that the only delays in forwarding supplies had come from lack of cars, and this shortage had always been speedily remedied. The Army of the Potomac was better supplied in all respects than the Union armies in the West, or any army in the world. It was the ultimate in praise for Stanton and his subordinates.

Both McClellan and Stanton were right on the question of supplies. McClellan exaggerated his deficiencies. Stanton mistakenly believed, in his methodical, civilian thinking, that all supplies listed as delivered to the Army of the Potomac got to their destination. He had failed to realize, until he sent an assistant to survey the supply situation, that rear-area troops appropriated substantial quantities of matériel consigned to combat forces. To Stanton's credit, he had immediately replenished the dwindled stocks and in good time for McClellan to move if he had wanted to do so.[6]

Stanton was so irate at Lincoln for not dismissing McClellan that he failed to notice signs that the President's almost infinite patience had about played out. McClellan unhurriedly crossed the Potomac at long

[5] Stanton to Greeley, Oct. 4, 1862, Lincoln Papers, IU; Halleck to wife, Oct. 7, 1862, in *Collector*, XXI, 53; *O.R.*, XIX, pt. 1, 8; pt. 2, 72; McClellan, *Own Story*, 613–14; Gorham, *Stanton*, II, 66; Flower, *Stanton*, 194–5; Morse, *Welles Diary*, I, 160–1; Andrews, *op. cit.*, 315.

[6] T. A. Scott to H. J. Jewett, Feb. 19, 1880, and to McClellan, same date, McClellan Papers, LC; Kamm, *op. cit.*, 148–9; *O.R.*, XIX, pt. 1, 7–9; pt. 2, 416, 492–3.

last, almost six weeks after being directed to do so, and then reposed again. When he allowed Lee to move toward Richmond unopposed, Lincoln resolved to remove him. But he decided to await the outcome of the fall elections.

By this time standpat Democrats looked to McClellan for leadership to "bestride these lilliputians" and to inaugurate a new, conservative era. The general listened to this theme in a receptive mood, writing to his wife on October 31 that "I think it will end in driving Stanton out. . . . If I can crush him I will—relentlessly and without remorse." To bring this about, McClellan authorized Barlow and the *World* clique again to "open your batteries" on Stanton "as soon as you please." But McClellan's dreams of vengeance were far afield from reality.

Lincoln was convinced at last that in addition to failing to crush Lee, McClellan as commander of the army was a threat to the survival of civil authority over the military. The last state election took place on November 5; the next day Lincoln directed Halleck to remove McClellan "forthwith, or as soon as he may deem proper." Stanton persuaded Halleck to act "forthwith," and an order went out by special courier after Burnside agreed to take the command.

McClellan and his soldiers took the dismissal with good grace, although there were a few spontaneous demonstrations. But only when Stanton felt sure that there would be no trouble did he release the announcement to the press. Halleck joined him in worriedly watching the effect of the news, and—of comfort to Stanton—in the conviction that McClellan's supersedure was "a matter of absolute necessity." "In a few more weeks," Halleck confided to his wife, "he would have broken down the government." [7]

The long joust between McClellan and Stanton had reached an end at last. How had Stanton acquitted himself? In his heart he knew that he need not be ashamed of his role. When his old friend the Reverend Heman Dyer asked Stanton whether there was any truth to the charge that he was willfully hindering McClellan, the Secretary, in evident distress of spirit, replied that there was not. He swore to God that he had entered Lincoln's cabinet as McClellan's "sincere friend," and though he soon began to doubt the general's ability, he "hoped on." The move to the Peninsula proved to be the most hazardous, the most expensive, and the most protracted that could have been devised, but

[7] Halleck in *Collector*, XXI, 53; Lincoln, *Works*, V, 486; Oct. 31, 1862, ms "Extracts from Letters to Wife," McClellan Papers, LC; T. J. Barnett to Barlow, Sept. 19, and Marcy to same, Sept. 21, 1862, Barlow Papers, HL.

not being a military man, he had acquiesced in the decision and done everything he could to aid him. When McClellan left Washington exposed to seizure by the enemy, however, Stanton had deemed it his duty to take measures for its safety. Otherwise, he had employed the whole power of the government to support McClellan's operations in preference to those of any other general.

Why should he wish to thwart McClellan? Stanton asked. His own reputation descended at McClellan's failures. He was suffering under a weight of vicious criticisms, yet his every effort had been expended to strengthen the general. For his acts in the efforts to sustain this government, Stanton expected to stand before God in judgment. He never altered his conviction that if "Little Mac" remained in command, the Union's efforts for survival would be wasted in inconclusive maneuverings, until war-weariness combined with growing disaffection in the North to terminate the war on the basis of a permanently severed nation.

These sentiments, despite their occasional grandiloquence, were wholly truthful so far as Stanton's official actions were concerned. That he was McClellan's "sincere friend" at the time he entered Lincoln's cabinet is debatable, however, and he had scarcely fostered "every confidence" in McClellan when he criticized him to persons outside the government. Stanton was discreet, rather than untruthful, in not admitting his efforts to have the general removed from command. But it was the Secretary's right, even his duty, to acquaint Lincoln and other officials who were responsible for the success of the war effort with his true estimate of McClellan, and to work for his removal once convinced that he was incompetent.

It has been charged that Stanton acted from political considerations in opposing McClellan and that he was the mouthpiece and ally of the radicals. The evidence fails to support such a charge. Though he shared many of the radicals' political opinions, he needed no prompting from them in trying to get rid of McClellan. It had been evident to Stanton from the time he entered the War Department that the North could win only by taking the offensive; the task demanded generals with the will to fight relentless, offensive war. And McClellan, who fought only when a battle was forced upon him, was simply not the man for the job.

No dearth of war materials handicapped McClellan, and whenever troops were withheld from him the decision was Lincoln's, not Stanton's. When Stanton stopped recruiting, it was through bad judgment, not treachery. Until Halleck came to Washington, Stanton counseled Lincoln on troop placements and strategy, but Lincoln often disagreed with him, and Lincoln called the shots. In whatever degree interference from Washington, rather than McClellan's own lethargy and incompetence, brought about the general's undoing, Lincoln, not Stanton, was at fault. On the personal side, McClellan had ample reason to complain of Stanton's conduct, but officially Stanton did his full duty.

Stanton was human enough to take pleasure in McClellan's fall from power, and he gloated over it to ordnance officer Balch. That soldier's wife, later repeating an account of this conversation, reflected Stanton's feelings in these terms: "How wonderfully McClellan has disappeared from public view! The *Herald* it is true and papers of that ilk cry him up, and will not allow good in any one else. But his day has passed, as that of Frémont and various others." [8] But, Stanton worried, would Burnside, Lincoln and Halleck's choice to succeed McClellan in command of the dispirited Army of the Potomac, be an improvement?

And would matters shape up better in the West as well? There, shortly before the ax fell on McClellan, Buell, in Kentucky, was also dropped. Like McClellan, his close friend, to whom he owed his appointment, Buell was a good organizer. But years of peacetime service in the adjutant general's office had smothered the fire in his heart and bound him around with system. Gruff and unapproachable, a rigid disciplinarian, he rarely praised his officers or men, and they detested him. No general in the Union Army showed a tenderer regard for slaveowners.

When Braxton Bragg invaded Kentucky about the time Lee penetrated Maryland, Stanton persuaded Lincoln to replace Buell, recommending General George H. Thomas, a Virginian and, like Stanton, a Democrat. But Halleck induced Lincoln to give Buell another chance. Buell caught up with Bragg at Perryville, where a bloody fight took place. Both sides claimed a victory. But when Bragg withdrew into eastern Tennessee, Buell, instead of following him, decided to return to Nashville and begin new preparations for an advance on Chattanooga. Halleck warned him that Lincoln would tolerate no further delay. When Buell ignored this admonition, Lincoln decided again to remove him, a move Stanton had advocated for two months.

Stanton had no voice in the selection of William S. Rosecrans as Buell's successor; the choice was Halleck's, seconded by Chase. The fact that the new general, an Ohioan and a West Pointer, who had

[8] Harriet Balch to her mother, May 4, 1863, George T. Balch Papers, UCB; to Dyer, in Gorham, *Stanton*, I, 426–32; Ropes memo, Feb. 1870, of conversation with Stanton, Sept. 1869, Woodman Papers, MHS, repeats the Dyer letter theme.

served with both McClellan and Grant since rejoining the Army, was an influential Roman Catholic layman and that his brother had recently been chosen Catholic bishop of the Cincinnati diocese, was not lost upon the political-minded Chase. Donn Piatt, who happened to be in the War Department when Rosecrans's appointment was announced, declared that Stanton, turning to him abruptly, snarled: "Well, you have your choice of idiots; now look out for frightful disasters." But like all of his recollections, this one too needs to be taken with a qualification that Piatt was prone to misstate facts and to distort personalities. In any case, Stanton did not oppose the Rosecrans appointment; he had met Rosecrans earlier that year, and the two men enjoyed a pleasant and lengthy interview, smoking and chatting intimately over a wide range of subjects. "You may consider this the beginning of good luck," Stanton had said, according to Rosecrans's account.[9] Whether these new appointments would bring "good luck" or not was now up to the generals, not to Stanton.

[9] Piatt, *op. cit.*, 81; Rosecrans to wife, April 11, 1862, Rosecrans Papers, UCLA; *O.R.*, XVI, pt. 2, 623, 652; XXIII, pt. 2, 552.

CHAPTER XI

DISCOURAGED
BUT NOT DESPAIRING

T HROUGHOUT the summer of 1862, Stanton's enemies had swooped in to press for his dismissal. They exploited the McClellan issue, the allegations of Stanton's inefficiency in providing adequate medical care and weapons for the armies, and, increasing in significance, the question of the fate of the Negro. Stanton's future depended entirely upon Lincoln's confidence in him. Stanton felt that the nation's future hinged on his ability to swing Lincoln toward a proper decision on the Negro question.

Lincoln's outstanding characteristic as President was his capacity for growth: adapting himself, other men, and a multitude of measures to altered circumstances. He never lost sight of his primary goal, a restored Union. In that clear vision he saw that there were alternate approaches to the question of the Negro's destiny. But he, like Stanton, sensed that there was no way to final success that must not first be hewed out by the Union's soldiers.

When Stanton joined the cabinet, Seward, Bates, Welles, Smith, and Blair were convinced that the Negro question must be avoided so far as possible in order to keep the support of Southern Unionists and Northern conservatives. Chase alone represented the radical wing of the Republican party, which insisted that it was senseless to combat a rebellion while upholding the evil that had caused it.

As a war Democrat, Stanton had made himself acceptable to Republican moderates and radicals alike. During his first few months in the war office members of both groups as well as his erstwhile Democratic friends thought that his views on the Negro problem were in accord with their own. What becomes more and more manifest, however, is that Stanton's rapport with the Buchanan-Breckinridge Democratic faction had been a marriage of convenience. Thus his natural inclination was to support Chase inside the cabinet and to cooperate with the Wade-Chandler-Stevens cabal in Congress, an inclination that took on the utility of expediency when the current of Northern opinion began to veer unmistakably their way, and because the co-operation of these congressmen was absolutely necessary if the Army was to get needed appropriations and recruitment legislation.

He certainly regarded the President as overly cautious on the Negro question. But Cameron's fate reminded him that it was expedient to conform, at least outwardly, to Lincoln's wishes. It was a situation to tempt this single-minded man, responsible for the primary instrument for the winning of the war—the Army—to see to this goal with every means at hand.

It was in the success and welfare of the Army that Lincoln and Stanton found their first identity of interest, and it became a lasting tie between the two men, although not the only one. Lincoln appreciated the fact that Stanton was also able to grow and yet bend his convictions to his chief's decisions. And, in different ways, both men were deeply mystical. Although Stanton gave an impression of stern practicality, he had after all grown up in an atmosphere of antislavery convictions and rapturous spiritualism. His early religious experiences and his reactions to family tragedies, the fact that it was in a church that he had met Mary Lamson and that another house of worship offered him his first view of Ellen Hutchison, should not be forgotten.

Now Stanton was pouring his acquired skills as an organizer into the growing Union armies. But, deliberately hidden from almost everyone, he was also pouring out his heart. Though he had once detested militarism, the Army to him came to achieve the same kind of mystical symbolism as the Union itself. News of the brutal murder of his friend General Robert McCook, the brother of his former law partner, who was seized by rebel guerrillas while he lay ill in an army ambulance and slain in cold blood, touched Stanton's deepest feelings. If Negro slavery impeded the forward march of Union troops, then he had no question in his mind or heart which must give way.

He quickly learned that wherever federal troops appeared in the loyal slaveholding states and in the enclaves of territory which Union arms had already wrested from Dixie, they acted as a disturbing and disintegrating force upon the institution of slavery. Northern soldiers, most of whom had no love for Negroes, equated slave ownership with disloyalty, coming thus simply to the heart of the matter. It was no accident that Stanton ordered the tracks of the vital Pennsylvania Railroad to be closely guarded in slaveholding Maryland, whereas the line in free-soil Pennsylvania was unprotected.

Stanton's estrangement from McClellan pushed him further along toward support of a strong policy concerning the Negro. McClellan had consistently asserted that the war must not alter existing race relations, that the Army must remain outside the controversy. But Stanton soon saw that it could not hold aloof.

Slaves brought the armies information and sought refuge in Union camps. The troops befriended and protected them whether their orders allowed it or not. Not that the soldiers for the most part were moved by humanitarian motives of racial equality. It was enough for the Union soldier that Negroes were valuable rebel property and that the South, deprived of their services, could not hope to win the war. The North, conversely, might win in less time and with less human cost if black laborers and black soldiers could add their strength to the effort. This attitude on the part of many Union soldiers received forceful expression in the matter of fugitive slaves.

During the early months of the war it was Lincoln's policy to have no policy with respect to runaway slaves who made their way into Union lines. This was a problem falling within the category of camp police regulations as defined by prewar practices, and each commander did as he chose about it.

Few followed McClellan's course of scrupulous regard for Southern property, human or otherwise. Sympathy for the Negro communicated itself from soldiers to their families, as well as through the reverse path, and thence to state officials and to members of Congress. General W. A. Gorman, for example, wrote Senator Wilson that "if rebels or anybody else get a slave returned to their master during this rebellion, they will have to find some other instrument to perform the work than myself. . . . Every fugitive slave that has come to my Brigade, has been fed & cared for, as we understand the order of the War Department." George Bancroft advised his son, an officer with McClellan, that "opinion is fast spreading that the negroes must be available in the service. If they come to you, use them, & reward them with freedom." And Lincoln's old friend Leonard Swett heard from an Illinois soldier that "the tendency of public opinion in the army is very radical. . . . You cannot be too ultra for the soldiers." [1]

---

[1] Gorman to Wilson, Dec. 22, 1861, Wilson Papers, LC; Bancroft to son, July 17, 1862, Bancroft-Bliss Papers, LC; to Swett, Oct. 1, 1862, in "Civil War Letters of

Stanton, aware of these developments, approved Butler's policy in New Orleans of declaring the fugitives to be contraband—property liable to confiscation under the laws of war—and using them as laborers. But this halfway position outraged Northern conservatives and failed to satisfy the radicals, while it put the loyal slaveholders of the vital border states into an awkward position. These considerations inspired Stanton and his cabinet colleagues, as Welles recalled, to put "no more . . . on paper than was necessary" concerning Butler's policy, and to use oral rather than written messages to other Union commanders when suggesting that they emulate it.

This clumsy compromise barely sufficed as policy in occupied rebel areas and was advisory, not mandatory, everywhere. But no approved course of action existed at all regarding runaway Negroes claimed by border-state owners willing to prove their loyalty by swearing to an oath of allegiance. Prewar federal law required—and the wartime predilections of some army officers, such as McClellan, Halleck, and Buell, inspired—the return of escaped slaves to their masters. The Union's armies could become slave-catching agencies if particular commanders wished them to. Popular concern over this subject reflected the realization that the real issue of the war was the Negro question.[2] Stanton, who like Lincoln could grow, came to understand that the question of the Army's role in relation to slavery could not be long avoided. McClellan rejected this view. Part of his conflict with Stanton rested on this base. And the interaction of the North's soldiers with the South's slaves brought the President and the War Secretary into substantial accord.

As the Army and Stanton moved closer to the radical position on the Negro, he tried to take Lincoln with him, even to the point of acting guilefully to put the President in a position where circumstances might force a consent to emancipation and the use of Negro troops. Something had to be done.

In July 1861, the House of Representatives had passed a resolution stating that no soldier need capture or return fugitive slaves. Then a Confiscation Act of August 8 authorized the seizure and condemnation in the federal courts of property put to rebel use, and declared forfeited all claims to the labor of slaves used in aid of the rebellion. But as

---

W. W. Orme," ISHS *Journal*, XXIII, 254. On McCook, see New York *Tribune*, Aug. 23, 1862.

[2] Welles, "The History of Emancipation," *Galaxy*, XIV, 839; Butler, *Correspondence*, II, 37–8; Flower, *Stanton*, 184; Randall, *Constitutional Problems Under Lincoln* (rev. ed., Urbana, 1951), 342–70.

interpreted by such cautious officers as Attorney General Bates, these enactments by no means voided the fugitive slave law. The executive branch of the government was clearly bringing up the rear on the Negro issue, with the Army as its only outthrust salient.

In default of executive action, Congress again took up the matter and on March 13, 1862, enacted a new article of war that prohibited officers, on penalty of dismissal from the service, from aiding in the capture or return of runaway slaves of disloyal masters. Stanton, as shall be shown, instigated a second Confiscation Act, which Lincoln signed on July 17, 1862, and it went further: fugitive, captured, and abandoned slaves of rebels were declared free, and the President could employ Negroes for the suppression of the rebellion, in such numbers and manner of organization as he judged necessary. It was a cautious way for Stanton and radical congressmen to empower Lincoln to enroll Negroes as soldiers and push him toward a willingness to use the power.

For the present, Lincoln chose to use them only as noncombatant laborers. To put arms in the hands of former slaves—to use black men to kill white men—had more explosive potentialities than emancipation itself.

Almost from the time he became Secretary of War, Stanton was far ahead of Lincoln in his thinking on the matter of utilizing Negroes in the war effort. As early as April 1862, newspapers reported that Stanton was considering the use of Negroes as garrison troops in the less healthful parts of the South, and that a colorful Zouave uniform, including scarlet trousers, had already been chosen for the "sable arm."

Soon after this, General O. M. Mitchell wrote to Stanton that in two instances he owed his own safety to the faithfulness of Negroes, and had thereupon promised protection to every slave who brought him information, regardless of orders to the contrary issued by Buell, his department commander. Stanton revealed his personal feelings in the matter by responding: "The assistance of slaves is an element of military strength, which, under proper regulations, you are fully justified in employing for your security and the success of your operations. It has been freely employed by the enemy, and to abstain from its judicious use when it can be employed to military advantage would be a failure to employ means to suppress the rebellion and restore the authority of the government." [3]

[3] The Mitchell-Stanton exchange, and the newspaper items, are in Dudley Taylor Cornish, *The Sable Arm* (New York, 1956), 31–3; Bates to Gov. A. W. Bradford, May 10, 1862, Letterbook B–5, 92, RG 60, NA.

As soon as Congress passed the second Confiscation Act, Stanton asked Francis Lieber, a German-born scholar devoted to the Union cause, now teaching law at Columbia College, to prepare suggestions on the use of Negroes "that come to our armies for support or protection." Lieber's study, submitted early in August 1862, concluded that Union policy and sentiment required a constructive, humanitarian employment of fugitive Negroes in the Union Army as armed menials, and insisted that the South would benefit from any delay in such utilization.

But Stanton was moving ahead of the idea of using Negroes only as soldierly laborers. Early in September, he had Holt appointed Judge Advocate General of the Army, and asked him to prepare an opinion on the government's rights and duties under the second Confiscation Act, to counter Bates's views and perhaps to have arguments at hand to bring Lincoln to his viewpoint. Holt had announced his conversion to emancipation before his appointment; his report to Stanton recommended an unqualified use of Negro troops as fighting men. Holt recalled years later that Stanton, "in one of those unreserved conversations which we occasionally had upon the absorbing questions of the day, . . . declared . . . with the vehemence which often characterized him in the discussion of such topics, that the war could never be successfully closed for the government, without the employment of colored troops in the field." Holt correctly felt that Stanton had been advocating such a policy for some time.[4] Indeed, Stanton had already allowed one Union general, David Hunter, to arm Negroes without Lincoln's knowledge and with his own implied consent.

In March 1862, Stanton had sent Hunter to take command of the Department of the South, where Union control was limited to Hilton Head, North Carolina, and the neighboring coastal area. Hunter's force was small, and, finding many brawny young Negroes within his lines and noting that his predecessor's orders from Secretary Cameron authorized the employment of "loyal persons" in any manner that circumstances might call for, he began arming and training colored soldiers, and then ordered that all slaves in his command be freed. It was the same sort of unauthorized action that Frémont had taken earlier in Missouri. The news of it reached Washington in mid-May and broke like a thunderclap. Without discussing the matter with the

---

[4] Holt in Wilson, "Jeremiah S. Black and Edwin M. Stanton," *loc. cit.*, 470–1; on Holt's abolitionism, Mary Bernard Allen, *Joseph Holt* (Ph.D. thesis, University of Chicago, 1927) ; Lieber's memorandum and a relevant letter to Halleck, Aug. 10, 1862, are in Lieber Papers, HL.

cabinet, Lincoln rescinded Hunter's order, and Stanton helped him prepare the text of the annulment.

Hunter's action brought him under the scrutiny of Congress. Venerable Charles A. Wickliffe, a Union Democratic representative from Kentucky, asked Stanton by private letter whether Hunter's enlistment of Negroes was sanctioned by the War Department. Receiving no answer, he wrote again, whereupon an assistant secretary responded that the query had been brought to Stanton's attention and would be answered in due course.

Still no reply was forthcoming; so Wickcliffe obtained passage of a resolution directing Stanton to inform the House concerning the acceptability of Hunter's policy to the War Department. Brought to bay, Stanton responded that he had no "official" information about Hunter's Negro regiment, and had ordered Hunter to report to him on the matter.

Hunter was delighted to make the occasion of his report to Stanton an excuse for an impudent apologia. No fugitive slaves were enlisted in his department, he reported. "There is, however, a fine regiment of persons whose late masters are 'fugitive rebels,'" which was eager to go "in full and effective pursuit of their fugacious and traitorous proprietors."

The general stated that it was his "painful duty" to assert that he had never received any specific authority from the War Department to issue clothes and arms to his Negro regiment. But he deemed himself authorized to enlist as well as outfit the regiment by Secretary Cameron's instructions to his predecessor. If other duties had not intervened, he concluded defiantly, he would have raised not merely one but five or six such regiments, for the experiment had been "a complete and marvelous success." By autumn he hoped to have 48,000 or 50,000 Negroes under arms.

Stanton communicated Hunter's response to Wickliffe without comment, which seemed a gratuitous insult to the congressman. The enraged Kentuckian denounced Stanton's uncommunicativeness as an implied endorsement of the general's sarcastic statements, and accused Stanton of complicity in a policy that would stamp the Union cause with infamy and call down the wrath of Christendom.

At this point Congressman Robert Mallory, of Kentucky, came to Stanton's defense. He felt sure that Hunter had acted without authorization, he declared, because only three or four weeks previously Stanton had informed him and two other border-state congressmen that he had ordered the arrest of an officer who had asked for authority to arm Negroes. Implacable Thad Stevens's jaw dropped in amazement at Mallory's statement; he had expected Stanton to assume full responsibility for Hunter's action and had evidently been misled concerning Stanton's opinions. Congressman Charles Ingersoll, of Pennsylvania, formerly an admirer of Stanton, hastened to inform Governor Andrew that such "miserable duplicity" as Stanton's "ought to damn any man however high," and the antislave Republicans should trust him no longer.[5]

Newspapers played a guessing game, seeking the truth of the matter; and editor James Gordon Bennett in the New York *Herald* speculated that cabinet differences respecting Hunter's proclamation might cause the ax to fall on Stanton for conniving with Hunter and trying to force the President's hand. The editorial elicited a reply from Lincoln.

Lincoln, marking his letter "private," assured Bennett that he was wrong about Stanton. "He mixes no politics whatever with his duties; knew nothing of Gen. Hunter's proclamation; and he and I alone got up the counter-proclamation. I wish this to go no further than to you, while I do wish to assure you that it is true."

But was it true that Stanton had known nothing about Hunter's proclamation—that he had no intimation that Hunter might be planning some such action? Some months before this, Hunter had written to Stanton, on January 29, from his previous command post at Fort Leavenworth: "Please let me have my way on the subject of slavery. The Administration will not be responsible. I alone will bear the blame; you can censure me, arrest me, dismiss me, hang me if you will, but permit me to make my mark in such a way as to be remembered by friend and foe."

Similarly, though Stanton may have had no "official" information that Hunter was arming Negroes, he had reason to know that something of that nature was afoot, for no sooner had Hunter arrived at Hilton Head in July than he asked for authority to arm "such loyal men as I can find in the country, whenever, in my opinion, they can be used advantageously against the enemy." Hunter left no room for doubt as to what he meant by "loyal men." It was important to be able to distinguish them, he said, and for that purpose he requested 50,000 pairs of scarlet pantaloons, "and this is all the clothing I shall

---

[5] Ingersoll to Andrew, July 7, 1862, Andrew Papers, MHS; *Congressional Globe*, 37th Cong., 2d sess., 3121–8; *Letter of the Secretary of War*, Sen. Exec. Doc. 67, 37th Cong., 2d sess.; Lincoln, *Works*, V, 219–23; Chase, *Diary*, 99; *O.R.*, ser. 3, II, 147–8, 196–8.

require for these people." [6] Stanton also received what amounted to official information of what Hunter was doing when copies of Hunter's order to enlist Negroes, accompanied by protests from Treasury agents managing plantations in the area, were forwarded to him by Chase.

After the war, Hunter asserted that he enlisted Negroes (and presumably issued his emancipation edict) on his own responsibility, for Stanton would not take an open stand or authorize pay for the black soldiers. But silence on the part of Stanton, after he had received Hunter's Fort Leavenworth letter and his request for scarlet pantaloons, might very well have been interpreted by the general as implied consent to go ahead. Furthermore, Stanton, in denying any complicity in Hunter's actions, in permitting Hunter himself to answer Wickliffe's queries, and in submitting Hunter's answer to the congressional inquiries without comment, allowed him to take full responsibility for his actions, as the general had promised to do. Nor is it without significance that Hunter chose to adorn his Negro soldiers with pantaloons of the same color that newspapers had credited Stanton with favoring for Negro soldiers only three weeks earlier. And, finally, while the tempest surrounding his actions was still at its height, Hunter had the temerity, or the confidence in Stanton's reaction, again to make a formal request to the War Department for authority to recruit "all loyal men to be found in my department" as an infantry force.

Further evidence of Stanton's sympathetic attitude toward Hunter is afforded by a statement of General Townsend, who claimed that in the early spring the Secretary showed him a military proclamation, in his own penmanship, declaring that all slaves and other property of persons in rebellion had been forfeited to the United States, and instructing all commanders to regard the slaves as free men. "There was so much commotion over military orders declaring certain blacks free," wrote Townsend, "that Mr. Stanton, wholly out of consideration for Mr. Lincoln, dropped his proclamation and instigated the [second] Confiscation Act which accomplished the same result with less friction."

On July 21, 1862, after this second Confiscation Act gave Lincoln legal authorization to use Negroes in any capacity he saw fit, Hunter informed Stanton that the withdrawal of a large number of his troops

[6] Lincoln, *Works*, V, 255; *O.R.*, VI, 263-4; ser. 3, II, 50-60; Hunter to Stanton, Jan. 29, 1862, Stanton MSS.

to reinforce McClellan had put him in a precarious position and again asked, as already noted, permission to recruit colored soldiers. Stanton brought up the request in a cabinet meeting, where Chase and Seward joined him in endorsing it. But Lincoln declared that he was not yet willing to arm Negroes.

The significant point is that Lincoln thought the moment, not the idea, unpropitious. Halleck, who joined in cabinet discussions on this subject immediately after arriving in Washington, remembered that all agreed that Negroes must serve in the Union cause. "And the only point of doubt," Halleck later informed Lieber, "was in regard to the *time* of doing this." Lincoln thought some delay necessary in order to assure the co-operation of white soldiers and to prepare the public mind. But this was not known to the public, and the Hunter affair seemed proof that Stanton was at odds with Lincoln.[7]

Actually, the President was contemplating a general emancipation as well as the mere employment of a limited number of blacks as soldiers, as he privately advised Stanton. On May 28, Stanton predicted to Sumner that a decree of emancipation would be issued within two months. While driving to the funeral of Stanton's baby with Welles and Seward on July 13, Lincoln brought the emancipation possibility up to them. Welles later remembered Lincoln's saying that this was "the first occasion when he had mentioned the subject to any one." But either Welles's memory played him false or else Lincoln, to prevent jealousy, did not want them to know that Stanton had been his earlier confidant on this subject.

On July 22, the day after Lincoln declined to approve Hunter's request to enlist Negroes, Francis Brockholst Cutting, a New York lawyer who had been a rabid proslavery Democrat, called on Stanton. The Secretary told him that slavery, the cause of sectional troubles, must be wiped out in order to weaken the enemy and to rally the ever increasing number of antislavery people in the North to a more vigorous support of the war effort.

Somewhat to Stanton's surprise, Cutting agreed with him. Stanton asked him if he would be willing to talk to Lincoln—a free expression of opinion from a onetime proslavery Democrat such as Cutting might go far toward convincing the President that loyal Northern Democrats were now more willing to support an antislavery program than was

[7] Flower, *Stanton*, 184; Chase, Diary, 96; *Report of the Military Services of Gen. David Hunter, U.S.A., during the War of the Rebellion* (New York, 1873), 20; *O.R.*, XIV, 363; Halleck to Lieber, Oct. 15, 1865, Lieber Papers, HL.

generally supposed. Cutting readily assented, and Stanton took him to Lincoln's office, where he left the two men alone.

Cutting talked with Lincoln for two hours. He pointed out the desirability of emancipation as a deterrent to recognition of the Confederacy by foreign governments, and the growing impatience of people of antislavery convictions, the group on which Lincoln must chiefly rely for support in winning the war. Lincoln urged the necessity of holding the border states in line. Cutting responded that they could never be relied on and were disloyal at heart; their congressmen would not even accept the offer of compensated emancipation that Lincoln had been urging upon them almost from the beginning of the war.[8] Apparently this meeting which Stanton arranged helped Lincoln reach a fateful decision.

The regular cabinet meeting took place later that day, and the question of arming Negroes was again brought up. "The impression left upon my mind by the whole discussion was," Chase wrote, "that while the President thought that the organization, equipment, and arming of negroes would be productive of more evil than good, he was not unwilling that commanders should, at their discretion, arm for purely defensive purposes, slaves coming within their lines." But on the matter of emancipation Lincoln was now ready to go further than most members of his cabinet had suspected. Taking a sheet of paper from his pocket, he read a proclamation that on January 1, 1863, all slaves in states still in rebellion were to be forever free.

Stanton favored Lincoln's issuing the proclamation at once. Chase, more surprised than anyone, said the measure went beyond anything he had contemplated. He thought it would be better to allow generals to organize and arm Negroes quietly, and to proclaim emancipation in local areas. Stanton recorded, in a memo he made at the meeting, that Chase "thinks it [emancipation] a measure of great danger, and would lead to universal emancipation," unsettling the government's fiscal position.

Seward favored enlisting Negro troops but argued strenuously against emancipation. It would induce foreign nations to intervene in the war, he said, because their cotton supply would be endangered. Lincoln should announce emancipation only when the war took a turn for the better, so that it might be heralded by a victory, attended by "fife and drum and public spirit."[9]

[8] Cutting to E. L. Stanton, Feb. 20, 1867, Stanton MSS; Sumner to Andrew, May 28, 1862, Andrew Papers, MHS; Morse, *Welles Diary*, I, 70–1.

[9] Nicolay and Hay, *Lincoln*, VI, 128; Chase, *Diary*, 99–100.

According to the unsupported testimony of Frank B. Carpenter, the artist, who claimed to have obtained the information from Lincoln himself, the President was so impressed by Seward's argument that he decided to withhold the proclamation until a more propitious time. Though Carpenter did not say so specifically, it has been inferred that Lincoln reached this decision before leaving the cabinet meeting. But there is evidence to indicate that Lincoln left the meeting undecided, chiefly because of Chase's opposition; that after giving the matter further thought he decided to issue the proclamation the next day; and that the delay afforded Seward an opportunity to bring a new influence to bear upon Lincoln in the person of Thurlow Weed.

Having talked to Lincoln before the cabinet meeting, Cutting saw him again that afternoon. Lincoln told him he intended to issue the proclamation the next day. But that night Weed got to Lincoln and persuaded him to change his mind, arguing that the proclamation could not be enforced and that it would be folly to make an empty gesture that would offend the border slave states.

A letter from Count Gurowski, a State Department translator, to Governor Andrew confirms Cutting's statement that the emancipation edict had been sidetracked through the interposition of Weed. Another letter, from Wolcott, who had, through Stanton, secondhand knowledge of what happened at the cabinet meeting, confirms the view that Chase, the most radical of all the cabinet members, was chiefly responsible for staying Lincoln's hand. Wolcott wrote Pamphila: "We all plied him [Chase] so vigorously, that he came round next morning, but Seward had worked so industriously, in the meantime that for the present at least,—that golden moment has passed away, and *Chase* must be held responsible for delaying or defeating the greatest act of justice, statesmanship and civilization, of the last four thousand years." [1] Whatever Chase or Stanton felt concerning freedom for the Negro, by the second year of the war it was only a matter of timing, and in the cabinet Stanton's position was clear.

With Lincoln reluctant to exercise the authority to enlist Negro troops which Congress had granted him, Union commanders continued to follow their own predilections. Having had his fingers scorched in Hunter's case, Stanton was now careful to keep his own counsel on the issue of colored soldiers. Lincoln maintained the policy

[1] Smith, *Garfield*, I, 238; Wolcott and Cutting in Wolcott MS, 186; Gurowski to Andrew, Aug. 5, 1862, Andrew Papers, MHS; Carpenter, *Six Months at the White House* (New York, 1867), 20–2.

of no policy; so Stanton, obedient to the President's wishes, dealt with each case on its merits, and held off impetuous radicals who insisted on the immediate employment of black soldiers throughout the Army.

When swashbuckling Jim Lane, commanding in Kansas, advertised in newspapers for black recruits and wired Stanton that he was "receiving Negroes under the late act of Congress," Stanton informed him that only Lincoln's authorization could permit the enlistment of Negroes and that the President disapproved of Lane's orders. But Lane ignored the rebuke from far-off Washington and by the end of October had two Negro regiments in being. Journalists persistently questioned Stanton concerning the fate of colored units forming in Kansas, Rhode Island, Massachusetts, and other places. He dodged the issue, stating that he would not muster them into service but that they might find employment in "some local use." [2]

Stanton authorized General Rufus Saxton, who had been assigned to Hunter's department to recruit a Negro labor force, to enlist 5,000 black volunteers to guard plantations and settlements within the Union lines and to protect Negro workers from attack by former masters. He reminded the general that by act of Congress all slaves entering the service of the United States, along with their wives, mothers, and children, were to be forever free: "You and all your command will so treat and regard them."

The Secretary wondered, however, how various generals would carry out the new policy. There was no simple answer. Modern concepts of administrative uniformity do not apply in the Civil War; the responsibilities of generals to the President and Secretary of War were ambiguous and exceedingly flexible. Scorn for the civilian Secretary had been a fixture of professional martial mores for seventy years, and Stanton's driving energy had not yet eradicated that attitude, although the presence in the army higher command of numerous recent appointees from civilian life had injected a whole new set of relationships between the military and the civilian authorities. No one knew with any degree of certainty what these relationships were.

Under Stanton's orders, Grant employed refugee Negroes as laborers, teamsters, and quartermaster workers. In Missouri, where Frémont's earlier activities had split Unionists into rival factions,

[2] *O.R.*, ser. 3, II, 445; Watson to Gurowski, March 22, 1863, Gurowski MSS, LC; Gurowski, *Diary*, II, 104, 133; Quarles, *op. cit.*, 113–14.

Stanton, for once disobeying Lincoln, who wanted to go very slowly on this tender issue, ordered that the confiscation legislation be enforced. Because local partisanship in that harassed state continually entangled the Army in personal and political quarrels, which no one in Washington could predict or prevent, Lincoln suspended the order.

One of Butler's generals, West Point graduate John W. Phelps, a hard-driving Vermont abolitionist, commanding near New Orleans, began to organize slaves as soldiers. Butler informed Stanton that Phelps "intends making this a test case for the policy of the government," and asked for instructions.

Stanton, again obedient to Lincoln, answered that the President held to the opinion that under the laws of Congress fugitive Negroes must not be returned to disloyal masters, and that the laws of humanity demanded that they be fed and cared for. Those capable of labor should be put to work and paid wages. "In directing this to be done," wrote Stanton, "the President does not mean, at present, to settle any general rule in respect to slaves or slavery, but simply to provide for the particular case under the circumstances in which it is now presented." [3]

Butler, a former Democrat, held the Negro in low esteem as a potential soldier, but Phelps, in defiance of both Butler and the War Department, went ahead with his plan of enlistment, and asked Butler to provide arms and accouterments. When Butler promptly denied Phelps's request and ordered him to stop drilling his colored recruits and put them to work cutting timber and digging trenches, the testy Vermonter resigned from the Army.

Meanwhile, public opinion in the North began to veer unmistakably toward the use of Negro troops, and with Chase's encouragement, Butler, a man who could change course quickly when the political winds shifted, made a deft alteration of policy. At the outbreak of the war, Governor Thomas O. Moore, of Louisiana, had organized a regiment of "Native Guards" made up of free Negroes, who were numerous in New Orleans, planning to use them in the service of the Confederacy. Persuading the members of this unit to transfer their allegiance to the Union, Butler proceeded to augment it with colored volunteers, not bothering to inquire too carefully whether a recruit had been a free man or a slave. But the idea persisted in Washington

---

[3] *Letter of the Secretary of War*, Sen. Exec. Doc. 67, 37th Cong., 2d sess.; *O.R.*, XIV, 377–8, 439–42, 486; XVII, pt. 1, 470–1; John M. Schofield, *Forty-Six Years in the Army* (New York, 1897), 57–8; Wolcott MS, 187.

that Butler still felt dubious about the fighting qualities of former bondsmen.

Stanton was not dubious. From the reports which crossed his desk he realized that the question of arming Negroes was interwoven with other issues—the status of fugitive slaves of loyal as distinguished from disloyal owners, and the Army's relationships with ostensibly loyal civil authorities in the border areas. But in his annual report for 1862, Stanton, undoubtedly with the President's approval, publicly repeated the argument which he had expressed to Lincoln in private conversations and in cabinet counsels—that rebel strength derived from slave labor and that the Union must turn black energy everywhere against the South in order to win.

If possessed of the power, Stanton would have used Negro troops in 1862 and the Army would have treated all fugitive slaves as free men regardless of the loyalty or disloyalty of the master. When a fifteen-year-old slave boy escaped in November from his "thorough loyal master" in Maryland, and army officers in the District of Columbia refused to return him, Stanton supported them. "The [Confiscation] Act of Congress," he wrote, "will not allow such an order to be given." The majority of the Union Army simply would not be slave catchers, Stanton was convinced.[4]

But individual Union commanders continued to decide local policies for themselves. Dix, commanding in Norfolk in December 1862, placed the necessity for re-establishing municipal civil government ahead of considerations of the Negro's status, and ordered that only white residents who swore loyalty to the Union might vote, and promised that the Army would protect oath takers in all their property. Dix's approach matched that of Lincoln, whose thinking at this time envisaged no change in race relations in ostensibly loyal areas and who was supporting a policy of financial compensation for slaveholders in the loyal states.

Such caution disgusted many Northerners. George Bancroft came to the real point involved when he wrote to his soldier son: "I do not approve of General Dix's proclamation, by which he saves the slaves of Norfolk . . . to their masters under the pretext of ordering an election . . . If Lincoln carries out all his projects he will leave the United States a very speckled sheep indeed, here a bit of black slave and here a bit of free."

[4] Cornish, *op. cit.*, 57–68; Stanton's endorsement in W. E. Cole to Stanton, Nov. 20, 1862, NYHS; Arnold, *op. cit.*, 573; Halleck to Lieber, Feb. 24, 1865, HL; *O.R.*, ser. 3, II, 910–12.

Stanton had but one "project"—to give his armies the power to win. Still, he now obeyed Lincoln on the question of Negro troops as in all else. But as Stanton told Edward Atkinson in June 1862, he had come to the conclusion that every day the war continued, force was added to the abolitionists' arguments. Any large number of black soldiers for Northern armies must obviously come from the border states and from the South, for the colored population of the free states was too insignificant to fill up large troop units. Thus, the labor corps of Secessia would diminish while the fighting forces of freedom grew in proportion. Southern white soldiers would be reluctant to go off to fight far from their homes from fear that the blacks about them would rise to arms under the national banner.

Accepting these arguments, Stanton passed them on to the President, ever cautious on the color question. Even as Lincoln debated the wisdom of emancipation in the South and the use of Negro troops as war policy, important Northern opinion was advancing to demand abolition in both the North and the South as a war aim.[5]

The Union Army marched in the van of Northern opinion, and Stanton and Lincoln could lose step with the preponderance of military sentiment only at the unimaginable risk of losing army support for civil policy. When a woman slave found refuge in Washington, and federal marshal Lamon jailed the hapless Negro as the first step in returning her to her self-proclaimed loyal Maryland master, the provost marshal of the District, Doster, led an infantry company to the prison and threatened to break it down. The two men took their quarrel to Lincoln, who refused to intervene, but Lincoln's guess "that if I wanted to take the woman, Lamon could not prevent it," resulted in freedom for the slave.

Minnesota soldiers on a train in "loyal" Missouri saw Negroes, under a provost guard, being taken back to masters who had sworn allegiance. The troops had no sympathy for provost marshals or for slavery; they overpowered the guard, freed the slaves, and were themselves arrested. Soon after, newspaper accounts of the incident brought on a congressional investigation. The Army in this case was caught in a squeeze. Would military discipline be upheld or must the administration suffer a deluge of public opprobrium?

Stanton saw to it that the disobedient Minnesotans were "im-

---

[5] Atkinson to "Ned," June 10, 1862, Atkinson Papers, MHS; Bancroft to son, Dec. 10, 1862, Bancroft-Bliss Papers, LC.

prisoned" in a comfortable St. Louis hotel on full rations, while he worked through his friends in Congress to have the whole unsavory matter dropped. The Negroes remained free, the soldiers were released without penalty or court-martial, but the basic question remained.

Army officers created various formulas in attempts to meet their own immediate, local needs, and indirectly complicated the question. General Buford, commanding at Cairo, Illinois, an important river junction in a deeply divided area, ordered his provosts not to receive applications from disloyal slaveowners for the return of slaves and other property. Loyal owners got army co-operation only if their slaves were willing to return to bondage. If the Negro was not willing, then the provost involved was to prevent the owner from regaining his human chattel.

Stanton approved Buford's policy, but it was only temporary and local and was unsuited to other areas and other times. He also approved Holt's decision which held that West Bogan, a Negro slave in Arkansas who murdered his master in self-defense, was responsible as a whole man for his act both under military and civil law.[6]

Little by little, the Army was making the institution of slavery a casualty of its needs. On the Negro question Stanton could go only as fast as Lincoln and the Army permitted him to proceed. But the soldiers' needs, and the need for soldiers, were pushing the North ahead on the decisions concerning emancipation and the employment of freed Negroes in military service, far faster than the radical political leaders could accomplish.

For example, the draft call of July 2 had failed to produce a sufficient number of troops; on August 4 a supplementary call was made. Stanton issued elaborate regulations for putting the draft into effect in those states that should fail to fill their quotas. The threat of conscription caused serious unrest.

One governor after another asked for a postponement of the hated draft, each of them assuring the War Department that he could fill his quota through volunteering, if granted a little more time. Stanton refused to defer the draft beyond August 15, the date originally set for it, but he permitted each governor to assume the responsibility for doing so himself. Actually, he had no alternative; he could not coerce the governors. One state and then another put off the draft—a month, two months, three months. States supplemented the federal bounties for

[6] Ms report on West Bogan, Holt Papers, LC; on Buford and the Minnesota soldiers, see *Letter of the Secretary of War*, Sen. Exec. Docs. 24 and 51, 38th Cong., 1st sess.; Doster, *op. cit.*, 26–7, on the Maryland slave.

enlistments with bounties of their own. Some of them, after exhausting all other alternatives, had to resort to a draft at last. With flagrant inequalities, the states tardily met the demands of both calls.[7]

It was becoming evident to Stanton and to Lincoln that if the war should be prolonged, volunteering and drafting by the states could not supply the needed manpower. The alternatives were a federal draft law and the enlistment of Negroes from occupied Dixie. As wars sometimes do, this one was getting out of hand. In the forge of the battlefield it was shaping the fate of the nation and of the Negro in ways which neither side had foreseen when it began. At the storm center Stanton could feel the irresistible pull of the winds, and as was his habit, he rode with them. So did Lincoln.

On Monday, September 22, it was certain that Lee had been halted at Antietam. Lincoln summoned the cabinet members to meet with him at noon. He brought along a book that the humorist Artemus Ward had sent him, and read them a chapter from it, chuckling appreciatively.

Stanton listened glumly. He felt that it was scarcely a time for nonsense. It did not occur to him that Lincoln, by relaxing for a moment, was steadying his nerves.

Lincoln put the book down and his face became grave. They all knew, he said, that for months he had been pondering the troublesome slavery question. Two weeks before, when the rebel army entered Frederick, he had made a silent promise to himself and—he hesitated —to his Maker that as soon as the enemy had been driven out of Maryland, he would issue the emancipation proclamation that he had been withholding since July. Lincoln drew a paper from his pocket. He did not want advice about whether to issue it or not, he said; he knew what each of them felt about it and had made up his own mind. True, he would have preferred a more decisive victory than Antietam with which to proclaim freedom, but he had waited long enough. He read the proclamation. It warned that in one hundred days—on January 1, 1863— all slaves in states still in rebellion were to be declared free.

Stanton offered no comment, but he undoubtedly was disappointed that Lincoln was still in favor of compensating "loyal" slaveholders and had not yet faced up to the need for employing Negroes in the Union's military services. Later that day, Watson grumbled to Dahlgren that the proclamation did not go far enough.[8]

[7] Shannon, *op. cit.*, I, 278–92; *O.R.*, ser. 3, II, 479–80.
[8] Dahlgren, *op. cit.*; Chase, *Diary*, 149–52.

McClellan, then under fire from Washington for not pursuing Lee with greater vigor, learned of the emancipation decision and thought of opposing it openly. He finally issued an order calling it to the attention of his troops, adding significantly, and with an eye cocked at a presidential nomination for himself, that in a democracy, where the civil authority was paramount, "the remedy for political errors . . . is to be found only . . . at the polls."

The War Department received reports of loud, disloyal talk around McClellan's headquarters, some of it attributed to the general himself. One of Horace Greeley's men sent Stanton accounts of these unsettling attitudes. Thanking Greeley, Stanton wrote: "The state of sentiment described by your correspondent has long been known to me & has been stimulated and fostered for twelve months against all my warnings and efforts." [9]

But the President, as already noted, decided to hold off a decision on ousting McClellan until after the fall elections were past, though Stanton argued that the administration would gain more votes than it would lose by kicking him out immediately. Stanton also insisted that Republicans everywhere would benefit if all the party's candidates stood foursquare against slavery. To that end he induced General James S. Wadsworth, a man of strong antislavery sentiments, to run for governor of New York, refusing him a field command so that he would accept the gubernatorial nomination.

Stanton was well advised in directing his attention to the state elections, for with the country sunk in discontent prospects looked bleak for the Republicans. In the Midwest this disaffection had reached a stage of near revolt, and in the southern counties of Illinois, Indiana, and Ohio, where a majority of the people were of Southern descent, secret "copperhead" societies began to work furtively and even openly against the government.

It was Lincoln's edict of emancipation that touched off this tinder pile of discontent, for although many of these people or their forebears had brought with them a hatred of slavery when they emigrated from the South, they also hated the Negro with equal vehemence. Perhaps the loosening of his bonds would permit him to come spilling as a cutthroat competitor for jobs across the Ohio into the Northwest. Stanton unwittingly gave substance to this fear when, notwithstanding a provision of the Illinois constitution forbidding the entrance of free

---

[9] To Greeley, Oct. 4, 1862, Lincoln Papers, LMU; Andrews, *op. cit.*, 315.

Negroes into that state, he ordered the commanding general at Cairo to colonize and find jobs for confiscated Negroes sent North by federal armies operating along the Mississippi.[1]

To combat this rising hostility to the government in the Midwest, Stanton authorized federal officers to arrest all persons attempting to discourage volunteering or otherwise affording aid and comfort to the enemy. As a result, hundreds of persons were taken into custody, and thus Stanton's reputation as a ruthless enforcer of internal security was cemented into history. These measures served to stiffen the attitude of resistance, and as almost all the victims were Democrats, the cry arose that the administration was attempting to stifle criticism and to destroy the opposition party. Even loyal Democrats considered Stanton's actions a threat to civil liberties and joined in the chorus of protest.

When some states found it necessary to impose a draft in order to obtain their enlistment quotas, the opposition to the administration reached a new pitch of intensity; and when decisions in state courts by certain Democratic judges threatened to render the draft laws inoperative, Lincoln, two days after issuing the preliminary Emancipation Proclamation, ordered that all persons discouraging enlistments, resisting state draft laws, or found guilty of any disloyal practice, be subject to trial by military court and denied the benefit of the writ of habeas corpus. The proclamation not only gave implied approval to the wide latitude that Stanton had already allowed himself in combating sedition, but by creating new and loosely defined offenses akin to constructive treason, gave him virtually unlimited power, subject only intermittently to the intervention of the humane and forgiving President.

It was not Stanton's nature to coddle treason. Henceforth an individual's liberty could hang on a stroke of his pen or a curt sentence from his lips. Yet although not hesitant to act sternly on mere suspicion of guilt, Stanton, except in moments of high excitement and crisis, acted with reasonable restraint. Appointing a new corps of civilian provost marshals throughout the country to enforce the new edict, he instructed them to arrest troublemakers only on the authority of a governor, a general commanding a military district, or the Judge Advocate General of the Army. His and Lincoln's harsh orders were

[1] Wood Gray, *The Hidden Civil War* (New York, 1942), 91–2, 99–100; Frank L. Klement, *The Copperheads in the Middle West* (Chicago, 1960), 1–39; Henry Greenlief Pearson, *James S. Wadsworth of Geneseo* (New York, 1913), 151; Chase to Hiram Barney, Oct. 26, 1862, Chase Papers, LC.

necessary and desirable, not only to secure adequate numbers of men for the Army but at least partially to centralize and to regularize the sprawling, undisciplinable, and irregular internal security apparatus bequeathed to Stanton by Seward and Cameron. The new regulations imposed a superficial uniformity upon Northern anti-disloyalty activities. Stanton still had to accept state and local participation in security administration, but this was a step upward from what had been in effect.

Many cases of unauthorized arrests of civilians still occurred. When they came to Stanton's notice, he ordered the parties discharged from custody. But under an authoritarian policy abuses were inevitable, frequent, and sometimes tragic. Personal animosities, political ambitions, and excessive zeal on the part of subordinates, and occasionally Stanton's own impetuosity, made innocent Americans suffer.

Early in November 1862, Stanton freed all civilian prisoners against whom no evidence existed and who were citizens of states that had filled their draft quotas, and he paroled individual offenders elsewhere on promise of good behavior. Defending his security policy, he said: "It has been the aim of the Department to avoid any encroachment upon individual rights, as far as it might be consistent with public safety and the preservation of the Government."

But the apprehensive and resentful Democrats could not see it quite that way, and during the election campaign they brought a steady drumbeat of complaint against the administration for its alleged assaults on civil rights. Many persons in the North found fault with the Emancipation Proclamation. A large number of Republican party leaders moped because of Lincoln's refusal to get rid of McClellan and for failing to prosecute the war more vigorously. As a result of the general discontent, the Republicans could scarcely have fared worse in the balloting. The Democrats took Ohio, Illinois, Indiana, New York, and Pennsylvania away from them, kept control in New Jersey, and gained a split in Wisconsin to increase their representation in Congress from 44 to 75. Stanton's hand-picked New York candidate, Wadsworth, lost decisively to Seymour. Even in those states that the Republicans carried, their majorities fell off sharply from those of 1860. They would still carry a narrow margin of 18 votes in the House, owing chiefly to Stanton's use of the Army in the border slave states to overawe opposition. It was a thundering defeat.[2]

---

[2] Lincoln, *Works*, V, 436–7; *O.R.*, ser. 3, II, 902–3; Randall, *The Civil War and Reconstruction* (New York, 1937), 600–1.

"Discouraged but not despairing," Stanton had once described himself to Greeley, and he shrugged off the despondency he felt at the Republican party's losses. At least McClellan and Buell were out of the picture, and the President had come to accept the need for emancipation.[3] Stanton hoped that oncoming events would regain for the Republican party the ground it had lost.

[3] To Greeley, Oct. 4, 1862, Lincoln Papers, LMU.

CHAPTER XII

MY WAY IS CLEAR

THE NEW commander of the Army of the Potomac, Burnside, claimed Stanton's primary attention. He was only thirty-eight years old. After graduating from West Point, he had served in the artillery near the close of the Mexican War, and then resigned from the Army to become a manufacturer and later a railroad official. Volunteering immediately on the outbreak of war, he fought at Bull Run, captured Roanoke Island on the North Carolina coast, then New Bern, and performed ably during Pope's Virginia campaign and at South Mountain. He had been slow getting into action at Antietam, through no fault of his own, Stanton believed. Friendly, open, striking in appearance, popular with fellow officers and with the troops, he seemed a promising man.[1]

On November 5, 1862, Halleck asked Burnside to report at once his plan of operations. The new commander answered that he would feint from Warrenton toward Culpeper and Gordonsville, then move his whole force to Fredericksburg and drive on to Richmond from there. Although Halleck, Stanton, and Lincoln all favored Burnside's advancing by way of Culpeper and Gordonsville, instead of merely feinting in that direction and attacking by way of Fredericksburg, Halleck on November 14 wired Burnside: "The President has just assented to your plan. He thinks that it will succeed, if you move rapidly; otherwise not."

Burnside arrived at Fredericksburg on schedule. Then a hitch

[1] Stanton's memo on Burnside, undated, *ca.* Oct., 1862, copy owned by the estate of Benjamin P. Thomas.

developed; pontoons for bridging the river had not come. It was no fault of the War Department; certain field officers had fouled things up. And Stanton heard that there were other indications that all might not be well.

After the battle of Antietam, General Joe Hooker, of Burnside's command, had been hospitalized in Washington. He was ambitious and fond of publicity. When he returned to the army, his corps was stationed near the United States Ford, some twelve miles above Fredericksburg. Hooker, on November 19, asked Stanton's permission to cross the ford and strike for Bowling Green before the enemy concentrated. He would avoid tarrying before the enemy's defensive works, "which, God knows, we had enough of under McClellan."

Hooker had no right whatever to bypass Burnside and take his case to Stanton, and his offense was all the more rank in that he had not even waited for Burnside to approve or disapprove his plan. Burnside, meanwhile, informed Hooker that he considered his plan premature. When heavy rains deluged the country, Hooker had reason to be thankful that he was not isolated on the far side of the river.

Burnside's pontoons began arriving on November 24, a week later than he had expected. The next day Stanton accompanied Lincoln to Aquia. Both of them warned Burnside that an attack at Fredericksburg would be hazardous now that Lee had concentrated his force. Burnside felt sure he would cross the river and defeat Lee, although he admitted the movement would be risky.

Their visit with Burnside favorably impressed Lincoln and Stanton, who liked his aggressive spirit. With Burnside taking hold in the East and Rosecrans ready to move decisively in Kentucky, the future seemed bright to Stanton.

But a second complaining letter from Hooker chilled Stanton's optimism. As soon as the enemy learned that the movement toward Gordonsville was no more than a feint, wrote Hooker, Burnside "should not have lost a moment in taking possession of Fredericksburg." The Union army would now be holding the town if Hooker had been allowed to have his way. Now Burnside faced a perilous undertaking.

Stanton learned that friends of Chase were rallying to Hooker as a general without political ambitions who would support Chase's aspirations to the presidency—whatever general could bring the war to a victorious close would have enormous influence. Hooker unquestionably wanted to command the Army of the Potomac and was furthering the intrigue by finding fault with Burnside. This, together with

Hooker's heavy drinking, counted against him with Stanton. But Burnside, not Hooker, received his full attention.[2]

On December 11, the Union army started to throw its pontoons across the river in the face of a galling fire. News came to the War Department on the morning of the thirteenth that the two armies had come to grips. Welles surmised from the strict censorship clamped on by Stanton that things were not going well, but little by little the news came out. Union troops had been slaughtered in futile charges against the formidable Confederate breastworks. The casualty list mounted to more than 10,000; the Confederates lost less than half that number. Burnside wanted to renew the attack the next day. His commanders argued that to do so would mean another appalling loss of life. Reluctantly he ordered the army to withdraw across the river.

Newspapers charged Stanton and Halleck with mismanaging the whole campaign by peremptorily ordering Burnside to cross the Rappahannock. Loud demands for a shake-up in the government were common.

Burnside frankly admitted that he had acted contrary to the advice of Lincoln, Stanton, and Halleck, and accepted full responsibility. The hostile press, however, asserted that Stanton forced Burnside to take the blame for the Fredericksburg fiasco. Diarist Strong, uncertain concerning the truth of this charge, feared that something would burst somewhere unless Stanton was speedily shelved. He noted that even loyal Republicans, mourning dead sons, relatives, and friends "sacrificed to the vanity and political schemes of this meddling murderous quack," felt that Stanton's "name is likely to be a hissing, till it is forgotten, and . . . Honest Old Abe must take care lest his own fare no better." [3]

Republican radicals, on the other hand, blamed Seward for the administration's shortcomings and, spurred on by Chase, met in caucus to consider a resolution calling for Seward's resignation, which they planned to present to the President. Conservative senators refused to support the resolution until, in amended form, it omitted specific mention of Seward and brought Stanton within its purview by calling for a reorganization of the cabinet. But the radicals obtained a majority of the committee that would present the resolution to the President, thus making sure that Seward would be the main target of their attack.

[2] Charles F. Benjamin, "Hooker's Appointment and Removal," *Battles and Leaders*, III, 239–43; Hooker to Stanton, Nov. 16, 19, Dec. 4, 1862, Stanton MSS; *O.R.*, XXI, 66–7, 773–4; Walter H. Hebert, *Fighting Joe Hooker* (Indianapolis, 1944), 151.

[3] Morse, *Welles Diary*, I, 191–2; *O.R.*, XXI, 66–7, 773–4; Strong, *Diary*, III, 281.

On learning of the action of the caucus, Seward tendered his resignation, and Stanton, not going quite that far, offered to tender his.

Lincoln listened to the complaints of the senatorial committeemen in a long morning meeting on December 20, then brought them back to the White House that night after arranging for all the cabinet members except Seward to be present. Neither group had expected to be confronted in person by the other. Lincoln defended the absent Seward and avowed (inaccurately) that in important matters the cabinet was consulted and acted as a unit. He asked the cabinet members to corroborate his statements. Chase, angry and embarrassed, but not daring to contradict the President in the presence of his cabinet colleagues, failed to support the senators' complaints as they had expected him to do. Blair and Bates vigorously defended Seward and denied the legislators' right to dictate to the President in the choice of his advisers. Stanton remained close-mouthed through the interview. To enter into the discussion would be to invite the conservative members of the committee to turn their fire on him.

Next morning, however, Stanton told Senator William Pitt Fessenden that the meeting "was the most impressive he had ever witnessed" and that he had been struck by the dignity and propriety exhibited by the senators and was disgusted with the cabinet; that what the senators said about the manner of doing business in the cabinet was true, "and *he* did not mean to lie about it; that he was ashamed of Chase, for he knew better." Stanton felt sure that Seward had brought about the change in the original caucus resolution in order to divert senatorial hostility to him. But he had not tendered his resignation, he said, and did not intend to be driven from the cabinet by Seward. His relationships with the Treasury head and the Secretary of State, once cordial, had noticeably cooled.

In claiming that he had not tendered his resignation, Stanton was stating the truth but creating a false impression, for he had offered to do so. And before the morning was over he would offer to do so again.

Welles was a witness to this second tender when he stopped by Lincoln's office. The President had stepped out and Stanton and Chase were there waiting for him. Welles stated emphatically that Lincoln should not accept Seward's resignation. Neither of the others offered any comment, though Welles thought "both wished to be understood as acquiescing." Lincoln came in. Chase said he was so distressed by the happenings of the previous night that he had prepared his resignation. Lincoln's eyes lighted and he reached out for the paper Chase held in his hand. Chase seemed reluctant to let go of it, but Lincoln pulled it away from him, and reading it hurriedly, stole a grin at Welles and said: "This cuts the Gordian knot."

Stanton said solemnly: "Mr. President, I informed you the day before yesterday that I was ready to tender my resignation. I wish you, sir, to consider my resignation at this time in your possession." Lincoln answered: "You may go to your Department. I don't want yours. This is all I want," and he held out Chase's letter. "This relieves me, my way is clear; the trouble is ended. I will detain neither of you longer." [4]

Lincoln saw his way clearly indeed. With the resignations of Chase and Seward in his hands he declined to accept either of them. He had foiled the scheme of the radicals, kept the factional balance of the cabinet undisturbed, vindicated his right to choose his own advisers, and won the grudging respect of the senators by his political astuteness. In short, Lincoln had performed a substantial political operation. But his patients—the cabinet, the Army, and the country—were still far from the best of health.

The intra-cabinet feuding was beyond Lincoln's power to prevent, but he let it go on much too long. Further, his willingness to let cabinet officers run their departments almost without supervision, except for the war office, had permitted vexatiously contradictory and independent policies to go on at the same time. Though Stanton and Seward had learned better, Lincoln's slipshod ways encouraged Chase and Blair to assume viceregal attitudes when it pleased them and their ambitions to do so. As an administrator, Lincoln had a long way to go to excellence and he never tried very hard to get there.

In Stanton's case this resulted in the Secretary's taking on a crushing burden of responsibility in default of Lincoln's or Halleck's assumption of it, yet having to bear with Lincoln's habit of deciding matters without consulting him. The President had brought Halleck into the Army's command structure, and though he had proved himself unwilling to lift his share, so that Stanton had to carry him in policy matters, Lincoln kept the general on. Stanton had been pressing for centralization in the command responsibility of the Army. Eight separate field forces existed. They were nominally under Halleck's control but actually were almost autonomous unless, like McClellan, the generals competed with Lincoln for power.

The Army needed a center for decisions and harmony in its command structure. While Lincoln and Stanton lacked full confidence in staff and field officers and therefore refrained from delegating total

[4] Morse, *Welles Diary*, I, 200–4; Fessenden, *op. cit.*, I, 248–9.

powers to any general, the civilians had to continue poking their noses into strategy matters. So long as no one knew what the functions of the President, Secretary of War, and commanding general were, then harmony was elusive.[5] However, the war was slowly, painfully, fitfully pushing the nation toward a military structure capable of exerting the concerted pressure needed for success.

Stanton had also continued advocating to Lincoln the need for the enlistment of Negroes into the Union armies as a military necessity and as a logical consequence of emancipation. By the end of November, Lincoln had come to agree with him. The President decided that on January 1, 1863, he would add to his Emancipation Proclamation the news that he was planning to put arms in the hands of the erstwhile slaves of rebel masters. Lincoln told his friend T. J. Barnett that he viewed this as a conservative move which by hastening peace might forestall more extreme proposals and more immediately succor loyal Southern whites. Therefore, Lincoln expected the Army's commanders to enforce strictly all the provisions of the proclamation.

Stanton saw to it that, as much as possible, generals were in command who would go along with Lincoln's policy once it was announced. This in part underlay his attacks on McClellan and other high officers, and explains the surprise move in mid-December, when Lincoln relieved Butler of command at New Orleans, putting Banks in his place. Butler had brought order to the city, but his highhanded methods nevertheless permitted corruption and had made him a controversial figure. Arriving in Washington, Butler proceeded to the White House. Lincoln received him cordially, but when Butler inquired why he had been recalled, the President referred him to Stanton. The Secretary was as close-mouthed as the President. Butler left his office bitterly aware of the swarm of rumors concerning the reasons for his dismissal. It seems most likely that he did not appear to Lincoln or to Stanton the proper man to administer the new policy with respect to Negroes.

Although the holiday season in Washington was saddened by Burnside's defeat, government officers opened their homes in traditional fashion on New Year's Day. Noah Brooks, a newspaper correspondent on close terms with Lincoln, wrote that at Stanton's "there was much elegance and profuseness of hospitality," and his "face wore no sign of

---

[5] David Davis to Leonard Swett, Nov. 26, 1862, ISHL, on cabinet; other data in Halleck to Gen. McPherson, Feb. 13, 1863, owned by Carl Sandburg; Rachel Sherman Thorndike (ed.), *The Sherman Letters* (New York, 1894), 204–5 (hereafter cited as Thorndike, *Sherman Letters*); Pendleton Herring, *The Impact of War* (New York, 1941), 151–2.

the worry that must have distressed him on that anxious, unfestive day." Emancipation and Negro enlistments were sweet words to Stanton.

Lincoln issued the proclamation, freeing all slaves in areas still in rebellion, and announcing that "such persons of suitable condition, will be received into the armed service of the United States to garrison and defend forts, positions, stations, and other places, and to man vessels of all sorts in said service." Butler, tarrying in Washington, let it be known that he concurred heartily in Lincoln's policy, and Sumner, learning this, imparted some information to him. "Mr. Stanton assured me last evening," said Sumner, "that had he known your real position with regard to the proclamation he would have cut off his right hand before he would have allowed anybody to take your place; that his fixed purpose was that on the 1st of January a general should be in command at New Orleans to whom the proclamation would be a living letter, and that, in this respect, it was natural, after the recent elections in Pennsylvania and New York, that he should look to a Republican rather than to an old Democrat."

After talking to Stanton, Sumner had gone on to see the President, who assured him that he hoped very soon to return Butler to New Orleans, thereby indicating that he and Stanton were in agreement on this matter. Soon afterward, Lincoln called Butler to the White House and proposed that he return to Louisiana and raise a Negro army there. But Butler did not wish to serve as a mere recruiting agent; he wanted to be restored to his old command.

Telling Stanton that he would like to send Butler back to New Orleans, if it could be managed without offending Banks, Lincoln remembered that Banks had wanted to lead an expedition into Texas. This would leave the way clear for Butler to take over again in New Orleans. Stanton went so far as to draw up orders effecting both of these objects. But Seward, because of the opposition of foreign governments to the general, objected so strenuously to Butler's reappointment that they were never issued.[6]

Meanwhile, fearfully shaken by the disaster at Fredericksburg, Burnside saw no way to redress it except by attacking again. But he

[6] Lincoln, *Works*, VI, 22, 73–4, 76–7, 100; *Butler's Book*, 533–4, 549–51; Butler, *Correspondence*, II, 563–4, III, 15, 20; *O.R.*, LIII, 546; Sumner to ?, Dec. 27, 1862, Meyers Collection, NYPL; same to J. M. Forbes, in Hughes, *op. cit.*, I, 353; Brooks, *Washington in Lincoln's Time*, ed. Herbert Mitgang (New York, 1958), 48; Barnett to Barlow, Nov. 30, 1862, Barlow Papers, HL.

had utterly lost the confidence of the men serving under him, and the discipline, morale, and efficiency of his army had completely broken down. Hooker talked loudly of Burnside's incompetence and of the administration's imbecility. He declared that the country needed a dictator. In view of the demoralization of the army, Lincoln told Burnside not to order a general advance without first letting him know.

Burnside came to the White House on New Year's morning and offered Lincoln his resignation. He told Halleck and Stanton in Lincoln's presence that they should resign, too, in order to restore public confidence. Lincoln calmed the excited Burnside and he returned to the army. But he insisted that the evasive Halleck either approve or veto his plan to attack again. Halleck continued to side-step until Lincoln finally wrote him: "If in such a difficulty you do not help, you fail me precisely in the point for which I sought your assistance." The rebuke offended Halleck and he tendered his resignation. He withdrew it when the harassed Lincoln withdrew the offending letter. Stanton, keeping his mouth shut, stayed out of the imbroglio.

With the halfhearted approval of Halleck, Burnside moved his army up the river to effect a crossing. The heavens opened, a torrential rain fell, and the army, bogging down in deep mud, finally floundered back to Falmouth.

Burnside came again to the White House and demanded that Lincoln either allow him to clean house by discharging Hooker and other complaining and intriguing officers or accept his resignation. On the morning of January 25, Lincoln called Halleck and Stanton to his office and told them he had decided to relieve Burnside and put Hooker in command. Both Halleck and Stanton would have preferred to transfer Rosecrans to the Army of the Potomac, but Lincoln did not ask for their opinion. He chose Hooker because that general had a reputation as a fighter and stood higher in popular esteem at that moment than any other eastern general. But in giving Hooker the assignment, Lincoln informed him frankly that he was "not quite satisfied" with him because of his loose talk about a dictatorship and his disloyalty to Burnside. A clerk in the War Department asserted that when Hooker was given command of the Army of the Potomac, Stanton's first impulse was to resign, but his sense of duty kept him at his post.[7] Perhaps Lincoln insisted that he stay, for at this time Stanton was deeply involved with his chief in a political plan of immense importance.

[7] Benjamin, "Hooker's Appointment and Removal," *Battles and Leaders*, III, 239–43; William Howard Mills, "From Burnside to Hooker," *MAH*, XV, 50–4; Nicolay and Hay, *Lincoln*, VIII, 206; *O.R.*, XXI, 941–2, 945, 1007–12.

Although the presidential election of 1864 was still a long way off, the Democratic bosses were already grooming McClellan, now in retirement, for that party's nomination. The catastrophic fall election of 1862 and the effects of the Fredericksburg defeat had almost convinced Lincoln that the Republicans were destined to lose control of the government, and the worried President hoped that if the Democrats did come to power, they would do so under leadership that would continue the war for the Union. He therefore took immediate steps, with Stanton's help, to dull the McClellan boom.

Lincoln broached a proposition to Thurlow Weed that Democratic Governor Seymour, of New York, be his successor in the presidential office. Weed's account of this incident has been discredited as a phantom of an old man's mind. But soon after, Stanton's friend Edwards Pierrepont offered Seymour the "entire force and zeal and vast energy of the War Department" to help secure him the Democracy's nod as its next presidential candidate. With Stanton's backing, Seymour would be sure to win, Pierrepont asserted, and then the Democratic party would unite the North as never before and in harmony with Republicans quickly bring the war to a successful conclusion.

Taken by itself, this letter would stamp Stanton with perfidy toward Lincoln in its promise to Seymour of War Department support. But in connection with Weed's assertion that Lincoln was in favor of Seymour as the Democratic leader most likely to continue the war, it indicates that the President and his "Mars" were working hand in glove.[8] Seymour soon began to exhibit such strong states' rights convictions, however, that Lincoln changed his mind about him. And, like most Republican leaders, Lincoln proved to be unwilling to lose power by default.

To stem the Democratic resurgence following upon Fredericksburg, Republican congressmen began what amounted to a campaign of extermination against Democratic generals. Stanton prompted and joined in on this politicians' vendetta. His co-operation with the legislators is explicable only when Lincoln's Negro enlistment policy is kept in mind. He was pleased when the powerful Committee on the Conduct of the War renewed an investigation of the Army of the Potomac and put McClellan, nervous and resentful, on the griddle. Stanton secretly provided information from Department files so that Republican sena-

[8] Thurlow W. Barnes, *Memoir of Thurlow Weed* (Boston, 1884), 428; Eisenschiml, "An Intriguing Letter," *Autograph Collector's Journal*, I, 13–14.

tors could launch a new smear campaign against West Point graduates. After Stanton relieved General Franklin of his command in the Army of the Potomac and sent him to the western frontier, it was widely rumored that other "McClellanite" officers were destined for similar treatment.

Goaded by the charges made in Congress against them, both McDowell and Buell asked Stanton for a court of inquiry. Stanton disliked McDowell intensely, but he granted the general's request and the court exonerated him. Yet Stanton never again employed him in the field.

In addition to disliking Buell, Stanton suspected him of conspiring to discredit Rosecrans in order to regain command, and he knew that Buell was opposed to the administration's emancipation policy. Not wishing to afford Buell the opportunity to put his case before the country, Stanton refused his request for an open court of inquiry, allowing him only a secret hearing before a military commission. It was a court-martial under another name. Though Piatt, whom Stanton chose to represent the government, lodged no charges against Buell, he unfairly impugned both his ability and his loyalty.

Another court-martial convicted Fitz-John Porter, McClellan's closest friend, of insubordination based on charges brought by Pope after Second Bull Run. Porter was dismissed from the service. To McClellan's supporters in the Army, as to more recent commentators, it was a rigged trial, although no evidence exists that Stanton packed these courts and Stanton's own notes indicate that he awaited the court's decision in the Porter case with considerable uneasiness and suspense.[9]

Stanton was also closely involved in the persecution of General Charles P. Stone, who had once stood close to McClellan. Far back in 1861, a detachment of Stone's troops had suffered a minor disaster at Ball's Bluff. Ugly suspicions of disloyalty began to center on Stone. The general played into the hands of his traducers when he forbade fugitive slaves from seeking asylum within his lines. Criticized in Congress for his tender regard for slaveowners, Stone insinuated that his detractors, especially Senator Sumner, were cowardly slackers. That was enough for the Committee on the Conduct of the War, which

---

[9] Stanton's notes, undated, copy owned by the estate of Benjamin P. Thomas; Eisenschiml, *The Celebrated Case of Fitz John Porter* (Indianapolis, 1950); Lincoln, *Works*, VI, 67; Jan. 30, 1862, Patrick ms diary, LC. In 1886 Porter had the decision reversed and he was reinstated; see his ms "Written History of the Fitz-John Porter Case," Porter Papers, LC.

soon gathered a mass of hearsay evidence suggesting that Stone was disloyal.

Chairman Wade presented this evidence to Stanton, who had just become War Secretary. It proved to Stanton that West Pointers like Stone were too solicitous concerning slavery and far too cavalier toward their civilian overlords. Stanton directed McClellan to place Stone under arrest. McClellan suggested that Stone be given a military trial, but Stanton would only allow him to appear before the committee.

Stone never had a chance. The committee would not reveal the charges against him or the names of his accusers. Stone's arrogance vanished. Rearrested, he was placed in solitary confinement. Stanton sent McClellan all pleas for mitigation of Stone's confinement or for a review of his case. But McClellan by this time was under heavy fire from the committee and deemed it inadvisable to antagonize the legislators by aiding Stone. Though no specific charges were ever made against Stone, he remained a prisoner for six months.

It required an act of Congress to pry Stone loose. Returning to Washington, he sought vindication. Lincoln, Stanton, and other officials listened to him with apparent sympathy, each blaming Stone's troubles on someone else. Stanton again refused Stone a court of inquiry, but he did permit him to appear before the Committee on the Conduct of the War.

Allowed at last to meet specific accusations, Stone acquitted himself on all counts and was restored to a minor command.[1] Unable to live down the accusations that had been brought against him, however, he soon resigned from the Army.

It never occurred to Stanton that a Secretary of War owed his officers greater protection from unfair army hearings or from overzealous congressmen than he accorded to Stone or the others. To be sure, all the generals who ran afoul of him had shown too much military arrogance and Democratic partisanship to enlist Stanton's sympathy. Still worse, in his reasoning, they formed the centers in the Army for pockets of conservative sentiment regarding slavery. By mid-1862, Stanton felt that this attitude was giving the enemy aid and comfort. Six months later, with Lincoln determined to have the Army accept Negro troops into its ranks and with the Democrats booming McClellan for President, Stanton looked on these officers as unworthy of any support. In championing McClellan they defied their commander in chief.

[1] Stone to Sumner, Dec. 23, 1861, Sumner Papers, HU; to Gen. S. Williams, Feb. 12, and J. F. Doyle to McClellan, March 7, 1862, McClellan Papers, LC; T. Harry Williams, "Investigation: 1862," *American Heritage*, VI, 171–2.

What it amounts to is that the war had brought the Army into politics. Only generals who won battles, Stanton felt, had a right to express themselves on policy matters, but even they, if overruled, must obey their constitutional superiors. Officers who time and again failed to gain victories had far less justification to presume to shape policy. No officer had the right to treat the President, the Secretary, or Republican congressmen with contempt.

Politics was a dangerous game with its own set of rules. Army officers who "indulge in the sport," Stanton wrote in a memorandum to Lincoln, perhaps to assuage the President's uneasiness concerning the Republican attacks on Democratic generals, "must risk being gored. They can not, having exposed themselves, claim the procedural protections and immunities of the military profession."

Apparently Stanton's argument convinced Lincoln. The President made no serious effort to soften the blows which rained down from Capitol Hill and from the War Department upon the heads of McClellan's friends in the Army.[2]

Lincoln's issuance of the Emancipation Proclamation and his consent to the arming of Negro troops wiped out all major differences of opinion on those subjects between him and Stanton. Both men now bent their efforts toward implementing the new policy. Stanton told Watson that his aim now was to "carry out the great scheme of emancipation so as to overcome the rebellion." The use of Negroes in uniform was to be another phase of the all-out war effort.

The government had scarcely announced the new policy of Negro enlistment when zealous Governor Andrew obtained Stanton's permission to recruit a colored regiment in Massachusetts. Unable to fill up the unit there because of the dearth of resident Negroes, Andrew asked Stanton for permission to recruit them in other states. Turned down by the Secretary, Andrew side-stepped by forming a private recruiting organization whose far-flung activities moved the Washington *National Intelligencer* to comment that its agents "will shortly turn

---

[2] Stanton's memorandum, dated Jan. 1863, was placed in his copy of Lieber's *Civil Liberty*, owned by Mrs. Van Swearingen. It is noteworthy that it represented to Stanton more than a mere justification for momentary partisanship. Stanton protected against Republican congressmen such generals as Meade, Grant, George Thomas, and Sherman, who met his criteria of victorious yet obedient officers. Later, Stanton slashed at Sherman for overreaching himself as a treaty maker. And when President Andrew Johnson played what Stanton felt was a wrong brand of politics *with* the Army, a worse offense in Stanton's judgment than playing politics *in* the Army, the Secretary helped Congress to subdue the offender.

up in Egypt, competing with Napoleon for the next cargo of Nubians."

A flood of messages came from other Northern governors, objecting to Andrew's activities and insisting that Negroes recruited in their states be credited to their own enlistment quotas. The border states were particularly averse to serving as a recruiting ground for Massachusetts, and it became evident that Negro enlistments, like the administration of the draft, must be under federal control. When Stanton's friend in Congress, Henry Wilson, of Massachusetts, proposed legislation empowering the loyal states to recruit Negroes in occupied portions of the South, Stanton, undoubtedly at Lincoln's behest, privately and hotly argued with Wilson against the measure, for it would simply permit a Northern white to stay home for every black obtained, augmenting the Army not at all, and the Secretary warned Wilson that he would resign the day after such a bill passed. Wilson dropped the matter, though Massachusetts and a number of other Northern states continued to recruit Negroes at times in the borderland and in the occupied South, over Stanton's, and later Grant's, opposition.[3]

With the field again clear for federal action, Stanton sent Adjutant General Lorenzo Thomas to the Mississippi Valley to supervise Negro recruiting, to enlist white officers who would be willing to serve in Negro regiments, and incidentally to watch Grant. Thomas reported almost immediately that he was "working like a Turk" to keep up with the influx of Negroes. Those who were unfit for military service he put to work on abandoned plantations leased by the government to loyal white men, who paid them wages, but he also organized 20,000 of them into regiments to protect these workers. The officers were drawn from Grant's army, and Thomas reported that Grant's men were now so favorably disposed toward the new policy that he could have obtained many more officers than he needed.

Assured that the new program would function, Stanton threw it into high gear. Negroes rushed to the colors in such numbers that Stanton found it advisable to organize a Bureau of Colored Troops in the War Department under the charge of Major Charles W. Foster, who at once proceeded to regularize and give central direction not only to the recruitment of Negroes but also to their training and welfare as soldiers. Owing largely to Stanton's efforts, the Negro from this time

[3] Pearson, *Andrew*, II, 71–3; Cornish, *op. cit.*, 108, for *Intelligencer*; Brooks, *op. cit.*, 104–5; Quarles, *op. cit.*, 189–90; Hesseltine, *War Governors*, 287–90, 297–304.

forth became an effectual counterpoise in tipping the scales for the Union. Cognizant also of the long-range aspects of the Negro problem, Stanton appointed Robert Dale Owen, J. McKaye, and Samuel G. Howe as commissioners to study the condition of the freedmen and the treatment that should be accorded them.

When the new bureau was established, William Whiting, solicitor of the War Department, advised Stanton that the law of July 17, 1862, provided no federal bounty for Negro enlistees and approved paying them only as laborers, not as soldiers. Under this ruling Stanton fixed their pay at ten dollars per month, three dollars of which would be paid in clothing, as compared with the thirteen dollars per month plus clothing that white soldiers received. Incensed at this discrimination, Governor Andrew made himself the champion of the Negro troops. He had an interview with Stanton, whose bearing he described as "very reprehensible," and concluded that it would be inadvisable to press him on the matter. "He is very sore," he wrote, "and behaves badly." It was probably Andrew's evasion of Stanton's ruling against the recruitment of Negroes for Massachusetts regiments in other states that had aroused the Secretary's ire, and Andrew knew he would soon cool down.

The Republican radicals were still indignant at the alleged rough treatment the administration had accorded Frémont, who had been relieved from duty after Jackson's Valley campaign, and the new policy with respect to Negroes gave Lincoln an opportunity to assuage the radical resentment by offering him a new assignment. He offered the general authorization to raise a colored force in Virginia of about 10,000 men, but Frémont declined the appointment. Nor did Stanton favor him for any larger duty, intimating to John Murray Forbes that what was needed for the Union's forces then amassing was a commander with an "organizing mind" who was "willing to spend and be spent."

Already, however, the enlistment of Negroes had proved to be a boon to the Union cause, and Lincoln advised Stanton that he wished to accelerate the program along the shores of the Mississippi. Abetting Lincoln's program, Stanton urged Congress to remove the wage and bounty discrimination against colored troops, but not until the end of the war did it do so.[4]

Stanton hoped to have 100,000 Negro troops organized by mid-

[4] *O.R.*, XVII, pt. 2, 421–4; ser. 3, III, 121, 252; Pearson, *Andrew*, II, 71–3, 81–5, 96–118; Lincoln, *Works*, VI, 242–4, 342; Hughes, *op. cit.*, II, 69–70; Quarles, *op. cit.*, 192–5; Townsend, *Anecdotes*, 76–81; Sumner to S. G. Howe, May 15, 1863, HU.

summer 1863, and he confided to Chandler that Lincoln was offering every support. The prospect of drawing on the black strength of the South as a sustenance for the North delighted the President, who believed with Stanton that the Confederacy, already employing all its white men in uniform and in war work, must go down to defeat.

Lincoln and Stanton, both Midwesterners, had long recognized the military, economic, and political significance of clearing the Mississippi River to its mouth. Stanton had urged Halleck and Butler to seize Vicksburg, a natural citadel high on the river bluff and now strongly fortified by the Confederates, when its capture might have been relatively easy; but neither general felt able to spare troops for that purpose, and the project was shelved by the pressure of events elsewhere. And so both Lincoln and Stanton were in a mood to listen when, back in October 1862, General John A. McClernand came to Washington with a proposal to complete the opening of the river.

A fellow townsman of Lincoln's, McClernand had served as a congressman for several years before the war. His influence among Illinois Democrats was very great. Accepting a brigadier general's commission at the outbreak of hostilities, he did a fine job counteracting proslavery and secessionist influence in southern Illinois. But his record as a field commander had not been brilliant, and he had shown a tendency to resent superior authority and to seek the limelight.

McClernand's success in recruiting troops made his proposal to enlist men in the Midwest for an expedition against Vicksburg seem plausible. He caught Stanton in one of his sour moods against West Pointers. Stanton said he hoped McClernand could show them what a nonprofessional soldier could do.

Halleck, suspicious of all amateur generals, was skeptical of McClernand's capabilities, and though unwilling to oppose Lincoln and Stanton openly, he kept a checkrein on the untried officer. McClernand busied himself with raising troops; then he heard that an expedition against Vicksburg was already under way. He wired Stanton asking whether he had been superseded. Stanton reassured him, though in somewhat ambiguous language. The Vicksburg operation came within Grant's department, he said, and McClernand would command one of the three corps making up Grant's army. Halleck informed Grant that Lincoln wished McClernand to command the attack on Vicksburg under Grant's direction. The whole business was loosely handled. McClernand assumed he was to have an independent command. Grant thought him one of his subordinates.

Postmaster General Blair, in cabinet meeting, alluded to McClernand's having been crowded aside, and of a "combination" to deprive him of command. Lincoln started from his chair and denied that any such maneuver could succeed. Stanton reassured the President. Everything was in order; he and Halleck had arranged matters.

But when McClernand reached Grant's army late in December 1862, his suspicions seemed confirmed. Sherman was in command of the troops McClernand had forwarded and was already on his way to Vicksburg by water. McClernand, hastening to join Sherman, wrote a scathing letter to Lincoln which blamed Halleck for contempt of superior authority in depriving him of his command.

Lincoln pleaded with McClernand not to involve him in another "family controversy"; Stanton wrote somewhat evasively that McClernand must know his own and Lincoln's sincere desire "to oblige you in every particular consistent with the general interest of the service." While this pot simmered, Sherman and Grant's winter-long efforts against Vicksburg resulted in a dismal failure.[5]

Stanton had been keeping close watch on Grant ever since Fort Donelson fell, and was warmed at the thought of this officer's habit of hitting hard at the enemy. But disturbing reports of tippling on Grant's part kept trickling into Washington. Worse, it was said that many of his officers discouraged runaway Negroes from coming into the Union lines and mistreated those who came. This was contrary to the wishes of the government, wrote Halleck, at Stanton's urging, and Grant must put an end to it. "The character of the war has very much changed within the past year," explained Halleck, writing with an unmistakable Stantonian flourish. "The North must conquer the slave oligarchy or become slaves themselves."

Grant replied that he and his officers knew their duty as soldiers. Even those who were unsympathetic toward Negro enlistments would conform to the new policy in good faith, and he himself would carry out "any policy ordered . . . to the best of my ability." It was the sort of declaration Stanton liked to hear from a general. Grant rose even higher in his estimation when he learned that the western commander had instructed his officers to aid not only in recruiting colored troops but also "in removing prejudice against them."

Now Stanton became desperate to know the truth concerning affairs at Grant's headquarters, and he did not trust Thomas's reports. Only a

[5] Morse, *Welles Diary*, I, 217; Stanton to McClernand, Oct. 29, 1862, McClernand Papers, ISHL; McClernand to Lincoln, Jan. 7, 1863, R. T. Lincoln Papers, LC; *O.R.*, XVII, pt. 2, 302, 332, 420, 579; Smith, *Garfield*, I, 238.

person of absolute discretion could serve his needs. Watson's health had completely broken down from overwork, and though Stanton convinced him not to resign, his assistant suffered from continuing illnesses. Then Wolcott died in January 1863 from sheer exhaustion, and Stanton was now bereft of a friend and his only complete confidant.

Early in March, Charles A. Dana agreed to serve as an assistant secretary, and Stanton soon learned that he was an able, conscientious administrator, who filled in the void left by Wolcott's death and Watson's feebleness. Confident that departmental affairs were in good order, Stanton took a short vacation in order to prevent a complete physical collapse. In mid-April he traveled to Gambier, where he relaxed in his sister's home; then he went to Steubenville and sat again on his favorite rocky perch overlooking the river. Although he tried to shut out the war, keeping his presence as secret as possible, the telegraph linked him to Washington, and from his old friends in Ohio he learned of their disturbance at the slowness and cost of the campaigns and the rumors of Grant's return to alcoholism.

Back in Washington by the last week of April, Stanton again fell ill. He had sent Dana to Grant's headquarters, ostensibly as a special commissioner to investigate the payroll service, but actually to check on Grant, with instructions to report daily by secret cipher but never to presume to interfere with military policy. Dana remained in the West until July, and his reports were increasingly favorable to Grant.[6]

Grant and his staff had made Dana welcome after their initial suspicion of him as Stanton's man lessened. Dana came to serve both Stanton and Grant as a liaison each could trust. When his relations with McClernand worsened, Grant was able to gain Stanton's sympathies through Dana.

Unable to take Vicksburg from the north, but determined not to admit defeat by turning back, Grant marched his army down the west bank of the Mississippi to a point well below the city. Admiral Porter ran his flotilla past the city's blazing defenses and ferried Grant's troops to the east bank of the Mississippi. Then Grant cut loose from the river, his only supply line, and living off the country, speedily interposed his army between the two Confederate forces that opposed him, one commanded by Johnston and the other by John Pemberton.

Dana, on April 25, reported that all the Union commanders except

---

[6] Watson to Stanton, June 7; Stanton to Dana, March 11, 1863, Stanton MSS; *O.R.*, XXIV, pt. 1, 31; pt. 3, 156–7; Dana, *Recollections of the Civil War* (New York, 1902), 20–1 (hereafter cited as Dana, *Recollections*); Benjamin P. Thomas (ed.), *Three Years with Grant* (New York, 1955), 60–2; Wolcott MS, 90–1.

McClernand had performed brilliantly. That general had failed to execute orders, could not control even his own headquarters, and in defiance of Grant's policy of mobility, encumbered his actions by having his bride along with him. By early May, Dana was advising McClernand's removal, Stanton replying that it was up to Grant, in whom he and Lincoln had full confidence and to whom they would extend all support, and both Dana and Stanton agreed that Grant should see their exchange of letters and telegrams.[7]

Grant drove Johnston out of the town of Jackson and forced Pemberton to withdraw behind the Vicksburg redoubts. McClernand was slow getting into action and performed poorly. When Grant assailed the Vicksburg fortifications, McClernand deranged his tactics by prematurely and falsely claiming to have captured two of the enemy's positions. Dana reported that Grant almost relieved McClernand on the spot, but having now decided to lay siege to Vicksburg, he let him retain command until the city surrendered, meanwhile watching him closely. After that, Grant hoped to induce him to take an extended leave of absence. According to Dana, McClernand should not even command a regiment—a verdict reflecting Grant's views almost entirely, but unfair to McClernand, who seems to have performed better than these reports allow, and who had run into the rigid antipathies of the West Pointers who now dominated the western armies.

McClernand did not last out the siege. On June 19, Grant reported to Halleck that he had relieved him for issuing a congratulatory address which publicly disparaged the achievements of all but his own troops. But it was clear that this was Grant's excuse. McClernand's sheer incompetency, as Grant saw it, was the reason for his removal. Grant was sorry only that he had waited so long to act; the fear that McClernand would succeed him were he disabled triggered the dismissal. Not unexpectedly, and with some truth, McClernand claimed that Grant's jealousy lay behind his removal. Stanton refused him a court of inquiry, alleging that it was inexpedient at the moment to withdraw field officers from combat duty to serve as judges. McClernand tried to enlist Montgomery Blair in a plot to oust Stanton from the war office and restore himself to command. But Blair, through Captain Wright Rives, a mutual friend, refused the bait, and McClernand dropped

[7] Gen. James H. Wilson to Adam Badeau, May 6, 1863, Wilson Papers, LC; Stanton-Dana exchange, April 25–May 6, 1863, Stanton MSS; Dana, *Recollections*, 33; *O.R.*, XXIV, pt. 1, 84; Bruce Catton, *Grant Moves South* (Boston, 1960), 407–13.

from the scene. Stanton was learning that amateurs were not necessarily better than West Pointers after all.

Dana played a large part in educating him to this fact, for Stanton trusted Dana's judgment. Stanton was impressed to hear Grant praised for possessing abilities and personal characteristics remarkably different from those of other senior officers he had encountered. Writing to a close friend, James S. Pike, about Grant's "splendid campaign," Dana set a theme he followed in his letters to Stanton on the general. Grant, Dana asserted, was like "Zack" Taylor; absolutely honest, doggedly determined, and direct in purpose. But he was more intelligent and better versed in military matters. As a bonus, Grant lacked political aspirations, "and I don't believe he could be brought to have any. I never knew such transparent sincerity combined with such mental resources," Dana wrote.

Through Dana, Stanton learned of Grant's orders to General McPherson concerning Vicksburg's Negroes, who, their former masters alleged, desired to remain with their "white families" rather than strike out for themselves. Grant ordered that army officers were to inform the Negroes that they were now free. If they wished to accompany white exiles into Confederate territory, they might do so. But, Grant added, if anyone suspected that whites were coercing Negroes to accompany them, then the blacks should be turned back "except such as are voluntarily accompanying families, not more than one to a family." [8] Here, Stanton realized, was a general who could fight, think, and grow. He was someone to keep in mind.

[8] To McPherson, July 7, 1863, DeCoppett Collection, PU; Dana to Pike, July 29, 1863, Pike Papers, CFL; on Blair, see Rives to McClernand, July 16, 1863, owned by the estate of Benjamin P. Thomas; *O.R.*, XXIV, pt. 1, 43, 169; Dana's dispatches to Stanton, April 25–June 19, 1863, Stanton MSS.

CHAPTER XIII

WAR IN GOOD EARNEST

$\mathbb{B}$OASTING LOUDLY of what he would do when the spring rains ended and the roads dried out, Hooker prepared for his promised assault. Then, in the first week of May, he had made his first large-scale contact with Lee, and seemed to be seized with indecision. Although outnumbered two to one, Lee resorted to daring strategy, sending "Stonewall" Jackson on a wide flanking movement to the left that would bring him in on Hooker's rear. Perfectly executed, the maneuver caught Hooker by surprise and crushed the Union right. The two main armies came to grips near the hamlet of Chancellorsville. Hooker imposed a strict censorship. For three days the War Department learned virtually nothing except that Hooker had been wounded and that his army was in a desperate plight. Then it became clear that Hooker's defeat was complete. Stanton's fears that he was only a mediocre commander, incapable of directing large numbers of men in battle, were proved distressingly correct.

On May 6 word came that Hooker, his wound not serious, had withdrawn across the river. But the Union losses would amount to 17,000 men. Lincoln paced his office, groaning: "My God, what will the country say?" And Stanton, as he checked the endless casualty lists, seemed crushed, admitting to a White House secretary that "this is the darkest day of the war." The Army of the Potomac, which he had so painstakingly supplied, which he felt was his own creation and had become his very idol, had failed again. Now military defeat, cabinet intrigues, and home-front disaffection kept Stanton "in a condition of a candle burning at both ends," a clerk recalled. But there was work to do.[1]

[1] *O.R.*, XXV, pt. 2, 148, 269–70, 300–1, 351, 435; Morse, *Welles Diary*, I, 293–4; A. E. H. Johnson, "Reminiscences of the Hon. Edwin M. Stanton," *loc. cit.*, 76–7;

Stanton tried to lift Northern morale and to deflect criticism from himself and from the Department by letting it out to the press that Hooker had suffered a mere reverse. He attempted to encourage Hooker, informing him that the public confidence in him was unshaken, and used the same line with Republican congressmen and other friends of the general, promising that Hooker should lack for nothing he could give him.

But Stanton, straight-laced as ever, was disturbed by reports that discipline in the Army of the Potomac had broken down and that the general's headquarters resembled a "combination of barroom and brothel." Stanton warned Hooker to ban liquor and women from his camps.

Much worse, however, was the bad feeling developing between Hooker and Halleck. It was, Stanton confided to Hitchcock, largely Lincoln's fault. The President often sent Hooker orders or suggestions without consulting Halleck. Whenever Hooker came to Washington, he talked only to Lincoln, ignoring both Halleck and Stanton. Hooker had never told them of his plans before or since Chancellorsville. Thus the Army's civilian head and ranking general were often wholly ignorant of what was going on. Perhaps it was under Stanton's prompting that Lincoln belatedly acted to clarify Halleck's status. On June 16 he telegraphed Hooker that "in the strict military relations to General Halleck," Hooker was "a commander of one of the armies," and Halleck was its chief general, expected to pass Lincoln's instructions to Hooker, who would obey them.[2]

By this time, however, the fat was in the fire. Lee's lean marchers were streaming toward the Potomac River on a second invasion of the North. And Stanton had to manipulate many of the strands of logistics that Halleck's hands should have grasped.

Stanton's reactions to the first reports of Lee's northern surge which filtered in to him on May 28 were quick and useful. There was no repetition here of the panic he exhibited, just after taking office a year earlier, at news of the *Merrimac*. Stanton had learned his job and now understood far better the power of men and arms. He had, above all, developed a confidence in the President and in the nation he served,

William O. Stoddard, Jr. (ed.), *Lincoln's Third Secretary: The Memoirs of William O. Stoddard* (New York, 1955), 173.

[2] *O.R.*, XXV, pt. 2, 437–8, 449, 504–6; XLV, 18; May 24, 1863, Hitchcock diary, William A. Croffut Papers, LC; Lincoln, *Works*, VI, 282; Chase to Hooker, May 23, 1863, Chase Papers, 2d ser., LC.

and in the steadfastness of the ordinary soldiers who served him, which he had not enjoyed in his first weeks as War Secretary.

Camping in the telegraph rooms, he concluded that Lee's thrust would take him into Pennsylvania, and hurriedly regrouped the training, administrative, and convalescent commands there, ordering them equipped to fight. On the twenty-ninth, Stanton issued a new call for troops to serve for three years or the duration of the war. Governor Curtin objected that men would refuse to volunteer for such long service and, in order to get troops quickly, asked for permission to call out 50,000 militia for sixty days. Stanton, out of patience with the Pennsylvania officials, who caused more trouble than those of any other state, refused.

Governor Curtin stood firm on his determination to call out shortterm militia instead of recruiting men for three years, and when Stanton displayed equal stubbornness, he appealed directly to Lincoln. The President compromised, calling on Pennsylvania, Ohio, Maryland, and West Virginia to provide 100,000 men for six months. Stanton, exasperated, refused to furnish uniforms for the Pennsylvania militiamen. But both Curtin and Cameron, the latter now back from Russia, interceded with Lincoln, and Stanton had to eat crow when Lincoln wrote: "I think the Secretary of War better let them have the clothes."

By mid-June all the North was uncertain and jittery concerning Lee's plans and progress. Both Lincoln and Stanton stayed close to the War Department's telegraph rooms, and Stanton forwarded copies of all available information to Hooker. Stopping in at Stanton's office, Welles found Lincoln anxious and Stanton fussing, while Halleck nervously puffed on a cigar. "There is trouble, confusion, uncertainty," Welles recorded, "where there should be calm intelligence." [3]

Things seemed to go from bad to worse. The Army of the Potomac, Stanton heard, was becoming dispirited as Hooker's incapacity manifested itself. According to General Patrick, still mourning for McClellan, Hooker "acts like a man without a plan, & is entirely at a loss what to do, or how to match the enemy, or counteract his movements." Patrick felt that since Chancellorsville, Hooker had taken on the role of a Micawber, waiting for "something to turn up." What turned up was news of more reverses for the Union forces and accounts of Lee's continuing northward advance.

[3] *O.R.*, XXV, pt. 2, 567; XXVII, pt. 1, 47–8; pt. 2, 567; XXVIII, pt. 3, 54–5, 76–7; Morse, *Welles Diary*, I, 328–30; Stanton to Capt. Ferguson, June 13, 1863, R. T. Lincoln Papers, LC; same to Gen. Couch, June 12, 1863, Letterbook II, Stanton MSS; Lincoln, *Works*, VI, 298; Kamm, *op. cit.*, 150–3.

Hooker began to exhibit the same failings that had caused McClellan's downfall. Fearing that he was outnumbered, though his force was superior to Lee's, he asked that all troops in the Washington area be put under his command. He complained that the government lacked confidence in him and was not properly supporting him.

As Lee's movement unfolded, Hooker wired Halleck that the Union garrison at Harpers Ferry would be mere bait for the rebels, and asked for authority to withdraw it and unite it with his command. When Halleck responded that he wanted Harpers Ferry held as long as possible, Hooker resentfully requested to be relieved from command. Halleck answered: "As you were appointed . . . by the President, I have no power to relieve you. Your dispatch has been duly referred for executive action."

On June 27, about eight-thirty in the evening, Halleck brought Stanton Hooker's request for relief from command. Stanton sent for Lincoln at once. The President read the dispatch with a wooden face. "What shall be done?" asked Stanton. Lincoln responded immediately: "Accept his resignation." President and Secretary of War consulted together and, without advice from anyone else, decided on General George Gordon Meade as the man to succeed Hooker.[4]

A strict, conscientious general who had performed creditably as a senior corps commander, Meade was a native Pennsylvanian; Lincoln thought he would fight well on his own dunghill, and he was physically in position to come to grips with the elusive Lee. But radical Republican leaders were bound to be unhappy at this choice. Meade was reputedly a Democrat and had been friendly with McClellan. Neither Lincoln nor Stanton worried over these imputations now. Battles took priority ahead of any other considerations.

Next day Lincoln and Stanton merely went through the motions of consulting the rest of the cabinet on the change in command. Stanton finally stated that orders were already on their way to Meade placing him in command. Chase, who had been Hooker's sponsor, was visibly upset. Hooker, like his predecessors in command of the ill-fated Army of the Potomac, blamed Stanton and Halleck for his own misfortunes and incapacity.

Years later, Stanton told diplomat John Bigelow that he had not been surprised at Hooker's resignation; rather he had been shocked at its

[4] *O.R.*, XXVII, pt. 1, 60–1; XLIII, 71; June 17, 1863, Patrick ms diary, LC; George S. Boutwell in Allen Thorndike Rice (ed.), *Reminiscences of Abraham Lincoln by Distinguished Men of His Time* (New York, 1888), 128; Benjamin, "Hooker's Appointment and Removal," in *Battles and Leaders*, III, 241.

selfish nature and unexpectedness. Total disaster faced the Union and it was almost precipitated by the unsettling effects of the general's request to be relieved.[5]

Meade on July 1 reported that his army had made contact with Lee's near the little Pennsylvania town of Gettysburg, and that a major battle seemed imminent. The next three days found Lincoln and Stanton almost constantly in the telegraph office, but the chattering instruments brought them little reliable news. Late at night on July 3, reports arrived that the suffering near the battlefield was terrible for want of food and medical supplies, and that barns, houses, and yards in the vicinity overflowed with the wounded and dying. Stanton hurried the recruitment of a group of civilian surgeons and got them off to the front, and arranged for a volunteer corps of Adams Express Company employees to be passed through the lines to help transport the sufferers to hospitals.

Not until July 4 could the weary, tense watchers in the War Department be sure of the outcome of the battle. That afternoon Stanton announced that Meade had won and Lee was retreating southward, and he privately urged Meade to cut Lee off.[6]

While Lee's fate remained undecided, close behind news from Gettysburg came Grant's announcement that he had taken Vicksburg. News of two great victories sent a wave of joy across the North. Stanton ordered Hardie to hang out the flags of the War Department to honor the "brilliant successes at the front." A huge crowd, after serenading Lincoln at the White House, moved on to the War Department, where Stanton responded to the roar of cheers with a rare public speech. He praised Grant, Meade, and Halleck, and predicted that the twin triumphs would send traitors and copperheads in the North "hissing to their holes."

Though Stanton sustained Meade in public, he, like Lincoln, felt deeply irritated by the general's reluctance to follow up his victory with a knockout punch. Floodwaters prevented Lee from crossing the Potomac to safety. Despite Lincoln's entreaties, Meade made no move to disturb him, but telegraphed on July 13 that all but one of his corps commanders advised against risking an attack. Next day, Stanton drew

[5] Morse, *Welles Diary*, I, 348–9; Gorham, *Stanton*, II, 101; Chase to David Dudley, June 30, 1863, Chase Papers, LC; Hooker to C. A. Stetson, July 4, 1863, autograph file, and Barnett to Barlow, June 19, 1863, Barlow Papers, HU; April 2, 1867, Bigelow ms diary, NYPL.

[6] *O.R.*, XXVII, pt. 1, 69–73; pt. 3, 504, 510, 519, 521; Stanton to Surgeon General W. A. Hammond, July 3, 1863, Letterbook II, Stanton MSS; Welles, *Diary*, I, 357.

Lincoln aside before the cabinet meeting opened to tell him that Lee's army had crossed the river unmolested. The faces of both men registered deep dejection. When John P. Usher, Smith's successor at the Interior Department, asked if there was bad news, Stanton, always reluctant to divulge such information, curtly answered: "No." But Lincoln, casting a mildly reproachful glance at Stanton, said they might as well know the truth.[7]

The truth, according to Stanton, was expressed in his letter to publicist McClure: "As long as General Meade remains in command, he will receive the cordial support of the Department, but since the world began no man ever missed so great an opportunity of serving his country as was lost by his neglecting to strike his adversary." For in the weeks after Gettysburg, Lee escaped to the South.

To the tired men of Meade's army, it seemed incredible that more was expected of them. *"We are satisfied with what has been accomplished & believe, as we did at Antietam ten months ago, that it was a mercy to us that the Rebels left as they did—We could not attack them safely," General Patrick, of Meade's staff, recorded in his diary. "The whole country is in an uproar," Patrick noted, "& it would take little to upset the Administration—which is known to be corrupt by all." But second thoughts, and his own growing animosity toward Meade, convinced Patrick that "a part of the fault is General Meade's, as he has never [before] been in command of men, . . . knows nothing of the wants of an Army, so far as the ranks & file are concerned, & does not seem to care much about them if he can avoid trouble."

But if Lee was not crushed the Union was safe. Gettysburg and Vicksburg, Watson wrote Stanton, at least silenced those persons who wanted McClellan restored to top command. Dana expressed similar mixed reactions to recent events: "Had Meade finished Lee before he had crossed the Potomac, as he might have done & he should have done, . . . we should now be at the end of the war." But realizing that Meade had acted according to the advice of his corps commanders, who were senior to him in rank, Dana did not blame the general alone. And the over-all military picture was now favorable. "The Mississippi is all regained & the rebels have been compelled to fall back. . . . Arkansas & Louisiana will very soon resume their federal relations with clauses in their constitutions prohibiting slavery," Dana gloated. Troops captured

[7] Stanton to James A. Hardie, July 5, 1863, Hardie Papers, LC; New York *Herald*, July 8, 1863, has Stanton's speech; Morse, *Welles Diary*, I, 365–71, on cabinet reaction to events.

at Vicksburg were disillusioned with the experiment in rebellion, and Dana guessed that the Confederacy was almost out of reserve man-power for its armies.[8] The pleasures of victory were adulterated in Washington, however, for while the nation's forces were stemming the rebel host at Gettysburg, and cracking the last Confederate stronghold on the Mississippi, another Union army and its general had been caus-ing endless trouble.

On assuming command of the Army of the Cumberland, Rosecrans, an excitable, moody man, had shown that all too common failing of Union brass—a reluctance to advance. But on the last day of 1862 he had closed with the Confederate army under Bragg in a three-day fight at Murfreesboro. It seemed that Rosecrans was defeated. His reported reverses, General Patrick noted, added to those of Burnside in Virginia, "have had a very chilling effect upon all of us, & . . . seems to add to our calamities about as much as we can bear."

But Bragg retreated southward and Rosecrans claimed a victory. It had come less than three weeks after Fredericksburg, when another outright defeat might well have broken the Northern will to continue the war. In a gush of gratitude, Stanton wired Rosecrans: "There is nothing in my power to grant to yourself or to your heroic command that will not be cheerfully given." Whereupon Rosecrans had begun to ask for so many things that Lincoln interceded, insisting that Stanton's promise, though "pretty broad," must have "a reasonable construction."

Meanwhile, Grant had brought Vicksburg under investment, and Lincoln, Stanton, and Halleck urged Rosecrans to keep pressure on the Confederates so that they could not send troops to raise the siege. Rosecrans came up with the surprising argument that to continue to at-tack would be to induce Bragg to send aid to beleaguered Vicksburg—reasoning which impressed Lincoln "very strangely." Stanton groused that Rosecrans's complaining telegrams were becoming a major item of expense to the War Department.

There was a vacant major-generalship in the regular army, and the friends of Rosecrans and other generals urged the claims of their favorites upon the War Department. Either Lincoln or Stanton hit upon the idea of awarding the promotion to whichever field commander should first win an important victory, a tactless means of goading

<hr/>

[8] Stanton to A. K. McClure, July 22, 1863, Letterbook II, Stanton MSS; July 13, Oct. 30, 1863, Patrick ms diary, LC; Watson in *O.R.*, XXVII, pt. 1, 92–4; pt. 3, 552–3; Dana to James S. Pike, July 29, 1863, CFL.

them into action, to be sure, though only Rosecrans of all the generals objected when Halleck informed them of it.[9]

Then came the twin Union victories at Gettysburg and Vicksburg. Stanton wired Rosecrans: "You and your noble army now have the chance to give the finishing blow to the rebellion. Will you neglect the chance?" The general reacted like a man deeply pricked by a thorn. A journalist reported that he had become convinced that Stanton and Halleck were his enemies, and voiced his opinion of them with such vehemence that "it really embarrassed me to listen to him."

Most of July slipped by with Rosecrans still inactive. He was making final preparations for an attack on Chattanooga but kept his intentions to himself. Stanton wanted to dismiss him, but Halleck begged that he be allowed a little more time and sent him a warning: "I have deemed it absolutely necessary, not only for the country but also for your own reputation, that your army shall remain no longer inactive."

When August came with Rosecrans still finding excuses for failing to do battle, Halleck sent him a peremptory order to advance and to report daily on the position of his army until it had crossed the Tennessee River. The general answered that he was now ready to order the army forward, but if he was to have no discretion as to where he should cross the river, he preferred to be relieved. Halleck told him to cross wherever he pleased, but to stop arguing and start moving. Rosecrans answered with a tirade against Stanton. Halleck responded that Stanton felt no personal animosity toward Rosecrans, although "many of your dispatches have been exceedingly annoying" and "conveyed the impression that you were not disposed to carry out the wishes of the Department, at least in the manner and at the time desired."

Rosecrans now directed his complaints to Lincoln. The President told him to forget bygones and try to move into eastern Tennessee before the fall rains came. Rosecrans could still get there, Lincoln wrote, but the question now was: Could he stay there? He assured the general that he still had confidence in him and was not watching him "with an evil eye."[1] Lincoln's cheering statement cloaked the deep concern Rosecrans was causing him and Stanton. But the civilians, though supplying Rosecrans with all they could, and patiently seeking to encourage him to greater activity, had a crisis closer to Washington to deal

---

[9] *O.R.*, XX, pt. 2, 306; XXIII, pt. 2, 111, 138; Lincoln, *Works*, VI, 138–9; Jan. 3, 1863, Patrick ms diary, LC.

[1] Lincoln, *Works*, VI, 377–8; *O.R.*, XXIII, pt. 2, 518, 592, 601–2; XXX, pt. 3, 110; Andrews, *op. cit.*, 438.

with. In the third year of the war, disaffection on the home front reached new heights, and threatened to upset everything.

A number of state elections had taken place in the spring of 1863, and the Republicans put forth a mighty effort to retrieve their losses of the previous autumn. Stanton furloughed several generals to stump Connecticut, and building on the lessons of the autumn elections of 1862, arranged to send home on leave as many Connecticut, Pennsylvania, and Ohio soldiers and clerks as could safely be spared. On the eve of the elections, he approved a scheme whereby the Ordnance Bureau suggested to Connecticut's munitions manufacturers that they put pressure on their workers to vote for William A. Buckingham, the Republican governor, who was seeking re-election. He won a sweeping victory.

In New Hampshire, Colonel Walter Harriman, a war Democrat, at Stanton's prompting resigned temporarily from the Army to run as an independent candidate for governor, and took enough votes away from the regular Democratic candidate to give victory to the Republican. The Secretary deserved the praise he received years later from N. G. Onleen, the Republican state chairman of 1863: "But for your aid the rebel yell of victory would have been heard among the white hills of New Hampshire." [2]

But westward, in Ohio, there was a less happy political picture, which illustrated the imperfections of the government's internal security arrangements. A lame-duck Democratic congressman, Clement L. Vallandigham, lifted his voice in repeated protests against the government's interferences in elections, the draft, arbitrary arrests of civilians, and the continuance of the war. Stanton had known Vallandigham during his Ohio years—had lent him money, in fact—though he had no use for him now. Lincoln decided that it was better to let Vallandigham blow off steam than to jail him, and neither Lincoln nor Stanton approved when word came that Burnside, now commanding the Department of Ohio, had clapped the agitator in jail and proposed to try him for treason before a military commission.

With Vallandigham in custody, the prestige of the government must suffer if he escaped conviction. Stanton feared that some United States or state judge might choose to disregard the blanket suspension of the

---

[2] N. G. Onleen to Stanton, Dec. 22, 1869, and Stanton to Buckingham, March 21, 1863, Letterbook I, Stanton MSS; Hesseltine, *War Governors*, 320; A. K. McClure, *Abraham Lincoln and Men of Wartimes* (Philadelphia, 1892), 241–2 (cited hereafter as McClure, *Lincoln*).

privilege of the habeas corpus writ and order the prisoner's release from military jurisdiction. He prepared an order suspending the writ privilege specifically in this case. Lincoln felt that Stanton's fears were unfounded and directed him to withhold the order.

The military commission found Vallandigham guilty and sentenced him to imprisonment for the war's duration, but on May 9 Lincoln had the agitator put beyond the Union lines. By thus releasing Vallandigham from prison and sending him to join "his friends" in the Confederacy, Lincoln and Stanton made him appear ridiculous to loyal Northerners.[3]

As Stanton had foreseen, however, Northern Democrats began to laud Vallandigham as a martyr. Ohio Democrats went over to the peace faction, and the state convention nominated the exiled politician for governor by a unanimous vote. Other friends of his tried to bring suit in his behalf before the United States Supreme Court, perhaps, as Bates supposed, to place "a peg on which to hang a denunciatory speech against the Administration generally and the War Office in particular."

Although fearing that the judges who had sustained the Dred Scott decision might decide against the government, Stanton was ready to meet the rebels in court as well as anywhere else, but Bates convinced him to drop the matter; at least not to make the government the initiator of a suit. Many of the government's policies were being questioned in state courts, and as Watson wrote Holt, "this Department stands no chance in a game of shuttlecock before disloyal judges." [4]

Stanton spared little attention for this concern. His primary worry was to secure enough soldiers from the North to increase the number of defeated rebels to the point where the Confederacy would collapse.

Successive manpower crises in 1862 had shown Stanton that the existing recruiting and internal security systems were inadequate, cumbersome, and inefficient. To be sure, the corps of civilian provost marshals which Stanton had created in September 1862 had been an improvement over the total lack of a system with which the government had struggled along before then. At Seward's suggestion, Stanton had appointed Simeon Draper, an able, hard-working merchant of New York City, as the civilian Provost Marshal General in the War Depart-

---

[3] Vallandigham to Stanton, June 26, 1848, Stanton MSS, on the loan. Stanton's habeas corpus order, May 13, 1863, is in the R. T. Lincoln Papers, LC. Other data in Klement, *op. cit.*, 87–97; Lincoln, *Works*, VI, 215; *O.R.*, ser. 2, V, 657.

[4] Bates to Stanton, Jan. 31, 1863, Jan. 19, 1864, Stanton MSS; Lieber to B. J. Lossing, April 21, 1863, Lieber Papers, LC; Lieber's memo on habeas corpus, HL; Watson to Holt, May 13, 1863, Holt Papers, LC.

ment. But Draper lacked authority from Congress and status in the Army, and he was unable to bring army commanders or state officials to heel in anti-subversion and recruiting matters.

At the very least, the 1862 experiment had proved to be a vexatious patronage chore for Lincoln; state governors nominated and dominated the special provost marshals. Largely free of centralized discipline, these provosts often played local politics and pursued personal ends in enrollment and security operations. Because the provost system was uncentralized and proved to be uncontrollable, it was fraught with danger to civil liberties and democratic government. Much of the criticisms leveled at Lincoln and Stanton for arbitrary arrests and interferences with civil processes, must be directed to the untamable civilian provost corps.[5] It had been the best Stanton could manage at the time. But it was not what he wanted, and he pushed Lincoln and his friends in Congress as hard as possible toward a security system which would be more efficient and humane because more centralized and controllable, and toward acceptance of the necessity for a federal draft. Volunteering had failed to keep the Union regiments at full strength, and state governors could not be relied on to comply promptly with requisitions for troops.

By the so-called enrollment act of March 3, 1863, Congress provided for a national draft to be administered by a military officer, a Provost Marshal General of the Army in charge of a separate bureau of the War Department, and Lincoln at Grant's advice named Colonel James B. Fry to that office. Fry divided the entire country into enrollment districts, corresponding roughly to congressional districts, and appointed military provost marshals in each. The long arm of the War Department moved close to every fireside; military provost marshals were now in control of conscription and internal security, and Stanton was their chief.[6]

Hooker, indeed, complained to Stanton that he had been arrested by a diligent provost marshal for traveling without a pass. The War Department's solicitor gave an opinion of the vast sweep of a provost's

---

[5] Morse, *Welles Diary*, I, 286; *O.R.*, ser. 3, II, 936–41, has Draper's report; U.S., AGO, *General Orders Affecting the Volunteer Force, 1861–4* (Washington, 1864), II, 120–1, has Draper's orders; and see Hyman, *op. cit.*, 165–6.

[6] Minute of the War Council, Jan. 1, 1863, Stanton MSS; L. D. Ingersoll, *A History of the War Department of the United States* (Washington, 1879), 348–67; Gerald I. Jordon, *The Suspension of Habeas Corpus as a War Time Political Control Technique* (Ph.D. thesis, UCLA, 1941). Note that each field army, except Sherman's, had a provost marshal organization independent of Fry's. But as combat units became occupation troops, field army provosts performed enrollment services for the PMG Bureau.

powers, which Lincoln and Stanton approved, that defined even "Standing mute" on the part of a civilian being questioned as an offense punishable by military arrest and trial, if obstruction of the draft was involved.

These were incredibly harsh regulations when judged by prewar civilian standards. Lincoln's approval of these stern measures indicates how far two years of civil war had twisted American traditions from their accustomed paths. He and Stanton realized, however, that the men already in uniform were looking on the draft as a test of the government's commitment to sustain them. For example, Rosecrans's ordnance chief, Horace Porter, wrote home from his Tennessee bivouac: "We are all anxiously waiting for the conscription to fill up our old regiments, which are dwindling rapidly. I hope it will clear the street corners of those idlers who ought to be here putting their shoulders to the wheel!" A few days before the new draft law was to go into operation, Porter was worried that "nothing can be done before it takes place. Who will enforce it? We are shooting deserters, hanging spies, & commencing to make war in good earnest here."

Short of losing the support of the soldiers, Lincoln and Stanton had no alternative but to make war in good earnest on the home front. But before Fry could even complete the organization of his personnel, the new draft system met its severest test.

Stanton had unsuccessfully opposed one feature of the enrollment act, not repealed for a year to come, which permitted a man to obtain exemption from the draft by paying $300 commutation or furnishing a substitute. Workingmen grumbled that this was a year's wages and that it was the rich man's money against the poor man's blood.[7] The commutation issue combined with other factors and erupted into a terrible orgy of violence.

The first drawing of names under the new act occurred in the New England states, and except for sporadic opposition in Boston, no trouble was experienced. On July 11, drafting began in New York City. At about noon, two days later, Stanton received word that a serious riot had broken out, an office of the provost marshal burned, and the adjoining block set on fire.

By nightfall much of the upper East Side was in the hands of the ruffians, who, having overpowered the police, looted jewelry stores and

[7] Hooker to Stanton, July 7, 1863, Stanton MSS; Whiting to Stanton, June 6, 1863, Policy Book, 7, RG 110, NA; Porter to mother, March 16, May 17, 1863, Porter Papers, LC; Stanton to E. D. Morgan, July 17, 1863, NYHS; *O.R.*, ser. 3, III, 166–7, 612–13.

liquor shops. Small mobs were reported "chasing isolated negroes as hounds would chase a fox," venting their blind rage upon the black men, whom they held responsible for the war. Confederate agents were suspected of organizing the uprising. Mayor Opdyke and prominent citizens telegraphed to Washington for troops.

Agreeing that the New York resistance to the draft had become a test of the national government's determination to enforce the conscription policy—indeed, of its intention to carry on the war with its uttermost energies—Stanton wired that "the Government will be able to stand the test, even if there should be a riot and mob in every ward of every city. The retreat of Lee's army, now in rout and utterly broken, will leave an ample force at the disposal of the Government." Of course, Lee was not "utterly broken." But Stanton was gathering the "ample force."

On the third day of the riot the crowds virtually controlled the city until, that night, the first detachment of regulars arrived. Stanton ordered Dix to take command in New York. He sent a telegram to Thurlow Weed, which was designed for publication, as an indirect appeal to the mob. Port Hudson, the last rebel stronghold on the Mississippi River, had just surrendered; a Confederate force at Helena, Arkansas, had been defeated. Gettysburg, Vicksburg, Helena, and Port Hudson— four Union victories in eight days! "Has New York no sympathy for these achievements won by the valor of her own sons?" asked Stanton. "Shall their glory be dimmed by the bloody riots of a street mob?"

By the fourth day, police, militia, and about eight hundred troops drawn from the forts in the harbor, the Navy Yard, and West Point brought the mob under control. But the riots, though suppressed, weakened the government's prestige. Rumors spread that the second draft call for New York, scheduled for August 19, would not be issued, that Lincoln was readying to withdraw the Emancipation Proclamation and to disband Negro units in the Army, and that Seymour was preparing a secession movement to take his state out of the Union. Already angry at the opposition to the draft, Stanton was infuriated by these accounts; Dana could assure an inquiring friend: "Of course the stories are false that the administration have entertained the idea of recalling & repudiating the [emancipation] proclamation. . . . No such thing will be done . . . & as a safeguard against such a calamity, hereafter, the work of subsisting and arming the Southern Negroes is being prosecuted with all possible energy."

And, Dana insisted, the second draft call would commence as planned. "There are troops enough there [in New York City] to render the Copperheads harmless. Besides, as the pinch comes Governor Seymour lacks courage for the revolution his friends have planned."

Stanton had every intention of enforcing the draft law as soon as order was restored in the city, although Seymour asked for a postponement and entered into a long correspondence with Lincoln. Now anxious to show the country that the national authorities were prepared to overawe all opposition, Stanton told Welles that he wished Lincoln would stop the letter writing.

On August 19, on schedule, the draft wheels began to spin again. No further disturbance took place, for Stanton had seen to it that the city was strongly guarded and that Dix had full authority to meet resistance if it came.[8]

Governor Seymour justified his docile attitude toward the rioters and his opposition to the draft on the ground that the conscription act was unconstitutional. Lincoln said he could not wait for the Supreme Court to decide that point; he needed soldiers at once. And Stanton wrote to Brady, his colleague in the Sickles trial: "If the national Executive must negotiate with state executives in relation to the execution of an Act of Congress, then the problem which the rebellion desired to solve is already determined. . . . The governor of New York stands to-day on the platform of Slidell, Davis, and Benjamin; and if he is to be the judge whether the Conscription Act is constitutional and may be enforced or resisted as he or other state authorities may decide, then the rebellion is consummated and the national government abolished."

Although it seemed at times that Seymour and other Democratic governors were determined to obstruct the government at every step, even those governors who were most loyal to the administration bickered endlessly over the accuracy of state quotas, credits for men already in service, bounties, and the alleged harshness and corruption of provost marshals. In the face of these protests, the government used the draft chiefly as a means of coercing the governors into filling their quotas with volunteers. Lincoln sometimes intervened when crisis threatened, but for the most part it was Stanton who had to deal with the complexities of the draft and try to placate the governors. Sometimes he was tactful; sometimes his temper flared. It was a duty scarcely calculated to increase his popularity.[9]

[8] Dana to James S. Pike, Aug. 18, 1863, CFL; *O.R.*, XXVII, pt. 2, 886–93, 915–21; Morse, *Welles Diary*, I, 399; Gorham, *Stanton*, II, 111–12; Stoddard, *op. cit.*, 182–90; Irving Werstein, *July, 1863* (New York, 1957).

[9] *O.R.*, XL, pt. 3, 345; Forbes to Andrew, Nov. 24, 1863, Andrew Papers, MHS; Gorham, *Stanton*, II, 109–12; Hesseltine, *War Governors*, 297–304; Jack F. Leach, *Conscription in the United States: Historical Background* (Rutland, 1952).

A lull in the pressure of events during the last days of August gave Stanton a chance for a much needed break in his grinding routine. After combining an inspection tour of West Point with a brief stop at a New Jersey seaside resort, he joined Ellen and the children at a mountain retreat near Bedford, Pennsylvania, in expectation that Lincoln would meet them there as planned, but the President could not leave Washington.

Stanton's oldest son had just graduated from Kenyon with high honors. The family toasted the youth's achievements. Young Edwin told how he had joined a military company formed in late 1862 to resist rebel invasions of Ohio. When the group arrived in Cincinnati, crowds came to see the son of the famous War Secretary. Almost every man of the Kenyon unit claimed to be Stanton's son, and the impression spread that this was indeed a large family. Kenyon had offered the boy a post as a tutor but he wanted to be his father's private secretary. Stanton refused to permit this, not wanting to taint his record for impartiality with any suggestion of nepotism, but later Eckert secretly appointed the boy to a Department clerkship and Stanton, faced with the accomplished fact, took him on as his confidential clerk.

During this pleasant, brief interlude, Stanton kept in touch with Lincoln and the Department by telegraph and through Eckert enjoyed continuous access to developments.[1] He returned to the capital on September 7, refreshed in mind and body, and ever more impressed with the reports that had come in regarding Grant's fighting ability, modesty, and common sense.

Now that the Mississippi was clear, Grant, who disliked being idle, proposed to take his army to Mobile and from there thrust northward into the vitals of the Confederacy. Stanton and Lincoln favored Grant's idea, but Halleck vetoed it, thereby making one of the major errors of the war.

As commander in chief of the Union armies, Halleck had fallen far below Lincoln's expectations, but Stanton, now again closest to Lincoln, although recognizing Halleck's deficiencies, maintained good relations with him on the whole, often using him as a buffer in his dealings with other generals. But Halleck was a desk man rather than a field soldier, and he waged war according to rules. And because the rules said that an invading army should spread out and occupy as much

---

[1] Bodine, *op. cit.*, 376; Stanton to Eckert, Sept. 1, and same to Prof. B. F. Lang, Sept. 20, 1863, Stanton MSS; Lincoln, *Works*, VI, 436.

enemy territory as possible, he now dispersed Grant's army instead of allowing him to carry out the design against Mobile. As a result, the Confederacy, groggy from the pounding it had taken during the early summer, was allowed time to recuperate.

Grant had risen steadily in Stanton's estimation ever since the fall of Fort Donelson, and he was primarily responsible for the general's rapid rise in rank and prominence. Stanton felt that Grant deserved a more significant role, and proposed that he should be given command of the Army of the Potomac. Halleck doubted whether Grant would want the job, and Dana, after sounding out Grant, persuaded Stanton not to press it. Grant had told Dana that, although he would always obey orders, he knew the men and the topography of his present command, and further did not want to become the target of the jealousy of eastern officers by being imported in over them. Mobile was still his target.[2]

Stanton thereupon sent Dana to Rosecrans's headquarters. That general had begun his long-delayed advance. By skillful maneuvering he forced Bragg to abandon Chattanooga. At the same time a small Union force under Burnside took Knoxville, one hundred miles to the north. At last the Union armies had a foothold in eastern Tennessee. By the time Dana arrived at Chattanooga, Rosecrans was preparing to continue his advance, heedless of the fact that Bragg, whose army had not been defeated but merely outmaneuvered, was preparing a heavy counterattack. Now that caution was demanded, Rosecrans moved recklessly.

On September 19, Dana reported to Stanton that a brisk battle had begun a few miles south of Chattanooga along Chickamauga Creek. Stanton felt a quiver of apprehension when he read: "Longstreet is here." It meant that Bragg had been reinforced from the Army of Northern Virginia.

Lincoln and Stanton hovered near the telegraph all through the next day; at 8 p.m. the telegraph began spelling out excited words from Dana: "My report today is of deplorable importance. Chicamauga [sic] is as fatal a name in our history as Bull Run." Forty minutes later a wire from Rosecrans stated: "We have met a serious disaster, extent not yet ascertained." Messages coming in throughout the night showed that what at first had seemed to be a wholesale panic of the Union army had been a partial rout. Dana reported that Rosecrans had

---

[2] Grant to Dana, Aug. 5, 1863, Dana MS, Ac. 2603, LC; Dana's reminiscence in *ANJ* (Jan. 1, 1870), 310.

shown little generalship at all, and had been caught up in the tangle of fleeing troops and swept back into Chattanooga. General George Thomas had made a desperate stand that saved the army from utter disaster, and Generals Thomas L. Crittenden and Alexander M. McCook, the latter a brother of Stanton's former Steubenville law partner, were being blamed for the defeat.

Stanton, like Lincoln, felt that possession of Chattanooga was vital to the Union cause. The Secretary summoned Meade to Washington to confer with him and with Halleck on ways to save the situation. Neither general had much to offer. Stanton, however, was again thinking of crushing rebel strength in the Mississippi Valley by concentrating overwhelming strength there.

Then reports from Tennessee became contradictory and confused. Dana warned Stanton that Rosecrans might abandon Chattanooga, a report that disturbed the Secretary mightily; but the next day—the twenty-third—Dana informed him that Rosecrans would stay there and fight. Dana thought he could last only fifteen or twenty days, and less than that if Bragg received more reinforcements. Rosecrans needed 20,000 to 25,000 men to secure his position. This message reached Stanton at nine forty-five that night.[3]

Stanton asked Hay to bring Lincoln to the War Department. Something must be done at once or Chattanooga would be lost; and Stanton had a plan. He summoned Halleck, Chase, and Seward to his office. To John W. Garrett, of the Baltimore & Ohio Railroad, S. M. Felton, president of the Philadelphia, Wilmington & Baltimore, and former Assistant War Secretary Scott, of the Pennsylvania, Stanton sent identical telegrams: "Please come to Washington as quickly as you can." He wired General J. T. Boyle at Louisville for immediate information concerning the condition and capacity of the rolling stock and the gauge of the railroad from Louisville to Nashville and from there to Chattanooga. By that time Halleck, Lincoln, Chase, and Seward had arrived at the War Department for the war's only cabinet meeting there. It was just past midnight. Watson, terribly ill, Hardie, and Colonel McCallum, director of military transportation, also attended the conference.

Opening the meeting, Stanton said: "I propose then to send 30,000 men from the Army of the Potomac. There is no reason to expect General Meade will attack Lee, although greatly superior in force; and

[3] Dana to Stanton, Sept. 8, 9, 20–3, and Rosecrans to Halleck, Sept. 20, 1863, Stanton MSS; Dana, *Recollections*, 106–7; Lincoln, *Works*, VI, 474–5; Kamm, *op. cit.*, 164; George G. Meade, *Life and Public Services of George Gordon Meade* (New York, 1913), II, 150; Andrews, *op. cit.*, 469–70.

his great numbers where they are, are useless. In five days 30,000 could be put with Rosecrans."

Halleck was dubious whether even western reinforcements could get to Rosecrans in time, and Lincoln, dolefully shaking his head, offered to bet that if the order were given at once, 30,000 troops from the Army of the Potomac could not even be put into Washington within five days. A long argument ensued. Lincoln and Halleck felt reluctant to weaken Meade, whereas Chase, Seward, and McCallum supported Stanton's proposal. It was finally agreed that two corps of the Army of the Potomac should be put under the command of Hooker and sent to Rosecrans at once. At 2:30 a.m. Halleck telegraphed Meade to have those corps ready to entrain for Washington within twenty-four hours, unless he contemplated an immediate forward movement himself. Stanton wired a promise to Dana that 15,000 infantry under Hooker would be in Nashville within five or six days. Without sleep that night, Stanton started them moving.[4] By noon the next day Felton, Scott, and Garrett were at the War Department poring over railroad maps spread across desks in Stanton's office, calculating distances and running speeds, ascertaining the locations of cars and locomotives, laying out a route for the fastest mass movement of troops in history.

The troops would entrain at Culpeper, then switch at Washington onto the tracks of the B & O, which would take them through to Benwood, on the Ohio River. There the soldiers would detrain and be ferried to Bellaire, Ohio. Connecting railroads would transport them to Indianapolis by way of Columbus. From Indianapolis they would proceed by still another railroad to Jeffersonville, Indiana, where they would again detrain and cross the Ohio River for the second time to Louisville. From there the L & N would carry them to Nashville. The last leg of the rail journey would be via the Nashville & Chattanooga to Bridgeport, Alabama, twenty-six miles across the mountains from Chattanooga.

Stanton authorized McCallum to superintend the loadings and the movement to Washington. From Washington to Jeffersonville, Garrett would be in charge. Scott would proceed to Louisville and manage the movement from there on. All army personnel were to obey the railroad officials. It was agreed that an order authorizing Hooker to take military possession of all railroads and equipment necessary to the operation, as provided for by Congress under Stanton's instigation, should

[4] *O.R.,* XXIX, pt. 1, 146–7; Stanton to Dana, Sept. 24, 1863, Stanton MSS; Hay, *Diaries and Letters,* 93; Chase, *Diary,* 201–3; A. E. H. Johnson in New York *Evening Post,* Feb. 13, 1887; Bates, *op. cit.,* 172–82.

go out in Lincoln's name. By nightfall the railroad men had separated to take up their assigned tasks.

Orders from Stanton began flashing over the military telegraph. By 5 p.m. on September 25, less than forty-eight hours after Dana's message had reached Stanton, the first trains were chugging through Washington. At eleven the next morning, Stanton learned that the first three trains, of more than 60 cars, carrying 2,000 men, had reached Martinsburg in good order. Nine more trains with nearly 5,000 men had passed the Relay House, thirty miles north of Washington, and swung onto the B & O's main line. Stanton sent "a thousand thanks" to the railroad men, and added: "If there is no hitch in the west all will go well, I hope."

By the morning of September 27, 12,600 men, 33 cars of artillery, and 21 cars of baggage and horses had passed through Washington, and the first four trains had reached Benwood, across the mountains, 412 miles away. No time was lost in crossing the river, for instead of using ferries, railroad personnel and soldiers built a bridge of scows and barges so that the troops could march across.

Stanton heard that the station agent at Grafton had received an order to hold a troop train until General Carl Schurz arrived. The Secretary dashed off a torrid wire to Schurz: "Major-General Hooker has the orders of the Department to . . . put under arrest any officer who undertakes to delay or interfere with the orders and regulations of the railroad officers in charge of the transportation of troops." The trains continued to move.

At 10 p.m. on the twenty-seventh, Stanton wired Scott at Louisville: "The whole force, except 3,300 of the Twelfth Corps, is now moving. The number will exceed 20,000." Stanton granted Scott's request to change the gauge of the Louisville & Lexington Railroad, and Scott impressed 8,000 Negroes and put them to work tearing up and resetting rails. The chugging caravan now extended from the Rapidan to the Ohio; the trains were carrying 20 per cent more men and 50 per cent more horses than the requisitions called for.

Not a single delay occurred until the trains reached Indianapolis. There the troops had to be detrained and reloaded because of the different gauge of the Jeffersonville Railroad. They had also exhausted their rations by this time; so during the stopover they paused for a hot meal. It meant a loss of six hours. Nevertheless, by September 29 trains were arriving and departing regularly at Louisville. At ten-thirty the next night the first troops arrived at Bridgeport. Seven days had elapsed since Stanton had put the operation in motion. Less than three days later, more than 20,000 men, 10 batteries of artillery with their horses and ammunition, and 100 cars of baggage had safely covered the 1,200 miles to Bridgeport. The first fifty miles, to Washington, had been over a railroad completely wrecked the previous autumn; the B & O, repeatedly torn up by the Confederates, had been partially rebuilt time and again; the two railroads spanning the last three hundred miles had often been disrupted by Confederate raiders under Morgan and Forrest. Stanton wired Scott at Louisville: "Your work is most brilliant. A thousand thanks. It is a great achievement."

Behind the troop trains came another puffing caravan carrying the necessary camp and field equipment for the two army corps—wagons, horses, mules, tents, baggage, supplies of every sort. Stanton urged Garrett not to relax until this movement had also been completed. Although Confederate forces belatedly raided the railroad, thereby causing some delay, all the supply trains came through safely, and Hooker informed Stanton: "If you projected the late movement . . . you may justly claim the merit of having saved Chattanooga to us."

Stanton had indeed performed one of the great feats of the war and was justly proud of his achievement. Sure that Hooker's troops would only have languished in Virginia, where Meade showed no disposition to attack, he had moved them to a position where they could render real service. Stanton sent Meigs to Chattanooga to solve the supply problem, providing him with what Meigs described as "the fullest powers & more money & means of war at my command . . . than any other man since Napoleon," with "no other instructions than to . . . help this thing through & he would put his name at the bottom of a sheet of paper & I might write over what I would." In a telegram to Meigs, Stanton jibed at the lethargic Meade: " 'All quiet on the Potomac.' Nothing to disturb autumnal slumbers. . . . All public interest is now concentrated on the Tennessee and at Chattanooga." [5]

Though Stanton had averted catastrophe at Chattanooga, Rosecrans's situation continued to be perilous. He could not be overwhelmed by superior forces, but he had many more mouths to feed. The Confederates planted guns on Missionary Ridge and Lookout Mountain, heights dominating the city. Their batteries commanded the river. All the Union supplies had to be brought in from Bridgeport under rebel harassment,

[5] Meigs to his father, Oct. 27, 1863, Meigs Papers, LC; *O.R.*, XXIX, pt. 1, 149–53, 161–2, 167–9, 187–8; pt. 3, 871; XXX, pt. 4, 78, 291. George Edgar Turner, *Victory Rode the Rails* (Indianapolis, 1953), 289–94, disposes of the argument that Chase should be credited with the train-lift idea.

by back roads winding through the mountains, where horses often floundered belly-deep in mud. The undernourished animals became too weak to pull the wagons; troops went on half rations.

Dana reported grave unrest among Rosecrans's officers. He deemed the removal of Crittenden and McCook to be imperative, and suggested that if Rosecrans was to be replaced, some western general "of high rank and great prestige like Genl. Grant for instance," rather than an Easterner, should be put in command. Three days later he reported that George Thomas's conduct in the late battle had won him the highest esteem, "and should there be a change in the chief command, there is no other man whose appointment would be so welcome to this army."

Stanton obtained an order from Lincoln removing Crittenden and McCook and ordering them to Indianapolis for a court of inquiry, which, despite fears that these two officers were to be made the sacrificial goats for Rosecrans's failure, exonerated them both. Replying to Dana's telegram, Stanton stated that he held Thomas in high regard, "and I wish you to tell him so. It is not my fault that he was not in chief command months ago." Thomas, however, sent word confidentially to Dana that he did not want it, from fear that a promotion would appear to be a result of intrigue against Rosecrans. But Dana reported that Rosecrans was definitely losing his grip: "There is no system in the use of his busy days and restless nights." He deemed the army "very unsafe" in Rosecrans's hands, prophesying that "catastrophe is close upon us." Unless communications could be opened within a fortnight, the army would be obliged to abandon the city or starve.[6]

Stanton blew up. "The tycoon of the War Department is on the war path," Hay confided to a friend; "his hands are red and smoking with the scalping of Rosey. . . . Prenez Garde." But Stanton's temper soon turned to more constructive channels.

Dana's warning that Rosecrans might abandon Chattanooga brought about a hasty consultation between Lincoln, Stanton, and Halleck. An order flashed to Grant, at Cairo, to go at once to Louisville, where an officer from the War Department would meet him with instructions. Stanton was soon rocketing westward on a special train; the engineer had orders to throw the throttle wide open, and dishes crashed off the tables when the train took the mountain curves. Fearing that the careening cars might leave the tracks, an army officer yanked the bell

[6] Dana to Stanton, Sept. 27, 30, Nov. 8, 10, 16, 1863, Stanton MSS; Anson McCook to George McCook, Oct. 8, 1863, owned by Mrs. McCook Knox.

cord for the engineer to slow down, but Stanton ordered the high speed maintained.

Arriving at Indianapolis, Stanton learned that the Louisville train, with Grant on board, was just about to pull out. He ordered it held, and hurrying down the long platform, he swung onto the last car. Grant greeted him cordially; the two men had never met before, and the general was still in the dark about why he had been sent for.

Stanton handed Grant two orders signed by Lincoln and told him he could accept whichever he preferred. Both orders put Grant in command of a new Military Division of the Mississippi, comprising all the Union armies west of the Allegheny Mountains except Banks's command in the southwest. One left the department commanders as they were; the other assigned Thomas to Rosecrans's place. Grant took the one replacing Rosecrans.

After a brief rest at the Galt House in Louisville, Stanton and Grant continued their conversations through the next day. The Grants went out that evening, and Stanton, feeling ill, retired to his room. He had caught cold the night before, and suffered from an immediate resurgence of his asthmatic complaint, which plagued him in an aggravated form for the rest of his life.

A messenger interrupted his troubled sleep with a telegram from Dana: Rosecrans had decided to abandon Chattanooga. Stanton became highly agitated and began a frantic search for Grant, bidding guests and employees of the hotel to send the general to him at once if they encountered him.

Grant returned about eleven o'clock, receiving Stanton's message from everyone he met while approaching the hotel. He hurried to Stanton's room and was inwardly amused to see the nervous, bearded Secretary clad in a low-reaching nightgown. Stanton read Grant the dispatch from Dana and declared that the retreat must be prevented. Grant immediately wired Thomas to take command at Chattanooga and to hold on at all costs. Thomas answered promptly: "We will hold the town till we starve." [7]

Rosecrans later charged that his removal from command was the result of a plot inspired by Stanton, of the sort he believed had cut off the careers of McClellan and Burnside. The evidence against this is convincing. General James B. Steedman stated that Stanton's only

[7] U. S. Grant, *Personal Memoirs* (New York, 1886), II, 17–27 (cited hereafter as Grant, *Memoirs*) ; Hay to Miles [O'Reilly], Oct. 24, 1863, Hay Papers, LC; A. E. H. Johnson in New York *Evening Post*, Feb. 13, 1887.

animus against Rosecrans was that the general was "a damned coward" at Chickamauga, but that the Secretary had supported Rosecrans up to that time. After the war, General James A. Garfield, of Rosecrans's staff, confided that Rosecrans had been seeking access more to the White House than to the enemy. "If the President hunters had left him alone," Garfield wrote, "he might have been at the head of our armies today but in the fatal summer of 1863 he was enveloped in clouds of incense—& visions of the Presidency were constantly thrust before him. . . . Certain it is that the War Department was ready to find fault with him from that time forward." Dana recalled that although Stanton no longer trusted Rosecrans, he never pressed for his removal. Lincoln made that decision; though Stanton was in favor of it.[8]

Five exhausting days after he had left Washington, Stanton telegraphed Watson: "I expect to leave for home tomorrow, . . . I will not make as quick time returning as I did coming here." His exertions had sapped his strength, and Stanton had to seek rest. He spent Thanksgiving Day in Steubenville with his mother, now nearing seventy, his son Edwin, and his sister Pamphila, who was shocked at his appearance and, remembering how her husband, Wolcott, had worked himself to death as Stanton's assistant, warned him to guard his health. He answered that were he to collapse, a hundred men could fill his place who might do better. Talk of his indispensability angered him, for it was not only untrue but insulting to others.

Meanwhile Grant, reinforced by Sherman's troops and with the supply problem well in hand, sent Bragg's army reeling southward from Chattanooga in defeat.[9] The Confederates had made Grant's task easier by sending part of their besieging force under Longstreet to fall on Burnside at Knoxville. With Chattanooga liberated, Burnside, in his turn, was hemmed in. But when Grant sent Sherman to relieve him, Longstreet drew off toward the Virginia border. The Union forces now had an unshakable hold on most of eastern Tennessee, owing largely to Stanton's strategic shifting of troops and his championship of Grant.

Though the Union victory at Chattanooga came too late to influence the autumn state elections, Republicans, campaigning under the name

[8] Stanton to Halleck, Oct. 20, 1863, NYHS; Smith, *Garfield*, II, 845–85, and Rosecrans to Dana, *ca.* 1882, Dana Papers, LC, on Rosecrans's accusations. Steedman's reminiscence in Cincinnati *Commercial*, Nov. 20, 1879; Garfield to Young, March 31, 1867, John Russell Young Papers, LC; Chase to Garfield, Aug. 17, 1863, Chase Papers, LC; and Dana in *ANJ* (Jan. 1, 1870), 310, offer other data.

[9] Dana, *Recollections*, 151–2; Wolcott MS, 193; *O.R.*, XXXI, pt. 1, 666, 684, 728; ser. 3, III, 910; Stanton to Dana, Oct. 22, 1863, Stanton MSS.

of the National Union party in order to attract the votes of loyal Democrats, found that wherever the outcome seemed uncertain the War Department threw its weight behind Union candidates. Stanton granted furloughs so that troops from doubtful states could go home and vote. In Maryland, provost marshals guarded the polls, forced prospective voters to take a state-drawn test oath, over the protests of Democratic Governor Bradford, and arrested some objectors; but it was clear enough that only Democrats suffered interference from the military.

In Delaware, New York, Kentucky, and Tennessee furloughed regiments arrived home in time to cast ballots, and to assert by their presence and comments that Democrats were akin to traitors. Provost marshals in Tennessee instigated a "get out the vote" campaign, stating that civilians who did not vote were explicitly denying the sovereignty of their nation and state. As voters had to swear to a rigid state oath of past loyalty, Tennessee Democrats, many of whom had supported the Confederacy in one way or another, were caught in a trap. They could neither ignore the election nor safely vote against Republican candidates.

The Midwest was the area of greatest concern. Reports of plots by copperhead societies to make the elections a signal for revolution came from Indiana's Governor Morton and others. At the request of Morton, Stanton granted General Lew Wallace and other Hoosier officers leave to make speeches in Indiana. Pennsylvania's Governor Curtin had ruffled Stanton no end, but the War Secretary helped to elect him by authorizing furloughs for several Keystone regiments.[1]

Midway in the campaign a scandal involving Stanton threatened to swing California into the Democratic column. The Supreme Court, deciding a case initiated by Stanton five years before, had found the New Almaden Company's title to its California mining lands to be "utterly fraudulent." The company, however, was continuing to occupy and work the properties, which, by reason of the decision of the court, belonged to the government.

Without fully examining the merits of the case, Lincoln immediately sent his close friend Leonard Swett to California armed with a writ authorizing the U.S. marshal to seize the mine and to use federal troops if resistance should be encountered. It was also decided that the gov-

---

[1] *O.R.*, XXIX, pt. 2, 394, 470; XXX, pt. 3, 722, 738; pt. 4, 31–2, 57; ser. 3, III, 967–81; Hesseltine, *War Governors*, 312, 321–3, 336–9; Gen. Robert Schenck, *To the Loyal People of Maryland* (n.p., n.d.), 1–2; Stewart Mitchell, *Horatio Seymour of New York* (Cambridge, 1938), 346–7; Report on Tennessee, Citizens File, Box 77, RG 109, NA.

ernment would lease the repossessed mine to the Quicksilver Mining Company. The matter began to smell bad.

Not only had Stanton taken action to dispossess the New Almaden claimants during his sojourn in California, but he had also been employed afterward by the Quicksilver Mining Company to represent it in a case before the Supreme Court. Now the Quicksilver Mining Company seemed likely to acquire the New Almaden properties. Men high in government, including Swett himself, were said to own Quicksilver stock, and Stanton was rumored to have been the person who obtained the writ of dispossession against the New Almaden Company; for this accusation no proof was ever adduced.

Republican prospects in the California gubernatorial election dimmed. Friends of the administration, however, claimed that Lincoln had been misled by his advisers or by financially interested persons, and pointed out that as soon as he had been undeceived he had taken steps to correct his error. Perhaps the political repercussions had been more frightening than the actual situation warranted, for the Republican candidate for governor was overwhelmingly triumphant.[2]

Most of Stanton's attention during the campaign, however, was centered on his native state of Ohio. John Brough, the Union candidate for governor, was opposed by the blatant copperhead agitator Vallandigham, who had made his way to Canada and was now campaigning from there. The real question at issue was whether the pivotal state of Ohio was willing to support the further prosecution of the war.

Stanton realized the crucial nature of the Ohio contest. He felt sure that the Army detested copperheads, and arranged for Ohio troops to vote in the field and for War Department clerks to go home on leave with free railroad passes. With the returns counted, Dana wired from Grant's headquarters that Ohio soldiers, almost 40,000 of them, had voted almost unanimously for Brough, who won by more than 100,000 votes. Union candidates took 29 of 34 seats in the state senate and 73 of 97 in the house.

And Stanton was especially pleased that Steubenville's "Bloody Fourth Ward," traditionally Democratic, had gone Union, and that on election night crowds had cheered for Lincoln and Stanton and christened the electoral district "Stanton's Ward." He wrote to an old friend there: "I am proud of my native town, and rejoice that the enemies of my country have been so signally rebuked." His own efforts during

[2] Leonard Ascher, "Lincoln's Administration and the New Almaden Mine Scandal," *PHR*, V, 38–51.

the critical summer and autumn of 1863 had in large part made possible the victories in battle and in the balloting.

Elsewhere the Union ticket swept to victory in a smashing reversal of the results of 1862, carrying every loyal state except New Jersey. Unblushingly using the power of the War Department on behalf of Union candidates, Stanton had helped bring about a stunning victory on the home front. When lame-duck Democrats in Congress tried to carry through a law forbidding military officers from interfering in civil elections and a censure resolution against Stanton for using military power at the polls to overawe opposition, he had no excuses, no explanations, no justifications to make. The proposed law and the censure attempt failed.[3] Most important to Stanton, the election results were in.

[3] *Report [No. 14] of the Committee on Military Affairs on Bill [Senate No. 37] to Prevent Military Officers from Interfering in State Elections*, Sen. Exec. Docs. 14, 29, 38th Cong., 1st sess.; Doyle, *op. cit.*, 205; Hesseltine, *War Governors*, 335.

CHAPTER XIV

TRAMPLED BY THE HOOF OF WAR

WITH Bragg's army driven off, the energetic Grant renewed his proposal to attack Mobile and then to use that city as a base to bring the remainder of Mississippi and part of Alabama and Georgia under Union control. He argued that the winter weather would enable him to hold his present line in eastern Tennessee with a minimum of troops, and that only by sending large numbers of men from northern Virginia could the Confederates hope to check his advance. If they did this, then the Army of the Potomac could crush a weakened Lee. The plan was the only one that could be carried out during the winter, and it might end the rebellion by spring.

At the White House, Halleck insisted that any weakening of Grant's forces in Tennessee would enable Longstreet to take Knoxville, Cumberland Gap, or some other strategic point. Stanton and Dana, advocating immediate approval of Grant's idea, felt that any Confederate pressure in the West could be overmatched if the Army of the Potomac in the East moved on Lee. But none of them, they acknowledged, trusted Meade to move in; he seemed to Stanton to be always "on the back track . . . without a fight." They thought of Sherman or William F. Smith to succeed Meade.

Lincoln hesitated, mindful of the possible resentment of the Army of the Potomac toward another interference from Washington, yet, as Garfield confided to Rosecrans, the President and Stanton were "immensely disgusted with the late operations of the Army of the Potomac." Finally Lincoln shelved Grant's plan because of lack of confidence in Meade and hesitancy in removing him, and the Union armies went into winter quarters. Grant moved his headquarters to Nashville, where big things were in store for him.

On February 29, 1864, Stanton flashed Grant the news that Lincoln had named him lieutenant general, a rank, in the history of American arms, enjoyed only by Washington and conferred by special brevet on Scott but now revived by Congress. Three days later he directed Grant to report to Washington to take command of all the Union armies.

In backing him, Stanton clearly was not acting as a servant of the radical leaders. From all that he knew of Grant's views on the Negro issue Stanton could be sure only that he and the general agreed with Lincoln that in order to win the war, the strength of black men must be added to the Union effort and denied to the Confederacy. But far more important to Stanton was his conviction that Grant was a fighting general.

On March 9, in a short ceremony at the White House, Grant received his commission from Lincoln in the presence of the cabinet and a few high-ranking officers. Halleck became chief of staff, in which capacity he would serve as a channel of communication and co-ordinator between Grant and the War Department on the one hand and the department commanders on the other, thus relieving Grant of paper work and Stanton of the need to oversee a thousand details of military administration. As one of Grant's subordinates, C. B. Comstock, commented: ". . . the programme is, Halleck here as office man & military adviser, Sherman to take Grant's place, McPherson Sherman's, Grant in the field." This arrangement, which Stanton helped to work out, gave to the Union a command system superior to anything theretofore achieved in modern war.[1]

Grant had planned to make his headquarters in the West, but he soon agreed with Lincoln and Stanton that his proper place was with the Army of the Potomac. Meanwhile the Committee on the Conduct of the War continued to urge the removal of Meade. But now, having entrusted Grant with the supreme command, the civilian leaders wished to give him a free hand. Grant persuaded Stanton to keep hands off, and asked Meade to stay. With Meade as the tactical commander and Grant close by to determine strategy and spur him into action, the Army of the Potomac hereafter would perform effectively.

[1] T. H. Williams, *Lincoln and His Generals*, 302–3. Other data in March 11, 1864, Comstock ms diary, LC; Garfield to Rosecrans, Dec. 9, 1863, Rosecrans Papers, UCLA; Dana, *Recollections*, 157; *O.R.*, XXIX, pt. 2, 537; XXXI, pt. 3, 349–50, 457–8; XXXII, pt. 2, 494; pt. 3, 13, 261; XXXIII, 663, 728; XLV, pt. 2, 246–7.

Lincoln and Grant between them worked out a broad strategic plan. Grant, with Meade directing the Army of the Potomac, would harry Lee relentlessly, always trying for a death grip. Sigel would push up the Shenandoah Valley and approach Richmond from the West, while Butler, advancing on it from Fort Monroe, would snarl the railroads from the South, thus severing Lee's supply lines and blocking his escape route. In the West, Sherman would drive for Atlanta, pommeling Bragg's old army, now under Johnston, and wasting Georgia's resources, while Banks, taking off from New Orleans, would carry out Grant's unfulfilled design of reducing Mobile and then push northward to join Sherman. The strategy of concerted attack which Lincoln had sought to employ from the beginning was in effect at last.

Stanton threw all the power of the War Department behind the gigantic undertaking. Manpower was again a matter of foremost concern and was more acute because the terms of the men who had enlisted for three years at the outset of the war would expire at almost the precise time that the big spring drive had been scheduled to get under way. These veterans now constituted the hard core of the Union forces, and Stanton doubted whether the war could be won without them. So while calling on the loyal governors to stimulate voluntary enlistments and ordering a new draft designed to bring a total of one million men under arms, he also offered every possible inducement to these seasoned troops to re-enlist—a federal bounty of $400 plus whatever a man's town, county, and state might be offering, a thirty-day furlough, a trim chevron designating a soldier as "a veteran volunteer," and the right of a regiment to keep its old number and organizational standing provided three fourths of the outfit signed up.

When a veteran regiment had obtained the necessary number of re-enlistments, it would parade smartly through the camps, flags flying, band blaring some patriotic air, and marching men and bystanders bursting into a roar of cheers. Under the contagion of this enthusiasm, and from their own consciousness of their indispensability, 136,000 battle-hardened troops joined up again to see the war through to the end, and Stanton could take satisfaction in having brought the government through one of its hardest tests.[2]

The War Department was a place of unceasing organized confusion as its orders assembled in Virginia and in the West huge quantities of weapons, rations, and medical stores; and great amounts of horses, mules, wagons, railroad iron, cars, locomotives, bridge timber, tele-

[2] Catton, *This Hallowed Ground* (New York, 1956), 317–19; Johnson, "Reminiscences of Hon. Edwin M. Stanton," *loc. cit.*, 84; Meade, *op. cit.*, II, 169–70, 178.

graph cable, and war materials of every sort. Stanton worked without letup through the early months of 1864, ignoring the wild rumors of quarrels between himself, Halleck, and Grant.

Such reports, Halleck assured Sherman, "are all 'bosh.' " He, Grant, and Stanton were working in efficient harmony. The commanding general kept away from Washington, drilling officers and troops, while Halleck and Stanton dealt with "the rascally politicians and shoddy contractors." Hay agreed that "the stories of Grant's quarreling with the Secretary of War are gratuitous lies. Grant quarrels with no one." And Grant wrote to Lincoln on May 1, with the big push about to begin: "From my first entrance into the volunteer service of the country to the present day I have never had cause of complaint, never have expressed or implied a complaint against the administration or the Secretary of War for throwing any embarrassment in the way of my vigorously prosecuting what appeared to be my duty. Indeed, since the promotion which placed me in command of all the armies, and in view of the great responsibility and importance of success, I have been astonished at the readiness with which everything asked for has been yielded, without even an explanation being asked. Should my success be less than I desire and expect, the least I can say is, the fault is not with you." It was a far different tone from that continually sounded by McClellan, Buell, and Rosecrans.

But already a hitch had developed. In April, Banks had moved up the Red River, expecting to win a quick victory and then move on Mobile. But he mismanaged the campaign so flagrantly and took such a drubbing that his army could be expected to be of little use for some time. Grant wired that Banks should be removed, and Stanton agreed. But Banks was Lincoln's personal friend and had the strongest kind of support in Congress, in the cabinet, and in Northern political circles as well. If Grant made the removal of Banks a matter of absolute military necessity and suggested the precise boundaries that a replacement would command, the President would act. Stanton would support Grant as soon as the general made his desires clear.

Grant recommended that Canby, Stanton's onetime aide, take command of Union troops in the southwest, with Banks having charge of New Orleans. Stanton added his approval to this proposition, and Lincoln issued the order. The new team was working.[3]

It had shaken down barely in time. On May 4, Stanton announced

[3] Grant to Lincoln, May 1, 1864, R. T. Lincoln Collection, LC; *O.R.*, XXXII, pt. 2, 407–8; XXXIV, pt. 3, 252–3, 293–4, 329–33, 409–10, 491; Ludwell H. Johnson, *Red River Campaign* (Baltimore, 1958) ; Hay, *Diaries and Letters*, 176.

that Grant had crossed the Rapidan and was advancing on Lee; Sherman had started to attack Johnston from Chattanooga; a third army was ready to start the next day.

Now began the tense waiting period, which Stanton most hated and which in the past had always presaged disaster for his beloved Army of the Potomac. He had done all he could; now it was up to Grant.

Lee melted away from the Rapidan, waited for Grant's army to enter the tangled, wooded region to the south of the river known as the Wilderness, and then struck viciously. The military telegraph to the War Department fell ominously, shatteringly quiet. It was as though the Wilderness had swallowed up Grant's army.

Tension mounted and strained at Stanton's nerves. Hitchcock noticed "that, in reaching for a piece of paper, his fingers showed a nervous tremor that I had never observed before," and wondered, as Stanton must have wondered, whether Grant, like McClellan, Hooker, Burnside, and Meade, had failed.

Then, on Friday evening, May 6, a message flashed in to the War Department from Union Mills, about twenty miles out of Washington. Henry Wing, a nineteen-year-old correspondent for the New York *Tribune*, wanted to communicate with Dana; Stanton took over at the end of the wire. Wing reported that he had just come from the battlefield, barely evading rebel cavalrymen, and wanted permission to wire a report of the battle to the *Tribune*. Stanton ordered him to divulge his information to the War Department. Wing refused to do so unless he was allowed to send his message to the newspaper. Wild with anxiety, Stanton threatened to arrest him.

Lincoln came in. "Ask him if he will talk with the President," he told the operator. Wing agreed to tell Lincoln all he knew provided he could send one hundred words to the *Tribune*. Lincoln consented to this condition and told the young reporter to put his message on the wire. Meanwhile, Stanton sent a special locomotive for him.

Wing arrived at Washington shortly after 2 a.m. and was brought at once to the White House. Lincoln and the anxious cabinet members learned only that both armies had suffered terrible slaughter. When Wing left the battlefield at the end of the first day, the outcome had still been doubtful, but he brought a message to Lincoln from Grant. "He told me to tell you, Mr. President," said Wing, "that there would be no turning back." Lincoln threw his arms around the boy and kissed him. He and Stanton visibly relaxed. The specter of a repetition of past sacrifices which had accomplished nothing was at last dissipated.

Two days later the first official reports arrived from the front. The battle had been a draw, but Grant, unlike all his predecessors in command of Union forces in Virginia, was still driving southward. Another bloody battle took place at Spotsylvania Court House, and Grant wired that "the result up to this time is very much in our favor." He would continue the campaign "if it takes all summer."

As Grant's messages arrived, Stanton relayed them to the country, ostensibly as reports to Dix in New York, although he gave them directly to the Associated Press. This innovation in public relations proved beneficent. Not even the endless casualty lists which followed Grant's reports dampened the general enthusiasm in the North or seriously unsettled business confidence.

Then fighting stopped as an unceasing downpour made organized movement impossible for five days. Grant assured Lincoln and Stanton that "the elements alone have suspended hostilities and that it is in no manner due to weakness or exhaustion on our part." The army was in the best of spirits and confident of success. Grant was grateful for the unfailing flow of men and supplies which had come to him from Washington. Stanton glowed with happiness, his secretary recalled, and the "fretfulness and impatience" which had so marked his behavior during the past three years lessened amazingly.

It was while Stanton was in this happy mood that a message arrived from Grant expressing the utmost confidence in Meade, and recommending that he and Sherman be made major generals in the regular army. The War Secretary, once so displeased with Meade, was now willing to accept him at Grant's estimate.[4]

Stanton could enjoy such peace of mind only briefly, for suddenly his safeguarding of home-front morale seemed undone.

Two rabidly anti-Lincoln newspapers in New York City, the *World* and the *Journal of Commerce*, printed a bogus proclamation, which they attributed to Lincoln, stating that the Virginia campaign was a stalemated failure and that military affairs everywhere were going badly, calling for 400,000 men for the Army, and appointing a day of national fasting, humiliation, and prayer. The total effect was that the Union cause was in dire straits.

Seward rushed to Stanton's office. It was "steamer day," and if other papers copied the item it would soon be all over Europe. Stanton

[4] *O.R.*, XXXVI, pt. 2, 369; pt. 3, 722; Croffut, *op. cit.*, 462; Grant to Stanton, May 13, 1864, owned by the estate of Foreman M. Lebold; Johnson, "Reminiscences of Hon. Edwin M. Stanton," *loc. cit.*, 76–7, 85–6; Ida M. Tarbell, *A Reporter for the Union* (New York, 1927), 41; Hay, *Diaries and Letters*, 180.

had just that instant learned about it. He ordered Dix to close down the two papers and arrest their editors at once.

Dix became convinced that the offending editors had been the victims of a hoax. Stanton answered sharply that Dix had been ordered only to arrest the culprits and close down their papers. Dix was one of Stanton's closest friends. But the grim Secretary had no time now for pleasantries. Dix hastily complied with the order.

Other New York papers, even those that detested the gullible victims, denounced Stanton for encroachment on freedom of the press. Later investigation showed that the bogus proclamation had been transmitted to Washington over the wires of the Independent Telegraph Company. When the manager of that firm refused to open his books, Stanton arrested the entire Washington staff, as well as its employees in other cities, and other journalists he suspected of complicity.

Dix finally learned that two reprobate newsmen had been at the bottom of the deception. They had hoped to make a killing on the stock market by publishing the adverse proclamation. Dix put them both in Fort Lafayette. The telegraph company had been wholly innocent, however, and Stanton immediately released its employees, permitted its offices to be reopened, and freed the inoffensive journalists he had arrested. He would have allowed the credulous editors to cogitate on their carelessness by spending a few more weeks in jail, but Lincoln ordered their immediate release.

Welles thought that the suppression of the offending newspapers was indefensible.[5] The hypercritical Navy Secretary somehow failed to see that the effects of this proclamation, if Stanton had left it to circulate unchecked, might have threatened the North's willingness to endure the growing casualties which Grant was reporting from Virginia.

At a strategic road hub, Cold Harbor, Grant flung his men forward in repeated assaults and saw his columns wilt away in the worst slaughter of the war. Since the beginning of the campaign he had lost a third of his army. Reading the interminable casualty lists, the nation sickened at the sacrifice.

Repulsed at Cold Harbor, Grant tried again to slip around Lee's flank. But the wily Confederate, moving on interior lines, always confronted him behind breastworks and refused to be coaxed out into the

[5] Morse, *Welles Diary*, II, 38; Louis M. Starr, *Bohemian Brigade* (New York, 1954), 315–20; Dix to Stanton, May 18, 20, 1864, CHS; Lincoln, *Works*, VIII, 13–14; Dix to Mrs. Stanton, April 16, 1864, owned by Mrs. Van Swearingen.

open field against Grant's superior numbers. Further frontal attacks meant a larger loss of life than Grant could now afford. So he again moved southward, across the James River, putting himself south of Richmond, and then drove west toward Petersburg, the key to Lee's communications. Lee got reinforcements to the city's thin defense lines just in the nick of time. Grant was once again repulsed with sickening losses, and he now saw no alternative to settling down to a siege. Long lines of parallel entrenchments curled south and east of Richmond as both armies dug in. Grant stabbed at Lee's fortifications, always keeping the pressure on, and at the same time probed westward, feeling for the railroads that brought Lee's supplies.

If the other Union armies in Virginia had carried out their assignments, Lee would have been smashed or in a more desperate condition by now. But Butler, soon after commencing his move on Petersburg, was neatly sealed up in a pocket at the confluence of the Appomattox and the James; and Sigel, whose appointment had been a sop to the German voters, was defeated at New Market and obliged to retreat down the Shenandoah Valley. With Grant and Lincoln's approval, Stanton found a less important place for Sigel at Harpers Ferry, though the choice of Hunter to succeed him was not much of an improvement. To get rid of Butler, however, was a more prickly proposition.

When Grant established his headquarters at City Point after bringing Richmond under siege, he informed Halleck that it might become necessary to remove Butler from command for incompetency, and because Butler and General William F. Smith, whose services Grant valued, could not get along together. Later, Grant suggested to Halleck that Butler be transferred to some department where he would be less likely to do harm. Halleck answered that it had been foreseen in Washington that Grant might be obliged to relieve Butler because of his total unfitness for a field command and his quarrelsome nature, but he promised to be an embarrassment anywhere. The best solution of the problem would be to leave Butler in nominal command of the Department of the James, while seeing to it that he remained at his headquarters, and to give Smith command of the troops in the field.

Grant acquiesced in Halleck's suggestion. Though it was an election year and resentment on the part of Butler might cost the administration votes, Lincoln approved the order and it was issued on his authority. Meanwhile, however, Smith had put himself in bad repute by loosely voicing unflattering opinions of certain of his brother officers. Because of this, and also because Grant had come to have misgivings about the workability of a divided command, he now decided to transfer Smith elsewhere and leave Butler in command for a while longer.[6]

On the same day that Grant commenced his campaign against Richmond, Sherman marched his army out of Chattanooga and directed it toward Atlanta. His route led through rugged country, where subsistence would be difficult; but his sole complaint was of a superabundance of supplies! Stanton liked this approach to war almost as much as he admired Grant's.

Sherman's adversary, Confederate commander "Joe" Johnston, took every advantage afforded by the seamy terrain. It became a campaign of thrust and parry between two skillful swordsmen, each trying to put his opponent at a disadvantage. But Sherman kept pressing. When he notified Stanton on May 14 that he had taken Dalton, the Secretary wired his thanks and his hopes for still greater success. "Your dispatches are promptly forwarded to General Grant," he said, "and the victorious shout of your army strengthens the hearts of the Army of the Potomac."

Now, with Grant in over-all command and with Sherman performing so creditably in the West, Stanton noticeably lost his earlier antipathy toward West Pointers and was warm in his praises of Sherman. An Ohioan, the brother of the influential Republican senator John Sherman, "Tecumseh" was related by marriage to the powerful Ewing family. After graduating from the Military Academy, Sherman spent thirteen years as a regular officer, with relatively little combat service even in the Mexican War. He resigned from the Army in 1853 and unsuccessfully entered the banking field, then the law, but hungering for the military life again, he took on the superintendency of a military college in Louisiana. With the secession winter, he returned North, and in May 1861, was once more in uniform.

Trouble had dogged him, and unscrupulous journalists whom he offended spread the rumor that he was insane. No doubt Sherman was unstable, but once he joined Grant's command he performed brilliantly as a constructive subordinate. A close relationship of mutual trust had developed between him and his commanding officer. Now Sherman, on his own, was living up to Stanton's estimation.

Sherman sensed a note of discouragement in the reports Stanton sent him about Grant, and he told Stanton not to lose heart: "If General

[6] *O.R.*, XXXVI, pt. 2, 652–3, 840–1; pt. 3, 177–8; XXXVII, pt. 1, 485; XL, pt. 2, 558–9; pt. 3, 31, 59, 69, 122–3; William D. Mallam, "The Grant-Butler Relationship," *MVHR*, XLI, 260–4.

Grant can sustain the confidence, the esprit, the pluck of his army, and impress the Virginians with the knowledge that the Yankees can and will fight them fair and square, he will do more good than the capture of Richmond or any strategic movements, and this is what Grant is doing." Sherman could have added that he was doing much the same good work in the West.[7]

While Grant's guns thundered at Richmond's defenses and Sherman moved doggedly toward Atlanta, Lincoln and Stanton continued working quietly to bring the subjugated areas of the South back into the Union, and the political managers on the home front shaped their strategy for the forthcoming presidential election. Lincoln's emancipation edict and his consent to the use of Negro troops had mollified the radicals to the extent of enabling the Republicans to present a united front in the state and congressional elections of 1863, but with the national nominating convention approaching, the party cleavages opened again. Now the troublesome issue was the terms on which the seceded states were to be allowed back into the Union.

From the very beginning of the war, Lincoln had held to reunion as the primary goal. His quickness of action in the slaveholding border states in 1861 and 1862 had kept them in the Union. Since then portions of Virginia, Arkansas, Louisiana, and Florida had been taken by federal armies. Lincoln's orders and congressional enactments concerning property and suffrage rights favored loyal men and imposed penalties on the disloyal in these occupied areas.

Stanton, as head of the Army, had known the need for an over-all occupation policy long before Lincoln determined upon one. As Union forces penetrated more deeply into Dixie, Northern soldiers had come to assume the role of occupation forces. They were singularly unfitted for the task, lacking any consistent military rules, traditions, or legislative enactments for their guidance, and Stanton had asked Lieber to prepare a codification of the rules of land warfare as a basis for coordination in military occupation policies.

Yet, even before co-ordination was possible, similar needs brought Union commanders, without concert or study, to similar actions. They had the dual duties of belligerent occupation and of the restoration of national authority; they had to govern as well as occupy. This complex task fell everywhere on officials who, Stanton learned, were becoming

[7] *O.R.*, XXXVIII, pt. 4, 19–20, 173, 260–1, 281–2, 294; pt. 5, 73; Thomas Ewing, Sr., to Ellen Sherman, Dec. 12, 1862, Ewing Family Papers, LC.

the work horses of the armies once the battlesmoke cleared—the provost marshals.

Provost marshals soon transcended their traditional role as disciplinarians over troops and assumed the multifarious tasks of determining who among the Southern civilians in their control should remain free or go to jail, stay at home or face exile, get scarce food, clothes, seeds, and tools, travel on the railroads, receive mail, or practice professions and trades. Military provosts enforced Treasury, postal, and conscription laws, put confiscation policies into effect, and prosecuted before military courts those civilians who broke regulations or who were caught aiding the South or allegedly intending to do so.

Everywhere provosts enjoyed the help of Negroes and of Southern civilians who claimed always to have detested the Confederate cause, who had assembled black lists of zealous secessionists, and now were ready to claim the fruits of their Unionist fidelity. And almost everywhere, provosts tested the allegiance of the conquered civilians in their jurisdiction by requiring them to swear to some kind of an oath of loyalty. Without a provost's receipt for a completed loyalty oath, Southern civilians inside Union occupation zones could barely exist.

Stanton's role in educating Lincoln in these facts of army life was a substantial one, as together the two men read over innumerable reports from provost units on Southern duty. Out of the Army's pragmatic institutional adjustments to occupation responsibilities, Lincoln shaped one keystone of his thoughts concerning a reconstruction. He desired, the President told Banks concerning Louisiana, "a tangible nucleus" of loyal Southerners around which "the remainder of the State may rally round as fast as it can, and which I can at once recognize and sustain as the true State government." Lincoln appointed military governors for the occupied areas—empowered by his authority and the muscle of the War Department to exercise both civil and martial powers—to work with the provosts and other officers of the federal army "in reinaugurating the National authority," as Lincoln described the mission of Military Governor Hamilton in Texas.[8]

Stanton, like Lincoln, was wholly dedicated to the defeat of the South as the war's purpose rather than to any primary concern for the future of the emancipated Negro. "The occupation of Texas by the military

---

[8] *O.R.*, XXII, pt. 2, 731–2; Lincoln to Banks, Sept. 19, Nov. 5, 1863, HL; Frank Freidel, "General Orders 100 and Military Government," *MVHR*, XXXII, 549; George L. Hendricks, *Union Occupation of the Southern Seaboard* (Ph.D. thesis, Columbia University, 1954) ; Wilton P. Moore, "The Provost Marshal Goes to War," *CWH*, V, 62–71; Hyman, *op. cit.*, 166–98.

forces, and its reconquest, is the end to be accomplished," Stanton noted to Horatio Woodman, and to this end, for every rebellious state, he improvised out of what was at hand.

The Army was at hand. But in the developing complexities of military occupation not all of its growing number of component parts could work together effectively, nor was Stanton ever able fully to control his vast creation, even with his monopoly of control over the telegraph. The new military governors, for example, got into continuous difficulties with the generals and the provost marshals of the uniformed commands. Stanton told Military Governor Stanley, of North Carolina, that his powers were limitless, that Stanley was to "be Dictator." But Stanley and General Burnside engaged in a running duel concerning status, prestige, and power, which Burnside usually won. Similar disputes engaged the attention of Rosecrans and Military Governor Andrew Johnson in Tennessee, and Halleck's vast learning and persuasiveness was needed to prevent serious incidents. In essence, Lincoln's injunction to General Gillmore in Florida—"You are Master"—rather than Stanton's to the civilian, Military Governor Stanley, held true in such arguments.[9]

Lincoln left it largely up to Stanton to deal with the endless details of military occupation. He was more interested in transforming conquests into reconstructed states. The President exploited the Army's experiences as an occupation force, which Stanton related to him, and combined the existing military realities with his hopes for a future political reunification of the Southern states to the Union.

Restoring the South fell within his sphere of authority under his war powers, Lincoln believed, and as a supplement to his annual message to Congress in December 1863, he announced a plan he had been considering with Stanton for some time. Excluding only a few major offenders from its lenient terms, it offered a full pardon with restoration of most rights to property, except in slaves, to all persons implicated in the rebellion who would swear thereafter to uphold the Constitution, the Union, the Emancipation Proclamation, and all laws pertaining to slaves. Anxious to quell sectional hate and make reunion palatable to the South, the President announced further that when, in any state, a number of voters equal to one tenth of those who had participated in the election of 1860 had taken this oath of future allegiance, they could re-establish a state government, republican in form, and he would recognize it and grant it federal protection. Lincoln declared that

[9] Stanton to Woodman, Sept. 27, 1863, Woodman Papers, MHS; on Texas, Stanley to Stanton, Jan. 10; Halleck to Rosecrans, March 20, 1863, Stanton MSS; Lincoln to Gillmore, Jan. 13, 1864, Nicolay Papers, LC.

307

any provision adopted by such a state government in relation to Negroes "which shall recognize and declare their permanent freedom, provide for their education, and which may yet be consistent, as a temporary arrangement, with their present condition as a laboring, landless, and homeless class, will not be objected to by the national Executive."

It amounted to a statement that Lincoln, hoping to seduce Southern whites from their support of the Confederacy, would allow them to solve the race problem, altered as a result of emancipation, in their own way, provided they were fair-minded about it and acted quickly. Lincoln did not set this December pardon proclamation as his own final policy, much less as the only one which the nation, Congress, or the political parties might consider, for he well knew that reconstruction had to be a political issue. He made it mild because he wanted it to be attractive to Southerners, and to mark a moderate path for his party to take. Almost as a necessary consequence, its terms repelled many Northerners.

Peace Democrats in the North condemned the December 1863 pardon and reconstruction plan as excessively harsh. Republican radicals had something far more stringent in mind for the South, and the kindly, lenient Lincoln was becoming an obstacle to their plans. Other Republican senators, though less vindictive than the radicals, feared that Lincoln's readiness to forgive and forget might very well enable an unrepentant South, in alliance with Northern Democrats, to regain its old ascendancy in the national government, circumvent emancipation by keeping the Negro in a state of voteless peonage, and undo all the gains that were being won at such bitter cost in the war. Out of their forebodings came a desire to keep the reconstruction process under the control of Congress, a desire that tended to push conservative Republican congressmen into the radical orbit, thus enabling the extremists to determine legislative policies. Support of or opposition to the President's reconstruction plan soon became one of the marks that identified the faction within the Republican party to which an individual adhered.

With a presidential election coming on, radical leaders, eager to jettison Lincoln, had commenced almost a year ahead of time to consider alternatives to him. They saw in Chase a man with views close to their own, and indications of a Chase boom were evident as early as midsummer of 1863. The Treasury Secretary listened appreciatively and craftily nudged the movement along. Smugly convinced of his own rectitude and inordinately ambitious to be President, he let it be known that his talents were available for whatever role he might be called to fill.

Rumors came to Washington that the 10,000 Treasury agents were organizing Chase clubs throughout the country. Newspapers willing to support Chase's candidacy were favored with Treasury advertising. Chase seldom attended cabinet meetings any more, and seemed to be avoiding the President. Stanton told Dana that although Lincoln knew full well what was taking place, he made no effort to stop it.

Postmaster General Blair, Stanton's unrelenting enemy, declared that Stanton "would cut the President's throat if he could," and fancied that the patronage of the State, War, and Treasury departments was being used against the President.[1] Blair's hatred of Stanton had become so vitriolic that he would believe nothing good of him. But Bates, a man of cautious legal mind who formed his judgments carefully, also suspected Stanton of working secretly for Chase.

The truth is that Stanton's approval of Lincoln and of the Lincoln reconstruction plan was unconditional, and he had nothing to do with Chase's sly maneuverings. Yet his personal relations with the ambitious Treasury head continued to be close, for soon after Lincoln announced his plan for the South, Stanton asked Chase to stand as godfather at the baptism of his baby daughter, Bessie.

Nevertheless, Stanton wholeheartedly supported Lincoln's reconstruction program, for in December 1863 and throughout 1864, it fit the Army's needs. The day after Christmas, Lincoln and Stanton visited the prison camp at Point Lookout, Virginia, where the amnesty proclamation had already enticed a sizable portion of the captured rebels into signifying their desire to become "galvanized Yankees." Stanton thereafter ordered cavalry units and Union spies to spread copies of the proclamation throughout the South, greatly adding to the effectiveness of the Union's propaganda. Combined with increasing Northern victories, the Lincoln reconstruction and pardon plan proved a powerful solvent of the Southern will to fight. Despite organized and unofficial Confederate attempts to combat it, it helped bring on the ultimate collapse of the rebellion. Stanton's acuity in recognizing the potency of the Lincoln plan as a war weapon must be given its due credit.[2]

[1] William E. Smith, *The Francis Preston Blair Family in Politics* (New York, 1933), II, 252 (hereafter cited as Smith, *Blair Family*); Morse, *Welles Diary*, II, 58; Hay, *Diaries and Letters*, 60–70; Bates, *Diary*, 310; Lincoln, *Works*, VII, 53–6.

[2] Hyman, *op. cit.*, 187–90; Lincoln, *Works*, VII, 95; Morse, *Welles Diary*, I, 536; Bates, *Diary*, 343; Stanton to Chase, Dec. 30, 1863, HSP.

Working through the War Department, Lincoln tried out his reconstruction plan in four of the states now partially controlled by Union armies—Louisiana, Arkansas, Tennessee, and Virginia. In the first three, Unionist constitutions were soon created and ratified by the required 10 per cent of oath-swearing voters. Then state officials from governors on down were installed under the protection of army bayonets, and these states sent representatives to Congress. In Virginia a Unionist minority under Francis H. Pierpont, which had set up a rump government at Alexandria, had previously won Lincoln's recognition as the rightful government of the state.

But in no case did Congress, dominated by the radicals, consent to seat the delegates elected by these states. To be sure, the new state governments rested on the shaky bases of Union Army support and the conversions of former rebels, whose sincerity in swearing oaths of future loyalty the radicals professed to doubt; and as will be seen, Lincoln himself came to distrust the regeneration of the residents in these "loyal" areas of the South.

Congress in July 1864 created a more drastic reconstruction measure as a product of radical pressure. Known as the Wade-Davis bill, it contradicted Lincoln's plan in every particular; asserted Congress's right to control the reconstruction process; and declared that reconstruction must wait until rebel resistance ceased, that the majority, not merely 10 per cent, of the voters in a Southern state must swear to an "ironclad test oath" of past as well as future loyalty, that ex-Confederates must be excluded from suffrage and officeholding unless Congress rather than the President pardoned them, and that slavery, along with the rebel war debt, was dead. The Wade-Davis plan obviously looked to substituting Negro voters for almost all Southern whites, for few whites could honestly claim the kind of unalloyed past Unionism that the test oath required.

Lincoln was hurt and angry at this open challenge by men who were leaders of his own party, especially as it was made in an election year. He killed the Procrustean Wade-Davis bill with a pocket veto, explaining to the country that its enactment would have snuffed out the free state governments already established in the South. But he admitted that he was not inflexibly committed to his own plan of reconstruction. If Southerners wanted to come back into the Union under the Wade-Davis terms, Lincoln would enforce its stipulations. Enraged by Lincoln's action, the sponsors of the bill drew up a manifesto excoriating the President.

Though co-operating fully with Lincoln in establishing these new state governments, Stanton remained on close terms with Wade and Davis.[3] The tenacious suspicion that Lincoln's "Mars" was supporting the radicals in their war upon Lincoln seems to gain a degree of credibility from Stanton's later testimony to the Senate Judiciary Committee that reconstruction was properly "subject to the controlling power of Congress." He had never doubted that his and Lincoln's efforts to create loyal state governments in the South were legal and necessary, he said, but added: "I supposed then and still suppose, that the final validity of such organizations, would rest with the law-making power of the Government."

In this view Stanton was not, however, as Welles and more recent commentators mistakenly assumed, at odds with Lincoln. The President also recognized that the two houses of Congress had the autonomous power to pass on the admission of their own members, and thus could determine the final step in reconstruction.[4]

Chase's self-appointed campaign manager, Senator Samuel C. Pomeroy, of Kansas, arranged for the public distribution late in February 1864 of a "strictly private" circular lauding the Ohioan's qualifications for the presidency and sharply criticizing Lincoln. Chase, embarrassed at the revelation of what appeared to be double-dealing on his part, hastened to disclaim all prior knowledge of the circular and submitted his resignation to Lincoln. The President chose to welcome his profession of ignorance and refused to accept the resignation. But the incident alerted Lincoln's partisans and moved them to counteraction.

Various Republican state conventions warmly endorsed Lincoln. And when a legislative caucus at Columbus announced that the Republicans in Ohio intended to support the President, Chase was left in the position of a candidate unable to obtain the backing of his own state. When news of this action in Ohio reached Washington, Welles overheard Seward and Stanton chuckling over Chase's misfortune. The next day Chase announced his withdrawal from the race.

With Chase ostensibly out of contention, some radical Republicans

[3] *O.R.*, XXVI, pt. 1, 694–5; William A. Russ, Jr., "Administrative Activities of the Union Army during and after the Civil War," *Mississippi Law Journal*, XVII, 71–89; Brooks, *op. cit.*, 156–7; Jonathan T. Dorris, *Pardon and Amnesty under Lincoln and Johnson* (Chapel Hill, 1953), 3–94.

[4] Wade to William Stanton, Feb. 5, 1864, owned by William Stanton Picher; Morse, *Welles Diary*, II, 247; Stanton's statement in George S. Boutwell, *Reminiscences of Sixty Years of Public Affairs* (New York, 1902), II, 90–3 (cited hereafter as Boutwell, *Reminiscences*).

tried to engineer Butler as a replacement for Lincoln, but the scheme failed to catch fire. A splinter group brought their discontent into the open by nominating Frémont. But the more astute radical leaders hesitated to oppose the President openly and preferred to play for time, trying unsuccessfully to postpone the Republican, or, as it was finally named, the National Union Convention.[5]

On June 7, the Republican convention met in Baltimore and Lincoln won in a walk. The politicians who would gladly have thrown him over had sensed that the people were solidly behind him, and masking their mortification, they bowed to the inevitable. Stanton was happy with the result, but he was displeased that Andrew Johnson, of Tennessee, had been nominated Vice-President. Distrusting all Southerners and by now most Democrats as well, Stanton would have preferred to see Hannibal Hamlin on the ticket again. The cabal against Lincoln had made Stanton very angry and he took special pleasure in Lincoln's success at the convention.[6]

Though the radicals had been able to offer little formal opposition to Lincoln's renomination, the harmony that impressed many persons was wholly on the surface. Scarcely had some of the delegates returned to their homes when they began scheming to sidetrack Lincoln before election time, if they could find a candidate more to their liking. Lincoln was about to perform some sidetracking of his own, for soon after the nominating convention he reached the end of the road with Chase.

The crisis came about over the job of Assistant U. S. Treasurer in New York City when Chase chose to ignore the wishes of both New York senators and attempted to give the post to one of his henchmen. Balked by Lincoln, he tendered his resignation, a move he had previously found effective in causing Lincoln to back down. But this time the President resolved to call Chase's bluff.

Chase submitted his resignation on June 29, and that night Governor Brough, of Ohio, who had just arrived in Washington, encountered Lincoln, who, after cautioning him to "remember that it is not public until tomorrow," proceeded to tell him of his intention to accept Chase's

---

[5] Donnal V. Smith, *Chase and Civil War Politics* (Columbus, 1931), 116–54.

[6] Hay, *Diaries and Letters*, 168. Some unreliable evidence exists to indicate that Lincoln and Stanton tried to have Butler nominated for Vice-President. Like Johnson, Butler was a war Democrat, and his submergence into politics would have relieved Stanton of the problem of removing him from a field command. Butler refused a second place on the ticket, and the move, if it was ever seriously made, came to nothing. A. E. H. Johnson's reminiscence in New York *Evening Post*, July 13, 1891; Butler, *Correspondence*, IV, 29.

resignation. Brough suggested that if Lincoln would delay action until morning and give him time to "get the Ohio men together," he might be able to straighten the matter out.

"But this is the third time he has thrown this resignation at me," Lincoln said, "and I do not think I am called on to continue to beg him to take it back, especially when the country would not go to destruction in consequence."

"This is not simply a personal matter," Brough responded. "The people will not understand it. They will insist that there is no longer any harmony in the councils of the nation and that the retiring of the Sec'y of the Treasury is a sure indication that the bottom is about to fall out. Therefore to save the country from this backset, if you will give me time, I think Ohio can close the breach and the world be none the wiser."

Lincoln answered: "I know you doctored the matter up once, but on the whole, Brough, I reckon you had better let it alone this time."

"Then I have but one more question to ask," said Brough. "Have you settled who is to be the successor, or is the matter open to advisement?"

Lincoln said somewhat hesitantly that he had someone in mind but would keep that to himself for the present. Brough said he intended to call on Stanton, and Lincoln admonished him: "Remember, Brough, not a word of this to any one."

Brough talked to Stanton for almost two hours, never divulging what he knew. The next morning he again called on Stanton, and while the two men sat talking a messenger brought each of them a note from Chase. Stanton opened his and read silently: "I felt myself bound yesterday to send my resignation to the President. I would have been gratified to be able to consult you, but I feared you might be prompted by your generous sentiments to take some step injurious to the country. Today my resignation has been accepted, and if you have not already been informed of it, it is due to you that I should give you the information as soon as received by myself."

Meanwhile, Brough, glancing through the note that Chase had sent him, learned that Lincoln intended to appoint former Governor Tod, of Ohio, to the Treasury post.

Stanton finished reading, slipped Chase's note in his pocket, and fell back in his chair with a groan. Brough rose to go, but Stanton gasped: "For God's sake don't leave me yet."

"I think," said Brough, "you have quite as much as you can digest today."

"What do you refer to?" asked Stanton.

"I mean that little paper in your pocket."

"What do you know about it?"

"Oh, I knew of it last night."

"You did, d—n you, and did not tell me of it? Is that being friendly?"

"I was under a pledge of secrecy which I could not violate."

"But what will we do, who can succeed him?"

"His successor is already appointed, and his name is sent to the Senate."

"Who is it?"

"Ex-Gov. Tod."

Stanton gasped when he heard this. "Then we are gone!"

Tod, while serving as governor, had co-operated splendidly with the War Department. But he was known as an extreme hard-money man and could scarcely be expected to continue Chase's policy of issuing paper money. Stanton, once a hard-money man himself, had come to accept paper money as the only means of keeping the war machine going and of avoiding the bankruptcy nightmare he had feared since Sumter. And he remembered the old Ohio campaign slogan: "Vote for Tod and the black laws." He feared that Tod would align himself with the Blair-Welles wing in the cabinet.

"Well, Stanton, I must go," said Brough, "but let me give you a bit of comfort: *that appointment will never be accepted.*"

"Then, remember," said Stanton, "that I hold you personally responsible for the result."

Moving on, Brough drove over to see Chase and frankly expressed the opinion that Chase had been in the wrong, then returned to the White House, where Lincoln confided that the feverishly excited members of the Senate Finance Committee were unalterably opposed to Tod and wanted him to withdraw the nomination. But he did not intend to do it. Brough predicted that Tod would resolve the difficulty by refusing to accept the appointment.

And that night, Hay brought Brough a note from Lincoln stating that Tod had declined to serve. Brough broke the news to Stanton. The Secretary exclaimed joyfully: "You may go where you please, Brough, I am going to bed to sleep. *We are safe for another day.*"

Early the next morning, Lincoln advised Stanton that an Ohio man must replace Chase, and that he was considering former Governor Dennison, a stiff-necked, energetic, antislavery man, whose administration of the state's finances at the outbreak of the war had been somewhat loose, and whose forceful war measures as governor had not been popular. Meeting Brough later, Stanton said: "You must help me defeat that, Brough, or we are lost. I would not remain Secretary of War an hour after such an appointment."

Brough found the President adamant on the point of giving Chase's place to an Ohioan. Stanton had suggested during his talk with Lincoln that Brough would be far better than Dennison, but Brough immediately refused the post and said Ohio would be better satisfied to have it go to someone of national reputation in matters of finance.

Just then a messenger entered and laid a card on Lincoln's table. Brough saw the name of William Pitt Fessenden, chairman of the Senate Finance Committee, on the card, and told the President: "There is your man."

"He will not accept," said Lincoln.

"The public will compel him to," said Brough. The President took Brough's advice and sent Fessenden's name to the Senate.[7]

Fessenden, an advocate of drastic wartime taxes and of Chase's financial measures, though accounted a radical, was far more moderate in his attitude toward the South than Chandler, Stevens, or Wade. Stanton regarded him as wholly satisfactory and urged him to accept the appointment. When Fessenden complained that the job would kill him, Stanton retorted: "Very well, you cannot die better than in trying to save your country." Fessenden's acceptance of the position pleased all factions of the party, and Welles, who, like Stanton, had feared that Chase's departure might excite unrest, noted that "it appears to give relief rather than otherwise."

In fact, Chase discovered that he had few real friends. On the day his retirement was announced, only Stanton and Fessenden of the cabinet called at his home. He found Stanton always warm and cordial. "No other Head of Dep't has called on me since my resignation," he later admitted to his diary, and on another occasion noted that he had "called on Mrs. Stanton. Nice children. Took tea with the family & spent evening." [8]

It took courage on Stanton's part to maintain public association with the discredited Chase, for their continued friendship inspired rumors that he too was on the way out. But Lincoln appreciated Stanton's worth. In addition, the President knew that Ohioans regarded Stanton as their

---

[7] Brough related his experiences to William Henry Smith almost immediately after returning to Ohio; ms "Private Memoranda—War Times," William Henry Smith Papers, OHS; and see Chase to Tod, June 20, 1863, Chase Papers, ser. 2, LC.

[8] Chase, *Diary*, 240; Sept. 16, 1864, ms diary, Chase Papers, LC; memo, undated, J. W. Schuckers Papers, LC; Fessenden, *op. cit.*, I, 320–1; Morse, *Welles Diary*, II, 62.

man and would have deplored his exit from the cabinet so soon on Chase's heels. Yet Stanton's intimacy with Chase, Wade, Davis, and other radicals does not mean that he was faithless to Lincoln. He seemed, rather, to be trying to bring them and the President somewhere closer to a middle position on reconstruction. Under either Lincoln's or the congressional reconstruction plan, the Army must play a primary role. Stanton had to know what was going on, and he was, as always, willing to dissimulate in order to stay on the inside track.

It is clear, however, that his own feelings at this time were far closer to Lincoln's than to the radical extremists'. Shrewd Samuel Bowles considered Stanton to be in "the extreme right of the Republican party" along with Lincoln, Chase, and Andrew, rather than of "the Wendell Phillips school." Furthermore, Butler, now a thoroughgoing radical, complained that Chase's departure from the cabinet had left that faction without representation among the President's official advisers.[9]

And so the sultry political vapors from the steam box that is Washington in summer, blew hot across the country, veiling the true feelings of the sphinxlike figure in the War Department toward the President and toward Chase, his friend of long standing. The rivalry that had long marked the relations between Lincoln and Chase might yet determine the next occupant of the White House, the outcome of the war, and the destiny of the nation; the Republican party, dedicated to repairing the shattered Union, seemed on the way to its own rupture. But the politicians were more strained than the political organizations.

For the first time in the war, the military and political situations were actually well under control. Writing to a friend abroad from Grant's headquarters at City Point, Dana commented on Chase's retirement and on Lincoln's renomination, and mirrored Stanton's feelings on events. The radicals were "desperately opposed to Mr. Lincoln," Dana asserted, "not only on account of his slowness in going ahead upon questions of principle, but especially on account of his persistent attachment to the Blairs, who are upon the whole, the most unpopular men in the whole country." But with the nomination once made, most men accepted Lincoln as the best choice.

The Democratic party, Dana continued, "seems to be hopelessly split" between the peace and war factions, and thus their convention was being delayed until August in hope of reconciling the two. McClellan

---

[9] George S. Merriam, *The Life and Times of Samuel Bowles* (New York, 1885), I, 390–1; Butler to G. Gooch, March 1, 1864, Butler Papers, LC.

would probably be the opposition candidate, he guessed, although the Unionist branch "is looking to Grant." He would not run, Dana was sure, and so Lincoln's triumph was certain.

Sherman was now "far forward into the centre of Georgia," closing in on Atlanta, destroying Jefferson Davis's last major rail links between the southeast and the Mississippi Valley. Grant has "a secure base, with short lines of communication" on the James, threatening Richmond and the eastern terminus of the Southern railroad system, such as it was. "It is a mere question of time and patience, though you need not be surprised at more brilliant and effective movements," Dana advised. Lee was no longer a threat except for nuisance raids and there would be no more full-scale invasions of the North. "All of his railroads have been broken up, all of northwest Virginia is destitute, deprived not only of supplies but of laborers, so that the harvests which have been put into the ground . . . cannot be harvested. . . . Indeed it would be difficult to form an idea of a territory more trampled and blasted by the hoof of war, than the greater part of Virginia. I have now been over the most of it, and it is a scene of desolation which beggars fancy, and it is becoming more gloomy from day to day." [1] The gloomier Virginia appeared to Dana, the happier Stanton became. This was the way to wage war.

[1] Dana to James S. Pike, July 10, 1864, CFL.

CHAPTER XV

A TOWER OF STRENGTH

ANA'S PREDICTION that the only way Lee could now harass the North was by means of raiding parties was accurate. Gray raiders broke loose in the Shenandoah Valley once again in the first week of July. Bald, stooped Confederate general Jubal Early commanded the raiders, but beyond this there was little reliable information. Stanton was taking all possible emergency measures, but he desperately needed accurate intelligence.

On July 8, Hitchcock called on Halleck. He was alarmed by the danger to the capital represented by Early's thrust, but Halleck was calm and passive. At Stanton's behest, Halleck had warned Grant of the situation, but Grant had recommended no course of action. Thinking it unwise to leave decisions affecting the safety of Washington to Grant far down in Virginia, Hitchcock hurried to see Stanton and repeated his forebodings. The Secretary calmly told him that everything was in Grant's hands.

Hitchcock was far from satisfied, and he decided to see Lincoln. He found him more depressed than he had ever seen him, "indeed quite paralyzed and wilted down," but nevertheless the President repeated what Halleck and Stanton had said. Hitchcock warned that if Stonewall Jackson were alive and in command of the rebel raiders, Washington would fall within three days. There was nothing to stop him. Stanton had told Lincoln the same thing, Hitchcock later learned. But neither of them could move the President. Hitchcock concluded that Lincoln, having been criticized before for interfering in tactical movements, had resolved to keep hands off Grant, and Stanton was obeying this decision.

The rebels crossed the Potomac. Lincoln, now spending every free minute at the War Department, told Hay that with good management the Union forces could annihilate any enemy detachments that ventured north of the river. Stanton agreed, provided that General Hunter would act vigorously. But Hunter had withdrawn too far westward and might not come up in time, and Sigel, Stanton knew, was inept.

Lincoln and Stanton were determined not to withdraw men from Grant, although they hoped that he would recognize their danger and decide to send some troops to Washington. The Secretary called on Pennsylvania and New York for 100,000 militiamen each to serve for 100 days. Governor Seymour responded handsomely, but Curtin was obstreperous, as usual, insisting that he control the Pennsylvania troops but that the federal government pay and supply them. Stanton scorned the proposition; unless these men were under army control they were useless. The governor finally backed down.[1]

Debouching from the Valley and swinging eastward toward Washington, Early's troops seemed to overrun western Maryland. Though Union general Lew Wallace dug in at the Monacacy River, Hunter, who might have come in on Early's rear, seemed paralyzed. Tardily recognizing the seriousness of the threat Early posed, Grant sent Rickett's division of the 6th Corps to support Wallace, but on July 9 the Confederates swept through this thin barrier. Washington lay before them. Grant wired Halleck that the rest of the 6th and part of the 19th Corps were hurrying to the rescue. Stanton, anxiously waiting for the reinforcements to arrive, had a new worry. He had reports that an unknown horseman was shadowing Lincoln's carriage; the Secretary increased the cavalry escort which, at his orders, had been guarding Lincoln for a year.

Early's marauders snipped the telegraph wires connecting Washington with the North. No trains entered or left the city. Refugees streamed in from the countryside, their household goods piled helter-skelter on any sort of conveyance they could lay their hands on. Pale soldiers from convalescent camps and ragtag District militiamen manned the capital's forts. War Department clerks worked with loaded muskets beside their desks, expecting momentarily to be ordered to the entrenchments.

Stanton became somewhat nervous, but managed to calm some bureau officers more agitated than himself. He had his secretary take $5,000 in government bonds and $400 in gold belonging to Ellen, now their entire personal fortune, from a War Department safe and carry

---

[1] Chase, *Diary*, 234; Hay, *Diaries and Letters*, 206; *O.R.*, XXXVII, pt. 2, 16–18, 37, 70, 91, 94; Hitchcock to Mrs. Horace Mann, July 14, 1864, Hitchcock-Mann Correspondence, LC, which is far fuller than the account in Croffutt, *op. cit.*, 463–4.

them home with him that night. The clerk hid them in his mattress.[2]

Toward midnight on July 10, Stanton sent for the Lincolns to come in from the Soldiers' Home in Georgetown, where the Lincolns and the Stantons had adjoining summer residences. Lincoln was irritated and came to the White House against his will. He was angrier when he learned that a gunboat was standing by so that the President might flee from the city. Lincoln later learned that it had not been Stanton who ordered the vessel readied, but Admiral S. P. Lee, who was later rebuked by Welles for contributing to the public panic.

On July 11, troops from the Army of the Potomac reached the city in strength. Early's men began to withdraw. Lincoln and Stanton hoped to cut them off, but they recrossed the Potomac loaded with plunder. Dana, for Stanton, wrote Grant the next day that everything had been at loose ends for want of a commander in the Washington area, and Grant should appoint one at once, because if the incompetent Hunter ever managed to get to Washington, he would be the ranking officer, "but he will not do." It was up to Grant to act now; mere advice or suggestions were insufficient. "General Halleck will not give orders except as he receives them; the President will give none, and until you direct explicitly what is to be done," Dana implored Grant at Stanton's behest, "everything will go on in the deplorable and fatal way in which it has gone on in the past week." Grant was clearly in top command.

But just as clearly, the Union chain of authority, weakened by Halleck's maidenly behavior, needed a link below Grant capable of independent action in the area north of the Army of the Potomac. Early's raid, to Grant, meant only that Lee was weaker by that many troops; to Lincoln and Stanton, it was a threat to the symbol of the Union.[3]

Montgomery Blair, furious at the burning of his home in Silver Springs by the raiders, commented openly that the army officials around Washington were incompetent poltroons, specially criticizing Halleck and Stanton. Halleck protested to Stanton that the slanderer should be ousted from the cabinet. Stanton referred the matter to Lincoln without comment; the Secretary agreed with Blair about the incompetent officers and wanted to dismiss Halleck, but Lincoln would not allow it.

---

[2] Grant to Halleck, July 9, 1864, R. T. Lincoln Collection, LC; William Whiting to A. C. Washburn, July 11, 1864, Washburn Papers, MHS; reminiscence of A. E. H. Johnson in Washington *Star*, Nov. 2, 1895.

[3] Brooks, *op. cit.*, 160; Hay, *Diaries and Letters*, 208; *O.R.*, XXXVII, pt. 2, 223; S. P. Lee to James R. Doolittle, Feb. 20, 1865, Doolittle Papers, LC.

Through the raid and the subsequent recriminations, Stanton kept his temper in check to a noticeable degree. He had been quiet and subdued through the whole affair, displaying little of the apprehension that he usually exhibited under stress. Stanton even claimed to William Henry Smith, an Ohio friend, a week after Early's threat was dispelled, "that the most comfortable time in Washington since the beginning of the war, was when cut off last week from the rest of the world." His son, who had been with his father every moment, wrote proudly to Pamphila: "You may be sure that father did his duty, humiliating as it was to witness persistent carelessness and blundering and discouraging as it was to be constantly hampered because some one's feelings might be hurt by supersedure, or for other paltry reasons." The War Secretary, young Edwin claimed, "was constantly vigilant," and Lincoln would have done well to listen to him.[4]

Stanton's mild behavior seems most attributable to his faith in Lincoln and Grant. He could face the world as he had never been able to do under that general's predecessors in command. Like Stanton, Grant distrusted Hunter, who finally asked to be relieved. Grant readily consented. He had already chosen Philip Henry Sheridan to command in the Shenandoah Valley. This mite of an Irishman, short, slight, ungainly, seemed too inexperienced to Stanton, but both he and Lincoln acceded to Grant's judgment, and Sheridan proved to be a terror in battle. Grant, like Stanton, wanted to supersede Halleck at this time, but Lincoln again vetoed the idea.[5]

By early August, however, Stanton was again exhibiting his well-known nervous pessimism, and this attitude is reflected in Dana's admission "that [the] last month has very much complicated the political as well as the military situation." Grant was stalemated near Richmond. The old evil of the Army of the Potomac—mutual recriminations among the officers—was reappearing. "At all this the country is deeply discouraged," Dana admitted, "and the party for peace at any price very active. Still more active, if possible, is the anti-Lincoln party among the Republicans, composed of all the elements of discontent that a four year administration could produce." The Democrats, happy at Republican discord, were, however, finding that their "candidate is missing after the most desperate search," but Dana again

---

[4] *O.R.*, XXXVII, pt. 2, 223; Stanton to Halleck, July 14, 1864, Letterbook IV, Stanton MSS; Browning, *Diary*, I, 675–6; Hitchcock to Mrs. Horace Mann, July 14, 1864, Hitchcock-Mann Correspondence, LC; memo, July 18, 1864, W. H. Smith Papers, OHS; Lincoln, *Works*, VII, 439–40; to Pamphila in Wolcott MS, 195–6; Smith, *Blair Family*, II, 274.

[5] Aug. 4, 1864, C. B. Comstock ms diary, LC; *O.R.*, XL, pt. 3, 357; L, pt. 2, 945–51.

prophesied that they must take on McClellan. Lincoln and Stanton saw the probable candidacy of McClellan on the Democratic ticket as a first move toward getting the Union Army to quit fighting, Dana reported, and to this end the peace faction was trying to restore the general to an active command before the election, "but I don't think it has had any influence on the mind of the President, or that there is any likelihood of his yielding to it."

Despite reverses and losses the South was "as defiant as at first," Dana admitted gloomily. The Wade-Davis manifesto had virtually served notice that the Republican extremists intended to desert Lincoln in mid-campaign and find some other candidate on whom the party could unite.[6]

Realizing the importance of making a show of strength on behalf of Lincoln and the Republican-Union coalition, Stanton had swung into action in Kentucky, the first state to hold an election after Lincoln's nomination. It was scheduled for August 1. Only certain county offices and an appellate-judgeship were at stake, but the Kentucky election was regarded as a bellwether for the voting of the other border states in September.

Lincoln declared martial law in Kentucky and suspended the privilege of the writ of habeas corpus. The Army, under tough young General S. G. Burbridge, a native son, tightened its grip on the state. Prominent Democrats were arrested and the name of a Democratic candidate for judge was stricken from the polls on the ground that he was disloyal. But Democratic party leaders made a substitute nomination for the judgeship, and their candidates swept the state.

Although the defeat in Kentucky made Stanton pessimistic, he never permitted his discouragement to become despair, and he turned his attention to Maine, another early-voting state. Governor Samuel Cony wanted men who had enlisted for coastal defense and in the Navy credited against the state's draft quota. If the people were denied this "pitiful favor," he warned Stanton, "you may look for political results agreeable neither to you nor myself." But Grant needed men. Stanton refused the governor's plea and another for a delay in the hated draft. In spite of this, Republican candidates came through with comfortable majorities, and Cony congratulated Stanton on this gratifying result.[7]

The Republican victory in Maine failed to end the search by some of

[6] Dana to J. S. Pike, Aug. 8, 1864, CFL.
[7] Hesseltine, *War Governors*, 375–6; *O.R.*, ser. 3, IV, 488–90, 544–5, 639, 688–90, 714.

the party's leaders for a better presidential candidate than Lincoln. Once started, the movement gained its greatest impetus in New York City, though it ramified elsewhere. On August 25, Republican National Chairman Henry J. Raymond and members of his committee, highly alarmed, hurried to the White House for a consultation with Lincoln. "Hell is to pay," wrote Nicolay. "The N. Y. politicians have got a stampede on that is about to swamp everything." Raymond thought the only way to silence Lincoln's critics and salvage the election would be to bring about a quick peace. He suggested that Lincoln send a peace commission to Richmond.

Inwardly Lincoln felt no more confident of his re-election than did Raymond, but he presented a bold front. And Seward, Stanton, and Fessenden—"the strong half of the cabinet," Nicolay called them— backed up his assertion that to sue for peace would be worse than losing the presidential contest, it would be to surrender it in advance, and argued that the people still had faith in Lincoln. The committee members, according to Nicolay, returned home "much encouraged and cheered up." [8]

Just at this time an incident occurred, however, that put Stanton in a bad light. The Democrats, capitalizing on the nation's war-weariness, claimed that the Lincoln administration would reject any overtures for peace; actually there was no chance of peace, except through military victory, unless it was to be on Confederate terms. With Lincoln adamant against negotiations unless they promised a restoration of the Union, Stanton found himself associated with a peace effort that reflected unfavorably on the administration.

The move was initiated by the erratic Horace Greeley, when he learned on dubious authority that two Confederate agents had arrived on the Canadian side of Niagara Falls with credentials from Jefferson Davis to treat for a cessation of hostilities. They were Clement C. Clay, of Alabama, and Jacob Thompson, late of Buchanan's cabinet, and their real purpose was to foment unrest in the North. But the gullible Greeley obtained Lincoln's reluctant consent to make contact with them. His efforts resulted in failure, as Lincoln had foreseen, but Jeremiah Black, no less credulous than Greeley, believed that if he could sit down face to face with his old friend Thompson, something might be accomplished. Stopping at Stanton's home one morning, Black told him

[8] Nicolay to Hay, Aug. 25, and to Therena Bates, Aug. 28, 1864, Nicolay Papers, LC.

what he had in mind. Stanton assented to his plan, not caring to counter Lincoln's earlier consent to Greeley.

Returning from Toledo, where he had found Thompson, Black wrote to Stanton on August 24 that he had gained the impression that the Southern people ardently wished for peace and would welcome an armistice, provided their domestic affairs would remain undisturbed and they would be allowed to honor their state debts and reward their soldiers. They now assertedly resented French and British attentions, and regarded the question of slavery in the territories as unimportant, Black reported; nor did he think they would demand a fugitive slave law.[9]

It was quite clear that the Confederates wanted things their own way, and Stanton answered Black tartly that he had no intention of conveying his advice to the President. Moreover, he resented Black's tying him in so closely with his visit to Thompson, as a result of which the newspapers were making it appear that Black had acted under authorization from the government. "The upshot of it all is," he wrote, "that you go for an Armistice, which is nothing more and nothing else than South Carolina wanted when the rebellion began; you and I then opposed it as fatal to the government and our national existence. I still oppose it on the same ground."

Black, in hot anger, challenged his former friend's veracity, going on for eight pages, defending the desirability of an armistice and carping at Stanton. With these amenities, their long friendship ended. Black had helped Stanton get his start as a Washington lawyer; they had worked hard and fruitfully together on the California cases and in Buchanan's cabinet; Stanton had loaned Black money to help his friend out of serious personal difficulties. Now it was over, and Black was to become one of Stanton's bitterest foes.[1]

So the hopes of victory that had budded so brightly in the spring wilted in the hot, dry summer. Grant was at a standstill. Early again erupted from the Shenandoah Valley. Sherman apologized for his slow rate of advance. Stanton, though weary, regained his unwonted mildness. He answered Sherman: "Do not imagine that we are impatient at your progress." The War Department would provide him

[9] Black to Stanton, Aug. 24, 1864, Black Papers, LC; Gorham, *Stanton*, II, 148–53; Ralph F. Fahrney, *Horace Greeley, and the Tribune in the Civil War* (Cedar Rapids, 1936), 172.

[1] To Black, Aug. 13, 1864, and Black to Stanton, Sept. 3, 1864, and on the loan, note of Nov. 17, 1859, Black Papers, LC; Edward C. Kirkland, *The Peacemakers of 1864* (New York, 1927), 121; Brigance, *op. cit.*, 119, 128–9.

everything he needed; "take your time," Stanton encouraged, "and do your work your own way."

But with most of the fall elections coming on, Republican politicians became fretful at the slow progress of the war. Chase made his peace with Lincoln. But the schism with the Frémont faction remained unhealed and many of Stanton's radical friends continued to scheme against Lincoln. Stanton himself remained wholeheartedly for the President's re-election. Some persons felt that Lincoln would improve his chances by dismissing his crusty War Secretary, but the President did not agree. Answering a petition inquiring whether the rumors were true that Stanton had resigned, Lincoln said that the reports were "all a mistake."

Most Union Republicans regarded Stanton as an indispensable asset to the President. One Ohio politician heard rumors that Stanton was resigning, and pleaded with him not to do so. "If, in this crisis, *you* should leave, *Ohio is gone*," he said. "For God's sake, stand to your post. Don't give an inch. Your name in Ohio is a tower of strength for Lincoln." [2]

The resignation rumors grew in certainty and detail. There was little real food for them to feed on, however, and Stanton would be "one of the very last to quit, and never except on compulsion," Welles thought.

Others were less contemptuous of Stanton. Samuel Shellabarger, onetime Republican congressman from the Columbus district, and now trying for a comeback, hoped that Stanton could make speeches in his behalf in Ohio, and a premature announcement that Stanton would campaign for Republicans in that state had, one party stalwart wrote, "created great enthusiasm." The Young Men's Republican Union and the General Committee of War Democrats asked him to speak in New York City to "accomplish vast good," and Sumner's aid was enlisted to get the Secretary there. Frank W. Ballard, secretary of a New York businessman's war association, thought a Stanton speech "would reduce McClellan's ratio in this city alone from ten or fifteen thousand votes" and "aid us in . . . exploding his gunboat." [3]

But Stanton had to decline these appeals for personal appearances

[2] For Sherman, see *O.R.*, XXXVIII, pt. 5, 390; Henry C. Wilson to Stanton, Sept. 12, 1864, Stanton MSS; Lincoln's endorsement on petition, July 27, 1864, Lincoln Photostat Coll., LC.

[3] Morse, *Welles Diary*, II, 102; Shellabarger to Stanton, Sept. 12, H. C. Page to same, Sept. 21, and C. S. Spencer to same, Sept. 26, 1864, Stanton MSS; Ballard to Sumner, *ca.* Sept. 30, 1864, George Fort Milton Papers, LC.

because of the pressure of war duties. His reticence convinced Mc-
Clellan, among others, that Lincoln and Stanton were close to a
complete break, which was not true.

It seems clear that most Northerners, Republican or Democrat, felt
that Lincoln and Stanton were for the same things and hoped to reach
their goals by agreed means. "Both of you rise and fall with the cause of
the country," Stanton heard from a New York supporter who believed
that the triad of Lincoln, Stanton, and Union were "inseparable" and
"unconquerable." Stanton was soon to show his devotion to the President and to the Republican-Union party, which he envisaged as the
political institution that would make the sacrifices of "his" Army
worth while.[4]

On August 29 the Democrats nominated McClellan, with George H.
Pendleton, of Ohio, as his running mate. The platform called for the
immediate cessation of hostilities and a negotiated peace on the "basis
of the Federal Union of the States." McClellan renounced the peace
plank but tried to reap benefit from the deep discouragement in the
North. Despite his refusal to endorse a peace-at-any-price policy, the
election would determine whether the war would be fought to a finish.
That was enough to stir Stanton to action, over and above his own
detestation of the Democratic candidate.

His energy further convinced Lincoln that "Stanton's familiarity
with all the existing complications in the War Department would
render [it] difficult to part with him at this juncture." Lincoln, in order
to placate the radicals who still smarted at Chase's dismissal, and to
show defiance to McClellan, who seemed to consider the presidential
race as a contest between himself and Stanton as well as with Lincoln,
decided that the radicals must be placated, and that Postmaster General
Montgomery Blair was more expendable than War Secretary Stanton.
The President dismissed Blair, naming Dennison to his place, and
Stanton's most active enemy was gone from the cabinet. Frémont
renounced his candidacy. The radicals reluctantly concluded that
Lincoln was their lone hope. Just in time, the Republicans achieved the
needed unity.[5]

---

[4] Stanton to Sumner, Oct. 3, 1864, HU; McClellan to Barlow, Sept. 21, 1864, Mc-
Clellan Papers, LC; C. D. Smith to Stanton, Sept. 21, 1864, Stanton MSS.
[5] Smith, _Blair Family_, II, 287; Blair, Sr., to Montgomery Blair, Sept. ?, 1864,
Blair Family Papers, LC; Morse, _Welles Diary_, II, 158; Wade to Chandler, Oct. 2,
1864, Wade Papers, LC.

Three pivotal Northern states—Ohio, Indiana, and Pennsylvania—had local and congressional elections scheduled for October 11, and the result of the presidential contest in November might hinge upon their outcome. The campaign in Ohio seemed placid compared with that of 1863, when Vallandigham ran for governor, but the determination of the Indiana Democrats to overthrow Governor Morton made the situation crucial in the Hoosier state. For more than a year now Morton had avoided calling the hostile legislature into session, fearing that the copperheads would gain control. As no appropriation bills had been enacted, he had been obliged, in order to pay state expenses and the interest on the state debt, to rely on gifts from loyal individuals and levies on certain counties plus the proceeds from the sale of the output of a state arsenal which Stanton bought at a high price for the federal government in order to ease Morton's financial stress.

These sources of state income proving insufficient, Morton had come to Washington to ask for outright federal aid. Lincoln referred him to Stanton. Back in July 1861, Congress had appropriated $2,000,000 for the President to spend to furnish arms to loyal citizens in states threatened with rebellion. The law was broad enough to enable Stanton to pay military expenses incurred by Morton, but not the interest on the state debt. But the Secretary threw legality to the winds and advanced $90,000 to Morton for military purposes together with a loan to prevent the state from defaulting on its interest payments.[6]

Complicating the election picture, Grant's method of warfare ground up manpower at an appalling rate. Lincoln issued a call for 500,000 more troops and set September 5 as the date when drafting would begin, to make up deficiencies in state quotas unfilled by volunteers. Throughout the North party officials complained to Stanton that a forced levy on the eve of the election would cost Lincoln the presidency.

Just at this juncture, Seward inadvisedly stated in a public speech that volunteers were filling the ranks so rapidly that no new draft would be needed. Stanton assured Grant that Seward's declaration had been "wholly unauthorized and most unhappy," having caused a sharp drop in enlistments. He had persuaded the President to refuse to delay the draft call, for he believed that if Lincoln modified it in the slightest degree, the Army would turn against him; a conviction supported by impressive evidence. The draft would not be postponed a

6 William D. Foulke, *The Life of Oliver P. Morton* (Indianapolis, 1899), II, 228–68; William F. Zornow, *Lincoln and the Party Divided* (Norman, 1954), 191.

single day, he promised Grant, at the same time asking the general to send him a telegram for publication urging the necessity of immediately filling up the Army by draft.

Grant readily came to Stanton's assistance, and in phrases which exactly mirrored the Secretary's views on the need for pushing the conscription through. All the men called for were needed, Grant wrote. "A draft is soon over, and ceases to hurt after it is made. . . . Prompt action in filling our armies will have more effect upon the enemy than a victory over them. They profess to believe, and make their men believe, that there is such a party North in favor of recognizing Southern independence that the draft cannot be enforced. Let them be undeceived." When, again at Stanton's instigation, Sherman protested that if the President should modify the draft "to the extent of one man," the Army would vote against him, Stanton forwarded his telegram to the northwestern governors as proof that conscription must be enforced.

Determined to go ahead with the draft, Stanton gave way to the protestants only to the extent of granting them a four-day delay to revise some state quotas and rearrange some draft districts. Department commanders were instructed to be ready to meet resistance, and special precautions were taken in Indiana. The firm policy paid off, and the opposition collapsed. Resistance was negligible.

But Morton was still extremely doubtful of how Indiana would vote, and to assure a Union majority, he and Schuyler Colfax, Speaker of the House of Representatives, asked Stanton to grant furloughs to 15,000 Indiana troops of voting age so that they could come home at election time. Former Governor Morgan, of New York, warned Stanton that a movement had been set afoot in the Empire State to corral the soldier vote for McClellan, and added: "You . . . will know how to apply the remedy better than I do." Stanton did. He dismissed twenty quartermaster clerks who had been touting McClellan. Answering a protest from one of them, he said: "When a young man receives his pay from an administration and spends his evenings denouncing it in offensive terms, he cannot be surprised if the administration prefers a friend on the job." Pro-McClellan talk in the Army became measurably muted.

Stanton meanwhile approved a levy upon the salaries of Department personnel for Republican party purposes. He and Holt, agreeing that only pro-Lincoln newspapers should enjoy government favors, combed reports of provost marshals and accusations by local Republican workers to sift the worthy faithful from the anti-Lincoln recipients of patronage. Stanton was determined that, from the Secretary's office on down, the Army was to support Lincoln if possible, or at least not to oppose him.[7]

The busy Secretary condoned Governor Morton's retention of volunteers in Indiana until after the election, and persuaded Sherman to furlough Indiana officers to make speeches there; General Logan spoke in Illinois; General Blair in Missouri. Convinced that the soldier sentiment was overwhelmingly Republican, Stanton sent home all sick and wounded Indiana troops capable of leaving the hospitals at election time, first promising Grant and Sherman that all these men would return as soon as they had cast their votes.

He had asked Grant's opinion of the desirability of allowing soldiers to vote in the field. The general favored it, feeling that men fighting the country's battles had more right to determine the choice of its rulers than the stay-at-homes. Stanton followed Grant's recommendations in prescribing rules for army voting.

Information came to the War Department that Confederate agents in Canada were planning depredations in the northernmost states of the Union to add weight to McClellanite charges of Union weakness, and were also slipping persons across the border and colonizing them at various points so that they could vote the Democratic ticket. Stanton ordered Dix, at New York City, and Hooker, now commanding at Columbus, to establish "a perfect cordon" on the Canadian border, "through which the miscreants will not be able to escape."

A sensational victory by Admiral Farragut in Mobile Bay and Sherman's capture of Atlanta lifted Northern spirits. Sheridan won two encounters at Opequon Creek and Fisher's Hill. Stanton sent him congratulations and the information that Lincoln had promoted him to brigadier general in the regular army, but this, too, was partially for its effect on the election. General Wool commended Stanton for the "electric" impact on the public of his telegram to Sheridan.[8] But was all this enough?

On the night of October 11, when the Ohio, Indiana, and Pennsylvania contests were to be decided, Lincoln walked over to the War Department to scan the returns as they came in on the military telegraph.

[7] Morgan to Stanton, Sept. 15, 1864, Stanton MSS; on soldiers' sentiments, see Col. Hazard Stevens's letters, May–Sept. 1864, UW; General H. W. Allen to J. H. Speed, Sept. 11, 1864, Holt Papers, LC; *O.R.*, XXXIX, pt. 2, 396–7; XLII, pt. 2, 370; ser. 3, IV, 709–12, 732.

[8] *O.R.*, XXXVIII, pt. 1, 154–5; pt. 5, 809; XLII, pt. 2, 1045–6; XLIII, pt. 1, 61; pt. 2, 170, 463–4; Josiah Benton, *Voting in the Field* (Boston, 1915); Gorham, *Stanton*, II, 158–9.

Stanton was highly excited; the President seemed serene as they sat alone in Stanton's office, where Eckert, passing through the crowded outer room, brought them numerous telegrams as they came off the wire. The early returns seemed encouraging. In the camps around Washington the Union majorities were running as high as ten to one, though at Carver Hospital, which Stanton and Lincoln passed daily in the summer on their way to the Soldiers' Home, the majority was smaller, only three to one. Lincoln said jocularly: "That's hard on us, Stanton—they know us better than the others."

At about eight-thirty Dana came into Stanton's office. Lincoln drew a thin, yellow-covered pamphlet from his pocket and asked Dana if he ever read Petroleum V. Nasby. When Dana claimed only slight familiarity with the work of the humorist, the President told him to pull up a chair and favored him with a reading. Lincoln and Dana enjoyed some good laughs, while Stanton, obviously disapproving, especially when Lincoln paid scant heed to Eckert's telegrams, glowered in a corner. When Lincoln finally put the book aside to read an especially important telegram, Stanton motioned to Dana to come into Eckert's room. He shut the door behind them.

"God damn it to hell," he burst out in a fury. "Was there ever such nonsense? Was there ever such inability to appreciate what is going on in an awful crisis? Here is the fate of this whole republic at stake, and here is the man around whom it all centers, on whom it all depends, turning aside from this monumental issue to read the God damned trash of a silly mountebank!"

Another occurrence soon caused Stanton to blow off again. A messenger brought in a card and handed it to the President, who said, as he passed it on to Stanton: "Show him in!" Stanton read the card and muttered to Dana: "God in Heaven, it is WHITELAW REID!" The Secretary so detested Reid, a correspondent of the Cincinnati *Gazette*, that he had instructed the doorkeepers to bar him from the War Department.[9]

By this time the returns showed a safe Union majority in Ohio. A dispatch from Indianapolis predicted that Morton would win by 30,000.

[9] Dana, *Recollections*, 261-2, attributed these incidents to the night of the presidential election on November 8. But Hay, *Diaries and Letters*, 228, states that it was on this night of the state elections that Lincoln read from Nasby, and the clinching fact is the presence of Reid, who told of being at the War Department the night of October 11 in a letter of that date to Edward McPherson (McPherson Papers, LC). Hay also makes Dana's account somewhat dubious by stating that Stanton enjoyed the reading of Nasby. Perhaps the Secretary pretended that he did until he got Dana alone.

It was signed "McKim." "Who is that?" asked Hay, who had joined the group. "A quartermaster of mine," said Stanton in smug satisfaction. "He was sent there to announce that."

Then, warming to this theme, Stanton recounted how he had assigned officers to attend all Republican meetings in Ohio and Kentucky to oversee the party loyalty of uniformed speakers and local workers. "A nephew of Brough's that I placed at Louisville and made a Colonel, I reduced to Captain and ordered him South the other day," Stanton smilingly admitted; "he was caught betting against Morton." A murmur of approval filled the room. Hay remarked that Colonel George B. Dandy's New York regiment was reported to be strongly pro-McClellan, and added that Dandy wanted a promotion. Stanton drew deeply on his cigar, puffed a long spiral of smoke heavenward, and said sarcastically: "He will get it." Hay observed to his diary: "Colonel Dandy's dream of stars passed away in that smoke." [1]

The complete returns, when compiled a few days later, showed that the Union ticket had won in all three states. In Ohio the party's majority amounted to 54,000. It took 17 of 19 congressional seats; three congressional districts had been gained by the soldier vote. In Pennsylvania the Unionists would now hold 16 congressional seats to 8 for the Democrats. The Union state ticket won by 13,000 ballots, with soldier votes contributing materially to the victory. Morton won in Indiana by more than 20,000, and the Unionists recaptured the state legislature.

In Maryland, meanwhile, a new state constitution prohibiting slavery was submitted to the people. The home folk rejected it, 29,536 to 27,541, but soldier ballots altered these figures to 30,174 for the constitution and 29,699 against it. Henry Winter Davis credited Stanton with helping to change the outcome of the balloting. [2]

The victory in the October state elections brought comfort to Republican leaders, but a charge of fraud in Indiana and the close vote in Pennsylvania chilled their optimism. Stanton was determined to make the most of the Unionist sentiment that prevailed in the Army in the November presidential election. Nevertheless, his temper flared when politics intruded on military security.

New York's legislature set up machinery to allow its thousands of troops to vote in the field. Arrangements were made for agents of each party to distribute and collect ballots and transmit them to each man's home precinct to be tallied. The procedure made it necessary for the

[1] Hay, *Diaries and Letters*, 228–9.
[2] Steiner, *op. cit.*, 314–15; Zornow, *op. cit.*, 191–204.

agents to know the whereabouts of New York regiments, and Chauncey M. Depew, the New York secretary of state, came to Washington to obtain the information from the War Department.

Day after day he called on Stanton only to be rebuffed in the most insolent manner. To divulge such information to a bunch of loose-mouthed politicians, said the Secretary, would be the same as giving it to the enemy. But Lincoln, who wanted those soldier votes so badly that he would be willing to take a carpetbag and collect them himself, intervened, and Stanton, all politeness now, called Depew to the War Department. That night the New Yorker left for home with a paper listing the location of every New York unit.[3]

Stanton, unperturbed, decided to gain advantage from this defeat. High army officers soon found themselves under pressure to aid the Republican state agents and to place obstacles in the way of Democratic vote-counters. Marsena Patrick, provost marshal general of the Army of the Potomac, an influential New Yorker and Democrat, received a telegram from Dana accusing him of favoring the Democratic agents. "The insolence of the Secretary and of the Administration generally, is intolerable," Patrick wrote in his diary, and pressured Meade to protest against what was going on, for when the New York agents reached Baltimore, the three Democrats among them were arrested for "gross frauds and forgeries."

Patrick now complained to New York's congressmen, who were unable even to see Stanton. Grumbling about the "systematic abuse" he was suffering, Patrick had to give up the unequal contest, for it was clear that army officers who supported McClellan were not going to get a fair hearing from the Department.[4]

Force was not the only weapon in Stanton's election battery. He assigned General John G. Barnard to write for the newspapers a history of the Peninsular campaign which would smear McClellan. The Secretary kept close watch over Barnard's work, making frequent and trenchant comments, and encouraged General Wool to take to the pen on a similar theme, to place McClellan's "generalship in a true light."

Six days before the election, Stanton ordered several commanders to furlough home all troops from crucial states who were in hospitals or otherwise unfit for the field but who could travel. Illinois, like Indiana, had made no provision for her soldiers to cast their ballots in the field.

[3] Depew, *My Memories of Eighty Years* (New York, 1922), 52–5; Benton, *op. cit.,* 155–6.

[4] *O.R.,* XLII, pt. 3, 435–6, 571; Oct. 30–Nov. 11, 1864, Patrick ms diary, LC.

For the Republicans to lose Lincoln's home state would be worse than a military defeat. So entire regiments were furloughed home; troops jammed trains from the Mississippi to the Atlantic. Dana recalled that "all the power and influence of the War Department . . . were employed to secure the re-election of Mr. Lincoln."[5]

News came to Stanton that Governor Seymour, "under a specious pretext," intended to order out the New York National Guard to supervise the polls on election day. Stanton suspected a plot to intimidate Republican voters. He immediately wired Grant to send "loyal, suitable officers" with adequate troops to reinforce Dix. "Western men should be sent if possible," he added, and Butler, who though a drawback in the field knew how to cow a city, might well accompany them.

Grant sent Butler to see Stanton, and the Secretary confided his fears to the general. Dix aspired to be governor of New York, he said, and would not act tough in a crisis. He did not want to displace his old friend, but he would feel better with Butler there, ostensibly under Dix's command. Butler accepted the assignment, and detachments from his Army of the James embarked for New York. A few days later Butler sent Stanton a dispatch stating simply: "The quietest city ever seen." Lincoln probably never knew what had been going on in his behalf.[6]

Lincoln, surprisingly, was alone at the White House on election day, for Seward, Usher, and Dennison had gone to their states to vote, Fessenden was raising money in New York, Bates and Welles were at their departments, and Stanton, his energy spent completely, was at home, seriously ill with chills and fever. At 7 p.m., Lincoln and Hay splashed through the driving rain from the White House to the War Department. Telegraph reports placed the President in the lead. One message announced a Republican victory in Steubenville. "Ah," said Lincoln, "it's all right; we have carried Stanton's town." In tribute to the absent War Secretary, the President proposed three cheers.

By midnight it was evident that Lincoln had won decisively. The completed tally gave him 2,203,831 votes to McClellan's 1,797,019. He had won every state except Kentucky, Delaware, and New Jersey, and his electoral vote would be 212 to 21 for the general. The men who were doing the fighting had voted for more of it in order to make

[5] T. H. Williams, *Lincoln and the Radicals* (Madison, 1941), 235; *O.R.*, XXXIX, pt. 3, 603; ser. 3, IV, 871–2; Dana, *Recollections*, 260–1.

[6] Hay, *Diaries and Letters*, 233; *Butler's Book*, 753–6; *O.R.*, XLII, pt. 3, 470.

their efforts worth while. Soldiers in the field gave Lincoln 119,754 votes to 34,291 for McClellan. When soldiers voted at home their ballots were not segregated, but the ratio must have been approximately the same. Without their ballots, Lincoln might have lost New York, Connecticut, Maryland, and Pennsylvania, and the arrest of New York's Democratic agents had helped to take that state. Furloughed troops swelled Republican totals in Illinois and Indiana, where soldiers also guarded the polls. All together these six states contributed 101 electoral votes, enough to elect Lincoln.[7]

Two nights later, a cheering crowd, gay with flags, banners, and lanterns, heard Lincoln give an impromptu victory speech, and then went on to Seward's house. Seward suggested that the celebrants go on to Stanton's; "he needs poking up, for he has been seriously sick, I hear, for several days past."

Indeed, this attack had almost been fatal, and Stanton had to remain in bed for three weeks, although he insisted over his doctor's protests that army matters be brought to him. The visible effects of the illness shocked everyone. Even his enemies seemed stunned into a degree of backhanded sympathy. Whitelaw Reid, for example, wrote that "no one had ever connected the thought of possible sickness with his burly form and bullying ways," and predicted that Stanton was about to resign from the cabinet.

It was a shrewd guess, if premature. The sick man, who knew how close death had brushed him, confided to Chase that he required "absolute rest and relief from labor and care. I long for, and hope soon to have [them]. Our cause is now, I hope, beyond all danger, and when Grant goes into Richmond my task is ended. To you and to others it will remain to secure the fruits of victory, and to see that they do not turn into ashes."

Stanton slowly regained his strength, and the knowledge that he had played a major part in helping Lincoln win re-election spurred his recuperation. A brief wire from Grant—"The election having passed off quietly, no bloodshed or riot throughout the land, is a victory worth more to the country than a battle won. Rebeldom and Europe will so construe it"—was far more precious to him than any of the exaggerated praises he received from Republican party spokesmen.

The real victors in the elections, Stanton insisted, were the Union and the Union soldiers, whose willingness to fight on against the re-

[7] Brooks, *op. cit.*, 195; Wolcott MS, 215; Hay, *Diaries and Letters*, 233–6; Hesseltine, *War Governors*, 380–4; Mitchell, *op. cit.*, 380.

bellion had rallied the Northern people to support Lincoln. But Stanton too had fought a good fight, and won.[8] Now he was awaiting only the final testament to his accomplishments, the defeat of all rebel forces and the surrender of the last vestiges of Confederate authority, to cast off the burdens he had long ago assumed at Lincoln's urging.

In less than six months the goal of Confederate defeat was to be realized. But fate had something far different in store for Stanton than the return to private life for which he yearned, and on which his health depended.

[8] Seward in Brooks, *op. cit.*, 200–1; Reid in Cincinnati *Gazette*, Nov. 18, 1864; Grant in *O.R.*, XLII, pt. 3, 581; Stanton to Chase, Nov. 19, 1864, in Maynard County (Ill.) *Times*, Oct. 25, 1877.

CHAPTER XVI

HIS IRON MASK TORN OFF

IN THE midst of what Lincoln called "the passion-exciting subject of the election," Chief Justice Taney died, and in private conversations Lincoln indicated that he had Chase in mind for the place. Since his resignation from the cabinet, Chase had been morose and bitter, but he had stumped for Lincoln against McClellan. Now Chase admitted to Stanton that if Lincoln offered him the vacated position, he felt inclined to accept it.

This was a blow to Stanton, for he had secret hopes for the appointment. His lawyer's mind was entranced by the vision of the nation's highest judicial post. Secretly concerned at the precarious state of his health and increasingly worried about his family's finances, Stanton would have welcomed the secure future which the Supreme Court leadership offered. Still, he did nothing himself to indicate this desire to the President, but, probably with Stanton's knowledge, his wife, who usually kept out of official matters, took a hand. At Ellen's request, Orville H. Browning, Lincoln's close friend, interceded with the President.

Browning was motivated more from distrust of Chase than from admiration for Stanton. Meeting with Lincoln, however, Browning professed real enthusiasm concerning Stanton's qualifications. The President admitted his own high regard for Stanton but offered no further comment.[1]

A number of Stanton's influential friends worked for his appointment with greater conviction than Browning displayed. Justice Rob-

---

[1] Browning, *Diary*, I, 687–8; Browning to Ewing, Oct. 17, Ewing Family Papers, LC; Ewing to Browning, Oct. 24, 1864, Ewing Letterbook, *ibid.*; Stanton to Chase, Oct. 13, 1864, Chase Papers, HSP; Chase to Stanton, Oct. 13, 1864, Stanton MSS; Lincoln, *Works*, VIII, 120.

ert C. Grier, of the Supreme Court, who was himself widely thought of as a probable replacement for Taney, offered Stanton every aid "to have you preside on our bench—I am sure you would be the *right man* in the *right place*." Methodist bishop Matthew Simpson, the President's favorite preacher, also called on Lincoln to urge Stanton's claims for the position. Simpson recalled that after he finished talking, Lincoln swung a long leg over his chair arm, ran his fingers through his hair, and said: "Bishop, I agree with every word you have said. But where can I get a man to take Secretary Stanton's place? Tell me that and I will do it." Soon after, Lincoln made a similar comment to Judge E. R. Hoar.

Weeks passed and the President made no move. Speculation increased. Alexander K. McClure, the Pennsylvania politician, concluded after talking with Lincoln that he was almost set on Stanton.[2] Other rumors had it that Stanton would become Chief Justice so that Lincoln could appoint Butler, Banks, or Montgomery Blair to replace him at the war office.

These possibilities horrified most Union Army officers. Meade wrote to his wife that "I should think it a great misfortune to see either Banks or Butler there." Hitchcock, no admirer of Stanton's personality, thought much less of Butler as a qualified replacement and was "afraid to say who may occupy his place in the War Department."

Stanton remained as "shut-pan" as Lincoln through all this intense jockeying. In mid-October, he and Fessenden went to Grant's headquarters for a tour of the Virginia front, and Stanton learned from Grant that he wanted him to stay in the war office.

When Stanton returned to Washington he had to decide whether to abandon hopes for the court post in order to continue to serve the Army, or to remain available and satisfy his own ambitions. While he struggled to choose and to get Lincoln re-elected, his illness came on, and Grant's fears of Butler as Secretary of War increased. Even General Patrick, who hated Stanton, agreed in conversation with Grant that Butler meant disaster. Patrick, on November 15, learned that Grant had decided to go to Washington and intervene personally.

Grant got Lincoln's promise to make no change in the war office without consulting him. Then he advised the President to keep Stanton where he was, as the best man by far for the job in hand. It appears,

---

[2] Grier in Gorham, *Stanton*, II, 469–70; on Simpson, see reminiscence of Edwin L. Stanton, Sept. 18, 1867, and A. E. H. Johnson's recollection in an undated news clip, both owned by Gideon Townsend Stanton. On Hoar, Rhodes, *op. cit.*, V, 182; and see McClure, *Lincoln*, 129.

too, that Grant and Stanton met the same day. When he returned to his headquarters Grant was able to assure the apprehensive Patrick that Stanton would not give up the Secretaryship.

Stanton, however, had made up his own mind before Grant came to Washington. William M. Evarts, himself a possible nominee for the post of Chief Justice, noted on November 16, before Grant reached the capital, that Stanton had decided to keep the war office, and Edwards Pierrepont, Stanton's close friend, informed Lincoln that Stanton almost a fortnight before had specifically told him that he no longer desired the judicial nomination.[3]

No one can say whom Lincoln might have chosen if Stanton had remained in the running. It may not have been a real sacrifice, therefore, for Stanton to withdraw from consideration. But by the same logic it was a genuine offering which Stanton made on the altar of patriotism, for as far as he knew in mid-November, Lincoln might have picked him.

All this was secret. Stanton meanwhile, bland and calm in the knowledge of his decision, was supporting Chase at every opportunity, encouraging him to keep courage and to retain his availability. Lincoln leaned more toward Chase, making light of the harsh things Chase had said about him, and asserted that as Chief Justice, Chase would be disposed to uphold the administration policies he had helped to frame. To a number of callers Lincoln said his sole doubt about Chase was whether his ambition for the presidency might govern his actions on the bench.

Chase was still disturbed at newspaper reports which favored Stanton for the judicial palm. He finally had to write to Stanton, asking what he knew of Lincoln's plans. On November 19, Stanton felt able to indulge in candor now that Grant had seen him and Lincoln. "I am not a candidate for it, do not want it, and this office has not been spoken of between the President and me," Stanton answered Chase, "except that I have given him a number of recommendations and solicitations for your appointment." The newspaper reports of his own candidacy were lies "invented by knaves for fools to feed on," Stanton insisted. Chase was overjoyed to receive this news from his "dear friend."[4]

[3] Nov. 15–28, 1864, Patrick ms diary, LC; Evarts to R. H. Dana, Nov. 16, 1864, Dana Papers, MHS; Meade, *op. cit.*, II, 239; Adam Badeau, *Grant in Peace* (Hartford, 1887), 80–1 (cited hereafter as Badeau, *Grant*); Butler, *Correspondence*, V, 168; Pierrepont to Lincoln, Nov. 24, 1864, R. T. Lincoln Papers, LC; Hitchcock to "My Dear Niece Mary," Nov. 17, 1864, Hitchcock Papers, LC.

[4] Stanton's Nov. 19 letter in Maynard County (Ill.) *Times*, Oct. 25, 1877; and see Chase to Stanton, Nov. 29, 1864, owned by Gideon Townsend Stanton. On Stanton's

On December 6, Lincoln gave Chase the nomination. Stanton and, through him, Dana were among the few who knew that "the appointment was not made by the President with entire willingness. He is a man who keeps a grudge as faithfully as any other living Christian, and consented to Mr. Chase's elevation, only when the pressure became very general, and very urgent." Montgomery Blair would have received Lincoln's nod, Dana believed, except for Grant's intercession and the fact that the Senate had clearly intimated that it would not take him for the high court because he was "a second rate man." In the interest of party harmony, Lincoln rose to the occasion and chose Chase. Stanton had done some rising on his own.[5]

Late in September, Sheridan had narrowly escaped disaster in the Shenandoah Valley. While he was returning from a war council in Washington, Early's reinforced Confederates struck his army at Cedar Creek and sent it reeling back in confusion. Sheridan heard the firing at Winchester, twenty miles away, and spurring forward, rallied the troops and won a decisive victory. The feat won him a promotion to major general and Stanton's gratitude.

But now, to end forever the vexatious uses the Valley afforded the enemy as a granary and a corridor of invasion to the North, Sheridan under Grant and Stanton's orders began a program of wholesale destruction, burning barns and fences, confiscating livestock, and destroying all the foodstuffs that his men were unable to eat. Stanton also adopted stern measures to protect the Manassas Gap Railroad from guerrillas, directing that every house within five miles of the tracks be destroyed, unless the owners could prove their loyalty, and that any unsworn civilian found within a similar distance of the tracks be assumed to be a robber or a bushwhacker.

So thorough was Sheridan's devastation of the Valley that starvation threatened the people, and he asked permission to issue rations to them. Stanton approved the proposal but only on an emergency basis. Loyal persons should be sent North, where they could earn a livelihood, he said, and the disloyal made to go South and "feed upon the enemy." While the men of Virginia were serving in the rebel ranks or as bushwhackers, he saw no reason for the federal government to support their wives and children. The tough policy toward the enemy that Stanton

---

support of Chase, see Whitelaw Reid in Cincinnati *Gazette*, Nov. 18, Dec. 12, 1864; Nicolay and Hay, *Lincoln*, IX, 391; Wolcott MS, 197.

[5] Dana to James S. Pike, Dec. 12, 1864, CFL.

had advocated since his entry into the war office was now being applied with full force.[6]

In the West, though Sherman had captured Atlanta, he had failed to destroy the Confederate army, now commanded by John B. Hood. An energetic, sometimes reckless fighter, Hood seized the initiative, sending his bold cavalry chieftains, Forrest and Wheeler, to harass Sherman's supply lines. To try to run down Hood would be useless, and Sherman, having no desire to remain on the defensive, proposed to send Thomas to Nashville with enough troops to defend Tennessee, and then, severing his communications and living off the country, march the rest of his army through Georgia to the seacoast, where a Union fleet could meet him and where he could establish a base. To walk a well-appointed army through the heart of the Confederacy would demonstrate the power of Union arms, he said, and the swath of destruction he proposed to leave in his wake would bring home to the Southern people the awfulness of war.

At first blush Sherman's daring proposal did not appeal to Grant. Hood, his army unimpaired, might be too much for Thomas. Or suppose he should follow Sherman? Could an army the size of Sherman's maintain itself in hostile country with an enemy nipping at its flanks and rear? Grant communicated his doubts to Lincoln and on October 12 learned from Stanton that though the civilian authorities were hopeful of seeing Sherman's plan put into effect, the decision was Grant's.

Meanwhile, however, Grant had become convinced that Sherman's plan was sound. Once again the Washington authorities deferred to his judgment. Within three weeks Northern newspapers were headlining Sherman's proposed movement. Stanton in hot anger dashed off a wire to Grant. Sherman's officers should keep their mouths shut, and Sherman himself was careless in giving out information. "Matters not spoken of aloud in the Department are bruited by officers coming from Sherman's army in every Western printing office and street." Grant proposed to ferret out the loose-mouthed culprits and consign them to the Dry Tortugas.

On November 16, Sherman's army of 65,000, mostly troops from the Midwest, wheeled out of Atlanta on the long march to the sea. Smoke clouds billowed behind them; everything of military value in the city was being sent up in flames. Hood did not follow Sherman, but chose to double back on Thomas. Schofield checked him in a bloody

[6] *O.R.*, XLIII, pt. 2, 348, 823–4; XLVI, pt. 2, 275–6.

fight at Franklin and then dropped back to join Thomas. Hood took a position on the high ground south of Nashville.

Knowing that Thomas had superiority of numbers, Grant, Stanton, and Lincoln all expected him to strike. But he was a methodical general, who wanted to achieve a knockout when he swung. His cavalry was not yet ready, and Thomas wanted his horsemen in prime condition to harass a routed enemy. When he still failed to attack, Stanton telegraphed Grant: "The President feels solicitous about the disposition of General Thomas to lay in fortifications for an indefinite period. . . . This looks like the McClellan and Rosecrans strategy of do nothing and let the rebels raid the country." Stanton told Grant to authorize Thomas to seize all the horses he needed, and to urge him to get on with the work; else: "If he waits . . . Gabriel will be blowing his last horn." [7]

Grant ordered Thomas to attack at once. When he still held back, Grant advised Lincoln to replace him. Though Lincoln and Stanton both had confidence in Thomas despite his seeming lack of aggressiveness, they had Halleck inform Grant that if he wished to remove Thomas, no one in the government would oppose his decision, but he would have to issue the order himself. Grant sent an order of removal to the War Department with instructions to forward it to Thomas, who meanwhile reported that a sleet storm in the Nashville area had halted all operations. Grant consented to withhold his order, but again becoming impatient, decided to go to Nashville and effect the change in command. Lincoln and Stanton tried to dissuade him, but found him immovable. Before he could leave, however, a telegram from Thomas announced that he had won a smashing victory at Nashville.

The message reached the War Department at 11 p.m. on December 15. Eckert took it off the wire, ran downstairs, leaped into an ambulance, dashed to Stanton's house, and pounded on the door. The Secretary stuck his head out of a second-story window. Eckert shouted the news. "Hurrah!" cried Stanton, and Eckert could hear Ellen and the Stanton children also shouting "Hurrah!"

The Secretary pulled on his clothes and hurried with Eckert to the White House. Hearing a commotion in the downstairs hallway, Lincoln tumbled out of bed and received the news in his nightshirt at the head of the stairs. His worn face gleamed with pleasure in the faint light of the candle that he held above his head.

[7] *O.R.*, XXXIV, pt. 3, 222, 239–40, 740, 749; XLV, pt. 2, 15–8, 84.

At midnight Stanton rushed off a telegram to Thomas, tendering his thanks for a stunning setback to the Confederacy. "We will give you a hundred guns in the morning," he told Thomas. Next morning Lincoln wrote Thomas to the thundering of the guns: "You have made a magnificent beginning; a grand consummation is within your easy reach. Do not let it slip."

Thomas began a resolute pursuit of Hood's retreating army, but the weather again turned bad and the streams became impassable. Then the skies cleared and Thomas proceeded to follow through. Pounding and slashing at Hood's demoralized army, he virtually annihilated it as an effective fighting force.

Stanton, his confidence in the dogged general vindicated, suggested to Grant that Thomas deserved a major general's commission. Grant unhurriedly assented to it. But Thomas, morbidly sensitive, had been cut to the heart on learning of the intention to remove him, although he did not blame Stanton. He considered the Secretary fair and just, and granted that the War Department had done everything he asked to assure the success of his army.[8]

Meanwhile Sherman had vanished somewhere east of Atlanta. For three weeks all that Washington heard about him came from Southern newspapers, which claimed that his army faced starvation and predicted it would soon surrender. Grant told Lincoln and Stanton not to worry; Sherman would reach salt water in good time. On December 13, Sherman gained the outskirts of Savannah, made contact with a Union fleet, and flashed reports to Washington. Senator John Sherman sent him a congratulatory wire, and noted that "I live next door to Stanton, and he favors me with the despatches when they come. By the way, he is your fast friend, and was when you had fewer."

Lincoln and all the cabinet had been torn with tension and worry ever since Sherman left Atlanta. News of Sherman's victory was a happier moment for them than the reports of Lee's surrender four months later. "Our joy was irrepressible," Hugh McCulloch recalled, "not only because of their [Sherman's army's] safety, but because it was an assurance that the days of the Confederacy were numbered. Every member of the cabinet knew, at last, that the war was won and the Union safe."[9]

On Christmas night, Grant wired Stanton that Savannah had sur-

---

[8] *O.R.*, XLV, pt. 2, 195, 265, 283, 295–6, 307, 561; Lincoln, *Works*, VIII, 169; Bates, *op. cit.*, 315–21.

[9] McCulloch to J. E. Remsberg, April 15, 1891, LNLF; Thorndyke, *Sherman Letters*, 240–1.

rendered; Sherman presented the city to Lincoln as a gift. Yet, despite Stanton's sincere appreciation of Sherman's accomplishment, it is evident that a distrust of Sherman had been building up in his mind for some time, notwithstanding the avowal of friendship for the general that he had made. For Sherman frankly disapproved of the government's policy toward Negroes, writing to Stanton that he opposed the enlistment of blacks. He preferred to keep the Negroes for some time to come in a subordinate position, he said, "for our prejudices, yours as well as mine, are not yet schooled for absolute equality." If Negroes did the fighting, advised the general, they would demand a voice in governing the country. He thought it preferable to use Negroes as laborers and to dragoon into the Army white men who stayed home for "trade and gain." "If, however, the government has determined to push the policy to the end it is both my duty and pleasure to assist," he wrote.

Now word came to the War Department that Sherman had driven fugitive slaves from his camps, in one instance leaving Negro refugees to be slaughtered by Confederate cavalry. Halleck, in a friendly warning, cautioned Sherman that he was gaining the reputation of having a "criminal dislike" toward "the inevitable Sambo." Abolitionist leaders were outraged and Lincoln was under heavy pressure to punish the offending general.

Stanton, aware of and sharing Grant's high regard for "Tecumseh," was more disturbed than anyone else in the administration. He asked Grant to impress upon Sherman the difficulty of securing more white replacements and the consequent advisability of organizing colored regiments. Grant replied that he had already done so, and suggested that Stanton explain to Sherman in person that the use of Negro troops for garrison duty would free white soldiers for combat.

Although he was still ill at the time he received this suggestion—he had had to leave his own New Year's reception and had been in bed since—Stanton decided to go along with Grant's idea.[1] He boarded the ship *Nevada* on January 7, 1865, in company with Meigs and other officers. The ostensible purpose of the trip was to provide a rest for Stanton and to untangle a snarl of conflicting Treasury and War Department policies concerning captured cotton. But the Negro question was uppermost in Stanton's mind.

On January 9 the ship reached Savannah, and although Stanton com-

[1] Jan. 2, 1865, Meigs ms diary, LC; *O.R.*, XXXVIII, pt. 5, 792–3; XXXIX, pt. 3, 428–9; XLIV, 806, 809, 836–7; pt. 2, 16; Robert K. Murray, "General Sherman, the Negro, and Slavery," *NHB*, XXII, 125–30, offers an extreme view of Sherman's Negrophobia.

plained of internal pains which he said would impel him to resign very soon, he plunged into a ceaseless round of activity. Sherman conducted the party on a tour of the city and of the Union army camps. At Stanton's request, which the sensitive Sherman felt to be a gratuitous insult, a meeting of twenty leading Negro churchmen was called. Stanton was interested to learn from the Negroes their goals now that they were free, their willingness to accept Union military service, and their views on whether white men would accept colored neighbors when peace came.

Then Stanton asked Sherman to leave the room, whereupon he asked the Negro leaders how their people regarded the general. He had been friendly and courteous, they said; they had complete confidence in him.

Stanton seemed impressed by the good order prevailing in Savannah and by the courtesy of the troops toward the inhabitants. On the surface, the Secretary's visit was pleasant for everyone. He invited Sherman and his staff as well as several naval commanders to dine on the *Nevada,* and he saw to it that he and Sherman faced each other across the table, so that they might continue their talks. "Sherman," navy man Dahlgren noted, "was evidently not pleased with some of the plans."

The general was more pleased when Stanton asked him to offer suggestions for handling the Negro question. Freedmen should colonize lands abandoned by rebels on offshore islands, Sherman insisted, and, isolated from exploitative whites, bridge the gap between slavery and responsibility. Stanton was interested. He and Sherman stayed up late developing the idea, to which the Secretary contributed suggestions and corrections and which Sherman put into practice the next month.

Their apparent harmony increased when Stanton and Sherman granted an audience to some white Georgians who came to Savannah during this visit to ask how their state could be readmitted to the Union. Wishing to increase disaffection among die-hard rebels, Sherman with Stanton's approval explained to the Georgians that under Lincoln's amnesty proclamation a full pardon had already been offered to all but a few Confederates. Stanton might have warned the general that certain radical Republicans in Congress spurned Lincoln's plan; in the case of Louisiana, where 20 per cent of the voters had acted in accordance with Lincoln's invitation, the radicals led by Wade, Davis, and Sumner had refused to seat the state's representatives because it had denied the vote to Negroes. A sharp difference in reconstruction policy was shaping up between Lincoln and Congress, but Stanton apparently did not explain the situation to Sherman, perhaps assuming (on the basis of considerable evidence) that Senator John Sherman had done so. Instead, he entreated him "as a soldier and patriot" to end the war with all possible speed because bankruptcy threatened the government.[2]

When Stanton boarded the ship for home after a four-day visit, Sherman's junior officers voiced their relief. "Stanton," one commented, "has been very bearish and boorish, as is his nature, and it will be a relief to everyone to have him out of the way." But Sherman was pleased at what he felt were the positive results of the Secretary's visit; the general was convinced, as he wrote to his wife, that Stanton "is cured of that Negro nonsense."

Stanton, on his part, professed to feel easier about Sherman's attitude toward the Negro, and so informed William Lloyd Garrison. But both men were dissembling.

On the day Stanton interviewed the Negro ministers, Sherman had written secretly to Halleck that though for the moment he seemed to be popular with Stanton, he would not deceive himself; a single misstep on the Negro question could "tumble down my fame into infamy." He appreciated Halleck's hint that he should act cautiously, and "will heed it as far as mere appearances go, but, not being dependent on votes, I can afford to act, as far as my influence goes, as a fly-wheel instead of a mainspring."

And Stanton was still unsure concerning Sherman's trustworthiness in regard to the Negro. En route home, Stanton wired Grant and asked him for a meeting "so as to communicate other matters that cannot safely be written." [3]

Stanton was still seriously ill, but some news he received before leaving Savannah changed his plans concerning a fast trip home. Wilmington, on the Cape Fear River, had finally been sealed off by the capture of Fort Fisher, losing to the Confederacy its last point of contact with the outside world. A previous attempt to take the fort had resulted in a fiasco, largely through Butler's bungling.

[2] Jan. 7–11, 1865, and dinner seating plan for Jan. 12, on flyleaf, Meigs ms diary, LC; *Memoirs of General William T. Sherman* (2d ed., New York, 1887), II, 242–52 (hereafter cited as Sherman, *Memoirs*); Dahlgren, *op. cit.*, 492; Lloyd Lewis, *Sherman, Fighting Prophet* (New York, 1932), 482–3 (hereafter cited as Lewis, *Sherman*); Oliver O. Howard, *Autobiography* (New York, 1907), II, 189–92; on John Sherman's propensity to advise his brother, see Gen. Manning Force, ms Personal Record, II, 131, UW.

[3] Maj. J. H. Gray to wife, Jan. 14, 1865, War Letters, 1862–5, MHS; M. A. De Wolfe Howe (ed.), *Home Letters of General Sherman* (New York, 1909), 327–30 (cited hereafter as Howe, *Sherman Home Letters*); Garrison, *op. cit.*, IV, 132–3; *O.R.*, XLVI, pt. 2, 157; XLVII, pt. 2, 36–7.

When Stanton learned in Savannah that Lincoln at Grant's urging had at last removed the maladroit Butler, and that Fort Fisher had surrendered, he decided to stop there on his way home, despite his painful illness. In the name of the President, Stanton thanked Admiral David D. Porter and the army commander, General Terry, for their victory, for the Confederate flag that had flown over the fort, and for ridding the administration of Butler. Going ashore, he watched working parties burying the dead and putting the wounded on shipboard. Still fatigued, Stanton dined with General Saxton and his wife. He grew animated as he saw the books in the confiscated house the officer was using. "Ah, here are old friends," he said of Macaulay's poems. Saxton read aloud "Horatius at the Bridge," and Stanton responded with "The Battle of Ivry." That night and the next day, Stanton was "in his most genial mood," quoting poetry, telling amusing anecdotes, sparking the conversation. "The Titan Secretary of War was replaced by the genial companion," Mrs. Saxton recalled.[4] With victory at hand, Stanton was at last relaxing.

He was in this happy frame of mind when he arrived in Washington, although his health was still troublesome. Stanton crossed departmental lines to compliment Mrs. Porter on her husband's "brilliant success." And he amused Lincoln by telling how a Union sentry challenged his party one day while they were on a river-borne survey of the Fort Fisher area. Informed that the Secretary of War and a major general were on board, the sentry responded: "We've got major generals enough up here—why don't you bring us up some hard-tack?"

Then the geniality vanished. Stanton had been under a fierce congressional attack during his absence, ostensibly for his arbitrary arrests, and this time the onslaught came from the radical Republicans, who were disgruntled at Stanton's enforcement of the President's reconstruction plan and feared that Stanton was now under Lincoln and Sherman's moderate influence concerning the Negro and reconstruction.

Stanton was faithfully executing Lincoln's policy on both subjects. But knowing more than any other man in the country how the President's plan for the South was working out, Stanton was becoming increasingly convinced that Lincoln's mild terms of December 1863 required rethinking. Dana wrote of the deficiencies of the "newly-tinkered states" of the occupied South, and regarding Kentucky, that the state

<hr/>

[4] *O.R.*, XLII, pt. 3, 1098–1106; XLVI, pt. 2, 29, 155–7; XLVII, pt. 2, 3, 69; Butler to Comm. J. M. B. Clitz, Sept. 25, 1865, Letterbook, Butler Papers, LC; on Mrs. Saxton, see W. H. Stanton, *op. cit.*, 137–8.

"is one great Golgotha filled with the bones of Union men whom the President has pardoned."

Except to Lincoln, Stanton kept silent concerning his inner doubts; they agreed to launch a full investigation of the way in which presidential reconstruction was actually working out in the Mississippi Valley, both to forestall a congressional inquiry and because Lincoln was beginning to doubt whether his was the best way toward reconstruction in practice. The war was still to be won, and even if Lincoln now chose to stick to the terms he had offered in 1863, there remained whatever time Stanton stayed on in his second administration in which he could try to persuade the President to a sterner course.

Stanton also realized that some congressmen who were criticizing him now were angrier over his rejection of their patronage requests, or over the ouster of Butler, than they were over nuances of reconstruction policy. Congress was feeling its oats now that the war was nearing its end. The first target for its attention was the Army, which must administer any reconstruction program.[5]

But more immediate events claimed Stanton's attention. On January 31, Grant wired that three Confederate commissioners were at his headquarters with instructions from Jefferson Davis to treat for peace, and wished to confer with Lincoln. Stanton felt that a satisfactory peace could come only with the destruction of Lee's army, and he feared that the kindhearted President might yield too much if he sat down with the commissioners. On his suggestion, Eckert went off to Grant's headquarters to learn what terms they proposed.

Finding that their instructions contemplated a recognition of Confederate independence, Eckert broke off negotiations at once. But Grant, convinced from private conversations with the emissaries that peace with union was attainable, urged Lincoln to confer with them. Lincoln answered that he and Seward would meet them at Hampton Roads. The conference came to nothing, as Stanton had anticipated, and Lincoln returned to Washington. But Stanton was surprised when the President proposed two days later in a cabinet meeting to recommend to Congress the remuneration of dispossessed slaveowners provided the Confederates would lay down their arms by April 1. With victory definitely in sight, with the Thirteenth Amendment on its way toward

[5] Dana to J. S. Pike, Dec. 12, 1864, CFL; Stanton to Mrs. Porter, Jan. 20, 1865, D. D. Porter Papers, LC; Brooks, *op. cit.*, 257.

ratification, Stanton and the other cabinet members saw no need for such magnanimity, and Lincoln reluctantly abandoned the idea.

On March 3, while the President sat in his office at the Capitol signing bills, Stanton brought him a telegram from Grant. Lee had suggested to Grant that the two of them attempt to end hostilities by means of a military convention which would embrace the bases of reconstruction. Lincoln had no intention of acceding, but before he could say anything Stanton implored him to refuse the suggestion. Only the President, Stanton pleaded, should negotiate peace or initiate reconstruction; otherwise he would be "a mere figure-head." After thinking for a moment, Lincoln, reaching for a sheet of paper, wrote: "The President directs me to say to you that he wishes you to have no conference with General Lee unless it be for the capitulation of Gen. Lee's army, or on some minor, and purely, military matter. . . . [And] you are not to decide, discuss, or confer upon any political questions. Such matters the President holds in his own hands; and will submit them to no military conferences or conventions. Meantime you are to press to the utmost, your military advantages." Then he turned to Stanton. "Now, Stanton," he said, "date and sign this paper and send it to Grant. We will see about this peace business."

Grant, wondering whether this message had been intended as a rebuke, assured Stanton that he would not relax his military efforts in the slightest until victory was achieved. Nor would he embarrass the government by exceeding his authority; it was because he had no authority to negotiate with Lee that he had asked for instructions. Stanton answered: "No apprehension is felt that you will ever exceed your authority, and your object in applying for instructions was understood." [6]

Taken all together, Lincoln and Stanton reposed full confidence in Grant, who "rules [military] matters when he really attempts it," in Rutherford Hayes's words. But the President and Secretary were determined that the civilian authority should exercise full control over political concerns, including the reconstruction question.

Stanton kept a firm grip on the Army's administrative affairs so that Grant might be free from distractions and run the field commands. It was a new civil-military relationship which was developing between Stanton and Grant. The general was in control of basic military policy;

[6] *O.R.*, XLVI, pt. 2, 311–12, 343–4, 365, 823–4, 841; Lincoln, *Works*, VIII, 330–1; A. E. H. Johnson in Washington *Star*, Sept. 3, 1892; Ward Hill Lamon, *Recollections of Abraham Lincoln* (Washington, 1895), 249ff., and in a fuller version in an undated memorandum, Lamon Papers, HL; and see Edward L. Pierce, *Memoir and Letters of Charles Sumner* (Boston, 1893), IV, 206 (hereafter cited as Pierce, *Sumner*).

the Secretary saw to it that he had the tools of war and virtual exemption from political interference. And Lincoln was now more free than ever before to concern himself with the reconstruction question. He left the endless administrative work of the war to his busy "Mars," who seemed indefatigable, but who was rapidly wearing out.

The strain of seeing to it that Lincoln was kept safe on the windy, raw day on which he took the oath of office for the second time, drained Stanton further. Abundant preparations insured that "we had no disturbances, no fires, no raids or robberies," Halleck wrote Lieber the next day. Detectives watched closely over the many hundreds of deserters from the rebel army who were in Washington, and gangs of rowdies from Northern cities were "completely overawed."

When he and the other members of the cabinet took their places in the Senate Chamber to hear Andrew Johnson swear the oath as Vice-President, Stanton sagged with weariness. Then, to everyone's amazement, Johnson launched into a tirade against secessionists and his personal political opponents. Welles whispered to Stanton that "Andy" must be drunk or crazy; Stanton muttered that something was surely wrong with him. "Stanton appeared to be petrified," a journalist recorded.[7] It came out later that Johnson had been ill and to brace himself for the ceremony had taken a stiff drink of whisky, which, in his weakened condition, had been too much for him. Leaving the chamber, the cabinet members took reserved seats on the platform that had been built in front of the Capitol, and listened while Lincoln, in his inaugural address, pleaded for a peace without malice and with charity for all.

To the south, Sherman moved up through South Carolina, intending to make a junction with Grant. His men, in spite of orders, burned and pillaged as they marched, avenging themselves savagely on the fractious little state that they blamed for causing the war. When they entered North Carolina the destruction stopped. By March 22, Sherman had reached Goldsboro, and Stanton, sending Meigs to make sure he was properly supplied, had him take along a florid congratulatory letter to Sherman. But Stanton's rapidly declining health temporarily robbed him of the buoyancy which good news usually inspired.

Stanton was done in. Soon after the inauguration, Surgeon General

[7] Halleck to Lieber, March 5, 1865, Lieber Papers, HL; Morse, *Welles Diary*, II, 252; Brooks, *op. cit.*, 212; Charles Richard Williams, *Diary and Letters of Rutherford B. Hayes* (Columbus, 1922), II, 569.

Barnes again ordered him to bed. Journalist Reid, who had no fondness for Stanton, attributed "the paroxysms of passion (daily growing more and more frequent) which have so often disgraced the war office," to the "lamentable results of enfeebled health." Stanton, he wrote, "is rather to be pitied than censured for what has thus befallen him in the country's service."

Grant had invited the President and Secretary to visit his head-quarters before the final drive began. Stanton's illness prevented him from making the trip, but Lincoln accepted the invitation and decided to take his wife and son Tad along.

Although Ellen protested, Stanton decided to bid good-by to the Lincolns at the wharf, but their ship pulled out before he arrived. Less than an hour later a violent gale struck Washington, unroofing houses, uprooting trees, and lashing the Potomac into a fury. Stanton, concerned for the President's safety, again left his sickbed to go to the War Department for news. Word came the next afternoon that all was well with the Lincolns. Stanton replied that Lincoln had gone to the "Sunny South" just in time; the Washington weather was cold and disagreeable following the storm. "I would be glad to receive a telegram from you dated at Richmond before you return," the Secretary stated.[8]

Except for the weather, Washington was unusually peaceful. Even Lincoln's political tormentors were quiet, and the army command seemed content at last with what the War Department was doing. Sherman came from Goldsboro to consult with Lincoln and Grant. Both generals felt confident that the Confederates were now fighting on determination alone. Grant was ready to begin his final drive as soon as Sheridan joined him from the Shenandoah Valley. His chief concern was that Lee might slip away, move southward to join Johnston, and play hare-and-hounds with the Union forces until he could again be brought to bay. Lincoln, sure that the end was near, and disturbed by Sherman's propensity toward severity for the South, made it clear that he wanted a soft peace, one which, abjuring revenge and reprisals, would enable erstwhile enemies to live in friendship again; but he and Senator Sherman, also present, predicted how politically difficult the reconstruction issue would become.

General Sherman left to rejoin his army, and Grant, bidding farewell to the President, began probing westward toward the railroads that supplied Lee's army and afforded a possible escape route. Grant

---

[8] *O.R.*, XLVI, pt. 3, 86–7, 96–7, 169; XLVII, pt. 2, 947–8; Reid in Cincinnati *Gazette*, March 18, 1865; A. E. H. Johnson in Washington *Star*, Feb. 15, 1896.

planned to smash heavily at Lee's overextended right flank. Lincoln wired Stanton that he felt he should return to Washington but wanted to stay on and watch Grant's movements develop.

Stanton urged Lincoln to remain, at least for a few days. The President's presence on the scene would spur the troops to take Richmond; "compared to that no other duty can weigh a feather." Only petty tasks waited in the capital. Lincoln decided to stay, and sent his wife back to Washington.

Shifting his troops to the endangered right wing, Lee gave Sheridan's horsemen a tough time at Five Forks. But the Union cavalry held, and infantry support arrived in time for Sheridan to strike back furiously. Lincoln informed Stanton that Sheridan, aided by Warren's 5th Corps, had carried everything before him. Grant had ordered an attack along his entire line. A breakthrough somewhere was imminent.

Stanton haunted the telegraph rooms in the War Department, forgetting to go home for dinner, and on the night of April 2 not going home at all. He heard from Lincoln that night that Grant had taken 12,000 troops. "This has been a blessed day for the country," Stanton exulted.

Early the next morning, Lincoln flashed Stanton the news that Lee had evacuated Petersburg. Grant, sure that Richmond was now undefended, was hurrying troops to cut off the retreating Confederates. Stanton sent Ellen a scrawled message: "Petersburg is evacuated and probably Richmond. Put out your flags," and her raising of patriotic bunting at their home set off a day of wild celebration at the capital.

Stanton feared that the President, near the battle lines, might expose himself unduly, and warned him not to risk capture by "a treacherous and dangerous enemy." Lincoln thanked him for his caution, but said: "I have already been to Petersburg, stayed with Gen. Grant an hour and a half and returned here. It is certain now that Richmond is in our hands, and I think I will go there to-morrow." [9]

A sixteen-year-old telegraph operator, W. E. Kettles, of Boston, was handling the wire when news that the Union troops had entered Richmond flashed into the War Department. The boy seized the dispatch, upsetting an inkwell in his eagerness, and ran with it to another

[9] Lincoln, *Works*, VII, 385, VIII, 377; Howe, *Sherman Home Letters*, 377; *O.R.*, XLVI, pt. 3, 109, 332, 346, 509; Stanton to Ellen, April 2, 1865, owned by Mrs. Van Swearingen; A. E. H. Johnson in Washington *Star*, Feb. 15, 1896; on Senator Sherman, Gen. M. Force, ms Personal Record, II, 131, UW. M. Blair to Barlow, April 26, 1865, Barlow Papers, HL, on General Sherman's severity at City Point.

telegrapher, who threw open the window and shouted into the street: "Richmond has surrendered!" The news spread fast, and people streaming from stores and offices speedily filled the thoroughfares. Cannons began firing, whistles tooted, horns blew, horsecars were forced to a standstill, the crowd yelled and cheered. Stanton came into the telegraph office, and picking Kettles up in his arms, lifted him to the window sill and shouted: "My friends, here is the young man who received the telegram which tells us of the fall of Richmond!"

A roar from the crowd answered Stanton. The Secretary was beside himself with joy. Work in the War Department was abandoned for the day, the first time such a thing had happened since Stanton took charge. He strolled about the building in an exuberant mood. But there was a hint of disappointment in the message he penned to his wife: "Lee and the remnants of his army escaped during the night. It is not known where Jeff Davis is gone, but Grant is pursuing Lee."

The night that Richmond fell, Stanton ordered two candles placed in every window of the many buildings now occupied by the War Department, with a man standing by to light each pair when a band crashed into the first notes of "The Star-Spangled Banner." Flags decorated the façade of the main War Department building. THE UNION IT MUST AND SHALL BE PRESERVED appeared in jets of flame, and beneath this motto an American eagle grasped in its talons a scroll labeled "Richmond." Flags, flowers, evergreens, and lanterns ornamented Stanton's residence.

Surging crowds accompanied by discordant brass bands passed from one house to another, demanding speeches from anyone of importance. Many persons who habitually avoided public speeches spoke that night, and Stanton's unplanned address, according to newsman Brooks, was the best of these "offhand" offerings, and was reminiscent of the President's talk at Gettysburg. Stanton, tears in his eyes, stopping several times overcome by emotion, asked the cheering crowd to thank God, to ask His blessings for Lincoln and the men in uniform who had brought them to this joyous day. "Henceforth our commiseration and our aid should be given to the wounded, the maimed, and the suffering," he said, his powerful voice clearly penetrating the din. He hoped for divine guidance so that the victorious nation could "be just in the hour of victory, and to help us to secure the foundations of this republic, soaked as they are in blood, so that it shall live for ever and ever." Cheers interrupted every line, and reached a new volume after Stanton read Grant's dispatch announcing the fall of Richmond. He introduced telegrapher Kettles to the crowd; the boy had dined with the Stantons that night and now, flushed with joy and embarrassment, could find no words.

Seward had been another dinner guest. He left it to the crowd "to judge what I ought to think of such a Secretary of War as this," and the response made the verdict clear. It was Stanton's night and he was happy.[1]

While Grant pushed rapidly westward in an effort to head off Lee, Lincoln remained in Richmond, where he consulted with Judge Campbell, Confederate Assistant Secretary of War, about the restoration of the Union. Fearful that the guileless Lincoln might surrender the fruits of victory, Stanton summoned his watchdog, Dana, and hurried him off to Richmond. Before Dana reached there, Stanton wired Lincoln that Seward had been thrown from his carriage and had suffered serious injuries. Lincoln started at once for Washington. But Dana learned that the President had authorized General Godfrey Weitzel, the Union commander in Richmond, to inform Campbell that he would permit the rebel legislature of Virginia to assemble for the purpose of withdrawing the state's troops from the Confederate armies and stopping resistance to the federal government. A committee of legislators had already met, reported Dana, to act on Lincoln's proposal.

Good news continued to pour in. "Sheridan defeated Lee yesterday," Stanton notified Ellen on April 7; "captured many generals and many thousand prisoners." The next day, he received Grant's wire predicting Lee's imminent surrender, and on the ninth, he hurried to the White House with the long-awaited news—Lee had capitulated.

Grant's terms had been generous, and had been restricted to military concerns. Reading Grant's telegram, the President and Stanton threw their arms around each other. One onlooker, Dr. Reid, of Steubenville, an old friend of the Secretary, recalled that Stanton, "his iron mask torn off, was trotting about in exhilarated joy."

Stanton that night wired joyfully to Grant of his gratitude to God and his thanks to the general and his men. Immediately after, he sent an order to every army command across the nation for a salute of 200 guns to be fired the next day, and characteristically, the text of the order ended: "Report on the reception and execution of this order is to be made to the Adjutant-General at Washington." That night the windows of the War Department again blazed with light; high up on the front in letters of fire appeared the word "Grant." Re-

[1] Wolcott MS, 200; Flower, *Stanton*, 262–3; Townsend, *Anecdotes*, 122–4; Brooks, *op. cit.*, 219–21; Washington *Chronicle*, April 4, 1865; *ANJ* (April 8, 1865), 517.

joicing to the thunder of the saluting guns the next day, the nation seemed in a delirium.[2]

Stanton gave Lincoln his letter of resignation the next day, as he had earlier told Chase he would do as soon as Richmond fell and Lee surrendered. Lincoln looked down on Stanton from his towering height, placed a hand on each of the Secretary's shoulders, and said: "Stanton, you have been a good friend and a faithful public officer and it is not for you to say when you will be no longer needed here." Stanton reluctantly agreed to stay on for a brief while longer.

Perhaps this decision was made easier for him, or made to seem necessary, by news that Dana sent from Richmond on the afternoon of April 10. General Weitzel had allowed the churches there to reopen but had backed down from his original stipulation that as part of the Episcopal ritual the ministers of that denomination must offer a prayer for the President of the United States—during the war they had included the President of the Confederacy in their prayers. As a result of Weitzel's leniency, not a single minister had asked God's blessing on the President, though they had prayed for "those in authority," a phrase Stanton suspected was meant to apply to rebel officials more than to the Union government. Stanton, determined that former rebels must respect federal authority, sent Weitzel a blistering reprimand, but Lincoln intervened on behalf of the general. It was another indication that the softhearted Lincoln needed watching. And Stanton was furious that the President's charity toward defeated rebels should be returned with contempt. "He expected," Stanton's secretary recorded, "that they would at least be equal to the President in . . . Christian qualities. . . . To him such an insult to his chief was indefensible."

Now worried, Stanton wished that Lincoln had not talked to Campbell in Richmond. The Secretary feared what the Virginia rebel legislators might do if the Union commander in Richmond permitted them to meet. He repeated several times to Lincoln that it had been a mistake to recognize them in the slightest manner, and urged over and over again that Lincoln revoke his instructions to Weitzel.

Confirmation of Stanton's forebodings arrived in a telegram from Dana. The committee organized by Campbell to call the Virginia legislature into session was going far beyond Lincoln's authoriza-

[2] Stanton to Ellen, April 7, 1865, owned by Mrs. Van Swearingen; *O.R.*, XLVI, pt. 3, 619, 640, 655, 663–4; A. E. H. Johnson in Washington *Star*, Feb. 15, 1896; ms journal of Dr. Reid, owned by Alexandra Sanford; Flower, *Stanton*, 270, and Hugh McCulloch to J. E. Remsberg, April 15, 1891, LNLF, deal with the reception of the news. Stanton's order is in New York *Times*, April 9, 1865.

tion to withdraw the Virginia troops from the Confederate armies. Assuming to act as a rightful governing body, these recent rebels were undertaking to treat for terms of peace, shocking even Campbell by their temerity. Encountering Stanton soon after he received this information, Sumner found him gravely concerned, and fearful that the Union was losing the fruits of its victories.[3]

Stanton was somewhat comforted that night, April 11, when Lincoln, speaking to a huge crowd on the White House lawn, defended the restoration policy he had followed in Louisiana and pleaded for the speedy acceptance of the Southern states into the Union, though repeating that he was not committed to any single plan of reconstruction. Directing his remarks to the advocates of Negro suffrage, Lincoln indicated that he had been moving forward on this question; he expressed his wish that the "reconstructed" state government in Louisiana enfranchise colored Union Army veterans and "the very intelligent" Negroes.

Encouraged by the tenor of this speech to believe that Lincoln was very close to his own position on the Virginia situation, Stanton the next morning, reinforced by the views of the new Attorney General, James Speed, continued his argument with the President. It carried over after lunch and late into the afternoon. To place such powers in the rebel Virginia legislature, Stanton insisted, "would be giving away the scepter of the conqueror." Lincoln's Virginia policy would bring trouble between the President and Congress. Reconstruction must encompass a new concept of suffrage in the South now that "the blacks were free," Stanton argued. Could Lincoln, in justice, leave the Negroes to the mercies of their former masters, or forget the human and material sacrifices which he and Stanton had demanded of the North?

He spoke as earnestly and persuasively as he knew how, and Lincoln listened attentively, then forbade the meeting of the Virginia legislature. Stanton always took great credit on himself for winning this concession from the President. But it seems doubtful whether Lincoln was influenced overmuch by his arguments. For Lincoln had slowly been coming to agree with Stanton on the question of the need for Negro suffrage; in Richmond he had been extremely careful not to recognize the Virginia legislature as a lawful governmental body. Now

[3] Lamon, *Recollections*, 234–5; Rhodes, *op. cit.*, V, 180; Wilson, "Edwin M. Stanton," *loc. cit.*, 15; Evan R. Jones, *Lincoln, Stanton, and Grant* (London, 1875), 121; Carpenter, *op. cit.*, 265–6; Flower, *Stanton*, 271, 310–11, on the resignation. Other data in Lincoln, *Works*, VIII, 405; *O.R.*, XLVI, 678, 684, 711; Sumner to Chase, April 12, 1865, Chase Papers, 2d ser., LC.

that Campbell's committee had gone far beyond what he had intended, he was ready enough to call off the whole thing, especially as Lee's surrender had since accomplished what he had had in view—the demobilization of the Virginia troops.[4]

Grant, years later, wrote that Stanton on his own authority countermanded Lincoln's orders concerning the Virginia legislature. "This was characteristic of Mr. Stanton," Grant stated. "He was a man who never questioned his own authority, and who always did in wartime what he wanted to do." But Grant, who knew from Stanton himself how seemingly difficult it had been to bring Lincoln to retract the instructions, misrepresented the situation.

Stanton's role in rejecting the Virginia arrangement was an important one. In no sense, however, did he, as Grant asserted, take "the liberty of countermanding the order." Nor did the Secretary, as Robert Stiles, one of the affected Virginia state legislators, concluded, deserve the "responsibility (or glory) of breaking up the policy of restoration." The Virginia situation was an impossible one for the victorious Union. Lincoln's arrangement there could never have won Congress's approval; indeed, his willingness to end it indicates that it had lost his own support. Lincoln, not Stanton, ended the matter.[5]

Despite this victory, when Sumner saw Stanton the next day he found him still highly excited. Stanton's concern resulted in his summoning Grant to Washington; he arrived late in the afternoon on April 13 and came to the War Department at once, where, Meigs noted, he "was welcomed and thanked by the Secretary with much emotion." Almost at once they agreed to order the cessation of drafting and recruiting and to curtail army purchases and remove military restrictions. After this conference, the Secretary and the general enjoyed a brief, pleasant interview with Lincoln.

That night the Stantons entertained the Grants. A band serenaded the party, and the Secretary and his guests came out on the steps to listen. Fireworks were popping everywhere, and a crowd gathered to cheer the distinguished gathering at the Stanton home.[6]

---

[4] Lincoln, *Works*, VIII, 399–405; Fawn M. Brodie, *Thaddeus Stevens* (New York, 1959), 209–13; A. E. H. Johnson in Washington *Star*, Jan. 11, 1896; Flower, *Stanton*, 271.

[5] Stiles, "Lincoln's Restoration Policy for Virginia," *MH*, XXII, 209–23; Campbell, *Reminiscences and Documents Relating to the Civil War During the Year 1865* (Baltimore, 1887), 43–4; Grant, *Memoirs*, II, 506–7.

[6] Sumner to Chase, April 13, 1865, ISHL; April 13, 1865, Meigs ms diary, LC. A drunken man, claiming to be acquainted with Stanton, tried to mingle with the party but was sent away. He was later identified, probably mistakenly, as Michael

After his guests had departed, Stanton worked on through the early morning hours of April 14 completing a provisional plan for the military government of the defeated South which Lincoln had asked him to prepare. Stanton had already given Lincoln a rough draft on the thirteenth; now he had Grant's thoughts on the matter and they agreed that the Army must temporarily "take over" the territory it had won. Lincoln had invited Grant to attend a cabinet meeting that day. Stanton's haste to prepare this plan is explained by the general's presence.

The April 14 meeting opened with an exchange of congratulations between the cabinet officers and Grant. Lincoln, cheerful and happy, rejoiced at the imminent prospect of peace and hoped that the passions of war would soon diminish. He expected momentarily to receive news that rebel general Johnston had surrendered to Sherman, for he had had his usual dream foreshadowing important events, which had come to him before Antietam, Murfreesboro, Gettysburg, and Vicksburg.

Near the close of the meeting, Stanton remarked that the establishment of civil government and the maintenance of order in the South, where the rebel collapse had ended all governmental stability, would be the administration's paramount problem, and at Lincoln's request he had drawn up a tentative plan for the cabinet's consideration.

Lincoln said that he had lacked time for a full study of Stanton's proposal but was glad to have it presented. He thought it essential to have a plan in operation before Congress reassembled in December, and asked Stanton to read his plan to the cabinet members.

It was in the form of an executive order, and applied to Virginia and North Carolina, making them a military department under a military governor, whose regulations were to be enforced by a new provost marshal corps under the central direction of the commanding general of the Army and the War Department, and employing martial law as the base of authority.

The military governor and the provost marshals were to establish order, so that the civilian branches of the national government could re-establish revenue offices, postal facilities, federal courts and attorneys, and land offices, and then self-government could recommence, although this final step was not then of concern to Stanton. Private citizens who remained obedient and peaceful were to be unmolested.

O'Laughlin, of whom more later. Benn Pitman (comp.), *The Assassination of President Lincoln and the Trial of the Conspirators* (facsimile ed., New York, 1954), 226–7.

Stanton had "left open" the question of whether Negroes should vote or not, for this was merely a projected plan for immediate army needs, and the Negro question, he knew, would require extended debate.

A pause ensued. Everyone seemed to agree with the Stanton plan. Then Welles spoke up. He concurred on the necessity for prompt action, but he objected mildly to the provost reform and more forcefully to combining two state entities under even a temporary form of government, especially a military one. Virginia was different from other rebellious states, he contended, in that the administration had acknowledged the Pierpont government there as legitimate, and that government had consented to the separation of West Virginia from the mother commonwealth.

Lincoln thought that Welles's objections were well taken; some of them had already occurred to him, he said. The President directed Stanton to redraft his document, making it apply separately to the two states, and to have copies of the new draft available for the cabinet members at their next meeting the following Tuesday.

The Navy Secretary did not, however, make an issue at this time of Stanton's proposed use of military forces in the occupation, although in later years he claimed the credit for exposing a sinister design on Stanton's part to overawe Southern states by martial power and to commit Grant to his ideas. At the April 14 meeting, the President and all the cabinet officers accepted Stanton's military approach with the exceptions that Welles had taken and in which Lincoln had sustained him. What was deferred was essentially the question of Negro suffrage, not, as Welles later asserted, the need for temporary military government, on which all agreed, or the reorganized provost corps, or the sanctity of Pierpont's puny Virginia state organization.[7]

That afternoon word came that Jacob Thompson, Stanton's erstwhile cabinet colleague in Buchanan's administration, and more recently a high Confederate official, was expected to be in Portland, Maine, that night to board a ship bound for England. Dana, once more in Washington, brought the telegram to Stanton, who immediately said: "Arrest

[7] F. W. Seward in Washington *Chronicle*, Jan. 25, 1875; Gideon Welles to son Edgar T. Welles, Jan. 28, 1875, Welles Papers, LC; Morse, *Welles Diary*, II, 280–2; his "Lincoln and Johnson," *Galaxy*, XIII, 525–7; and his letter to Johnson, July 27, 1869, in Beale, *Welles Diary*, III, 714–17. Lincoln and Chase were at this time in correspondence on a plan of restoration, using military force as a primary step, which was very similar to Stanton's; see Lincoln, *Works*, VII, 399–400. On need for martial law, see Roswell Marsh to Stanton, April 10, 1865, Stanton MSS.

him." Then, as Dana was leaving, Stanton said: "No, wait; better go over and see the President."

Dana found Lincoln washing his hands in a room off his office. Looking up, he said: "Halloo, Dana! What is it? What's up?" Dana read the telegram from Portland, whereupon Lincoln asked: "What does Stanton say?" "He says arrest him," answered Dana, "but that I should refer the question to you."

Lincoln said slowly, drying his hands: "Well, no, I rather think not. When you have got an elephant by the hind leg, and he's trying to run, it's best to let him run." Back at the War Department, Stanton asked Dana: "Well, what did he say?" Dana told him. "Oh, stuff!" grumbled the Secretary.

Down in Charleston Harbor an impressive ceremony, which Stanton had arranged, was taking place that same day. Stanton had conceived the idea that at the proper time he would order General Anderson to replace the flag that he had been obliged to haul down four years earlier. Now the Sumter flag was going up again, and among the guests were Henry Ward Beecher and William Lloyd Garrison, there at Stanton's invitation. The Secretary had hoped to attend himself but, unable to leave the capital, had sent Holt to represent him.[8] When the flag had descended in 1861, the war had begun. Its ascent in 1865 meant that the war, except for spasmodic rebel resistance, was won.

[8] Dana, *Recollections*, 273–4; *O.R.*, XLVII, pt. 2, 536, 581.

THE MISFORTUNE OF THAT STATION

WITH Lee's surrender foretelling an early end to the war, Stanton took on stature as the organizer of victory. He had made a far greater impact on the public consciousness than any of his predecessors and had lifted the office of Secretary of War out of obscurity. His countrymen knew his name as they recognized Lincoln's and Grant's, and his popularity was close to theirs, although then as now Americans understood better how to evaluate and reward the services of generals and Presidents than to judge the achievements of an appointed official. It is therefore even more remarkable that Stanton should have achieved the wide recognition that he did.

Only the terrible, revolutionary nature of the war can explain this. To Stanton's generation it was a shocking experience; the cost in lives and money was unprecedented. War needs had prescribed that the Negro must go free. Battles had stricken secession from the remedies available to a state in the federal union. Blood and suffering had kept the nation together, although the question of the further purposes for which that centripetal force had been exerted was still unanswered.

Was Stanton's contribution to Union victory as extraordinary as the nature of the conflict? Persons close to Stanton believed that it was. Dana was sure that the Union would have lost its fight without him. Admiral Porter, who privately wished that Stanton rather than Welles controlled the Navy, concluded that "Lincoln's Mars" was "the man for the times." From the vantage point of his cosmopolitan education and career, Francis Lieber adjudged that democratic government, a new idea in history, had seemed doomed in 1861. The Union's first efforts to save itself had been fitful, awkward, and inadequate. Then Stanton had helped to release the nation's energies. From a people not subject to a consolidated government and with a strong anti-militarist tradition, he organized armies through volunteering and conscription. He sternly overbore the many active sympathizers with rebellion who infested the North, maintaining adequate internal security with a minimum of trespass on civil liberties. At the same time, Lieber wrote, he kept down "the arrogance of the sword," yet never let "the chariot of war . . . run in the mere rut of routine." A stern pilot, Stanton was the only one who could have brought the ship of state into the safe harbor of victory.

Other commentators were more restrained in their judgments on Stanton's accomplishments. George W. Payne, an obscure government clerk, estimated that "there is nothing of a remarkable . . . character" in what Stanton had achieved, considering the expert assistants who ran the War Department. And of course Stanton's detractors —the Blairs, McClellan, Frémont—insisted that he had delayed rather than spurred victory. Ironically, Stanton's great enemy, the publisher of the New York *World*, Manton Marble, came close to a part of the truth when he editorialized that Stanton "could not have made a great figure in ordinary times." Stanton would have agreed with him.[1]

He was not a great man. But unlike the Blairs or McClellan, he never deluded himself with the idea that he was. Stanton recognized his own simple abilities and grave limitations. Provost Marshal Doster, from his intimate associations with Stanton, drew a perfect description of the man. "Stanton," he wrote, "was an able, overworked Pittsburgh lawyer suddenly called on to play the combined roles of Carnot and Fouché, apparently utterly ignorant of both roles, and equipped with no special talent . . . other than the professional ones—ability to work, dogmatic temper, a bullying propensity. . . . As in his law office, red tape, papers, precedents, decisions were his business here. As there he knew he could abuse his client as much as he chose, provided he won his case, so here he knew, no matter what he did, all would be right, if he secured the verdict." No good lawyer ever gave up a case, Doster continued; nor would Stanton. "So he went on working up his case . . . in a perennial passion. . . .

[1] *World*, Dec. 25, 1869; Payne's ms sketches, CHS; Porter's ms Journal, I, 411–13, Porter Papers, LC; Lieber's ms essay on Stanton, HL. Stanton in Nov. 1865 refused to let Lieber publish it because it might seem like a bid for the presidency; Lieber **to** ? (probably Benson J. Lossing), Dec. 25, 1865, Lieber Papers, LC.

The verdict—victory—the suppression of the rebellion were the goal. Nothing else mattered."

A new America was being forged by men of these characteristics even before the cannon crashed at Fort Sumter. By 1865, entrepreneurs of Stanton's drive and inventiveness were reaping fortunes through their vast midwifery of industrial production and communications. The wonder is that he should have chosen to serve the Union instead of garnering the share of this outpouring wealth that his abilities would certainly have earned him.

Stanton's idealistic streak had brought him to the bypass of selfless government service. His talents, combined with a puritanical standard of official and personal honesty, were precisely what were required when he took over the war office, and George Templeton Strong, a man of insight, though a critic of the Secretary rightly placed him in a "reputation of honor as Lincoln's right-hand man." From his often unpleasant experiences at the war office, Strong concluded that Stanton combined good and evil in his character. "He was honest, patriotic, able, indefatigable, warm-hearted, unselfish, incorruptible," Strong judged, as well as "arbitrary, capricious, tyrannical, vindictive, hateful, and cruel." [2]

Taken together, these characteristics, when joined with the personal loyalty he offered to Lincoln, enabled Stanton, the second-rate man, to serve greatly. He *was* the man for those extraordinary times, and he did a titanic job in the face of immense difficulties.

Never, except for temporary shortages which no wartime government has ever learned how to prevent, had the far-flung Union armies lacked the essentials of war after he took office. During 1861, his predecessor, Cameron, had spent approximately $40,500,000 for supplies, and a great deal of this was misspent. In Stanton's first year as Secretary, army expenditures for matériel tripled; a year later they more than doubled again. When Lee surrendered, Union supply depots held enough matériel to support another three years of war at the heavy current rate of consumption. Whole fleets of ships, railroad cars, and wagons, vast droves of cattle and horses, moved about constantly to keep the augmenting armies supplied. Quartermaster General Meigs rightly asserted that nothing like it had ever been done before. "You may well be proud of this record," Stanton's friend Pierrepont wrote

[2] Strong, *Diary*, IV, 266; Doster, *op. cit.*, 116–17.

to him, "as the country will be of a Secretary who made such a report possible." [3]

If supplies were plentiful, the quality of the soldiers' food left a great deal to be desired, despite the exorbitant prices the government was forced to pay for it. But notwithstanding the complaints about "salt horse," no army up to that day had eaten so well as the Union's forces after Stanton took over. Shoes, uniforms, and the many miscellaneous articles of equipment improved measurably in quality as well as in quantity under his vigilant eye. The word "shoddy," a common epithet of 1861, had largely dropped from soldiers' letters by 1865, and there was no "carnival of fraud" in the purchase and distribution of supplies.

Stanton appointed special commissioners to oversee the standards of manufacturers of military supplies, and these vigilant men did effective work. To oversee the commissioners, as well as to supervise army morals, Stanton resuscitated an almost defunct army bureau, the Inspector General's Office, and making it responsible only to himself, used it as a watchdog. But this unit lacked prestige and influence. Its personnel hesitated to submit reports adverse to comrades. Stanton therefore, in order to get inquiries into accusations of fraud, turned repeatedly to special investigating commissions, usually staffed by a general and a civilian, with the backing of Stanton's authority to compel testimony.

More than this he could not do. The best men of the North were attracted to business, the Army, and elective politics; there were few like Stanton who would submerge their talent, energy, and honesty in the profitless blind alley of appointive office. Once a friend urged him to dismiss a War Department civilian official of high rank, who had accepted bribes. Stanton bitterly replied: "I know all you say is true— He is a d—d scoundrel—But who will do the daily work that he has charge of, who is an honest man? Will you?"

Because the answer was almost always negative, Stanton plugged ahead with the best human material he could find, and burned himself out seeking to oversee the work of many subordinates whom he mistrusted but for whom no better replacements were available. Similarly, if Congress's ambiguous laws on captured cotton and trading permits opened the way to defalcations, embezzlement, and trickery in

[3] Weigley, *Meigs*, 265, 311–20; Pierrepont to Stanton, Nov. 28, 1865, Stanton MSS; editorial, *ANJ* (May 27, 1865), 636–7.

Stanton : The Life and Times

the Treasury Department, he was powerless to intervene. Except to fuss and threaten, there was nothing he could do.

But Stanton himself remained untouched by financial dishonesty. The only "graft" he accepted was the professional services of an army doctor. The government gave Stanton his salary, and that was everything material he took from the war.[4]

Though Stanton was ever vigilant against fraud, even here it is dangerous to generalize about him. At least one time he concealed financial wrongdoing for the sake of his party and a friend.

In 1864, the captain of a captured Confederate blockade runner implicated Republican Senator William Sprague, Chase's son-in-law, in a venture of running guns through the blockade into Texas, where they were exchanged for cotton. Chase, during his service as Secretary of the Treasury, had been accused of laxity and favoritism in granting permits to trade in cotton. If it had come out, just after his appointment as Chief Justice, that his son-in-law had profited from a treasonable enterprise, Chase would have faced political ruin and Lincoln and all Republicans would have suffered immeasurably from the scandal. Submerging his standards of honesty in the Union's need for faith in the Republican leaders, Stanton hushed up the matter, and the damning evidence disappeared from the Department's files.[5]

Perfection would have been impossible to achieve in his position, and Stanton never strove for it. There were many things which he could not change or even correct very much. In his efforts to keep the armies up to the mark in manpower, Stanton found himself encumbered by the fact that at the outset of the war state authorities and the War Department had tried to encourage enlistments through the payment of bounties. By 1864, Congress had authorized bounties of $300 for each new recruit and $400 for each veteran who re-enlisted. To escape the "ignominy" of a draft, states, counties, and municipalities paid ever larger bounties to volunteers as the war wore on until this practice reached fantastic proportions.

[4] Stanton's comment is quoted in Barlow to M. Blair, April 29, 1865, Letterbook XI, 329–33, Barlow Papers, HL; Johnson, "Reminiscences of Hon. Edwin M. Stanton," *loc. cit.*, 79; Henry S. Olcott, "The War's Carnival of Fraud," in A. K. McClure (ed.), *Annals of the War* (Philadelphia, 1879), 705–16; J. Duane Squires, "Some Enduring Achievements of the Lincoln Administration, 1861–1865," *ALQ*, V, 191–7; A. E. H. Johnson to J. Tweedale, May 2, 1886, Sec. War Correspondence File, Box 321, RG107, NA.

[5] Thomas Graham Belden and Marva Robins Belden, *So Fell the Angels* (Boston, 1956), 57–62, 141–6, 159–60; *Letter of the Secretary of War*, Sen. Exec. Doc. 10, 41st Cong., 3d sess.

The extravagant system was self-defeating in a sense, for men held back from enlisting in the hope of obtaining even larger bounties by waiting, and it encouraged desertion and the vicious practice known as "bounty jumping." Desertion became one of Stanton's major headaches, for other factors besides the lure of bounties induced men to slink off from the armies. Stanton dealt harshly with deserters and others guilty of breaking regulations whenever he had his way, but his sternness was often tempered by Lincoln's intervention, thereby causing Stanton to grumble that the President was imperiling discipline.

Stanton cannot be blamed for the inadequacies of the bounty system. One phase of administration where he fell woefully short, however, was his failure to make efficient use of the regular army. The difficulty of recruiting regulars in competition with new volunteer regiments should have suggested the desirability of making every qualified private of the regulars a drill sergeant of volunteers and also of dispersing the regular officers among the many raw, new units, instead of maintaining the standing army as a separate organization.

In July 1861, Congress authorized such use of regular army officers, but first Cameron's ineptitude and then Stanton's distrust of career soldiers, and political considerations of prime importance to Lincoln, kept it in abeyance. This preference for nonprofessionals drastically lowered military standards and perhaps resulted in prolonging the war unnecessarily at an enormous cost in lives and money.

But Stanton, if admittedly deficient in this regard, compensated in part by learning quickly to hold on to able officers, whether volunteers or regulars. This was no gentleman's war, he informed Sumner when the latter's friend, a lieutenant, requested an extended furlough in order to practice law; he was too valuable to accommodate. Chase met the same answer when he interceded for a colonel who wished to resign; "I found Stanton so averse to losing good officers that I gave up the attempt," Chase wrote.[6]

There was an all too prevalent feeling at the outbreak of the war that no special training was needed to command troops. Even Lincoln in a moment of discouragement had thought of taking the field in person. The notion had its roots in the American tradition of retaining civilian control over the military, a tradition to which Stanton was so unwaveringly committed that Grant met a sharp rebuke from the Secre-

[6] Ella Lonn, *Desertion during the Civil War* (New York, 1928). Upton, *op. cit.*, 235–7; Sumner to Horace Gray, Dec. 30, 1863, Gray Papers, LC; "Some Letters of Salmon Portland Chase," *AHR*, XXXIV, 554.

tary when he tried to assume control of the military telegraph. This idea of civilian fitness also created confusion in the conduct of the war at the top level. Lincoln continually interfered in shaping strategy and determining troop placement until Grant became the chief field commander, and continued to offer advice afterward. Though it was a necessity forced upon him by the lethargy and inefficiency of his generals and by Halleck's reluctance to make decisions, and though it probably averted disaster until Grant emerged, it frequently put the military and the civilian authorities at cross-purposes.

It must be said for Stanton that he never tried to dictate strategy except in bringing his influence to bear on Lincoln in opposition to McClellan's Peninsular campaign. Had Stanton been allowed a free hand, he would probably have centered the control of army operations in the War Department. Greater military efficiency might have been achieved that way, but there would have been a loss in flexibility. It may have been all for the best that Lincoln maintained close watch over war operations and was in many particulars his own Secretary of War. For Lincoln plowed around obstructions, thereby avoiding abrasions, whereas it was Stanton's habit to meet them head on. The Secretary would have shivered many a plowshare without the President's restraining guidance.

No doubt Stanton's early lack of appreciation for West Point training contributed to the poor leadership that so often plagued the Union armies. But the system of allowing state governors to choose officers up through the rank of colonel, and Lincoln's practice of granting commissions for political reasons, contributed even more to inefficiency. Stanton's aversion to West Pointers dissipated under the acid test of war, and on the whole his judgment with respect to the choice of top commanders turned out to be good. Grant and George Thomas were his personal protégés, and Grant in turn brought forth Sherman and Sheridan. Stanton inherited Buell and McClellan, erred in recommending Pope and in seconding a vicious policy toward Southern whites living inside that general's lines, had no voice in the selection of Burnside, disapproved of Hooker and Rosecrans, endorsed Meade, and seems to have been noncommittal in the selection of Halleck.

No matter how much Stanton at first distrusted West Pointers, he always had to rely on their advice in matters involving the Army's bureau administration. He was barely settling into the war office when he faced the question of reorganizing the Army Medical Bureau. Officials of the United States Sanitary Commission, a civilian organization dedicated to healing wounded soldiers and sustaining their morale, pressured Stanton to replace old, ossified Surgeon General C. A. Finley with Dr. William Hammond and to modernize the Medical Bureau altogether. Heeding Hitchcock's advice against stripping the Army's bureaucratic gears through overrapid reforms, and sharing Lincoln's disquiet at the political meddling indulged in by the Commission's leaders, Stanton opposed the action. Congressmen favorable to the Commission thereupon forced Stanton to appoint Hammond.

Stanton got his back up. Although he fully appreciated the humanitarian work that the organization was doing, he hated interference and became antagonistic to its leaders. Soon the heads of the Commission had linked up with the Blair family and the New York *World* in a resolute attack to cause Stanton's downfall.[7]

This confirmed Stanton in his dislike of pompous, bumptious Hammond, who, like most Commission officials, was a friend of McClellan. Meanwhile, Hammond initiated a whole series of constructive though expensive reforms in the Medical Bureau. Stanton curtailed these expenditures and hand-picked a committee to investigate the Bureau. The investigators turned up enough evidence to satisfy Lincoln that Hammond should be brought before a military court for trial.

Defending Hammond, Commission leaders persuaded a number of prominent physicians, educators, literary figures, and scientists to sign a remonstrance accusing Stanton of treating the accused man unjustly. This tipped over a beehive in Congress. Most of the eminent signatories beat an undignified retreat when Stanton threatened to summon them to Washington for an investigation.[8]

Neither Stanton nor Hammond would back down, and the trial began in January 1864. Hammond had two days in which to answer charges that took six months to prepare. Certain letters vital to his defense disappeared from his files. A new Judge Advocate, John A. Bingham, Stanton's former opponent in politics in Cadiz, subjected Hammond to a "blanket tossing"; the court found the doctor guilty of improper conduct and dismissed him from the service. Lincoln refused to intervene in the case.

---

[7] George W. Adams, *Doctors in Blue* (New York, 1952), 32–5, 76, 85–7; William Q. Maxwell, *Lincoln's Fifth Wheel* (New York, 1956), 9, 140–3; Strong, *Diary*, III, 248–53; McClellan, *Own Story*, 545.

[8] Strong, *Diary*, III, 314, 353, 359, 385; Maxwell, *op. cit.*, 179, 236–7, 333; Sumner to Henry W. Longfellow, Jan. 12, 1864, Longfellow Papers, Craigie House, Cambridge; Thomas Hill to S. Hooper, Jan. 12, 1864, Hill Letterbooks, Archives, HU.

With Hammond deposed, Stanton chose Acting Surgeon General Joseph K. Barnes to head the Medical Bureau. Once more master in one part of his own house, Stanton now bent his efforts toward improving the Bureau's effectiveness in line with Hammond's earlier recommendations, granting it exclusive control of camp and general hospitals and generously rewarding members of the Medical Corps with brevets.

The Sanitary Commission would continue to do mighty work throughout the war, notwithstanding Stanton's aversion to its leaders. In this the Secretary may have had more justification than has been supposed, for all accounts of his relationship with the Commission have been based upon its own records or represent the views of its leaders, who, though high-minded and well-intentioned, were also domineering and opinionated, and thus not easy to work with. After the war the official historian of the Commission easily obtained full confirmation of Stanton's unfavorable disposition. But he added significantly: "I am still unable to place my finger upon telling facts which will prove in what special cases this animus was exerted to our manifest injury." [9]

As with the Medical Bureau, Stanton was seriously hampered by bureaucratic inertia in equipping the Army with the tools of war. Though antiquated weapons soon gave place to better and more modern arms, no one in the War Department gave much encouragement to inventors except on Lincoln's intercession, and it took Stanton a long time to find subordinates who were open-minded and genuinely interested in weapons development.

Hitchcock's early advice to Stanton to avoid unsettling existing bureau procedures and supervisors wherever possible, plus the Secretary's uncertain and unforgiving temper, may also account for his toleration of hidebound General James W. Ripley as Chief of Army Ordnance—that together with the fact that he entrusted Watson with the supervision of technical ordnance matters and that Lincoln himself kept an eye on weapons experiments. The breech-loading rifle, for example, failed to win adoption until a relatively late date. And it may be that Stanton leaned somewhat to Ripley's point of view—that it is better to depend on old and tested weapons for which production facilities are in existence than to experiment with "newfangled" items which, even if they promise a great deal, may never get off the drawing board in time to be of use. To strike a reasonable and safe balance between

[9] Maxwell, *op. cit.*, 241–4; Strong, *Diary*, III, 393–4, 418, 439–42; Duncan, ". . . Surgeon General Hammond," *loc. cit.*, 252–61; Nevins, "The United States Sanitary Commission and Secretary Stanton," MHS *Proceedings*, LXVII, 402–19.

the tried and the promising is the perennial problem of the armed services in wartime. Though greater boldness and initiative in the War Department would have brought an earlier increase in the Union Army's firepower, yet, considering all the complications involved, Stanton's officials met that problem reasonably well.

Ripley finally proved to be such an obstructionist that he had to be removed at last. Over Stanton's objections, Lincoln selected as his successor General Ramsay, who had disobeyed Stanton's order to remove the weapons from the Washington arsenal at the time Pope met disaster. To his discredit, Stanton hamstrung Ramsay by appointing Captain George T. Balch, nominally as Ramsay's assistant, but virtually as his overseer. Finally, in General Alexander B. Dyer, a choice of Watson and Stanton, the Ordnance Bureau came under the supervision of a man well qualified for the job, and with his advent the Bureau would be more sympathetic toward the development of better instruments of war.

Stanton's performance in relation to the medical and ordnance organizations fails to reflect the highest credit on him. To be sure, Hitchcock and Halleck, who were sometimes hidebound in accepting changes, must share with Stanton the blame for hesitating to inject new methods and abler personnel into the two moribund bureaus. But the final responsibility remains his. Bravely inventive in most matters, he permitted the overcaution of his advisers, his own impatient temper, and the pressures of a multitude of competing demands for his attention, to get the better of his good sense.[1]

In other respects Stanton clearly contributed greatly to the success of the Union effort. He organized the country's telegraph and railroad industries into effective instruments of warfare. Frederick Seward described him as "the master spirit of the contest," shuffling men and supplies on a vast chessboard visible only to himself. In order to insure that his control over the telegraph would be absolute, Stanton determinedly kept the Department's telegraphers in civilian status and under his orders alone, outside the control of the Army's Signal Corps. His monopoly of telegraphic communications often placed Stanton in a bad light. Orders went out from Washington under his name which were in fact signed by subordinates. Bureau heads could sometimes convince the overbusy Secretary that a complex policy was necessary

---

[1] Bruce, *op. cit.*, 265–6, 275–7; Roscoe Pound, "Bureaus and Bureau Methods in the Civil War," MHS *Proceedings*, LXVII, 420–35.

and secure his approval for it after it was already in effect. Stanton took the blame for errors and excesses in such circumstances, and he took it without flinching.

Railroad communications developed under his encouragement into an integral part of the Northern military machine. Only such co-ordination made possible the salvation of Rosecrans's army at Chattanooga, in the greatest transportation feat in the history of warfare up to that time. Stanton's director of railroads did not hesitate in 1864 to use the Secretary's name in threatening to draft striking railroad engineers and replace them with soldiers. The strikers resumed work.[2]

Stanton also understood the power of the press and tried to gain favorable treatment in newspapers. Feeling that the Associated Press, under Democratic control, was untrustworthy, he hindered its agents as much as he could. He turned to smaller, country newspapers not serviced by the A.P. wires, favored them with Department advertising and printing, and by these means helped good Republicans and Union Democrats to start newspapers. Stanton did not find it objectionable that anti-war newspapers were often lost in transit and sometimes excluded from army camps. Provost marshals created endless difficulties for Democratic journalists, and military telegraphers favored the correspondents of Republican newspapers.

Although Stanton detested generals who divulged plans to journalists, he did not hesitate to leak stories to favored correspondents and sometimes wrote them himself. He commanded the services of such men as Horatio Woodman, Crosby Stuart Noyes, Lieber, and the representatives of the potent Loyal Publication Society. Their work was reinforced by speeches, sermons, and articles by federal place holders, army officers, and ministers. The administration received inestimable assistance through the efforts of these persons. Stanton, in recruiting and sustaining them, performed an effective public relations function for the War Department and the Union.[3]

On the western waters, Stanton's enterprise created an Army-run flotilla of river steamers, a ram fleet, and a corps of "marines" to do work which the Navy at first disdained to perform. He supported the creation of the Congressional Medal of Honor, conscription, the Provost Marshal General's Bureau, and absentee voting for soldiers, and

---

[2] Grant, *Memoirs*, II, 105–6; Pound, "The Military Telegraph in the Civil War," *loc. cit.*, 202–3; Seward, *Reminiscences*, 243; Haupt, *Reminiscences* (Milwaukee, 1901), 165; T. H. Parker, "A Glimpse of the Railroads during the Civil War," *WPHM*, XX, 20.

[3] Newbold Noyes, "Crosby Stuart Noyes," ColHS *Records*, XL, 207.

wrestled the moribund army bureau structure toward a staff organization. Like Lincoln, Stanton realized that war in the modern manner must be directed toward the destruction of the enemy's total resources.

In the field of policy, Stanton had pushed strongly for emancipation and the enlistment of colored troops, and some 180,000 were now in the Army, although few saw combat service. But the enlistment of Negroes as soldiers intensified a problem that had remained unsolved since the beginning of the war—that of exchanging prisoners.

There were two complicating factors. First, the North refused to enter into any agreement on this subject that might be construed as a recognition of the Confederacy. Second, many captured rebels did not want to be exchanged for Northern prisoners held by the Confederacy, but preferred to stay in the North if released.

One of Stanton's first objectives on becoming Secretary had been to relieve the plight of Union prisoners. He ordered that their pay and allowances be continued during their captivity. But his efforts to achieve a general exchange of prisoners and to supply some of the wants of the South's captives could not surmount the obstacles of the Confederate government's desire for recognition and the more important goals of the Union government, to which Stanton had to give his first attention.

Reports of horrible conditions among Union prisoners in the South brought a barrage of criticism against the Lincoln administration and demands that humanity be given priority over all other considerations. Consequently, on July 12, 1862, Stanton authorized Dix to reopen negotiations for a general exchange, "observing proper caution against any recognition of the rebel government," and exchanges were satisfactorily effected for several months.[4]

By early 1863, the Union had the majority of prisoners, thousands of whom did not wish exchange, but desired to remain in the North. Agreeing with Lincoln that it was inhumane to force these captives to return to Dixie, Stanton set a new policy for would-be defectors which blended perfectly into the President's developing thoughts on reconstruction.

Stanton conceived a system by which captured rebels might be screened and the most promising defeatists among them culled out to

4 *O.R.*, ser. 2, III, 192, 222–4, 230, 778–9, 783–4, 790–1; IV, 174, 266–8; Hesseltine, *Civil War Prisons* (Columbus, 1930), 7–31 (hereafter cited as Hesseltine, *Civil War Prisons*); Lincoln, *Works*, V, 449; Nicolay and Hay, *Lincoln*, X, 44.

serve the Union cause as turncoats. He did not expect his program to change all captive rebels into pure Unionists. Stanton planned it, rather, to open the way to freedom for a small minority of prisoners, those who were politically significant and intelligent and whose conversions would have the effect of spurring defeatism among their neighbors when, newly sworn to Unionism, they returned to communities in the border states and in occupied Southern areas.

Confederate authorities, resenting the success of Stanton's policy, used it as an excuse to hesitate on regular exchanges of the Northern soldiers they held. Stanton was taken to task for cruelly and deliberately keeping good Yankee troopers in terrible Southern captivity. But the basic policy was part of Lincoln's larger vision of finishing the war. Stanton carried it out better than the administrative structure of the War Department would seem to permit, in a workable and effective, if primitive, form of psychological warfare.[5]

The actions of certain field officers of both armies further complicated the prisoner problem. On taking command at New Orleans, Butler had caused a citizen to be executed for tearing down a Union flag. For this and other offensive actions, President Davis declared Butler and his officers felons "deserving of capital punishment," and announced that no more Union officers would be released on parole until Butler had been punished for his "crimes." In retaliation, Stanton, after consulting Lincoln, ordered all exchanges of Confederate officers stopped.

Davis had also warned that any Negroes taken in arms, together with their white officers, would be dealt with according to the states' statutes for the suppression of slave insurrections, in effect making Union officers commanding Negroes liable to the death penalty for inciting blacks to revolt, and virtually condemning Negro troops to death or slavery. With the Confederate government bound to treat the black man as a chattel and Stanton determined to release no more Confederates until all Union soldiers were guaranteed protection under the laws of war, exchange virtually stopped.

Then the Confederate cavalry commander Nathan Bedford Forrest swooped down on Fort Pillow, a small Union post on the Mississippi garrisoned by Negro troops. He refused to accept the surrender of the defenders and, according to restrained, careful subsequent investigators, slew them without mercy along with their white officers.[6]

[5] Hyman, "Civil War Turncoats," *MA*, XIII, 134–8.
[6] Flower, *Stanton*, 235–6; Hesseltine, *Civil War Prisons*, 210–14; Lincoln, *Works*, V, 128, 940–1.

Perhaps as a gesture of appeasement for Forrest's brutal act, or more likely because the Confederacy was powerless to alleviate conditions in its prison camps, the South offered to surrender some hopelessly ill or wounded Union prisoners without an equivalent return. Stanton accepted the offer. When the prisoners were delivered, he arranged for them to be photographed and inspected by a committee of Congress. "There appears to have been a deliberate system of savage and barbarous treatment and starvation," he said, and as a measure of retaliation, he ordered the rations of Confederate captives, hitherto the same as the Union Army ration, reduced by 20 per cent. When properly distributed the reduced ration was sufficient to maintain health. But when mismanagement or vengefulness on the part of prison keepers entered into the picture, hunger and disease ensued.[7]

Though exchanges were blocked, Confederate troops in many instances continued to be paroled. The North broke out in wrathful indignation upon learning that many of these parolees, under promise not to take up arms again, had again been captured in the fighting at Chattanooga. Bitterly accusing the South of bad faith, Stanton prohibited further paroles.

With paroles as well as exchanges halted, both sides were under the necessity of guarding and supporting an increasing host of captives. Even in the more prosperous North the compounds became filthy and overcrowded. In the South conditions became intolerable.

Appalled by reports of mass starvation in Southern prison camps, Stanton ordered Hitchcock, now improved in health and in charge of prisoners, to put Southern captives on a corresponding diet. Hitchcock protested that such action would be inhumane, and, just before asking Stanton to reconsider his decision, the general confided to a friend: "I expect to have no difficulty in turning the attention of the Secretary to a better view."

Stanton rescinded the order. To alleviate the condition of Union prisoners, he ordered 24,000 rations sent to Libby Prison, in Richmond. False reports that the rations had been devoured by the Confederates circulated freely in the North. Incensed at these "abusive accusations," the South discontinued the arrangement, angering Stanton in turn. Retaliation led to counter-retaliation.[8]

Through it all, Stanton endured a mounting chorus of criticism di-

[7] Lincoln, *Works*, VII, 345–6; *O.R.*, ser. 2, VII, 110–11, 1504.
[8] *O.R.*, ser. 2, V, 691; VI, 314–15, 489, 504, 523–4, 625, 686, 1014; VIII, 800–1; Hitchcock to Mrs. Mary Mann, Nov. 25, 1863, Hitchcock-Mann Correspondence, LC; Bates, *Diary*, 314.

rected against him from the South and from Northerners who believed that he was the heartless ogre responsible for the sufferings in the prison camps. He took comfort from the fact that Grant sustained him in his opposition to exchanges. Grant admitted that "it is hard on our men held in Southern prisons not to exchange them, but it is humanity to those left in the ranks to fight our battles. Every man we hold, when released on parole or otherwise, becomes an active soldier against us at once either directly or indirectly. If we commence a system of exchange which liberates all prisoners taken, we will have to fight on until the whole South is exterminated. If we hold those caught they amount to no more than dead men."

The general and the Secretary were in perfect agreement. Soon after Grant took over-all command, Stanton prepared a confidential memorandum for his attention, pointing to the fact that the South, its white manpower draining away, and refusing to arm its slaves, must benefit disproportionately from whatever activity an exchanged or paroled soldier engaged in once he returned from the North. Thus the war would be prolonged, with infinitely more suffering to both sides than the relatively few prisoners must endure because of the stoppage in exchanges and paroling. At the bottom of this memorandum, Stanton penned in a joyous scrawl: "The general presented the same argument to me before I could advance it to him." [9]

All this confirmed Stanton in his belief in the barbarity of Southerners, yet he would have been a man without pity to be unmoved by the plight of Northern prisoners. There was little he could do to aid them. Even after the war, however, the Democrats would continue to accuse him of heartlessness. To meet these attacks, the Secretary's friends in Congress asked Stanton for an explanation of his course, which Stanton provided.

He had made unceasing efforts to liberate and relieve the prisoners, he claimed, but it had been impossible to obtain an agreement for a general exchange on Southern terms. In the beginning, this would have meant a virtual recognition of the Confederacy, and later the abandonment of Negro troops and their officers to vengeful punishment. His task had been made still more difficult, Stanton explained further, by the Confederacy's refusal to release noncombatant prisoners captured in loyal states, by its releasing from parole and restoring to military service some 40,000 rebel soldiers taken at Vicksburg and Port Hudson, and by what he believed to be a deliberate attempt to starve

[9] Stanton's memo, undated, copy owned by the estate of Benjamin P. Thomas; Beale, *Welles Diary*, II, 168–71; *O.R.*, ser. 2, VII, 607, 906–14, 926, 929, 1070–3.

Union prisoners. This justification of his actions was never made public. Nor did Stanton cite Grant's opposition to exchanges as a reason for the failure to effect a general release of Northern prisoners. He took the buffeting himself.[1]

He also took a major share of the criticism that arose because of the Union's internal security policies. Civil liberty did suffer in the North. Even Lincoln, though deeply reverential of constitutional guarantees, would not allow himself to be unduly impeded in the exercise of power by doctrinaire conceptions of civil rights. Stanton, a man of far less breadth of vision who focused on immediate objectives, frequently used the power of his office in ways ordinarily barred to American government. This came about in some degree from his relish of power, but a more compelling factor was the magnitude and imminence of the peril the nation faced. The enemy not only threatened the ramparts; he also skulked inside the gates.

Stanton's widespread dragnet often ensnared the innocent along with seditionists. In Stanton's name, army officers, state militiamen, home guards, police chiefs, and vigilantes arrested persons for disloyalty. The great fault of the internal security apparatus, Provost Marshal Doster recalled, "was that it operated like a rat-trap—there was only a hole in but no hole out." Few of the many officials empowered by Stanton to prevent disloyalty would risk discharging a prisoner until the threat was clearly past. This made it inevitable that Stanton would be blamed for every excess. Five years after Stanton died, Chase and his friend John Schuckers met a small-town Wisconsin editor, Democratic in politics, who on Stanton's authority had been unjustly jailed for disloyalty. "His hostility was unappeasable," Schuckers recorded. "Speaking to me of Stanton . . . he broke out . . . 'He's in hell, God damn him—I know that he's in hell.' "

Yet Stanton, with Lincoln, sought to restrain the exercise of despotic power when it was possible. But he could not oversee the daily security work of all the army commands. Many civilians were imprisoned on false or trivial charges. The fact remains, however, that most of the civilians who were arrested for disloyalty and tried before military commissions on that charge, were found to be guilty.

Stanton almost invariably acted swiftly in ordering releases for the far greater number of persons whose arrest had been clearly unwarranted; nor were many whose arrest had been merely precautionary

[1] Hesseltine, *Civil War Prisons,* 222–3; New York *Times,* Dec. 27, 1864; Flower, *Stanton,* 238.

kept in prison once the need for precaution had passed. Most prisoners gained release merely by swearing allegiance and promising not to hold further communication with the Confederacy and not to sue for damages.

But Stanton did insist on the most severe penalties for those against whom the evidence of disloyalty was strong. Similarly, any captive who, freed after swearing loyalty to the Union, violated the pledge and again fell into Stanton's hands, could expect the fullest penalties in his power to apply. And Stanton could not abide a suspect who lied to him. A Confederate spy captured by Stanton's agents once offered him erroneous information, later boasting to Barlow: "Stanton was humbugged; he believed my statements & acted on them." But Stanton unearthed the deception and saw to it that the trickster remained in a military jail even after the war ended. To Stanton, the internal security problem was deadly serious and intensely personal.[2]

On the whole, control of the press was singularly lax. Only news sent by telegraph came under direct government scrutiny; letters circulated freely without examination; couriers were normally allowed to come and go at will; and papers not only printed detailed information on military plans and troop movements but criticized the government freely, in numerous instances carrying their opposition to the point of disloyalty. The problem of maintaining secrecy in the face of so much journalistic freedom plagued the Union Army throughout the war.

War correspondents with the troops did come under military jurisdiction, however, and the 57th Article of War gave Stanton a weapon against journalistic irresponsibility by making anyone holding correspondence with or giving intelligence to the enemy liable to death or such other punishment as a court-martial might prescribe. Though Stanton was often careless of the First Amendment, and subjective and arbitrary regarding excessively frank scribes, offenders rarely suffered punishment. Now and then a general excluded a correspondent from his lines and in a few cases the War Department denied passes to culpable journalists. But the brash and ingenious newsmen were not easily muzzled, and throughout the war the Confederates could obtain copious information merely by scanning the Northern papers. Stanton's action against the New York *World* and the *Journal of Commerce* for printing the bogus Lincoln dispatch is a rare instance of the suppression of

---

[2] Schuckers Papers, LC, memo, *ca.* 1875, on the Wisconsin editor; G. S. L. Grenfell to Barlow, Jan. 13, 1868, Barlow Papers, HL; Hyman, *op. cit.*, ch. 7; Randall, *Constitutional Problems*, 155; K. A. Bernard, "Lincoln and Civil Liberties," *ALQ*, VI, 380–94; *O.R.*, ser. 2, LV, 380–425.

newspapers. There were numerous other episodes in which the military arm moved against offenders, but such shutdowns were always temporary.

The mistaken zeal of subordinates often outran the intentions of the War Department and the President, and when Burnside suppressed the Chicago *Times* for criticizing his arrest of the quasi traitor Vallandigham, Stanton revoked the order at Lincoln's behest, adding: "The irritation produced by such acts is . . . likely to do more harm than the publication would." Had the impetuous Stanton been allowed to have his way, the policy might have been tougher. But press control was a matter over which Lincoln exercised close personal supervision. The result was that with few exceptions the policy of the government was tolerant rather than oppressive, and it often endured torrents of abuse in the press without attempting retaliation.

Most of the newsmen's shafts were directed at Stanton. They hated him "as they do Original Sin," wrote Noah Brooks, Lincoln's journalist friend, "for he is as inexorable as death, and as reticent as the grave. He is very arbitrary, and shuts and no man openeth, or opens and no man shutteth." Only Louis Koerth, a convalescent combat veteran who was serving as Stanton's clerk-bodyguard, knew how deeply hurt the Secretary was when he overheard newsmen muttering: "There goes old bulldog." Information on Stanton as press censor derives largely from the accounts of these journalists. It is little wonder that he appears in the worst possible light.[3]

Careless of his own popularity, seldom afraid to say no, working like one of his lowliest troopers, Stanton plunged ahead, implacably intent and not easily turned aside from his purpose. With all his blind spots, he administered his office with commendable efficiency. Method, system, and irresistible driving energy characterized his performance. Impulse, prejudice, and reluctance to admit error marred it.

He seemed to invite enmity by his sheer impatience. Laboring like a giant in a position in which he had to make enemies, any man would have become irritable. Stanton tended in that direction because of his asthmatic malady, which worsened until twice in 1864 he was overcome by fits of strangulation, and a liver ailment also grew more severe. He watched the fate of Union armies like a mother who has entrusted her sons to strangers, and his wrath at incapacity, at error, or at what he

[3] Brooks in Sacramento *Union*, May 2, 1863; Koerth in New York *Commercial Advertiser*, March 24, 1903; Randall, "The Newspaper Problem in Its Bearing upon Military Secrecy during the Civil War," *AHR*, XXIII, 302–23.

Stanton : The Life and Times

thought were more sinister reasons for reverses, was always unrestrained. Obliged to contend with incompetent generals, wolfish contractors, and arrant and furtive traitors; working his brother-in-law to death and himself close to it; and feeling the loss of thousands of men in battle who he felt were better than those who came to him for favors, Stanton became an impatient man, prone to quick, often unjust suspicions.

"My chief is narrow-minded," Hitchcock once confided, "full of prejudices, exceedingly violent, reckless of the rights and feelings of others, often acting like a wild man in the dark, throwing his arms around, willing to hit anybody, so he hits somebody, and makes a big stir. His idea of energy is altogether physical. He is coarse in his use of language, and his dislikes are mere prejudices—not founded upon any proper knowledge of character or . . . of the profession of which he is the legal head." Yet Hitchcock admitted that in all matters of substance he agreed with the irascible Secretary.

Too often Stanton administered rebukes with unpardonable severity. Department underlings hid when bad news came in from the front, and mere trifles would send him into a tantrum. Many persons felt the whiplash of his tongue. Stanton's trouble, often, was that he just did not realize that he had been cruel or unjust. He had once suspected young General James H. Wilson of incapacity. Information from Grant changed his mind, and thereafter Stanton supported the cavalryman. Learning of this after the war, Wilson reflected: "I would rather be opposed by Edwin M. Stanton than by any other man in America. I regard Mr. Stanton [as] the greatest civilian of the day."

Provost Marshal General Patrick, of the Army of the Potomac, had a far lower opinion of Stanton. Patrick's rugged sense of duty and Democratic party principles often put him in opposition to Stanton's orders concerning travel passes, trade permits, fugitive Negroes, and arrests of civilians. It is noteworthy that Stanton's growing irritation with Patrick never interfered with that officer's promotions.

Early in 1865, Patrick decided to have a showdown. He and Stanton retired behind the locked doors of the Secretary's office. "I never talked more plainly to any man in my life," Patrick recorded; "I will do him the justice to say that he behaved well. He heard me patiently, said what he had to say, and gave me the key to much of the mischief that has been going on." [4]

---

[4] Jan. 30, 1865, Patrick ms diary, LC; Hitchcock to Henry Hitchcock, April 25, 1862, MoHS; Wilson to Badeau, Aug. 5, 1865, James H. Wilson Papers, LC.

General Lorenzo Thomas, a man of limited ability and narrow views, was often the target of Stanton's hostility. Thomas confessed that "Stanton is an enigma to me. He has no manners, and treats persons rudely, and yet at times he appears kind." When Stanton was able to oblige petitioners, Thomas acknowledged, it was only after he had determined that the Army's needs were first met. But with that hurdle overcome, the Secretary was happy to grant favors which could mean life or death, happiness or despair, to someone.

But he often had to submerge the impulse to oblige supplicants in the galling necessity to say no, and he rarely confessed the deep distress he felt on these frequent occasions. In a moment of release, Stanton poured out his heart to Mrs. Isabella Beecher Hooker, a relative of Henry Ward Beecher, who thanked him for a favor done. "In my official station I have tried to do my duty as I shall answer to God at the great day," he wrote her, "but it is the misfortune of that station—a misfortune that no one else can comprehend the magnitude of—that most of my duties are harsh and painful to someone, so that I rejoice at an opportunity, however rare, of combining duty with kindly offices." [5]

Those who suffered from Stanton's outbursts of temper or who ran afoul of his policies looked upon him as a power-mad tyrant, and Gideon Welles added that he was a sycophant as well. More charitably, one of Black's friends ventured this "true solution" of Stanton's character: ". . . he had no head for abstract ideas; but great faculty for concrete things." Stanton was no thinker, but an "actor" cloaked in power.

These erroneous judgments have satisfied most subsequent commentators on Stanton. A far more accurate description emerges from the recollection of Stanton's chief clerk, Charles Benjamin, who observed his busy superior every day for seven years, and who admitted the defects of Stanton's impetuous, erratic behavior in the same critical terms employed by Doster and Hitchcock. "Yet such a man would apprehend deeply where he apprehended rightly," Benjamin wrote; "his ardor of mind would inspire him with confidence in the means, and trust for the end; his free-handed energy would open otherwise undiscoverable paths to fortune; his sense of humor would tend to link him to sober views of men and things; his furtive heartiness would win strong

[5] To Mrs. Hooker, May 6, 1863, in R. B. Hayes scrapbook X, HML; F. B. Carpenter in Los Angeles *Herald*, April 28, 1901; Thomas to Cameron, March 18, 1863, Cameron Papers, LC.

friends, if few; . . . his inherent love of orderly courses would strip absolutism of its worst excesses and consequences; and his supernaturalism would endow him with a calm and persistent courage."

Stanton, in Benjamin's estimation, was never the cold, feelingless, fact juggler most persons believed him to be and which the Secretary desired to seem. Rather he was "intuitive rather than logical, and romantic rather than realistic; . . . his firmness often meant sheer obstinacy," and his "ardor" resulted in "raw haste." [6]

The journalist Sylvanus Cadwallader, no admirer of Stanton, has left proof of the acuity of Benjamin's perception. Cadwallader once dared criticize Stanton to his face for not attending the funeral of a combat officer who had been a friend of the Stanton family. The Secretary heard the reporter's harsh observations through without commenting. Cadwallader belatedly realized that he had not known of the casualty.

"At the news," the journalist recorded, Stanton slumped heavily on his high desk, "body leaned forward, his golden bound spectacles thrown upon his forehead, & with a tender sorrowful faraway look of countenance which I had never before seen him exhibit till then, & one rarely seen on this stern official. . . . I left Mr. Stanton's office in a softened mood, suspecting there was, contrary to my former opinion, an unexplored region containing some drops of human kindness, under the unexplored exterior of the unloved Secretary of War." [7]

[6] Benjamin, "Secretary Stanton: The Man and His Work," _JMSI_, VII, 240–1; J. Ashton to Black, Jan. 3, 1870, Black Papers, LC; Welles to Andrew Johnson, Jan. 4, 1870, Johnson Papers, LC; Jessie Benton Frémont, _Souvenirs of My Time_ (Boston, 1887), 146.

[7] "My Four Years with Grant," ms, ISHL; and see Lewis Stanton in New York _World_, Dec. 6, 1886.

CHAPTER XVIII

STANTON'S LINCOLN

JOURNALIST Cadwallader's phrase—"the unloved Secretary of War"—would have been accepted as accurate by almost everyone of that generation and by most subsequent commentators as well. But one time in his life, apart from his relations with his family, and except for his intimacy with Chase years before, Stanton opened his heart to another person and found acceptance and reciprocal affection. Because Lincoln was a great man, Stanton reached in his service a plane far higher than his more prosaic spirit could have touched.

History records few instances when two men of more disparate outward characteristics were brought together in positions requiring mutual trust, complementary talents, and capacity for quick growth. Despite the differences in their natures, Lincoln and Stanton had much in common. They shared memories of a boyhood spent in the great river valleys that divide yet knit together the great plain west of the mountains. Both had come up from lowly origins, although Stanton had the advantage of a middle-class upbringing and a superior formal education. Each sought success through the practice of the law, but Stanton achieved far wider professional renown than Lincoln, driving ahead in his humorless, undeviating way toward the lucrative practice he enjoyed when Lincoln gained the pinnacle of politics.

Stanton was more closely attuned than Lincoln to the immediate present; he was in many ways a "modern" man-in-a-hurry, never tempering the inadequacies of his nature with the sweet sensitivity of soul that Lincoln brought to his experiences. Life was a way to material success for Stanton. Yet Lincoln, by offering Stanton his trust, by feeding the sense of nationalism already sparked in Stanton's breast by service in Buchanan's cabinet, and by matching Stanton's temper with his quietude of spirit, received in return the devotion of a man who was content to be his servant.

Something in Lincoln's calm, warm, mystical character drew Stanton out of the self-centered shell which he had built around his life. Lincoln's shrewd judgments on men and exploitations of power impressed Stanton. His devout concern for human beings echoed far back into Stanton's youth. Lincoln's conviction that the American experiment in democracy was worthy of survival and sacrifice brought Stanton to action to sustain the conviction. Stanton's early contempt for Lincoln gave way to respect, and then to love.

The deep relationship that grew between them was apparent only to those few persons who knew both men well. Lincoln's secretary, John Hay, soon after the war ended wrote to the War Secretary: "Not every one knows, as I do, how close you stood to our . . . leader, how he loved you and trusted you, and how vain were all the efforts to shake that trust and confidence, not lightly given & never withdrawn. All this will be [known] some time, of course, to his honor and yours."

Hay delighted Stanton by recalling that "there are many meddlers whose knuckles you had rapped, many thieves whose hands you had tied, and many liars whose mouths you had shut for a time by their prompt punishment, who had occupied themselves in traducing you. That is all over now. . . . It is already known, as well as the readers of history a hundred years hence will know, that no honest man has cause to quarrel with you, that your hands have been clean and your heart steady every hour of this fight, and that if any human names are to have the glory of this victory, it belongs to you among the very few who stood by the side of [Lincoln] . . . and never faltered in your trust in God and the People."

Hay's confident prediction that history would cast a gentle light on Stanton's career as War Secretary, and correctly illuminate the nature of the relationship that existed between Lincoln and his "Mars," was one with which Lincoln agreed. The President told his journalist friend T. J. Barnett that Stanton "is utterly misjudged . . . at present, the man's public character is a public mistake." A friend of Seward's, after a lengthy sojourn in Washington, reflected that Stanton "justified the high encomiums you bestowed upon him. I am satisfied that Mr. Stanton merely desires to know what is right and then has both the inclination and the nerve to do it. Much prejudice exists against him —but ultimately the country will do him justice—tardily perhaps— but surely."

Not so surely. For Stanton deliberately obscured his real feelings in order to carry out his responsibilities as Secretary. Thus, even General N. P. Chipman, who worked closely with Stanton and admired him, had to confess that "well as I felt that I knew him, yet he is a stranger to me." [1]

And a stranger he remained, except to Lincoln. The two men grew together. In 1862, a shrewd Ohioan, William T. Coggeshall, likened Lincoln to "a boy carrying a big basket of eggs." "Couldn't let go his basket to unbutton his breeches—was in sore distress from a necessity to urinate—& stood dancing, crying—What shall I do?" The cabinet, Coggeshall continued, "is like a collection of powerful chemicals—each positive, sharp, individual—but thrown together neutralize each other & the result is an insipid mess."

By 1865 Lincoln was no longer dancing in agonized indecision, and of the cabinet officers, Stanton had emerged into brilliant prominence. The war had developed both men to an almost incredible degree. Their relationship had steadily become warmer and warmer, until by 1865 it had evolved into an understanding partnership on official matters and a firm personal friendship. Nothing could have been further from the truth than Manton Marble's assertion that Lincoln was convinced that there was not an honest hair on Stanton's head. [2]

To be sure, Mary Lincoln and Ellen Stanton did not like each other, and this prevented social exchanges beyond those required for official decorum. But as things worked out this was no great impediment in the way of the increasingly affectionate feelings of the two men for each other. They arranged things so that they spent as much time in each other's company as possible, only in part to facilitate discussion of the endless matters of war and politics.

For example, when in late June 1863 the heat of Washington became intolerable, Ellen Stanton went off to the cooler highland of Bedford, Pennsylvania, after first exacting a promise from Lincoln that he and her husband would join her there for a long weekend. Each week the two men hoped to be off. But in August, Stanton admitted to her that "some thing always turns up to keep him or me in Washington. He is so eager for it that I expect we will accomplish it before the season is over." They were never able to get away together, however.

---

[1] Hay to Stanton, July 26, 1865, Stanton MSS; Barnett to Barlow, Nov. 30, 1862, Barlow Papers, HL; W. H. Robinson to Seward, June 13, 1864, Seward Papers, UR; Chipman in Supreme Court, *Eulogies*, 47–9. See also Gamaliel Bradford, *Union Portraits* (Boston, 1914), 165–96.

[2] Oct. 23, 1862, Coggeshall ms diary, owned by the estate of Foreman M. Lebold; New York *World*, Aug. 8, 1863.

The preceding year they had arranged to take adjoining summer cottages on the shaded grounds of the Soldiers' Home in suburban Georgetown. Often, Stanton could not get out there, though Lincoln could, and the President would go out of his way while driving to the White House from the Soldiers' Home to stop at Stanton's town residence. While the cavalry escort which Stanton insisted accompany Lincoln waited, the Secretary would come out of his house and talk with the President in his carriage. Sometimes, their discussion of official matters was interrupted by the shouts of the crowd at nearby Franklin Square when a baseball game was in progress.[3]

Often they could get out to the Soldiers' Home retreat together, and it became a common sight in the last two summers of the war to see the President's plain open carriage leaving the capital for this suburban haven of relative coolness, carrying the tall, lean frame of Lincoln slouched next to the heavier, squat, erect body of his War Secretary. The two men talked incessantly in low tones so that the drivers and the escorting cavalrymen would not hear, and jotted notes on scraps of paper from the time they left Pennsylvania Avenue, but they visibly relaxed as they approached their destination.

Here their children took over, shouting, jostling the two tired men, and cajoling until a game was granted. One day, telegrapher Bates, bringing a message to Stanton from the War Department to the summer home, found the Secretary engaged in a spirited game of "mumble-the-peg" and was himself dragooned into it.

Lincoln and Stanton more than liked each other's children, and neither man could resist the blandishments of the young. A friend of Stanton's youngest daughter remembered how she and other youngsters would loiter around the Stanton home to enjoy his gentle stories to them. Though Stanton never accepted gifts for himself, he could not remain unbending where his children were concerned. An anonymous friend sent young Lewis Stanton a white pony and a colorful Zouave uniform. Stanton ferreted out the donor's identity, but by this time the children were in love with the pony, and the wire Stanton sent, instead of saying that he would return the beast, read: "Lou is on his back and don't believe he will ever get off."

Someone had given the Stanton children a flock of peacocks. When they persisted in flying off, soldiers at the Home hit on the expedient of tying a stout cord, with a piece of wood attached, to a leg of each

<hr />

[3] Stanton to Ellen, Aug. 25, 1863, owned by Gideon Townsend Stanton; Allen C. Clark, "Abraham Lincoln in the National Capital," ColHS *Records*, XXVII, 36–7.

bird. These devices were light enough to permit the peacocks to fly into the trees to roost, but heavy enough to prevent their leaving the grounds. Lewis recalled: "One evening . . . just before sunset, Mr. Lincoln and my father arrived at the cottage. They at once noticed the peacocks who were roosting in a small cluster of cedar trees with the ropes and sticks caught in the many small branches and recognized the dangerous and uncomfortable position when on the morrow they would attempt to fly to earth. The two men immediately went to work, and I can see them now dressed in their long black coats and beavers solemnly going to and fro unwinding the ropes and getting them in straight lines and carefully placing the small pieces of wood where without catching they would slide off when in the morning the birds flew down." [4]

Lincoln spent more time with Stanton than with any other cabinet officer. This close association aroused the jealousy of Welles, Blair, and Chase, and perhaps this subdued but intense competition for first place in the President's heart accounts for some of the acrimony that existed among the cabinet officers. Almost every man who served Lincoln loved him; that Stanton received the warmest response was his treasured and private reward for his efforts.

To be sure, Lincoln's preference for Stanton's company may have been due in part to his desire to oversee his volcanic "Mars," and also to the monopoly Stanton kept over the military telegraph. Lincoln was at the War Department as often as he could be, and at critical times he and Stanton rarely left the place. The President was a familiar sight to the guards Stanton kept posted around the White House—striding in his long, awkward gait to the rickety turnstile that separated the two buildings, hurrying back to a reception or dinner he had deserted in order to slip over to see Stanton and read the dispatches.

Though the relationship between them was not as amiable as that between Lincoln and Seward, it was more intimate. Stanton and Lincoln virtually conducted the war together, whereas Seward had a free hand in managing the State Department except when a diplomatic crisis threatened. Lincoln, Seward told diplomat John Bigelow in 1867, "was the War Minister, and a very good one."

Lincoln was calm, unruffled, careless with secrets, forgiving, inclined to tell a joke to place matters in perspective; Stanton was seem-

---

[4] On children, see letter of Mrs. Wylie to Craig Wylie, April 11, 1937, owned by Craig Wylie; Bates, *op. cit.*, 397–8, on the game; Utica (N.Y.) *Morning Herald*, May 17, 1886, on the horse; and on the peacock incident, the ms recollection by Lewis Hutchison Stanton, owned by Gideon Townsend Stanton.

ingly merciless, secretive, implacable with error, furious at reverses. Congressman Dawes observed of them: "The one sorrowed over the calamities of war; the other sorrowed that more was not achieved by it." Heart and head of the war, was the way telegrapher Bates thought of the two men, and he insisted that they never really were at odds. "Stanton required a man like Lincoln to manage him," Grant said years later. Lincoln dominated Stanton by "that gentle firmness." Sometimes too forbearing, Lincoln was frequently saved from error by Stanton's strict sense of duty. There were times when Lincoln overrode Stanton, as in appointing officials to the War Department and officers to the Army. Other times the President found himself imposed upon. Yet the two men worked well together on the whole, and counterbalanced each other's faults.

This harmony was desperately needed if the Union's effort was ever to achieve co-ordination. Back in the dark days of September 1862, Chase, talking to Garfield, had spread out his fore and middle fingers to form a V, of which the forefinger represented Stanton, "full of impulsive energy, strong and sincere, but impatient of delay and restraint and feeling at times completely disheartened by the complexities of his position." The middle finger was Halleck—intelligent, "cold as a stone, cares not one penny for his work, only as a professional performance." At the junction between the two was Lincoln, "with a great and noble heart." Then, after heartbreaking failures and frustrations, the addition of Grant to the command structure proved adequate to bring on the defeat of the rebellion.

Lincoln and Stanton were alike in most important respects, Meigs realized. They asked for action, progress, and achievement. Not receiving them, they were "urgent when patience failed under costly inaction." [5]

Whenever affairs came to an impasse between them, it was Lincoln's will that controlled, and the phrase "I yield to whatever the President may think best for the service" is in one form or another widely distributed through more than three years' accumulation of memoranda and notes between the two men. When Stanton saw a specific order in

[5] Typescript, "1861–5," Dawes Papers, LC; Feb. 28, 1867, Bigelow ms diary, NYPL; A. E. H. Johnson in Washington *Star*, Nov. 23, 1895, and in New York *Evening Post*, July 13, 1891; Bates, *op. cit.*, 129–30, 621; Grant, *Memoirs*, II, 380–1, and quoted in John Russell Young, *Around the World with General Grant* (New York, 1879), II, 354, 358–9 (cited henceforth as Young, *Around the World*); Smith, *Garfield*, I, 240; Meigs to his brother, *ca.* 1888, owned by Edward S. Corwin; Current, *op. cit.*, 162.

Lincoln's handwriting, he knew that his own objections to an appointment, a contract, or a policy had been overruled, and though he fretted, he did not fail to comply with the President's decision. Until that moment, however, he felt free to try to sway Lincoln as much as he could, and to insulate him if possible from too persuasive petitioners.

A typical instance involved a group of captured Confederates who, prompted by a Pennsylvania recruiting agent, offered to take the oath of allegiance, enlist in the Union Army, and serve against the western Indians. Lincoln ordered that their wish be granted, that they receive the usual bounty, and that they be credited against Pennsylvania's draft quota.

Stanton refused to carry out the order. Provost Marshal General Fry immediately sided with Stanton, pointing out that the prisoners already belonged to the Union and to allow them bounty would be a waste of money. Pennsylvania deserved no credit for their enlistment, Fry insisted, and to permit such an error would deprive the armies of needed manpower from that state. Stanton said: "Now, Mr. President, those are the facts, and you must see that your order cannot be executed." Lincoln, sitting on a sofa in Stanton's office with his legs crossed, answered firmly: "Mr. Secretary, I reckon you'll have to execute the order." Stanton snapped: "Mr. President, I cannot do it. The order is an improper one, and I cannot execute it." Lincoln looked Stanton straight in the eye and said with determination: "Mr. Secretary, it will have to be done."

"Stanton then realized," wrote Fry, "that he was overmatched. He had made a square issue with the President and been defeated, notwithstanding the fact that he was in the right. Upon an indication from him I withdrew and did not witness his surrender. A few minutes after I reached my office I received instructions from the Secretary to carry out the President's order."

In a letter to Grant, however, Lincoln admitted that Stanton had been right. "I send this as an explanation to you, and to do justice to the Secretary of War," he wrote. "I was induced, upon pressing applications, to authorize agents . . . of Pennsylvania to recruit in one of the prison depots . . . ; and the thing went so far before it came to the knowledge of the Secretary that, in my judgment, it could not be abandoned without greater evil than that which would follow its going through. I did not know, at the time, that you had protested against that class of thing being done; and I now say that while this particular job must be completed, no other of the sort will be authorized, without an understanding from you, if at all. The Secretary of War is wholly free of any part in this blunder." [6]

But it was only rarely that Lincoln had to say "I am the President" in order to get something done. He usually found a way toward solutions with which Stanton might disagree but against which the blunt War Secretary would not take an adamant stand. This subtle relationship between the two men deceived many persons. Insensitive, credulous Donn Piatt, for example, asserted after observing Lincoln and Stanton for three years that the President "is weak and timid and the indomitable will, intellect, and energy of Mr. Stanton controls him."

Stanton never controlled Lincoln, but the President's customary method of dealing with his cantankerous War Secretary—through tact, calm but firm explanations, and frank statements of his own embarrassments in a particular situation—was rarely visible on the surface of affairs. This is well illustrated by Lincoln's advice to Stanton concerning the complex question of captured rebel soldiers who did not wish to be exchanged.

Adverting first to the matter of Confederate prisoners of war whose homes had been brought within the Union lines and who wished to take the oath of allegiance and be discharged, he wrote that "none of them will again go to the rebellion, but the rebellion again coming to them," some of them might rejoin it, though not enough to do much mischief, and to release them would not only assuage distress in a number of deserving cases but also "give me relief from an intolerable pressure. I shall be glad therefore to have your cheerful assent to the discharge of those whose names I may send, which I will only do with circumspection."

Lincoln went on to state: "In using the strong hand, as now compelled to do, the government has a difficult duty to perform. . . . While we must, by all available means, prevent the overthrow of the government, we should avoid planting and cultivating too many thorns in the bosom of society. These general remarks apply to several classes of cases, on each of which I wish to say a word."

Two surgeons had been dismissed from the service. One, needing some lumber in the performance of his duties and unable to get it in any other way, had made out a false certificate. Another surgeon had

[6] Nicolay and Hay, *Lincoln*, V, 146–7; Lincoln, *Works*, VII, 530; VIII, 17; Lincoln to Stanton, July 12, 1862, Lincoln Papers, NYPL; memo, July 14, 1864, W. H. Smith Papers, OHS; Fry in New York *Tribune*, June 28, 1885.

employed two of his sons as servants. Lincoln observed that dismissal was too harsh a penalty in cases involving neither incompetency, intentional wrong, nor real injury to the service, and offered the opinion: "In such cases it is both cruel and impolitic, to crush the man, and make him and his friends permanent enemies to the administration if not to the government itself."

Lincoln next directed Stanton's attention to the fate of the family of a civilian who had killed a recruiting officer in Maryland; they had been driven from their home "without a shelter or crumb." Of course, there had been no justification for killing the officer, wrote Lincoln. But this is past. What is to be done with the family? Why could they not occupy their old home, unless it was needed for the public service, and excite much less opposition to the government than the manifestation of their distress was now doing?

Having made these objections and suggestions to Stanton, Lincoln brought up another specific case in which the two of them had sharply disagreed. A civilian government employee in charge of refugee Negroes at Cairo, Illinois, found guilty of turning over one of his charges to his loyal master in Kentucky, had been sentenced to five years at hard labor by a military court. Lincoln had drawn up a pardon for the offender on the solicitation of his neighbors, but had delayed issuing it until he could learn Stanton's views; and Stanton had offered the opinion that Lincoln could make no greater error and do no greater injustice to the colored race, to whom he had promised protection, than by releasing the man. "His crime in my judgment is greater than that of the African Slave Trader," protested the angry Secretary, "and his pardon will in my opinion injure the government in the eyes of all civilized nations and destroy the faith of the colored race in the government."

Owing to Stanton's opposition, the pardon had been withheld, and now Lincoln, in a letter setting forth his objections to some of the Secretary's procedures, presented his view of the case. The offender was an old man of unquestioned patriotism, he said, and though undoubtedly guilty, had fallen afoul of a new law. His action would have been "perfectly lawful only a short time before, and the change making it unlawful had not, even then been fully accepted in the public mind." The conclusive point with Lincoln, however, was that the severe punishment of five years at hard labor in the penitentiary was not necessary to prevent the repetition of the crime by the offender or by others. "If the offense was one of frequent recurrence the case would be different," he admitted, "but this case . . . is the single instance which has come to my knowledge. I think that for all public purposes, and for all proper purposes, he has suffered enough." And in each matter Stanton came to obedience.[7]

Lincoln's sense of humor and his utter lack of toploftiness facilitated his relations with the plain-spoken Secretary. Once when Lincoln sent a petitioner to Stanton with a written order complying with his request, the man came back to report that Stanton had not only refused to execute the order but had called Lincoln a damn fool. Lincoln, in mock astonishment, asked: "Did Stanton call me a damn fool?" Being reassured on that point, the President remarked drolly: "Well, I guess I had better step over and see Stanton about this. Stanton is usually right."

He and Stanton each realized that what one said of the other would be rapidly circulated. The President knew that Stanton was "terribly in earnest," and Stanton knew that until Lincoln decided on a matter, he could protest as outspokenly as he wished. Lincoln was willing to circumvent the stubborn Stanton in matters which he felt were important enough, knowing that the War Secretary would finally accept the decision. Robert Lincoln and Ward Hill Lamon, Lincoln's old friend, remembered the unwritten understanding between the two men—each could veto the other's acts, but Lincoln was to rule when he felt it necessary. Important and importunate demands that Lincoln could not refuse, he turned over to Stanton, who accepted the onus of saying no.

On the other hand, when Stanton received meritorious requests that he ached to grant, but feared that an unbearable precedent might thus be set, he referred them to the White House. A Baltimore delegation asked him for the release of a clergyman imprisoned for disloyalty, on the grounds that the man's pregnant wife would die unless her husband was released. Stanton sent the Marylanders to see Lincoln, knowing that the President would be touched, as he had been, and order the release. In such instances Stanton deliberately kept his harsh reputation, but pointed the way to mercy.

Informed Washingtonians knew how to bypass Stanton. When Savannah was taken and starvation faced the inhabitants, New Yorkers assembled relief supplies and Treasury officer Chittenden approached Stanton for a pass to forward the materials to Georgia. No, the Sec-

[7] Piatt to Rosecrans, Feb. 25, 1865, UCLA; Lincoln, *Works*, VII, 255–7; Eugena Jones Hunt, "My Personal Recollections of Abraham and Mary Todd Lincoln," *ALQ*, III, 250–1.

retary replied; the war was not yet won: "To exhaust the supplies of the enemy is one of the objects we are trying to accomplish; it is one of the most effectual means of making war. . . . Why do you ask me to do what you would not do yourself in my place? I will not do it. If the people of New York want to feed anybody, let them send their gifts to the starving prisoners from the Andersonville stockade."

Chittenden "could not answer the Secretary," but previous encounters had taught him what to do. He went to Lincoln.

"Stanton is right," the President decided, "but the Georgians must not be left to starve, if some of them do starve our prisoners." And so the supplies went off; although, in order not to "offend Stanton unless I can make something by the transaction," Lincoln had Chittenden accompany them to report on the attitudes of the newly conquered Southerners toward the victorious North.

The President's sensitivity to subtle stimuli that the War Department ignored seemed to drive Stanton to distraction. Lincoln's propensity to delay important decisions as long as possible rubbed harshly against Stanton's taut impatience. Lincoln often clothed in seeming ambivalence his hopes that grave public matters might, by the passage of time, resolve themselves without official interference. He "talks as many ways as he has fears, impulses, & fancies," newsman Barnett reported. These habits of the President sent Stanton into pungent rages. But the important element for their relationship, and for the nation, was that Stanton cooled as quickly as he had ignited. Lincoln had his way, and Stanton adapted his own desires to the wishes of the great man he served.[8]

Now Stanton felt his task was largely done. But still he could not relax. Perhaps he had forgotten how. Unlike Lincoln, he could never immerse himself in outside affairs and so briefly forget official matters. Stanton pursued Lincoln to the theater to "buttonhole" him on pressing business. Even at his home, Stanton could rarely find peace.

During the early years of the war, Ellen had pretensions to social leadership. The Stantons lived in splendid style, and under her urging, entertained frequently and lavishly. She impressed visitors, and Lincoln came to like her. Ellen is one of three persons who are

---

[8] Lamon, *Recollections*, 234; on Robert Lincoln, ms recollection of Lewis Hutchison Stanton, owned by Gideon Townsend Stanton; D. R. Barbee, "President Lincoln and Dr. Gurley," *ALQ*, V, 11–12; Chittenden, *Personal Reminiscences, 1840–1890* (New York, 1893), 246–9; T. J. Barnett to Barlow, Oct. 27, 1862, Barlow Papers, HL.

known to have received a copy in his hand of William Knox's "Mortality," the favorite poem of the President. Noah Brooks remarked that Stanton "has a little, aristocratic wife, lives in handsome style, consuming much of his large fortune, probably, in his ample and somewhat gorgeous way of living."

Brooks was right. The fortune that Stanton's law practice had brought him by 1862 was gone by 1865 and he was perilously close to personal bankruptcy. But always feeling that the war could not last for any great length of time, and anticipating the rich private practice he would resume with enhanced reputation as soon as he could leave the government's service, Stanton had denied nothing to his beloved Ellen, though he worried over the unceasing outflow of their capital, which she replaced with impressive furnishings, delicate linens, and spectacular table services. The costs of the older children's education mounted, and, as always, he saw to the support of his mother and Pamphila and helped more than a dozen nieces and nephews. Ellen never begrudged them these contributions, though she preferred that her in-laws live at some distance.[9]

Stanton would have preferred simpler living. His major contribution to their ornate home was a set of high bookcases which he had ordered built in 1864, in preparation for retirement from the war office. He designed these cabinets to come apart with the removal of a few pins, thus providing ease of transport. They now sheltered more than 2,500 volumes; lawbooks in the main, but supplemented since 1862 with works on military strategy and the laws of war. In the secluded study where these texts offered him some isolation from the grinding pressures that awaited him each day, Stanton sought brief comfort.

But Ellen drew him forth to dinners, theatricals, card parties, and dances, and once to a White House reception for "General" and Mrs. Tom Thumb. His heart was never in it. One night at the home of Attorney General Bates he remembered some unfinished matter, rose abruptly from his seat, and said to Ellen: "Come . . . let's go home." Fellow guests thought that his behavior was more that of a rural boor than an eminent statesman.

It was Ellen, however, who finally reduced their social standing. Her personality created enmities. Hay thought her a pretty woman, "white and cold as marble, whose rare smiles seemed to pain her," and a

[9] Leonard Grover, "Lincoln's Interest in the Theater," *Century Illustrated Monthly Magazine*, LXXVII, 945–6; Brooks in Sacramento *Union*, May 27, 1863; Ellen's copy of the poem is owned by Mrs. Van Swearingen; property list and financial details owned by Craig Wylie.

visiting Iowa lady wrote that "she is very handsome, but much complaint is made of her freezing manner and repellent address."

Most persons assumed that Ellen's unpleasantness was due to Stanton's tyranny over her. The fact was, however, that she was not well. Stanton was worried that she might succumb to consumption. Since the birth of their last child, Bessie, in 1863, Ellen's thinning hair embarrassed her. Her temper grew waspish and uncertain, and by early 1865 she had cut their entertaining to a minimum and taken to collecting autographs.

Their troublesome wives were another bond between Lincoln and Stanton. Like the President with his Mary, Stanton remained deeply in love with Ellen. When she and the children were away he was intensely aware of her absence. "All is silent and lonely," he wrote her on one such occasion, "but there is consolation in knowing that you and the children are free from the oppressive heat and discomfort in Washington." [1]

For Stanton, his patriotism and his feeling for Lincoln made all the sacrifices worth while, and sustained him as he bore the burden of his position. He was happy in the prospect of final victory. Busy as always with the multitude of demanding matters that came to his attention each day, Stanton felt that all the dangers to the nation's survival, and to Lincoln's personal safety, were ending.

Ever since his young manhood Stanton had had a morbid fear of death in any form. All during the war, he had been conscious of the possibility of assassination, and had received several threats that attempts would be made against his person. But his greater fear now was that die-hard Confederates or their Northern sympathizers might seek to avenge Southern defeats or halt ratification and execution of the Thirteenth Amendment by an attack on Lincoln.

The President long before had determined that "he would not be dying all the while," as he had remarked to Senator Cornelius Cole, of California, when Early's raid posed an assassination possibility. He shrugged off Stanton's pleas that he take care of himself, and only grudgingly accepted the cavalry escorts and sentries which Stanton assigned for his protection.

---

[1] To Ellen, Aug. 25, 1863, owned by Gideon Townsend Stanton; Oella Stanton Wright to Ellen, June 24, 1864, on health; and Stanton's bookcases are now owned by Mrs. Van Swearingen; Hay, *Diaries and Letters*, 45; "An Iowa Woman in Washington, D.C., 1861-1865," *Iowa Journal of History*, LII, 85-6; Jasper A. Conant, "A Visit to Washington in 1861-1862," *Metropolitan Magazine*, XXXIII, 315.

Shortly before the second inauguration day, word reached Stanton of a plot to kidnap Lincoln. The tip, one of many of that kind which Stanton received, came indirectly from a War Department clerk, Louis J. Weichmann, who lived at a boardinghouse kept by Mrs. Mary A. Surratt on H Street. Weichmann told Captain D. H. L. Gleason of furtive conversations he had overheard at the Surratt place. Gleason hurried to Stanton's office, for although he felt that the Secretary "was no favorite with the soldiers, who considered him overbearing and cold-blooded," he also knew "that all felt that he was a man of judgment as well as iron will . . . who could be depended on in a pinch."

Gleason found Stanton "rather explosive in his language, a trifle imperious, and overbearing in his temper, and not a lovable man to meet socially." But this was no social call. After hearing Gleason, Stanton increased the guards protecting Lincoln, over the President's protests. With the war coming to a victorious end, there was no reason to do more.

Precautions for Lincoln's safety had been taken early in the war, when mounted guards were posted at the carriage entrances of the White House and sentries at the foot gates. Lincoln protested that the presence of armed guards smacked too much of imperialism, and the arrangement had been discontinued. Later, however, against Lincoln's wishes, Stanton had detailed a cavalry detachment to accompany him on his trips between the White House and the Soldiers' Home and on his rides around Washington. An infantry company encamped on the grounds of the Executive Mansion guarded the building. A special officer of the Metropolitan Police Force was to accompany Lincoln when he attended the theater.

But the President disliked these arrangements too, and sometimes evaded the guards. Stanton cautioned him to beware. When Lincoln ignored the warning and continued to walk alone from the White House to the War Department in the dead of night, as he had done since the beginning of the war, the Secretary gave orders that he must never be allowed to return alone. A sergeant recalled that one dismal, rainy night Lincoln, emerging from the side door of the War Department, remarked to his escort: "Don't come out in this storm with me, boys. I have an umbrella, and can get home safely without you."

"But, Mr. President," a soldier objected, "we have positive orders from Mr. Stanton not to allow you to return alone. You know we dare not disobey his orders."

"No, I suppose not," agreed Lincoln. "If Stanton should learn that

394

you had let me return alone, he would have you court-martialed and shot inside of twenty-four hours."

Ward Lamon was another who pressed Lincoln to take better care of himself. He later told Stanton that Lincoln "thought me insane upon the subject of his safety." In December 1864, Lamon threatened to resign his position as Marshal of the District of Columbia when Lincoln, as he had done on several previous occasions, dismissed his escort and went unattended to the theater. Lamon wrote Lincoln that "you know or ought to know that your life is sought after and will be taken, unless you and your friends are cautious."

Lincoln's theatergoing had become more rather than less frequent during the latter days of the war. Worn by his labors, he welcomed escape from reality. And he thought it important, as he told Cole, "that the people know I come among them without fear." [2]

At the close of the excited, joyous meeting with Grant and Stanton on April 13, Lincoln invited them and their wives to accompany him and Mrs. Lincoln to Ford's Theater the following night to witness a play. Grant accepted, but his wife later told Mrs. McCulloch that she had said to him: "You know that Mrs. Lincoln was not very agreeable at City Point; she was very much excited because the wife of one of the Generals rode on horseback by her husband's side, while she was escorted in a carriage with us." In reply, Grant said they need not go to the theater; "we will go visit our children . . . and this will be a good excuse." At the reception the Stantons gave for the Grants that night, Ellen and Mrs. Grant decided that neither would go unless the other did.

Midway through the next afternoon Ellen went to the War Department to consult her husband about the invitation. He told her to decline if she wished; he had frequently rejected similar invitations from Lincoln in order to discourage his theatergoing. That afternoon the Grants went off to visit their son in New Jersey. Shortly before Stanton left the Department for the day, Lincoln came in and asked Stanton whether Eckert, whom Lincoln liked, could accompany him to Ford's that night. Again wishing to discountenance the President's going at all, Stanton asserted that Eckert had work to do. Lincoln said

[2] Cole, *Memoirs* (New York, 1908), 214; Gleason, "Conspiracy Against Lincoln," *MH*, XIII, 59–65; Lamon to Lincoln, Dec. 10, 1864, and to Stanton, April 27, 1865, Lamon Collection, HL; George S. Bryan, *The Great American Myth* (New York, 1940), 60–6, 68–73; Eisenschiml, *Why Was Lincoln Murdered?*, 46; reminiscence of Louis Koerth in New York *Commercial Advertiser*, March 24, 1903.

he would ask the colonel himself, but Eckert supported Stanton, and Lincoln decided to ask Major Henry R. Rathbone and his fiancée to join him. The President left, and shortly afterward Stanton went home to a late dinner.[3]

After the meal, Stanton called on bedridden Secretary Seward, who lived near by on another side of Franklin Square. The air had turned cold and raw; fog blurred the gas lamps along the street. Stanton found that Seward had guests, and chatted with them until he heard music and remembered that War Department clerks were to serenade him that night. Hurrying home, he met a group of army officers and invited them to join him. He then made a short speech to the serenaders; a little after nine o'clock the torchlit crowd moved off to quench their thirst at the Falstaff House and to await Lincoln's exit from Ford's Theater in order to cheer him.

As the celebrants disappeared, Stanton invited the officers to join him in the house. The servants had gone out, and the officers soon left.

About ten o'clock he locked up the house and went upstairs with Ellen. She entered the nursery to look after the children and he went into the bedroom.

He had almost finished undressing when he heard Ellen cry from downstairs: "Mr. Seward is murdered!" "Humbug," answered Stanton, "I left him only an hour ago." But he pulled on his clothes, hurried downstairs, and questioned the man who had brought the message. The room filled with people, some of them saying that Lincoln, too, had been assassinated. Hearing this, Stanton, in sudden high excitement, started out the door, but a man threw his arms around him and shouted: "You mustn't go out. . . . As I came up to the house I saw a man behind the tree-box, but he ran away, and I did not follow him." Stanton refused to stay and went out into the misty night. A hack stood at the door. He leaped in and told the driver to go to Seward's.[4]

Just as Stanton drove up, he met Sergeant Koerth, who had been at Ford's that night, and from him learned the first confused details of

[3] Reminiscence of Susan Man McCulloch, owned by Hugh McCulloch; Fry, *op. cit.*, 291; Badeau, *Grant*, 362; Bryan, *op. cit.*, 160–1; Bates, *op. cit.*, 366–8. Eisenschiml's account, in *Why Was Lincoln Murdered?*, 38, 61–3, and Roscoe's, *op. cit.*, 145–6, 189–95, *passim*, offer conclusions from these facts which seem unsupportable.

[4] Ms diary of an anonymous War Department clerk, Lincoln Photostat Coll., LC; Browning, *Diary*, II, 20; Flower, *Stanton*, 279; M. A. De Wolfe Howe (ed.), "Dickens, Stanton, Sumner, and Storey," *AM*, CXLV, 463–5, has Stanton's account. Edwin L. Stanton thought that there never was a man outside the Stanton home; Wolcott MS, 200.

the attack on Lincoln. Welles arrived; Stanton ordered Koerth to find some soldiers and to set guards around the homes of all the cabinet officers and the Vice-President. The two Secretaries pushed through the crowd of people in the lower hallway of the Seward home and went up to the blood-spattered third-floor room, where a doctor was examining the stricken Secretary of State. Stanton and Welles moved into an adjoining room, where young Frederick Seward, like his father suffering from stab wounds, lay paralyzed.

Stanton decided to go to Ford's, and Welles agreed to accompany him. At the doorway they met Meigs, who urged them not to attempt it. Welles thought Stanton hesitated. But he stuck to his decision. They found another carriage, and with Meigs and Judge David K. Cartter, of the District Supreme Court, were under way toward the theater when Eckert rode up. He, too, tried to persuade them to stay away from the neighborhood of Ford's Theater. Thousands of frenzied people were milling through the streets, he said. But they agreed that they must go, and Meigs shouted to some passing soldiers to accompany them.

Tenth Street, in the vicinity of the theater, was jammed with wild-eyed people. The officials left their carriage and pushed through the crowd with difficulty. They learned that Lincoln had been carried from the theater to a house across the street. There they found him, stretched diagonally across a bed because of his great length. He was unconscious and breathing heavily. This labored respiration was the sudden, bitter, shocking proof to Stanton that death must come; his infant son had sounded that way when he died in his arms.

While the guards outside struggled to keep back the surging crowd, the room where Lincoln lay became more and more crowded. A number of physicians were attending him, and several congressmen and other cabinet officers arrived. Overcoming his mounting grief, Stanton sent an armed guard for Vice-President Johnson, who arrived soon afterward. But when Mary Lincoln, who had been sobbing in a nearby room, asked to see her husband, Senator Sumner, knowing how she detested Johnson, suggested that he should not remain, and at Stanton's request he left. Though Stanton disliked Mrs. Lincoln, he now treated her tenderly.[5]

While Lincoln's life ebbed away, Stanton set about avenging the deed. Moving into the parlor, he ordered Corporal James Tanner, a

[5] Koerth in New York *Commercial Advertiser*, March 24, 1903; Morse, *Welles Diary*, II, 284–7; Howe, "Dickens, Stanton, Sumner, and Storey," *loc. cit.*, 463–5; "Mrs. Lincoln and Mr. Stanton," in Boston *Transcript*, Jan. 7, 1870.

shorthand clerk in the Ordnance Bureau, to take testimony from witnesses of the terrible moments in Ford's Theater. They soon identified the assassin as the actor John Wilkes Booth.

At midnight, Stanton alerted all military forces in the Washington military district; the long roll of alarm drums snapped thousands of troops into formation; railroad passenger travel to points south was stopped, and fishing vessels on the Potomac were forbidden to touch shore south of Alexandria. Dana wired Grant to return to Washington, and to see to his safety.

Soon after midnight, a bay horse, saddled, bridled, and sweating and quivering after a hard ride, was found standing on a byroad less than a mile from the city. A liveryman named John Fletcher identified the saddle and bridle as belonging to one George A. Atzerodt, and testified that he had rented a horse that night to a certain David E. Herold, who had ridden into Maryland preceded by another horseman.

Fletcher may have revealed that Atzerodt had stayed at the Surratt boardinghouse. Or John Mathews, a friend of Booth's, may have told the police that the actor often visited that place to talk with John Surratt, the landlady's son. It is unlikely that the police knew about the boarder Weichmann, through whom the War Department had learned indirectly of the earlier plot to kidnap Lincoln. But in any event, at about 2 a.m. on the fifteenth, a police squad entered the Surratt house and searched it for Booth and John Surratt. Finding nothing suspicious and eliciting little information, they went away.[6]

While all this was going on, Stanton, realizing that the nation had to know what had occurred, was dictating a description of the events of the night to Dix at New York for release to the press, which, owing to mechanical difficulties, which were of common occurrence, or to the confused rush of events, did not go out until 2:15 a.m. Stanton assembled a logical narrative of the attacks on Lincoln and Seward from the incoherent accounts he had heard. He thought both men must die from their wounds, and ended with a bitter description of Lincoln's happiness at the last cabinet meeting: "The President was very cheerful and hopeful; spoke very kindly of General Lee and other members of the Confederacy, and the establishment of government in Virginia." Now happiness had turned to horror, and Stanton never forgot the moment or forgave its perpetrators.

In the dark morning hours a War Department detective searched

---

[6] *O.R.*, XLVI, pt. 3, 756, 766; David Miller DeWitt, *The Assassination of Abraham Lincoln and Its Expiation* (New York, 1909), 59–61, 270–2 (cited hereafter as DeWitt, *Assassination*).

Booth's trunk in his room at the National Hotel and discovered a letter addressed to the actor which indicated that the murder plot had been spawned in Richmond. By 3 a.m. Stanton had become convinced that Booth was the murderer, and word went out to arrest him. The hours passed by, full of activity on Stanton's part, yet each one endless and nightmarish.

At dawn a cold rain set in, drenching the waiting, unmoving crowd outside. Tanner finished transcribing his notes and went into the room where Lincoln lay. He approached the bed, and from between Halleck and Meigs he glimpsed Stanton, visibly moved, trying to keep control of himself.

The unconscious figure breathed with shuddering gasps. At least ten doctors were attending the President now. But there was little they could do. The end was very near. At 7:22 a.m., Surgeon General Barnes folded Lincoln's arms across his chest and looked significantly at the Reverend Phineas D. Gurley, pastor of the New York Avenue Presbyterian Church, which the Lincolns had attended. The minister lowered his eyes in the heavy silence, now empty of the murdered man's heavy breathing, and uttered a short prayer. A long moment of quiet followed his "Amen." Then Stanton, openly weeping at last, murmured that Lincoln now belonged to the ages.[7]

While preparations were being made to remove the President's body to the White House, the cabinet members, with Seward and the new Treasury Secretary, Hugh McCulloch, absent, convened in the back parlor to sign a letter prepared by Attorney General Speed informing Andrew Johnson that the duties of the presidency now devolved upon him. Speed and Welles were delegated to take the letter to Johnson. Stanton, Welles thought, showed chagrin at being passed over. It seems doubtful, however, whether any of these exhausted men were perceptive enough at this moment to measure subtle reactions with any accuracy. Stanton may merely have wanted to see how well his orders of the night before, setting up a guard around Johnson and all the cabinet officers, were being carried out.

By this time, Stanton and most of the other men in the sad room

---

[7] The evidence on what Stanton said is surveyed in Eisenschiml, *Why Was Lincoln Murdered?*, 482–5, and Bryan, *op. cit.*, 186–90. There seems little doubt that Stanton made some such statement; this is one of the few times on record that his prose style transcended the pedestrian. Other data are in *O.R.*, XLVI, 775, 780–1; Pitman, *op. cit.*, 236; and see Robert T. Lincoln to Edwin L. Stanton, Dec. 24, 1869, owned by Gideon Townsend Stanton, on the Secretary's emotion and kindness to the President's family.

were convinced that Lincoln's murder was the result of a vast con-spiracy "planned and set on foot by rebels under pretense of avenging the rebel cause"; and this is what Stanton released to the press. Police, military detectives, and whole regiments of troops were scouring southern Maryland trying to pick up the trail of the accomplices. Stan-ton called in Colonel H. S. Olcott, of the Secret Service, the chief of the New York Police Department, and Colonel Lafayette C. Baker, top War Department sleuth, to aid in the search. Journalist George A. Townsend noted how Washington was "full of Detective Police" when he arrived there the next day to cover events.

At Stanton's order, Fry ordered all provost marshals in the North to scrutinize persons trying to leave the country for Canada or Europe. Later all this was to seem like panic on Stanton's part. But on the grim morning that Lincoln died, no one thought that these were exces-sive precautions.[8]

For the moment, everything that could be done was taken care of. In the bright morning hours of Saturday, April 15, the weary men who had waited for Lincoln to die went to their homes for what rest they could get. But the church bells of the capital, tolling the Presi-dent's death, prevented even an hour's sleep. At 11 a.m., when the cabinet assembled to witness Johnson take the oath of office as Presi-dent of the United States, everyone sagged with physical and mental exhaustion.

Still, a sense of urgency pervaded them, Stanton above all, for he had the immediate responsibility for the security of the country, and the war was still not ended. As the cabinet members assembled to hear Johnson, they may have seen copies of a throwaway broadside which was widely scattered in Washington that day. Entitled *Epilogue*, its anonymous author, after vividly describing the wild night of the as-sassination, concluded that there was no need for panic. "Today Stanton's powerful hands seize the direction and transmit it to the hands of the new President," the writer continued; "Stanton is up to every emergency."

And Stanton's behavior was proving the assertion correct. Always before, death close at hand had unsettled him close to the point of im-balance. Now he seemed calm, grim, decisive, in complete outward

[8] Townsend, "The Crime of Lincoln's Murder," ms owned by George A. Bonaven-ture; Eisenschiml, *Why Was Lincoln Murdered?*, 194; DeWitt, *Assassination*, 57–8; Morse, *Welles Diary*, II, 288–9; *O.R.*, XLVI, pt. 3, 783–5; XLVII, pt. 3, 221.

control of himself, and intensely curious about the man who was taking the oath as the new President.

Johnson was relatively unknown. Not for weeks to come was Stanton or most others to know much about him as a person or about his opinions on public matters. Even as he raised his hand to swear the oath, some Washingtonians speculated on how Stanton and Johnson would get along. One government official, George W. Payne, mused that "it remains to be seen whether Andrew the 2d will be Commander in Chief or a Subordinate. Time proves all things. *Nous Verrons.*" Stanton, like America, had to wait and see.

Johnson, now President, asked the cabinet to meet briefly with him at noon. He remarked that the country was in the grip of fear and panic. Stanton was later to be blamed for contributing to this unease. But much occurred for which he was not responsible. For example, one of the men who carried Lincoln's wounded body from Ford's Theater was Captain E. E. Bedee, of the 12th New Hampshire Volunteers. He gave Stanton some papers that had dropped from the President's pocket. Hay, not knowing this, concluded that Bedee had stolen them, and got General Hardie to arrest Bedee, under Stanton's name. Bedee spent five miserable days in a military prison, fuming at Stanton, who was completely ignorant of the whole affair. When the Secretary learned of Bedee's plight he released him immediately and ordered Hardie to make a public statement exonerating the captain. But it was Stanton who received the blame.[9]

Stanton, meanwhile, temporarily abandoning his plans to retire from his office, was indeed in virtual control of the government. He had charge of the Army, Johnson was barely sworn in and vastly unsure of himself, and Congress was not in session. With a civil war not yet fully won and with the excitement of assassination momentarily justifying almost any action he might want to take, Edwin M. Stanton could do much as he liked. In mid-April 1865, the American experiment in democracy, the American tradition of civilian control over the military institutions, was again on the brink of extinction.

[9] *Epilogue* (n.p., April 15, 1865) ; Payne ms biographical sketches, CHS; the Bedee affair is in the James A. Hardie Papers, LC.

CHAPTER XIX

SHERMAN'S TRUCE

"ALL WAS vague and uncertain," Welles remembered of the noon cabinet meeting on Saturday, April 15. Johnson told the tired men before him that he would announce his policies in due time, but in all essentials they would be the same as Lincoln's. He asked the cabinet members to stand by him in his difficult and responsible position, and with the others, Stanton numbly agreed. Over the weekend, Republican congressmen, drawn to the capital by news of the assassination, met with Johnson and were largely satisfied that his policies toward the South, and concerning the need for the Negro to vote there, were in substantial accord with their own.

When the new President again met with his cabinet, on Sunday morning, the sixteenth, Stanton, as was his responsibility, brought forward the plan of reconstruction he had presented at the last meeting of Lincoln's cabinet. In accordance with the dead President's request, he had now made separate provisions for North Carolina, where a new government had to be established, and for Virginia, where the loyal Pierpont government, though commanding the allegiance of only a fraction of the people, might become the basis of a restored commonwealth. He did not, however, have copies of the document ready; it was to be printed confidentially by trusted workers at the Treasury, and he wanted cabinet agreement on its contents before entrusting the plan to the typesetters. But the general tenor of the paper was clear to the assembled cabinet. There was little discussion; too much else remained to be done at that moment.

Welles thought that his earlier objection against the section of Stanton's plan which had proposed setting up a centralized provost marshal organization in the Army to stablilize conditions in the South until civil government came in, had been successful, for Stanton omit-

402

ted this clause from the current version of his plan. But Welles was merely betraying his ignorance of the realities of military occupation. Stanton knew that the army field commands with their existing provost units would be the immediate occupation force in the South regardless of whether his proposed new organization was approved, and in any case a new army bureau was something for Congress to deal with. No matter what proved to be the nature of the more permanent reconstruction that the President might wish to follow or that Congress would insist on, Yankee soldiers were going to run things in the South for a time.

Therefore, what was really important at the moment was less the civilians' plans for final reconstruction than the ability of the civilian institutions to direct the Army. Stanton's responsibility, the day after Lincoln's death, remained what it had been before that event—to bring the war to its close and to see to it that the military machine moved in obedience to its civilian superiors.

Only from the vantage point of retrospect, when the events of later years had distorted his memory of what was truly the case in April 1865, could Welles assign to Stanton a Machiavellian role in having a "tough" reconstruction plan at hand. The document that Stanton read to the cabinet on April 16 was neither a finished blueprint for reconstruction nor an essay in the radical philosophy of Southern war guilt. It was precisely what Stanton's responsibility required him to have ready—a sketch, an outline for immediate use, to guide the President, the cabinet, and the Army.

That evening Welles, at Stanton's invitation, called at the War Department, and the two men chatted until Sumner, Dawes, Colfax, Gooch, and Covode, of Congress, came in. Meigs also joined the group. Stanton took from his desk the newly printed copies of the plan he had outlined that afternoon to the cabinet, and read it to the group before him. Welles later professed to be shocked to find Stanton divulging cabinet secrets to outsiders; Stanton always insisted that as this was the plan Lincoln had already approved in substance and that Johnson had promised to follow, there was nothing amiss in this procedure. He was merely emulating Lincoln's habit of testing the reaction of congressional leaders before acting on a proposal—for their approval must ultimately be necessary, as Lincoln had acknowledged, before reconstruction could be completed.[1]

---

[1] Beale, *Welles Diary*, III, 291, needs supplementing by Welles's letters to Johnson, July 27, 1869, and to Joseph Fowler, Nov. 9, 1875, in *ibid.*, 714–21, 733, and to

Therefore, Stanton had prepared an outline to guide himself at this meeting with Sumner. He knew how respectful Lincoln had been to the powerful senator's opinions, and vividly remembered that Lincoln, only five days before, had publicly advocated Negro suffrage. No doubt Sumner would bring up the subject now.

Stanton had not finished reading his proposal when Sumner asked him what provision he had made for Negro voting. Stanton replied that he had purposely avoided raising the question for fear of causing a split in the Union-Republican party. But, Sumner insisted, freedom for the Negro would be a mockery without the right to vote. He would not support any plan of reconstruction, he declared, that failed to grant the black man his rights. Again Stanton deprecated the necessity of intruding this burning question at this moment; again Sumner insisted. Most of the others, including Welles, now left. Sumner and Colfax were then able to persuade the hesitant, exhausted War Secretary to insert a clause in his plan for North Carolina stating that all "loyal citizens" would be allowed to vote.[2]

Meanwhile, Lincoln's death still dominated Stanton's thoughts. He helped arrange the funeral details, and on April 19, during the stirring services in the Capitol Rotunda, Stanton was barely able to contain himself.

A talk with Mary Lincoln confirmed Stanton's own resolution that nothing concerning the dead President should be exploited commercially. Stanton had instructed General Townsend, who accompanied the funeral party as his representative, to allow no photographs to be taken. In New York, however, his injunction was disregarded. The Secretary sent Townsend a stiff reprimand, and ordered the plates seized and destroyed, along with all prints that had been made, warning Townsend that he would hold him personally responsible if any more pictures were taken.[3]

M. Blair, *ca.* Feb. 1877, HL. See also Frederick Seward in Washington *Chronicle*, Jan. 25, 1875; John A. Dodds, "Honest John Covode," *WPHM*, XVI, 181; Dawes, "Recollections of Stanton under Johnson," *AM*, LXXIV, 495–7; Julian, *op. cit.*, 225, 257; April 16, 1865, Meigs ms diary, LC; George Fort Milton, *Age of Hate* (New York, 1930), 169.

[2] Stanton's notes, dated April 16, midnight, describing these events, copy owned by the estate of Benjamin P. Thomas, makes it clear that there was no prearrangement between him and the legislators as Welles always insisted. See Pierce, *Sumner*, IV, 244; Beale, *Welles Diary*, III, 719–21, 733; Welles, "Lincoln and Johnson," *Galaxy*, XIII, 528–30, 666.

[3] *O.R.*, XLVI, pt. 3, 952, 965. Dix informed Stanton that his order had been carried out with respect to a large plate that had been made, but that he had

Two days later, Stanton and Welles met by prearrangement at 6 a.m. to pay their last respects to Lincoln before his remains started on the funeral journey to Illinois. Later in the day, at a cabinet meeting, mercifully brief, everyone but Welles seemed willing to let slide for the moment the question of Stanton's reconstruction order—all were drained emotionally by their reactions to two weeks which had seen Lee's surrender and Lincoln's murder.

Then, about 6:30 p.m. on the twenty-first, Grant rushed into the War Department. He brusquely asked B. M. Plumb, the clerk on duty, whether Stanton was expected back that night. Barely waiting for Plumb's reply—that he did not know—Grant hurried downstairs, where he hastily penned a note to the Secretary and sent it to his home by mounted courier.

Stanton was at dinner when the breathless messenger arrived. He opened the note and read: "Sir,—I have just received . . . dispatches . . . from General Sherman. They are of such importance that I think immediate action should be taken on them, and that it should be done by the President in council with his whole cabinet . . . and the meeting [should] take place tonight."

Within thirty minutes Stanton arrived at the War Department in a state of high excitement. Seizing pen and paper, he dashed off a note, and ordered Plumb to make copies of it and to rush one to each cabinet officer by mounted messenger. The note stated that "by direction of the President" a cabinet meeting was called for eight o'clock that night. Stanton and Grant, after conferring about Sherman's dispatches, went to Johnson's temporary residence to tell him of the meeting. Grant remained with the President while Stanton went on to pick up Welles.

They drove back to the War Department, and Welles waited downstairs while Stanton, in his office, called telegrapher Bates in and dictated a memorandum to be read to the cabinet. The Secretary was so excited that Bates, "a rapid penman," could not keep up with the "sentences that came tumbling from his lips in an impetuous torrent."

---

retained a smaller plate, thinking the Lincoln family might want it. He sent the Secretary a print made from this plate. Stanton answered that the family objected to publication and Dix should also destroy the smaller plate, as ordered. Stanton evidently kept the print, however, and a few years ago a reproduction of it turned up in the Nicolay Papers, ISHL. Other data in Lamon to Stanton, April 12, 1866, HL; Morse, *Welles Diary*, II, 292–3; Browning, *Diary*, II, 23; order, April 18, 1865, Garrett Family Papers, LC; G. M. Dodge, *Personal Recollections* (Council Bluffs, 1914), 28.

Rereading the document, Stanton corrected Bates's errors and omissions in his heavy, tight scrawl, and then at a more moderate pace dictated a new copy. He confessed to Bates that indignation at General Sherman had caused him to speak so rapidly and incoherently.

The President and the cabinet assembled promptly on the hour, along with Grant and Preston King, former New York congressman, Republican political leader, and personal adviser to Johnson. At Stanton's request, Grant proceeded to read the communications from Sherman. The first was a letter stating that Sherman had entered into an agreement with rebel general Johnston which, if approved by the President, would bring peace from the Potomac to the Rio Grande. It had already been approved by John C. Breckinridge, Secretary of War of the Confederacy, "in his capacity as major general," Sherman explained, and it provided for the surrender of the last of the rebel forces. This much had been expected. But Sherman also promised the recognition of existing Southern state governments once their personnel swore allegiance to the Union. Where conflicting state or local governments existed, the United States Supreme Court was to decide which was legitimate. The agreement further provided for the re-establishment of federal courts in the South, for franchise and property rights for peaceful Southerners, and for a general amnesty. Sherman and Johnston pledged themselves to "promptly obtain the necessary authority" from their superiors "to carry out the above programme."

Those present listened to Grant with a sense of shock and incredulity, for when Sherman had begun negotiations with Johnston a week before, he had informed Grant and Stanton: "I will accept the same terms that Grant gave General Lee, and be careful not to complicate any points of civil policy." But now Sherman had done precisely what he had promised not to do. The agreement, far from being a mere military convention terminating hostilities, was a virtual treaty of peace. It recognized the legality of the insurrectionary state governments, promised immunity to all persons who had taken part in the rebellion, and permitted the Confederate troops to deposit their arms in their respective state arsenals, thus providing Southern state governments with a supply of war material. It put in question the legitimacy of all Union state governments where rival state authorities existed, as in those areas of the South where Lincoln's reconstruction policy was in operation, and the clause specifying arbitrament by the Supreme Court betrayed Sherman's ignorance of American institutions, for the Court had no role to play in deciding such political questions. Conflicting state governments in the South would make new strife probable. It left a possibility of recognizing the rebel war debt. And it might even be construed as recognizing the right to property in slaves.

All of those present at the cabinet meeting condemned Sherman's action; the President, Stanton, and Speed were the most emphatic, though Speed expressed friendship for Sherman, and Grant, though strongly opposed to Sherman's course, refrained from censuring him. Everyone agreed that generals in the field had no authority to settle political questions. Stanton, Johnson decided, should immediately inform Sherman that his action was disapproved and that hostilities should be immediately resumed after giving the Confederates the forty-eight hours' notice required to terminate the truce.[4]

Grant quickly secured Stanton's permission to go in person to Raleigh, where Sherman had established his headquarters, and take with him Stanton's order stating that Johnson disapproved of the convention, that Sherman was to resume hostilities, that Lincoln's views to Grant of March 3, 1865, forbidding conference except on military matters, applied to Sherman, and that Grant should take charge of operations against the enemy. Johnson was later to claim that the only part of this order that he authorized was the disapprobation he felt concerning the truce; Stanton, in the name of the President, was virtually removing Sherman from command. If so, it is remarkable that Grant made no protest either to Stanton or to Johnson on this score. To be sure, everything was done in haste, and all the officials concerned had little time in which to consider the implications of their words and action. But if Grant, as his biographer suggests, went to Raleigh "to soften the blow," part of the responsibility for its harshness is his.[5]

Another factor in the situation rasped Stanton's strained nerves. After the fall of Richmond, the Confederate officials had fled to Greensboro, North Carolina. Sherman, confident that his peace terms with Johnston would be approved, had ordered General Stoneman to withdraw his troops from the railroad leading south from Greensboro and join him at Raleigh.

On April 22, Halleck, who had recently been put in charge of

[4] Memo of Plumb, NYHS; Elizabeth Blair Lee to Adm. S. P. Lee, April 17, 1865, Box XII, Blair-Lee Papers, PU; *O.R.*, XLVII, pt. 3, 221, 243–4, 263; Morse, *Welles Diary*, II, 293–5; Johnson to Speed, April 21, 1865, Johnson Papers, LC; Bates, *op. cit.*, 395–7, 424–5.

[5] Anna S. McAllister, *Ellen Ewing, Wife of General Sherman* (New York, 1936), 304; Hesseltine, *Ulysses S. Grant, Politician* (New York, 1935), 51–2 (hereafter cited as Hesseltine, *Grant*); the order is in *O.R.*, XLVII, pt. 3, 263; Johnson's claim in M. Blair to Barlow, April 26, 1865, Barlow Papers, HL.

Virginia and that part of North Carolina not occupied by Sherman's troops, wired Stanton from Richmond of rumors that Jefferson Davis had taken a large store of specie with him in his flight from the fallen rebel capital. Halleck was concerned that the Confederates might try to make terms with Sherman, or some other Union commander, by which they might be permitted to flee abroad with this plunder. Not knowing of Sherman's terms with Johnston, Halleck wondered whether Sherman had not opened an escape route for the refugee rebel officials by withdrawing Stoneman from the railroad. Stanton impulsively leaped to action.

Announcing to the press the terms that Sherman had offered Johnston and the action taken with respect to them by the President and the cabinet, Stanton stated that Sherman had deliberately disobeyed Lincoln's instructions to Grant of March 3 after those instructions had been approved and reiterated by President Johnson as a definition of the authority of military commanders in negotiating with the enemy, and asserted that the withdrawal of Stoneman's force might open Davis's path of escape with the specie. With this dispatch Stanton sent a nine-point explanation, also for publication, and solely on his own responsibility, of why Sherman's action had been repudiated. It amounted to a castigation of Sherman and virtually accused him of disloyalty.[6]

Stanton knew that he was risking his own career in releasing this statement. Next to Grant, Sherman was the most popular general with the public, and Grant had supported his favorite subordinate many times before Lincoln, the War Secretary, and Congress. The general's brother, John, the influential Ohio senator, and, through General Sherman's wife, the potent Ewing family would inevitably be involved in his criticism of their relative.

But too much was at stake now for Stanton to hesitate. He knew that Sherman had disagreed with him and the Lincoln administration concerning Negro troops, and also that the general had been contemptuous of the political implications of military actions and had simply ignored occupation responsibilities as much as he could. For example, Sherman's was the only major command which never developed a provost marshal system—which other officers used as occupation administrations—into anything more than military police units. Having helped immeasurably to win the war, Sherman was now presuming to structure

[6] Morse, *Welles Diary*, II, 309–10, III, 247; *O.R.*, XLVII, pt. 3, 277, 285–6; A. E. H. Johnson in Washington *Star*, Sept. 3, 1892.

the peace. Stanton never denied Sherman's martial achievements, but he could not feel that the general possessed equal political acumen.

Although Sherman professed contempt and resentment for politics, Stanton knew that Democratic politicians had great interest in the general. He knew, too, that Sherman had little understanding of or even sympathy for political democracy, and had recently admitted that he preferred monarchy as a ruling system. It seemed to Stanton that if he hesitated at rebuking Sherman, there might develop a popular movement to support the convention terms with Johnston, along with a copperhead drive to elevate Sherman into the White House. "I think father never managed anything so well," Stanton's son wrote at this time to Pamphila. "Had there been any delay a powerful opposition might have been organized, and all might have been lost."

Two months earlier when defeatist peace rumors were abroad in the North, Lieber had pleaded in a letter to Halleck that Stanton and Lincoln avoid any movements toward an armistice. "The very word makes me grave," Lieber asserted. "An armistice would be the death to our cause. . . . We want the peace of the lands, but this implies the submission of the revolted states. An Armistice was one of the very points of the detestable [Democratic] Chicago Platform, & *no armistice*, one of the distinct points on which Mr. Lincoln was re-elected."

From Stanton's reaction to the news of Sherman's truce, as he advised Dana, it is obvious that he saw it as an armistice involving all the implications Lieber stated. Secretly, President Johnson agreed with Stanton, although he never admitted his distrust of Sherman, which dated back to his Tennessee military-governorship, to anyone but his intimate friend and adviser Sam Milligan. Johnson preferred to let Stanton chastise the popular general.[7]

As reports of the nature of Stanton's dispatch spread over Washington and the country, alert politicians hurried to learn what it was really all about. Montgomery Blair, characteristically, was the first to see Johnson, who quickly convinced him that Stanton was solely responsible for everything the wire contained, that all Johnson had wanted transmitted was a disapproval of the truce terms. While the two men were talking, Senator Chandler came in. He intruded the blunt comment that Sherman "was the coming man of the Copperheads & this blunder had come just at the right time to destroy him." Blair claimed

[7] Thorndike, *Sherman Letters*, 241; Russ, "Administrative Activities of the Union Army," *loc. cit.*, 84–5; Lewis, *Sherman*, 553; Wolcott MS, 200–1; Ida Tarbell's memo of conversation with Dana, Allegheny College; Lieber to Halleck, Feb. 4, 1865, Lieber Papers, HL; Milligan to Johnson, April 29, 1865, Johnson Papers, LC.

to be insulted and left. The President then proceeded to condemn the Sherman-Johnston convention in more violent terms than even Chandler felt free to use.

Stanton meanwhile confided to Browning that in his opinion Sherman had "given up all for which we had been fighting, and threw away all the advantages we had gained from the war." Even now, Jefferson Davis might be escaping with the Confederate treasure because of the Sherman truce, Stanton asserted.[8]

The Sunday-morning headlines blazoned the startling story for the country at large to ponder over. Stanton worried most about how the Army would take all this. That Sherman's own men, who had followed him through victory across half the country, would support their leader, was inevitable. But Sherman's was not the only army of the Union. Grant and Halleck agreed with Stanton, and General Patrick, who had been critical of Stanton for three years, was now unreserved in his support of the Secretary's stand. Sherman had been "playing the fool," Patrick felt on reading the Sunday newspapers; his acts were "astounding and humiliating. Sherman must be crazy." No one seemed able to account for Sherman's behavior, and in the eastern commands there was "universal surprise" at it, Patrick wrote.

Hitchcock, too, thought Sherman insane for agreeing to the truce, and even some of the western troopers accorded a grudging assent to Stanton's policy. The weight of informed opinion was heavily with Stanton. So the President remained quiet and let events develop.[9]

On April 24, Grant informed Stanton that Sherman had obeyed instructions and had given Johnston notice of the termination of the truce, and that Sherman was not really surprised at the order. Since signing the truce with Johnston, he had heard that Grant had withdrawn permission for the Virginia legislature to meet. But Sherman believed that he had followed Lincoln's program as prescribed in the past and the one that the dead President would have wanted in force at the present. Writing to Stanton directly the next day, Sherman admitted his "folly" in mixing civil and military matters, but he felt that they were "inextricably united." Sherman had thought that Stanton at Savannah had implied that the financial difficulties of the North "demanded

[8] Smith, *Blair Family*, II, 183–4; E. B. Lee to Adm. S. P. Lee, May 18, 1865, Blair-Lee Papers, PU; Morse, *Welles Diary*, III, 247; Chandler to wife, April 23, 25, 1865, Chandler Papers, LC; Browning, *Diary*, II, 24; M. Blair to Barlow, April 28, 1865, Barlow Papers, HL.

[9] April 24, 1865, Patrick ms diary, LC; same date, Hitchcock ms diary, GI, which differs significantly from the account in Croffut, *op. cit.*, 476–7; Milligan to Johnson, April 29, 1865, Johnson Papers, LC.

military success, and would warrant a little bending to policy," and insisted that he had emulated Grant's terms to Lee, and Weitzel's invitation to the Virginia legislators to assemble. He still felt that the rejection of his terms to Johnston was an error, "but that is none of my business," he wrote, and concluded by saying that he would obey orders.

Sherman's tone infuriated Stanton. In informing the press that the truce with Johnston had been terminated, Stanton supplied only the first part of Grant's dispatch, omitting his explanation of why Sherman had granted the Confederates such liberal terms and completely ignoring Sherman's own explanation. In fact, he did not even acknowledge it. On the same day Stanton received it, April 25, he wired Grant: "The arrangement between Sherman and Johnston meets with universal disapprobation. No one class or shade of opinion approves it. I have not known as much surprise and discontent at anything that has happened during the war. . . . The hope of the country is that you may repair the misfortune occasioned by Sherman's negotiations."

So far Sherman had not learned of Stanton's "nine reasons" for repudiating his actions. When he read them in the newspapers without having been officially informed of them, he in turn felt outraged, particularly because he thought that Stanton had given the public the impression that he had previously been furnished with a copy of Lincoln's March 3 instructions to Grant, and that Stanton "gave warrant" to the impression that he had been bribed from the rebel treasure hoard to let Jeff Davis escape.[1]

Sherman's rage reached a new pitch, however, when Halleck, on Grant's secret instructions, interjected himself into the situation. Halleck ordered Meade, Sheridan, and Wright, of Sherman's command, to send troops into North Carolina irrespective of any "truce or orders" of Sherman's, and to "push forward, regardless of any orders save those of Lieutenant-General Grant, and cut off Johnston's retreat." A second dispatch of Halleck's ordered Thomas, Stoneman, and Wilson, also of Sherman's command, to disregard their chieftain's orders. To Sherman, Halleck's orders were gratuitous insults which Stanton further aggravated by releasing all the details to the press; the peppery warrior "exploded *instanter*" at their mention, Dahlgren recorded.[2]

---

[1] April 25, 1865, Comstock ms diary, LC; *O.R.*, XLVII, pt. 1, 34–6; pt. 3, 296, 301–2, 345–6; Sherman, *Memoirs*, II, 349–73.

[2] Wilson to Badeau, May 13, 1865, Wilson Papers, LC; Halleck-Lieber exchange, June 3, 4, 16, 1865, HL; *O.R.*, XLVII, pt. 1, 29–48; pt. 3, 334–5, 345–6, 410, 435, 634–7; Dahlgren, *op. cit.*, 510–11.

If Grant could have had his way, the troublesome affair would have stopped at this point. He had achieved what he had set out to do in his hurried trip to Raleigh. His mere presence there had quieted the western troops, one of them, General Manning Force, noting that "Grant is here, and it is his judgment, and who would question that?" The truce was disavowed and Grant's reputation was secure. But Sherman, now angered beyond control, feeling that he could never forgive Stanton's publication of selected portions of the pertinent correspondence and Halleck's vexatious order, refused to remain quiet. He never learned of Grant's role.

"I am not a politician," he wrote Grant, "never voted but once in my life, & never read a political platform." He was "hurt, outraged, & insulted by Mr. Stanton's public arraignment of my motives and actions. . . . I respect his office but I cannot him personally, till he undoes the injustice of the past." Sherman also wanted Grant to tell the President that the rumors of his own political ambitions were groundless.

Along with Grant, Senator Sherman wanted Tecumseh to accept the censure as a due penalty for overstepping the limits of military functions. The senator wrote to Stanton that he felt "distressed beyond measure" by the terms his brother had offered Johnston, but he also felt that grave injustice had been done. The worst that could be said against General Sherman was that, like Lincoln, he had been too lenient toward the rebels, and had trusted them too far, "while we know that to arm them with the electoral franchise . . . is to renew the war." He did not want his brother to be unjustly treated, however, if only because to do so might drive the general into an alliance with the copperheads.[3]

But the Sherman-Ewing clan soon took a different tone, and commenced to pressure Stanton to retract his criticisms, which he refused to do. Then, on April 28, word came that Johnston had surrendered on the same terms Lee had accepted. Immediately, the tide of opinion that had set so strongly against Sherman began to turn in his favor as his great war services were remembered. Meanwhile, Stanton's enemies hurried to feast on his latest difficulty.[4]

[3] W. T. Sherman to Grant, May 28, 1865, HL; John Sherman to Stanton, April 27, 1865, Stanton MSS; Young, *Men and Memories*, I, 436; Force ms Personal Record, II, 181, UW.

[4] Grant to Sherman, May 6, 1865, W. T. Sherman Papers, LC; Thorndike, *Sherman Letters*, 249, 365; McAllister, *op. cit.*, 304; William Stanton to H. H. Marlcham, June 1, 1904, Willis Weaver Papers, LC; A. E. H. Johnson in Washington *Star*, Sept. 3, 1892; *O.R.*, XLVII, pt. 3, 311.

A scheme to oust Stanton from the cabinet had already been initiated behind the scenes, and now the plotters came cautiously into the light, drawn by the opportunity which the Stanton-Sherman rift offered. It was fomented by friends of Ben Butler, with allies among other radical Republicans who felt that Johnson needed men in the cabinet who fully agreed with them, and Stanton was not accounted a radical. The intrigue involved Chase, who expressed every support for Tecumseh; but to President Johnson, the slippery Chief Justice agreed with the War Secretary's analysis, though in milder terms.

What Chase hoped to gain by getting Stanton out of the cabinet at this time is unclear; perhaps he feared Stanton and Sherman as possible political rivals in 1868 and hoped that, if both men were egged on, each would kill the chances of the other. Stanton suspected what was going on, and though deeply hurt at the undeserved knife in the back from his friend, had already countered the plot, though unknowingly. On April 28 his son wrote to Pamphila: "A faction in favor of Sherman is reported as being organized here under the leadership of Chase and Butler; the object of course being to break down father." But the War Secretary's promptness in acting against the Sherman-Johnston truce, and President Johnson's quiet support of Stanton, had ruined the plot. "They are too late," the younger Stanton wrote.[5] As the Secretary had acted to disavow the truce before he learned of this plot to unseat him, this fortuitous result must be accounted as a bonus for his stern and unswerving, if untactful, devotion to his duty.

Though Sherman had justification in feeling bitter toward Stanton, he had brought his troubles on himself, and someone in Washington had to intervene. His assurance to Stanton that he would negotiate with Johnston solely on military matters showed that he realized that there were limitations on his authority as a military commander. True, Stanton should have informed Sherman of Lincoln's instructions to Grant of March 3, and of Lincoln's revocation of his order to Weitzel to allow the Virginia legislators to assemble. But the Secretary's remissness gave Sherman no warrant for overstepping his authority. Stanton had given Sherman no authorization to deal with political matters when he visited him in Savannah, and Grant's terms to Lee at

[5] W. B. Matchett to Butler, April 22, and J. W. Shaffer to same, May 14, 1865, Butler Papers, LC; Thorndike, *Sherman Letters*, 247–8; Chase to Johnson, May 7, 1865, Johnson Papers, LC; Wolcott MS, 200–1.

Appomattox afforded no precedent for Sherman's action. Though Sherman had stipulated that the terms of his agreement with Johnston must be ratified in Washington, he had announced them the next day to his army as though ratification were certain, thus forcing the administration to act quickly and decisively in disavowing the terms of the truce. Sherman, contemptuous of politicians and distrustful of democracy, probably thought that generals were better qualified than civilians to act as peacemakers.

And Sherman was not, as he had thought, following the path toward peace terms which Lincoln had blazed. Lincoln's thoughts on this matter were pragmatic and dynamic, not ideological and fixed. Sherman's inability to understand this was shared by many Americans in 1865 and later, and was to produce tragic consequences.[6]

On the other hand, Stanton had acted toward Sherman with his customary bluntness and disregard of personal feelings, and his "nine reasons" for revoking the truce, combined with the crude orders from Halleck to Sherman's subordinates to disregard the orders of their commander, had put the general in an unnecessarily bad light. But Grant's and Halleck's roles in issuing these orders indicate that the responsibility for them must be shared. Stanton's error was to publish them.

It was planned to hold a great review in Washington before the volunteers put off their uniforms. The armies moved toward camps near the capital. Sherman received a note from Halleck inviting him to stay at his home while in Richmond, and also informing him that Halleck had arranged to review his troops there. Sherman curtly declined the invitation. His men would not parade for Halleck, he declared, and suggested that Halleck go into hiding when his army marched through Richmond; he might find himself insulted if seen by Sherman's angry troops.

Informing Grant of his actions, Sherman declared: "I will treat Mr. Stanton with like scorn & contempt, unless you have reasons otherwise, for I regard my military career as ended, save and except so far as necessary to put my army into your hands. Mr. Stanton can give me no

---

[6] Lewis, *Sherman*, 536–44; Raoul S. Naroll, "Lincoln and the Sherman Peace Fiasco—Another Fable?" *JSH*, XX, 459–83; Murray, "General Sherman, the Negro, and Slavery," *loc. cit.*, 125–30; Harry W. Pfanz, "The Surrender Negotiations between General Johnston and General Sherman, April 1865," *MA*, XVI, 61–70; Hesseltine, "Abraham Lincoln and the Politicians," *ALQ*, VI, 55.

orders of himself. He may, in the name of the President, and those shall be obeyed to the letter; but I deny his right to command an army. . . . Subordination to authority is one thing, to insult another. No amount of retraction or pusillanimous excusing will do. Mr. Stanton must publicly confess himself a common libeller or——but I won't threaten. . . . He wants the vast patronage of the military Governorships of the South, and the votes of [the] negro[es] . . . for political capital, and whoever stands in his way must die. Keep above such influences, or you will also be a victim. See in my case how soon all past services are ignored or forgotten."

With the Ewing family and John Sherman now rallying to his support, cocky Tecumseh seemed, as he assembled his veteran troopers at Alexandria, to be having things his own way. Stanton kept quiet, in conformity with Thurlow Weed's advice: "The Shermans are overacting. You can afford to be silent." [7]

Sherman's troops gave free expression to unflattering opinions of Stanton in Washington's hotel lobbies and barrooms. Rumors that Sherman planned to take over the government flew around Washington. The Committee on the Conduct of the War became disturbed and decided to put Sherman on the carpet, asking him to appear before it with Grant. Both generals pleaded pressing duties elsewhere, but the members would not be denied. Wade wanted to know particularly whether Sherman, in offering his lenient peace terms, had acted under previous confidential instructions from Lincoln, and at his request Stanton ordered the two generals to appear.

Presenting himself before the committee, Sherman answered Wade's questions in a curtly defiant manner. His terms, he said, conformed to Lincoln's well-known wishes for a quick and humane peace, and though not specifically authorized by Lincoln, would, in Sherman's opinion, have been upheld by him, had he lived. Sherman then told the committee members that Stanton was a two-faced scoundrel.

Sherman's testimony confirmed the suspicions of certain of the radicals that his peace terms had been intended to put him in the running for the presidency, and they thought that his criticisms may have damaged Stanton. At Stanton's suggestion they summoned Meade and Grant to testify concerning the manner in which he had conducted the War Department. Under Wade's questioning Meade asserted that he

[7] *O.R.*, XLVII, pt. 3, 454–5; Sherman to Grant, May 10, 1865, W. T. Sherman Papers, LC; Thomas Ewing, Jr., to Sr., May 12, 1865, Ewing Family Papers, LC; Weed to Stanton, May 27, 1865, Stanton MSS.

Stanton : The Life and Times

had no cause for complaint, and when prodded further, declared that Stanton had shown "great ability." Grant, waxing more enthusiastic, said with emphasis that Stanton had performed "admirably," and in response to further questions from Wade, asserted that there had never been any misunderstandings between him and Stanton, nor had the Secretary ever interfered with or obstructed his plans. D. C. Chipman, a Steubenville friend, wrote to Stanton that with the two generals thus on record, "you need have no solicitude about your fame." [8]

Many persons were intent upon observing what would occur when Sherman came face to face with Stanton. On May 23, the Army of the Potomac led off the Grand Review. Spic and span, in perfect alignment, the troops swung down the avenue through the wildly cheering crowd, flags flying, horses prancing, field guns rumbling a heavy undertone to the cadence of the marching feet, the officers saluting smartly and the colors dipping when the various units passed the reviewing stand. This was a far cry from the defenseless days of 1861, and the nation took pride in its power and hurrahed in happiness that the bloodletting was finished.

Sherman's western army paraded the next day. The tall, lean men from the Mississippi Valley followed their commander in rhythmic tread, lines straight, heads held high, stepping off smartly in their long, rolling stride. After passing the reviewing stand Sherman swung out of line, dismounted, and strode up the steps. Onlookers—some, like newsman Noah Brooks, equipped with field glasses—watched each motion of the men on the stand. Sherman saluted the President and took his proffered hand. Stanton stood next. He started to extend his hand to Sherman, but realized that the general intended to ignore it and allowed his hand to fall. According to Brooks, "Stanton's face, never very expressive, remained immobile." But Sherman flushed deeply, either in anger or exaltation, deliberately walked past Stanton, shook hands with Grant, and turned to watch the marching men. [9]

Sherman had publicly snubbed the Secretary. To Senator Lyman Trumbull, reading exaggerated newspaper accounts of the episode, this was a shocking breach of democratic principles. He urged Stanton to stay in the war office regardless of the rash of reports, touched off by the incident, that the Secretary was about to resign. Stanton's mail

[8] Fessenden to Stanton, May 23, Chipman to same, May 30, 1865, Stanton MSS; Flower, *Stanton*, 387; *CCW*, I, 38, 523–4, III, 4–14; Julian, *op. cit.*, 258; *O.R.*, XLVII, pt. 3, 576, 581–2.

[9] Brooks, *op. cit.*, 278; Dana, *Recollections*, 288–90; Grant, *Memoirs*, II, 379; *O.R.*, XLVII, pt. 3, 586.

brought him similar reactions from across the nation and—to his mind, most important—from many men still in uniform.

To Republican-Union party leaders, it was vital for Stanton to stay on. As Lieber commented to Sumner: "His resignation at present would be an unfortunate support of 'the Blairs' and look like a justification of Sherman's conduct on the part of the Administration—a great mistake—should it happen." To prevent it from happening, President Johnson, now head of the Union coalition, specifically asked Stanton to retain his portfolio, and, Barlow informed Montgomery Blair after an interview with the President, Stanton had reluctantly agreed.[1]

Despite all the fuss, Stanton always felt ready to forgive Sherman. He retained a conciliatory attitude toward the general, as he informed William Stanton. Yet proud, stern, stubborn Tecumseh, though more angry with Halleck than with Stanton, refused a reconciliation.

On the morning after the review, young Edwin L. Stanton answered a ring at the door of his home. Mrs. Sherman had sent a bouquet of choice flowers for his mother as a "mute appeal for forgiveness" for the general's discourtesy; and Mrs. Sherman told Lincoln's old friend Orville Browning that she wanted to call on the Stantons but was worried about the propriety of her doing so. Browning advised her to go, and serving as mediator, expressed his regret to Stanton at the difficulty that had arisen. Stanton replied that there was no difficulty so far as he was concerned, and that he entertained no hard feelings toward the general. Browning said that Mrs. Sherman would be glad to pay her respects to the Secretary and Mrs. Stanton, if a call from her would be acceptable; Stanton responded that it would be most agreeable. A few evenings later, at Mrs. Sherman's request, Browning accompanied her to the Stanton home, where they spent a pleasant half hour.[2]

The general, however, continued to nurse his resentment. And the Secretary, without animus but convinced that Sherman had been foolish in his terms of peace with Johnston, would forgive but not retract. It went against the grain with Stanton to make amends to anyone publicly, and he was not convinced that in proportion to Sherman's misdeeds he had handled the general ungently.

---

[1] Trumbull to Stanton, May 25, 1865, Stanton MSS; Lieber to Sumner, June ?, 1865, HL; Barlow to Blair, June 16, 1865, Letterbook XI, 522–5, Barlow Papers, HL.

[2] Willis Weaver, *Edwin M. Stanton and the Sherman-Johnston Terms of Peace* (n.p., 1927), 19, and see the ms memoranda in the Weaver Papers, LC. See also Morse, *Welles Diary*, II, 309–10; Browning, *Diary*, II, 30, 40; Wolcott MS, 213; A. E. H. Johnson in Washington *Evening Star*, Sept. 3, 1892.

More was involved in this than either man's personal feelings. It tied in with their differences over policy, with the question of what attitude the government should adopt toward the conquered South and the rights that should be accorded to the Negro. This was a controversy in which Sherman and Stanton were irrevocably at odds; so the feud continued to smolder.

CHAPTER XX

JUSTICE

GOVERNMENT AGENTS meanwhile had again swept down on the Surratt boardinghouse and arrested everyone in the place. But the raid netted them only Mrs. Surratt, her daughter Anna, and some female boarders, all of whom, except Mrs. Surratt, were soon released. Just as the agents were about to take their prisoners away, a knock sounded at the door. Standing there was a rough-looking individual dressed like a day laborer, with a pickax on his shoulder. Arrested on suspicion, he proved to be Lewis Payne, the man who had attacked Seward.

Two more suspects were arrested elsewhere—Samuel Arnold and Michael O'Laughlin. Then Atzerodt fell into the net. He had been detailed to murder Andrew Johnson but had lost his nerve. Edmund Spangler, a scene shifter at Ford's Theater, joined the swelling number of apprehended conspirators. Booth's pursuers arrested Dr. Samuel A. Mudd, who had set the actor's broken leg. It was now clear that Booth had headed south, and information from Detective Britton A. Hill confirmed Stanton's erroneous but persisting belief that the murder plot had originated in Richmond.

Stanton ordered Payne, O'Laughlin, Spangler, and Atzerodt confined below deck on the monitor *Montauk*, which was anchored close by the Navy Yard. The other male prisoners were placed in the hold of the monitor *Saugus*, riding near by. Each prisoner had an iron ball attached to his leg by a heavy chain and wore handcuffs joined by an iron bar. Later, for better security, Stanton ordered a canvas bag placed over each man's head and tied around his neck. A hole in the device allowed the prisoners to breathe and eat, but they were unable to see.

As the summer heat descended physicians attending the prisoners reported that these hoods might drive them insane. Stanton promised to have the hoods removed, to allow the prisoners to exercise daily, and to provide them with reading matter, but none of these promises was kept. Mrs. Surratt was never subjected to the ordeal of the hood, however, nor was she ever placed on a monitor. She remained in the Carroll Annex of the Old Capitol Prison until shortly before the trial.[1]

Booth was still at large. On April 20, Stanton issued a proclamation offering $50,000 reward for his apprehension, with additional amounts of $25,000 each for the capture of Herold and John Surratt. Information indicated that young Surratt had escaped to Canada, and as the days passed with Booth's whereabouts still unknown, Stanton became despondent from fear that he, too, had eluded the authorities. He wanted Lincoln avenged.

Then, on April 26, while Stanton was at home, resting on a sofa, Colonels Baker and E. J. Conger rushed into the house. "We have got Booth," Baker shouted.

Stanton slowly put his hands to his eyes, and for a long moment remained silent. Then he rose deliberately and put on his coat. Meanwhile, Baker had placed a number of articles on a table—a belt, pipe, knife, compass, diary, two pistols, and a few other effects which had been taken from Booth's body.

The murderer had been taken near Port Conway, Virginia; Booth and Herold had been hiding in a tobacco barn, where a cavalry detachment had found them. When the fugitives refused to come out, the soldiers had set fire to the barn. Contrary to orders, one of the soldiers, Sergeant Boston Corbett, had shot Booth, who died shortly afterward. Herold was captured alive, and in company with Booth's body, was aboard the steamer *John S. Ide* headed for Washington. Conger, on a faster ship, had brought the effects of the dead man which Baker showed to Stanton.

The Secretary ordered Baker and Eckert to intercept the *Ide* and take her directly to the Navy Yard. There, under cover of night, Herold and the body of Booth were transferred to the *Montauk*. Early the next morning, Baker, Holt, Dr. Barnes, and other officials boarded the *Montauk*. Word of the capture had spread rapidly and a crowd watched them from the shore. On a carpenter's bench under an awning

---

[1] Guy W. Moore, *The Case of Mrs. Surratt* (Norman, 1954), 18–24; Eisenschiml, *Why Was Lincoln Murdered?*, 178; Hill to Stanton, April 16, 1865, Stanton MSS; DeWitt, *Assassination*, 73.

on the *Montauk*'s deck, lay Booth's body, wrapped in canvas. Barnes directed an autopsy on the dead man, and identified Booth beyond a possibility of doubt.

Stanton knew that every hair of Booth's head would be prized by Confederate partisans. One worshipful woman had already succeeded in boarding the *Montauk* and snipping off a strand. The Secretary resolved that Southern sympathizers should have no opportunity to transmute the murderer into a martyr. On a promontory where the Eastern Branch emptied into the Potomac, stood a onetime federal penitentiary that had become part of the Washington arsenal. Near the western end of this building was a large room with a brick floor. After studying a plan of this structure, Stanton directed the commander of the arsenal to bury Booth there in secret.

Late at night, as enlisted men dug a grave, other soldiers placed Booth's body in a musket case and transported it to the arsenal. Eckert and Baker were in the building as Stanton's representatives, but neither of them witnessed the interment, which was conducted without ceremony. The arsenal commander reported to Stanton that Lincoln's murderer was buried in a secret, unmarked, and unhallowed grave.[2]

While the dragnet had been closing, Holt, who was also head of the Army's Bureau of Military Justice, had been busily collecting evidence against the conspirators. Some of it confirmed Johnson and Stanton's belief that high-placed Confederate officials had been involved in the murder plot, and on May 2 the President proclaimed that Jacob Thompson, Clement C. Clay, "and other rebels and traitors . . . harbored in Canada" had conspired with Jefferson Davis to commit the outrage. Thereupon Johnson offered a reward of $100,000 for Davis's apprehension and $25,000 for the capture of each of the others.

Though many Northerners were astounded at the proclamation, Stanton always believed that the evidence Holt had shown him justified the action, even though it might not satisfy the requirements for

---

[2] DeWitt, *Assassination*, 67–8, 86–7; Eisenschiml, *Why Was Lincoln Murdered?*, 198; *O.R.*, XLVI, pt. 3, 963; Baker, *History of the United States Secret Service* (Philadelphia, 1867), 540–2. *Impeachment of the President*, House Rep. 7, 40th Cong., 2d sess., 409 (cited hereafter as *Impeachment Report*), contains Stanton's testimony explaining to the House Judiciary Committee the reasons for the "mystery" surrounding Booth's burial—to prevent a hagiography from growing. Stanton later pardoned Corbett for his act; Byron B. Johnson, *Abraham Lincoln and Boston Corbett* (Waltham, Mass., 1914), 36–8.

conviction in a civil court. Dana, privy to all this, realized that Stanton, Holt, and Johnson—already convinced that Davis and his subordinates had been guilty of starving Union prisoners, plotting to poison the water supplies of Northern cities, setting fires in New York City, and sending hostile forces into the North from Canada, as in the raid at St. Albans—became easily assured that they had inspired the murder of Lincoln; and Stanton and Holt never changed their minds.[3]

Clay surrendered to the Union Army on May 11, having learned of Johnson's proclamation, and on the same day federal troops arrested Alexander H. Stephens, Vice-President of the Confederacy. Two days later electrifying news reached Washington. Jefferson Davis, supposedly the archconspirator, had been captured in southern Georgia, and rebel Postmaster General Reagan also fell into the government's hands. John Campbell, who had tried to negotiate with Lincoln after the fall of Richmond, was being held under arrest at his home. Destitute and broken in health, Campbell elicited the sympathy of loyal men, owing in part to his known hostility to Davis during the last part of the war. Campbell now petitioned for a parole, and Halleck asked what should be done with him.

Stanton was sure that Campbell had deceived Lincoln at Richmond, and he had seen a letter addressed to Campbell while he had been Confederate Assistant Secretary of War, in which the writer proposed to assassinate Lincoln. On Stanton's orders, and with the President's assent, Campbell, as well as Davis, Clay, Stephens, Reagan, R. M. T. Hunter, and James A. Seddon, went to prison.

Mrs. Campbell, who had known the Stantons in prewar days, begged him to parole her husband. "And now Mr. Stanton," she pleaded, "at the risk of wearing out your patience—permit me to refer you back to . . . October 1863 when you rendered to myself and daughter, then in Washington, marks of kindness and consideration, I have never ceased gratefully to remember. . . . You said, I think in the last interview I had with you, what I quote to you now, 'I am sure, Judge Campbell would have no desire to separate me from my wife and children—and I have no desire to keep him apart from his. . . .'

---

[3] The reward for W. C. Cleary was $10,000; *O.R.*, XLVII, pt. 3, 301; XLIX, pt. 2, 566–7; ser. 2, VIII, 549, 552; Morse, *Welles Diary*, II, 299–300; Seymour J. Frank, "The Conspiracy to Implicate the Confederate Leaders in Lincoln's Assassination," *MVHR*, XL, 631. Allen, *op. cit.*, 136, suggests that Johnson more than Holt or Stanton inspired the second proclamation as well as the initiative for the military trial of the assassins; confirmed in Dana to James S. Pike, May 10, 1865, CFL.

Oh, Mr. Stanton, let the thought of your own family plead for us."

As time passed, Stanton became disposed to treat Campbell leniently, but except for Seward, the other members of the cabinet and the President distrusted the former Supreme Court judge. Six weeks after receiving Mrs. Campbell's plea, Stanton was obliged to tell her that the President and cabinet had decided that Campbell must remain in prison for the present.[4]

Though the civil courts were functioning, Stanton wanted to try the alleged culprits at once before a military commission, where the rules of evidence would be less constricting and punishment was more likely to be stern and swift. He agreed with his friend Brady that this was the only plausible moderate course, for if the assassins got off or if President Johnson appeared to be weak toward them, then the "half-crazy abolitionist mind of the North" might whirl around to join with copperhead Democrats in opposition to constructive reconstruction measures.

So, in cabinet, Stanton pressed his arguments for the utility of a military commission. He had wanted the trial begun before Lincoln was buried, but failing in that, wanted no more time lost, and President Johnson was on his side. Attorney General Speed seemed reluctant to agree at first on the legitimacy of a military tribunal, but he soon succumbed to the argument advanced by Stanton and Holt that a trial by a military commission would be legal under what Holt termed "the common law of war." [5]

A large segment of the press continued to insist that military proceedings were unconstitutional. Former Attorney General Bates wrote a powerful argument to this effect which received wide newspaper circulation. Though Stanton had never had a very high opinion of Bates, he was worried that the President might accept his reasoning and terminate the trial. At Stanton's suggestion, Speed published a lengthy counterblast to Bates's criticism.

The weighty opinions of Bates and Speed fanned the fires of journalistic abuse. Greeley leveled such a barrage of criticism at Stanton that he contemplated bringing suit against the *Tribune* for

[4] Mrs. Campbell to Stanton, May 28, 1865, Hitchcock Papers, LC; same to M. Blair, July 17, 28, 1865, Blair Family Papers, LC; Morse, *Welles Diary*, II, 306, 331–2; *O.R.*, ser. 2, VIII, 550–4, 559–62, 576–7, 703.

[5] Brady to Stanton, May 14, 1865, Stanton MSS; Morse, *Welles Diary*, II, 303–5; Eisenschiml, *Why Was Lincoln Murdered?*, 468; Henry L. Burnett, "Some Incidents in the Trial of President Lincoln's Assassins," in James G. Wilson and Titus M. Coan (eds.), *Personal Recollections of the War of the Rebellion* (New York, 1891), 189.

trying "to incite assassins to finish their work by murdering me." Although no suit was pressed, personal animosity endured between the two men.[6]

Stanton was not, as Welles supposed, the originator of the plan whereby the trial would be conducted secretly. This was Holt's idea. The Kentuckian was convinced that he had a God-given mission in life to avenge Lincoln's murder. For his part, Stanton had wanted an open military trial from the beginning, but Holt convinced him that secrecy was the better way. News that the trial was to be held behind locked doors mysteriously leaked out, and it brought such voluble protests that Stanton had to rescind the order.

So far as Stanton was concerned, the trial of the conspirators was Holt's responsibility from beginning to end. His own official concern with it was finished when the assassins and conspirators were caught, although he continued to play a significant part in collecting evidence and examining witnesses. He did not, however, predetermine the outcome.

With Speed now convinced that a military trial for the assassins was legal, Stanton had General Townsend select the officers who would constitute the court. Townsend learned that some officers, despite the Attorney General's ruling, were skeptical of the legitimacy of the proceedings. C. B. Comstock, for example, was one of the original choices for the commission. "Wish I could get off," he wrote in his diary. "They ought to be tried by civil courts." Comstock was delighted when, suddenly, orders from the Secretary of War relieved him of this unwelcome assignment, along with one other, unnamed officer. Stanton took care to tell Grant that no fault was to be imputed to Comstock, but that as Grant had been a target for assassination himself and the two officers were members of his staff, it seemed best to substitute other men. It is obvious, however, that this alteration cleared from the roster of the officer-judges at least one man who doubted the validity of the court of which he was a member.

Stanton designated Holt as Judge Advocate to present the case for the government, with Congressman Bingham, Stanton's old Cadiz friend, and Colonel H. L. Burnett as his assistants. The accused were

[6] Stanton to Pierrepont on the suit, in *O.R.*, XLVI, pt. 3, 1141–2, 1149; R. Marsh to Stanton, June 2, 1865, Stanton MSS, on Bates. Bates's argument reprinted in Washington *National Intelligencer*, Jan. 3, 1867; and see Bates, *Diary*, 481–3; Speed, *Opinion on the Constitutional Power of the Military to Try the Assassins of the President* (Washington, 1865). Note that Montgomery Blair accepted the legality of the commission; see Barlow to him, Aug. 21, 1865, Letterbook XI, 955, Barlow Papers, HL.

allowed to employ civilian counsel. Under the rules of procedure in a
military court, it was incumbent upon the prosecution not only to obtain
convictions wherever they were warranted but also to present all
evidence bearing on both the guilt and the innocence of the accused
and to see to it that their rights were respected.[7]

The military commission began its sitting on the morning of May 9.
Next day the prisoners were led in to hear the charges and specifica-
tions, which were drawn also against the other Confederates whom the
President had accused of complicity in the assassination in his recent
proclamation. To Stanton and Holt, it seemed no less important that
the guilt of these officials be established than that the prisoners be
convicted. Throughout the trial the Secretary was on the alert for
evidence against them.[8]

By May 23, Holt, Bingham, and Burnett had brought 123 government witnesses before the military court; after this the defense produced its witnesses. A summation by each side followed. Then the
court went into private session to deliberate.

Holt relied chiefly on three witnesses to link Davis and other
Confederate leaders to the murder plot. They were Sanford Conover,
Richard Montgomery, and Dr. James B. Merritt, all of whom claimed
to have had intimate contact with the Confederate agents in Canada.
For "prudential reasons" the commission went into secret session for
their testimony, but Benn Pitman, the chief court reporter, allowed
part of Conover's testimony to reach the press. It created such a stir
that the government felt obliged to corroborate it by releasing the
testimony of the others. Counterevidence brought forward impugned
the witnesses' veracity, and they soon became enmeshed in a web of
falsehood.

To Jacob Thompson and Jeremiah S. Black, all this proved that
"the vindictiveness of our old colleagues at Washington knows no
bounds," and that Stanton and Holt were indulging in personal spite
against Thompson by accusing him of complicity in Lincoln's murder.
But if this was true in whole or in part, the fact remains that Stanton,
who had no role in selecting the government's witnesses, was far
from being the only official in Washington who was convinced of the

---

[7] William Walsh to Holt, April 21, 1865, Holt Papers, LC; May 8–10, 1865, Com-
stock ms diary, LC; Burnett, "The Controversy Between President Johnson and Judge
Holt," in Wilson and Coan, *op. cit.*, 203; Stanton to Hancock, June 19, 20, 1865,
Stanton MSS; Moore, *op. cit.*, 24–6; Morse, *Welles Diary*, II, 303–5.

[8] *O.R.*, XLVII, pt. 3, 534, 541; Pitman, *op. cit.*, 46–7; Stanton to Seward, June 1,
1865, Seward Papers, UR.

existence of a conspiracy, born in Richmond and in Canada, to kill Lincoln and other high government personages.[9]

While the military commission weighed the evidence in seclusion, speculation ran riot concerning what the decision would be. It was the consensus that Payne, Herold, and Atzerodt were doomed. But Arnold, O'Laughlin, and Spangler seemed only remotely implicated in the murder plot, and Dr. Mudd and Mrs. Surratt seemed to stand a chance of acquittal. Working against Mrs. Surratt, however, was the fact that her son was a fugitive. The government hoped to force him out of hiding by imperiling the life of his mother.

Stanton, according to his private secretary, had no personal connection with the trial of Mrs. Surratt aside from subjecting her boarder, Weichmann, to a stiff cross-examination. Weichmann's testimony, by showing that Booth had frequently visited and talked to his alleged accomplices at the Surratt boardinghouse, laid the basis for the charge that the plot had been hatched there. Taken in connection with statements of John M. Lloyd, who kept a tavern for Mrs. Surratt, it also clearly implicated her. It also counted against her that the assassin Payne had been arrested while seeking entrance to her house, and there were other complaints against her. But she might have escaped conviction if it had not been for the testimony of Weichmann and Lloyd.

Weichmann, too, might very well have been accused of complicity in the plot, and two years later, at the trial of John Surratt, Lloyd not only contradicted some of the statements he had made at the conspiracy trial but admitted that he had been subjected to both promises and threats.[1] That Weichmann was subjected to the same sort of intimidation by Stanton, in the private cross-examination, seems likely from the statement made by John T. Ford, owner of the celebrated theater. Ford, imprisoned with Lloyd and Weichmann, became convinced from what they told him that Mrs. Surratt was innocent and that the two witnesses had been coerced. "Many yet living recall their fright," Ford wrote, and asserted that Weichmann had told him that "Secretary Stanton had, in a threatening manner, expressed the opinion that his [Weichmann's] hands had as much of the President's blood on them as Booth's."

Weichmann, testifying at the John Surratt inquiry in 1867, said he

---

[9] Thompson to Black, July 6, 1865, Black Papers, LC; Frank, "The Conspiracy to Implicate the Confederate Leaders in Lincoln's Assassination," *loc. cit.*, 633–9.

[1] We have not tried to retell the story of the trial, but rather to trace Stanton's role in these events. Pitman, *op. cit.*, 292–6; Benjamin, "Recollections of Secretary Stanton," *loc. cit.*, 766.

had been "nervous" at the previous trial, and contradicted some of his previous statements, thereby putting Mrs. Surratt in a more favorable light. At this second trial, which in some respects amounted to a re-hearing of Mrs. Surratt's case, Louis Carland, a former customer at Ford's Theater, testified that Weichmann had told him in 1865 that if he had been "let alone . . . it could have been quite a different affair with Mrs. Surratt than it was," that his statements had been written out for him, and that he had been threatened with prosecution as an accessory if he refused to swear to them. Weichmann, under examination, denied that he had made this confession, but admitted that he had talked to Carland.

John W. Clampitt, one of Mrs. Surratt's lawyers, a number of years after the trial wrote that Weichmann, after testifying, had been stung with remorse because he had committed perjury in implicating Mrs. Surratt in Lincoln's murder. Certain "authorities of the War Department" had threatened to prosecute him as an accomplice in the conspiracy against Lincoln if he refused to offer testimony, Weichmann claimed, according to Clampitt. Holt had rejected the first statement Weichmann had prepared with the remark that "it was not strong enough," whereupon, still under threat of prosecution, Weichmann had written a second and stronger statement, the substance of which he subsequently swore to on the witness stand. The man to whom Weichmann made this confession, wrote Clampitt, was refused permission to testify.[2]

Just how severely Stanton worked Weichmann over in private cross-examination must remain a matter of conjecture. But Stanton was not the only one who put the young clerk on the griddle. Passions were high, and this was a period when even civil courts employed standards of procedure which today seem shockingly low. Promises as well as threats helped loosen Weichmann's tongue, as they had with Lloyd. Later, on Stanton's and Holt's recommendations, Weichmann was given a clerk-ship in the Philadelphia customhouse, and he kept his government post for more than twenty-five years, writing in 1900 that except for the continuing intercession of Burnett and Bingham, "I would long ago have fallen by the wayside." But he also asserted at this time: "I believe that both Mrs. Surratt and her son were deeply involved and if they had done their duty as Christian people they could have saved the life

---

[2] Clampitt, "The Trial of Mrs. Surratt," *NAR*, CXXXI, 233–4; Ford, "Behind the Curtain of a Conspiracy," *ibid.*, CXLVIII, 484–5; *Trial of John H. Surratt in the Criminal Court for the District of Columbia* (Washington, 1867), I, 290, 444–5; Moore, *op. cit.*, 79–89.

of Mr. Lincoln." On his deathbed he signed a statement attesting to the truth of "every word" he had uttered at the assassination trial.

Throughout the trial the government tried to minimize the fact that Booth had concocted two separate plots against Lincoln. The first was to kidnap the President, and it was not until the very day of the assassination that Booth had resolved to kill him. This fact was made evident in the diary that had been taken from Booth's body and subsequently turned over to Stanton. Strangely enough, this diary, which would have shown that Arnold, O'Laughlin, and both Surratts, though participants in the abduction plot, were ignorant of Booth's design to murder, was never introduced in evidence by either side. In this the prosecution was remiss in its duty to present all the facts. But the government was in no mood to draw fine distinctions. To the prosecuting authorities, complicity in the one scheme amounted to participation in the other. A President, after all, was dead; the abduction plot alone warranted severe penalties.

That the defense attorneys failed to call for the diary is far more remarkable than that the government did not produce it. They were singularly inept or, at best, incredibly forgetful. Though the diary was in the War Department archives, the New York *Times* of April 27 and the *World* on the next day had referred to its being found.

It was not part of Stanton's responsibility to see to it that the diary appeared at the trial. There is no evidence that he was a party to its suppression, if, indeed, the document was suppressed at all in the sense of a deliberate withholding of it. But this was to be added to the arsenal of historical weapons which Stanton's enemies were to launch at him as a result of later developments.

Another abstruse feature of the trial was the failure of the Judge Advocate to attempt to trace Booth's movements from the time he left Dr. Mudd's house after having his broken leg set until he crossed the Rappahannock River at Port Conway—a period of nine days. Stanton's offer of a reward for Booth's capture had been accompanied by a warning that anyone harboring or aiding the fugitive would be tried as an accomplice in his crime, and a number of persons were known to have aided Booth during this phase of his flight. But though some of these persons were arrested and questioned, no charges were brought against them. Yet the government knew Booth's route.[3]

The military commission reached a verdict on the last day of June.

[3] Eisenschiml, *Why Was Lincoln Murdered?*, 136–7; Moore *op. cit.*, 94; Mary W. Porter, *The Surgeon in Charge* (Concord, N.H., 1949), 17.

It found all the prisoners guilty of conspiring with the Confederates named in the proclamation to murder Lincoln, Johnson, Seward, and Grant, and sentenced Payne, Herold, Atzerodt, and Mrs. Surratt to be hanged. O'Laughlin and Dr. Mudd were sentenced to hard labor for life, Spangler for six years.

According to the rules governing the commission, it could impose the death penalty only by a two-thirds vote. In Mrs. Surratt's case this was obtained on condition that five members of the commission be permitted to petition President Johnson for a commutation of her sentence from death to life imprisonment by reason of her age and sex. This petition was attached to the findings and sentences by Burnett after he had taken the court record to Holt's office. Its existence was kept a strict secret from the public.

There is no doubt that Stanton, like President Johnson and the other members of the cabinet, felt that Mrs. Surratt was guilty. Welles, writing to Johnson in 1873, "thought then and think now, [that] she was deserving of punishment as any of those implicated." Welles asserted that "my impression of her guilt was derived chiefly from Mr. Stanton, who denounced her as most deserving of punishment." But Welles, who hated Stanton, never implied that the War Secretary engineered her death sentence.

Nor did Stanton prevent her from receiving the President's clemency. The commission reached its decision at a time when both men were severely ill. The sick President and the sick War Secretary saw each other only momentarily if at all during the first week of July.

Holt was able to obtain an interview alone with the ailing President on the afternoon of July 5, and he brought to the White House "a formal brief review of the case" and the secret record, though not the voluminous testimony. He was not circumventing Stanton. Existing procedures involved direct communication between the Bureau of Military Justice and the President; there was no reason for Holt to go through the office of the Secretary of War.

No one else was present when Holt laid these papers before Johnson. Johnson did not read them; Holt merely briefed him on them. The sentences in the case of Herold, Atzerodt, and Payne were considered and approved. What happened next, however, in the case of Mrs. Surratt, became the subject of a heated controversy between Johnson and Holt in later years.

The President claimed that "no recommendation for a commutation of her punishment was mentioned or submitted to me." Holt maintained, on the other hand, that he "drew the President's attention specially to the recommendation in favor of Mrs. Surratt, which he read and freely commented on." Both men agreed, however, that the matter of clemency for Mrs. Surratt was discussed, and Johnson never denied that they were at one in the opinion that her age and sex furnished no ground for modifying the sentence of the court and that she deserved to die. Thus it seems unlikely that Johnson would have been moved by the petition, whether or not he saw it.[4]

Johnson made a telling point against Holt in their later controversy by calling attention to the fact that Pitman's record of the trial contained no reference whatever to the petition for clemency, though Stanton had stipulated that Burnett should be responsible to the Bureau of Military Justice for its "strict accuracy." The President accused Holt and Stanton of engineering the omission of the petition, maintained that he had never seen the petition, and in a campaign speech in 1873, when he was electioneering for a U. S. Senate seat, stated that Mrs. Surratt had been executed by trickery and that Stanton eventually committed suicide in remorse for this deed.

There was evasion, but the trickery was not of Stanton's making. The whole question of the accuracy of the Pitman trial record needs evaluation, for example. Pitman himself described his transcript as "a great heap of rubbish." But this is not the major point.

Holt's excuse for not including the petition in Pitman's authorized printed record of the trial—namely, that "recommendations to mercy by members of military courts do not in law constitute any part of the records"—would appear to be pure evasion, inasmuch as Pitman's book is as much a history of the trial as an official record of the court proceedings, and contains many documents and papers far less pertinent to the subject than the omitted petition. In the "formal brief review of the case" that Holt submitted to President Johnson on July 5, no mention is made of the petition. Nor did Holt mention it in his formal report of the proceedings to Stanton.

Thus the conclusion seems inescapable that Holt, determined that the major conspirators should die, willfully concealed the contents of the petition from the President. And the question then arises: Was Stanton a party to the subterfuge? The evidence seems to exempt him from this charge.

----

[4] Welles to Johnson, Nov. 5, 1873, Johnson Papers, LC; Holt, *Rejoinder to Ex-President Johnson's Reply to His Vindication of 26th August Last* (Washington, 1873), 10–11; Speed to Lieber, July 5, 1865, HL, on Stanton's illness. The assertion in Roscoe, *op. cit.*, 487, that Stanton instigated a deception on Johnson is not sustained by evidence.

Toward the conclusion of his July 5 interview with Johnson at the White House, Holt wrote an order approving the sentences imposed by the court and naming July 7 as the day for the execution of the four death sentences. Johnson affixed his name to it. Holt gathered up all the papers and went directly to the War Department. "I happened to be with Mr. Stanton as Judge Holt came in," Burnett recalled years later. "After greetings the latter remarked, 'I have just come from a conference with the President over the proceedings of the military commission.' 'Well,' said Mr. Stanton, 'what has he done?' 'He has approved the findings and sentence of the Court,' replied Judge Holt. 'What did he say about the recommendation of mercy of Mrs. Surratt?' next inquired Mr. Stanton. 'He said,' answered Judge Holt, 'that she must be punished with the rest; that no reasons were given for his interposition by those asking for clemency, in her case, except age and sex. He said her sex furnished no good ground for his interfering; that women and men should learn that if women committed crimes they would be punished; that if they entered into conspiracies to assassinate, they must suffer the penalty; that were this not so, hereafter conspirators and assassins would use women as their instruments; it would be mercy to womankind to let Mrs. Surratt suffer the penalty of her crime.' "

Similar testimony is offered by Clampitt, who went with Mrs. Surratt's daughter on July 6 to Holt to ask him to plead with the President for mercy to the mother. Holt met them at the White House and told them that Johnson "is immovable." The President, according to Holt, had reviewed the trial proceedings and findings "and has no reason to change the date of the execution, and you might as well attempt to overthrow this building as to alter his decision." [5]

If Burnett's and Clampitt's recollections of these conversations are substantially correct, then Holt was giving every impression that Johnson had seen the petition for clemency. Stanton would have had no reason to question the inference that Holt had shown it to the President. No direct evidence incriminating Stanton in Holt's dissimulation has ever come to light, and Holt alone may have been blameworthy.

[5] Pitman to T. Ewing, Jr., July 11, 1865, Ewing Papers, LC; reminiscence of Col. W. M. Nixon, May 17, 1929, George Fort Milton Papers, LC, on 1873 suicide claim. Other data in Burnett, "The Controversy Between President Johnson and Judge Holt," in Wilson and Coan, *op. cit.*, 220–1; Clampitt, "Trial of Mrs. Surratt," *loc. cit.*, 240; R. A. Watts, "The Trial and Execution of the Lincoln Conspirators," *MHM*, VI, 105–6; and Roger J. Bartman, O.F.M., *The Contribution of Joseph Holt to the Political Life of the United States* (Ph.D. thesis, Fordham University, 1958), 255–96.

On the other hand, Holt would have been a bold man indeed to deceive Stanton in a matter of such importance. Nor does it seem likely that the petition could have been omitted from Pitman's published record of the trial without Stanton's knowledge and consent. And complicity in the one implies complicity in the other.

Yet Welles, who made a profession of dredging up facts and fancies critical of Stanton, confessed in 1870 that "my impression is and always has been that Holt was the companion and coadjutor of Stanton, yet I have no positive proof of the fact, and I should not, therefore, feel justified in [so] placing him before the public." David Miller DeWitt, whose study of the conspiracy trial has been amplified but never superseded, believed that Stanton first connived with Holt, Bingham, and Burnett to secure the death sentence and then helped see to it that Johnson never learned of the petition for clemency. But no one knows what took place in the secret session of the military commission, and DeWitt's conclusion rests on conjecture. Guy W. Moore, who had access to documents that were unavailable to DeWitt, could find nothing, except by unverifiable inference, connecting Stanton with the decision arrived at by the court.

The only attempt by Stanton to bring the facts out into the open was made more than a year later when he asked the cabinet to approve Holt's request for a court of inquiry to deal with the widespread rumors concerning the Surratt mercy petition. But President Johnson refused the request.

Shortly before Stanton died he evoked a promise from Bingham to keep forever secret what both men knew of the Surratt case. Years later, Bingham confessed to Holt only that Stanton's "advice" was "to await the final judgment of the people." The nature of their information, then, is still secret. But it appears from the fragmentary evidence that Stanton died convinced that Mrs. Surratt had been guilty, and he had no remorse over her punishment. Coming to believe that Holt had used him as well as the President for the fulfillment of his own sense of mission, Stanton refused to reveal publicly what he felt was the truth. If this surmise is accurate, then Stanton's reticence saved, rather than injured, Holt's reputation.[6]

---

[6] Welles to Johnson, Jan. 14, 1870, Johnson Papers, LC; DeWitt, *op. cit.*, 233–4, 255; Moore, *op. cit.*, 105, 113–18; Holt to Bingham, Feb. 18, 1873, owned by Milton Ronsheim; Browning, *Diary*, II, 95–6; Burnett, "Assassination of President Lincoln and the Trial of the Assassins," in James H. Kennedy (ed.), *History of the Ohio Society of New York, 1885–1905* (New York, 1906), 614.

The news reached the public on July 6 that Mrs. Surratt was to die the next day. Friends and sympathizers began last-minute efforts to save her from the gallows. Father Walter, pastor of St. Patrick's Church, who had declared his belief in Mrs. Surratt's innocence, secured a pass from the War Department to visit her. That afternoon, General Hardie went to the priest and informed him that the pass given to him was invalid because Stanton had not signed it, and added: "I want you to make me a promise to say nothing of Mrs. Surratt's innocence, and I will give you the necessary pass." Father Walter declared indignantly that he would proclaim his belief as he chose to, even if Stanton would have him hanged for it. But as Hardie prepared to leave, the priest said: "I cannot suffer Mrs. Surratt to die without administering the sacrament." He agreed to keep silent, whereupon Hardie presented him with a pass already signed by Stanton.

When the incident came to light a few days later, it caused a stir in the press, and the onus immediately fastened upon Stanton. Hardie hastened to explain that he had gone to the priest in a "friendly and kindly" spirit to request that he desist from talking about the matter because of turbulent public sentiment. His visit had been unofficial and not suggested by or known to Stanton. Walter had become so denunciatory, said Hardie, that he had thought of obtaining another priest for Mrs. Surratt, but when the father calmed down, he had decided to give him the pass. Stanton had "made no condition" as to its issuance, Hardie insisted.

It became known still later, however, that as a precautionary measure General Hancock had been sent to call on Walter's superior in Baltimore, who had admonished Walter to "observe silence." Under this injunction, Father Walter attended Mrs. Surratt until she went to the scaffold. In later years, he always insisted that she had been innocent of the crime.[7]

In a last desperate effort to save Mrs. Surratt, her counsel appealed to Stanton's friend Judge Alexander Wylie, of the Supreme Court of the District of Columbia, for a writ of habeas corpus. He issued it on the morning of the day set for the execution. But President Johnson sent an order to Hancock suspending the privilege of the writ. The hammering continued on the scaffolds.

[7] *O.R.*, ser. 2, VIII, 696–700; Clampitt, "Trial of Mrs. Surratt," *loc. cit.*, 240; New York *Tribune*, July 17, 21, 1865; Moore, *op. cit.*, 65–9.

That same morning General Hartranft informed the President by letter that the assassin Payne had made a statement to him absolving Mrs. Surratt of complicity in both the assassination and the abduction plot. A certain John S. Brophy brought a letter to Holt in which he stated that he had heard Weichmann admit to giving false evidence and that Weichmann would make a written confession if assured that it would be handed to Johnson personally and remain a secret. An endorsement on Brophy's letter affirms that it was presented to the President. If so, he paid no heed to it, or to Hartranft.

Outside the President's office Mrs. Surratt's daughter went into hysterics on being denied access to him; Johnson had ordered all suppliants referred to Holt. Behind the closed door Johnson, in a consultation with Stanton, Harlan, and one or two other members of his cabinet, was talking informally of the advisability of commuting Mrs. Surratt's sentence. According to Harlan's recollection, Stanton argued against mercy in terms so much like Johnson's statement of July 5, as reported by Burnett, that either Stanton and Johnson had identical ideas, which may have been the case, or Harlan was putting his memory of Johnson's words into Stanton's mouth.[8]

Shortly after one o'clock on the afternoon of July 7, the condemned prisoners were hanged. The next day Anna Surratt petitioned Stanton for her mother's body, but, still feeling that the total responsibility for the conspirators was Holt's, Stanton referred the petition to him, and he refused to grant it.

Johnson had at first directed that the other convicted prisoners be committed to the Albany Penitentiary. But Stanton, aware that efforts were under way to have federal judges review the legality of the culprits' military trial, persuaded the President to send the prisoners outside the jurisdiction of all civil courts. Stanton felt no mercy at all for these men; they had helped to kill Lincoln and should pay the price. On this recommendation Johnson ordered them to the sun-baked Dry Tortugas, off the Florida coast.[9] For this concern over jurisdiction, which for Stanton was part of larger problems involving the Army's ability to function in what he still felt was an emergency situation, he was to receive public condemnation.

Stanton also became the target for popular censure for his closing

---

[8] Clampitt, "Trial of Mrs. Surratt," *loc. cit.*, 235, 240; DeWitt, *op. cit.*, 139, 286–7; Moore, *op. cit.*, 62–4; Eisenschiml, *Why Was Lincoln Murdered?*, 472–3; Pitman, *op. cit.*, 250.

[9] Morse, *Welles Diary*, II, 334; *O.R.*, ser. 2, VIII, 700; New York *Tribune*, July 17, 1865; Anna Surratt to Stanton, July 8, 1865, Stanton MSS.

of Ford's Theater. Determined that nothing connected with Lincoln's murder should serve to glorify that deed or become a shoddy commercial exploitation, Stanton, soon after the assassination, had posted guards at the theater. He planned to confiscate it to prevent it from ever again being used for public entertainment. Bates thought that this was another example of Stanton's tyranny, and many others agreed with him. But the President and McCulloch, Welles, and Harlan in the cabinet concurred with Stanton on the necessity for the move, all fearing that riots and violence must ensue if it reopened as a theater. And army spokesmen afforded Stanton some comforting support. The *Army and Navy Journal* editorialized that if Ford "did not know enough, of himself, to close its career as a playhouse, it is fortunate that there is a man in Washington competent and spirited enough to give the instruction." [1]

[1] Ford and the Henry Winter Davis family worked out a lease arrangement by which the government paid $1500 a month to keep the theater closed, and later Congress provided $100,000 compensation; Davis to Stanton, July 19, 1865, Stanton MSS; Sec. War Correspondence File, Box 318, RG 107, NA; *ANJ* (July 29, 1865), 777; Bates, *Diary*, 491; Morse, *Welles Diary*, II, 331–2; Browning, *Diary*, II, 37–8.

CHAPTER XXI

DISCORD

NOW THAT Lincoln's assassins had been brought to justice, Stanton again contemplated resigning from the cabinet. But a sense of duty not yet completed compelled him to accede to the new President's request and hang on for the present. There was still a great deal to be done in connection with the vast military machine he had helped to create.

An immediate question was the speed with which it should be pruned of its volunteers. The impatient Republic demanded that all its citizen-soldiers be allowed to return home, but too many uncertainties faced Stanton concerning the nature and extent of the Army's responsibilities during the coming months. With Congress not in session, it would be impossible to raise new regular regiments at once. Therefore, he decided, a portion of the highly trained volunteers, especially the officers, must stay in service.

During the spring months of 1865, Stanton returned a large share of the wartime enlisted volunteers to civilian life. Substantial demobilization was achieved so smoothly that it surprised many contemporaries. When Lieber inscribed a copy of his book *Civil Liberty* to Stanton, he noted that the returning veterans, "instead of threatening liberty," were strengthening it by contributing their skills and energies to the spectacular growth of the nation. A military class had not developed out of the war, as Lieber had feared it might, and it was to Stanton's credit that civilian authority had retained its control over the wartime military galaxy.

Stanton now had to reorganize the Army; from the single wartime task of crushing the rebellion, it had to turn to the varied needs of peace. One part of the Army would have to deal with training and ceremonial chores in the North. A second, larger portion of the troops must grapple with the western Indians, grown obstreperous as a result of the wartime efforts by the Union and the Confederacy to recruit them and now armed with surplus weapons.

Mexican affairs were another concern. Napoleon III of France, taking advantage of the Civil War, had placed a royal puppet on the throne of an unwilling Mexico. One Sunday afternoon soon after Lee had surrendered, Stanton, his tongue loosened after some wine, denounced Napoleon for his imperialism "and fairly made the air blue and sulphurous with his fearful oaths," one of his listeners recalled. Stanton was going to send Sheridan to the Texas border with an impressive force, and was ready if necessary to order him south and "drive those —— Frenchmen into the sea and drown them like a lot of blind pups!"

With these thoughts in mind, Stanton closely observed the regular officers who came through his office seeking reassignments in the spring of 1865. Young, spectacular George Armstrong Custer, proudly wearing his two stars, remembered that when he went to pay his respects to Stanton, a fellow townsman, the Secretary asked him to stand at attention. Then Stanton walked, with head bowed, in a circuit of the room, peering over his glasses at the youthful general, who was soon on his way westward to help subdue Kirby Smith's last rebel forces and under Sheridan's command to impress the French in Mexico.[1]

Then there was the question of the Army's role in the South. Here the military were expected to retain powers and functions undreamed of in prewar America. In assuming the responsibility for occupying the South, Stanton and the Army faced their knottiest postwar problem. The Army's problems in the South were not only different from those confronting it in the North and the West; they were unique in the American experience. Now American soldiers would regulate the lives of millions of other Americans. Only the lessons learned since 1861 were at hand to guide Stanton and Grant in administering the occupation, and these might not be relevant in peacetime.

In reality, Stanton was now the head of a peacetime military establishment consisting of two armies, each with its own purposes. The pacification of the West and the occupation of the South were their primary separate missions, and prescribed different organizations for each. This duality, though obscured by political crosscurrents, was to

[1] Mrs. Van Swearingen owns the inscribed Lieber volume. On Mexico, Hamilton G. Howard, *Civil War Echoes* (Washington, 1907), 226–8; Jay Monaghan, *Custer* (Boston, 1959), 267; *ANJ* (May 13, 1865), 600, surveys army problems.

be recognized in Congress's reconstruction statutes two years hence, when the southern army commands were placed under legislative control, and the President was permitted to retain command only of the northern and western sections. But in the first months of Johnson's presidency, what political future impended for the Army or for the nation was unknown.

No matter what policies the President and Congress had in mind for the South, Stanton had to bring stability to the war-torn area quickly. The South was a vacuum, bare of legitimate authorities, verging in some sections on anarchy. The Army moved in because no one else could do the job.

In the provost marshal units developed during the war years by every army field command except Sherman's, the Army had ready to hand an apparatus capable of taking on the complex occupation tasks. But the provosts of each military level—army, corps, division, regiment, and in some instances down to the company—were responsible only to their immediate superior officer, were independent of one another, and were capable only in theory of executing a general policy.

Stanton, knowing this, had included in his first reconstruction proposal to Lincoln the suggestion that there be established a centralized provost organization. Although this section was tabled, at Welles's suggestion, as a threat to democracy, events were to prove that centralization in reconstruction was needed for uniformity and consistency in policies, regardless of whether President or Congress set the goals. But even in their unreformed administrative arrangement, the provosts offered the best tool the Army had for immediate use in the South.

In the first weeks of peace, Union provosts disarmed Confederate veterans, restricted travel, enforced liquor prohibition decrees, put Negroes to work on roads and bridges, set up provost courts to try ordinary criminal cases, applied loyalty tests, established priorities in food distribution, supervised the repair of municipal sewage facilities, and drew up maximum-price schedules for scarce commodities. Because of their wartime experience, the provosts were able to take on these multitudinous tasks in addition to traditional military police functions, and this ability made it possible for them to bring about a swift transition from shooting war to nominal peace. In most cases in the South, provosts became the locus of both military and civilian authority. "I would rather act as Provost Marshal myself," wrote General H. M. Judah, commanding in Georgia in midsummer 1865, "than make a mistake in the appointment."

Stanton kept the Army engaged in this kind of essential housekeeping and out of politics as much as possible. When Provost Marshal Patrick presumed to reinstate civilian municipal government in Richmond, the Secretary blistered him. Such matters, he insisted to Patrick, were outside the business of the Army.[2]

The South was in the soldiers' hands. Neither the President nor Congress had thus far set a line of policy for the Army to follow in the defeated rebel states. Any reconstruction plan, however, needed the Army to see to its execution. The Army's central role was not, as historian William A. Dunning later described it, the "mere accidental feature of the general issue . . . throwing over the situation a sort of martial glamour." Nor was the military's importance due to the mere fact that Stanton was War Secretary and Grant the ranking general. They, and the Army as an institution, had to become entangled in events because they came to differ with the new President on what the war had meant and on what the peace should bring.[3]

For the first few eventful weeks after Lincoln's death, Andrew Johnson had remained a shadowy figure to Stanton, but now the War Secretary was able to take time to evaluate the Tennessean whom tragedy had catapulted into the White House. He saw a man of vigorous physique and tremendous moral courage who, stubbornly struggling to rise above a mudsill origin, had dared to defy the secessionists of his state and speak out boldly for the Union.

Orphaned at the age of four, Johnson had been bound out as an apprentice to a tailor, and yet had become a man of comfortable means. His flair for oratory, coupled with conscientious study of politics and government, had enabled him to become the spokesman of the artisans, mountaineers, and small farmers of his eastern Tennessee neighborhood. Elected first to the state legislature, he had gone on to Congress, become governor of Tennessee, and then a United States senator.

At Lincoln's urging he had risked political suicide and even death itself to serve as Military Governor of Tennessee; then, a delegate to the Union National Convention of 1864 as a war Democrat, he had become

---

[2] Judah to Gen. Grosvenor, Aug. 9, 1865, in Army Commands, IX, 34, RG 98; a survey of provosts' duties is in Union Provost Marshal File, Miscellaneous, Box 78, RG 109, NA; June 8, 1865, Patrick ms diary, LC.

[3] Dunning, "The Impeachment and Trial of President Johnson," AHA *Papers* (New York, 1886–91), IV, 479–80; Hyman, "Johnson, Stanton, and Grant; A Reconsideration of the Army's Role in the Events Leading to Impeachment," *AHR*, LXVI, 85–100.

the party's choice for Vice-President because as a loyal Southerner he could lend balance to the ticket. Throughout his political life he had been faithful to the principles of the Democracy.[4]

Johnson's allegiance to Jacksonian principles and his own stern struggle to rise in life had instilled in him a hatred of monopoly and privilege. He shared Stanton's biting scorn for the planter aristocrats and came to the presidency breathing threats of fire and slaughter against them for bringing on the war. But no one knew that Johnson had never fully overcome the "poor white's" feeling of inferiority, and he was soon to succumb to the flattery of his erstwhile social superiors. Although he opposed slavery, he hated abolitionists. His private secretary, Colonel William G. Moore, judged that Johnson sometimes "exhibited a morbid distress and feeling against the negroes," and was quite willing to remand them to the custody of their former masters with only such protection as the Thirteenth Amendment afforded.

Furthermore, Johnson was irrevocably committed to the doctrine of states' rights. To him, the Constitution was still, as it had been when he first entered politics, a compact between sovereign states; the war had not changed this relationship at all. From that postulate he soon concluded that reconstruction amounted to no more than a resumption by the revolted states of their rights and duties under the Constitution, and he stressed rights more than duties.

Lincoln had felt somewhat the same way about the status of the seceded states, but whereas Lincoln, in advancing his plan of reconstruction, had declared that he did not mean to rule out other plans and had confessed that events controlled him to a greater degree than he could control them, Johnson, after forming an opinion, proved obstinately averse to modifying it; nor would he, when unable to have his way in full, concede whatever might be necessary at the moment in order to obtain as much as he could. His strength was not pliant like Lincoln's, and he was often blindly stubborn, mistaking rigidity for constructive consistency. Trusting and confiding completely in no one, never happy "unless he had some one to strike at or denounce," Johnson was of "the same materials that martyrs are made of," his friend Hugh McCulloch wrote later.

It was not only that Johnson lacked Lincoln's temperament and sensitive tact. He lacked his predecessor's statesmanship and stature.

---

[4] Claude G. Bowers, *The Tragic Era* (New York, 1929), 30; Curtis Nettels, "Andrew Johnson and the South," *SAQ*, XV, 55–7.

Johnson never realized that Lincoln's 1863 reconstruction and amnesty proclamation was primarily a flexible, skillful wartime weapon designed to hasten the coming of peace, but not necessarily of equal worth in prescribing the final form which that peace must assume. There is every reason to believe, as Harrison Gray Otis noted, that Lincoln would have adapted his concepts of reconstruction, of the need for the disfranchisement of Southern whites, and of the role of the Negro, to the changed circumstances of 1865. Johnson could not advance beyond 1863.[5]

Yet to the Democratic concept of a weak national government, Johnson inconsistently added Lincoln's theory of the strong "war powers" belonging peculiarly to the President, from which it followed that only he was constitutionally authorized to administer the reconstruction process. This elevation of the executive at the expense of the legislative branch of the government, though promoted by Lincoln during the unprecedented emergency of the war, went contrary to the long course of Anglo-American constitutional history and the habits engendered by the weak Presidents after Jackson. The congressional opposition that Lincoln had encountered even at the height of the struggle should have warned Johnson of what to expect now that hostilities had ceased. But instead of re-examining his constitutional assumptions, he was to allow them to lead him to an extreme and exposed position. And he ended up by contending that whereas the President could declare the war ended, Congress could not say it continued; that whereas the President could employ soldiers for reconstruction purposes and issue pardons wholesale, Congress could not prescribe martial law for the South or pass an act of amnesty; that whereas the President could say who could and could not vote for members of constitutional conventions in the seceded states which were to initiate the reconstruction process, Congress could not modify the list; that whereas the President could prescribe the ratification of the Thirteenth Amendment as a condition for the restoration of a state to its normal position under the Constitution, Congress had no power to make the adoption of the Fourteenth Amendment a similar condition. In short, Johnson came to magnify his part of the national authority as a shield to protect state autonomy. But none of this was visible in April 1865.

[5] Otis, "The Causes of Impeachment," *CM*, LXXXV, 192; Brodie, *op. cit.*, 228; Feb. 19, April 9, 1868, Moore notebook, Johnson Papers, LC; McCulloch, *Addresses, Speeches, Lectures and Letters upon Various Subjects* (Washington, 1891), 143–6; Eric L. McKitrick, *Andrew Johnson and Reconstruction* (Chicago, 1960), 85–92, *passim*.

Johnson, often vehement in his language, had denounced "treason" and "traitors" with such malevolence during the war that even some tough-talking radicals had thought his language unseemly. Northern Democrats of the Vallandigham and Barlow stripe looked upon him as a deserter from their party. While Johnson was serving as Military Governor of Tennessee, Stanton had frequently been drawn into controversies between him and the Union commanders over their respective spheres of authority. But these had not been serious difficulties compared with what occurred in other occupation commands, and Halleck, in April 1865, could write of Johnson: "I like him very much, and I think he will be a firm and judicious Chief Magistrate. He was the only civico-military Governor of a rebel state who gave us no trouble, and who had the good sense to act always right." Halleck guessed that Johnson would be more severe toward rebels than Lincoln had been, "but perhaps, after all, it may be the better."

Stanton agreed with this estimate of the new President. Like Johnson, he had detested West Point and glorified the volunteer generals, but he had overcome this prejudice by the end of the war. Johnson had not. For his part, Johnson had once thought Stanton too lenient toward secessionists. Late in 1864, the Secretary had ruled that attorneys pleading before military commissions on behalf of imprisoned civilians in Tennessee, need not swear to the "ironclad test oath" of past loyalty, because, in many areas, there were no lawyers who could swear that oath without committing perjury. As a lawyer, Stanton felt obliged to grant accused persons the protection of proper legal procedure, and once Tennessee was safe, he had relaxed the oath requirements over Johnson's opposition. On the whole, however, the wartime relations between the two men had been good.[6]

Though he could guess no better than anyone else what course Johnson would choose to follow regarding the South, Stanton, however he mourned Lincoln, was encouraged by what he thought were the true characteristics of his successor. After talking with Stanton, Dana wrote that "the probability of any serious division in the Republican [Union] party seems to be entirely removed by the accession of President Johnson. For the present he commands the undivided support not merely of the party, but of the country in general."

Dana predicted that Johnson would move cautiously on all matters, and "especially upon the all important question of the readmission

---

[6] Halleck to Lieber, April 18, 1865, HL; James B. Steadman to Johnson, April 15, and A. Lovering to same, April 24, 1865, Johnson Papers, LC.

into the union of the seceded revolutionary states. Upon this subject there is a very great division of opinion, and men are very zealous upon all sides of it. Mr. Johnson is, however, evidently disinclined to any precipitate action, and I judge that neither Virginia, the Carolinas, Georgia, Alabama, Mississippi, nor Texas, will get back into the union until they are thoroughly regenerated." Dana also thought that on the question of punishing rebel leaders Johnson's vindictiveness was exaggerated.

This was close to what Stanton, Halleck, and Grant thought were the President's views toward the South. The promise of harmony on this essential question augured well for the continued political success of the Republican-Union coalition.

Since 1863, Stanton had formally supported this war-born alliance of the Republicans with former Democrats who wished to exert every effort to crush the rebellion. So had Johnson. It is clear that, unlike many wartime Union Democrats who were already returning to the regular Democratic fold, Stanton considered his own divorce from the party an irrevocable one. He wanted the Republican-Union coalition to succeed, and he agreed with his friend Brady that Johnson would find a natural political home with "sensible Republicans and . . . War Democrats" like themselves.

To Stanton, the Democratic organization was permanently tainted with treason. He had resented the Democrats' wartime criticisms of the administration's policies on internal security, conscription, emancipation, and Negro enlistment. Once a hard-money Jacksonian, Stanton had become converted to newer economic doctrines. He feared that if the Democrats succeeded in repudiating the government's wartime monetary measures, the abyss of bankruptcy would loom frighteningly close. The Army's occupation activities were costing almost as much as the conduct of the war itself. A drastic retrenchment in appropriations for the military, which Democrats were already demanding, would mean that there would not be enough soldiers to enforce whatever reconstruction policy was finally agreed on.

To be sure, the Democrats, though quickly restored as a national party, lacked leadership. But the Republican coalition, with Lincoln's moderating influence gone, was embarrassingly rich in would-be leaders, each of whom controlled powerful factions in Congress and in the Northern states. Stanton was worried that the precarious unity within the Republican organization would suffer unless President Johnson, now head of the Republican-Union alliance, could quickly gain enough

443

prestige within the party to keep differences muted. The obvious way for Johnson to gather laurels was for reconstruction to proceed quickly and effectively in the South. Stanton was determined that the Army would aid the President in this need.

Stanton felt that his own position, in relation to the various Republican factions, was a moderate one. He was "in betweenity," and he told James S. Scovel, a New Jersey Republican leader, that he wanted to "unite the conflicting interests of the republican party." [7]

Therefore, Stanton was particularly alert to opportunities for advancing these goals when on May 8 his plan of reconstruction came up as the principal order of business before the cabinet. Stanton knew that Welles was in opposition to many of its features, but he expected support from Kentuckian James Speed, the Attorney General since 1864, and from Blair's replacement as postal head, William Dennison, an old Ohio acquaintance. The new Treasury Secretary, Hugh McCulloch, of Indiana, was an unknown quantity. Fellow Hoosier John P. Usher was due to relinquish the Interior portfolio within a week; Stanton hoped that Usher's successor, James Harlan, of Iowa, would prove to be an ally. Seward was still painfully recuperating and it was not yet known whether he would be able to resume his responsibilities at the State Department.

Whatever the cabinet members thought, decision was up to the new President. And so Stanton reintroduced his proposal for a centralized provost marshal corps less in the hope that Johnson would approve the suggestion than from a desire to educate him and the cabinet concerning the nature of the Army's problems in the South. The Secretary had also separated his proposal for Virginia from that for North Carolina. He had received word from Halleck that even the Virginia Unionists regarded the Pierpont government as a sham. Stanton proposed using it only as a medium for calling and supervising an election to choose new state officials.

Stanton's proposal was designed merely as an interim arrangement, to build on what the Army was already doing without a plan while waiting for higher authority to give purpose, direction, and meaning to its occupation of the South. He had no conception of his draft as a sophisticated or complete scheme, and he was committed to almost none of its provisions. It was a sketch, not a blueprint.

[7] Stanton and Scovel's testimony, *Impeachment Report*, 35, 403, 622; Dana to J. S. Pike, May 10, 1865, CFL; Brady to Stanton, May 14, 1865, Stanton MSS; McKitrick, *op. cit.*, 42–84.

Welles, ever suspicious of Stanton, saw his plan as a design for extending permanent military control over Virginia. But when he again objected to the proposed reform of the provost marshal organization, and to the abandonment of the Pierpont government, and persuaded other cabinet members to sustain these objections, Stanton, after defending the need for the provost reform, surprised him by surrendering with "alacrity and cheerfulness." The War Secretary thereupon amended his proposal so as to commit the federal government to aid Pierpont, and the provost matter was cut from the text.

Stanton's plan for North Carolina again came before the cabinet the next day, and the members studied it carefully, for whatever was adopted for North Carolina would probably become a pattern for the other states. Following the plan worked out by Lincoln and put into effect in Louisiana, Tennessee, and Arkansas, Stanton proposed that the President appoint a provisional governor for North Carolina. It would be the duty of this official, acting under the protection of federal troops, to see to it that delegates were elected to a convention to draw up a new or revised state constitution providing for a republican form of government. The state could then resume its proper relationship to the Union.

Stanton proposed to allow all "loyal citizens" to vote in this election, and he included Negroes in this category, as he had promised Sumner that he would, in order to break the deadlock between the White House and the Republicans in Congress that had so far balked the reconstruction process. Stanton did not know that Johnson had already told young Frank Blair that he "meant to . . . make the [Southern] states qualify their own voters." When Stanton asked for a poll of the cabinet officers to determine whether the majority were for or against Negro suffrage in the Southern states, Welles, who, like Johnson, never realized that this issue could not remain static, objected that Lincoln had already decided this matter in the 1863 reconstruction proclamation. The President nevertheless called for a vote. The cabinet divided equally. Stanton, Dennison, and Speed favored Negro suffrage; Welles, Usher, and McCulloch opposed it. On returning to the cabinet after his close call with death, Seward lined up against votes for the blacks.

Johnson took no part in the discussion. He said he would reserve his decision pending further study of the question. It soon became evident that he had no intention of forcing Negro suffrage on the South. Stanton had fulfilled his promise to Sumner that he would include a pro-

445

vision for Negro voting in his proposal. But Stanton's conviction on the issue was still plastic. He knew that Grant did not favor votes for Negroes and he recognized that the President's mind was fixed. Stanton made no attempt to change it.[8]

During the next two weeks, Johnson, with some advice from Stanton and Grant, worked out two proclamations dealing with reconstruction and amnesty. The Secretary and the general agreed that almost anything was better for the Army than the present rudderless drifting; the President's proposals would certainly serve as a stopgap until Congress met.

On May 29, Johnson put his plan into effect by proclaiming the appointment of William H. Holden as provisional governor of North Carolina. Every member of the cabinet assented to his exclusion of Negroes from voting for delegates to the state constitutional convention, which in turn was to determine the qualifications for future voting and the eligibility of persons to hold office.

At the same time that he issued this proclamation, Johnson issued another granting amnesty and pardon, with certain exceptions, to all persons who had taken part in the rebellion. To obtain this pardon a person had only to swear that he would henceforth be loyal and would abide by all laws and proclamations relating to emancipation.

Johnson excluded from the benefits of the proclamation certain civil and military officers of the Confederacy, disloyal Northerners, all persons who had taken the oath of allegiance under Lincoln's 1863 proclamation and had subsequently violated it, and Southerners owning property valued at more than $20,000 who had voluntarily aided the rebellion. This reflected Johnson's conviction that the planter class should pay for its sins. He left a way open for even the excluded classes to obtain relief, however, by allowing anyone denied the benefits of the proclamation to petition him individually for pardon. His policy was based upon an expansive view of national executive power, and the Army was the keystone of the President's mechanism.

Meanwhile Johnson also announced the recognition of the Pierpont government in Virginia. In the course of the summer he extended his reconstruction policy to encompass Mississippi, Georgia, Texas, Ala-

---

[8] Elizabeth Blair Lee to Adm. S. P. Lee, May 18, 1865, Box XII, Blair-Lee Papers, PU; Welles, "Lincoln and Johnson," *Galaxy*, XIII, 521–3, 530–2; Welles to Johnson, July 27, 1869, in Beale, *Welles Diary*, III, 717–21, and see 733; *ibid.*, II, 301–3; memo, Jan. 22, 1866, Chase Papers, LC; *Impeachment Report*, 401; *O.R.*, XLVI, pt. 3, 571, 939.

bama, South Carolina, and Florida. He also confirmed the so-called "ten per cent" governments that Lincoln had instituted in Louisiana and Arkansas, and the government that he himself had inaugurated in Tennessee during the war.

Thus the reconstruction process, furthered by the Army, moved forward rapidly, and showed signs that it might be fully in operation before Congress assembled in December. Stevens, Wade, and Sumner, among many other legislators, became increasingly dissatisfied with the lenient terms that Johnson was offering the South, and unsuccessfully urged him to either call a special session or refrain from going any further until Congress met. Even men of moderate views complained that the President was usurping legislative powers.

Stanton and Johnson, however, seemed to be in substantial agreement on the course of affairs. The Secretary, Sumner learned, was convinced of the desirability of a moderate policy concerning the South.[9] That Sumner's information was correct is evidenced by a cabinet discussion on the subject of the "ironclad" test oath.

In 1862 Congress had prescribed that all federal officials must swear to this attestation of past loyalty as a requirement for employment. The "ironclad" oath was becoming a symbol of the radical Republicans' views on what a proper reconstruction should be, for its enforcement in the South would exclude almost all Southern whites from participation in government.

Late in June, McCulloch reported that he could not find qualified Southern whites to fill the great number of reopened revenue offices there. Stanton agreed with the President that McCulloch should modify the oath so that it would amount only to a promise of future loyalty or waive it altogether. Similarly, Stanton paid out of army funds the salaries and expenses of the provisional governors and the subordinate officials whom Johnson had chosen to lead the Southern states back into the Union, though none of those men could qualify for any federal position under the "ironclad" oath's stipulations concerning past loyalty. Each of the Southern governors had received a pardon from the President for their participation in the rebellion. In mid-1865, Stanton thought that when Congress assembled, the legislators would accept reconstruction as an accomplished and desirable

---

[9] *Impeachment Report*, 831–6; Richardson, *Messages and Papers*, VI, 310–14; Stevens to Sumner, May 10, June 3, 14, and Hooper to same, May 22, 1865, Sumner Papers, HU; Pierce, *Sumner*, IV, 235; Stevens to Johnson, May 16, and Johnson to Stanton, June 3, 1865, Johnson Papers, LC.

fact and would sustain the executive officers in their evasion of the oath law.[1]

Whether such swift forgiveness for the defeated rebels marked the course of wisdom depended on the sincerity of the South's repentance and the quality of the state governments set up by Lincoln and Johnson. According to some observers, the Southerners were thoroughly whipped and knew it. They were ready to rejoin the Union in good faith, recognize the new status of the Negro, and deal justly with him.

Other observers, however, saw conditions as less idyllic. To be sure, they reported, the erstwhile rebels had been humble in the hour of defeat, when they feared Northern vengeance, and had been most friendly for a while with the triumphant federal soldiers and the Unionists and seemed disposed to accept their leadership. But once convinced that they had nothing to fear, their attitude had stiffened. Unionists, Negroes, Yankee veterans now living in the South, and occupation soldiers were being ostracized, if not worse. Treason, far from being odious, was becoming the badge of social acceptability.[2]

In his office at the War Department, Stanton found himself daily more and more enmeshed in the realities that lay behind these generalizations. He thought for a while that the Freedmen's Bureau, established as an autonomous unit of the War Department by Congress on March 3, 1865, would afford the Southern Unionists and Negroes adequate protection. On May 10, Stanton named one-armed General O. O. Howard, "the Christian soldier," as head of the Bureau, an appointment that Lincoln had wanted made. The Bureau became a sort of welfare agency for Southern blacks, and it also took over the administration of justice in cases where the rights of Negroes were involved, as well as control of abandoned and confiscated Southern lands.

Howard was a conscientious, high-minded man, but some of his subordinates were not always capable, discreet, or even honest. Northern Democrats professed to believe that the Bureau was only a Republican job-making machine, whereas Southerners regarded it as a "foreign" agency supported by an army of occupation. Bureau officers reported on unfriendly Southern reaction to their work, and through Howard, Stanton saw these accounts. He also received news from army

---

[1] Morse, *Welles Diary*, II, 318–19; Hyman, *Era of the Oath* (Philadelphia, 1954), 95–118.

[2] Chase to Johnson, May 17, 1865, Johnson Papers, LC; same to Stanton, May 20, 1865, Stanton MSS. See also Walter S. Fleming, *Documentary History of Reconstruction* (Cleveland, 1906–7), I, 46–62; Francis Butler Simkins, *A History of the South* (New York, 1953), 255.

occupation commands of increasingly serious jurisdictional conflicts between the Bureau's special tribunals, provost courts, and the state civil courts now revived by the Northern soldiery. Stanton took no sides in this dispute at first; the Bureau was the radical Republicans' pet and he and President Johnson were careful, at this point at least, to stay in a middle course.[3]

But the situation in the South worsened as the summer of 1865 advanced. Army commanders were irked that Bureau personnel by-passed them and reported directly to Howard. Bureau officers professed to believe that most regular army men were anti-Negro. Southern state government officials damned them both.

Grant and Stanton tried to work out these conflicts as they arose, but the Secretary was becoming convinced from the reports he received that Southern whites were unregenerate. Army officers complained that the civil officials of the restored state governments which they were nurturing on their bayonets, had little gratitude; state officers were refusing to protect Union Army personnel and veterans now living in the South from insults and, in many instances, from actual physical assaults by civilians. Stanton endorsed one such report from Florida: "Look into this; see the Gen." Grant agreed with the Secretary that it was intolerable that American soldiers and veterans should be so rudely handled by the former enemy. They agreed, too, that authenticated reports of Southerners defiling the graves of fallen Northern troops, of deliberately plowing up Union Army cemeteries, mutilating the corpses, and destroying markers, could not be ignored. But the President, receiving these reports, apparently did nothing about them.[4]

The progress of Johnson's pardon and amnesty program became the most telling argument to Stanton that the President was on the wrong track. After the amnesty proclamation was issued, Stanton ordered army personnel in the South to administer the loyalty oaths as prescribed. Many soldiers were disgusted at the sight of prominent former rebels rushing to swear loyalty to the Union they had tried to destroy. "Now the scramble is to who shall get down first and lowest," Badeau wrote. Most Union Army officers felt that Southerners were knowingly perjuring themselves by their oath taking.

[3] O. O. Howard, *op. cit.*, II, 207–8; George S. Bentley, *A History of the Freedmen's Bureau* (Philadelphia, 1955); IGO, Extracts of Reports, 1865–8, II, 297, RG 159; Army Commands, Department of Georgia, VIII, 11–12, RG 98, NA.

[4] Bureau of Freedmen, Refugees, and Abandoned Lands, AAG, Vol. XLIV, 202, 290, RG 105; Army Commands, Provost Marshal, Virginia, Vol. XXXVI, 29–30, RG 195; Union Provost Marshal File, Miscellaneous, Box 70, RG 109, NA; Sheridan to Holt, April 28, 1866, Sheridan Papers, LC.

President Johnson, ignoring criticisms of his policy, continued to pardon rebels in an increasing volume. The business of securing these prized pardons became a scandal in Washington, and Stanton grew offended at what he saw daily in the capital. So far as is known, however, he protested only once to Johnson concerning a pardon petition. After reviewing the petitioner's contributions to the rebellion, Stanton wrote: "It shows that if the rebellion were any crime his guilt is without apology." But Johnson granted the pardon.[5]

Stanton was not, however, at one with the radicals, who did not, in any case, have a cohesive position for him to agree with. But he did have a professional dedication to his work and a personal loyalty to the military institution. Johnson's pardon policy, he began to fear as the summer wore on, must return to power in the South the very men for whose downfall the Union armies had shed so much blood. Stanton admitted to Chase in mid-August that he was becoming apprehensive that Johnson would accede to the demands of the Southern provisional governors for a complete withdrawal of Union troops.

At his fingertips were the facts of what was going on in the South. Although the provisional governors reported directly to the President, the army commanders in the South and the Freedmen's Bureau officials sent their accounts to the War Department. Stanton did not like what he saw, and he confided some of his misgivings to Lieber under the strictest injunction to secrecy.

In addition to being disturbed by Southern developments, Stanton disliked the fact that in Washington the President was cold-shouldering the Republicans who had elected him to office and favoring advocates of a soft policy toward the South, Democrats in the main. But though uneasy, Stanton was still honestly in support of Johnson. He deplored any talk of a break between Johnson and the Union party.[6]

Johnson, taciturn to the point of secretiveness, found that he was displeasing extremists in both political camps. Conservative Democrats condemned him for authorizing the use of any military force in the South at all and for sustaining the sentences of the Lincoln conspirators and war criminals such as Henry Wirz. They conspired to oust

[5] Badeau to Gen. J. H. Wilson, July 24, 1865, Wilson Papers, LC; IGO, Extracts of Reports, 1865–8, II, 331, RG 159, NA; Chase to Johnson, May 23, 1865, John Russell Young Papers, LC; Stanton to Johnson, June 18, 1865, Johnson Papers, LC; Jonathan T. Dorris, "Pardon Seekers and Brokers: A Sequel of Appomattox," *JSH*, I, 276–92; Hyman, "Deceit in Dixie," *CWH*, III, 65–82.

[6] Chase to Sumner, Aug. 20, 1865, Chase Papers, 2d ser., LC; Lieber to same, July 28, 1865, HL; for reports, see Sec. War Correspondence File, Box 318, RG 107, NA; and on party alignments, McKitrick, *op. cit.*, 70–6.

Stanton from the cabinet as the first step in redirecting the President's course. And they dangled before Johnson the lure of the headship of a Democratic party reunited in its Northern and Southern branches and again capable of sweeping the polls against any contenders that the young, faction-ridden, and sectional Republican party could pit against it. For the present, Johnson held aloof.

Radical Republicans were equally perturbed. Not only was reconstruction proceeding in defiance of their expressed views, but party conventions, both Republican and Democratic, dominated by moderates, which met during the summer in various Northern states, pledged support of the President's reconstruction program.

Inside Johnson's cabinet, the moderates who hoped that the Union party coalition would assume a permanent postwar form, and who favored Negro suffrage for the South—Stanton, Speed, Dennison, and Harlan—concluded that the majority of the people in the North would not support votes for the black man. Stanton, in addition, heard opinions from Grant, Garfield, and others that the Army's professional officers, rapidly replacing the wartime volunteers in command positions, were advocates of white supremacy and were unsympathetic to the Republican politicians' plans for raising the Negro to the ballot box in the South. Temporarily accepting this conclusion, although he later became convinced of its error, Stanton shared his friend Pierrepont's belief that the President was sincerely concerned with advancing the Negro's welfare.

To differ with Johnson might drive him completely into the hands of the Democrats. At the very least it would lead to a split among the Republicans. There was no conclusive reason yet for Stanton to believe that the President's basic assumptions concerning reconstruction were in error, though details were going awry. So Stanton and the others continued to support Johnson's policy—or, more accurately, they did not oppose it—and Sumner complained that the cabinet "had turned into a company of courtiers." [7]

Meanwhile, however, the trend of events in the Southern states strengthened the hands of Stevens and Sumner. When Johnson's provisional governors began calling elections for delegates to state constitutional conventions, and it became evident that not many of the men chosen in the seceded states could qualify for political office without a

[7] Sumner to Stevens, July 12, 1865, Sumner Papers, HU; Barlow to M. Blair, April 21, May 10, 1865, Letterbook XI, 284, 369–71, Barlow Papers, HL; Jacob D. Cox to Garfield, July 21, 1865, Garfield Papers, LC; Pierrepont to Stanton, April 27, 1865, Stanton MSS.

pardon, Johnson continued to grant pardons freely. He let it be known, however, that the state conventions would be expected to take action formally abolishing slavery, renouncing the ordinances of secession, and repudiating the Confederate war debts. Johnson also wired Governor Sharkey, of Mississippi, whose convention was the first to assemble, that he hoped the delegates would grant voting privileges to Negroes who were able to read and write or who owned real estate worth $250, so as to "completely disarm the adversary and set an example the other States will follow."

Though very few Negroes could have voted under such a provision, neither Mississippi nor any other state saw fit to follow the path of political wisdom by granting this or any similar concession. Northern moderates found reason for suspicion when a number of Southern states repudiated their rebel war debts only with extreme reluctance and worded their resolutions so as to make it clear that not they but the national government had abolished slavery.[8]

In the Southern state elections that followed the conventions, so many unpardoned rebels were elected to local offices and to Congress that even Johnson began to lose patience. As President, he could pardon individual past acts of rebellion. But in 1864 Congress had extended the provisions of the "ironclad" test oath to its own members. Few of the men that the South chose as delegates to Congress could swear to their past loyalty to the Union without perjury. Some stood charged with treason against the United States.

Johnson, again forgetting his theories concerning the autonomy of the states, pressured the South to choose men for Congress who could swear to the test oath. By selecting officeholders from among white Unionists like himself, the former Confederate states could have found representatives qualified for admission to Congress on the basis of past loyalty to the Union. Such strategy would have forestalled Republican claims that the South was unregenerate, made it impossible for the radicals to gain the support of moderate Republicans in excluding Southern delegations from Congress, and helped to convince most Northerners, Stanton included, that Negro suffrage was unnecessary in the South.

But instead of heeding Johnson's sage advice, Southerners persisted in choosing their wartime leaders to represent them in Congress. In addition to being abysmally poor politics, this was an arrogant as-

[8] Milton, *op. cit.*, 249–65; Rhodes, *op. cit.*, V, 535–9; W. D. Shipman to Barlow, Aug. 29, 1865, Barlow Papers, HL.

sumption that the only fault in the South's treason had been its failure. Southerners, it appeared, expected to suffer no consequences at all for the rebellion. In Louisiana the Democratic platform called for Congress to grant compensation for the emancipated slaves and appealed for a general amnesty and prompt restitution of confiscated property. It seemed to Stanton, as to many other Northerners, that the South's supplications were becoming demands. The South's insensitivity to the fact that it had recently been in rebellion, and to the opinion of moderate Northerners, played directly into the hands of the Republican radicals.[9]

Equally unsettling to Stanton and other distrustful Northerners were the "Black Codes" being enacted by Southern state legislatures. To be sure, new state laws, now that Negroes were no longer property, were needed to stabilize the restless, wandering hordes of freedmen. In every Southern state, the codes uniformly acknowledged that slavery was ended, recognized the marriage relationship between Negroes, and allowed them to assume responsibility for their children.

Certain other aspects of these codes, however, struck Northerners as unfair and discriminatory. Negroes could sue and be sued and testify in court, but only in cases involving other Negroes. In all instances the codes put black workers into a status less than free if no longer slave, barred Negroes from jury duty and forbade their bearing arms, and in many cases prescribed harsher penalties for Negroes than for white men committing the same crime.[1]

Stanton was becoming increasingly disgusted by the evidence that the South had learned nothing from its experiment in rebellion, and that the Southerners returning to power intended to continue their exploitation of the Negro. "Every day reveals the deplorable results of war on our own people and the degeneracy that follows in its train," he wrote in mid-August to a friend. "I am still toiling away in the Department, but hope only for a little while."

He was desperately tired; his serious attack in July, combined with the emotional strains of the past few months, had worn him down. Ellen, herself not well, badgered him to resign. Speed noted that "Stanton's friends have been pressing him to go away and take some rest. I think if he does not he is likely to be a great sufferer."

Stanton decided to take the much needed vacation. It might restore

[9] Stanton to Dana, August 10, 1865, copy owned by the estate of Benjamin P. Thomas; Hyman, *Era of the Oath*, 83–8; Fleming, *op. cit.*, I, 229–30; *O.R.*, ser. 2, VIII, 818.

[1] Lieber to Stanton, July 30, 1865, Stanton MSS; Fleming, *op. cit.*, I, 273–312.

his dissipated strength, and would at least offer him an opportunity to think about his own future. If he decided not to leave the war office, then he must also come to some decision concerning his views on reconstruction.

Ellen's mother came to Washington to care for the younger children. Eckert and the oldest boy, Edwin Lamson Stanton, received the Secretary's detailed instructions on maintaining telegraphic communication with him. On August 21, Stanton and Ellen started north in search of cooler weather. A Department telegrapher accompanied the party, for Stanton would not cut himself off completely from his work.

Reconstruction concerns followed him. In Mississippi, Governor Sharkey began to recruit state militia forces from among pardoned former rebels. General H. W. Slocum, commanding in Mississippi, issued orders prohibiting the formation of such units, considering them violations of the paroles of former rebels and patent threats to the freedmen. Johnson supported the governor.

Army officers were angered at this new example of Southern temerity and resented Slocum's humiliation. General Manning Force, on duty in Mississippi, wrote: "If it were not that good faith to the colored people requires the government to defend their interests a while, the simplest course would be to withdraw all troops at once." And he wondered: "How far are we bound in honor, to supervise the state laws [in the South] upon the . . . freedmen?" [2]

Stanton kept out of this affair. His party remained for a blissful week at a New Jersey seaside resort to enjoy the surf, delaying a scheduled inspection of the Military Academy. "The tyrannical old Turk was hourly expected at the Point . . . but he did not appear," recorded George T. Strong. While in New Jersey, Stanton heard from his son that little of importance was transpiring in Washington. But Grant wired him for permission to remove a general from duty with the Freedmen's Bureau in Georgia because of his "prejudices in favor of color." Stanton ordered Eckert to comply with Grant's request; he and the commanding general were by no means committed to radicalism.

By prearrangement, Seward also kept watch on events for Stanton; the two men, though drifting apart in politics, kept a respect for each other based on their shared affection for Lincoln. Eckert called on the

[2] Speed to Lieber, July 5, 1865, HL; Stanton to J. L. Bates, Aug. 14, Schurz to Stanton, Aug. 29, Slocum to same, Aug. 29, and Sharkey to Johnson (copy), Aug. 30, 1865, Stanton MSS; Force, ms Private Journal, II, 220-2, UW; Force to Bliss, Aug. 25, 1865, Bancroft-Bliss Papers, LC; on the trip, Bates, *op. cit.*, 401-2; *ANJ* (Sept. 16, 1865), 49; McKitrick, *op. cit.*, 163-4, 192-5.

President daily to ask for instructions, and then sent on Johnson's requests for Stanton's opinions. Stanton, incapable of thorough vacationing, asked Eckert to check with the President and the cabinet on whether anything required him to return to Washington at once; in reply, Eckert assured Stanton that he could finish his trip, for Johnson and Seward thought no crisis was at hand and Speed had said: "Stay and enjoy your rest, while you can."

Each day, Stanton sent off to Eckert a long wire containing decisions on pending matters and inquiries on others. But Stanton had so impressed himself on the Department that bureau officers held up many matters until he returned. However, despite the numerous items of business that followed them on their vacation, the Stantons enjoyed themselves. They reached West Point on September 4 after inspecting a half-dozen forts around New York City, where the Secretary interviewed imprisoned Stephen Russell Mallory, former Confederate Navy Secretary, and concluded that Mallory still had not altered his convictions. A telegram from young Edwin told them; "All is well. . . . Bessie very bright. You better not return until this boiling weather subsides, the thermometer is 90 out here at the Point of Desperation in the City." Another wire, from Seward, assured Stanton: "I am watchful & I shall remain here. You need not return this week." [3]

While inspecting the Military Academy, Stanton learned that Montgomery Blair, who had publicly returned to the Democratic party, had scathingly denounced him, accusing him of pro-secession sentiments in 1860 and of now playing butcher at the guillotine whenever Thad Stevens ordered a campaign of decapitation. Along with this news, however, came reassurances from Eckert: Johnson had expressed to Seward full trust in Stanton, saying that "he would not listen to so offensive remarks from Mr. B. or any one else."

Thus advised, Stanton decided to continue the trip, for Ellen was still not herself. At West Point, Surgeon General and Mrs. Barnes joined the Stantons, and the party moved on to Newport, Rhode Island, where they were lavishly entertained. Stanton enjoyed his first experience at sailing; "a charming ride on a calm clear sea, with bright blue skies above us." But criticism hit at him even here.

A reporter of the Newport *Daily News* asserted that a luxurious steamboat had been chartered by the government in order to transport the Stanton party up the coast. The fact was, as the editor of that paper

[3] Strong, *Diary*, IV, 30; Edwin L. Stanton to Stanton, Aug. 29, Sept. 4, Grant to same, Aug. 3, Stanton to Eckert, Sept. 1, 2, and to Seward and reply, Sept. 4, 1865, Stanton MSS; Hardie to Col. F. I. Lippitt, Sept. 4, 1865, Hardie Papers, LC.

admitted in a retraction the next day, that the ship had been under government charter since 1861; it would have come to Newport in any case. In a personal letter of apology to Stanton, the editor assured him that no one who knew his services to the nation believed this canard.

Despite this unfortunate incident, the Stantons enjoyed Newport. "Mrs. Stanton looked very pretty, while the Secretary [was] . . . civil to everybody," wrote Mrs. George Bancroft, and she added that he had told her, concerning her son's marriage to a Southern girl he had met during his Union Army service: "I am glad that you are extending your ties southward." [4] He was less sure concerning the kinds of ties with which the President was seeking to bind the former rebels to the war-weary nation, and he wondered whether Blair had had "the left-handed assent of Johnson to make the attack" on him, or whether Johnson saw Blair's speech as an onslaught against the President as well as the Secretary. But Stanton worried most over Johnson's inconsistencies, and concluded that he was "trying to ride two horses and he probably means to join the party which finally [wins]." If this was true, and Johnson hoped to go along with the prevailing wind once its strength and direction were clear, then, it seemed to Stanton, it was his task to help steer events so that the President would tack the right way.

Whether or not the black man voted in the South would determine the issue.[5]

[4] *ANJ* (Sept. 16, 1865), 57; Eckert to Stanton, Sept. 5, 9, Stanton to Mrs. I. Bell, Sept. 12, and G. T. Hammond to Stanton, Sept. 15, 1865, Stanton MSS; Newport *Daily News*, Sept. 14, 15, 1865; Mrs. Bancroft to "Lundy," Sept. 15, 1865, Bancroft-Bliss Papers, LC; Blair, *op. cit.*, 15–16.

[5] W. D. Shipman to Barlow, July 14, Aug. 29, and Barlow to Shipman, Oct. 25, 1865, Barlow Papers, Letterbook XI, 226–8, HL, recounting conversations with Stanton at Newport.

DECISION

$\mathbb{C}$ONTINUING their trip, the Stantons came to Boston at the beginning of the third week in September, and stayed at the home of Congressman Samuel Hooper. Sumner was an intimate of the Hooper family, and the Secretary and the senator saw a great deal of each other in those long autumn days. Through Sumner, Stanton came to a crucial judgment concerning his course.

Although he had created a reputation for independent thought and action, Stanton had always been suggestible to stronger personalities. In his youth the preachments of Kenyon professors had firmly set his attitudes toward religion. Subsequently his impressionable nature was further demonstrated by the impact that the elder Tappan, Chase, Black, and, above all others, Lincoln, had on his professional career and on his social views. Now Sumner irrevocably affected him.

Back in April, Sumner had convinced him that Congress would demand Negro participation in the rebuilding of the Southern state governments, though Stanton had chosen not to press the matter then. During the intervening months, the deficiencies he had observed in the working out of the President's reconstruction plan had altered Stanton's views on the Negro as a citizen. Earlier he had distrusted the black man's ability to function as a voter and officeholder. Although he was by no means converted to an appreciation of the freedman as a social equal, Stanton now inclined to the belief that Sumner had been prophetically correct on the need for the Negro to vote in the South if the North's victories on a hundred battlefields were to be perpetuated.

During Stanton's visit in Boston, Sumner delivered the keynote address at the Massachusetts Republican state convention at nearby

Worcester. His theme was the right of all Negroes to "irreversible guarantees" of equal status with whites and a condemnation of the policy of the President. Congress should control the reconstruction process. Ample time should be taken to determine the terms to be offered, he said, but in all events the Constitution should be amended so as to prevent the denial of the suffrage to anyone on grounds of race or color.

Referring directly to Stanton, the senator said that there was still need for his energy in the government. The region that had been won to Union and liberty by the victory he had organized must not be abandoned to its ancient masters. "Let it be held by arms until it smiles with the charities of life," he urged. "A righteous government cannot be founded on any exclusion of race." According to Sumner, the Secretary told him that he had read the address and approved every word of it, thanked him for his complimentary references, and "asked him to do only what he wanted to do." [1]

Thus, in September 1865, Stanton apparently accepted Sumner's goals. But he wanted to hold to a middle course in achieving them.

With Ellen visibly improving in health, he decided to cut their trip short. The Stantons had to decline a good many invitations, and he hated to miss a chance to see William Lloyd Garrison, but he began to feel anxious to return to Washington. During a stopover in New York City, they were sumptuously entertained by Senator Morgan, who gave a party attended by more than 400 guests, and the New York *Times* noted "the entire absence of political dodgery and popular fishing" by the Secretary. Stanton, the writer rather incredulously concluded, was after nothing but a good time.

Seward was told that Stanton was "entirely restored to health. He has received great attention and marks of respect every where. . . . He says he goes home now to give you an opportunity to come." [2]

True to his word, Stanton's return to Washington permitted Seward to go on vacation, and Stanton kept in touch with him as Seward had done while Stanton was away, by means of the War Department telegraph. Late in October, Seward publicly extolled Stanton as the

---

[1] Freidel, "Francis Lieber, Charles Sumner, and Slavery," *JSH*, IX, 75–93; Pierce, *Sumner*, IV, 258; Morse, *Welles Diary*, II, 394; Sumner, *Complete Works* (Boston, 1900), IX, 437–89.

[2] Stanton to Gen. E. D. Townsend, and to Mrs. I. Bell, Sept. 17, 1865, Stanton MSS; Garrison, *op. cit.*, IV, 152; *Times*, Sept. 23, 1865; R. M. Blatchford to Seward, Sept. 23, 1865, Seward Papers, UR.

Danton of the Civil War. Stanton rather enjoyed reading the criticisms of the hyperbolic speech and of himself which quickly appeared in the press, and he asked Ellen to keep these poetic comments:

STANTON AND DANTON

If souls transmigrate, as we are told,
By all the Pythagorians old,
I'm sure the bloody soul of Stanton
Came from the carcass of old Danton.

STANTON THE IMITATOR

What a grotesque tyrant is Stanton,
Who with infinite, laughable pains
Imitates all things in Danton,
Except the old butcher's brains.

Stanton could afford to be amused. His current annual report summed up the impressive achievements of the war, and he felt rightly confident that informed opinion would credit his accomplishments.[3]

Once settled again in the war office, he started to put into practice his new conviction of the need for protecting the Negro. When Schurz proposed to make an inspection tour of the South on Johnson's invitation, but also under secret radical auspices, Stanton urged him to go. Schurz's reports, said the Secretary, though they might not change the President's views, would be of vital interest to the next Congress. This comment could only mean that Stanton hoped that Congress would intervene to modify Johnson's policy. He similarly tipped his hand in a letter to Schuyler Colfax, scheduled to be the next Speaker of the House of Representatives, welcoming him back to Washington— "The next session will be of deep interest and fraught with consequences to the Government."

The wisdom of Stanton's decision received another confirmation when Provisional Governor Parsons, of Alabama, came to Washington in November to consult with political leaders on sectional reconciliation. He had been one of the most co-operative of the temporary governors, and Stanton commended him to Sumner and to other New England Republicans as "a loyal and patriotic man." But Parsons told Sumner that he would emigrate rather than allow Negroes to vote.

[3] Stanton to Seward, Oct. 14, 1865, Seward Papers, UR; Washington *National Republican*, Oct. 23, 1865, for Seward's speech; Morse, *Welles Diary*, II, 383–4; poems owned by Gideon Townsend Stanton; *ANJ* (Dec. 23, 1865), 277.

"What can we expect for the future when such a spirit leads?" Sumner asked Stanton. It was a question which the Secretary had already been propounding to himself.[4]

His mind now made up, Stanton proceeded to support the Freedmen's Bureau in its contest with the army provost marshals for jurisdiction in the South. He had long known that the provost organizations were inefficient, for they lacked a single head. As a result, in the words of Provisional Governor Perry, of North Carolina, "the Provost Marshals decide the same questions differently in almost every district." Perry as well as other Johnson appointees had pressured Stanton to suppress the Topsy-like provost apparatus, though not, of course, to assign its manifold functions to the Freedmen's Bureau.

By report, many provosts were anti-Negro in comparison with Freedmen's Bureau personnel. Yet everything indicates that Stanton opposed the provost units primarily to achieve a desirable administrative reform. Stability in the South was no longer a daily gamble. Substitution of a relatively centralized agency like the Freedmen's Bureau for the unsystematic provosts was a necessary improvement, quite apart from the political significance of the move.

In the last weeks of 1865, after consultations with Grant, Stanton ordered the Bureau to assume the provosts' functions. Bureau officers, deriving their authority from Congress rather than from the now uncertain President, would supervise the military courts in the South which had taken jurisdiction away from the state courts in cases involving Negroes. In effect, the Bureau's agents, as one unhappy Virginia editor noted, "are to be invested with the duties of Provost Marshals." [5]

A second factor, of more importance than the need for a mere administrative reform, convinced Stanton that the provost system was inadequate in the South. For he had come to the conclusion that the entire reconstruction process begun by Lincoln and continued under Johnson was a tragic farce, thwarting the purposes of the Presidents and involving the Army in disgraceful corruption.

In December 1864, Lincoln, becoming uneasy over the manner in

[4] Schurz, *Speeches, Correspondence, and Political Papers* (New York, 1913), I, 264-7, 271-4; Stanton to Colfax, Oct. 16, 1865, IndHS; Sumner to Stanton, Nov. 5, 1865, Stanton MSS; Stanton to Sumner, Nov. 6, 1865, Sumner Papers, HU.

[5] Perry to Johnson, Aug. 20, 1865, Johnson Papers, LC; O. O. Howard, *op. cit.*, II, 225-8, 258, 390; Final Report, Provost Marshal, Jan. 13, 1866, Army Commands, Georgia, IX, 78, RG 98, NA; Harrisonburg (Va.) *Register and Advertiser*, Feb. 2, 1866.

which reconstruction was working out in practice, had ordered an investigation of the civil-military administration of the Mississippi River region. As finally arranged, a special committee composed of General William F. Smith and James Brady, Stanton's colleague at the Sickles trial, headed the investigating group. They concentrated their work in Louisiana, the most highly developed product of the wartime executive reconstruction policy. Their final report, given to Stanton when he returned from his 1865 vacation trip, was a scathing indictment of the army provost marshal and provost court systems there and of the civil administrations built on the foundations of Lincoln's 1863 amnesty proclamation.

According to the Smith-Brady report, the entire civil government in Louisiana was "a vast scheme of fraud enforced by military rule, by means of which, a few political tricksters have taken the reins of government into their own hands." Provost marshals, in collusion with the "popularly-elected" civilian officials, had made a racket out of trade and travel permits. Treasury agents, in on the graft, slithered through loopholes in army and Treasury regulations to pad their own pockets. The supposedly loyal white population was unregenerate despite their oaths of allegiance, and the few white Unionists, along with the thoroughly loyal but mute Negroes, groaned under harsh exactions. Elections under this travesty of a representative system were attended with fraud, terrorism, and corruption. Though the Lincoln reconstruction plan had effectively weakened the will of Southerners to continue fighting a war, it was by no means equally effective as a blueprint for postwar reconstruction.

Stanton had brought this report to the new President, and he and Johnson, along with Grant, had studied it carefully. They realized that it was laden with political dynamite. Its publication must inevitably condemn by inference Lincoln's whole Southern policy and affect the morale of the Army, for the report blistered almost every officer connected with the western command since 1862. It also brought the value of Johnson's state governments in the South into the most serious question. Johnson, Stanton, and Grant agreed to suppress the report. But Stanton could not suppress his certainty that the continuation of reconstruction in its present course, in which the Army had to sustain men against whom it had fought and who involved it in sordid corruption, was against the interests of the soldiers and of the nation.

Therefore, he curtailed the provosts as a move toward closing the channels of graft and improving the existing reconstruction process.

Stanton : The Life and Times

Stanton still hoped to convince the President of the need to alter the route that reconstruction was taking so that it would include Negro voters and thus could rest on a wider, firmer base. What he knew of the President encouraged the Secretary in his conceit that Johnson might swing his way. "Johnson was at that time hanging in the wind," a visitor at the White House, J. C. Derby, recalled, and Stanton and his friends were trying "to bring him right." [6]

Stanton also tried to bring the President and the cabinet "right" on the problem of what to do with the still imprisoned Jefferson Davis. Hoping to find evidence that would implicate Davis in Lincoln's assassination, Stanton had employed as archivist his old wartime counselor, Lieber. Although Lieber found much useful material in the captured Confederate official papers, he failed to unearth evidence connecting Davis with the murder.

At Holt's suggestion, Stanton had also agreed to the employment of Sanford Conover as a government agent. Conover had already shown himself to be a perjurer in the trial of the Lincoln conspirators, and almost at once he came up with a number of affidavits and witnesses involving the Confederate leaders in the assassination plot. But all of them proved to be as shady as Conover himself.

Therefore, Stanton had come to favor trying Davis for treason, for he knew that his evidence was insufficient to implicate the Confederate President in Lincoln's murder, even though he was reluctant to admit it. He still hoped that, with a little more time, he would find something incriminating, and on his insistence the matter was allowed to hang fire. Stanton also let his own resignation hang fire, so that the search for positive evidence against Davis would continue. [7]

In December, however, as the members of Congress began straggling back to Washington, Stanton's thoughts again turned to a return to private life. He was weary and still far from well, and Ellen joined with their friend Pierrepont in urging him to resign and form a law

[6] Derby, *Fifty Years Among Authors, Books, and Publishers* (New York, 1884), 472. In May 1866, Congress asked for the Smith-Brady report. Stanton refused to turn it over, and, remarkably, the congressmen acquiesced in this decision; see *Investigations at New Orleans*, House Exec. Doc. 96, 39th Cong., 1st sess.; Smith-Brady Commission Testimony and Report, ms, RG 94, NA.

[7] Freidel, *Francis Lieber: Nineteenth-Century Liberal* (Baton Rouge, 1948), 369–75; Morse, *Welles Diary*, II, 337–9, 362–3; Pierce, *Sumner*, IV, 253; *O.R.*, ser. 2, VIII, 847–67, 890–2, 931–45; Frank, "The Conspiracy to Implicate the Confederate Leaders in Lincoln's Assassination," *loc. cit.*, 641–4.

partnership in New York City. But he was dissuaded from this course by the pleas of the men he most respected—Sumner, Grant, Lieber, Brady, and others—that he stay at his post.

To collect his thoughts concerning his future, Stanton left on a trip to Steubenville before the congressional session started. He found the train ride invigorating in the crisp winter weather, with sparkling snow covering the mountains and everything frozen tight. As before, he kept in touch with affairs by telegraph, and Eckert, left in charge in Washington, supplied him with daily summaries of events. From Steubenville he went on to Gambier, where Pamphila was now living, to be with his mother on her birthday, and to learn whether his contributions to their support, which had diminished since 1862 as a result of his reduced income, would continue to be adequate if he remained in the war office. Grateful for the chance to relax, he enjoyed talking to members of the Kenyon faculty, and spent quiet hours reading Dickens, his long-time favorite, while taking his ease on the sofa in Pamphila's parlor.

Although the Gambier trip rested him physically, Stanton remained uneasy in his mind about his personal future and the drift of political affairs. His discerning sister, taking pleasure in his enjoyment of reading aloud from *Little Dorrit* and *David Copperfield*, realized that "his anxieties . . . exceeded all he had known before." He warned her to burn all his future letters containing references to public matters, but he did not alarm his family by telling them that he was facing financial disaster as a result of the cumulative drain on his capital occasioned by his diminished income since 1862.

With these burdens to trouble his thoughts, Stanton returned to Washington in time for Christmas and to observe the early weeks of the first postwar Congress. The ordinarily flinty War Secretary was always mellow on family occasions, enjoying the festive tree and the Christmas gifts with Ellen and the youngsters. "Our children are rejoicing over a Christmas tree as vigorously as if the wax-tapers and trinkets that have made it so glorious to behold, were not the same that have done duty the last three years," he wrote to Pamphila, and pridefully recounted how his home was crowded with well-wishers and friends of the Stanton youngsters. True, he wrote to his mother-in-law in Pittsburgh, the Washington weather was so thick, foggy, and disagreeable that "Ellen finds everything, like Mrs. Gummidge, 'going contrairey.' But for all that the children are happy and noisy. Ellen thanks you for the portfolio, & [Eleanor] for her work box. Lewis sends his thanks to you . . . for the gifts he got. But Bessie caps them all for wild fun and pigeon pie." [8]

Stanton knew that this was a happy calm before the storm. Among the elected delegates to Congress now crowding the capital were members from all the late rebel states except Texas, where the President's reconstruction program had been delayed. The Republican leadership, prepared for this moment, had arranged that the rolls of the House and Senate remain bare of the names of delegates from the South. Excluded from their seats, the Southern members would have to keep knocking on the doors of Congress until a new joint committee of fifteen, dominated by Republicans, chose to decide all matters relating to reconstruction; nor would either house admit new members until this committee had reported that the Southern states were entitled to congressional seats. In all this, the Republican leaders hoped that the President would come to see things their way.

Johnson, though indignant at this parliamentary maneuver, had by no means decided to pit himself against his party's chieftains. On December 5, the President had read his annual message to Congress. Written by the historian George Bancroft, it was a dignified and forceful speech. Appealing to the North to forget the past, Johnson declared that although each house could judge the qualifications of its members, ratification of the Thirteenth Amendment by any Southern state should be sufficient indication of its sincere desire for peace and union to permit its representatives to be seated. The President denied that the federal government had any right to control suffrage in the states, but the freedmen must be secure in their liberty, their property, and their right to enjoy a just return from their labor, and if they showed "patience and manly virtues," the vote, too, might be theirs in time.

But inaction held little appeal for the altruistic Sumner or the tough-minded Stevens, and about the time that Stanton returned from his visit to Gambier, the forthright Pennsylvanian rose in the House to take issue with the President in a bitter speech. Reiterating a program of land distribution in the South which he had worked out during the previous summer, Stevens announced his belief that the safety of the nation depended on the continuance of the Republican party in office, and this in turn, Sumner insisted, depended on giving the Southern Negro the vote.

[8] Badeau, *Grant*, 139; Wolcott MS, 205–7; Stanton to Eckert, Dec. 16, 1865, Stanton MSS; to Mrs. Lewis Hutchison, Dec. 25, 1865, owned by Gideon Townsend Stanton. McKitrick, *op. cit.*, 3–250, best surveys the political scene and events of late 1865.

Stanton still displayed his capacity for friendship with men of vary-ing opinions. He privately favored Stevens's ideas, Stanton admitted to Chase, but he kept this as a private opinion, never seeking it as a political end, perhaps because he realized that it could not pass. Votes for the Southern Negro was as far as he would go.[9]

Justice for the freedman, whether political or economic, seemed far from the desires of Southerners, according to the testimony of witnesses before the reconstruction committee. This testimony, although un-reliable in part, was enough to confirm Stanton's suspicions that the newly elected officeholders in and from the South were a prejudiced and stiff-necked lot, intent on keeping the Negro "in his place" and re-gaining control of the national government. When it was rumored that Johnson planned to end the military occupation of the South, the army commanders in that area complained that such action would leave white Unionists and Negroes exposed to rebel vengeance, and the House rushed through a resolution protesting against the removal of troops until Congress "shall have ascertained and declared their further presence there unnecessary." It was said in some quarters that Stanton had prompted this resolution, which in Welles's opinion was "pur-posely offensive" to the President.

Showing his displeasure by appointing the West Point cadets-at-large without consulting Stanton—he had sought Stanton's advice the year before, and Lincoln had consistently done so earlier—Johnson also transferred the responsibility of paying the Southern state governors from Stanton to Seward. This was admittedly less efficient for all concerned, but Seward's views now seemed to be much closer to those the President held.[1]

Though it seemed to Welles that Stanton was clearly adrift from the President, Stanton's real position at this stage of the developing crisis was that of a prospective compromiser. John Binney, who had spoken to Stanton in New York City, understood Stanton's purpose when he wrote to Thad Stevens: "It is of great importance that you & the other Radical leaders should keep up communication with the President, if it is possible;—so that you may adjust your measures more harmoniously for practical cooperation. This you can manage,

[9] Ms memoir by A. S. Chambers, NYHS; ms memo, Jan. 2, 1866, Chase Papers, LC; and see Richardson, *Messages and Papers*, VI, 353–71; Ralph Korngold, *Thaddeus Stevens* (New York, 1955), 282–31.

[1] See Grant's reports on the South, Jan. 11–20, and G. W. Childs to Johnson, Jan. 11, 1866, Johnson Papers, LC; Morse, *Welles Diary*, II, 413; E. M. Pease to Stanton, Jan. 12, 1866, Sec. War Correspondence File, Box 318, RG 107, NA, on the payments, and Stanton to J. R. Hawley, May 10, 1866, Hawley Papers, LC, on the cadets.

I should suppose, through Mr. Stanton, . . . who is a most faithful & true friend of the cause. I believe the President will be in favor of the measures, if they are wisely conducted, & presented in practical statesmanlike shape." Israel Washburn, former governor of Maine, also regarded Stanton, along with Seward, as a moderating influence in the party, and advised the latter that though the President and Congress had become so antagonistic that he sometimes feared they could never work together again, yet "so long as you & Stanton remain in the Cabinet I shall have hope."

Other moderate Republicans also hoped for party harmony and foresaw only disaster in pushing Johnson to a showdown on the question of Negro suffrage in the South. Charles Ray, former editor of the Chicago *Tribune,* wrote Senator Trumbull that Johnson would capitalize on Northern race prejudice and become "cock of the walk" if Congress took an uncompromising stand on Negro suffrage. With the war emotions dying, Ray wrote, "people are more mindful of themselves than of any of the fine philanthropic schemes that look to making Sambo a voter, juror and office holder." Ray asserted that most Northerners wanted only to protect the Negro's civil rights and assure him a livelihood in the South.

Trumbull had recently drawn up two bills designed to accomplish that very object, and Ray believed that the Republican party should stand on that program and let Negro suffrage come with the march of time. If the President would support Trumbull's bills, compromise was more than possible, and there would be no necessity for a rift with him. Stanton could bring his own views into perfect accord with these.[2]

One of the bills that Trumbull was sponsoring provided for the continuation and extension of the Freedmen's Bureau, thus providing military protection for Negroes under legislative authority but with executive enforcement. The other proposal was designed so that national civil rights laws would more permanently safeguard the Negro's civil rights against state action. Trumbull was an upright, scholarly man whose opinions were far more moderate than those of Stevens and Sumner, and the Bureau expansion bill, the first of the two to be passed by Congress, was described by Senator Fessenden as a product of the best thought of an extremely able committee.

At Johnson's request Fessenden spent a morning discussing the bill

[2] Binney to Stevens, Jan. 5, 1866, Stevens Papers, LC; Washburn to Seward, Jan. 13, 1866, Seward Papers, UR; Dawes, "Recollections of Stanton under Johnson," *loc. cit.,* 499; Ray to Trumbull, Feb. 7, 1866, Trumbull Papers, LC.

with him, and he came away convinced that the President would agree to it and that it would be the means of bringing him and Congress together. The next day, when Fessenden told Stanton about this interview, the Secretary expressed great relief. He had feared that Johnson would veto the bill and felt pleased at the prospect of harmony.

Surprisingly, however, Johnson did not discuss the measure with the cabinet until, on February 19, he read the members a veto message that he proposed to send to Congress the next day. None of them dissented, as the President had already made up his mind; but Welles correctly concluded that Stanton was unhappy about what appeared to be a change of heart on Johnson's part.

It would not have been conceding much to Congress if Johnson had signed the Bureau bill. His refusal to do so tended to drive the moderate Republican sponsors and supporters of the measure toward the camp of the extremists, though for the moment enough Republicans chose to stick with Johnson, still the titular head of their party, to defeat an attempt to override his veto.

Johnson in his veto message not only disapproved of the Bureau bill but questioned Congress's right to legislate on matters vital to the Southern states while they remained unrepresented; he thus denied the entire moderate Republican position. It seemed now even more vital to many incensed Republicans that the freedmen be protected by the national government, and Stevens pushed through a resolution which stated that only Congress could declare a state entitled to representation. Thus, as a result of the President's intransigence, Republican party strategy which had excluded the Southern delegates the preceding December now became the announced policy of both houses of Congress. The legislators had declared that Johnson had made executive leadership in reconstruction unacceptable. It was a high price to pay for the veto.[3]

Stanton so far had kept quiet about his own feelings. He deliberately avoided making public speeches; at his request Bancroft substituted for him in offering a eulogy on Lincoln and an oration for Washington's birthday. On the latter occasion, a group composed mostly of Democrats applauded Johnson's veto of the Freedmen's Bureau bill and then moved on to the White House to salute him. Stirred by the crowd's enthusiasm and flushed with what he held to be a triumph, the President came out on a portico and gave vent to some impassioned oratory,

[3] Fessenden, *op. cit.*, II, 34–5; Morse, *Welles Diary*, II; 434–5; Benjamin B. Kendrick (ed.), *The Journal of the Joint Committee of Fifteen on Reconstruction* (New York, 1914), 230–1.

calling the Joint Committee on Reconstruction "an irresponsible central directory," denouncing Stevens and Sumner as traitors to the fundamental principles of government, and even accusing his political enemies of plotting his assassination. His outburst could not encourage those who still hoped for party harmony. "Whether the difference [between Johnson and Congress] is radical or only in degree," Meigs wrote the next day, "I don't feel competent to judge yet. But I deplore the breach which puts our President in an attitude . . . with all the copperheads and rebels and all the weak-kneed on his side." Here, Stanton's opinion is clearly reflected.[4]

There was still a hope of reconciliation if Johnson would approve the civil rights bill, the second measure that Trumbull had introduced. Friends of this measure expected Johnson to approve it. Designed to emasculate the "Black Codes," it classified the Negro as a citizen, gave him the right to acquire and hold property, make contracts, go and come at pleasure, teach, preach, and testify in court, and brought these privileges under the protection of the national government. It decreed equal status in law for blacks and whites and made anyone who deprived any citizen of equal rights in law subject to punishment under the exclusive jurisdiction of the federal courts.

Trumbull evidently intended it as a conciliatory measure, in line with some of the President's statements in his December message to Congress. But on March 24 Johnson informed the cabinet that he intended to veto it, and he wanted each member to express his opinion before he did so.

Stanton, exhibiting an intimate familiarity with the proposal, explained that he disliked some of the enforcement features of Trumbull's bill that were modeled on the Fugitive Slave Law of 1850, but that under existing circumstances Johnson should approve it. His reasoning, and his evident liaison with the Trumbull wing of the party's moderate leaders in Congress, carried no weight. Johnson had set himself unalterably against the bill, and the bid for compromise which it signified. It granted the black race safeguards beyond anything ever enjoyed by the white race, he complained in his veto message, and in encroaching on powers rightfully belonging to the states, it was a step toward unwarranted centralization of governmental authority. And again the President objected to the passage of a law affect-

[4] Stanton to Bancroft, Jan. 9, 24, 1866, Bancroft Papers, MHS; and Bancroft to Stanton, Feb. 7, 1866, Stanton MSS; Meigs to father, Feb. 23, 1866, Meigs Letterbooks, LC.

ing all the states while Congress denied representation to eleven of them.

Within two weeks both the Senate and the House had passed the bill over Johnson's veto, the first time in the nation's history that such action had been taken on a major measure, though the Republican leaders had to resort to desperate expedients to push the repassage through. It seemed that the party breach had now become irreparable, as Johnson would yield nothing, for the sake of harmony, to moderate Republican sentiment, though the rich prize of the support of the middle-roaders was well within his reach.

Discerning, troubled Northerners, such as the diarist Strong, veered away from Johnson. "I fear that these vetoes shew Johnson's sympathies and prejudices to be wrong and dangerous," Strong wrote. "I am losing my faith in him." This was coming about through no logical process, the diarist confessed, but through an instinctive distrust of a man in whom so many copperhead and erstwhile rebel newspapers showed such unbounded faith. Strong thought the Republicans were fully justified in insisting upon the establishment of certain safeguards before restoring home rule and full recognition to the South. He shuddered when people asked him: "Would you make the South another Poland?" But he answered inwardly: "By all means, if it be expedient." The same sort of thoughts and misgivings must have passed through Stanton's mind.

Welles was ready to believe that Stanton had been guilty of lining up votes to undo Johnson's veto, and Johnson heard from other sources that Harlan and Speed as well as Stanton were disloyal to him.[5] A clamor for the War Secretary's removal that had been intermittent since the preceding December grew louder. But leading Republicans, though puzzled as to why Stanton remained silent on the political issues of the moment, pressured him to retain his office. His friend Pierrepont, still nominally a Democrat, received the first definite word that the War Secretary would stay on, and signaled the information to the public at a dinner speech in New York City that was later directed to the President's attention in the newspapers.

Stanton was pleased at this evidence of bipartisan support, but he did not think it impossible that the President would ask him to resign, although he wrote to Ellen in March that the newspaper rumors that described a change in the war office "were no doubt got up for specu-

[5] See *Harper's Weekly*, X, 226; Strong, *Diary*, IV, 76; Morse, *Welles Diary*, II, 463–4, 479–80; Browning, *Diary*, II, 65; Fleming, *op. cit.*, I, 197–200.

lating purposes." He hoped that "[General] Sherman will be my successor and this I would prefer to any arrangement likely to be made."

Stanton was not acting the politician. He was Secretary of War, and he placed this responsibility ahead of party purposes. Sherman was in accord with the President's reconstruction proposals, and Stanton knew that the general still hated him because of the unhappy events of the year past. Yet Stanton wanted him as his successor rather than any of the partisan candidates who so coveted the post, because he thought that Sherman would know how to run the Army and how to shield it.[6]

In his mediating position in the cabinet, Stanton had not gone any further than to criticize certain proposed actions of the President and in each instance he had finally acquiesced in them. Nor had he ever opposed Johnson's policies publicly. The President's suspicions that Stanton was divulging administration secrets to high-ranking Republicans were based only on the fact that the War Secretary stood high in their favor.

Stanton ranked high in the estimation of most persons. In an administration which was rapidly losing the support of the Republican-Union party, he was so much a symbol of the solidity which the public thought had existed under Lincoln that Johnson hesitated to break with him. Stanton was also, Johnson realized, the best administrator among the cabinet officers.

The Johnson administration still had three years to run. Neither man wished to precipitate a rupture that must involve their personal futures, the fate of what they still thought of as their common Union party, and the destiny of the Southern region and of the nation. Stanton still desired to serve as an adjustor between the President and Congress. He would not destroy what might be the last bridge to accommodation by resigning from the cabinet. And though he was reasonably sure that Grant felt as he did about events, Stanton was not positive. Until he knew that the Army's interests were safe, he could not abandon the war office; he was afraid that his successor might be someone who would overawe the seemingly simple, malleable commanding general.

[6] Detroit *Post, Chandler*, 299; Pierrepont speech in New York *Evening Express*, Jan. 12, 1866; Stanton to Ellen, March 19, 1866, owned by Gideon Townsend Stanton.

CHAPTER XXIII

THEY MUST MUSTER ME OUT

$\mathbb{A}$FTER Appomattox, Grant had feared that Stanton might try to dominate him in the internal affairs of the Army. For his part, Stanton was at first worried that the immensely popular Grant would bypass him in the way that prewar commanding generals had flanked former War Secretaries. By the end of 1865, however, though they had a few minor disagreements, the two men settled into a comfortable and complementary relationship. Grant made the commanding general's office more important than the war office in army administration, as it had been in prewar days—a development which Stanton favored in the interest of peacetime efficiency.

Stanton relied on Grant's opinions on basic army policy and military relations with the public. They agreed fully on problems of demobilization, army reorganization, surplus property disposal, civilians' claims against the military, and the desirability of army rather than Interior Department jurisdiction over the western Indians. Together, Stanton and Grant proposed early in 1866 that Congress establish a new permanent provost bureau in the War Department to deal with recruiting and desertion matters. But when the matter became enmeshed in a personal feud between General Fry and Congressman Conkling, and Grant shied away from a contest with the powerful legislator, Stanton followed his lead and let the matter drop. Years later, Grant remembered how "every day . . . we grew better and better friends." [1]

---

[1] Young, *Around the World*, II, 358; Grant to Stanton, Jan. 29, 1866, Stanton MSS; Badeau, *Grant*, 86; Hesseltine, *Grant*, 66–7; Fry, *The Conkling and Blaine–Fry Controversy in 1866* (New York, 1893), 17, 158–9; Stanton to House Military Affairs Committee, Feb. 19, 1866, Sec. War Correspondence File, Box 317, RG 107; and same to

So far as politics was concerned, Grant's position was even more ambiguous than Stanton's, and the general carefully kept secret his vaulting ambition for high elective office. Grant could appear as a supporter of Johnson and thus appeal to Democrats and Union party conservatives. Backed up by Stanton in matters of army policy, he saw to it that the soldiers executed their duties in the South and that the influence of the Army there fell into line with the plans of the congressional Republicans of moderate and radical bent, as in the supersedure of the Army's provost courts by the equally military Freedmen's Bureau tribunals. No wonder that Senator Cole, of California, could agree with a description of Grant in this period that argued: "Now Grant, somehow or other, seems to have a conservative odor about him, and at the same time a slight dash of radicalism will exhibit itself, which makes him not entirely one thing or the other." [2]

Wherever Grant was in politics, he was first a soldier. And, like Stanton, he was disgusted and resentful that with the war at an end hundreds of Northern civilians were suing army officers, especially wartime provost marshals, for damages. According to the claimants, these officers had arrested innocent persons, employed perjured witnesses and *agents provocateurs*, and deliberately ordered needless arrests in order to extort money from their victims. The law of Congress of March 3, 1863, dealing with the suspension of the writ of habeas corpus, exempted officials from suits for acts done in legitimate pursuit of their duties but was no immunity against charges of exploiting official powers for base ends or personal gain.

Lincoln had set a policy of having the Attorney General defend the few army officers who were sued during the war by civilians. But now that department of the government was too understaffed to cope with the flood of postwar litigation, and as a result of the rash of suits, army officers generally were becoming timid in the execution of their duties.

At the same time, however, officers were angered that plaintiffs in these suits were in many instances former slaveowners from border areas and Northerners who had been convicted of disloyalty by military courts on what seemed to soldiers to be adequate grounds. Now these untrustworthy miscreants—for this was how army personnel viewed them—were maliciously striking back at those who had justly

---

Grant, March 15, 1866, HQA, Letters Received (WD), 77 AUS1866, Box 102, RG 108, NA; S. Hooper to H. Woodman, July 13, 1866, Woodman Papers, MHS.

[2] T. Campbell to Cole, Feb. 11, 1868, UCLA; O. O. Howard, *op. cit.*, II, 284–5.

punished treason, and were demanding the return of confiscated property as well.

These damage suits, entered in state courts, inevitably brought about conflicts of jurisdiction when writs were issued on army personnel. To raise army morale, Stanton ordered that the Bureau of Military Justice supply free legal counsel for officers being sued by civilians if the Attorney General could not, so long as the Bureau was convinced that the charges were groundless. But he also authorized courts-martial for officers found to have been justly accused. At the same time, "to allay uneasiness and prevent litigation," Stanton had issued an order early in March 1865 directing army personnel to heed only the actions of federal courts. This order was in accord with legal and historical precedents, and with the current view of the War Department solicitor as well as the Attorney General, but because it was Stanton who issued it—as Grant had convinced him that he must in order to sustain the sagging morale of the Army's officers—he received the fullest share of public criticism.

One case may illustrate how Stanton stood as a buffer between the Army and indignant Northern civilians. In February 1865, the provost marshal of Cleveland, Captain F. A. Nash, was accused of taking bribes from men he had certified as unfit for military duty. A state grand jury, packed with angered patriots and jubilant copperheads, brought an indictment against Nash. Stanton's March order transferred jurisdiction to the federal court, where the grand jury confirmed the indictment. Freed on bond, Nash faced a court-martial that Stanton had ordered personally. The local army commander arrested the editor of the Cleveland *Leader* for publishing details of the court-martial proceedings. Stanton ordered his immediate release. Late in May, the military court found Nash guilty and prescribed a stiff sentence. But throughout, the press of the Ohio Valley saw Stanton as the villain of the piece.[3]

For years now Stanton had worried about what the civil courts would do in connection with the wartime emergency arrests and trials of civilians by the military, and the property confiscations performed by soldiers obeying his, the President's, and Congress's orders. In

---

[3] Bates to G. A. Coffey, May 5, 1862, Letters Sent, RG 60; AGO files 267 and 588EB 17, Sec. War Correspondence File, Box 322, RG 107, NA, deals with damage suits, Lincoln's policy, and Stanton's March 1865 order. On precedents and contemporary cases, see U.S., W.D., *Digest of the Opinions of the Judge Advocate General* (Washington, 1866), 189–90, and *O.R.*, ser. 2, VII, 441; the Nash case is in the Cleveland *Leader*, Feb. 8–May 25, 1865.

1864, the Supreme Court had squirmed out of having to take on this hot issue, when it denied Vallandigham judicial review of the sentence a military commission had imposed on him. One of the major reasons Lincoln had appointed Chase to the Supreme Court was that, as Dana phrased it, "if any law is needed at this special juncture he will make it."

But Lincoln had become alarmed, early in 1865, when he learned that Chase now believed that the President, and thus Stanton and the Army, had no right to suspend civil processes, that it was a function only of Congress. "Such an opinion from the Supreme Court," Dana wrote, "would have been a very injurious blow to Mr. Lincoln's administration," and Attorney General Speed, with Stanton's support, persuaded the Court to postpone consideration of pending cases involving this issue. This arrangement had only held off the problem, but any respite was a blessing.[4]

Then, just before he took his brief Gambier vacation in December 1865, Stanton learned that Joseph E. Maddox, of Baltimore, was claiming $30,000 damages from him because during the war he had been arrested on what he claimed were false charges of disloyalty.

Soldiers had found Maddox in possession of confiscated tobacco. He asserted that Lincoln had granted him a permit to trade through the blockade but that a military commission nonetheless sent him to prison. Stanton had freed Maddox after he had been in prison for some months, but had retained the tobacco for the government.

Maddox entered his suit against Stanton early in December in the New York City and County supreme court. Strong anti-Army sentiment had prevailed in New York City ever since the draft riots, and in 1864, in a suit against General Dix, a New York judge had declared the exemption provisions of the Habeas Corpus Act unconstitutional. As his counsel, Maddox employed Caleb Cushing, prominent Massachusetts Democrat, intimate of President Johnson, and an old enemy of Stanton's. The War Secretary, realizing the difficulty of proving that the extraordinary wartime internal security actions had actually been taken under specific presidential or legislative authority, had the government hire Pierrepont, who had been counsel for Dix in the 1864 case, to defend him.

From the first, Stanton had been apprehensive about the Maddox case; Browning noted after talking with him about it that "he was a

---

[4] Dana to James S. Pike, May 10, 1865, CFL; *Ex parte Vallandigham*, 1 *Wallace* 243, 244–5 (1864) ; and see *Walker* v. *Crane*, Federal Cases 17067 (1865).

little crusty in his manner, and, I think, suspected we wanted to make a point on him." Stanton had Lafayette C. Baker, former head of the army secret service, go to work to learn what he could about Maddox. Meanwhile, Cushing tried to compromise the affair out of court, for he was soon convinced that Maddox had no real case. By early June, Cushing was advising his client that "only honorable suits are wise ones" and that "the continued prosecution of the Secretary has the necessary effect of embarrassing the action of the War Department." He had learned that Marble, Black, the Blairs, and Barlow were behind Maddox as part of their drive to oust Stanton from the war office. Cushing, though unfriendly to Stanton, shied off from using the law for such blatantly partisan ends.

Although Stanton at first could barely give credence to Baker's reports that his political foes were willing to wreck the United States Army in order to get at him, the sleuth was soon able to bring him proof. The Secretary was outraged, albeit still terribly worried over the personal disaster that would befall him if the suit succeeded.

Cushing continued secretly to pressure Maddox to drop his claim, but the Marylander was fearful of the reaction of his backers if he did so. While he struggled to decide upon a course of action, Stanton could do nothing but sit tight. He kept the Maddox matter as quiet as he could in order to avoid worry for his family and his official subordinates. Stanton could not resign now if he wanted to, for except for his salary he was virtually without funds. As War Secretary, he presumably enjoyed the broad indemnity prescribed by the 1863 Habeas Corpus Act for acts performed by government officials in suppressing the rebellion; also the government's funds were behind him in such suits, and the Attorney General himself would defend him if asked.

Stanton knew that if Maddox won, the Army would become paralyzed as an effective force in the South, for similar suits would multiply against many officers. On merely hearing of the suit, army personnel were losing confidence regarding their legitimate powers. A great deal more than his own pocket was involved, and Stanton was determined to fight.

It may have been that the President wanted Maddox to win. This was the opinion of Washington commentators who kept their ears close to the ground around the White House. Logic supports the surmise. If Maddox succeeded, then Johnson need not issue an order he was preparing, limiting the Army's powers in the South. A victory for Maddox might transform the influential War Secretary into a bankrupted, subservient instrument of the President's will, and bypass the political repercussions that must attend a request from Johnson that Stanton resign, which the President's intimates were pressing him to make. All this gained without risk to himself, Johnson might yet bridge on his own terms the gap opening between the White House and the congressional leaders of the Republican party. For without the Army's willingness to enforce legislation protecting the rights of Negroes, further argument on that sore subject became meaningless. Not for the last time, Johnson hoped to win a political victory in the courts.

These potentialities forced Stanton and Grant to turn for help to the dominant Republican element in Congress. Because Ben Butler had evidence in his possession vital to the government's side, Pierrepont made peace with him on behalf of Stanton. Generals Grant and Fry, James Wilson, of Iowa, chairman of the House Judiciary Committee, and Henry Wilson, of Massachusetts, chairman of the Senate Military Affairs Committee, worked closely with Stanton, and a resolution calling for better protection for government officials emerged from the Senate early in February. "Stanton knows that a Radical Senate will sustain him," noted Democratic diarist William Owner.[5]

While waiting for Congress to act on his and the Army's behalf, Stanton, together with Grant, Fry, and Holt, had taken more immediate administrative action to deal with similar suits emanating from the South. On January 3, 1866, Grant issued to the Army General Order No. 3, "To protect loyal persons against improper civil suits and penalties in the late rebellious States."

By the terms of this order, present military and civil officers of the national government, as well as holders of confiscated property, occupants of abandoned lands, and Negroes who asserted that the civil courts of the South offered them no fair redress, were to have any suits against them transferred to federal courts or to the tribunals of the Freedmen's Bureau. This general order reflected Stanton and Grant's desire to protect the Army, not to push the Army toward supporting Republican political tenets. The order had the latter effect, of course, but this was neither Stanton's fault nor his intent.

But General Order No. 3 applied only to the South and to present government personnel. In addition to the Maddox case, more than fifty

---

[5] Browning, *Diary*, II, 17–18; entries, Jan. 3, Feb. 12, 15, 1866, Owner ms diary, LC; *Maddox* v. *Stanton*, in Cushing Papers, LC; Henry Wilson to Stanton, March 2, 1866, Stanton MSS; Pierrepont to Butler, Feb. 18, 1866, Butler Papers, 2d ser., LC; ms record in HR 39A–F13.7, "Protection of Federal Officials, Including Members of the Provost Marshal General's Office, from Local Vindictiveness," RG 21, NA, examined by permission of Hon. Ralph Roberts, Clerk of the House of Representatives.

suits against the wartime actions of former army officers were then pending in the state courts of Vermont, Indiana, and Kentucky, as well as in New York. Stanton and Grant requested the Attorney General to defend the officers and the veterans involved, and the War Department paid the expenses of each defense. This policy served from January through early May 1866 as an interim buffer designed to give confidence to the Army's officers that the government would sustain them. Then, on May 11, Congress amended the 1863 Habeas Corpus Act, providing for federal court jurisdiction in suits against soldiers and for the aid of the government's legal department to all current and former public officers for acts done under orders during and since the war. The immediate crisis was past.[6] But no one could say what might yet happen if Maddox won his case, if other courts took the government to task for exercising emergency powers during or since the war, or if the Supreme Court declared the Habeas Corpus Act and its amendment void.

Meanwhile Southerners continued their protests to the President against trials of civilians by military tribunals and Freedmen's Bureau courts. Stanton, at Grant's behest, had insisted in cabinet that the creation by the President of provisional civil governments in the conquered Confederacy did not end the Army's right to employ martial law there, and General Order No. 3 assumed this right. On April 2, 1866, however, Johnson proclaimed that the rebellion was everywhere ended and that the Southern states were now back in the Union.

Almost simultaneously, the Supreme Court issued a preliminary verdict concerning the wartime arrest of Lambdin P. Milligan, a subversive Indianan. The jurists ordered him and his accomplices freed from military custody, and promised that at the next term of court, in December, they would issue a more detailed opinion on the broader constitutional issues involved in the question of the exercise of martial law in noncombat areas. That forthcoming opinion would undoubtedly place another checkrein on army authority, and in anticipation, Johnson ordered a halt to military trials of civilians in the South.

By implication, the President's April proclamation on the South and the Court's predictable judgment on the exercise of martial law in the

---

[6] Townsend to Jeremiah S. Black, Sept. 4, 1866, HL; memo of Henry Stanbery, Feb. 22, 1867, Stanton MSS. On Northern cases, J. H. Ashton to H. H. Harrison, Letterbook E, 40C, RG 60; Policy Book, pp. 148–56, RG 110; WD, Executive Letters, LXXV, RG 107, NA. Other data in AGO, *Index of General Orders, 1866* (Washington, 1867); *ANJ* (June 16, 1866), 687; XIV *Statutes at Large* 46.

North, cast into confusion Congress's legislation on civil rights and the Freedmen's Bureau, as well as the War Department's regulations concerning the military occupation of the South. Army commanders pleaded for guidance. But neither Stanton nor Grant was yet able to provide it.

Stanton could not contain his disgust at the President's April peace proclamation. It was, he said to a friend, additional evidence of the politicians' willingness to sacrifice the best interests of the Army, and only if Johnson could resurrect the 300,000 Union dead would the nation accept the proclamation. His temper soon cooled, however, and on May 1 the War Department issued General Order No. 26, which, because "some military commanders are embarrassed by doubts," prescribed that in the South military trials were to give way to civilian state tribunals, where the latter existed. It seemed like utter triumph for Johnson's position.

But on April 9, three weeks earlier, Grant and Stanton had issued a secret circular of instructions to military commanders in the South which placed the Army there in the middle position of complying with the President's proclamation while retaining in reserve the martial authority which Congress had vested in it in the Habeas Corpus, Freedmen's Bureau, and Civil Rights acts. The confidential circular informed army commanders that Johnson's policy "does not remove martial law [but] it is not expedient . . . to resort to military tribunals where justice can be attained through the medium of civil authority." Each officer was, however, to retain the discretionary responsibility to determine the adequacy of justice attainable in Southern civil courts in each case, and Stanton—for the style of the message is his—also reminded army commanders of the existence of the Freedmen's Bureau courts and of the Civil Rights Act. Military personnel, and Negroes who claimed that they could not receive fair treatment in civil courts, would keep the mantle of the military tribunals around them; indeed, Sheridan and Holt agreed that General Order No. 3 not only was still in force but extended to veterans now living in the South.

Therefore, however it encouraged Southern whites and Northern Democrats, the effect of Johnson's April proclamation and his order concerning military trials was to force the Army a further step away from its traditional reliance on executive support and into further dependence upon legislative backing. The President's Southern policies were adding to Congress's strength, although Johnson thought himself a champion of executive power. Grant and Stanton and most military officers were moving with the Army into an unplanned and informal accord with Congress in order to keep down the harassments of the President's Southern supporters. To the men running the War Department, these were actions of self-defense, not attack.[7]

Though the Army was inexorably being drawn into the struggle developing between the President and Congress, there is every reason to believe that Stanton was not committed to radical politics. For example, when a group of Alabamans petitioned him to transfer a detachment of Negro troops away from their community, he gracefully obliged and received their thanks. Horace White, the Chicago *Tribune* publicist, was confident that Stanton was still in essential harmony with Johnson in mid-March, and pleaded with him to try to persuade the President to follow a different path. Radical leaders such as Butler knew that Stanton was by no means their man.[8]

Events, however, kept pushing Stanton further into open sympathy with Congress. On April 30, the Joint Committee on Reconstruction introduced a proposed Fourteenth Amendment to the Constitution, comprising five sections. The first was designed to prevent racial discrimination by states and permanently to nullify the "Black Codes." In framing section two, the committee had acceded to Johnson's contention that suffrage was a matter for the states to decide. It did not impose Negro voting on the South. But the war, by ending slavery, had also increased the South's representation in the lower house, almost as a reward for rebelling, by making obsolete the three-fifths clause in the Constitution. And so the plan of the committee provided that when a state denied the vote to any of its male citizens, except for participation in rebellion or other crime, its representation in Congress should be proportionately decreased.

Section three declared that all persons who had voluntarily aided the rebellion should be excluded, for approximately four years, from voting for representatives in Congress or for electors for President and Vice-President. Sections four and five repudiated all debts in-

[7] AGO, *General Orders, 1866* (Washington, 1867), No. 26; secret circular in Box 102, RG 108, NA; Sheridan-Holt exchange, April 28, 1866, Sheridan Papers, LC; S. Klaus (ed.), *The Milligan Case* (New York, 1929), 43–7; Flower, *Stanton*, 307; *ANJ* (Sept. 9, 1865), 40. See also *Letters from Lloyd Lewis* (Boston, 1950), 52; King, *Davis*, 251–8.

[8] "Many Alabamans" to Stanton, April 21, 1866, Sec. War Correspondence File, Box 315, RG 107, NA; Stanton to Johnson, March 10, 1866, Johnson Papers, LC; White to Stanton, March 15, 1866, Stanton MSS; L. Cowper to Butler and the latter's endorsement, April 25, 1866, Butler Papers, LC.

curred in aid of the rebellion and claims to compensation for loss of slaves, and afforded Congress powers of enforcement through appropriate legislation.

The amendment was not a product of radical vindictiveness; Stevens protested that it did not go nearly far enough. The cool and cautious Fessenden had taken a leading part in framing it, and he admitted that the third section of the proposed amendment was the weakest of all; it was "worse than useless, & was adopted against my judgment," he wrote. "Probably it may be stricken out & something better inserted in its place."

Whatever its weakness, the amendment proposal was the outcome of numerous compromises among the Republican committee members. It represented the moderate view. If Johnson accepted it, peace might still prevail between him and Congress.[9]

On May 1, while the proposed amendment was still pending in the House, Johnson brought it before the cabinet. On a poll of the members, Stanton, after seeming to avoid a commitment, said he could not approve it in its present form and believed some modifications would be worth attempting if the President might thereby be induced to approve it and thus come to agreement with Congress.

Welles denounced the congressional plan as an outrage and a wrong. Stanton interrupted to complain that Welles opposed all efforts to get along with Congress, and was "ironclad" on reconstruction and had not only leveled his fifteen-inch guns on Congress but proposed to ram them with his prow. Welles denied being unreasonable. The Constitution prescribed the terms on which states should be represented, said he, and Congress had no constitutional authority to impose additional conditions. Neptune was confused here. Congress was proposing to amend the Constitution, an action it had full power to initiate.

When Stanton unfolded his newspaper the next morning, he was astounded to see a full report of what had supposedly been a private meeting of the cabinet spread out in cold print. Though the news report allegedly came from "a Cabinet member," it turned out that Johnson had given it to his friends with the Associated Press, and it exaggerated Stanton's disapprobation of the reconstruction committee's proposal, while neglecting to mention his expressed belief that Congress and the President were "not so far apart that they could not

[9] Fessenden to George Harrington, May 12, 1866, HL; Joseph B. James, *The Framing of the Fourteenth Amendment* (Urbana, 1956), 67–9; McKitrick, *op. cit.*, 326–63.

come together." But the pro-Johnson press, which had been demanding Stanton's resignation, now seized on the distortion to claim the War Secretary as the President's staunch ally, and it pleased "Old Gideon" that Stanton must "content himself with the exposition made or openly deny it."

Stanton did not want to be put in this position. He tried to let the tempest pass, saying nothing publicly in rebuttal, and taking a long weekend trip to "get a little relaxation and mountain air" in company with Senator Morgan and Congressman Hooper.

Meanwhile, however, the President let it be known that he wanted each cabinet officer to state his position publicly. To force the War Secretary to a public choice, the National Union Club of Washington, composed largely of pro-Johnson officeholders, planned to serenade the President and the members of his cabinet on May 17, but Stanton absented himself, offering no reason. On the twenty-third, however, the tactic of the Johnson supporters was successful. A warm night and the Marine Band brought out a crowd of about 1,500, which, after listening to brief remarks from Johnson at the White House, moved on to the house of each cabinet officer in turn. Welles, McCulloch, and Dennison, the only other members who were at home, made short, extemporaneous speeches; but it was Stanton whom the paraders really wanted to hear, and the War Secretary, knowing that he would be facing a potentially hostile audience, had written out his remarks.[1] Appearing at his doorstep and bowing politely in response to the shouts of the paraders, he read his address, a man on either side of him holding a lighted candle, while stenographers, employed by newspaper correspondents, took down each word.

What he said in substance was that in its early stages Johnson's plan of reconstruction had, in addition to restricting "the exercise of the organizing power" to the people who were "loyal to the United States and no others," also required certain guarantees from the Southern states as "evidence of sincerity in the future maintenance of the Union." And this plan had "received the cordial support of every member of the Cabinet." To be sure, some members had thought it advisable to secure the right of suffrage in some form to the colored inhabitants of those states, and he himself had inclined to that view; "but after calm and full discussion, my judgment yielded to the adverse arguments resting upon the practical difficulties to be encoun-

---

[1] Morse, *Welles Diary*, II, 495–601; Browning, *Diary*, II, 74–5.

tered in such a measure, and to the President's conviction that to prescribe the rule of suffrage was not within the limited scope of his power."

Likewise, declared Stanton, what Johnson had said in his message of December 1865 in recognition of the right of the houses of Congress to judge the qualifications of their members, had received then and continued to receive his hearty support. He had welcomed the President's further assertion that "good faith required the security of the freedmen in their liberty and property, their right to labor, and the right to claim the just return of their labor," and had deemed the Freedmen's Bureau bill an honest effort on the part of Congress to meet the President's wishes in that matter, and had advised him to approve it. The President had not chosen to do so, however, and consequently it was no longer "the subject of debate or differences of opinion"; and the civil rights bill, having been passed over Johnson's veto, had likewise ceased to be a subject for argument.

That brought Stanton to the proposed amendment, and he could not give his assent to it, he said, because of the disfranchising provisions of the third section. Here Stanton echoed Fessenden's moderate view. In Stanton's judgment, "every proper incitement to union should be fostered and cherished, and for Congress to limit its own power by constitutional amendment for four years might be deplorable in its results." He made it clear that in his opinion the legislative body had an unquestionable right to participate in the reconstruction process. And this, in the state of affairs at the moment, was the crux of the reconstruction controversy. His speech ended, Stanton awaited the reaction; extremists on both sides were sure to be unsatisfied.

Some newspapers favorable to Johnson tried to make it appear that Stanton had unreservedly seconded the President's course.[2] But Stanton had not endorsed Johnson's position. Besides explaining his own course of action with respect to the President's reconstruction program, and objecting as had several moderate Republican congressmen to one phase of the congressional plan, he had thrust into prominence certain acts and statements of Johnson's that tended to endorse the congressional program, in order to show that a reconciliation might still be possible. Now, however, his remarks were being twisted in order to align him with Johnson, and this, added to Johnson's deliberately distorted report to the press of what he had said in cabinet

[2] Browning, *Diary*, II, 77; Gorham, *Stanton*, II, 302–10.

meeting, roused his anger against the President and led him to reassure his friends as to where he stood.

On May 28, Republican Congressman Samuel Shellabarger, of Ohio, wrote confidentially: "Secty Stanton called me into his private room a day or so ago to talk of reconstruction. He is heart & soul with us and I write this note that our friends in Ohio may know it as I see the Johnson people still claim *that* serenade speech to be [for] Johnson. As he said to me it is [for] Johnson but it is the Johnson we nominated and elected not that apostate who is now in sympathy with the traitors.

"He loathes the present Johnson movement as much as you do and if there is any ambiguity in his position it is owing to the fact that good men demand him to stay in the Cabinet. . . ." [3]

If there was any ambiguity in Stanton's position, the President was not deceived; nor had Stanton sought to deceive him. Since the cabinet meeting of May 1, Johnson knew clearly that Stanton's position was with Congress but not necessarily against the President. Johnson could not have failed to read the serenade speech as anything but a repetition of Stanton's insistence on compromise, strengthened by a shrewd highlighting of some of Johnson's words and deeds which had seemed to go toward that middle way. As the Milwaukee *Sentinel* aptly noted on May 26, and as he had stated to Shellabarger, Stanton had indeed endorsed the President, but it was the Johnson of the previous year he supported. Why, then, did not the President, aware of his hostility and able to demand his resignation at any time, insist that he resign now?

Part of the answer is in Johnson's hope that the Maddox suit would hogtie Stanton and the Army. A second reason rested in the approaching congressional elections. The President, secretly burning for approval at the polls, did not want to publicize the disunity in his administration. After speaking with Stanton, Lieber advised Halleck that were Johnson "to turn out the members of the cab. who do not go with him at present, it would probably turn the elections against him—but if the elections give him anything like a foothold in Congress, Blair will be in the cabinet."

Further, though Johnson was heartily distrustful now of Stanton, as he had every reason to be, he still perversely valued the Secretary's

[3] To Gen. J. M. Comly, Comly Collection, IV, Item 190, OHS.

judgment on administrative matters above that of any other cabinet member. And last, the President was struck by the weakness of Stanton's most vociferous detractors, the Blair-Barlow-Bayard cabal. These men had bungled with McClellan in 1864, had proved unable to sustain conservative Democratic candidates in their states a year later, and were unbearably rapacious in pressing claims for preferment upon national authorities. To be sure, Barlow insisted to Johnson that so long as he kept Stanton, "influential men . . . will make this a test of their support." But, the wily man in the White House wondered, what was this support worth? [4]

Soon the President was to construct a disingenuous portrait of his relations with Stanton as an excuse for not having removed him. By Johnson's later depiction, which his supporters accepted uncritically, Stanton was a devious obstructionist, who was employing the influence of his department in order to hamstring Johnson's policies, and required the kind of pressure which he had recently experienced from the White House before he would declare himself. Now the President presumed from Stanton's speech that the War Secretary was with him. It was a gross error on Johnson's part.

As for Stanton, he decided to stay on for a while in the war office, in part because he had not yet made up his mind whether the President was completely lost to reason. The shrewd journalist Cadwallader noted that since the May serenade speech nothing substantial had happened to force Stanton from the position he had outlined then. Stanton felt that Johnson might still be swayed from the course he had taken during the past year.

It was Johnson, not Stanton, who had not yet announced his position with respect to the proposed Fourteenth Amendment. Until he chose to reject it publicly there was always a chance, however remote, that he and Congress could be brought together. So Stanton, though now in virtual antagonism to the President, stayed on in the cabinet.

Remaining in the war office was also a measure of self-protection because of the Maddox suit. Linked with this was Stanton's concern for the fate of the Army. As Secretary, he was at the epicenter of the reconstruction process. Here he could give warning of dangerous designs on Johnson's part. With a complaisant man in the War Department, the President might appoint new officers in the Army and the Freedmen's Bureau, take over the military telegraph monopoly

[4] July 14, 1866, W. G. Moore notebook, Johnson Papers, LC; Barlow to M. Blair, July 16, 1866, Letterbook XIII, 133-6, Barlow Papers, HL; Lieber to Halleck, May 23, 1866, Lieber Papers, HL.

Stanton enjoyed and publish or suppress the reports that came into the Department, and refuse to permit the Attorney General to defend army officers in damage suits. "The Army would be very much disgusted to have one of the Blairs in the War Department," Halleck confided to Lieber, who replied that the rebel archives which he had collected under Stanton's orders "will all be dilapidated—destroyed" if a Blair came in. The German-born philosopher hoped that Stanton still meant what he had said to him in February of that year: "They must muster me out."

Only if Grant were to replace Stanton, General James H. Wilson wrote, would the Army welcome a change in the war office. But Grant, determined to remain behind the scenes as long as he could, told General Sherman that he was quietly discouraging all such talk.[5]

Patriotism was the compelling reason that induced Stanton to hold on. He along with many other Americans saw grave peril in the country's situation, and Stanton now identified the national purpose with the military institution. Envisaging himself as the civilian overlord of the martial arm, and as the defender of many men who had died but whose principles endured, Stanton was in a mood of conscious self-sacrifice. Two days after his fateful speech, he admitted to a friend: "Of late, my own mind has experienced strange sensations—present things are losing their hold; and dwelling on past events, especially of the last few years, my heart yearns toward those who have been, as it were, soldiers by my side, and are gone, or are going, forward to the front as an advanced guard. They will soon meet, or have already joined, Mr. Lincoln and others of that glorious army of martyrs, many of whom we have known here on earth."[6]

In early June 1866 there was still hope for those, like Stanton, who thought that Johnson would acquiesce in the proposed constitutional amendment. Stanton and Fessenden worked together on its objectionable third section, and when the document emerged from the Senate, it no longer restricted the voting privilege for tens of thousands of past rebels, but instead disqualified from holding federal or state office only the relatively few persons who, by engaging in rebellion,

[5] Lieber to wife, Feb. 24, to Halleck, March 20, and Halleck to Lieber, April 16, 1866, HL; Wilson to Badeau, July 18, 1866, Wilson Papers, LC; Grant to Sherman, July 21, 1866, Sherman Papers, LC; Cadwallader, ms, "My Four Years with Grant," 796–801, ISHL.

[6] Stanton to M. Odell, May 25, 1866, R. B. Hayes Scrapbook, X, 65, HML; Pierce, *Sumner*, IV, 288.

had violated an oath to support the Constitution, although it provided that Congress could remove even this disability by a two-thirds vote. Its leniency as a punishment for rebellion was almost unprecedented.

Meanwhile other matters occupied Stanton's attention. He had been worried that certain groups of Irish Americans, hoping to strike at Great Britain by invading Canada, might actually create a war, and he had pressed for a proclamation from the President to quell the insurgent "Fenian" organizations. But Johnson's advisers warned him that Stanton really wanted the proclamation issued in order to turn Irish voters away from the administration.

Not only is there no proof to support this assertion; there is every indication that Stanton was merely trying to meet his responsibilities by requesting the President to act. Johnson's delay, however, encouraged the foolhardy Fenians to essay an invasion of Canada, where militiamen speedily routed them.

Stanton was overworking himself as usual, even on relatively minor concerns. His friend Senator Henry Wilson sent him a copy of a new textbook on infantry tactics with the Senate's permission for Stanton to buy 10,000 copies at $1.25 each for free distribution. After studying the book intensively and comparing it with others, he wrote Wilson that he would not order it, even though Grant had written the preface. "Almost every . . . publisher & bookseller who risks his capital on . . . publication hopes for a 'sure thing' by getting the government to purchase & give [it] away — The recommendation of General Grant & other distinguished officers will help the sale of the book to those who want it, but affords no good reason for the government to give them away." [7]

It was always important to Stanton that the Army keep to a high level of fiscal morality. The War Department had received several hundred claims from Northern civilians who insisted that they had been appointed as special provost marshals during the war. Many of these claimants for compensation offered sketchy proof of service. "If a precedent is established allowing these claims," Stanton worried, "this department will be flooded with them for the next twelve months." Congress must set standards in these matters, and he would hold the fort of administrative responsibility until the legislators attended to this need.

Not only must Stanton protect the nation's funds; it appeared that

[7] Stanton to Wilson, June 13, 1866, Sec. War Correspondence File, Box 317, RG 107, NA; Helen Springer, "James Speed, The Attorney-General," *Filson Club Historical Quarterly*, XI, 182–3.

he must also shield the Army's and the nation's honor. Stanton and Grant were sickened when the showman Barnum offered the War Department $500 for the "dress" in which Jeff Davis had allegedly been captured.

But it was the South, always the South, that provided the knottiest problems and posed the gravest threats to the smooth, honest operation that Stanton sought for the administrative apparatus. A vast carnival of fraud seemed ready to erupt from Dixie, as thousands of claims poured in to the War Department from purportedly loyal owners of various kinds of property which the Army had used during the war. Stanton was convinced that many of these claimants had not been loyal. "How will the . . . Government be protected against the immense fraud that will be attempted & perpetrated under the head of loyalty?" he asked.

He was more repelled by news in May of a race riot in Memphis. A mob of whites, aided by police and other municipal officers, most of whom were Confederate veterans pardoned by Johnson, indulged in what Grant described as "murder, arson, rape, and robbery, in which the victims were all helpless and unresisting negroes. . . . The only protection the sufferers had was from the military forces of the United States . . . which was inadequate for putting down the riot speedily."

Even Grant, who had gained a reputation as a tender man toward the former enemy, hardened his heart. When L. McLaws, of Kentucky, appealed to him to countermand the orders of army officers there excluding McLaws from a state office because of his past service in the Confederate Army, Grant merely endorsed the petition: "Cant do anything." He could have, but he no longer wanted to. Stanton received a trustworthy report of an incident at Knoxville. A Negro sentry halted a former rebel colonel, as his orders required. When the civilian drew a pistol, the soldier shot him in the arm. A mob then invaded the army post and hanged the sentry while the local authorities stood by in support. "God damn it," Stanton scrawled on the report of the incident.[8]

Under such strains Stanton's health again gave way. On June 6 he appeared as a witness in the House investigation of the Conkling-Fry dispute; then he collapsed. Surgeon General Barnes ordered him

[8] On provost marshals, file of J. G. Anderson, Box 326; on property claims, A. G. Hobson to Stanton, Oct. 19, 1866, Sec. War Correspondence File, Box 316; on murder of the soldier, Box 315, all RG 107, NA; McLaws file, Box 97, RG 108, *ibid.*; on Memphis, Grant to Stanton, July 7, 1866, CG Letterbooks, 1866–8, RG 108, *ibid.*; on Barnum, undated entry, Hitchcock ms diary, GI.

to bed. Disobeying his doctor, Stanton stayed on the job until Barnes two weeks later "laid an embargo" on his leaving his home. "He is much better," the physician wrote Seward, "but ought to be kept very quiet for a day or two." [9]

Quiet was a luxury which Stanton and the nation needed. A suspension of all programs and policies, leaving the situation more or less as it was until a popular decision at the polls set reconstruction goals, might after all have served the interests of all regions and races most beneficently. But neither men nor measures would hold. As Stanton recuperated in the intense summer heat, new problems impended.

[9] Barnes to Seward, June 22, 1866, Seward Papers, UR; *Conkling and Provost Marshal General Fry*, House Report 93, 39th Cong., 1st sess., 38.

CHAPTER XXIV

FRUITS INTO ASHES

IN mid-June, Johnson began to show himself willing to break away from the Republican-Union coalition which had elected him Vice-President, and to assume the leadership of a new party, which, pledged to support his ideas on reconstruction, might handily link up with the Democrats. The President endorsed a convention to consider this maneuver, scheduled to meet in Philadelphia on August 14.

Meanwhile the Fourteenth Amendment proposal reached the form in which it stands today. Moderate Republicans were ready to accept it as a last word in the reconstruction process and to seat congressmen from the South as their states ratified it. But on June 22, Johnson publicly announced his disapproval of the amendment.

Nevertheless, it went out from Congress to the states, and Stanton, through inaction, tried to help its passage in at least one instance. Die-hard Democrats in the Tennessee legislature sought to block its ratification by boycotting the sessions to prevent the presence of a quorum. General Thomas, commanding at Nashville, asked the War Department by telegraph whether he should arrest the balky legislators and compel their attendance. For three days Stanton delayed answering Thomas's dispatch, no doubt hoping that he would act without orders. When he did inform the President of the situation, Johnson admonished him to keep the Army out of civil affairs.

During the delay two Tennessee members were brought to the legislature by state officials and made to attend, thus securing the quorum and insuring ratification. But despite the assertions of Johnson's supporters, it was the state authorities, inspired by "Parson" Brownlow, a bitter enemy of the President, who made the arrests. Whatever Stanton might have wanted the Army to do, his role in this incident was that of a passive, perhaps too passive, observer.[1]

The President's opposition to the amendment proposal, and the power exhibited by the Republicans of Congress in pushing it forward, moved Stanton and Grant to action. They had become convinced that the troops in the South needed a frank indication that if the soldiers set themselves against the President's peace policy, they would be assured of support from their superiors in the Army and from Congress. The occupation forces desired protection against retaliation from the White House and from harassment in state courts. Stanton and Grant provided for these needs.

On July 6, Grant issued General Order No. 44, strengthening No. 3 of the past January and openly countering the President's April peace proclamation. It empowered all army commanders in the South, down to the post level, to arrest civilians charged with crimes against military officers or against "inhabitants of the United States, irrespective of color, in cases where the civil authorities have failed, neglected, or are unable to arrest and bring such parties to trial." Those arrested were to stay in military confinement "until such time as a proper judicial tribunal may be ready and willing to try them." In substance, this order informed Johnson that the Army disagreed with his policy and that his estimate of Southern conditions was unreal and unfair to army personnel.[2]

Johnson thereupon let the cabinet know that he was at work on another proclamation, this time to decree not only that the rebellion was at an end but that civil authority was ascendant over the military everywhere in the country. Stanton voiced his frank opposition. He and Grant had approved the actions of Sheridan, in charge of Louisiana and Texas, and of Sickles, commanding in the Carolinas, who were holding civilians under sentences of courts-martial. Johnson knew that reports on Southern conditions from Sheridan and Sickles had sustained radical claims of the unregeneracy of Southerners. The President confided to his private secretary his opinion that Sickles was "a conceited cuckold" and ignored the general's views.

He should have afforded greater attention if not respect to these on-the-scene reports from the South. The fact that he did not presented Stanton with another proof of the accuracy of Sickles's assertion that

[1] Morse, *Welles Diary*, II, 528–31, 533–5, 538–41, 554–5; Howard K. Beale, *The Critical Year* (New York, 1930), 105.

[2] AGO, *General Orders, 1866* (Washington, 1867), No. 44; Jonathan Worth to Johnson, July 30, 1866, Sec. War Correspondence File, Box 317, RG 107, NA.

the President was making moderates into radicals by opposing everything Congress proposed. The Freedmen's Bureau, its life extended for another two years over another Johnsonian veto, would collapse without the Army to back it up, Sickles wrote, and "with a statesman of reactionary views in the War Department, the rebellion can never be morally eradicated."

As if to underline the truth of Sickles's views, in mid-July the governor of Virginia prepared to reactivate the state militia. Grant learned that the militia commissioners were all former rebels and that white Unionists and Negroes were excluded from the lists. He asked Stanton whether he had authorized the militia organization. Stanton assured him that he had not. "I must see the President on this," he replied to Grant, and then reported that Johnson declined to interfere in what he insisted was a matter of internal state authority.[3]

Irked at the passage of the amendment and at the War Department's refusal to conform to his wishes, the President decided to force a showdown in the cabinet. He had Senator Doolittle, one of the leaders of the movement for a new party, request an endorsement of it from each cabinet member. Stanton and the other dissenters would now be forced to declare themselves.

The stratagem brought resignations from Speed, Harlan, and Dennison. Faced with the same option, Stanton made the same decision. On July 16 he wrote a scathing letter to Doolittle, condemning the President's new party, "consisting mainly of those who carried on the rebellion . . . and those in the Northern states who sympathized with them." Stanton professed his already open support of the Fourteenth Amendment in its improved form and his desire to secure the suffrage right for Negroes in the South.[4]

There it was at last—a forthright endorsement of Congress's primacy in reconstruction and a clean break with the President. Stanton would now be obliged to resign. And he would have walked out of the cabinet and into the pages of history a hero in the sight of most of his countrymen and a man whose honor showed only minor blemishes.

But Stanton never sent the letter, though Ellen urged him to. For

---

[3] July 5, 1866, Moore notebook, Johnson Papers, LC; Sickles to Grant, March 7, 1866, and Grant to Stanton, with endorsements, July 21, 1866, HQA, Box 97, RG 108, NA; Sickles to Stanton, July 21, 1866, Stanton MSS; Sheridan to Grant, May 4, 1866, Sheridan Papers, LC; New York *World*, July 11, 1866.

[4] To Doolittle, Stanton MSS; Speed, *Speed*, 93–5. Alexander W. Randall succeeded Dennison; Henry Stanbery became Attorney General; and Browning replaced Harlan.

he knew that the Republicans in Congress were preparing a joint resolution declaring Tennessee restored to its proper place in the Union. It was issued on July 18. Though Johnson quibbled at the way Tennesseans had ratified the amendment, and criticized Stanton's part in the proceedings, he signed the resolution. To all appearances, the moderate Republicans had found a method—ratification of the amendment by the former rebel states—by which their position on reconstruction could be attained without serious obstruction on the part of the President.

And, too, the Maddox case had come to a head. On June 12, Cushing had notified Stanton that his client intended to drop the suit, although he would pursue his claim for the confiscated tobacco. Stanton had been immensely relieved. But, answering Cushing, he struck a brave pose. "This intelligence does not surprise me," he wrote, "for I never supposed he would bring the case to trial. Whatever may have been his object in bringing on the suit, or abandoning it, will make no difference in any official action of mine."

Stanton did not know, nor did he ever learn, that Grant had secretly informed Maddox that an army board would favor the claim for the tobacco if he dropped the damage suit against Stanton. But the general's elation at having headed off similar suits against army officers, and the Secretary's relief at being rid of the threat of bankruptcy, were brief indeed.

Two weeks after Maddox dropped his suit, William T. Smithson lodged a similar one against Stanton in the Supreme Court of the District of Columbia. In 1863 a military commission had sentenced Smithson to ten years' imprisonment for disloyal dealings in Confederate money. A year later Lincoln had pardoned the miscreant. Now, in July 1866, Smithson demanded $35,000 damages from Stanton. The nightmare of personal disaster, and of perpetual timidity on the part of the Army's personnel, had returned.

His friends rallied to him. James Brady had already offered to defend him, without fee, for any of his official acts, and Stanton accepted his aid in the Smithson case rather than test whether or not the President would do as the law required and provide funds for special counsel, as in the Maddox suit, or assign the Attorney General to his defense. Out of regard for Grant's good will, Johnson did place the new Attorney General, Henry Stanbery, who had served as War Department special counsel in similar cases, at Stanton's disposal. Brady and Stanbery entered a plea of not guilty to the charges.

Chief Justice Cartter, of the District Supreme Court, was a radical

Republican in politics and he and Judge Wylie were close friends of Stanton. They put the Smithson suit further back on the docket, and three years were to pass before it came up for trial.[5] The purpose of the delay was plainly to insure that the case was not decided until a Congress was in power that would sustain the indemnity provisions of the Habeas Corpus Act. So Stanton still had an impelling personal reason to remain in office, in addition to his other convictions, and the letter to Doolittle remained unsent.

Johnson's stubbornness on the Fourteenth Amendment had depressed Stanton terribly. He now was worried that the President, once he had gained Democratic support by the new-party maneuver, might lead a revolutionary movement to use the Army for the purpose of unseating the Republican congressional majority. Confiding his apprehensions to former Governor Morton, of Indiana, who was about to enter the Senate, Stanton advised him that Grant and Pope shared these fears. Morton insisted that Stanton must continue to protect the army personnel who had assumed such titanic responsibilities, and told him that the Republican-Union party would labor "unceasingly to throw the shield of the national protection around you." Learning from Stanton his decision to stay, Morton leaked the information to trusted mutual friends, and, later, Theodore Tilton remembered how men across the land "felt that the country was safe so long as the key to its arsenals was in Mr. Stanton's hands." [6]

By withholding his reply to Doolittle's letter, Stanton had still avoided making known his attitude toward the forthcoming Philadelphia convention. This was an omission that Welles proposed to make Stanton rectify at the first opportunity, and his chance came at a cabinet meeting on August 7, when Stanton commented facetiously that the War Department had been asked to furnish bunting to decorate the convention hall. Not having any, he had referred the request to the Navy, said Stanton, with a sidelong smirk at Welles. Neptune responded tartly that he always showed his bunting and it would be well for Stanton to show his. The War Secretary colored, but merely repeated that he had no bunting for the convention.

"Oh," Welles said disgustedly, "show your flag."

"You mean the convention?" Stanton asked. "I am against it."

[5] On Maddox, Cushing Papers, Ac. 5221, LC; *Smithson* v. *Stanton*, No. 2724, RG 21, NA; Stanton to Brady, March 23, 1867, Stanton MSS.

[6] Morton to Stanton, Dec. 31, 1866, Stanton MSS; Pope to Grant, July 24, 1867, in Sec. War Correspondence File, Box 327, RG 107, NA; Tilton, *op. cit.*, 215.

"I am sorry to hear, but glad to know, your opinion," Welles said.

"Yes, I am opposed to the convention," Stanton repeated.

"I didn't know it," Welles persisted. "You did not answer the inquiry like the rest of us."

"No," said Stanton. "I did not choose to have Doolittle or any other little fellow draw an answer from me."

That evening Welles asked Johnson whether he had previously known of Stanton's opposition to the convention. Johnson answered that Stanton had given him no previous intimation of it. Welles commented that the administration could not "get along this way." "No," replied Johnson, "it will be pretty difficult." But he still showed no disposition to ask Stanton to resign.

So Stanton stayed on, and because the President assumed a pose of innocence, the War Secretary, in the view of persons predisposed against him, was easily cast in the role of designing villain. "I see the President has the 'old man of the sea' still strapped on his back in the shape of the Secretary of War," the younger Frank Blair wrote his father.[7] But the straps could have been untied at a word from the President.

Meanwhile Congress had adjourned on July 27, and three days later a terrible massacre of Negroes occurred at New Orleans. The trouble began when certain so-called Union men proposed to reconvene the constitutional convention of 1864, which had adjourned subject to call, with the idea of having it impose Negro suffrage on the state so that they could dominate it themselves. Former Confederates had gained control of all the important offices in Louisiana except the governorship, which was held by James Madison Wells.

In the absence of Sheridan, General Absalom Baird was in charge of the federal troops in New Orleans. Louisiana's attorney general, Andrew J. Herron, and Lieutenant Governor Albert Voorhies, both former Confederates, informed him that in their opinion the proposed convention was illegal. If it assembled, the sheriff would arrest the delegates and the grand jury would indict them. Herron and Voorhies trusted that Baird would not intervene. Baird answered that he saw no harm in the projected meeting, for in the opinion of Governor Wells it was legal, and that he would tolerate no interference with it except on orders from Washington. He promised to telegraph for in-

[7] Morse, *Welles Diary*, II, 523, 573–4; Blair, Jr., to Sr., Aug. 7, 1866, Box XXVI, Blair-Lee Papers, PU; Barlow to W. D. Shipman, Aug. 22; to James Hughes, Nov. 8, 1865, Letterbook XI, 278–80, 1013–15, Barlow Papers, HL.

structions, however, and suggested that Herron and Voorhies also inform Washington of what was happening.

Consequently, the two men warned Johnson by telegram of the high state of excitement in the city, particularly among the Negroes, who were being harangued by agitators. They asserted that it would be impossible to execute civil process against the convention delegates without causing a riot and asked: "Is the military to interfere to prevent process of court?" Johnson answered: "The military will be expected to sustain and not to obstruct or interfere with, the proceedings of the court." The President, forgetting his states' rights views, also telegraphed Governor Wells demanding to know by what authority he had reconvened the 1864 convention and by what authority it presumed to act for the people of the state.

Stanton received his first intimation of trouble the same day, when Baird wired him a description of what had transpired in Louisiana and asked for instructions by telegraph. Baird evidently considered the situation crucial. But Stanton neither answered his telegram nor brought it to the President's attention, and it was not until ten days afterward that Johnson learned about it.[8]

When Johnson's telegram stating that the military would be expected to sustain and not obstruct the civil authorities reached New Orleans, Mayor John T. Monroe hastened to show it to Baird, informing him that he proposed to disperse the convention by arresting the delegates unless Baird approved of the meeting. The general was disturbed and puzzled at not receiving any answer from Stanton, and decided to arrest any person who interfered with the delegates, unless he received orders to the contrary.

At noon on July 30, some 26 delegates assembled inside the Mechanic's Institute. About 150 spectators, mostly colored, gathered in and around the building. Somehow Baird had got the idea that the convention would not meet until 6 p.m. and his troops were still at Jackson Barracks. Everything went off peaceably, however, until a procession of colored men came toward the convention hall. White men began to jeer the marchers. Someone fired a pistol, and, finally, a slaughter of the Negroes by the police and by other whites resulted. Before Baird's troops succeeded in quelling the violence, about 40 persons were killed and 160 wounded, the victims being mostly Negroes.

---

[8] "Notes of Colonel W. G. Moore, Private Secretary to President Johnson, 1866–1868," *AHR*, XIX, 102; *The New Orleans Riot*, House Exec. Doc. 68, 39th Cong., 2d sess., 4–5 (hereafter cited as *New Orleans Riot*).

On August 3, Stanton divulged what information he had been able to gain about the riot to the President and the members of the cabinet. He prefaced his remarks with a summation of reports he had received from army commanders in the South, who at Grant's orders had been surveying public opinion there; the conclusion was that the President's policies were encouraging unregenerate whites to hope for revenge against Unionists and Negroes. Then, repeatedly referring to Herron and Monroe as "pardoned rebels," Stanton implied that Johnson's flaccid reconstruction program had given rise to the New Orleans bloodletting.

In a statement to a friend and, almost in the same words, to Congress, Stanton later explained his own alleged remissness in informing Johnson of Baird's telegram. He wrote: "There was no intimation in the telegram that force or violence was threatened by those opposed to the convention or that it was apprehended by General Baird. Upon consideration, it appeared to me that his warning to the city authorities was all that the case then required, for I saw no reason to instruct him to withdraw protection from the convention sanctioned by the Governor, and in the event of any attempt at arrest, General Baird's interference would bring up the case with all the facts for such instructions as might be proper, and in the meantime under his general authority, he would take measures to maintain the peace within his command."

His explanation scarcely seems sufficient, however, in view of the urgency in Baird's dispatch and his specific request for instructions. Stanton was not so unscrupulously heartless as deliberately to provoke a riot for political advantage by withholding instructions from Baird, but that he had a political objective in mind seems highly probable, especially in view of his earlier delay in answering General Thomas's request for instructions concerning Tennessee. He was by no means unaware of the explosive situation at New Orleans. Baird's expressed intention to prevent interference with a Unionist convention, no matter how questionable its auspices, accorded with his own wishes. Stanton knew also that Johnson had no sympathy with the sponsors or the purposes of the convention and that if he was informed of a threatened clash of authority in New Orleans, he would order Baird to support the local authorities. Consequently, he withheld Baird's telegram from the President, but at the same time, not venturing to cross Johnson openly by endorsing Baird's resolution to protect the delegates, he simply neglected to answer the general's telegram.

This silence enabled his enemies to blame the massacre on him. He had wanted trouble to happen, they said, in order to discredit Johnson's policy. The accusation has never been sustained by proof. To be sure, Stanton had no scruples about discrediting Johnson, and his sympathies were wholly with the Unionists in Louisiana; but he had not intended to encourage bloodshed. Baird was, as Stanton said, already under orders to preserve the peace in New Orleans, and his failure to do so came about through no defect in his instructions. The police were responsible for the massacre, and neither Baird nor Stanton could have anticipated that troops would be needed to prevent local law enforcement officers from reveling in a blood bath.

Johnson, on the other hand, had helped to foment the trouble. When the Louisiana officials informed him of their intention to arrest the delegates unless Baird interfered, he had encouraged them to go ahead, assuring them that the military would be expected to sustain and not hinder them. In making this implied promise, however, he was acting in direct contradiction to the doctrine he had earlier instructed Stanton to lay down for General Thomas—that the duty of the United States forces "is not to interfere in any controversy between the political authorities of the state." For the supporters of the Louisiana convention not only claimed to represent the people by as good a warrant as their opponents, but also enjoyed the sanction of the duly elected governor of the state.

The President's worst fault had consisted, however, in ignoring the regular military channels and using a private telegram to local city and state officials as a means of communicating his wishes to a general of the national army. In defending himself privately to Sumner, Stanton made the point that if he had not communicated with Johnson, neither had the President communicated with him. And he implied that whereas his own inaction could have had no part in causing the riot, the President's failure to advise him of the intentions of the state's lieutenant governor and attorney general had allowed the situation to get out of hand. In Stanton's partisan opinion, Johnson was the "author" of the riot.[9]

Johnson seemed to learn nothing from events. While radical spokesmen were trumpeting exaggerated reports of anarchic Southern conditions based on the New Orleans tragedy, he stolidly went ahead with his plans to proclaim that peace was restored everywhere.

[9] Stanton to T. D. Eliot, Jan. 30, 1867, Stanton MSS, and testimony on May 18, 1867, in *Impeachment Report*, 398. See also *New Orleans Riot*, 6–7, 13, 22–3, 36–43, 273–5; Morse, *Welles Diary*, II, 596–70; Pierce, *Sumner*, IV, 298.

In the cabinet, Stanton frankly opposed the issuance of the general peace proclamation, as he had not done, through lack of opportunity, when the President had given the partial pronouncement to this effect in April. But though Welles saw this as evidence that "the Radical [now] stood out distinct and clear at a time when he flattered himself it was disguised," he misread Stanton's course. In April, Stanton had not enlisted under the radical banner; by August, he had almost come to that decision.

Johnson issued the proclamation of peace on August 20, and the next day Welles noted that it "takes well with the people." It did not, however, "take well" with the Army, for once again the commanders in the South were thrown into confusion. Almost immediately after the announcement, in Virginia a Union veteran was beaten severely by two former rebel soldiers, and then the victim was arrested by Norfolk police for disturbing the peace. But the War Department, Holt concluded reluctantly, was powerless to interfere, despite General Orders No. 3 and 44, which had become the main reliance of army officers in the South. Sheridan, who had received Grant's authority to continue martial law in Louisiana after the riots, wrote to him asking what effects the President's peace pronouncement would have there. "If civil authorities are to be looked to for justice," Sheridan asserted, "I fear that the conditions of affairs will become alarming." [1]

How alarming may be judged from a report of an army commander in Florida, General J. G. Foster, who wired Grant to learn whether the President's August proclamation had really been intended to "deprive me of the exercise of command." Did it restore habeas corpus privileges and establish the precedence of state laws over Congress's enactments on civil rights? Foster, reporting late in September, complained that on the day after reports of the President's policy were received in Tallahassee, municipal and county police began to arrest army personnel and Freedmen's Bureau agents for minor infractions of civil laws. He had ordered this harassment stopped, but he feared another "New Orleans" unless Washington provided clear guidance.

Now, after a year of secret skirmishing on the issue, Grant seemed ready to surrender the Army to the President. On October 17, he replied to Foster that General Orders No. 3 and 44 were clearly superseded by the President's proclamation. But that same day Grant in-

---

[1] Stanton to Jonathan Worth, Aug. 7, 1866, Johnson Papers, LC; Morse, *Welles Diary*, 580–1, 583; Holt to Stanton, Nov. 16, Sec. War Correspondence File, Box 318, RG 107; Grant to Sheridan, Aug. 3, CG Letterbook C, p. 153, RG 21; Sheridan to Grant, Oct. 6, 1866, HQA, Box 98, RG 108, NA.

formed Sheridan that those orders were not actually "revoked" any-where, but were left to each commander to employ or not as he deemed best, and that Sheridan should adopt the position that he had never "officially received" the President's peace proclamation.

Grant was straddling. Five days before his contradictory communi-cations of October 17, he had written confidentially to Sheridan: "I regret to say that since the unfortunate differences between the Presi-dent & Congress the former becomes more violent with the opposition he meets until now but few people who were loyal to the Government during the Rebellion seem to have any influence with him . . . un-less they join in a crusade against Congress & declare their . . . acts illegal & indeed I much fear that we are fast approaching the point where he will want to declare the body itself unconstitutional & revolu-tionary." Grant warned Sheridan that "commanders in Southern States will have to take good care to see, if a crisis does come, that no armed headway can be made against the *Union*." He advised Sheridan to prevent the civil authorities of Texas from calling out the state militia on any excuse, and Holt seconded a decision that the peace announcement did not cancel court-martial sentences imposed since its issuance, as some troubled officers feared.

Only in late November, after the congressional election results were in, would Grant formally inform Stanton that, as commanding general, he had finally interpreted the President's proclamation to mean that General Orders No. 3 and 44 were still in effect in order that the Army might employ martial law and so execute the will of Congress. "It is evident to my mind," he then wrote to Stanton, "that the provisions of the Civil Rights Bill cannot be properly enforced without General Order No. 44 or a similar one." [2]

So far as the public was concerned, the wildly popular Grant was above parties and politics. Stanton, however, knew that Grant as well as the majority of the Army's senior officers sympathized as he did with the Republicans' goals for the South. But the Secretary also knew of Grant's conflicting instructions to Foster and Sheridan. He could not be sure that Grant was trustworthy or firm.

Stanton was not privy to the secret sentiments that Grant had ex-pressed to Sheridan. The Secretary had been franker with Grant re-garding his views than the commanding general had been with him.

[2] Foster to Grant, Sept. 18, and Grant to Foster, Oct. 17, 1866, HQA, Letters Sent, Box 98; Grant to Stanton, Nov. 22, 1866, CG Letters Sent, 1866–8, RG 108, NA; Hes-seltine, *Grant*, 77; Grant to Sheridan in Badeau, *Grant*, 51; Sheridan to Grant, Oct. 6, and Holt to Sheridan, Sept. ?, 1866, Sheridan Papers, LC.

But even if Stanton had been aware of the communication to Sheridan, there would have been little reason for Stanton to expect that Grant would be willing to live up to them in the open.

After almost five years in the war office, Stanton needed no reminder that whichever end of Pennsylvania Avenue won the political fight over reconstruction, the Army would translate policies into action. How the soldiers would use their weight in the dispute between President and Congress depended largely on Grant.

Knowing that the Army went with Grant, and not with him, Stanton had to suppress as best he could his uncertainty concerning Grant's reliability. Grant, nursing his ambitions for office yet maintaining the appearance of aloofness from the political cauldron, if called to account could always claim to have been misled by Stanton. The fact was that he was directing the War Secretary, who could do nothing with the Army without the general's assent.

Stanton, trapped in his office by the intensity of his convictions, did not realize that he had become the prisoner of the institution he was determined to protect. The champion of civilian control over the military, Stanton was developing into a front man for Grant. All that Stanton knew was that he was in an exposed and frustrating position. He blamed the President and the Democrats for bringing him to it, and for exposing the nation to perils as great as those of 1860. After talking with Stanton, aging General Hitchcock wondered: "Have we run our race as a Republic? I hope not—but fear it."

Expressing unqualified optimism, Johnson's supporters assembled in mid-August at Philadelphia in a convention dominated by Democrats. Every one of the states was represented. The convention endorsed Johnson's policies and called for the election of a Congress pledged to support him. With the recriminations over the New Orleans tragedy at their height, the convention and subsequent pro-Johnson assemblages expressed the wishes of administration supporters and editors all over the country that Stanton be dismissed. But even with this kind of support, Johnson refrained from ousting Stanton. Senator Cole judged that the perplexed President "fears the effects of removals upon pending elections and is in doubt about what Congress intends to do in his case. Some of the Cabinet have shut down a little." [3]

[3] Sept. 1866 folder, containing marginal comments on a copy of the *Atlantic Monthly*, Hitchcock Papers, LC; petition to Johnson, Sept. 18, 1866, Johnson Papers,

Stanton's "shutdown" was due to his worry that Grant and Johnson were about to "suck at the same quill." He wrote to Congressman Ashley, of Ohio, that Grant was never a steady weight and his frequent visits to the White House were enough to cause concern. But Stanton hid his doubts and expressed his faith that "the head of the armies cannot ultimately be corrupted." Meanwhile he would keep a weather eye on Grant.

The President was also maintaining a sharp lookout over the general. Johnson and his supporters saw the importance of the Army as clearly as Stanton did, though they chose to hamstring the soldiers. Not knowing Grant's secret views regarding the South, and patronizingly contemptuous of the seemingly simple general, the President still hoped to enlist Grant on his side, and, as the general would bring the Army with him, to leave Stanton and the Republicans adrift and rudderless. To this end, Johnson during 1866 had taken to dealing directly with Grant, bypassing Stanton in army appointments, promotions, and contracts. It seemed to Stanton by the autumn of the year that the President was very close to success. Discouraged, Stanton was ready to quit.

He was again unwell, and his suppers ran to mush and milk. Strain and overwork had taken their toll. And Ellen, too, was ill; a persistent cough so weakened her that Stanton feared tuberculosis and sent her to visit her family in Pittsburgh, thus sparing her the turbulence of Washington at election time.

Before she left Washington she made Stanton promise to resign. "As yet I have said nothing about leaving the Cabinet to the President," he wrote Ellen in early October, "but am only waiting to finish some business." [4] Grant, he thought in his innocence, was the unfinished business.

Johnson was close to the double-barreled success of achieving Grant's co-operation and Stanton's resignation. But the President's supporters pushed Grant too hard and too fast. The Blair adherents in Missouri swore out writs under the Civil Rights Act to have the Army enforce that law against the state's Republican organization. Boasting that he had "hornswoggled" Grant into serving Democratic interests,

LC; Stanton to Speed, Aug. 14, 1866, Stanton MSS; Cole to wife, *ca.* Sept. 6, 1866, Cole Papers, UCLA.

[4] To Ashley, in Flower, *Stanton,* 310–14; to Ellen, Oct. 3, 1866, owned by Edward S. Corwin.

the younger Frank Blair failed to realize that the general was no one to be treated in this cavalier manner.

Then, in the first days of October, Johnson sent Grant a request for 10,000 stands of arms for Virginia's militia. Grant was furious. He had earlier protested that no Southern militia should form at all. Now the President intended to put the Army's weapons into the hands of men who Grant felt were unregenerate, a move that would permit assaults much worse than any thus far experienced.

Again, as in the matter of the Army's orders on martial law, Grant waited until the results of the congressional elections were in. Then, answering the President properly through Stanton's office, he advised Johnson that "I would not recommend the issue of arms for the use of the militia of any of the states lately in rebellion in advance of their full restoration and the admission of their representatives by Congress." [5]

Knowing in advance of Grant's reaction to the request for arms for the militia, Stanton again took heart. To be sure, one victory did not win the campaign. Johnson might yet oversway Grant's judgment, or get him out of the way on some pretext. Therefore, Stanton's business in the cabinet remained unfinished. He would stay on as Secretary so that Grant, who he felt was a shaky but essential prop to the Republican position, might receive the backing Stanton could provide through friends in Congress, and so that he might see to it somehow that the President did not replace Grant with a more malleable commanding general.

Meanwhile a barrage of appeals from influential Republicans, urging him to stay on as a patriotic duty, and thus feeding his need to feel himself wanted and in the right, confirmed his altered verdict to hold. News from Pittsburgh that Ellen's health was improving made easier another decision not to resign, although his doctor warned him that he could not drive his body at this pace much longer with safety. He wrote Ellen on October 6, to still her protest over his broken promise to her, asserting that Johnson was circulating stories that he was ill in order to "deep him before the public." The new Attorney General, Stanbery, had decided to "neither rent nor purchase [a Washington residence] at the moment, while things are so ticklish and uncertain. He firmly believes that Johnson will be impeached, and I think dreads it, as bringing on fresh troubles." For himself, Stanton did not believe that impeachment would come out of the next session of Con-

[5] To Johnson, Nov. 9, 1866, Sec. War Correspondence File, Box 323, RG 107, NA; F. Blair, Jr., to M. Blair, Dec. 21, 1866, Box XXVI, Blair-Lee Papers, PU.

gress, which he predicted would go overwhelmingly to the Republican radicals.

He wrote Ellen of how he missed her and the children, and gathered flowers to send her, "but they will be withered before they reach you." His brief moments of free time he filled with calls on Mrs. Grant, playing whist with Seward, and taking young Fannie Seward for drives.[6]

With the elections almost at hand, Johnson dared not press Stanton to leave the cabinet. He feared an explosive reaction if he obviously appeared to be reaching for control of the Army. If he removed Stanton he must have as a replacement someone who commanded the unquestionable confidence of Northern moderates and radicals and who would be acceptable to the Army as well. General Sherman was the logical choice to replace Stanton. Once this would not have displeased the Secretary, but that time had passed by. All the rumors that he had submitted his resignation "are from the old 'mint' & like their predecessors utterly false," Stanton advised Fessenden. Of other insistent suggestions that he was to take a diplomatic post abroad, Stanton wrote that "no earthly power could induce me to go to Spain or any foreign country whatever. My removal from the Department will gratify no one so much as myself. But it is only the forerunner of efforts to get Grant out of the way." Meanwhile, Grant, silent on public issues, was still permitting his devoted servant John Rawlins to depict him to the President as a thoroughgoing conservative, in full accord with Johnson in all essential matters.

In October, with "Tecumseh" Sherman's arrival in Washington, Johnson, preparatory to ousting Stanton, made an effort to clear Sherman's way into the War Department by inducing Grant to put aside his uniform and accept a trumped-up mission to Mexico, and thus to remove the obstacle presented by a situation in which Sherman as War Secretary would be giving orders to Grant, his superior in army rank. But Grant backed out when he realized the real purpose of the mission. Johnson finally sent Sherman on the diplomatic errand. Sherman had refused the President's request that he become War Secretary in Stanton's place, while Grant persisted in his unwillingness to replace Stanton himself.

Grant was now being mentioned for President; nor was he unresponsive to that tempting call. To immure himself in the War Department or to become too closely aligned with or against Johnson would

[6] Communications urging Stanton to stay in office, Sept.–Dec. 1866, in Stanton MSS; Stanton to Ellen, Oct. 2, owned by Gideon Townsend Stanton; and Oct. 6, 7, 11, 13, owned by Edward S. Corwin; Stanton to Seward, Oct. 17, 1866, Seward Papers, UR.

be to dim his prospects. He wrote to Admiral Daniel Ammen early in November to cancel a vacation they had planned. "I shall not be able to leave Washington this winter, . . . affairs have taken such a turn as to make this course necessary. I cannot explain in a letter."

Behind Grant's fearful reticence lay his knowledge that the President, though denying that the use of troops was legitimate in the former rebel states, had toyed with a Blair-inspired scheme to use federal soldiery to cow Baltimore's Republicans in local elections just past, though Maryland had never seceded. The plot had not come off, but that Johnson should even consider it seriously was enough to concern the War Department. At the same time, the President was expressing a concern that armed secret organizations were ready to overturn the government in Washington. No wonder that Grant, with his ambitions for the White House, feared to leave the capital.[7]

With Grant and Sherman refusing, for their different reasons, to replace him, Stanton resolved to hold the fort at least until Congress convened in December, as Fessenden and many others urged. Meanwhile he would attract as little attention to himself as possible and so perhaps hold off a decision between himself and the President. This explains why Stanton made no protest when Johnson bypassed him in trying to rig the Maryland election and when he transferred General George Thomas out of his Tennessee command. Stanton's addiction to silence made him refuse a chance to defend the course he had chosen in the *Atlantic Monthly*. He answered the publishers' offer: "In the grave and solemn condition of public affairs now existing, it is not likely that I shall seek to draw the attention of the people from what so deeply concerns themselves by any personal consideration or explanation."

There were other reasons also why Stanton did not wish to attract attention to himself. He was probably instrumental in organizing a Loyal Union Convention, which met at Philadelphia, on September 3, to counteract the Johnson convention, and in arranging for an anti-Johnson Soldiers' and Sailors' Convention at Pittsburgh in late September. But shortly before this latter convention assembled, he heard reports that the delegates planned to issue a resolution asking him to keep on at the war office. "It must be obvious to you, as it is to me,"

[7] Stanton to Fessenden, Oct. 25, 1866, HL; Browning, *Diary*, II, 103–4; W. T. Sherman to T. Ewing, Sr., Jan. 25, 1867, Ewing Papers, LC; Thorndike, *Sherman Letters*, 381; Ammen, *The Old Navy and the New* (Philadelphia, 1891), 533–4; Hesseltine, *Grant*, 77–9. On Baltimore, F. Blair, Sr., to E. B. Lee, Nov. 3, 1866, Box 8, Blair-Lee Papers, PU; Grant to Johnson, Oct. 24, 1866, CG Letterbook, RG 108, NA.

Stanton advised Congressman J. K. Moorhead, of Pennsylvania, "that any personal allusion to me would be prejudicial to any good influence I may be able to exert." He pleaded that the convention issue no "personal compliments . . . for which I have no taste." As a result, none were forthcoming.

Johnson's supporters were sure that the silence on Stanton's side represented weakness.[8] Indeed, Stanton felt strong enough to remain in office, if at all, only until Congress assembled, as he advised Sickles. Congress could tie Johnson's hands so that he and his supporters could not wreck the country or bring on another revolution, "although they have gone so far already," Stanton gloomily wrote, "that no statutes can prevent their acts from bringing on a reign of chaos and bloodshed in the South that will horrify the civilized world." To his friend and former colleague Watson, Stanton confessed his pessimism: "Public affairs are very gloomy; more so, and with more reason than ever before—not excepting the dark hours of 1860–1." [9] He still did not know how Grant would choose to act if matters moved to decision.

Early in October, President Johnson had requested the members of the cabinet, Grant, Farragut, and other celebrities to accompany him on a "swing around the circle" of the major Northern cities to bolster the prospects of the congressional candidates pledged to support his policy. Stanton, though he had urged Johnson to make the trip, perhaps thinking it would enlighten him concerning the true state of Northern opinion, begged off from accompanying him on the grounds of his wife's poor health.

Johnson addressed large crowds, and at first, while pulling no punches against his opponents, he kept his remarks in good taste. At Cleveland, however, some severe heckling, which seems to have been prearranged, caused him to lose his temper, and he broke into a tirade against Congress. From then on his political enemies harassed him almost every time he spoke, and all too often he bandied coarse language with his hecklers. Stanton deplored the manner in which Johnson was demeaning himself and his office, and later confided to the journalist Cadwallader the partial untruth that the reports of the President's conduct on his campaign tour were what finally decided him to oppose Johnson. Still, Stanton had resolved to stay in the cabi-

[8] Fessenden to Stanton, Oct. 20, Ticknor and Fields to same, Sept. 9, and H. Wilson to same, Sept. 15, 17, 1866, Stanton MSS; Stanton to Henry Wilson, Sept. 20, 1866, owned by Ralph G. Newman; Flower, *Stanton*, 309.

[9] To Sickles, in Gorham, *Stanton*, II, 339; Flower, *Stanton*, 312–14, to Ashley and Watson.

net until December, and so when the President returned from the tour, he was on hand along with the rest of the department heads to greet him and, according to Cadwallader, "was unusually gracious." [1]

Soon after returning to Washington, Johnson began a political purge of federal officeholders who had shown signs of hostility to him. Stanton retaliated by depriving pro-Johnson newspapers of War Department advertising, thereby causing the editor of the Philadelphia *Universe* to complain to Johnson: "The War Department Quartermasters have advertisements every week; but we never hear from them."

Meanwhile, the political outlook became darker for Johnson. Almost all of the Republican congressional candidates took the Fourteenth Amendment as their platform; and although party extremists such as Stevens and Sumner regarded the amendment as merely a step toward "complete justice" and wanted to impose additional conditions on the South, most Republican spokesmen and a majority of the Northern people were ready to accept the amendment as a "finality."

Seldom have revolutionists been offered remission on more generous terms—the establishment of equal civil rights for everyone regardless of race and a guarantee that for a reasonable time the national government would continue under the control of the party that had won the war. If the seceded states had accepted this settlement, the punitive doctrines of Stevens would have found small favor in the North. But Johnson's unflagging adherence to rigid constitutional theories and his denunciations of Congress encouraged the Southern states to resist, and in the weeks before the election some former rebel states refused to ratify the amendment. With that the tide of Northern sentiment set strongly away from Johnson and turned in the direction of the radicals, and now no one knew where it would stop. In the rank emotionalism of the times, people were even led to believe that Johnson was in league with traitors. It all worked for Republican success. A month before the election Stanton wrote to Ellen: "Both parties will be very much astonished if the elections do not go overwhelmingly for Congress. Everyone that I see expresses that belief." [2]

The belief was amply warranted and Johnson suffered a thundering defeat. The Republicans won better than a two-thirds majority in

---

[1] Morse, *Welles Diary*, II, 587; Flower, *Stanton*, 310–14; Browning, *Diary*, II, 115; Cadwallader, ms, "My Four Years with Grant," 795–801, ISHL.

[2] To Ellen, Oct. 6, 1866, copy owned by Edward S. Corwin; Beale, *op. cit.*, 317, has the Philadelphia *Universe* complaint.

both houses of Congress. And Republican and radical were now virtually synonymous. The overwhelming defeat suffered by the administration was in a sense an endorsement of Stanton, and in a moment of triumph it was not his nature to be humble. Long since out of harmony with the administration's program, he now became disdainful of it as a political force.

CHAPTER XXV

THE ROOT OF BITTERNESS

HIS OWN poor health and his concern for Ellen's temporarily more serious condition competed with politics for a share in Stanton's thoughts during October and November. He still feared that she was succumbing to "rapid consumption," and on the advice of Surgeon General Barnes she remained in Pittsburgh, leaving the children in Washington. As always, he was lonely without her, especially now that the older children were occupied with parties and the theater. He wrote Ellen of how little Bessie, their youngest and favorite, was "standing by his side having finished her breakfast and says tell Mama 'good morning' and tell her to come home. She is obstinately bent on writing . . . and jumps up and down impatiently waiting for me to 'git out [of] there.' " For himself, he was as busy at his work as ever. To comfort Ellen and perhaps to reassure himself, he asserted that political developments held no immediate threat to him.

So long as Ellen remained unwell he hid his worries behind pleasant domestic details. "I am in the Library," he wrote, "Lewis stretched out on the sofa reading—Ellie prying around among the books, Bessie leaning over the table saying 'tell Mama I want her to come home after breakfast' and singing 'red, white & blue,' her face as bright as the morning sun beam—here she stops my writing to give me a kiss." Stanton made it appear that his chief concern of the moment was the choice of costumes for a masquerade ball which the Grants were giving for the children of Washington's official elite.

By late November, Ellen's condition greatly improved, and he wrote her that his hour for resigning must still be delayed. She undertook to visit his mother and sister at Gambier, even though she and they disliked each other, in order to relieve her husband's mind concerning their ability to get along on the diminishing amounts he was able to send them. Since he had taken on the war office in 1862, he had contributed 10 per cent—$800—of his annual income to their support. But in 1866 the exceptional costs of Ellen's illnesses and the effects of inflation forced him to reduce his offering to $300, which sufficed only to pay the rent on his mother's home. Even this was more than he could safely afford and he was immensely relieved at Ellen's report that his mother and sister could get along, though barely, on less. Stanton budgeted all he thought he could spare for 1867—$80— as his contribution to them, a measure of his conviction that he must stay in his office regardless of the sacrifices this entailed.

Despite his considerate protection of Ellen from political concerns, Stanton knew that a storm was gathering. He felt with most moderate men that the President should have learned the lesson of the November elections, and should encourage the Southern states to ratify the amendment. From Washington, Grant penned a note to Sheridan to warn him that "things have changed here somewhat since the last election," but he could not predict the nature of the change and he was afraid to commit to paper all he knew.[1] Until Johnson spoke up, no one could do more than guess at the effects of the elections on his thinking.

Clearly, the decision for or against compromise must come from the White House rather than from Capitol Hill. Favorable action by only three Southern states was needed to add the Fourteenth Amendment to the Constitution. If Johnson signified his wish in the matter, Southerners would have to comply, despite the fiction of Southern state autonomy which he had created.

But stubborn, secretive, taciturn Andrew Johnson had no intention of supporting the amendment. He wasted time and thought on an absurd scheme, originating in North Carolina, of a constitutional amendment counterproposal that included a heavily qualified Negro suffrage and a general amnesty for the soldiers of the Union armies as well as for rebels; and listened to the suggestion of Jeremiah Black that Johnson again appeal to the people, as though a popular mandate had not just been expressed, on the constitutional principles which the Republicans were asserting.

Johnson's retention of Stanton in the cabinet continued to disturb

[1] Stanton to Ellen, Dec. 4, 6, 1866, owned by Edward S. Corwin; financial details in Pamphila Stanton Wolcott to A. Wylie, Oct. 18, 1870, owned by Craig Wylie; Stanton to Watson, in Flower, *Stanton*, 314; Grant to Sheridan, Nov. 15, 1866, Sheridan Papers, LC; Thorndike, *Sherman Letters*, 283–4.

extremist Democrats. Manton Marble heard from a Washington correspondent that if the vexing War Secretary stayed on as a spy for the radicals, then conservative opposition to alterations in federal-state relations or in the status of the Negro would have been wasted. Johnson must stand firm, the journalist insisted, so that Democrats of the right could isolate the radical Republicans from all moderate support. "If the President will give us a good pretext for fighting under *his* banner," the reporter urged, "we can get them mad, widen the breach by an exciting debate, and all will come out right." [2]

There was not the slightest possibility of success for these curiously unreal and insensitive Democratic projects. The war had made forever impossible a return to where the nation had been when Sumter was bombarded, or even to where it had been when Lee surrendered. Johnson had lost touch with the dominant trends of the time. Republicans in Congress were not going to debate any longer the desirability of the Fourteenth Amendment or whether they or the President should lead in reconstructing the South. The elections just past had decided these questions.

Johnson still had the choice of co-operating with Congress in working out the execution of its policies, or, if he preferred, he could stand by without interfering while it proceeded without him. If he chose to block Congress, however, then the legislators would have their way. But, blinded by an inflexible constitutionalism and betrayed by his racial prejudices, Johnson mistook the threats in the situation for opportunities.

Having convinced himself that he was carrying on Lincoln's policies in the South and practicing the same fine art of executive leadership, Johnson was now unwilling to admit that reconstruction in the South had always rested its constitutional justification on the Army's bayonets. By the end of 1865 he had professed to the nation that the Southern states were self-sustaining civil institutions, at a time when most of the officials of those states were still on the payroll of the federal government. Realizing that the North would not countenance withdrawing the troops, he kept the Army on duty in the South, but weakened the soldiers' effectiveness as occupation forces by limiting their power to employ martial law. Now, at the end of 1866, against the voters' opposite verdict, he had come to the position that the Army had no proper role in the South at all, and perhaps never had had one

---

[2] "J.C." to Marble, Dec. 2, 1866, Marble Papers, LC; Black to Johnson, Jan. 22, 1867, Johnson Papers, LC; Gorham, *Stanton*, II, 346; Fleming, *op. cit.*, I, 238–9.

after Appomattox, even though his own orders had sent the troops there. In Johnson's view, the nation had plenary powers over the South, yet was faced with ineluctable states' rights restrictions. He failed to see the contradictions in these positions. Worse, he could not believe that persons of different views could be either correct, sincere, or patriotic.

At the administrative heart of reconstruction, Stanton knew how casually Johnson cast constitutional consistencies aside whenever it suited him to do so.[3] But he clung to the hope that the elections just past had educated the President.

On November 30, the President had his secretary read to the cabinet a draft of the annual message he intended to deliver to Congress five days later. It did not include approval of the Fourteenth Amendment. Stanton raised a lone voice to object to Johnson's omission, and said he wished that the President had seen fit to support the adoption of the amendment "as the best solution of our difficulties, and [for] restoring the proper relations of the states, and the general government."

This occasion called merely for cabinet opinion on proposed presidential policy, not for a debate. Stanton's position was frank and open. Until Johnson delivered the message to Congress there was a chance that he might change his mind.

An uncertain and suspenseful lull gripped Washington during the first days of December. "The town is very quiet," Stanton wrote to Ellen the night before Johnson was to deliver his annual message; "very few strangers here, and the news so dull that the letter writers will have to take another turn at the Secretary of War, and ring the changes on his resignation or removal, or starve." Then Johnson read the message; he had not incorporated any part of Stanton's suggestions.

Stanton's private reaction to Johnson's message was bitter and unrestrained. On the day after the President apprised Congress of his position, the Secretary answered a petition he had received from Greeley asking that he pardon a Southerner convicted by a military commission. Stanton asked Greeley "how to secure a reciprocal benefit to those in the South who are exposed to persecution in rebel communities. Reports from military commanders press this necessity as urgent and represent that no spirit of forbearance and forgiveness

[3] Laurence Oliphant, *On the Present State of Political Parties in the Union* (London, 1866), 12–13, analyzes the Johnsonian inconsistencies in an essay based upon information supplied by Stanton; see this correspondence, owned by the estate of Benjamin P. Thomas. Their friendship stemmed from wartime days in Washington.

exists and that loyal persons for loyal acts during the war, are pursued with relentless hate." He opposed pardons for individuals and a general amnesty, therefore, "because of this want of reciprocity in forgiveness. How can it be secured?" [4] To thousands of Northerners, this was the heart of the matter.

Ellen now took on her first political assignment since she had sought the office of Chief Justice for her husband two years earlier. Going to New York, she met with their friend Pierrepont, who had tried to moderate the differences between the factions of the Union party and had worked for Johnson during the 1866 campaign. Pierrepont was now ready to abandon the President and the renascent Democrats in favor of the Republican-led Congress, and wanted Stanton to come to New York to talk over the matter and to meet important persons who were still uncommitted on political issues. Ellen insisted that he come. She wanted him to enjoy a change and she looked forward to socializing in the metropolis. Stanton procrastinated. He turned aside her impatient letters with sweet words and with descriptions of their adored Bessie, who was "as lively as a cricket." He could not leave Washington at this critical juncture, for a new, exposed flank had developed in the Army's lines. [5]

During 1866 the President had leaned increasingly toward the position that the Army had to stop employing martial law within the "reconstructed" states. Grant and Stanton had insisted that the Army must retain this power. Their reports concluded that the Army had aided the state authorities, not hindered them; nevertheless, state officials and Southern civilians were persecuting the nation's soldiers, not the other way around. Soldiers must be able to protect themselves if civil institutions unrecognized by Congress, and staffed by pardoned recent rebels, chose not to keep order. Martial law was the only way. [6]

Stanton had little hope that the President would extend the application of martial law, even in the peculiarly anarchic case of Texas.

---

[4] To Ellen, Dec. 4, 1866, owned by Gideon Townsend Stanton; to Greeley, Dec. 5, 1866, Stanton MSS; Morse, *Welles Diary*, II, 627–8; Browning, *Diary*, II, 113–14. See also *Violations of the Civil Rights Bill*, Sen. Exec. Doc. 29, 39th Cong., 2d sess., 17–37, for widespread echoes of Stanton's concern.

[5] Pierrepont to Stanton, Dec. 9, 1866, Stanton MSS; Stanton to Ellen, Dec. 11, 1866, owned by Edward S. Corwin; Stanley Coben, "Northeastern Business and Radical Reconstruction: A Re-examination," *MVHR*, XLVI, 88.

[6] Stanton to Johnson, Dec. 8, 1866, WD, Executive Letters, LXXV, 77, RG 107, NA; Grant to Johnson, Jan. 29, 1867, Johnson Papers, LC; Browning, *Diary*, II, 115–16.

Part of the pleasure Stanton took in the results of the November 1866 elections derived from his certainty that the augmented Republican phalanx in Congress, faced with executive inaction, would now supply authority for the Army to employ martial law in the South when necessary.

The Secretary was terribly concerned when he learned in early December that Johnson had acquired a potentially powerful ally. For the Supreme Court of the United States was readying its final pronouncement on the Milligan case, involving the question of martial law, which presumably would give added strength to the White House. If the Court decided that Milligan's contentions were correct, that the Army had never properly employed martial law even in the wartime North, then the Army and the Freedmen's Bureau by implication were rendered powerless in the postwar South. Congress's Civil Rights Act would become unenforceable, not only by reason of Johnson's policies but also because of the added weight of an adverse judicial decree. During 1866 Congress had overcome presidential vetoes and the Army had bypassed Johnson's peace policies. The Milligan case posed the question whether President and Court together might be too powerful for the legislators and the soldiers, and might thus overturn the verdict of the 1866 elections.

If Johnson had been willing to advocate support of the Fourteenth Amendment in his annual message, and thus permit disfranchisement at least of the leading rebels while providing for Negro suffrage, Stanton and most moderate Republicans would gladly have left the Milligan matter alone. Stanton was at this time considering the case of a Confederate provost marshal, G. E. Pickett, who after the war had ended was tried, convicted, and sentenced to death by a United States Army court for hanging Union prisoners in his charge. Pickett appealed to the "reconstructed" state courts, which ordered the Army to transfer him to civil jurisdiction. Stanton refused to obey this order; at the same time he held off executing Pickett, over the objections of Holt, who wanted to send Pickett to the gallows without delay. On December 10, Stanton advised Johnson that because of rumors of the Court's decision in the Milligan case, he was delaying action in all similar matters. "The magnitude of the offences alleged against Pickett," Stanton wrote, "is such that there should be no room to contest the jurisdiction of the tribunal to whom the trial may be committed." [7]

[7] Stanton to Johnson, Dec. 10, 1866, WD, Executive Letters, LXXV, 81–2, RG 107, NA; Klaus, *op. cit.*, 43–7; King, *Davis*, 251–8.

The possibilities inherent in the Milligan case made Grant more than ever the vital center of the situation. Johnson, of course, would happily abide by a Supreme Court decision which nullified the Army's power. Would Grant obey the President's probably ensuing orders taking away from soldiers in the South the last hope for protection? What would happen if Johnson, encouraged by a Court decision in favor of Milligan, decided to replace Grant, and the commanding general refused to give up his office to a successor who would co-operate with the White House and end martial law in the South? The least dreadful result would be the splitting of the Army into two opposing factions. It required no seer to envisage the possible result of this move—another civil war and the permanent collapse of the republic.

If these were improbable imaginings, Stanton was far from being the only one to dream them. What is more important, he proceeded in his characteristic manner to prevent them from becoming real. In his mind, the partisan advantages that might come from allying the Army with the Republican majority in Congress were inextricably mixed with patriotism and with his loyalty to the military arm.

Co-operation with friendly legislators had always paid dividends for Stanton and for the Union. By war's end Stanton was convinced that there should be permanent institutional channels connecting the cabinet with Capitol Hill, providing efficiency and harmony instead of the clumsy, discordant traditional practice. During 1865 he was busy with other things, but in early 1866 he and Speaker of the House Colfax agreed to provide each other with advance information on executive requests and legislative enactments concerning the Army. Inevitably, their accord was strengthened by the growing strains over reconstruction. Stanton followed this pathway when he sought a means of evading the impending Court decision on Milligan.[8]

As congressmen converged on Washington to attend the opening of the new legislative session in December, Stanton advised Colfax and George S. Boutwell, of Massachusetts, of his fears and of a solution he had worked out. His plan required Congress to make the commanding general the funnel through which Johnson must send all orders to army officers, and to specify that the President must not move Grant from

[8] Duff Green to Johnson, Feb. 2, 1867, Johnson Papers, LC; and see the exchange of letters between Colfax and Stanton, Dec. 1866 through Jan. 1867, in Sec. War Correspondence File, Box 325, RG 107, NA.

Washington without its consent. Last, the President had to disband the militias of the Southern states. The congressmen agreed, and Stanton excitedly interrupted Grant at one of the general's crowded receptions to tell him about it. Doubtless with Grant's approval, an army appropriations bill bearing the Stanton riders went smoothly through Congress, and Johnson later had to sign it in order to keep the government functioning.[9]

Stanton was satisfied that he had built a safe temporary barrier for the Army and given Johnson a dig for having bypassed him during the New Orleans tragedy. He did not realize that he had set the basic pattern for Congress's forthcoming onslaught on Johnson—the isolation of the President from control of vital segments of the administration, especially the Army. With Grant's safety assured, Stanton felt that he could join Ellen in New York City. There were some questions he wanted to ask his friend Pierrepont.

Between the social gatherings that Pierrepont arranged in his honor, Stanton and he talked over the implications of the Milligan matter. They agreed that ample precedent existed for disregarding or overturning a Supreme Court decision; Lincoln had felt the same way about the Dred Scott case. The two men again touched on the possibility of Stanton's resigning and joining Pierrepont in a law partnership in New York, which was what Ellen still wanted her husband to do. Then she again fell ill. They cut the visit short, and left the city convinced that the elite of society, business, and politics supported him. Stopping overnight at Philadelphia, Stanton had General Meade, who was in command there, secure them tickets for the theater so that they might become acquainted with the work of the actress Adelaide Ristori, their children's idol.

Ellen was still far from well when they returned home. During the height of the Washington social season, Stanton escorted his niece to the President's brilliant New Year's Day reception. Later that day, Stanton opened his home to visitors, as was customary for cabinet officers, and hundreds of military, naval, and diplomatic officials came to exchange greetings. Two weeks later, Ellen had recovered enough to join Stanton at the first state dinner of the year at the White House. But in the main she returned to the virtual retirement from society which had characterized her life during the past three years. She could take satisfaction, however, in her contribution to her husband's politi-

[9] Boutwell, *Reminiscences*, II, 107–9; Hesseltine, *Grant*, 82–3.

cal strength and personal confidence, for Pierrepont's support was significant not only in political terms but because Stanton saw in his friend's agreement a needed sign that he was on the right path.[1]

The Stantons had barely returned to Washington when the Supreme Court announced its opinion in Milligan's case. It realized Stanton's worst fears. Although disagreeing on some points, the jurists unanimously concluded that martial law was unwarranted where civil courts functioned. Though the case at hand dealt with wartime Indiana, its implications now supported the President, the Democrats, and the former rebels of the South. It cast into deepest doubt the legitimacy of the Army's actions in the South during the preceding year and a half. Most fatefully, the decision encouraged the extremists of the South and of the Democratic party to jubilant expressions of victory, and spurred radical Republicans into more determined efforts to come to a final clash. Congress, under radical control, now had to surrender or else move ahead by ignoring, circumventing, or overcoming the Court as well as the President.

Then the Court threw additional "important stumbling blocks in the course of congress," as Jeremiah Black exultantly described it. In two 5-to-4 decisions, a majority of the jurists condemned the loyalty oath tests with which Republicans were building permanent political machines in the border states and which they hoped to continue using to bar former rebels from voting and holding state and federal offices. *Cummings* v. *Missouri* involved a priest-teacher of that state who refused to swear to a required test oath as a prerequisite for teaching. The Blair family had helped him take the case to the Supreme Court in the hope that a verdict condemning the oath, which faced Missouri's officeholders and voters as well, would crack the Republican strangle hold on political power there. *Ex parte Garland* concerned an Arkansan who had practiced before the federal Supreme Court before the war, served as a rebel officer and legislator after secession, then received a presidential pardon and asked to resume his prewar profession. Congress had required that its "ironclad test oath" be sworn to by all attorneys seeking to practice in the federal courts as well as by judges and jurors. Garland insisted that the executive pardon he held from Johnson exempted him from the

---

[1] Stanton to Meade, Dec. 14, 1866, HL; Washington *National Intelligencer*, Jan. 3, and *National Republican*, Jan. 12, 1867; Stanton to Rev. Dr. Hall, *ca.* Jan. 15, 1867, CHS.

congressional oath requirement, as well as from all other penalties for his treason and rebellion.

In these cases, the Supreme Court seemingly took a firm stand in defense of civil liberties. Taken together, the Milligan, Cummings, and Garland decisions are noble assertions of the limitations on the government, brave condemnations of unbridled martial power, and intelligent criticisms of corrupting test oaths—in the abstract. To Stanton, to most Republicans, and to the United States Army, however, they meant that former rebels, waving the certificates of pardon which Johnson had issued so freely, would now flood the federal and state courts, to become attorneys, jurymen, and court officers, and perhaps gain federal employment as judges and even army commissions. The Army's efforts would not only be nullified; its personnel, facing judges and jurymen who were former rebels, must surely collapse under damage suits. The potential effect of these decisions would be to nullify the congressional achievements and the Army's regulations of 1866, if Congress permitted them to.

Stanton saw the Court's verdicts as tragedy. Along with most moderate Republicans, he was cast into despair at these prospects. Almost as soon as the decisions were known in the South, army commanders reported to him that civilian authorities were more than ever contemptuous of national authority, outspoken in their laments for the lost cause, and brazen in their assaults on soldiers, Yankee veterans now living in the South, white Unionists, and Negroes. The army officers did not know how to protect these people or themselves.

As things stood, the Army was in a hopeless situation. Presidential orders had placed the soldiers on occupation duty, then weakened their power to punish civilians who broke national laws but escaped prosecution in the state courts. Now the Supreme Court had knocked out all the props. The Army must either cease trying to function as an occupation force or get a new lease of power. Army officers could not long continue in the limbo into which the Milligan verdict cast them. According to the *Army and Navy Journal,* one of "the fruits of the Milligan Case" was the fear felt by all officers who had sat on military commissions in the North since 1861 or in the South since 1865 that they would now be sued for damages by persons they had convicted of offenses. Some such suits were already lodged in Southern state courts, and, the *Journal* editorialized, "officers will be exposed to endless worry and expense." Military personnel needed assurance that they would not suffer from doing their duty; otherwise, they would not perform it. Congress must "vindicate the National authority," and protect its military servants from vindictive harassment from civilians who had recently been rebels in arms against the nation.[2]

In his testimony to a congressional committee late in January, Stanton asserted that the Supreme Court had rendered the Army powerless to punish the murderers of Union soldiers in the South. State authorities there were demanding that the Army release all civilian prisoners from its custody. To prevent jurisdictional collisions between national and state powers, Stanton ordered the disputed prisoners transferred to Fort McHenry, but a writ of habeas corpus from a federal judge had secured their release.

He saw no remedy but to reinstitute martial law and military commissions in the South. Milligan had been properly convicted, and so had the civilian prisoners still in custody. Soldiers and Negroes could not secure justice in Southern courts unless the test oath shield was replaced. The Supreme Court's views were unsound and need not bind Congress, he asserted.[3]

But Congress had not yet proved itself capable of protecting the Army. Stanton did not know which end of Pennsylvania Avenue now held the solution to the soldiers' dilemma. He had to wait for events to unfold. So long as he held on to the war office he could try to mitigate the worst effects of executive and judicial policies he could not control. For example, he secured for army officers the assistance of federal attorneys in the rash of damage suits that now sprang up. Confused, hesitant, impatient for matters to settle down so that he could resign, Stanton again decided to hang on until the Army was assured of a better fate than serving as a pawn in a contest for power.

Buoyed up by the judicial decisions, Johnson commenced the new year in a confident mood. Seeking to capitalize on the effects of the Court's pronouncement, he wanted to force Stanton out of the cabinet. Therefore, at a cabinet meeting on January 4, with Grant present at the President's invitation, he asked the Secretary's opinion on a bill giving the vote to Negroes in the District of Columbia and disfranchising former rebels there by means of a test oath. Stanton supported the

[2] *ANJ* (Jan. 19, 1867), 332, 342; Stanton to Stanbery, Jan. 25, 1867, WD, Executive Letters, LXXV, 142, RG 107, NA; S. T. Glover to F. P. Blair, Jr., Jan. 4, 1868, Box XXVI, Blair-Lee Papers, PU.

[3] Testimony in *Murder of Union Soldiers*, House Report 23, 39th Cong., 2d sess., 34–6; see Union Congressional Executive Committee, *Review of the Decision of the U. S. Supreme Court in the Cases of Lambdin P. Milligan and Others* (Washington, 1867), 1–9; Klaus, *op. cit.*, 45.

bill. Congress, after all, had plenary powers to set suffrage standards in the federal district. Negro suffrage had to be tried, Stanton stated, and it might as well begin in the District as anywhere else. All the other cabinet officers supported Johnson's determination to veto the bill.

Johnson's plan for the January 4 cabinet meeting to force Stanton out of the cabinet, and impress Grant with the harmony of opinion among the other cabinet members, failed. Grant saw nothing wrong in Negro voting or in disfranchising disloyal persons by means of loyalty oaths or otherwise. But still determined to avoid open commitment, he had contributed little to the cabinet discussion, saving for his private correspondence a description of the disgust he felt at the efforts being made to push him into one partisan corner or the other. "But to leave now would look like throwing up a command in the face of the enemy," he wrote Sherman. Stanton also would not quit under fire, but, unlike Grant, he could not afford the luxury of silence.[4]

The President, to keep pressure on Stanton until he resigned, brought up the futile plan to counter the Fourteenth Amendment proposal with the one from the South. On January 8 Stanton spoke out. He hoped only that it meant that Southerners were ready to drop their damage suits against army personnel. Johnson then sprang what he thought was a trap, hoping that Stanton would fall into it. He asked for opinions on Thaddeus Stevens's heavily publicized plan to throw the South into a territorial status.

Attention fixed on Stanton. He did not hesitate, but interrupted Browning, who had started to speak out of turn, and demanded his proper priority. Stanton said that he had supported and administered both Lincoln's and Johnson's policies in the South, though he had felt free to criticize openly what he felt were errors in the ways in which they worked out. He had not seen Stevens's proposition, he said, "and did not care to, for it was one of those schemes which would end in noise and smoke."

For once, accord reigned in Johnson's official family. Perhaps there was still a chance, the President believed, that Stanton might be regained for his own side, further buttressing the strength apparently building at the White House since the Court had spoken out.

But all Stanton had done was to express a frank opinion, as was his habit. When he appeared two days later before the House commit-

---

[4] Grant to Sherman, Jan. 13, 1867, W. T. Sherman Papers, LC; Stanton to Johnson, Jan. 4, 1867, Stanton MSS; Morse, *Welles Diary*, III, 3–5; "Notes of Colonel W. G. Moore," *loc. cit.*, 104; Browning, *Diary*, II, 122. The bill was passed over the veto.

tee inquiring into the arrest of John Surratt, he assured the chairman, his friend Boutwell, that Johnson and the other cabinet officers had in no way obstructed the prosecution.

His frankness was again apparent eight days later. Congress proposed admitting Colorado and Nebraska as states on the condition that they include in their constitutions a clause providing for universal male suffrage. Johnson was outraged at Congress's daring to set fundamental conditions, but Stanton saw no reason why the legislature should not require what it wished. In any case, it was a question of law. He did not feel that Johnson should veto the bills merely because of his lack of sympathy.

Riding home with Welles that day, Stanton said that he was sick of the constant wrangling and wished that "this matter of the vetoes might be over." For the moment, Welles, like Johnson, felt that Stanton was reclaimable, and was not a radical spy, but honestly occupied a position on important questions that differed from the President's.[5]

This was true. But Welles and the President misread Stanton's habitual frankness as a plea for forgiveness. Stanton had merely been continuing his attempts to bring Johnson to a reasonable course of cooperation with Congress. The President, however, joyous at the Supreme Court's decisions, overestimated the strength the jurists added to his position. He was in no mood for co-operation.

Neither were the Republicans. In the first week of the new year, Congressman Ashley introduced in the House a resolution to inquire into Johnson's conduct as a preliminary to impeachment for alleged usurpations of power. John Sherman started a reconstruction bill through Congress which provided for precisely what the Court had condemned. Most Republicans, indeed most Northerners, were less interested in inflating the civil liberties of former rebels than they were concerned over justice to soldiers, Unionists, and Negroes.

Stanton openly supported Sherman's proposals. He asserted that the Court's decisions had been the final straw that pushed him completely over to the side of Congress. But he was not, he insisted, in sympathy with the radicals. He joined with John Sherman, Bingham, and Fessenden, all moderates, and with Grant, in keeping extreme reconstruction proposals in check.[6] Bingham, especially, was responsi-

[5] Morse, *Welles Diary*, III, 9–12, 17, 22–3, 26–7; *John H. Surratt*, House Exec. Doc. 9, 39th Cong., 1st sess.; *ibid.*, House Report 33, 39th Cong., 2d sess., 3–4; Browning, *Diary*, II, 123–4.

ble for the provision that the President would retain executive responsibility in the reconstruction bill that finally emerged.

In Montgomery Blair's warped analysis, the purpose of the congressional debate was only to throw dust in Johnson's eyes "by having Bingham . . . *pretending* to make war on Stephens [*sic*]." Stanton, according to Blair, was "carrying water on both shoulders but nobody but the President seems to be his dupe."

Johnson was nobody's dupe, and certainly Stanton at no point concealed his position. The President meanwhile brought Jeremiah Black to the cabinet room to help work out veto messages and asked Frank Blair, Jr., to draw up a new cabinet slate. But Congress was now moving at high speed.

While the debate on the reconstruction bill continued, Congress on January 22 took control of its sessions out of Johnson's hands by resolving to meet again immediately at the close of the current session in March, rather than in December. On February 8, the legislators enumerated the eleven states of the former Confederacy and excluded their electoral votes.

At this juncture all seemed to want to stop for a breath, as though suddenly fearful of the unknown hazards that might be encountered if they continued on the trackless path they were treading. Johnson tried to build bridges to the hesitant, conservative Republicans. "The fact is Andy is 'wooling' some of our naturally *'Democratic'* friends," California's Republican Senator Cole wrote in mid-February. "He is making progress; more progress than Congress." These maneuverings convinced some onlookers that Johnson was pausing rather than suffer himself to be impeached.[7]

One evening during these uncertain maneuverings, John Hay met Sumner, and the Massachusetts senator derided critics of Stanton who demanded that he leave the cabinet so that harmony might reign there, and insisted that "it was often the duty of a patriotic Minister to remain in the counsels of a perverted administration as a 'privileged spy.'" He felt that Congress must make it impossible for Johnson to remove Stanton. This, of course, was Sumner's point of view, and there is nothing to indicate that Stanton shared it at this time. He

[6] D. L. Eaton to Stanton, Jan. 9, and T. D. Eliot to same, Jan. 19, 1867, Stanton MSS; Klaus, *op. cit.*, 45.
[7] M. Blair to John A. Andrew, Feb. 18, 1867, Andrew Papers, MHS; Cole to Judge E. Burke, Feb. 13, 1867, UCLA; R. H. Stanton to Col. W. C. Breckinridge, Feb. 13, 1867, Breckinridge Family Papers, LC; "Notes of Colonel W. G. Moore," *loc. cit.*, 105.

was his own agent, not that of Congress. He was a partner to the legislative leaders only when he felt it necessary to curb Johnson's activities.

Mostly he attended to his departmental and personal business. Worried about the health of General Meigs, who was grieving over a son killed by rebel guerrillas in the war, Stanton sent him on a tour of Europe to compare supply procedures of foreign armies. Meigs was the bitterest foe of Johnson's policies in the Army. He refused even to correspond with pardoned former rebels concerning army contracts, much less grant any to them. Stanton sent him off nevertheless. The Secretary had to appear more than a dozen times in February before various congressional committees, and the testimony he gave was restrained and careful. He and Ellen gave several dinners and receptions, and their guests included persons of all shades of political opinion.[8] But despite the surface appearance of harmony, his official position was now disagreeable in the extreme. Stanton knew that no matter what he did, Johnson and the President's supporters in the cabinet would see no good in it.

This became strikingly evident on February 15. The Senate had asked Johnson to report on all instances of failure to enforce the Civil Rights Act. Stanton submitted a memorandum assembled by Grant and O. O. Howard, which listed hundreds of acts of violence on Negroes and soldiers. According to Welles and Browning, this was an "omnium-gatherum" of rumors. Over the opposition of almost everyone in the cabinet, Stanton insisted that Johnson add this report to his communication to the Senate. Looking earnestly at Welles, Stanton said that "he was as desirous to act in unison with the President as any one, no matter who; that this information seemed to him proper, and so . . . it seemed to General Grant, who sent it to him; but if others wished to suppress it they could make the attempt, but there was little doubt that members of Congress had seen this—likely had copies."

The report was finally given to the Attorney General for "investigation." Hardly able to contain themselves, Welles and Browning met the next day and decided that Stanton's "treachery" was so great and patent that Johnson must know their opinion of it. Polonius-like, Welles hurried through a heavy rain to the White House.

Johnson listened and seemed to agree with everything Welles said.

[8] Feb. 5, 6, 1867, Meigs ms diary, LC; Weigley, *Meigs*, 343; Colfax to Stanton, Feb. 8, and James Wilson to same, Feb. 9, 1867, Stanton MSS; *Impeachment Report*, 183–6; Thayer, *Hay*, I, 260–1.

Then the President made the incredible assertion that all that kept him from immediately calling Grant to the White House to learn how far the general was involved, was the fact that it was raining!

This starkly revealing episode illuminates more concerning the mood of the President and of his cabinet supporters than it does Stanton's alleged duplicity. Regardless of whether or not he was in sympathy with the administration's goals and practices, it was incumbent upon Stanton to reply fully and candidly to the Senate's request for information, for his was the department which enforced the Civil Rights Act. Undoubtedly, Stanton's report would embarrass Johnson. But Stanton had long since let the President know that White House policies were embarrassing the Army and the laws.

Welles and Browning, seeing only more proof of collusion, ridiculed the report on sight as untrustworthy, though it bore Grant's and Howard's names, and to cast aside so lightly the integrity of both officers was not merely ridiculous but stupid. The truth seems to be that Johnson and his advisers were by now in a mood to ignore disagreeable facts. They found it more pleasant to dream up a fiction of a conspiracy and to believe it themselves.

Stanton's distress over his divided position was becoming increasingly apparent. He tried to prove to Johnson that he was not set against him. In mid-February, Stanton saw to it that an account of his ideas reached the Washington *Chronicle*. The report stressed his alarm over the movement toward impeachment, which he likened to "revolution and anarchy." Congress and the President were wrecking the nation, and he called a plague upon both: "I aided to place two millions of men in the field to put down the rebellion; three hundred thousand have bitten the dust and an equal number are crippled throughout the land, and yet with all this tremendous effort and corresponding sacrifice, the country, in my judgment, is shadowed with the gloom of a darker hour than was incident to any crisis of the war."

This is authentic Stantonian prose. Whoever gave the text to the *Chronicle* either copied it verbatim during the interview or, what is more probable, received it directly from Stanton. There is no reason to doubt the reporter's concluding sentence: "The Secretary seemed completely unmanned as he uttered the last remark, and abruptly turned from his visitor to conceal his emotions." [9]

[9] *Chronicle*, Feb. 15, 1867; Morse, *Welles Diary*, 42–6; Browning, *Diary*, II, 130; memos in Stanton's hand, Feb. 9, Johnson Papers, LC, and Feb. 14, 1867, Stanton MSS.

During the following week, Congress hammered out its reconstruction bill, the legislators consulting Grant at every step. The bill prescribed the reinstitution of martial rule in the South under the command of five generals, who were to be named by the President. Loyal men only, black and white, were to begin anew the state-building process, and though the bill did not obliterate the Johnson state governments, it presumed that they would wither away, and they did. Under army protection, the electorate was to create new state constitutions and ratify the Fourteenth Amendment. When delegates-elect to Congress received admission, the process was completed.

There is no evidence that Stanton had any hand in evolving this measure beyond helping to block more radical proposals. He was to support it openly in cabinet deliberations and advise against a presidential veto. Yet Welles and the Blairs, somehow, were convinced that Stanton was "deep in the radical intrigues." They thought that he dominated Seward and that together the two Secretaries managed to "confuse and bewilder" the President. In the Blairs' view, Johnson should not only veto the bill but if it passed over his protest he should forbear from executing it. Stanton and Seward, they grumbled, were swinging Johnson away from the line of pure opposition that they would have hewed.

To be sure, Seward was advising Johnson to go more slowly than he had been. Seward respected the fact that Stanton voiced sentiments that were widespread in the North and had powerful friends. Like Stanton, he was fearful that the impeachment inquiry, added to other strains, could wreck the government, and that presidential defiance of the reconstruction bill might make impeachment certain. But Seward was not a tool of Stanton's. And Stanton was an ally, not a lackey, of the radical Republicans.

On February 22, Johnson asked his cabinet for their opinions on the congressional reconstruction plan. Only Stanton advised him to approve it. His stand was perfectly consistent with his words and deeds since Johnson had taken office. Stanton had openly insisted that martial law was necessary in the South even if it meant defiance of the Supreme Court. Now Congress was ready to impose military primacy after the executive had removed it and the judiciary had condemned it, and he was for it. A presidential veto of this bill might provoke impeachment, and he had already made public his fears concerning the possible effects on the nation of such an unprecedented attack on the presidency.

Stanton saw nothing in the congressional reconstruction bill for Johnson to veto. Granting that some Republicans were more conscious of material and party gains in all this than they were motivated by sincere concern for the welfare of the Negro, their plans for the South were far from ferocious. There were to be no executions of rebel leaders, and even Jefferson Davis was soon to be released from military custody to await a civil trial for treason which never came off. Congress envisaged no mass exiles or property confiscations, no imprisonments of high rebel officials, not even an attempt to establish by the law perpetual national supervision over Southern affairs or permanent Republican supremacy in politics. Reconstruction was still to be a moderate process, considering the alternatives Congress had.

But the President ignored Stanton's admonitions, and set Stanbery and Black to work preparing a veto message. Stanton was not surprised at this, but he was alarmed when some of the cabinet members suggested that if Congress impeached Johnson, he ought not to submit to such a "revolutionary" proceeding.[1]

The cabinet also had before it on February 22 a bill regulating the tenure of civil offices. This measure, a retaliation against Johnson's purges of officeholders, provided that persons holding appointments from the President and Senate should continue in their posts until the Senate sanctioned their removal by the President, but that when the Senate was not in session the President might temporarily suspend an officer, reporting the reasons for doing so to the Senate within twenty days after its convening. It also provided that cabinet officers "shall hold their offices . . . during the term of the President by whom they may have been appointed, and for one month thereafter, subject to removal by and with the advice and consent of the Senate."

Frank Blair, Jr., proposed that Johnson circumvent the intent of the tenure-of-office bill by making "a clean sweep" of all the cabinet incumbents while there was still time. Johnson, as usual, seemed to agree, but he did nothing.

When the cabinet met on Monday, February 25, Johnson took Welles aside and, referring to Stanton's support of the reconstruction bill, "alluded to the . . . pitiful exhibition which Stanton made of himself,

---

[1] John L. Motley, *Four Questions for the People, at the Presidential Election, Address at the Music Hall, Oct. 20, 1868* (Boston, 1868), 31–2, echoes Stanton's views. See also Browning, *Diary*, II, 131; Morse, *Welles Diary*, III, 47–9; John Bigelow, *Retrospections of an Active Life* (New York, 1909), IV, 42–4 (hereafter cited as Bigelow, *Retrospections*); F. Blair, Jr., to M. Blair, Dec. 6, 1866, Box XXVI, Blair-Lee Papers, PU.

and wondered if he (S.) supposed he was not understood. The sparkle of the President's eyes and his whole manner betokened intense though suppressed feeling." Most of the cabinet concocted fanciful schemes by which Johnson could resist impeachment by force, while the tenure question slid by. Meeting on Tuesday, the entire cabinet, with Stanton the most vociferous, and seeming "glad to be in accord with his colleagues," as Browning recorded it, advised Johnson to veto the tenure bill.

Johnson jumped at another chance to embarrass Stanton. He asked the War Secretary to prepare the veto. Stanton demurred, pleading lack of time and rheumatism. Seward accepted the task on condition that Stanton assisted him, and the Secretary of State contributed the lion's share of the resulting veto message. Stanton, as Johnson later told the Senate, referred to constitutional precedents, congressional debates, and judicial decisions which supported the veto position. "To all these," Johnson stated, "he added the weight of his own deliberate judgment and advised me that it was my duty to defend the power of the President from usurpation." The President had no doubts in February 1867 that his Secretary of War was sincerely opposed to the tenure-of-office bill. Six months later, Stanton invoked the protection of the measure, which had by that time become law over the President's veto.

Stanton was equally sincere and consistent when he counseled Johnson to approve the reconstruction bill and when he advised him to veto the tenure measure. Apart from his views on the constitutionality of the tenure proposal, Stanton had suffered too often from being unable to discharge officers whom he thought were inept or untrustworthy to support a legislative restriction not only on the President's power but on his own. For the common assumption then, shared by Johnson, Welles, and such observers as J. A. Trowbridge, was that the tenure bill protected all appointed and commissioned officials, including army officers and Freedmen's Bureau personnel, who would enforce the reconstruction measures then being created. Stanton did not want to hogtie the Secretary of War, whether himself or a successor, in the event that he wished to remove any officer who proved inadequate.

To be sure, Republican legislators intended that the tenure bill cover Stanton. But this was their purpose, not his. Earlier, Senator Howe, of Wisconsin, arguing that a cabinet belonged not to an incumbent President, but to the people, and that disagreement on vital issues might be the very reason why a cabinet minister should stay in office, told the Senate that Stanton knew nothing of this effort in his behalf. Then, while the tenure bill was pending in the House, Stanton instructed his friend Bingham that he did not desire the protection which the measure seemed designed to extend to him. Considering Stanton's intention to resign at the earliest possible moment, his statement has the ring of truth.

After all, it was far from sure that the tenure bill covered holdovers from Lincoln's cabinet. During a Senate debate on the measure, John Sherman had specifically stated that it did not. Stanton thought the tenure proposal was undesirable as well as illegal. He neither believed that its provisions covered him in his office nor expected to remain as Secretary long enough to need this or any other protection. No one in February 1867 could anticipate that the events of the succeeding six months could alter the situation so greatly that everyone's estimations would go awry.[2]

In view of these facts, it appears most improbable that Stanton, by advocating that the President veto the tenure law, while knowing that Congress would override the veto, was playing a Machiavellian role designed to lull Johnson into a false sense of security or to provide a means for later impeaching the President. Of course, it is possible that Stanton was concealing his hope that the bill covered him. Perhaps, on the other hand, Johnson was hiding a fear that this was true. Logic balks, if this is the case, at Johnson's retention of Stanton in his cabinet until the tenure bill became law. But the President made no move at all to rid himself of Stanton before it was too late.

Whatever the real, hidden, undiscoverable thoughts of the participants in these events concerning the coverage of the tenure-of-office law (Congress on March 2 overrode the vetoes on it and on the reconstruction bill), the belief that it covered Johnson's cabinet members grew increasingly widespread. Stanton came to see the law as a vote of confidence from Congress, carrying an injunction to hold on to his office and to harmonize its administration with the legislature's decrees. When he later claimed the protection of the law he had once declared to be unconstitutional, he was back in the position of a lawyer and he merely selected from an opposite body of evidence on

---

[2] Welles's notes on the tenure bill, in Beale, *Welles Diary*, III, 736; *ibid.*, 49–54, on cabinet proceedings; Browning, *Diary*, II, 132; Bancroft, *Seward*, II, 465; Blair to Johnson, Feb. 24, 1867, Johnson Papers, LC; "Notes of Colonel W. G. Moore," *loc. cit.*, 110; Flower, *Stanton*, 315; Pratt, *Stanton*, 448; Trowbridge, *A Picture of the Desolated States and the Work of Restoration, 1865–1868* (Hartford, 1868), 610–11; Richardson, *Messages and Papers*, VI, 492–8.

the question in order to protect the interests of a new client, Congress.

On the other hand, the President later claimed to believe that he could test the legitimacy of the tenure law by refusing to execute it or by violating its provisions. Yet Johnson faithfully executed other reconstruction acts in which he professed to have as little faith and which he had also vetoed, and which Congress enacted into laws over his condemnations. No President up to the time of Johnson's decision to violate the tenure law ever suggested a view of presidential power giving the executive a right to enforce only the laws he approved and to ignore or to violate others. War needs justified Lincoln in many extreme acts, but Johnson's was the most insistent voice heard after 1865 that the war was finished.

Knowing that the reconstruction law would be only as strong as the willingness of the executive arm to enforce it, Stanton's decision to keep his office was now based on his fear that Johnson would fail to fulfill the intention of Congress as expressed in its reconstruction bill regarding the South. In February 1867 the tenure-of-office proposal in Stanton's thinking was irrelevant, and its meaning very uncertain.[3]

The veto of the reconstruction bill penned by bitter Jeremiah Black boded ill for future stability, and the subsequent need for three more reconstruction acts, each designed to push the President and Southern whites to obedient action, indicates that Stanton's fears were founded on substantial reasons. Stanton did not trust Andrew Johnson unless he or Grant was on the scene.

On March 1, Seward gave Johnson the veto message he and Stanton had prepared on the tenure bill. The Secretary of State told John Bigelow that the South would be readmitted within a year and that the 1868 elections would kill "the root of bitterness upon which everybody nowadays seems to be chewing." Johnson sent the veto, along with the one on the reconstruction bill, to Congress.

Grant, now in close agreement with Stanton on essential matters, rejoiced next day at the overriding of the veto on the reconstruction act. Writing confidentially to his friend and backer Elihu Washburne, Grant condemned "the most ridiculous veto message that ever issued

---

[3] The entire question of the status of a cabinet officer was recently reviewed, and the Senate has left still unclear the matter of the autonomy of these presidential servants; see *Nomination of Lewis L. Strauss to be Secretary of Commerce*, Senate Executive Report 4 [Committee on Interstate and Foreign Commerce], 86th Cong., 1st sess.

from any President . . . It is a fitting end to all controversy (I believe this last [reconstruction] measure is to be a solution unless the President proves to be an obstruction)." Like Stanton, Grant did not trust Johnson to execute the law, and he shared the War Secretary's derisive view of Johnson's theory of presidential strength and practice of executive weakness. Stanton would have been vastly relieved to know that Grant and he were in basic agreement.

Johnson had removed more patronage appointments in the War Department from Stanton's control and tried to steer army printing and advertising contracts toward newspapers and publishers who sustained the administration. Congress countered on March 2 by requiring that the Government Printing Office do all departmental work. If it could not, the Clerk of the House, faithful radical Edward McPherson, was to farm out contracts. Avoiding another veto, Congress by joint resolution on the same day prohibited the payment of claims against the government to any person unable to establish consistent wartime Unionism, deliberately contradicting the implications of the Supreme Court's decision in the Garland case. Stanton distributed copies of this resolution through the Army as quickly as possible. Point by point, Johnson was forcing the Army into an utter dependence upon Congress.[4]

On March 4, Johnson and the cabinet met at 10 a.m. at the Capitol to deal with the last remaining bills of the congressional session. The President wanted to make a last-ditch stand against the army appropriations measure, containing Stanton's riders on the commanding general's functions and location, still unsigned before him. Again Johnson polled the cabinet. Browning had a veto message prepared, but Seward and Stanton convinced the President that a veto was unwise. Johnson said he would sign it but intended to add a protest. He turned to Stanton and asked him whether he was in favor of a protest. "I make no objection to it," Stanton replied, according to Colonel Moore. "But," said the President, "I wish to know whether you approve of a protest?" Stanton replied: "I approve your taking whatever course you think best." Johnson signed it, added the protest, and the historic Thirty-ninth Congress came to an end.

But at 1 p.m. the legislators met to form the Fortieth Congress.

[4] Grant to Washburne, March 4, 1867, ISHL; Bigelow, *Retrospections*, IV, 44–5; March 1, 1867, S. P. Chase Letterbook, LC, on appointments; on patronage and printing, J. L. Dunnig to Stanton, March 5, and Stanton to McPherson, March 7, 1867, McPherson Papers, LC; AGO, *General Orders, 1867* (Washington, 1868), No. 22.

Stanton and Grant, among others, had pleaded that the congressmen not disperse. Uppermost in their minds was uncertainty concerning Johnson's willingness to execute the reconstruction enactment.

Somewhat to the surprise of extremists in both camps, Johnson soon made it clear that he would execute the reconstruction law. He knew that the Republican radicals were watching his every move in the hope that he might trip himself. Johnson became touchy, and when, on March 8, McCulloch suggested that he quickly appoint the military governors in order to prevent impeachment, "the President got very angry," according to Browning, "and swore vehemently, and said they might impeach and be d–m–d—he was tired of being threatened —that he would not be influenced by any such considerations, but would go forward in the conscientious discharge of his duty without reference to Congress, and meet all the consequences." [5]

But despite his brave words, Johnson kept to his decision to obey the letter if not the intent of the reconstruction law. When the cabinet met on March 12, Johnson took Stanton aside, and while Welles writhed in impatient inability to eavesdrop, the President and War Secretary talked together for more than fifteen minutes. "At the close," Welles recorded, "Stanton was unusually jubilant, had a joke or two with McCulloch, and could not suppress his feelings." For Johnson had told him to name the military governors, and the jubilation Welles noticed derived from Stanton's relief on learning that the President was going to execute the law and by so doing was avoiding the crisis that must come from defiance. Impeachment, as Henry Dawes noted, "is very much under a cloud, and if nothing is done to give it new life it will die of two much nursing." [6] Johnson was at last trying to dam the tide of political extremism.

Morning newspapers the next day announced the names of the generals who by Stanton and Grant's selection were to be the governors of the South. Schofield in the First District, Virginia; "a Conservative Republican when the war broke out," the *Army and Navy Journal* described him, who "did not grow any more radical until his recent experiences in Virginia. He is a safe man." Pope—"a moderate Republican and an excellent administrator"—had the Third District,

---

[5] Browning, *Diary*, II, 134–5; Morse, *Welles Diary*, III, 59–63; memo, March 5–11, 1867, Welles Papers, LC; "Notes of Colonel W. G. Moore," *loc. cit.*, 106.

[6] Michael J. Cramer, *Ulysses S. Grant, Conversations and Unpublished Letters* (New York, 1897), 66–7; Sheridan to Grant and Grant to Johnson, with Stanton's endorsement, March 8–10, 1867, Johnson Papers, LC; Morse, *Welles Diary*, III, 64; Dawes to wife, March 8, 1867, Dawes Papers, LC.

Georgia, Florida, and Alabama. Ord took the Fourth District, Arkansas and Mississippi, and the *Journal*'s editor worried a bit over the fact that he was a conservative Marylander, though withal a just, reliable officer. Sheridan was assigned to the Fifth District, encompassing Louisiana and Texas. According to the *Journal*, he "had traveled far" toward radicalism since the war days, when he had thought that "the abolitionists and secessionists ought to be hung together." Welles worried most over the assignment of Sickles to command the Second District, the Carolinas, because that officer was Stanton's friend. "The slime of the serpent is over them all," Welles grumbled.[7]

A half year later, the younger Frank Blair explained the "spectacular uniformity" of these five generals. "They have their instructions . . . from Stanton," he wrote, "& it is this evil genius of our country who has corrupted the mind of Grant & whispered to him the prospect of absolute & permanent power." Stanton, Blair felt, was trying to be "a Bismarck to our King William [Grant]," and the War Secretary had secured a kingdom in the South for Grant to rule.

The Blairs' hatred of Stanton, intensified by their bitterness at Grant's refusal to go along with the President, had blinded them to realities. For Northern opinion generally approved of the choices for the military-governorships. Stanton and Grant had probably insisted only on Sheridan and Sickles; personal friendships bound the four men together in intimate confidence. The President had been free to specify the others. He learned that ranking army officers, almost to a man, were out of sympathy with his policies in the South. This was not Stanton's doing, or Grant's, but Johnson's.

It became quickly apparent, however, that the reconstruction machinery was not working to the satisfaction of either its congressional creators or its uniformed administrators. The first essential step was the compilation of registers of loyal voters. Die-hard Southerners refused to register and by means of threats made white and Negro would-be voters absent themselves from the polls. Ambiguities in the text of the statute, especially in the sections prescribing standards for disfranchisement, confused every district commander.

Therefore, on March 23, Republican leaders in Congress pushed through a supplemental reconstruction act, again overcoming the paper sword of another veto from Johnson. This supplement gave the army commanders in the South authority to initiate registrations and the constitutional conventions that were to follow them, and specified

[7] Morse, *Welles Diary*, III, 65; *ANJ* (March 30, 1867), 514.

a test oath designed to exclude most former rebels from participation in politics. Feeling that the situation was in hand, congressional leaders then adjourned until July 4, over the protests of Stanton and Grant, who wanted Congress to stay on and continue to keep watch over Johnson.[8]

Tension eased as the legislators left. Washington relaxed from a pitch of activity too intense to bear without relief. Stanton occupied himself with the upsurge of department business occasioned by the reconstruction laws. Cabinet officers shifted their attention to the Alaskan treaty with Russia and the troublesome Indians of the West. Tempers were restrained on these matters and the cabinet officers disagreed without questioning one another's integrity.

The Southern question was different. Johnson's acquiescence in executing the reconstruction laws had not changed the forbidding political fact that, as Senator Dixon phrased it to John Bigelow, "the President made no effort to ease the position of Northern [moderate] Senators and compelled them to vote either with the radicals or with the rebels."

So the emotional calm following the passage of the first two reconstruction acts in March was not a harbinger of peace. Stanton knew that the basic questions remained unanswered, and that old issues were being revived to exacerbate tempers. The Blairs were still searching for ways to push Johnson into outright championship of extreme Democratic tenets, and their first step, as always, was for the President to oust Stanton from the cabinet so that the seemingly manageable Grant, replacing Stanton, would work with the administration. The next step toward calamity was not long delayed.[9]

[8] F. P. Blair, Jr., to Sr., Aug. 2, 1867, Box XXVI, Blair-Lee Papers, PU; A. N. Rankin to Edward McPherson, March 19, 1867, McPherson Papers, LC; Morse, *Welles Diary*, III, 74; Randall, *The Civil War and Reconstruction*, 755-6.

[9] Smith, *Blair Family*, II, 382; Bigelow ms diary, March 28, 30, 1867, NYPL.

OFF THE SHARP HOOKS OF
UNCERTAINTY

$\mathbb{D}$URING March, Johnson opened a new battle line. His cabinet supporters asserted that Congress had designated the troops in the South a special corps, responsive only to the White House and therefore independent of the untrustworthy War Secretary and the uncertain commanding general. So far as the South was concerned, Johnson decided to ignore them both.

In bypassing the war office, Johnson plotted to thwart the clear intentions of Congress and to augment the powers of the presidency. His strategy assumed that Stanton and Grant had nothing to do with reconstruction beyond paying and supplying the soldiers assigned to occupation duties. By ordering the military governors to interpret the reconstruction law in a limited fashion, so far as the disfranchisement of former rebels and the status of Negroes were concerned, Johnson intended to soften the impact of the law on the South, and keep in office the men now controlling the Southern states. By appearing to execute the reconstruction act, however, Johnson could avoid dangers to himself. He might also, Welles suggested, establish control over the troops in the South and so have an obedient military force to act as a counterweight in the event of impeachment. In short, the President would employ the Republicans' laws for his purposes.[1]

He did not even pay Stanton the respect of concealing these intentions. Instead, Johnson displayed his plans at cabinet assemblies as though on signal flags. He should not have been surprised to find that Stanton read the message and took steps to counter the danger.

---

[1] Morse, *Welles Diary*, III, 59–63; memo, March 5–11, 1867, Welles Papers, LC.

Stanton and Grant conferred on this new menace to stability. They agreed on a strategy that, though paralleling the President's in some details, fit better with the facts of the time. In their thinking, Congress's reconstruction law had created a second, separate army of the United States, and its officers received their authority from the legislators rather than the President. In respect to this second "army," Congress had placed certain limits on the President's commander-in-chief function, left unlimited in the Constitution but not therefore unlimitable. He must appoint the district commanders, and he could remove any who failed to perform properly the responsibilities set down by Congress. But, Stanton and Grant concluded, neither the President nor any of the cabinet members could interpret the reconstruction law. Congress had delegated this power to the military governors alone.

To be sure, by this theory Stanton and Grant seemingly agreed with Johnson that the war office was bypassed. But this was of little concern to the Secretary and the commanding general—or, rather, was of great advantage. Grant maintained unofficial channels of communication with the army's ranking officers, with whom he enjoyed warm friendships and who shared with him a sense of professional solidarity. He could therefore secretly advise and influence the military governors. Enjoying the certain shield of the Army Appropriations Act, he could counter what he felt were destructive White House policies while furthering his own political ambitions. With the occupation commanders to brave Johnson's displeasure if they took issue with the President's views, and with Stanton to take on the cabinet infighting, Grant nestled in a safe haven of apparent neutrality.

As always, Stanton was out in the open. He accepted this exposed position because only in this way could Johnson's strategy be blocked without triggering the crisis that Stanton so feared. If the theory he and Grant had conceived could be sustained against the counterattacks which the President was sure to launch, then it no longer mattered so greatly if Johnson ousted Stanton or replaced Grant with his champion, or how the President, through Attorney General Stanbery, chipped away at the reconstruction law by restrictive analyses. Perhaps, therefore, Stanton could feel free to resign. The autonomous occupation commanders, independent of the White House as well as of the War Department, would still hold the fort.

The defenses came up barely in time. In the first application of a power of a district commander under the reconstruction law, Sheridan on March 27 removed several municipal and state officials of

Louisiana from their offices. Grant, while maintaining silence in public, secretly encouraged Sheridan. "It is just the thing," he wrote, "and merits the approbation of the loyal people at least." Then, retreating even in private correspondence to his neutral corner, Grant added: "I only write this to let you know that I at least approve what you have done."

Johnson asked Stanbery to determine whether a district commander could remove civil officials or set standards for voters, and ordered Sheridan to defer further removals until Stanbery's opinion was available. On April 3, Grant obediently transmitted this order through regular army channels. But two days later he sent Sheridan a private message, warning him that "there is a decided hostility to the whole Congressional plan of reconstruction at the 'White House,' and a disposition to remove you from . . . command. . . . Both the Secretary of War and myself will oppose any such move, as will the mass of the people." Grant "suggested," however, that Sheridan at his own discretion hold off further removals of state officials until Stanbery's opinion was in.

Then Grant sketched his and Stanton's novel view of civil-military relationships. "There is nothing clearer in my mind than that Congress intended to give District Commanders entire control over the civil governments of these [Southern] districts," he wrote, "and only recognized present civil authorities within these districts at all, for the convenience of their commanders, to make use of, or so much of as suited them, and as would aid them in carrying out the Congressional plan of restoring loyal, permanent governments." Grant was positive that Congress "contemplates that District Commanders shall be their own judges of the meaning of its provisions. Any opinion from the Attorney General should be weighed, however. The power of removing District Commanders undoubtedly exists with the President, but no officer is going to be hurt by a faithful performance of his duty. . . . I will keep you advised officially or otherwise of all that affects you." [2]

Stanton's subtle, complex position confused some of his friends, who could not understand why he stayed on in a turncoat administration. A movement of some strength was developing to make him the Republican presidential nominee in 1868, but as the Cleveland *Leader* editorialized, "his present cabinet position weakens him as a Republican party man." While Republican leaders pondered the Stan-

[2] Badeau, *Grant*, 60–1, 102; exchange between Johnson, Stanton, Grant, and Sheridan, March 27–April 13, 1867, Johnson Papers, LC.

ton paradox, he made it clear that he did not want the nomination. He was in politics, but only to see the Army through the dangers ahead, and to warn the President of limits beyond which it was dangerous to go.

Stanton overestimated his abilities as a pacificator. In his logical, lawyerlike way, he still assumed that Johnson would follow a rational political course. He did not comprehend that the President was bitterly emotional regarding the frustrations he had suffered, and now blamed all his troubles on the War Secretary. Stanton failed to anticipate that Johnson and his supporters would misread almost every event as a favorable augury for the White House and for the Democrats. For example, Welles exulted that a minor Democratic victory in Connecticut on April 1 was "the first loud knock which admonishes the Radicals of their doom." Unimpressed by the Democrats' prospects for widespread majorities at the polls, Stanton was concerned over more immediate menaces.

Mississippi officials, encouraged by Black, had alleged that the reconstruction acts were unconstitutional, and had petitioned the Supreme Court for an injunction forbidding the President to enforce them. Republicans steeled themselves for the worst. "I imagine that at no time in our history have there been so many ears pricked in all parts of our country for a coming decision of a tribunal," Lieber commented to Sumner.

When the cabinet assembled on April 5, Stanton joined in the unanimous opinion that the President was not subject to the Court's jurisdiction. But he was the only one to recommend that Johnson keep out of the affair and wait to learn how the jurists treated the petition. Stanbery argued that the President should be represented in the case as *amicus curiae*, which Johnson agreed to, and then Stanton merely stated that he would defer to the common judgment.[3]

Stanton wanted to keep Johnson aloof from the Mississippi matter in order that the President might avoid antagonizing the Republican leaders in Congress. The irritations of the Milligan and test oath decisions were still raw in Republican minds. The Attorney General's appearance in court would be enough to convince suspicious Republicans that the President was conspiring with the untrustworthy jurists

---

[3] *Leader*, May 6, 1867; Morse, *Welles Diary*, III, 77–8; April 5 (misdated July 5), 1867, Moore notebook, Johnson Papers, LC; Lieber to Sumner, April 15, 1867, Lieber Papers, HL; Browning, *Diary*, II, 142; Bigelow, *Retrospections*, IV, 57; *Mississippi v. Johnson*, 4 *Wallace* 475 (1867).

they were planning to remove more Johnson appointees from civil offices in those states. Grant encouraged the generals by restating to them his position regarding their independence from executive oversight, and assured them of his and Stanton's support. He advised them, however, to suspend state officers rather than remove them, in deference to the attitude Stanbery would obviously take, and to have them tried immediately by military courts, which deferred neither to presidential opinions nor to the Supreme Court's Milligan decision. In the same vein, he suggested to Sheridan that the test oath provision of the second reconstruction act was a proper mode for the "disfranchisement of a class of citizens that ought always to be disfranchised," although the Court had condemned such oaths. And he comforted Sheridan, writing: "I think your head is safe above your shoulders at least so that it can not be taken off to produce pain." [7]

Stanton attended every cabinet meeting in spite of his increasing illness. Determined to avoid a clash with the President, he kept quiet. His silence only infuriated Johnson, who decided to bring matters to a head. Without asking for opinions from Stanton or Grant, the President ordered Sheridan to suspend an order limiting voting to a fifteen-day period, in order to keep balloting going until Stanbery's forthcoming opinion opened a door through which white Southerners might perjuriously make their way to the polls. Still Stanton said nothing. Desperately trying to keep the peace, he obeyed each order from the President. Grant, he knew, would see to the execution of the substance of the reconstruction laws.

Similarly, though crudely goaded by Johnson, Stanton avoided commenting when the President released Jefferson Davis from military custody so that the rebel leader might face a civil trial. Again, when the mystery of certain missing pages from the Booth diary hit the headlines, and Johnson leaped to the conclusion that Stanton had hidden the torn leaves in order to conceal his guilt in the railroading of Mrs. Surratt to the gallows, Stanton forbore from fighting back either at cabinet meetings or in newspaper columns.

To be sure, Stanton knew that he would quickly have his chance. His friend on the House Judiciary Committee, Henry Wilson, arranged to have Stanton give testimony on the Booth papers soon after the headlines had appeared. But these were side shows in relation to Stanton's major concern, the issue of the powers of army commanders in the South.

[7] Sheridan to Grant, April 21, 1867, Johnson Papers, LC; Badeau, *Grant*, 65–8.

Then, in the second week of May, General Ord, commanding in Arkansas and Mississippi, threatened to disperse the "Johnson" legislatures of both states.[8] Inspired to hurry by the news of Ord's contemplated action, Stanbery on May 14 presented the cabinet with a first installment of his opinion on the reconstruction laws. No one was surprised to learn that it limited the powers of the district commanders, or that Stanbery would open the polls in the South to former rebels barred by Congress's laws. Stanton, however, was readying his lawyer's skill to match the best that the Attorney General could offer.

A week later, Stanbery offered a second chapter of his opinion. Stanton, tenacious and in deadly earnest, insisting that interpretation was out of their hands, countered him on point after point. Then, on May 23, after hearing the third part of the serial draft, Stanton made a desperate bid for compromise.

"I dissent from the whole opinion," he informed the President and his cabinet colleagues. Expanding on the reasons for his disagreement, Stanton followed the main line of his and Grant's interpretation of the President's insignificant functions under the reconstruction laws. Then he departed from the position he and Grant had agreed on. On his own initiative, he agreed with Stanbery that minor country and municipal officials in the South were subject to the relatively mild disfranchising standard of the Fourteenth Amendment, which he had helped to write, rather than to the far more inclusive pattern set in the reconstruction laws. Further, registering officers must accept the proffered loyalty oath of a would-be voter, even though they felt it was perjured. In short, Stanton was asking the President to accept the moderate Republican view that only the few thousand Southerners who had held state or federal offices before the war and then joined in rebellion, should be excluded from participating in reconstruction. He was prepared to reject the radical demand, symbolized by the test oath, that everyone in the South who in any way had aided the rebellion should be disqualified from voting or holding office.[9]

Here was a chance for Johnson to gain Stanton's aid in bridging the

---

[8] Johnson-Stanton-Grant exchange, May 7–14, 1867, Stanton MSS and Johnson Papers, LC; Stanton to Ord, May 11, 1867, HQA, Box 104, RG 108, NA; Morse, *Welles Diary*, III, 90–1; "Notes of Colonel W. G. Moore," *loc. cit.*, 99, 106; Boutwell to Butler, May 16, 1867, Butler Papers, LC; Eisenschiml, *Why Was Lincoln Murdered?*, 143–4.

[9] Stanton's minutes of the May 23 meeting, written in the flyleaf of a volume of army general orders, ISHL. Other data in Beale, *Welles Diary*, III, 93–4, 96, 98, 737. In part by 1868 and fully by 1871, Congress accepted Stanton's standards regarding federal officeholders' loyalty requirements; see Hyman, *Era of the Oath*, 121–34.

gap between the White House and Congress. He must acquiesce in the verdict of the 1866 elections, submit to congressional leadership, as he could not overcome it, and leave the South in suspended animation for the remainder of his term. But the President was no longer sensitive to moderate nuances. He thought that Stanton was pleading from weakness rather than bidding from strength, and rejected his appeal.

Johnson leaked accounts of these proceedings to friendly newspapers. Southern whites, encouraged by the implications of Stanbery's interpretation, intensified their harassment of soldiers and Negroes. Stanton and Grant thereupon circularized all Southern commands, cautioning officers to "great vigilance . . . for the prompt suppression of riots and breaches of the public peace." Pope removed more civil officials in Alabama. Sickles, despairing of the willingness of a South Carolina sheriff to punish offenders, threatened to arrest the offender and try him before a military court. Sheridan reported that he was preparing to oust more state officeholders in Louisiana.

Rumors grew that the President was on the point of removing Sheridan from his command as a sign to all the military governors to halt their interferences with state personnel. Sheridan had been the most outspoken of the high army officials in supporting the congressional policies for the South, and he was known as Grant's protégé. Grant wrote encouragingly to him: "You have to the fullest extent the confidence of the Secretary, the loyal people generally, and myself. Removal cannot hurt you if it does take place, and I do not believe it will. You have carried out the acts of Congress, and it will be difficult to get a general officer who will not." [1]

Trouble loomed closer to home. A District of Columbia municipal election was scheduled for June 3, and riots were feared now that Negroes could vote. Stanton ordered soldiers to duty, but one situation almost thwarted his security measures. A quartermaster captain of Democratic convictions refused to allow colored laborers time off to vote, and arranged with Negrophobe friends to block the roads and canal routes from his suburban supply depot into Washington. District Negroes, hearing of this plot, started out to free the coerced laborers. Stanton learned what was going on. He hurried Adjutant General Thomas off to investigate "in order that those who deserve to exercise the franchise have leave to do so without intimida-

---

[1] To Sheridan, Badeau, *Grant*, 66, 102; other data in Stanton to Grant, May 18, 1867, WD, Military Book, LVIII, 342, RG 107, NA; Browning, *Diary*, II, 146-7; Morse, *Welles Diary*, III, 99-100.

Stanton in his office at the War Department, 1865.

THE MEN AT THE SCRATCH.

FIRST KNOCK DOWN FOR ANDY.

ANDY SHIES HIS CASTOR INTO THE RING.

ANDY DISCHARGES HIS RIGHT AND HIS SECRETARY.

ANDY THINKS THE LAST ROUND NOT ON THE SQUARE, AND PROPOSES TO SETTLE THE MATTER OVER GRANT'S SHOULDER.

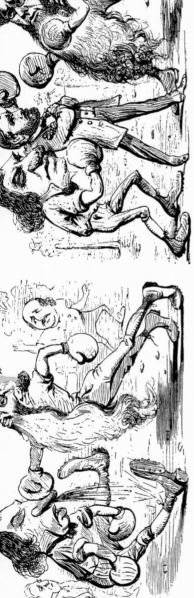

THE SECRETARY PUTS IN HIS "TENURE OF OFFICE," AND CAROMS ON ANDY'S BILL.

AWAITING THE REFEREE'S DECISION—THE SECRETARY A LITTLE AHEAD.

BOTH COME UP CHEERFULLY AND NOT AT ALL GROGGY.

"*A Fight for the Championship.*" *From Frank Leslie's Illustrated Newspaper, February 15, 1868.*

Probably the last photograph of Stanton, 1869.

tion or interference." By noon the belligerent captain was behind guardhouse bars. Army wagons were hurrying his jubilant employees to the polls. What might have been a bloody riot was transformed into a celebration. Though Welles saw in the Republican victory only evidence of managed black votes, Stanton took pleasure in the effective way he had enforced the new suffrage law.[2]

In the first week of June, Johnson went off on a trip, after ordering that Sheridan extend indefinitely the registration period for voting in New Orleans. The general obeyed this command, but disregarding the implications of Stanbery's views on the reconstruction laws, excluded from the polls all residents with rebel pasts, despite tenders of oaths claiming unalloyed past loyalty. Again, Grant secretly applauded his actions. Sheridan then discharged some levee commissioners. Governor Wells, of Louisiana, wired the President requesting that he revoke Sheridan's order; the President did so. But after reinstating the levee commissioners, Sheridan removed Governor Wells. Speculation increased as to what the President would do to Sheridan when he returned to Washington, and administration newspapers distorted the meaning of Stanton's bid for compromise to insinuate that the War Secretary was now with the President.

Grant was also absent from Washington; because he distrusted the President, he would leave the capital only when Johnson did. When the Sheridan story broke, Stanton sent Grant a code message: "You are needed here." Grant hurried back to Washington. After a conference with the anxious Secretary, Grant on June 7 wrote confidentially to Sheridan: "I know Mr. Stanton is disposed to support you not only in this last measure but in every official act of yours so far. He can not say so because it is in the Cabinet he has to do this and there is no telling when he may not be overruled and it would not be in keeping with his position to announce beforehand that he intended to differ with his associate advisers." Grant assured Sheridan that the President had earned the distrust of army officers, apart from any question of politics, by this cowardly thrust at Sheridan during Grant's absence.[3]

During the fortnight spanning his compromise offer of May 23 and the thwarting of Johnson's plans for Sheridan on June 7, Stanton lost

[2] June 3, 1867, Sec. War Correspondence File, Box 325, RG 107, NA; E. R. S. Canby to Stanton, June 2, 1867, Stanton MSS; Morse, *Welles Diary*, III, 102.
[3] To Sheridan, June 7, 1867, Sheridan Papers, LC; Badeau, *Grant*, 86, 103; Hesseltine, *Grant*, 85; Morse, *Welles Diary*, III, 104; Gorham, *Stanton*, II, 357–8, 381.

faith in the possibility that moderation might stabilize the course of events. He now joined irrevocably with Grant in sustaining the absolute powers of the military commanders in the South under Congress's laws. Hearing that Sickles was refusing to obey writs of habeas corpus issued by United States courts in the Carolinas requiring the general to turn over civilian prisoners convicted by military tribunals of murdering Union soldiers, Stanton telegraphed him: "You will neither give up the prisoners nor submit to arrest, but take into custody any and all persons attempting either." [4]

The President had returned to Washington and was on hand for the cabinet meeting on June 11, when Stanbery offered his greatly polished argument restricting the powers of the army commanders. Stanton dissented from every point, without any suggestion of compromise. Three days later, after hearing a final draft of Stanbery's opinion, the President decided to postpone for a while a direct assault on the Army, and to swivel his guns on Stanton, who Johnson mistakenly felt was weakening and might be coerced into submission or into resigning.

When the cabinet assembled on June 18, Johnson adopted a disingenuous pose of an innocent seeking guidance. He wanted, he said, "to avail himself of all the light which could be offered by . . . members of the Cabinet, to enable him to see that these [reconstruction] laws be faithfully executed, and to decide what orders and instructions are necessary to be given to the Military Commanders," as well as to be instructed on the wider question of his authority over the generals in the South. It was very important, the President continued, to have unanimity of opinion in the cabinet, and he wanted to scotch the rumors that accord did not exist.

Johnson and Stanbery rigged their trap by asking each cabinet officer's opinion on a curious catalogue of insignificant and unimportant matters, few of which were directly concerned with the major issues the President had stressed in his opening remarks. Not surprisingly, cabinet unanimity did exist on the questions of age and residential requirements for voters, the responsibility of registrars to maintain records, and the propriety of disfranchising Southerners who had held national commissions and thereafter joined the rebellion.

On points of greater substance, however, Stanton stubbornly stood alone. He was not dismayed by the President's portentous tone, and

---

[4] Sickles to Stanton, June 16, 1867, Stanton MSS; exchange, Sickles, Stanton, and Johnson, June 9–15, 1867, Johnson Papers, LC; Bowers, *op. cit.*, 166–7.

perhaps the Secretary courted dismissal at this time, when he was ready to justify his position before the cabinet and the country and yet avoid the consequences to himself that he feared would come if Johnson continued to reach out for control of the Army.

So Stanton cast dissenting votes all through the long afternoon. Registrars, he held, must be able to reject voters whom they suspected of perjury in subscribing the required loyalty oath. Members of secession conventions, state militias, and home-guard units, county and municipal officials, attorneys (as they were court officers), and even large contributors to rebel charities were as guilty of treason as front-line rebel soldiers and should not vote or hold office in the South. Aid to the rebellion must have been voluntary to warrant disfranchisement, Stanbery insisted. Stanton held that it was impossible to establish what was voluntary and what was coerced.

When dusk fell, the weary men prepared to adjourn. Stanbery announced that on the next day he would bring up for discussion some drafts of the interpretation of the reconstruction laws which he was preparing for the guidance of the army commanders.[5] But when the cabinet reassembled on June 19, and Stanton asked Stanbery whether his drafts were ready, Stanbery lamely replied that he had not had time to prepare them.

He had had, however, time enough to assemble another set of "interrogatories" and to get them printed, and now passed out copies to each cabinet officer. Stanton objected to this "string of general questions" to which "gentlemen were required to make immediate answer." The questions were plain and simple, and anyone should be able to give an opinion on them without preparation, Stanbery retorted, ignoring the fact that he and the President had carefully prepared answers as well as inquiries.

Stanton lost patience with the farce. He commenced reading a statement he had carefully prepared, supporting Congress's plenary powers in reconstruction and the independence of the generals in the South from the President. Although Johnson and Stanbery tried frequently to interrupt him, Stanton would not halt. Then, as soon as he had finished, each of his cabinet colleagues derided his assumptions and conclusions. Stanton refused to be drawn into a useless debate. The past week of exhausting arguments had shown him only what he

[5] Stanton's ms memos, June 11, 14, 18 meetings, Stanton MSS; Gorham, *Stanton*, II, 360–1; Morse, *Welles Diary*, III, 107–11.

Stanton : The Life and Times

already knew—that he was isolated in the cabinet. He also knew, better than the President and his supporters, that Congress held the reins of power and was prepared to lash out at Johnson for adequate cause. Stanton was convinced that the worst thing that Johnson could do was to fail to heed the danger signals so prominently flying, and Stanbery's advice was leading the President toward that extreme position.

Therefore, Stanton, having presented his brief, refrained from arguing further with his cabinet brethren, who after all were merely spectators. He would save his energy for the judge and jury on Capitol Hill, for the verdict must come from Congress. His position was on record, and he supposed the President could not now assert that there was unanimity of opinion in the cabinet.

But Johnson was determined to carry on the play, and so the inquisition resumed the next day, when the President sprang a set of special questions on Stanton. Couched in such artful simplicity that both yes and no answers were equally meaningless, they were designed to confuse the public and to push Stanton to the point of saying that the President had absolutely no powers left over the Army in the South.

Stanton refused to be trapped. Of course, he stated, the generals must obey presidential orders, so long as those instructions fitted in with Congress's laws. The legislators had intended the army commanders to modify or abolish the laws of the Southern states; therefore, the President might not forbid the generals to exercise this power, but rather should see to it that Congress's will was done. Resorting to the argument of unreal horrors, Johnson asked whether the general could modify decisions of state and federal courts. This had not happened, Stanton pointed out bitingly, but a general had the same power over a state court as over all other parts of the civil administration in the South.

Once again Stanton underestimated Johnson's stubbornness. The President still hoped to gain from the cabinet members a formal expression of unanimity of opinion in his favor. If he succeeded, then the officers on occupation duty, becoming confused concerning Stanton's position despite Grant's assurances, might well defer to orders from the White House from fear that protection from the War Department was too uncertain to depend on. Johnson suggested that a preamble to the order he intended issuing to the generals in the South, asserting that he and all the cabinet were in agreement on its terms, would be appropriate.

Attention fixed on Stanton. He spoke up without hesitation. The cabinet was not agreed, he said. Did not a majority vote constitute agreement, Johnson asked? Not in the cabinet, Stanton quite correctly retorted, for it was merely an advisory body and the head of one department could not be bound by the opinions of other cabinet officers, whose responsibilities were in other areas of government.

On this last point, Seward agreed with Stanton. Encouraged, Stanton said that he would not transmit such a preamble to the Army even if Johnson insisted on it. And so, after five weeks of steady pressure on Stanton at the cabinet table, the President lost. Stanton refused to abandon his ramparts. Retreating, Johnson lodged a final and petty shaft. He assigned Stanton to work with Stanbery on the presidential instructions to the generals in the South.[6]

By noon the next day the instructions were completed, and Stanton released them for transmission to the Army and to the press. The President went off on a trip, and Stanton collapsed.

His physical deterioration, combined with reports of the cabinet squabbling, inspired new rumors that he was resigning, which Greeley's *Tribune* denied on the basis that Stanton was one of a breed that "rarely die and never resign." Indeed, Stanton had no thought of quitting now. After talking with him, Hay recorded that "he said the newspapers must have their little item now and then. I don't think he is going just yet."

Meanwhile Johnson was touring the Democratic strongholds of the northeast, and from the reception he enjoyed he concluded that he had gained public favor. He also thought that his instructions to the occupation commanders, even without the suggestion of cabinet unanimity, had won the obedience he desired from them. Grant, however, was countering him secretly by advising the district commanders to shrug off the restrictive opinions from the White House.

Therefore, the generals were not confused, as Johnson had hoped they would be. But they were angry at being forced to disobey either him or Congress. Sheridan was most outspoken in his bitterness. Grant advised the youthful officer to comply nevertheless with the President's instructions and thus "silence all charges of attempting to defeat the Attorney-General's construction of the Reconstruction Act."

[6] Ms minutes of June 19–20 meetings, Stanton MSS; and see Gorham, *Stanton*, II, 362–71; Flower, *Stanton*, 316–19. Welles wanted no order issued at all, for it implied that Johnson now accepted the validity of congressional reconstruction: Morse, *Welles Diary*, III, 109–14.

But he also advised Sheridan to procrastinate. "In the meantime," Grant wrote, "Congress may give an interpretation of its own, differing possibly from those given by the Attorney General." [7]

The President then made a grave error. His friends in the War Department supplied him with a copy of a private communication that Sheridan had sent to Grant. In it, the younger officer vilified Johnson and derided Stanbery's opinion as a "broad macadamized road for perjury to travel on." Johnson released this to the Democratic press. Now taking care to guard his lines of communication from the President's spies, Grant had General Horace Porter write encouragingly to Sheridan that "Congress . . . will undo the mischief that has lately been done," and predicted that Stanbery's opinion "will therefore have no more weight than that of any other good lawyer."

In the first days of July, with Johnson returned from his tour and Stanton back at work, the cabinet considered Sheridan's publicized communication. Although Stanton agreed that it was disrespectful, he argued that Sheridan could say what he wished in private correspondence, and the Secretary wondered how the offending missive had come out of the War Department's files. Johnson, irresolute and afraid to come to blows with Congress, let slide this chance to remove Sheridan from command. And he still made no move to demand Stanton's resignation.

Working closely with Grant, Stanton prepared a bill designed to embody their views on the President's lack of power to direct army officers on reconstruction duty, and which would counter Stanbery's opinion on the standards for disfranchisement. Republican congressmen hurried it through both houses, whereupon Johnson blasted it in a veto message as an incitement to insubordination in the Army. But Congress easily surmounted this weak obstacle. On July 19, Stanton's measure became law, whereupon Congress adjourned. This third reconstruction act specifically gave district commanders the independence of the White House that Stanton and Grant had claimed derived from the first two laws, and implicitly recognized the existence in the South of a separate army under Congress's control. [8]

Stanton and Grant were satisfied that they had warded off crisis while at the same time protecting the nation's and the Army's interests.

[7] To Sheridan, June 24, 1867, Sheridan Papers, LC; Badeau, *Grant*, 83; Gorham, *Stanton*, II, 380; Hay, *Diaries and Letters*, 284.

[8] Draft of bill in Stanton's hand, Stanton MSS; Porter to Sheridan, June 25, 1867, Sheridan Papers, LC; Richardson, *Messages and Papers*, VI, 536–45.

At last the President seemed cowed. He uncomplainingly returned the troublesome Sheridan letter when Stanton, at Grant's request, asked for it. It seemed that an equilibrium had been achieved. Perhaps Johnson was ready to serve out the remainder of his term without seeking to alter his present relationship with Congress and the Army.

Things grew so quiet as the torpid midsummer heat blanketed the capital that Stanton returned the War Department to the prewar schedule of working hours, the last government agency to relax from the wartime tempo. He proudly hung the honorary Doctor of Laws degree which Yale awarded him next to the one he had previously received from Kenyon. Ellen and he, knowing what little interest he had in elective office, were amused but flattered at assertions that, after Grant, he was the front runner for a Republican presidential nomination.

Now that the district commanders could openly proceed in their disfranchising policies, Grant decided to go off on a vacation. The general, concerned over Stanton's health, insisted that Stanton seek recreation in turn when he returned to Washington. "Things might have been so different now," Grant noted regretfully to the Secretary, if Johnson had gone the right way "and given repose to the country and consequently rest to all interested in administering the laws."

Stanton's relationship with Grant had grown exceedingly close. They agreed that the President, though seemingly submissive, was still not to be trusted. Therefore, though Stanton did plan to take a vacation as soon as Grant was back in the capital, he would keep the war portfolio for another six months. If by the year's end Johnson had maintained his present tractability, then Stanton would feel free to resign.[9]

Andrew Johnson had other plans. Rejecting clear evidence that he had lost the game, politically weak yet thinking himself strong, Johnson still thought he could turn matters to his own advantage.

Stanton, the President concluded, had been directing Grant. He felt that he understood and could control men with ambition, and all Washington now understood that Grant was bent on the presidency. Johnson saw no reason why, if Stanton were gone, he should not pick up the reins and maneuver the general. Once in control of Grant, the

---

[9] Notes on a memo in Stanton's hand, undated, of conversations with Grant, *ca.* July 15, 1867, owned by the estate of Benjamin P. Thomas; ms memo, Grant to Stanton, June 13, 1867, Johnson Papers, LC; Gorham, *Stanton*, II, 374–5, for Grant's letter. Other data in Morse, *Welles Diary*, III, 123, 131–2; Cleveland *Herald*, July 11, 1867.

real center of the Army, Johnson could throw Republican strategy back on itself. And he guessed that, with Grant in apparent sympathy with him, the general's suitability as a Republican standard-bearer must diminish, and his own increase in the eyes of the Democrats, an outcome he deeply desired.[1]

Passion added its blinding effects to Johnson's conceits. Revived talk of Stanton's alleged duplicity in the Surratt clemency petition, of the Secretary's participation in drafting the third reconstruction act, and of Sheridan's publicized impertinence, proved to be more than the President could stand. He hinted about that he was ready to relieve Sheridan, but he told no one as yet that Stanton, too, was to go.

Army officers were distressed by the rumors concerning Sheridan. General George Thomas wrote Stanton that "the relief of Genl. Sheridan will be sure to revive the energies of the opponents of reconstruction . . . and in a like proportion embarrass the efforts of his successor." Grant cut his vacation short and hurried back to Washington.

There, on the last day of July, the President summoned him to the White House, and told him that Stanton as well as Sheridan was to be ousted. Johnson wanted Grant to take over the war office. Grant hedged. The next day he wrote Johnson asserting that the tenure law protected Stanton. "The meaning of the law may be explained away by an astute lawyer," he warned, "but common sense and the views of loyal people will give to it the effect intended by the framers." Why, he asked, had the President delayed a decision on ousting Stanton and Sheridan until just after Congress adjourned? Grant, in frank, outspoken terms, told Johnson that loyal men in both the North and the South might not submit "to see the very men of all others who they have expressed confidence in, removed."

This admonition made Johnson hesitate, and he brought some of the cabinet members and a few other intimates into his confidence. Seward reminded him of the respect in which Stanton was held across the country and revived Johnson's concern over impeachment. But Welles spurred him on, and Chief Justice Chase, whose political ambitions had long since cut the ties of friendship that had once bound him to Stanton, also encouraged the President. Johnson decided to push.[2]

[1] July 14, 1867, Moore notebook, Johnson Papers, LC; "Notes of Colonel W. G. Moore," *loc. cit.*, 103–4; July 31, 1867, Bigelow ms diary, NYPL, and see his *Retrospections*, IV, 92.

[2] Thomas to Stanton, July 4, 1867, HQA, Letters Received, Box 105, RG 108, NA; Badeau, *Grant*, 20–2; Morse, *Welles Diary*, III, 147–50; O. B. Matteson to Seward, Aug. 7, 1867, Seward Papers, UR; Robert B. Warden, *An Account of the Life and Public Services of Salmon Portland Chase* (Cincinnati, 1874), 669–70.

And so, on the hot, sticky Monday morning of August 5, 1867, the President's secretary appeared at Stanton's office with a message for the war minister: "Public considerations of a high character constrain me to say that your resignation as Secretary of War will be accepted." Stanton was not surprised. Grant had told him of his interview with the President six days before, and Stanton had urged Grant to take on the war portfolio if Johnson carried through his determination. But Stanton had scarcely believed the threat would ever come to pass. Nevertheless, he was prepared for it. Later that morning Stanton sent his reply to the White House. In accordance with his earlier confidence to Grant, he refused to resign before the next meeting of Congress in December.

Reading Stanton's reply, the President boasted that he would leave the stubborn Secretary "hanging on the sharp hooks of uncertainty for a few days, and then suspend him from office." But unless Grant was willing to take over in Stanton's place, Johnson could gain nothing from suspending Stanton except the pleasure of his absence from August to December. For it was certain that the Senate would confirm no one in Stanton's place except Grant. After a conversation with the President on August 10, Montgomery Blair admitted to his wife that "I hardly know what to advise. He [Johnson] is a very unhappy man & in a very helpless pitiable condition. I told him to send for Grant." [3] Blair and Johnson were to regret this suggestion.

At the war office, Stanton wrestled with the unsettlement in army circles caused by the President's request for his resignation. Johnson had already taken advantage of his absence from the cabinet to shift from the Army to the Interior Department the responsibility for control of the western Indian tribes. Pope and George Thomas had white Southern civilian prisoners in their charge awaiting trials before military commissions. The generals feared that any successor Johnson appointed to the war office would share Johnson's views on reconstruction and that consequently military trials would be rendered uesless.

Outwardly Stanton maintained his habitual icy demeanor. But in private he exhibited a turbulent emotional stress. Hitchcock realized that he was deeply wounded by the vitriolic journalistic treatment of the cabinet crisis, especially as many of the articles came from men who had fallen afoul of wartime security arrangements and were now

[3] Welles to Johnson, *ca.* Aug. 3, 1867, HL; Aug. 5, 1867, Moore notebook, Johnson Papers, LC; "Notes of Colonel W. G. Moore," *loc. cit.*, 107–8; Morse, *Welles Diary*, III, 152–8; Blair to wife, Aug. 10, 1867, Blair Family Papers, LC.

gaining revenge. Grant and Senator Wilson, talking with him about some abusive newspaper articles, saw the Secretary suddenly break into tears.[4]

It was not the contumely he experienced that depressed Stanton. His distress was occasioned by contradictory fears and hopes. He was eager to leave a cabinet situation that had long been irksome and was now impossible. Learning that Montgomery Blair, now a frequent White House caller, might replace him, Stanton again pressed Grant to take on the war portfolio if Johnson discharged him, in order to prevent such a national disaster.

Yet Stanton wondered why Grant seemed so eager. He became suddenly distrustful of the general. Stanton jumped to the conclusion that Johnson would never suspend him unless Grant were willing to step into the war office. Perhaps, after all, Johnson might overawe the general once he came into the administration. Then all the risks and efforts of years might be undone.

Stanton was incapable of expressing these fears to Grant. In turn, the general, as secretive and indrawn as ever, kept to himself his conviction that he had no choice but to safeguard the Army's welfare and the nation's interests by moving into the war office if Stanton moved out. Grant recognized that accepting a place in Johnson's cabinet might wither the political laurels he coveted. Failing to share his own fears with Stanton, he did not suspect that the Secretary questioned his motives.

The suspense was becoming unendurable for Stanton. Then, on Sunday morning, August 11, the President summoned Grant to the White House and offered him an interim appointment as War Secretary while continuing in his status as commanding general. Grant said he would obey orders, and disavowed any personal antipathy toward the President. Both men avoided the unpleasant subject of their differences of opinion on reconstruction. Johnson then went happily off to church.[5]

[4] Stanton to H. Woodman, Aug. 6, 1867, Woodman Papers, MHS; undated entry, *ca.* Aug. 7–10, 1867, Hitchcock ms diary, GI; Wilson, "Edwin M. Stanton," *loc. cit.,* 17; Pope to Holt, Aug. 10, 1867, Holt Papers, LC; on Thomas, Stanton to Johnson, Aug. 8, 1867, Johnson Papers, LC.

[5] On Aug. 10, Stanton confided his fears about Grant in a letter to his wartime associate Watson, but never sent it; copy of this letter owned by the estate of Benjamin P. Thomas. It fits in with and clarifies all other evidence. Other data in Badeau, *Grant,* 90; Hesseltine, *Grant,* 97; C. A. Dana and James H. Wilson, *Life of Ulysses S. Grant* (Springfield, 1868), 379–84 (hereafter cited as Dana and Wilson, *Grant*) ; Morse, *Welles Diary,* III, 167; Aug. 11, 1867, Moore notebook, Johnson Papers, LC, and "Notes of Colonel W. G. Moore," *loc. cit.,* 109; Gorham, *Stanton,* II, 405–7.

All during that long hot Sunday, Stanton had been speculating with Ellen and their guest, Pierrepont, concerning the probable course of events. After dinner they took seats by the open front door of the Stanton home to enjoy the twilight coolness. Grant appeared in the doorway. He seemed hesitant, and awkwardly asked Stanton for a private interview in the library.

Fifteen minutes passed. Both men reappeared, flushed with emotion and uncertain in their attitudes toward each other. After brief pleasantries, Grant left. His "good evening" had barely been uttered when Stanton told Pierrepont that the President next day would suspend him from the war office, in conformity with the tenure law.

Stanton lost control. He admitted to Ellen that she had been right in advising him for two years to leave the cabinet and take up private legal practice. Now he faced an uncertain future, with his private fortune gone and his health ruined. But at least the months of suspense were ended.

Next morning, his outward composure regained, Stanton went to his office to wait for what he knew was coming. Colonel Moore arrived at ten o'clock and gave Stanton a letter from the President suspending him and ordering him to transfer all records and authority to Grant. Stanton slowly read the brief text. "I will send an answer," he told Moore. The colonel went on to Grant's room. After reading the order assigning him to Stanton's place, Grant said: "Very well," and dismissed the President's agent. He then penned a note to Stanton expressing his "appreciation of the zeal, patriotism, firmness, and ability with which you have ever discharged your duties as Secretary of War."

Meanwhile Stanton prepared his answer to Johnson. He denied the President's right to suspend him without the Senate's prior approval. But as Grant was now his successor as well as commanding general, "I have no alternative but to submit, under protest, to superior force."

As always, he tried to shield Ellen. "I congratulate you," he wrote her immediately after dispatching a messenger to the White House with his rejoinder; "I am out of office and Grant is in. We can now make such arrangements for our northern trip as you may desire." Later that day, after he had left the War Department perhaps for the last time, Stanton and Ellen began to prepare for a lengthy vacation. He tried to convince her that he was happy and confident.

She knew better. As a chorus of opinions on the legality, morality, and wisdom of his ousting filled the nation's press, Stanton became moody. He brooded on the accusations hurled against him and worried over Grant's trustworthiness. The Washington *Intelligencer* hit closer to home than its pro-Johnson editor knew when he wrote:

> *Now is the winter of my discontent,*
> *For Andy seems upon my ruin bent,*
> *And Grant and Seward, whom I thought were friends,*
> *Have lent themselves to carry out his ends.*
> *Farewell, a long farewell to all my greatness,*
> Sic transit gloria *Stanton.*[6]

[6] *Intelligencer*, Aug. 23, 1867; to Ellen, Aug. 12, 1867, owned by Gideon Townsend Stanton; Aug. 12, 1867, Moore notebook, Johnson Papers, LC; "Notes of Colonel W. G. Moore," *loc. cit.*, 109; Badeau, *Grant*, 139–40.

IN SUSPENSE

U NABLE to believe that Johnson would actually force him from office, Stanton had made no preparations. He had $4.76 in cash remaining from his salary of the preceding month and no other ready money. Desperately needing rest and wanting to escape from the pressures of Washington until the December meeting of Congress decided his fate, Stanton borrowed $3,000 from friends, and with Ellen and Bessie headed north.

They aimlessly toured New England. He enjoyed a steamer excursion on Lakes Champlain and George and a visit to the fashionable spa at Saratoga Springs. Late in August the Stantons reached Congressman Hooper's Cape Cod home at Cotuit Point and were blessed with perfect weather. Stanton sported like a child in the bracing surf, delighted in picnics on offshore islands and a visit to an Indian village, and basked for hours on the sun-drenched beaches. He slept better than he had in years, and exulted to a hostess: "I can breathe! See, I can breathe!" She recalled that "all the sternness and severity of his countenance passed away. He joked and laughed . . . and . . . told us stories of the war."

Using the excuse of the seaside therapy he was enjoying, Stanton declined the large number of invitations to make speeches that came in. But Hooper guessed that the more important reason for his guest's reticence was that "there are things he does not wish to say nor omit to say." [1]

Better than Hooper, Ellen knew that Stanton was far less happy than he pretended. His hypochondria had returned, and from a morbid interest in afflictions he sought nostrums to cure his own and others'

[1] Hooper to Woodman, Aug. 23, 29, Sept. 2, 1867, Woodman Papers, MHS; Flower, *Stanton*, 324–5.

Stanton : The Life and Times

ailments. Seeking to conceal his inner depression, however, Stanton wrote his son, still employed at the War Department, that he intended to leave public cares to others, and that "every day increases my satisfaction at being out of Johnson's administration and the mode of leaving it could not have been approved more highly."

Young Edwin accepted his father's words at face value. He told Lieber that "it is indeed gratifying to have such thinkers and patriots as yourself . . . speak well of my father." To Stanton, Edwin continued, this was "immeasurably better than noisier applause from the crowd."

Truly, Stanton did not want or need public plaudits. Welles, as usual, misread the man's character when he happily recorded that Stanton must be sorely disappointed at the absence of "an earthquake" because of his removal from office. Equally incorrectly, Stanton's biographer Flower described Stanton as being content with the manner in which his successor in the war office was holding the fort on behalf of shared principles.

For Stanton's uneasiness of spirit was caused by Grant. Feeling cast aside by the stream of events, unsure to the point of illness over Grant's capacity to withstand Johnson's wiles, Stanton was bitter over the fact that the general completely ignored him.

"Your father is in very bad spirits," Ellen admitted to their son late in September; "the least thing upsets him. . . . I think one interview with General Grant could do more to set matters right than all the letters that could be written." But there were no letters from Grant, much less a suggestion for an interview.[2]

Hoping to cheer her husband, Ellen took to censoring his mail, removing the abusive and profane letters that came each day, so that he read only those which might lift his spirits. There were plenty of these, typified by an appreciation from Conkling, who thought that Stanton had managed with "credit and good effect," and Bigelow's "hearty appreciation of your course." Ellen clipped articles from newspapers which extolled Stanton's wartime achievements and postwar policies, and she made sure that he saw the numerous suggestions that he seek the Republican presidential nomination in 1868. She knew that he would not take the latter seriously, but hoped that they might amuse him.

Her efforts were futile. As momentous events transpired in Washington, and were reported and distorted in newspaper accounts, Stan-

---

[2] To Edwin L. Stanton, in Gorham, *Stanton*, II, 410; on nostrums, Stanton to Henry Wilson, Sept. 11, 1867, Wilson Papers, LC; E. L. Stanton to Lieber, Sept. 4, 1867, HL; Morse, *Welles Diary*, III, 173; Flower, *Stanton*, 325–6.

ton's despondency over Grant increased. Stanton learned only of the most forbidding omens, and in his pessimistic way he accepted them.[3]

He was left in ignorance of the fact that Grant was trying to thwart the President by every means at hand, including, as before, some surreptitious ones. Now that Stanton's oversight over army communications was unavailable, Grant distrusted the military telegraph. On the day he took over the war office, he had a friend, General James Forsyth, advise Sheridan to hurry an impending election in Louisiana, "in case the President insists upon your removal, that whoever may be assigned to your command, can be directed by General Grant to carry out the Military Reconstruction Acts as interpreted by you, and foreshadowed by your orders—in fact, General Grant wants things in such a condition of things in Louisiana that your successor (in case you are relieved) will have to carry out the Law as you have viewed it; and without the opportunity to change your programme."

Then, two days later, Forsyth transmitted to Sheridan Grant's prediction that the President had "about given up the idea of relieving you." Grant believed that Johnson, by letting Sheridan stay on, was trying to show that he was deferring to his new War Secretary.

But Grant had guessed wrong. The President, sharing the contempt that Welles and Browning felt toward Grant, decided to remove Sheridan despite Grant's protest and the opposition of all the cabinet. Grant flashed a secret warning to Sheridan, along with the advice "to go on your course exactly as if this communication had not been sent you, and without fear of consequences. That so long as you pursue the same line of duty that you have followed thus far . . . you will receive the entire support of these Headquarters."

By "these Headquarters" Grant meant himself as commanding general. In this capacity he felt independent of the President by virtue of congressional laws, and responsible to Congress for the safety of "its army" in the South. As War Secretary, however, Grant was far less buffered from the White House, as Stanton had learned. Nothing he could say could persuade Johnson not to transfer Sheridan from reconstruction duties.[4]

[3] Conkling to Stanton, Aug. 14, 1867, owned by Gideon Townsend Stanton; Bigelow to Stanton, Aug. 16, 1867, in Bigelow ms diary, NYPL, and see his *Retrospections*, IV, 94.

[4] Forsyth to Sheridan, Aug. 12, 14, 1867, Sheridan Papers, LC; Badeau, *Grant*, 104; Morse, *Welles Diary*, III, 169–73; Browning, *Diary*, II, 158.

Sickles was next to fall under the President's ax. The generals' homeward ways after Johnson relieved them became triumphal processions in Northern cities. Grant's backers interpreted these tributes as rebukes to their favorite for serving Johnson in the war office. The general, fretful over his dimming political prospects, was also angry because Johnson had not bothered to consult him about Sickles, or when he summarily dismissed the archivist Lieber. "You know that I have been eliminated," Lieber informed Sumner. "Young Stanton . . . knew nothing of this thing until he saw it in the papers. He feels indignant." So did Grant.

And yet the President believed that this treatment was making a friend of Grant. Johnson agreed with Frank Blair, Jr., that "Grant will ultimately come to us." [5]

Gaining inside information about these events only in letters from his son and from Sumner, which Ellen's censorship rendered more incomplete and fragmentary, Stanton became even more discouraged. He was increasingly positive that Grant was ineffectual as a block to presidential policies, and worried over Democratic boasts that Grant approved the removal of Sheridan, Sickles, and Lieber and supported the White House's attacks on Holt. Reading newspaper accounts of Hancock's relatively lenient course as Sheridan's successor, and of the growth of Klan outrages everywhere in the South, Stanton felt that his own removal had inspired Johnson's supporters with new courage. To the weary, dispirited man trying to rest at Cape Cod, further hurt came from reports that Grant was "ripping out Stanton's toadies and parasites" from the War Department, as one of Butler's correspondents described it. [6]

Stanton did not stop to think that Grant kept Edwin Lamson Stanton on as an assistant. Early in September, Stanton advised his son: "While you remain in the Department it is proper to render such aid as you can, and without taking any responsibility give General Grant what assistance may be in your power, but do not overtask yourself, or relieve others from such responsibility as properly belongs to them." Thus Stanton cut off by his own injunction a source of inside information which Grant had made no move to close.

[5] F. Blair, Jr., to M. Blair, Aug. 22, 1867, Box XXVI, Blair-Lee Papers, PU; Lieber to Sumner, Aug. 28, 1867, HL; Grant to Sickles, Aug. 24, 1867, CG Letterbook C, 29607, RG 107, NA; Hesseltine, *Grant*, 93–4.

[6] J. D. Andrews to Butler, Aug. 26, 1867, Butler Papers, LC; Lieber to Sumner, Aug. 25, 1867, HL.

In truth, Grant's accession to the war office produced changes only in superficial matters. Now that Grant sat in Stanton's chair, the Department's personnel relaxed. Courtesy replaced Stanton's notorious impatience. Subordinates no longer feared an inquisition when reporting to the Secretary. The general was quiet, undemonstrative, and patient. He substituted a small hand bell for the ferocious-sounding one that Stanton had used to summon officers and clerks. "I got along better with Grant," clerk Benjamin recalled years later.

But in substantive matters Grant continued Stanton's policies; indeed, he stressed economy even more than his predecessor. Like Stanton, Grant kept a tight clamp on damage claims, and men such as Barlow, Ward, Lamon, and Butler, who had thought that Grant's accession would mean opportunity to press claims that Stanton had rejected, were disappointed.[7]

If Stanton had known of Grant's adherence to his political ideas and administrative standards, he would have been vastly relieved. But Grant left him ignorant and Stanton's injured pride made him judge the general too harshly. Hooper communicated to Sumner the sense of Stanton's pessimism regarding Grant, and the senator added this judgment to the growing number of reports which asserted that the general had plotted with Johnson to oust Stanton and the others.

Grant's friends took alarm. Washburne hurried to Boston, and at Senator Wilson's home insisted that Stanton and Grant had "a perfect understanding." Stanton, learning of this, denied the existence of any formal agreement between himself and the general. This was picked up by the newspapers as another indication that Grant was now a White House servitor.

It was unfair to both men and dangerous for the nation. Since Stanton's suspension, sectional and partisan tempers had risen markedly. Hooper judged that Lieber was not far wrong "when he says that the Governors at the North may have to call for armed Loyalty to sweep down on Washington & Maryland." And it was through Hooper that Stanton received most of his information.

Meanwhile, Johnson worried over the fact that Grant, as commanding general, still felt himself to be the agent of Congress rather than the executive. Grant shrugged off the patronizing lectures on constitutional law, designed to persuade him to an opposite conclusion, which he suf-

[7] Stanton to son, Sept. 4, 1867, Pratt Collection, CU; William Conant Church, *Ulysses S. Grant* (New York, 1897), 97, 355; Hesseltine, *Grant*, 97; Lamon to Butler, Aug. 12, 1867, Butler Papers, LC; Charles Benjamin to Horace White, June 1, 1914, ISHL.

fered from Welles and the President.[8] On September 2, Grant, as chief general, issued an order to Southern army units forbidding appointments to state offices of men whom previous military commanders had removed. This obviously referred to Sheridan and Sickles, and implicitly criticized their successors, Hancock and Schofield, and the President.

In Texas, General Griffin removed civil officials "because of their known hostility to the General Government." Grant sustained Griffin and refused Johnson's request to restrict him from further removals. With Grant's secret encouragement, General Ord, boasting that he was following the path Stanton had earlier set, ordered registrars in Mississippi and Arkansas to bar all past rebels from voting. Assuring Chandler that Johnson could not cow him so long as the War Department was immune from Democratic control, Ord promised the Republican leader that "there will be a convention in both my states & then you gentlemen will control results."

Grant confided to intimates that he had taken Stanton's place only to prevent Johnson from making a clean sweep of the occupation commanders and substituting "obstructionists" like Hancock. Accepting this assertion, John Sherman, Lieber, and Holt spread the word around that Grant was fixed on Republican principles after all. Lieber advised Sumner that since this was the case, Stanton could rest assured. Grant would hold the war office in a proper manner until Congress assembled in December, in order to prevent Johnson from filling it with anyone else. Then Stanton could pick up the portfolio again. Stanton's spirits soared at the news.[9]

Though happier, Stanton could no longer remain in seclusion. He was running out of money and was restive from inaction. Through his friend Albert Gallatin Riddle, who had earlier served him as a special War Department counsel, Stanton secured a client to plead for before the United States Supreme Court. For the first time since 1862 he began to prepare a private case. He and Ellen planned to return to Wash-

[8] Hooper to Sumner, Sept. 2, 1867, Sumner Papers, HU; same to Woodman, Aug. 29, 1867, Woodman Papers, MHS; E. J. Sherman to Butler, Sept. 9, 1867, Butler Papers, LC, on the Wilson quote; Hesseltine, *Grant*, 96; Morse, *Welles Diary*, III, 186–90.

[9] Grant to Pope, Sept. 9, 1867, CG Letterbook C, 298; on Griffin, M. H. Royston to Johnson, Sept. 19, 1867, Sec. War Correspondence File, Box 329, RG 107, NA; F. Ballard to Holt, Aug. 29, 1867, Holt Papers, LC; Lieber to Sumner, Aug. 30, 1867, HL; Ord to Chandler, Sept. 16, 1867, Chandler Papers, LC; Grant to Chase, Oct. 21, 1867, Chase Papers, LC; Morse, *Welles Diary*, III, 193.

ington by the last week of September so that he might rest before the arguments began, but while en route southward he again fell ill. They stopped at Pierrepont's home near New York City for recuperation. On October 8 the Stantons reached Washington, and there was more good news for him.

Earlier that day Grant had invited Hooper for a drive. Talking with complete candor, the two men ranged over many subjects, including the presence in Washington of General Sherman, who had come at the President's request, perhaps to take over the War Department. They also discussed Grant's opinion of the President and his high estimation of Stanton. That evening, visiting Stanton to welcome him home, Hooper revealed the gist of Grant's disclosures. Writing later that night to Sumner, Hooper noted that Stanton "seems well and in good spirits," even though Grant still did not seek him out personally.[1]

At the same time that Grant was convincing Stanton's Republican friends that he was trustworthy, he was depicting himself to General Sherman as a storm-tossed victim of unprincipled men who cared for neither the Army's nor the nation's interests. He regretted the day he had taken on the war office, Grant insisted to his wartime companion, and confided to Sherman that he wished to be rid of the responsibility. Sherman advised him to keep himself and the Army clear of politics.

Learning of this through Sherman, the President, still resentful at Grant's recent behavior, again offered Sherman the post of War Secretary. Sherman made it clear that he would not climb over Grant's shoulders. At Sherman's suggestion that a meeting of minds was needed, the President talked with Grant.

He pointed out that elections in Northern states early in October had substantially reduced Republican majorities where they did not produce Democratic victories. Stanton's return to the capital so long before December, the President suggested, meant that he was preparing to resign all claims to the war portfolio before Congress assembled, thus relieving Johnson of any concern over the tenure law.

Nevertheless, the Republicans might still seek an impeachment. Supposing, Johnson asked, the legislators ordered his arrest during an

[1] Ellen to ?, *ca.* Aug. 30, 1867, owned by Mrs. Van Swearingen; Pierrepont to Marble, Oct. 1, 1867, Marble Papers, LC; Hooper to Sumner, Oct. 8, 1867, Sumner Papers, HU; same to Lieber, Oct. 13, 1867, HL; Sumner to Stanton, *ca.* Oct. 12, 1867, Stanton MSS; Dawes, "Recollections of Stanton under Johnson," *loc. cit.,* 504.

impeachment trial; what would Grant do? What if Stanton, despite rumors to the contrary, demanded the return of his office; would Grant comply?

Grant assured the President that he would not support an attempt by Congress to arrest him, or give Stanton back the keys to the war office short of a court order requiring the return, and in any case not without notification to the President. He convinced Johnson and Sherman that he was moderate in his political views, that he had no ambitions for the presidency, and that he held the war office only to keep the Army out of politics.[2]

Stanton, comforted by his renewed faith in Grant's Republicanism, decided to go visiting in Ohio. His health had again worsened and plans for resuming active law practice were necessarily postponed, which aggravated the financial problem. There was some real estate near Steubenville that might be salable, and he could visit his mother and sisters again while avoiding the tensions of the capital until after the beginning of the congressional session, when his case would come up before the Senate.

A spontaneous public demonstration formed in his honor when he reached Columbus on October 15, exhilarating and pleasing him. But the unseasonably hot, humid weather was uncomfortable, and the dust, "stifling on the roads," was hard on his asthmatic condition. "Already I am anxious to get home," he wrote Ellen, "or to the mountains where I can breathe. . . . I am weary and homesick."

Suddenly the weather changed, and, just as the congressional session opened, a great snowfall promised to trap Stanton in Columbus. "Not for several years have I witnessed such inclemency as there is here," he told his wife. "Snow and sleet cover the earth—everything is hard frozen—and it is growing colder by the hour. The river is closed with ice. It is fortunate that good coal abounds here but the suffering at other places must be very great."

Then he learned that the son of his late brother, Darwin, had died. Stanton hired a team and sleigh, and braving the harsh weather, plunged through to Steubenville to arrange for the burial. His feelings, as always, were at low ebb in the presence of death, and uncer-

[2] Grant to Sherman, Sept. 18, 1867, W. T. Sherman Papers, LC; Sherman to Grant, Sept. 25, 1867, HQA, Box 104, RG 107, NA; same to T. Ewing, Sr., Oct. 18, and Ewing, Jr., to Sr., Sept. 17, Oct. 12, 19, 1867, Ewing Family Papers, LC; Morse, *Welles Diary*, III, 234–4; Paul I. Miller, *Thomas Ewing, Last of the Whigs* (Ph.D. thesis, Ohio State University, 1933), 307.

tainty about his future increased his depression. He wrote Ellen that "your love is the only solace that supports me in despondency, and ill health, and many cares." Stanton was worried that she might become ill: "When I think of the dreadful consequences to our beloved children if you should be taken away from them, and how unlikely it is that I should remain long to give them even the little care and assistance that would be in my power, . . . the thought of such calamity to them overwhelms my soul with grief."

After the funeral, Stanton went on to Gambier to spend his fifty-second birthday with his mother and Pamphila. There was no celebration. He read from the Psalms and the Morning Prayer for Families, walked through the deep, quiet, snow to see the familiar scenes of the town, and visited old friends.

A letter came from Ellen confessing that she was deeply discouraged over their being "all adrift" and that she was "suffering anxiety and perplexity of mind about our present domestic conditions." He chided her, telling her that always before she had sustained him in adversity: "Why then, dear love, are you discouraged now?" His concern for Ellen, and the magnetic attraction of the events transpiring in the national capital, hurried him back to Washington.[3]

Ever since the President suspended Stanton in August, the country had waited for the reassembling of Congress. Beyond the probability that the Senate, invoking the tenure law, would send Stanton back to the war office, everything was uncertain.

While political leaders and presidential hopefuls maneuvered to gain advantage from whatever might occur, Stanton had kept silent. He knew that his star was rising in the shifting sweepstakes for the Republican nomination. Considering that he was making absolutely no effort to be advanced to a candidacy for which he had no ambition or interest, the seriousness with which he was mentioned is impressive. As a martyr, Stanton was enjoying more popularity than he had ever known before. His friend Lieber, among others who were hopeful that he would seek a nomination, was worried that he planned to abandon this advantage and "resign immediately after the Senate shall have shown that it rejects Stanton's suspension. I do not like it."

It was precisely Stanton's intention to regain the war office as a vindication for his career and then to resign immediately. But he confided his decision to no one except Ellen and Pamphila. "Why is

[3] Oct. 18, 31, Dec. 11, 19, 1867, owned by Gideon Townsend Stanton.

Stanton so over-reticent, so totally silent, to his best friends?" complained Lieber.[4]

Republican strategists also had to worry about the possibility that Johnson would not receive Stanton back into the cabinet even if the Senate refused to concur in the suspension. Grant's position was critical. If he thereafter kept the war portfolio at Johnson's behest, and added his vast popularity and his control of the Army to the President's strength, then the Republican position was destroyed and the tenure law rendered futile.

The nation had paid careful attention, therefore, to the President's message to Congress on December 3, hoping to find in it a hint of Johnson's intentions toward Stanton. But the only reference to the tenure law was a complaint that it prevented the President from discharging corrupt government agents. Nine days later, as the tenure law required, Johnson reported to the Senate on his suspension of Stanton. The senators thereupon referred the message to a committee and adjourned until the new year.[5]

Johnson's first impulse had been to send to the Senate a message stating that long before August 1867 he had lost confidence in Stanton, who not only differed with him but "employed the power, authority, and influence of the War Department to thwart measures from which, in Cabinet council, he alone dissented." In this draft, Johnson asserted that he let Stanton remain in the cabinet in the hope that the War Secretary would realize his unacceptability and leave of his own accord. The request for Stanton's resignation which he sent him on August 5, 1867, was merely a spur to achieve this result, but the Secretary, taking refuge behind the tenure law, refused, and so suffered suspension.

But this approach, the President realized, pictured Stanton as an honest, open opponent of White House policies, and Johnson wanted to create an opposite image. In the report which went to the Senate, Johnson portrayed Stanton as a conspirator who had advised vetoing the tenure-of-office bill and now insisted upon obedience to its restrictions; supported the initial steps of reconstruction under Johnson's program in 1865 and 1866, and then exerted secret efforts to nullify the success of that program; failed to prevent the New Orleans riot

[4] Wolcott MS, 209–11; Lieber to Martin R. Thayer, Nov. 20, 1867, and same to Sumner, Jan. 10, 1868, HL; Willard H. Smith, *Schuyler Colfax* (Indianapolis, 1952), 261 (cited hereafter as Smith, *Colfax*).

[5] Lieber to Sumner, Jan. 2, 1868, HL; Richardson, *Messages and Papers*, VI, 558–81; Morse, *Welles Diary*, III, 186–90, 240, 244.

and refused to accept the blame for its occurrence. It was an effective, powerful document.[6]

Immediately upon his return from Ohio, Stanton set to work preparing a counterblast to submit to Senator Howard, of the Military Committee, and the Christmas holidays passed almost unobserved as he completed the retort. In it he admitted that he had openly opposed the tenure law in the cabinet. Not only that, but he had asked congressmen, while the bill was in passage, to stipulate that he was not protected by it. Yet it was now law and he felt that he and the President must abide by it. On the question of reconstruction policy, Stanton accurately described how, in 1865, Johnson had employed the essential portions of the plan the Secretary had drawn up for Lincoln, and then tried to make it over in a manner which the country clearly felt was injurious to its interests and insulting to the war dead. Stanton asserted that the President had violated the democratic process when he sought to nullify Congress's reconstruction laws through obstructive interpretations. Johnson had forgotten, Stanton tellingly observed, that until mid-1865 his own statements had noted the provisional character of presidential reconstruction and the dominant role of Congress in the final step of admitting Southern states to representation, which was Lincoln's position throughout the war. After that Johnson had shifted away from this view to one of plenary executive power, and the trouble had started.

Concerning the New Orleans massacre, Stanton sarcastically agreed that he could not exculpate the President. No one could. Only Johnson's encouragement to intransigent whites, who were determined to prevent Negroes from exercising rights guaranteed by Congress, had made it possible.

For long months he had stood forth alone in the cabinet, openly opposing the President's policies. He had forborne from making any reply to the criticisms the President's supporters had cast on him. Now that Johnson wished to reduce to a matter of personal antagonisms what was truly an opposition of principles, Stanton wished to correct the record.[7]

But Stanton, despite the assertions of his biographers, never sent his reply to Capitol Hill. Shortly after the new year, he told reporters only that he had no reply to make as an individual to the President's charges. He was holding himself in check, he confided to his son, be-

[6] Undelivered draft in message vol. IX, Johnson Papers, LC; Richardson, *Messages and Papers*, VI, 583–94.

[7] Gorham, *Stanton*, II, 413–26.

cause Johnson had offended Congress and the nation, not merely himself. To reply to the President's assertions would be to dignify them beyond their worth. The Senate and Congress as a whole were going to fight on his behalf, or Stanton would wage no contest at all.

Another reason impelling Stanton to silence was the failure of the impeachment resolution against the President which the House of Representatives had wrestled with for a year. With this encouragement, Johnson proceeded to insist upon the removal of Generals Pope and Ord from their Southern commands and, according to Chandler, to predict victory in the coming struggle with the Senate over Stanton. Taking all this into account, Stanton held off from increasing the dangerous tensions already existing.[8]

A third factor holding Stanton back from publicizing his rejoinder to Johnson's message was the effectiveness of the President's communication to Congress. Even the *Nation* and the Cleveland *Leader*, firmly in sympathy with Republican tenets, admitted the impressive characteristics of the Chief Executive's statement and expressed the hope that it might not begin a mere squabble in print between Stanton and Johnson. Better, these influential journals stated, that Stanton let the Senate do his pleading for him.

And last, Grant was paying attention to him again. Grant's secretary, Adam Badeau, visited the Stanton home on New Year's Day and left a copy of the *Military History of U. S. Grant,* inscribed in affectionate and respectful terms. Probably Badeau also left with Stanton Grant's advice to keep silent in order that, together with their allies in Congress, they might answer the President with greater force than Stanton could muster alone. As he had done since Appomattox, Stanton accepted Grant's leadership, and a few days later the *Intelligencer,* a Johnson organ, was worriedly reporting that Grant, Stanton, and Senator Howard were meeting secretly with other Republican congressmen.[9]

At one of these meetings Stanton gave Howard his rebuttal to Johnson's accusations against him. It became one of the sources for the senator's report on the suspension. Howard leaked Stanton's defense to the newspapers before his committeemen saw it, so that Stanton,

---

[8] Stanton to E. L. Stanton, Dec. 26, 27, 1867, Pratt Collection, CU; James R. Doolittle, "Correspondence," SHA *Publications,* XI, 6–9; Detroit *Post, Chandler,* 295; Flower, *Stanton,* 330; Pratt, *Stanton,* 451; Rhodes, *op. cit.,* VI, 99n. The impeachment attempt failed on December 7, 1867; *Congressional Globe,* 40th Cong., 2d sess., 68.

[9] *Nation* (Dec. 19, 1867), 493; *Leader,* Dec. 13, 1867; Mrs. Van Swearingen owns the inscribed Badeau volume; *Intelligencer,* Jan. 11, 1868. Documents are in *Removal of Hon. E. M. Stanton and Others,* House Exec. Doc. 57, 40th Cong., 2d sess.

after all, got his views before the public without initiating a personal exchange between himself and the President.

Grant, meanwhile, was resisting terrific pressure to take sides openly. Writing to Fessenden, to whose opinions Stanton was always respectful, John Binney felt that the general was wise in keeping silent. "Should he give any disclosures of his views on reconstruction prematurely, his political enemies would endeavor to destroy him as a Presidential candidate," Binney asserted. "Besides, in his present position as General of the Armies and Secretary of War, it is better that he should interfere in politics as little as possible." [1]

Grant was interfering, and on a large scale, but secretly. He could still jump whatever way became necessary. Of all the major participants in this unsavory situation, Grant was the only one who could not lose. Stanton could not win.

Still holding to an exalted view of his opportunities, the President and his close advisers again looked to the Supreme Court in the first days of 1868 to serve their political purposes, and to defend in the name of civil liberty their conservative principles. The Court, Johnson hoped, would follow the clear line of the Milligan decision and declare the reconstruction acts unconstitutional. As the least result, Grant would surely abandon his flirtation with the Republicans. "He will feel that the foundation of radical reconstruction is gone," prophesied Senator Doolittle, the Democratic leader.[2]

It is difficult to understand how the President arrived at a judgment that he and the Court could overmatch the legislators, even if the jurists might be willing to stand up and defy Congress. Since the Milligan and test oath decisions a year before, the Republicans had subjected the Court to an intense barrage of criticism. Proposals to limit the jurisdiction of the tribunal, to require that two thirds of the judges be in agreement before a verdict could be reached, to reduce its membership, even to abolish it altogether, though not enacted into law, reflected the passionate temper of the congressmen. The jurists were to prove their sensitivity to these threats.

Johnson was less sensitive, even though Congress had severely limited his control over large segments of the government. The President might have gauged his weakness by the existence of the tenure act, the legislation restricting his control over the Army's commanding

[1] Dec. 30, 1867, Fessenden Papers, LC.
[2] To Marble, Jan. 2, 8, 1868, Marble Papers, LC.

to wreck Congress's laws. This might precipitate the crisis that Stanton was trying to fend off.

As things worked out, the jurists, more sensitive than the President to the legislators' wrath, later refused even to entertain the Mississippi petition, as well as a similar one from Georgia directed against Stanton and Grant, much less to pronounce that the reconstruction laws were invalid. Johnson would have been wiser to accept Stanton's advice, which was based on firm precedents, and to keep the White House out of the picture.[4]

Stanton and Grant feared most that the President, through Stanbery, would manage to water down Congress's reconstruction laws by means of narrow interpretations. Writing to Washburne, Grant predicted that "all will be well if Administration and Copperhead influences do not defeat the objects of the [reconstruction] measure," and asserted that Sheridan and the other district commanders were "carrying out the measures of Congress according to the spirit of their acts." Grant advised Sheridan to go on as he had been, interpreting the reconstruction legislation as he thought best. Whatever Stanbery decided, Grant suggested, it was up to the generals in the South to make up their own minds.[5]

The question of how far the President might direct the army commanders in the South kept crisis always in the offing. Stanton could only delay it; he could not keep it from occurring. He knew that when the chips were down he would have to follow the line that Grant was drawing.

Stanton's attention snapped away from politics in mid-April. A telegram announced that his mother was dangerously ill. He sped to Gambier on a special train. Mrs. Stanton was much improved when he arrived, but he fell ill in turn. However, he rested only three days in Gambier, for there was news of more trouble in the South. He returned to Washington on April 20, suffering as never before from asthma and in desperate need of quiet and rest. He found turbulence and strain instead.[6]

Sheridan in Louisiana and Pope in Georgia had informed Grant that

[4] *Georgia* v. *Stanton*, 6 *Wallace* 50 (1867); *McGhan* v. *Clephane*, in WD, Letters Received, CLXIII, 175, RG 107, NA, surveys precedents, with which the President had earlier agreed.

[5] To Sheridan, April 7, 1867, Sheridan Papers, LC; Badeau, *Grant*, 62.

[6] Stanton to John H. Clifford, May 7, 1867, NYHS; T. Shankland to Holt, April 30, 1867, Holt Papers, LC.

general, the autonomy of the army units in the South under the reconstruction laws, and the statute of July 1866 that prevented him from appointing new members to the Supreme Court in the event of vacancies. Notwithstanding, Johnson jumped at the first opportunity to force the issue of the constitutionality of the reconstruction laws, and to seek a judicial verdict that would nullify the popular will.

The chance came in late 1867 when a Mississippi editor, William McCardle, a former Confederate colonel, libeled General Ord and was tried before a military commission. McCardle sought a writ of habeas corpus from a federal judge in order to bring his case before a civil tribunal. Denied this, McCardle's counsel, Stanton's former associate Jeremiah Black, exploited a provision of the law Stanton and Grant had obtained from Congress to protect army officers in the South against the actions of civil courts, and thereby secured a Supreme Court hearing for an appeal on behalf of McCardle. In his appeal, Black alleged that Congress's exercise of martial law in the postwar South was as offensive as executive sponsorship of military rule in the wartime North, which the Court had condemned in Milligan's case.

Johnson blundered in permitting Black, his confidential adviser, to take on the McCardle appeal; Black's presence linked the White House with the attack on Congress and the Army. The President made a more serious error when he and Stanbery refused to provide Ord with a federal attorney to conduct his defense, as long-standing policy and recent legislation required.

Grant asked Stanton and Senator Trumbull to conduct Ord's defense, and Stanton brought in Matthew H. Carpenter, of Wisconsin. These three very able lawyers commenced work on a brief sustaining the legitimacy of the reconstruction laws. Congress, meanwhile, began preparing a measure of self-defense against the Court.[3]

Months were to pass before the Court made a decision on McCardle. But the effects of the case were significant in January 1868. Grant, angry with the President because of his treatment of Ord, advised Stanton to abandon the self-restraint which had characterized his demeanor since his return to Washington. Across town, where the debate

---

[3] Exchanges on McCardle between Grant, Ord, Stanton, and Stanbery, Dec. 31, 1867–Jan. 20, 1868, AGO, RP 670220, RG 94, NA. Other data in Flower, *Stanton,* 326–7n.; Brigance, *op. cit.,* 173; King, *Davis,* 262–3; Carl Brent Swisher, *American Constitutional Development* (2nd ed., Boston, 1954), 324. Subsequently, Johnson sought to appease Grant by authorizing federal attorneys to defend Ord. Grant refused, and the special counsel was used.

on Stanton's suspension was under way in the Senate Military Committee's rooms, Doolittle was reviving the old charges that Stanton had deliberately sabotaged the wartime prisoner-exchange system. Unwilling to remain quiet under this attack, Stanton sent to Senator Fessenden copies of the official documents on that vexed subject, though not those that would reveal Grant's role in formulating the Union policy. In a powerful blast at Stanton's Democratic critics, delivered while the Senate was in executive session, Fessenden defended the War Secretary. Stanton arranged to have the speech made public, and he wrote that it "has delivered me from revilers and persecutors who sought to destroy my good name and has covered them with confusion." [4]

Another effect of the McCardle appeal was the encouragement it afforded the President. Having convinced himself that every move the Republicans made must redound in his favor, Johnson shrugged off Doolittle's warning on the morning of Saturday, January 11, that the Military Committee was ready to recommend that the Senate order the return of Stanton to the cabinet; indeed, he seemed pleased at the opportunity for battle.

Events that day offered further corroboration of Johnson's lack of realism. Probably through Stanton, Grant for the first time became aware that if the Senate sustained Stanton under the tenure law, and he refused to turn back the war office to him, a $10,000 fine and a five-year prison term could result. Hurrying to the White House, Grant told the President that he was not going to run the risk. He would give up the portfolio to Stanton the moment the Senate voted in his favor.

For an hour Johnson pleaded with Grant, even offering to pay the fine himself and serve any sentence the general might incur by retaining the war office. Grant would not budge.

By this time neither man really heard the other. Johnson finally terminated the meeting with a request that Grant return to the White House on Monday, the thirteenth, to continue the discussion, and always insisted later that Grant acquiesced, implying also that he would not give up the war office without notice to the President. It appears most likely that Johnson misinterpreted as agreement what

---

[4] To Fessenden, Jan. 13, 1868, HL; Fessenden, *op. cit.*, II, 149–50; Stanton to Gen. E. S. Sanford, Jan. 8, 1868, Lincoln MSS, HU; to Mrs. Lucy Stanton, Jan. 8, 1868, CHS; Gorham, *Stanton*, II, 426–7.

Lieber called "that awful silence upon which Grant prides himself." [5]

Confused, Grant spent Sunday with General Sherman. There emerged from this meeting a plan to have Johnson nominate Governor Jacob Cox, of Ohio, as War Secretary before the Senate decided on Stanton's suspension. As a moderate Republican, Cox should gain quick bipartisan confirmation and the Senate would not vote on Stanton at all. Grant could then resign the temporary portfolio, retaining, of course, his army commission, and avoid all the pitfalls yawning before him. Johnson would gain the services of the popular and perhaps pliant Cox, who would add luster to his tarnished administration. Sherman would achieve his object of withdrawing his friend and the Army from politics. Only Stanton would be left without benefit, thrown over, ridiculous and humiliated. If the Senate approved a substitute for him, or failed to vote on his suspension, then it indirectly sanctioned his removal and, by implication, the charges Johnson had leveled against him.

The President had nothing to lose by trying out this plan. He had, however, no time to spare if he intended to make the experiment, for even as the men talked the Senate was moving toward a decision on Stanton. Yet, on Sunday, when Sherman underscored to Johnson the desirability of the plot he had helped to hatch, the general was surprised at the lack of interest on the part of the President. Sherman did not know that Johnson, confident that it was Grant's intention not to surrender the war office to Stanton whatever the Senate decided, and that the Republicans would not dare to proceed against the idolized Grant, felt that there was no need to placate moderate opinion by advancing Cox's nomination. [6]

Of the weekend plotters, only Grant sympathized with Stanton's political views and professed at least to respect him. No one, however, thought to warn Stanton of what they were conceiving, doubtless feeling that he would thwart Senate approval of a nomination of Cox through his friends in Congress. But it was Johnson, not Stanton, who, through inaction, destroyed the Cox scheme. On Monday morn-

[5] Lieber to M. R. Thayer, *ca.* Jan. 16, 1868 (misdated 1867), HL; Hesseltine, *Grant*, 107–8n.; Dana and Wilson, *Grant*, 394; Browning, *Diary*, II, 169; Morse, *Welles Diary*, III, 255–7.

[6] Badeau, *Grant*, 111; Lewis, *Sherman*, 590; Hesseltine, *Grant*, 104–5; and Rhodes, *op. cit.*, VI, 100–2, offer interestingly different interpretations of the Sunday negotiations, of which Rhodes's is the most accurate. But none take Stanton into account; nor do any of his biographers cover this weekend. See also Ewing, Jr., to Johnson, Jan. 12, 1868, Johnson Papers, LC, and Howe, *Sherman Home Letters*, 364–5.

ing, when Sherman went to the White House, the President made no mention of it, and he exhibited no anxiety or irritation over the fact that Grant did not appear.

During these critical days, Stanton was nervously aware that something was going on. Apart from the uncountable rumors that floated around the capital, however, his only source of information was a soldier on duty as a White House guard. The extent of the "secrets" he was able to transmit to Stanton was the names of persons calling on the President and the duration of their visits. So Stanton knew that Grant had been closeted with Johnson on Saturday and Sherman had followed the next day. This information shocked him. His pessimistic uncertainty concerning Grant's reliability returned. But there was nothing he could do but wait for the Senate's action and trust that the general would keep faith.

On Monday evening a messenger hurried from the Capitol to the Stanton home. The Senate had ordered that Stanton return to the cabinet. A flood of telegrams and callers followed during the evening, and Stanton found himself hosting an unplanned celebration party.

At another party in Washington that night, General Sherman told Browning that the President, by rejecting the plan to appoint Cox, was responsible for Stanton's success in the Senate. The President, greeting Grant at a White House reception, strangely did not ask him why he had not come to see him that day, as he later insisted had been promised. Grant did not tell Johnson that he had his resignation from the cabinet already written.[7]

At nine o'clock Tuesday morning, January 14, Grant appeared at the War Department. He locked the Secretary's office and, taking the key with him, went to his nearby rooms. An hour later Stanton entered the building. Smiling, he pushed through the throng of well-wishers and headed directly for his old office. Learning that Grant had the key, he sent for it, meanwhile waiting in the anteroom where so many persons had waited to see him. Although he refused to answer questions advanced by importunate journalists, Stanton was obviously in fine spirits.

Adjutant General Townsend came in with the coveted key, and in a mock "present arms" delivered it to Stanton. Stepping into the familiar office, Stanton began to deal with the unceasing stream of callers. He drew the $3,000 due him as salary for the period of his

[7] Hesseltine, *Grant*, 105; Sen. Edmunds to Stanton, Jan. 13, 1868, Stanton MSS; Browning, *Diary*, II, 173; Flower, *Stanton*, 331; H. G. Howard, *op. cit.*, 228–9.

suspension, and dictated a circular to Grant and the bureau heads stating that he was again in the Secretary's chair.

Despite his busyness, Stanton was filling in time. He wondered whether Grant was going to stand by. And what would the unpredictable President do now?

At noon Grant sent the President a message stating that, owing to the Senate's action, he was retiring from the Interim War Secretary appointment. Then, assuming that an earlier invitation from Johnson that he attend a cabinet meeting early that afternoon was still in effect, Grant went to the White House.

The excited cabinet officers were surprised to see him. Johnson, as usual thinking of himself as a manipulator of men and, paradoxically, as an injured innocent, directed a barrage of questions at Grant to which he insisted on mere negative or affirmative replies. The President confused and unnerved the general, making it appear to the cabinet members that Grant had proved false to his trust. Their impression was that Grant had promised the President to return the preceding day but had deliberately failed to do so, had broken his promise to warn the White House that he was giving up the war office, and had throughout plotted with Stanton, a view to which they were predisposed.[8]

Johnson lost a slim chance to keep Grant with him when he released slanted accounts of the Tuesday cabinet meeting to his friends of the press, impugning the general's veracity. He ignored all indications that there had been no plotting between Stanton and Grant concerning the return of the war office.

There had not been prearrangement. Before going to the stormy cabinet assembly on Tuesday, Grant had a lengthy talk with General William S. Hillyer, one of the few officers in the higher ranks who enjoyed the confidence of both the President and the commanding general. That evening Hillyer wrote a long letter to Johnson, the point of which was that there had been no collusion. Hillyer was convinced that Grant "never expected that Stanton would resume the duties of the War Office." Rather, Grant had believed that Johnson would prevent the occurrence, Hillyer wrote, referring to the scheme to nominate Cox.[9]

[8] Morse, *Welles Diary*, III, 259–62; Browning, *Diary*, II, 173–5; Hesseltine, *Grant*, 105–6.

[9] Hillyer to Johnson, Jan. 14, 1868, Johnson Papers, LC. Of all the authors treating these events, only Rhodes, *op. cit.*, VI, 100n., caught the significance of the

To be sure, Johnson did not receive the Hillyer letter until after the Tuesday altercation at the cabinet meeting. But Grant's appeal to Hillyer proves that he greatly desired that his honor not be contemned. The President acted without waiting for proof of either Grant's duplicity or his trustworthiness. By convincing the cabinet that Grant was a scoundrel, and blaring this to the world through the press, Johnson increased his sense of innocence. But he lost the only ally who might have made virtue, as the President defined it, triumph.

At the war office that Tuesday afternoon, Stanton, who had no way of knowing that the taciturn general was resigning the temporary appointment as Secretary, was finding it increasingly difficult to maintain an air of bland confidence. His slim store of patience became exhausted. He sent an officer to Grant's rooms with a peremptory summons to report. Grant arrived still sore from the lashing he had suffered at the White House, and disgruntled at the curt tone of the summons. When Sherman looked in on Stanton's office, he found the two men in close conversation.

Later that afternoon Sherman talked with Stanton. The Secretary tried to flatter him, Sherman wrote to his wife; "all very loving, and I told him simply that I should not recall the past, but wanted the Army to be kept out of politics, etc., etc." None of these "et ceteras" referred to conversation on the tenure law, Sherman disappointedly admitted. He had expected Stanton to ask his opinion "of his present status," and Sherman was ready to tell him to resign at once; this is probably why Stanton did not ask him.

Next morning all Washington read of Grant's resignation and of Johnson's attacks on his integrity, and Stanton, visiting at the Trumbull home, exulted in the reports that Johnson had "sworn and kicked the chairs around at a great rate" and that he and Grant had almost come to blows. But, reading on, Stanton learned that Grant during the preceding weekend had conspired to throw him over. He told Mrs. Trumbull that he no longer trusted the general. Once more Johnson was to pay a stiff price for having released these stories to the press, for Stanton's renewed distrust of Grant cost the President the voluntary resignation of the War Secretary.

Grant also read the newspapers that morning. Sherman, trying to

---

Hillyer letter. See also "Notes of Colonel W. G. Moore," *loc. cit.*, 115–16; Welles to Johnson, Feb. 5, 1868, HL.

pacify his bitter and angry friend, accompanied him to the White House, where the President untruthfully insisted that he had had no part in the newspaper onslaught. There seemed to be a lessening of tension, and some surface cordiality returned. The meeting ended with Grant and Sherman agreeing to try to persuade Stanton to resign at once now that the Senate had vindicated him. Perhaps Grant knew that this had been Stanton's intention.

Grant, however, had lost much of his influence over the Secretary. In his disappointment over what he felt was Grant's betrayal, Stanton was in no mood to listen to suggestions from him that he give up the war office. Perhaps Grant sensed this, for it was Sherman who undertook to feel Stanton out on the matter. Stanton rebuffed his awkward attempts to introduce the subject. Reporting to Grant, Sherman admitted that "I soon found out that to recommend resignation to Mr. Stanton would have no effect, unless it was to incur further his displeasure; and, therefore, did not directly suggest it to him . . . I would advise you to say nothing to Mr. Stanton on the subject of resignation unless he asks your advice. It would do no good, and may embarrass you." [1]

Stanton had rebuffed Sherman out of pique with Grant, not because he had abandoned the idea of leaving the war office at once. Then, on January 18, he wrote Pamphila that, although his vindication in the Senate had been "full and complete, . . . the Republican members of Congress insist on my remaining."

The conclusion seems inescapable that on January 15 Stanton had every intention of giving up his portfolio within the week. But during the next three days the Republican leaders, especially Trumbull, capitalized on his anger with Grant and persuaded him to stay on. They argued that until the general's trustworthiness was again established, Stanton could not feel free to abandon the war office to Grant or to anyone else Johnson might appoint to it. [2]

Stanton was easily persuaded by the deputations, the petitions, the telegrams and letters that urged his retention of the war office, to make the personal sacrifices necessary and accede to the requests. Even news from Pamphila that their mother was ill could not make

---

[1] Sherman, *Memoirs*, II, 421–6; Howe, *Sherman Home Letters*, 365; Hesseltine, *Grant*, 107; Mrs. Trumbull to Walter Trumbull, Jan. 16, 1868, owned by the estate of Benjamin P. Thomas; J. B. Stillson to Barlow, Jan. 27, 1868, Barlow Papers, HL; *Correspondence—Grant and the President*, House Exec. Doc. 149, 40th Cong., 2d sess.

[2] Wolcott MS, 210; Mrs. Trumbull to Walter Trumbull, Jan. 18, 1868, owned by the estate of Benjamin P. Thomas; Flower, *Stanton*, 336–8.

him leave the capital to visit her. He answered Pamphila on the eighteenth that he intended to stay on as Secretary only during the few remaining weeks of the winter. Then he planned to return to the life of a Steubenville lawyer, a career that he felt was within his physical resources and offered the best probability of swift prosperity. "I do not want to remain a day in the Department," he wrote, "but do not feel at liberty to give up immediately." He would wait out these few weeks in the expectation that the President would see the need for a moderate course and would appoint an acceptable successor.[3]

So he kept quiet in the war office. He received no direct communications from the White House and attended no cabinet meetings. The Army was now tied to the presidency only by the frayed strand represented by Grant, and by the official need of some of the cabinet officers for army records and the Army's co-operation in a number of matters.

Seward needed Halleck's confidential reports on British Columbia; McCulloch asked for troops to convoy gold shipments near the turbulent Mexican border; Randall wanted cavalry to patrol postal routes in northwestern Texas, where banditry was rife. These matters could not wait until someone decided who properly held the war office. McCulloch, therefore, had to pay Stanton's salary and to approve his drafts on the Treasury if he expected co-operation from the War Department, and Johnson made no objection.

Thus, Grant's protest to the President on January 30 that it was impossible for him to ignore orders from Stanton, as Johnson had instructed him to do, was not, as Johnson later alleged, conspiracy on the general's part. Rather it was an accurate reflection of the facts of intra-governmental needs. The Secretary of War had less power to initiate policies in the Army than the commanding general did. But he did have administrative resources with which to obstruct army operations if he chose, and he could adversely affect the functioning of other departments as well. Johnson, Grant felt, had instructed him not to obey Stanton in order to embarrass the Secretary. The effect, however, was to face Grant and, through him, all the Army's officers with the poor choice of insubordination either to the President or to the restored Secretary of War.[4]

The President misinterpreted the weaknesses of the situation as an-

---

[3] Wolcott MS, 210–11; and see accurate rumors on Stanton's plans for resignation in Washington *Intelligencer*, Jan. 20, 1868.

[4] Grant to Johnson, Jan. 30, 1868, CG Letterbook C, 328–9, 333–4, RG 107; Stanton to Seward, Jan. 24, 1868, Box 110, RG 108, and WD Executive Military Book, LIX, RG 107, NA, *passim*; Lewis, *Sherman*, 591; Howe, *Sherman Home Letters*, 369.

other opportunity to strengthen his own position. He still felt sure, he told Welles, that Stanton would quit, but if this surmise proved wrong Johnson was willing to push matters by forcing the Secretary out. Fearing this, Grant and Sherman tried to persuade Johnson not to precipitate the crisis that must follow any attempt on his part to eject Stanton from the war office. "If he will not [resign]," Sherman advised the President, "then it will be time to contrive ulterior measures. In the meantime it so happens that no necessity exists for precipitating matters."

Sherman was right. The existing situation, awkward as it was for all, at least maintained an uneasy equilibrium that presumably could have endured until another popular verdict was rendered in November. But the President would not wait. He was encouraged by reports of bad feeling between Stanton and Grant, and "he thought he would let them fight it out." Yet, still convinced that Grant had conspired to let Stanton return to the war office, he continued to fan the fires of this controversy in the partisan press.[5]

Grant was indeed angry with Stanton; he confided to Schofield that the Secretary's attitude was rude and officious. It was common gossip in Washington that Stanton did not use some of the clerks who had served Grant, for he thought that they might be spies for the general and perhaps for the President. Young Eddie Stanton now became his father's assistant, and Eckert assumed a second place of power in the Department. According to Charles Benjamin, a clerk who was displaced in the shuffling, Eckert and Eddie Stanton "imitated Stanton's arrogance, and both were petty tyrants instead of big ones, like their model." Stanton had the volumes of wartime telegraphic dispatches placed in Ford's Theater, which was still under armed guard. But Grant could also see that, except for these manifestations of distrust for everyone on Stanton's part, army administration was going on as before.[6]

Therefore, though Stanton and Grant nursed a resentment toward each other, they both distrusted the President more, and Johnson's unthinking assault on Grant's veracity pushed him and the Secretary back into accord. By the end of January, Grant was convincing Re-

---

[5] Morse, *Welles Diary*, III, 263, 267–8; Sherman, *Memoirs*, II, 423–6; "Notes of Colonel W. G. Moore," *loc. cit.*, 116–17.

[6] Schofield's reminiscence on Grant, to Hamlin Garland, Box 49, Garland Papers, USC; Benjamin to Horace White, June 1, 1914, ISHL; Johnson, "Reminiscences of Hon. E. M. Stanton," *loc. cit.*, 74; *General Orders—Reconstruction*, Sen. Exec. Doc. 342, 40th Cong., 2d sess.; Gorham, *Stanton*, II, 428–30.

publican leaders that the President was in error, if not lying, concerning a conspiracy on Grant's part to return the war office keys to Stanton. He had Rawlins go nightly to the home of General G. M. Dodge so that Dodge's guest, Senator Wilson, might examine beforehand Grant's replies to Johnson's unending accusatory letters. Through Wilson, Stanton's confidence in Grant increased, though their former cordiality was never regained.[7]

Social life functioned at an accelerated pace during these tense weeks. The Stantons joined the Grants at receptions in private homes. Sumner was now Stanton's particular friend in Washington, and he invited the Stantons to a small dinner party on February 2 in honor of Charles Dickens, then visiting the capital to offer readings of his popular works. Moorfield Storey, Sumner's young secretary, was a bemused witness to the scene, and recorded that "Mr. Stanton came out wonderfully and Mr. Sumner said that he had never seen him so agreeable, and that I might meet him for a winter without getting any but the very shortest replies from him."

Stanton's tongue loosened in the warm glow of his admiration for the visitor. He showed off his familiarity with the author's works by accurately quoting from memory long passages from *Pickwick*, which he said had provided an invaluable source of diversion during the worst days of the war. As the men sipped brandy and the candles flickered lower, Stanton at Dickens's request offered his recollections of the nightmare night when Lincoln was shot.

It was an impressive gathering of talent, young Storey remembered. "Mr. Dickens, whose nature is emotional, sensitive; Mr. Sumner, the man of intellect and principle; Mr. Stanton, the intensely energetic and practical." They were "as different types as could be imagined." His impression of the controversial War Secretary was not totally pleasant. "Stanton strikes me as a man of coarse mental fibre, not a man of sentiment or impressionable. There is something in his voice, thick and with a suspicion of the nose about it, a drawl at the end of words, that sounds unpleasantly," Storey recalled, in reaction to Stanton's nasal tone of speech caused by his asthmatic complaint and his flat midwestern accent, which grated harshly on an ear attuned to the New England way. "In fact he is not a refined or cultivated man," Storey continued, "but he strikes you as a man of energy, and firmness, and perhaps the very dullness of his nervous

[7] Cramer, *op. cit.*, 99–100; Dodge, *op. cit.*, 100; Sherman to Reverdy Johnson, Feb. 1, 1868, Reverdy Johnson Papers, LC.

organization enabled him to stand the tremendous wear and tear of the war, for after all it is the vibration rather more than the strain which snaps a string." Sumner and Dickens were far higher types, Storey concluded.

Yet the Massachusetts senator and the Englishman took pleasure in Stanton's company, and Dickens, years later, remembered the meeting in fond terms. The three men walked through the streets of the capital so that Dickens could see the sights, and Washington hostesses envied Ellen her husband's success with the social prize of the season.[8]

The pleasant interlude of the Dickens visit failed to relieve Stanton's uncertain tension. Still contemplating resigning the war office within a few weeks, he considered a speculation in Nebraska lands. In mid-February the promoter wrote that the deal was ripe, and to spur the hesitant War Secretary to a decision, needled him: "I see that if the official party can throw you out of the War Office they intend to do it & I venture to say you have not made enough in this war to keep you above want for time to come." If Stanton wanted to participate in the lucrative scheme, he had to decide immediately to pull up stakes in Washington and head westward. But Stanton answered that he could not take part. By this time Congress had taken a hand, and Stanton decided to hold on a while longer; he could not, as Bigelow realized, be tempted "to enter into any covenants."

On February 3 a joint congressional resolution asked for the correspondence between Grant and the President on the return of the war office, and Stanton sent along copies supplied to him by the commanding general.[9] Replying to the resolution, Stanton contented himself with informing Congress that he had had no communications with the White House since the past August 12; he was content to let the Grant-Johnson exchange speak for itself.

It spoke loudly enough to initiate a second attempt to impeach the President, which failed to get out of committee but which might have warned Johnson to practice self-restraint. There was a measure pend-

---

[8] M. A. DeWolfe Howe, *Portrait of an Independent: Moorfield Storey, 1845–1929* (Boston, 1932), 66–9 (hereafter cited as Howe, *Portrait of an Independent*) ; Howe, "Dickens, Stanton, Sumner, and Storey," *loc. cit.*, 30–3; Morse, *Welles Diary*, III, 277–9; Sumner to the Stantons, Jan. 21, Feb. 1, 1868, owned by Mrs. Van Swearingen; Mrs. John A. Logan, *Reminiscences of a Soldier's Wife* (New York, 1913), 227–8; Young, *Men and Memories*, I, 128.

[9] N. C. Roswell to Stanton, Feb. 14, 1868, Sec. War Correspondence File, Box 334, RG 107, NA, on business deals; Stanton to Grant, Feb. 8, 1868, *ibid.*, Box 337, on reports to Congress, and see Morse, *Welles Diary*, III, 269–70, 274, Bigelow, *Retrospections*, IV, 94.

ing in the Senate reorganizing the entire South into a single military district under Grant's command, and the day after the vexed correspondence was published, John Binney advised Fessenden that "after the hot and irritable correspondence . . . it would be imprudent to press this measure through the Senate in present circumstances, and besides, it may not be necessary."

The President made it unnecessary. Congress, instead, over Johnson's veto, passed another law, which put into Grant's hands all the executive authority that the reconstruction acts had heretofore entrusted to the White House. The Republicans now were confident of Grant, and Stanton, though he was still unsure of the general's reliability, made no protest.[1]

Unable to let bad enough alone, Johnson approved Hancock's dismissal of Negro aldermen in New Orleans whom Sheridan had earlier placed in office. Grant ignored the President's wishes in this matter and ordered Hancock to restore the Negroes. Over Sherman's protests the President pushed ahead with a plan to establish an eastern army command with headquarters in Washington and to give Sherman, as its commander, rank equal to Grant's. It was an obvious gambit to pit Sherman against Grant and to groom him for the post of Secretary of War.

Each of these egregious moves further antagonized Grant and pushed him and Stanton back into rapport. This had the effect of making Stanton, day after day, postpone resigning. He could not desert his post under fire from the White House. Johnson was succeeding only in isolating himself.[2]

The President's inability to sense the fact of his weakness is best evidenced by his determination to rid himself of Stanton once and for all, not caring that this must unleash another impeachment attempt and was precisely what the radicals were hoping for. Johnson seemed to court impeachment. He was going to pit himself against Congress and the Army, at a time when the White House had been discredited, against the institutions that enjoyed the strongest possible evidence of popular support and wielded the real weapons of governmental power.

Like the President, Stanton held an exalted view of his office and of his influence as Secretary. Actually, Stanton was out of touch with what was going on and was utterly powerless to control the actions of

[1] Binney to Fessenden, Feb. 5, 1868, Fessenden Papers, LC; Stanton to Colfax, Feb. 4, 1868, Sec. War, Reports to Congress, XI, 105, RG 107, NA.

[2] Hesseltine, *Grant*, 108–11; Lewis, *Sherman*, 592–3; Morse, *Welles Diary*, III, 278.

the men who were deciding his official fate. He held an office with power only to obstruct policies, earned an inadequate salary, lived in a region that worsened his health, and was involved in a situation that rasped at his strained nerves. It would be difficult to imagine a set of circumstances more poorly calculated to serve his self-interest. All he could do was wait. Merely standing on the side lines as he was doing required a full share of dogged, unyielding courage.

It was not easy for him to hold on to a cabinet post in defiance of a President's wishes. Only the most imperative convictions could have kept him at his post now that the Senate had sustained his right to it. Stanton agreed with John Hay that it was to be regretted that the fight against Johnson was pushing Congress into dependence on the Army. But Stanton pointed out that the issue facing the nation was not the theoretical trustworthiness of the Army in general, but rather the specific convictions of the Army's generals. He was confident that Congress and the country were in no danger from the military class. The threat to stability emanated from the White House, and Stanton feared that if Johnson gained control of the war office and the Army, then political democracy was in peril.[3]

Clearly, Grant alone could not prevent the President from frustrating the purposes of the reconstruction laws. Events during Stanton's suspension from the war office had proved the need for a stronger checkrein on the White House than army headquarters provided. Grant could stand firm against pressure from Johnson only if supported by a strong War Secretary. Therefore, Stanton reasoned, it was his responsibility to hold the war office against anyone the President might send to take it, until Congress and Grant indicated that the replacement was satisfactory.

There can be no doubt that Stanton saw himself as the savior of the nation's best, most patriotic interests. This man of unheroic mold was now, in his own mind, a knight engaged in struggle with a despised dragon of reaction. A man of Stanton's temperament, warmed by this self-image and flattered at the numerous messages of support he received, was capable of bravery transcending the physical. To be admired as a hero he found even more gratifying than the popular respect accorded him during the war as the organizer of victory.

So Stanton, day after day, kept postponing his moment of resigna-

---

[3] Thayer, *Hay*, I, 262–3; Dawes, "Recollections of Stanton under Johnson," *loc. cit.*, 499–500.

tion although Ellen nagged at him to realize that the imbroglio must lead to disaster for him. She begged him to give up, and to repair his health and attend to their financial wants. Instead of resigning, he wrote to Pamphila and told her that his contribution to her welfare and their mother's support this year must be nothing at all.

The materialism that had dominated Stanton in prewar years had gone into a complete decline during his six years of public service. He was now ruled by an idealism capable of denying to his wife and to his beloved mother and sister a minimal standard of living. Few who knew him would have guessed that he placed anything ahead of his family. Yet he was unable to pay the tutors who instructed the younger children and he had to borrow again to meet Ellen's medical expenses and other personal obligations.

He still wanted wealth and was cold to political ambitions. But he believed that he must preserve the sacrifices which he and the nation had invested since 1861 in remaking the Southern society. Stanton saw himself as an indispensable warrior blocking the perverted policies of the White House.[4] Andrew Johnson thought him a scarecrow, leagued in an unholy conspiracy with Grant.

Despite Johnson's fulminations, Stanton had not been part of a conspiracy. He and Grant had stumbled along separate but roughly parallel paths, wanting the Johnson administration to finish its remaining year without a crisis, so long as the White House showed restraint concerning the Army's work in the South.

The best advice that the President received was Sherman's—to let things alone, and by doing nothing, so to embarrass Stanton as to force him to resign from his ridiculous and personally ruinous situation. Stanton had intended to do just that, and still planned to resign when matters had settled down.

In ordering Stanton returned to the war office, the Republican senators had set as the price of peace that Johnson must accept the fact of the Army's insulation from the White House, and leave Stanton alone until a mutually satisfactory replacement could be named. Congress and the press focused unwavering spotlights of attention on the war office. The failure of earlier attempts at impeachment indicated clearly that short of reaching out again for control of the Army, the President was safe on that score. "Congress has stiffened up very much," young

[4] Wolcott MS, 210–11; Pamphila Stanton Wolcott to Alexander Wylie, Oct. 18, 1870, and financial details, owned by Craig Wylie. Requests, too numerous to cite, that Stanton stay on, in Stanton MSS.

Storey wrote, "and if Johnson issues any proclamations about Stanton, . . . he will be impeached instantly. He knows it, unfortunately, and he is too cautious to take any such step."

But Johnson was not cautious at all. Still casting about for a man whom he could dominate as War Secretary, yet who would be acceptable to the Senate, and who had the courage to take the chance, the President now resorted to a ridiculous possibility. On February 13 he had his secretary approach the chief clerk of the War Department, John Potts, to sound out this functionary on his willingness to become Secretary of War ad interim "until Genl. McClellan or some other suitable person could be nominated and confirmed by the Senate," as Colonel Moore recorded the President's plan.

Potts begged off. He wanted no part of a plot to bypass the tenure law in order to get Stanton out of the war office. Johnson, therefore, had to continue looking for the man to stand up to Stanton.[5] That the President could even contemplate nominating the obscure Potts as a man adequate to force Stanton out of office so that the spectacular McClellan might become his replacement, is the measure of Johnson's unreasoning partisanship.

[5] Howe, *Portrait of an Independent*, 58; "Notes of Colonel W. G. Moore," *loc. cit.*, 119; J. B. Stillson to Barlow, Feb. 7, 12, 1868, Barlow Papers, HL.

CHAPTER XXVIII

NO ONE WILL STEAL IT NOW

T WAS amusing to see how afraid everyone was of the War Office," one of General Sherman's friends remarked later. In mid-February, however, the President saw nothing to smile at.

After the humiliating refusal of chief clerk Potts to serve as a sacrificial lamb by becoming War Secretary ad interim, Johnson cast about for other possibilities. Welles, always eager to strike at Stanton, suggested that the President order Adjutant General Lorenzo Thomas to return to his titular post. The adjutant's duties, though secondary in importance to Stanton's and Grant's, included responsibility for personnel assignments and records. Having Thomas in charge of these matters would confront Stanton and Grant with an important Department functionary who, long out of favor with the Secretary and commanding general, would be dependent for support on the White House. In addition, bringing Thomas back would reduce the status of the acting chief adjutant, "Stanton's man," General Townsend. Johnson seized on the suggestion.[1]

Thomas, however, was a frail reed to employ as a staff. Except for field duty in the Seminole and Mexican wars, this sixty-three-year-old West Point graduate had spent his military career as a Washington desk soldier. Tall, thin to the point of gauntness, with a shock of white hair and a scraggly beard, Thomas was known in the Army as a tippler and an eccentric. He enjoyed very little popularity and almost no personal influence with his fellow officers, and up to this time was unknown to the public. If the President expected Thomas to rally any sub-

[1] S. Van Vleit to Sherman, May 29, 1868, W. T. Sherman Papers, LC; Morse, *Welles Diary*, III, 278–80.

stantial popular support to the White House in a crusade against Stanton, or to amass opposition to the vast prestige and influence Grant possessed in the Army, then he had committed a great blunder.[2]

Ignoring Thomas's known limitations, the President decided to use him in a grander way than Welles had suggested, and to attack on two fronts at once. He matched his order sending Thomas to resume charge of the adjutant bureau with another on February 12 calling Sherman to Washington to head the proposed new eastern command, despite Tecumseh's earlier expression of unwillingness to have anything to do with such an assignment. Sherman, the President hoped, would bring to his cause the distinction that Grant offered to his congressional champions and that Thomas so evidently lacked. If Sherman soon thereafter accepted the war office portfolio, as the President still planned for him to do, then Grant's power among the army hierarchy and popularity with the public might be countered. Further, Grant would be sandwiched helplessly between Sherman as Secretary and Thomas as adjutant controlling army records and officer assignments. The scheme might have succeeded, for with elections hovering within the year, probably few senators would have dared to refuse approval of a nomination of Sherman to the war office. Johnson should have made sure, however, that Sherman was willing to play his game.[3]

But the President was following the dictates of emotion rather than the guidelines of logic. He could no longer stand the thought of Stanton in the war office and was determined to remove him regardless of the Senate's ruling. Johnson confided to Colonel Moore that "self-respect demanded it; and . . . if the people did not entertain sufficient respect for their chief magistrate to uphold him in such a measure then he [Johnson] ought to resign."

Thomas took over the adjutant duties on the fourteenth without incident. The President was happy that "Aunt Nancy" Townsend now knew that "Brute Stanton has a superior, whose orders he must obey," as Johnson's daughter phrased it. But when he issued the order elevating Thomas, the President had not heard from Sherman concerning the general's willingness to accept an eastern command and so be on hand for the larger play.

A letter from Sherman arrived at the White House later that same

[2] W. T. Sherman to T. Ewing, Sr., Feb. 22, 1868, Ewing Family Papers, LC; Morse, *Welles Diary*, III, 289.

[3] Feb. 17, 1868, Moore notebook, Johnson Papers, LC; Morse, *Welles Diary*, III, 281.

day after clearing through channels at the War Department, where obviously Grant and Stanton had read it. Sherman absolutely refused the eastern assignment and the promotion in rank that went with it; he wanted no part in Johnson's plan. The President could do nothing but revoke his order.

Now knowing that Sherman, the only general who could act as a counter to Grant, would not play his game, that Stanton and Grant were aware of Sherman's refusal to enlist, and that Thomas was a lightweight, the President recklessly persisted in going ahead with the part of his plan that concerned Thomas. He would not backtrack. But it is difficult to see what safe advantage he hoped to gain from advancing now that he was shorn of his major weapon.[4]

On the nineteenth, Thomas, in his indiscreet, bumbling manner, further warned the opposition. He asked Townsend to look up the records on the tenure law and told him confidentially that the President intended to supersede Stanton and place Thomas in the war office. The records Thomas wanted were filed in an open room of the adjutant's division, where the activity of the clerks assigned to obtain them was clearly apparent. Johnson might as well have hoisted a signal.

Yet no one could believe that Thomas's assertions were true or that the President relied on this man. Stanton, sharing the contempt for Thomas that was common in army circles, and having convinced himself that the existing equilibrium, however unpleasant, would continue until Johnson finished his term, underestimated the intensity of the President's emotions.[5]

Johnson called Thomas to the White House at nine o'clock in the morning on Friday, February 21, and calmly lectured him on the tenure law. Then he gave Thomas two orders, one ordering Stanton to vacate the war office and the other naming Thomas to succeed him as Secretary of War ad interim. With an officer of the adjutant division accompanying him as witness, Thomas hurried to the War Department, informed Townsend of the change, then moved on to the Secretary's room. It was almost eleven o'clock when he knocked at the closed door and heard Stanton tell him to enter.

Stanton was seated on the worn leather couch near the window.

[4] Mrs. Martha Johnson Patterson to Johnson, Feb. 10, 1868, Johnson Papers, LC; Morse, *Welles Diary*, III, 282; "Notes of Colonel W. G. Moore," *loc. cit.*, 119, 120; April 9, 1868, Moore notebook, Johnson Papers, LC; Townsend, *Anecdotes*, 125; McCulloch, *op. cit.*, 143–6.

[5] W. T. Sherman to T. Ewing, Sr., Feb. 22, 1868, Ewing Family Papers, LC; Morse, *Welles Diary*, III, 289; Townsend, *Anecdotes*, 125.

Striding quickly across the long room, Thomas came close to him and said: "I am directed by the President to hand you this." A long, silent minute passed as Stanton read the brief text of the message removing him from the war office. He looked up at Thomas and asked in a bland voice: "Do you wish me to vacate at once, or am I to be permitted to stay long enough to remove my property?" Thomas replied: "Certainly, at your pleasure," and then let Stanton read the order naming him as the new Secretary. "I wish you to give me a copy," Stanton said. Agreeing, Thomas walked happily back to Townsend's room and had that officer make a copy of the text, certifying to it himself as Secretary ad interim.

While Thomas was busy with this clerical diversion, Stanton called Grant in. The two men quickly decided to hold Thomas off. Encouraged to find that Grant, on whose attitude everything depended, wanted him to keep the war office, Stanton was waspish when Thomas returned. "I want some little time for reflection. I don't know whether I shall obey your orders or not," Stanton snapped, and forbade Thomas to issue any orders as Secretary until he decided.

Somehow Thomas missed the point. When he returned to the White House shortly after one o'clock, he failed to mention to Johnson the final acid exchange with Stanton. The President, presuming that Stanton was ready to vacate without a fight, told Thomas to take over the war office the next day. Jubilant, Thomas went off to celebrate. Meeting with the cabinet soon after, Johnson informed the surprised officials of what he had done, gloating that "Stanton seemed calm and submissive," and sent a message off to the Senate with the information that he had replaced Stanton with Thomas.[6]

At least he thought he had. Johnson shared with most of his cabinet supporters the belief that Stanton was a cowardly bully who would quit under direct attack, and that Grant was an inept, untrustworthy self-seeker whose ambition would prevent him from making a public stand. But the President failed to explore the consequences that must stem from wrong estimates of the two men.

Up to the time that he was roughly ordered out of the war office, Stanton was useful to the President and the Democrats. Their supporters could malign him as a ridiculous functionary who was drawing pay without providing services. But with the ouster order, Grant moved to support Stanton in order to protect the Army from unbearable

---

[6] Morse, *Welles Diary*, III, 284; "Notes of Colonel W. G. Moore," *loc. cit.*, 120–1; Washington *Chronicle*, Feb. 22, 1868; Hesseltine, *Grant*, 113–14.

strains and to further his own ambitions. To Republican spokesmen, the War Department became a bastion of liberty resisting the encroachments of a tyrannical executive, with Stanton holding firm the ramparts and with Grant serving as a self-effacing savior keeping violence in check by his mere presence. Johnson threw both men irrevocably into the hands of the radical Republicans. They had no other place to go. Most Northerners made the same shift.

And while the President gloated over an easy victory, his supposedly cowed adversary built defenses. Messengers sped to Capitol Hill from the War Department bearing Stanton's accounts of the morning's events, creating uproars in both houses of Congress. Covode moved a resolution in the House to impeach the President, and even before Johnson's message to the Senate arrived, that body was in executive session considering Stanton's ousting.

Again Stanton was nervous, unsure of what the results would be, and doubtful of success. He sent his oldest son to Congress to obtain quick and reliable reports of his fate. At three o'clock that afternoon the youth wrote that "Senator Edmunds and Mr. Boutwell both say not to give up the office; . . . Senate in Executive Session now . . . Mr. Edmunds, Fessenden, Frelinghuysen, and all . . . say you ought to hold on to the point of expulsion until Senate acts." Meanwhile, Stanton's office was crowded with congressmen who had hurried up Pennsylvania Avenue to encourage the Secretary.[7] Senators and other supporters sent notes to the war office, and the terse word from Sumner— "Stick!"—became famous.

This was what Stanton needed—a clear indication that Congress would stand by him. Without it he was helpless, both because he had no power in his own right and because, in order for him to hold a position, he had to feel that it was respectable and legitimate. As the weak midwinter sun illuminated the excited group of men gathered around him in the war office, Stanton decided to accept Johnson's challenge. He wrote out an order to Grant calling for the military arrest of Thomas "for disobedience to superior authority in refusing to obey my orders as Secretary of War."

As soon as Grant received this order he hurried to the Secretary's room. Moving out of earshot of the onlookers, he and Stanton talked for almost half an hour. Neither man ever divulged what transpired,

[7] Horace White, *The Life of Lyman Trumbull* (Boston, 1913), 308–9; David M. DeWitt, *Impeachment and Trial of Andrew Johnson* (New York, 1903), 346–7 (hereafter cited as DeWitt, *Impeachment*); E. L. Stanton to Stanton, Feb. 21, 1868, Stanton MSS.

but Grant destroyed Stanton's order to arrest Thomas and returned to his office, where, for the rest of the afternoon, he refused callers.[8]

The news spread quickly. Incredulity was the dominant reaction. Even Welles privately thought that "this whole movement . . . has been incautiously and loosely performed without preparation. The Cabinet was not consulted. His [Johnson's] friends in the Senate and House were taken by surprise."

Dusk fell. At the Senate, bright windows showed that the executive session concerning Stanton was still under way. Tension mounted as wild rumors of violence circulated in the capital and flashed across the wires to all parts of the country. At a dinner party that evening in Washington, young Edgar Welles was shocked to hear his host, General William Emory, commander of the local garrison, order all officers to their posts. Republican senators, hotly debating a reply to the President's message on Stanton, were thrown into confusion by reports from journalists that Thomas was threatening force and that Stanton had already vacated the war office. "What are the facts? We desire to know," Senator John Conness scrawled hurriedly, and sent the note off to the War Department. Stanton replied: "I . . . mean to continue in possession unless expelled by force. Lorenzo Thomas is not, so far as I know, issuing any orders as Secretary of War." [9]

But what if the rumors concerning Thomas were true? Probably at Stanton's suggestion, a committee of Republican senators hurried to Grant's office to ask his intentions. "He asked," Sumner told Bigelow later that night, "how or when the President would get the . . . soldiers to remove Stanton [by force], implying that his orders could not be obtained for such a purpose." Grant was safe.

Embellished accounts of Thomas's bellicose intentions soon reached Stanton. Again fearing that the President would employ force against him, and feeling sure that Thomas would test the issue the next morning instead of waiting out the holiday weekend, Stanton, at nine o'clock Friday night, sent an urgent message to his Senate supporters. "I am informed that . . . Thomas is boasting that he intends to take possession of the War Office at 9 tomorrow morning," he wrote. "If the Senate does not declare its opinion of the law, how am I to hold

[8] Messages to Stanton, Feb. 21, 1868, in Stanton MSS; Townsend, *Anecdotes,* 133n.; other data in Flower, *Stanton,* 333–4; Washington *Chronicle,* Feb. 22, 1868.

[9] Morse, *Welles Diary,* III, 289; Conness, *Some of the Men and Measures of the War and Reconstruction Period* (Boston, 1882), 18–20; Gorham, *Stanton,* II, 440; U. S. Senate, *Trial of Andrew Johnson* (Washington, 1868), I, 663–5 (hereafter cited as Senate, *Trial*).

possession?" Less than an hour later the Senate by a party vote resolved that Johnson could not legally oust Stanton or replace him with Thomas.[1]

Now in possession of the Senate's sustaining resolution, Stanton announced his intention to stay in the war office night and day until some decision was reached. Any attempt to eject him by force, or to remove the seals of the Department from his charge, must lead to confusion and inevitably to violence, if troops under orders from Thomas and the President clashed with other soldiers obeying Grant and himself. Stanton would hold possession in order to forestall a contest by arms.

There were other ways to fight. Ever the lawyer, Stanton willingly entered the arena of the courts, where Johnson always after claimed to have wanted the affair to go. Stanton knew that Grant would not sanction a military arrest and court-martial for Thomas, for that would pit the Army against itself. The civil courts were another matter. Calling in his friend David Cartter, the partisanly Republican Chief Justice of the District's Supreme Court, Stanton issued a complaint against Thomas for violating Congress's tenure law and asked Cartter to invoke the penalties the law prescribed for the violation.

Stanton's action indicates the absence of any conspiring on his part to avoid a judicial test of the tenure law. He and Cartter, while filling out the complaint, discussed the probability that the President, through Thomas, would seize the opportunity that Stanton was now offering, to allege the unconstitutionality of the statute. And it was Stanton who insisted that they go ahead.[2]

It was one o'clock Saturday morning, the twenty-second, when the judge left with the paper. Of the crowd that had filled Stanton's office all day, only Nebraska's Senator John M. Thayer, who had volunteered to stay, remained to share the first long night of what promised to be a siege of uncertain duration.

The stillness oppressed Stanton. He nibbled nervously at a light meal which an armed soldier brought in, then abandoned it to peer anxiously out the windows at the sentries Grant had stationed around the buildings. Stanton asked Thayer whom he thought the commander of the guard, General E. A. Carr, would obey if contrary orders came from Thomas or the White House. Thayer realized that Stanton was really

[1] Senate, *Trial*, I, 210, 220–3; Gorham, *Stanton*, II, 439.

[2] Ms notes by Stanton on conversation with Cartter, dated "12:30 A.M., Feb. 22, 1868," owned by the estate of Benjamin P. Thomas; Gorham, *Stanton*, II, 441; Senate, *Trial*, I, 427–8.

inquiring whether Grant would stick or jump again to Johnson's support; a question "uppermost in the minds of all," Thayer recalled. The senator decided to test the matter by inquiring of Carr what he would do in the event of contradictory orders, and Carr, in what Stanton took as a good omen, replied that he would obey Grant and Stanton. Thereupon the Secretary wrote a request for Grant to give Carr permanent responsibility for the security of the War Department building and army records.

It was now almost two o'clock in the morning. A soldier brought in the card of Methodist bishop Simpson, whose sermons had delighted Lincoln and Stanton during the war years. Stanton had the minister admitted. He was gratified when Simpson asserted that the Secretary had the support of the "God-fearing portion of the people," and told of a dinnertime conversation with Grant the evening before in which the general was unreserved in his compliments to Stanton. With this the Secretary was "in fine spirits," Simpson recorded. They had a "very long religious talk . . . with prayer," and after a final benediction for Stanton's well-being, the bishop left.

Now elated, but soon oscillating between deep depression and buoyancy, Stanton failed to find the sleep he needed. He started from the couch where he lay at the sound of marching feet outside and wakened the dozing senator with a whispered warning: "I believe the troops are coming to put me out." Thayer peered at his watch. It was four o'clock, and the noise came from the changing of the guard in the chill dark. He and Stanton gave up the attempt to sleep and talked until dawn. Something was sure to happen.[3]

Many men slept poorly that night. Deducing from reports in the late evening newspapers on Friday that Stanton was giving up the war office, Johnson's secretary, Colonel Moore, had retired, thinking the whole affair finished. About two o'clock Saturday morning, a messenger from the White House got him up, for the President was worried by reports that Thomas was talking and drinking too much. Moore promised to stay with Thomas constantly the next day to keep him in check, slept awhile, then breakfasted hurriedly and rushed to Thomas's home, where he learned that the general "had gone away with two gentlemen." The frustrated colonel returned to the White House to learn what was going on.

[3] Thayer, "A Night with Stanton in the War Office," *McClure's Magazine*, VIII, 441–2; Robert D. Clark, *The Life of Matthew Simpson* (New York, 1956), 259.

General Thomas, too, had little sleep. He had returned early Saturday morning from a dance and was suffering from the early stages of hangover when, at eight o'clock, a district marshal and a deputy, the "two gentlemen" Moore heard of, wakened him with an order from Judge Cartter calling for his arrest. Thomas notified the President of this development. Appearing breakfastless before the judge, Thomas learned that he was subject to imprisonment for violating the tenure law but that $5,000 bail, in the form of surety pledges, was acceptable to guarantee his appearance in court the following Wednesday. The general's lawyer, Richard T. Merrick, who heard of the arrest as the news spread swiftly through the city, arrived too late to do more than witness Thomas's signature on the bail agreement.

Moore, after reporting to the President that he could not find Thomas, went out again in search of the elusive general. He missed him at Cartter's rooms, for Thomas, after leaving there, had gone to his attorney's office, where Moore found him. The two officers hurried to the White House. Thomas gave the President the details of his arrest, and Johnson said: "Very well, that is the place I want it in—the courts." Johnson was later to allege that the purpose of his next move was to force the constitutional issue now that Thomas's arrest made possible a resort to the courts. He sent Thomas to the Attorney General. Stanbery advised the general to return to the War Department that day and assume the office of War Secretary, and provided Thomas with a kind of script to follow.

According to Johnson, sending Thomas to eject Stanton again was the deliberate first step toward achieving a court test of the tenure law. But this argument strains the fabric of chronology and the logic of events. There could be a judicial test only so long as Stanton held the office, not if he gave it up to Thomas. The weight of evidence leaves little doubt that the President was in earnest about removing Stanton. He hoped that Stanton would yield the keys to Thomas, and did not behave as though he expected Stanton to disobey. Johnson's plans led to the war office, not the courtroom.

Only after it was clear that Stanton would not give up the war office, and impeachment again threatened the President for having made the attempt to force him out, did Johnson seriously consider a judicial test of the tenure act. He thereafter dignified the moves he had made to oust Stanton since August 1867 by claiming they were part of a pre-arranged pattern of constitutional maneuvering.[4]

[4] Feb. 22, 1868, Moore notebook, Johnson Papers, LC; Senate, *Trial*, I, 427-8.

Even assuming that Johnson was sincere in his protestations, his strategy was unsound. He claimed to have expected that the Supreme Court would take jurisdiction in the matter, expand the issue from a contest between Stanton and Thomas to the question of the constitutionality of the tenure law, and then declare the law invalid. Considering that the Court at this time was intelligently backing away from involvement in related explosive issues, it is doubtful that Thomas could have got it to take jurisdiction of an appeal.

The fact remains that the President never really tried for a Supreme Court hearing. He and the cabinet later discussed the desirability of securing a writ of quo warranto from the Court, which would bring Stanton and the tenure law into the jurisdiction of the high tribunal, but Johnson did not apply for that writ because it involved a lengthy procedure. A year might pass before the Court acted upon an application. During that year, precisely the remainder of Johnson's term, Stanton would hold the war office and perform as Secretary. The quo warranto procedure remained unused because the President wanted action, not litigation.

Johnson's rationale, young Moorfield Storey mused, "was an afterthought, a contingency arising unexpectedly, and could have formed no part of his intention when the order of removal was issued." For unless Johnson was bent on ousting Stanton, he had no reason for naming Thomas to the interim position and choosing a permanent nominee to succeed Thomas. And Johnson now had a plausible successor in mind as a permanent Secretary. Thomas Ewing, Sr., he planned, would replace Thomas once the general had finished serving as an expendable tool and had pried Stanton loose from the War Department. Obviously the Senate would not confirm Ewing if Stanton still held the office. No wonder the President castigated Thomas to newsman Stillson for "not holding on" at the war office "when Stanton was really scared." On Saturday morning, February 22, 1868, Johnson's attention, like that of the nation's, was fixed on the War Department, not the courts.[5]

By eleven o'clock Saturday morning Stanton's office was again crowded with friends; they were seated in a long arc with Stanton in

[5] Stillson to Barlow, Feb. 22, 1868, Barlow Papers, HL; Howe, *Portrait of an Independent*, 95–7. Lloyd Paul Stryker, *Andrew Johnson* (New York, 1929), 566; and R. W. Winston, *Andrew Johnson* (New York, 1928), 424, like most authors treating these events, accept Johnson's assertions uncritically.

the center facing them. Except for their conversation the building was quiet, for the clerks were away on the holiday weekend. Then Thomas's voice was heard. Stanton called for him to enter. Everyone said "good morning." Thomas read from the note that Stanbery had supplied him: "I am ordered by the President of the United States to take charge of the office." A hush fell on the assembled men.

Then, breaking the silence, Stanton ordered Thomas to return to his adjutant duties. Thomas repeated his first statement, adding: "I shall not obey your orders." Again Stanton ordered Thomas to abandon his presumptuous demand. "I shall not do so," Thomas replied. "Then you may stand there, if you please," Stanton answered, wagging his finger at Thomas; "but you cannot act as Secretary of War; if you do, you do so at your peril." Thomas again insisted that he was the Secretary, then moved to Inspector General Edmund Schriver's adjacent office and closed the door, whereupon most of the spectators left. Stanton followed Thomas. Privacy relaxed the men in Schriver's room. Stanton laughingly asked Thomas whether he really presumed to act as Secretary. The general replied affirmatively. Playing Thomas as a good trial lawyer maneuvers a not too bright witness, Stanton shifted the mood of the conversation to a light plane. He asked after Thomas's health, noting that the general looked worn. Thomas swallowed the lure: "The next time you have me arrested," he told Stanton, "please do not do it before I get something to eat."

Stanton laughed aloud, and said that he had fasted also. He placed an arm around the general's shoulders and ran his fingers through Thomas's hair. Turning to Schriver, who was discreetly out of hearing of the conversation, Stanton called out: "Schriver, you have got a bottle here; bring it out."

Admitting that he kept a little whisky on hand for a dyspeptic ailment, Schriver produced it; Stanton and Thomas divided the meager contents equally and each drank his share at a swallow. Stanton sent a messenger to his home for a full bottle of liquor and while waiting for it the two men chatted amiably for a half hour. They opened the new bottle and had several drinks, joking and smiling the while. Grant peered in rather incredulously, made an inconsequential comment, and withdrew. Meanwhile, Thomas's attorney and Moore were trying to get into the Department building to see what their charge was up to, but sentries refused them admission. Noon sounded on nearby church bells; a half hour later Thomas emerged and started back to the White House. It had, he later recalled, become a rather pleasant day.

Even while "Ad Interim" Thomas jousted with Stanton, the President was preparing to cast him aside, despite the fact that the aging general had, on Johnson's behalf, made himself ridiculous and exposed himself to legal penalties. The nomination of Ewing to the post of War Secretary went off to the Senate. But it was too late. The senators had adjourned early that day after a brief session. Ordering Moore to return to the Senate on Monday with the Ewing nomination, the President, showing "some anxiety," Moore recalled, turned to other matters.

Welles had told him about the incident of the preceding night, when General Emory had summoned his officers to their posts. Johnson called Emory to the White House and indirectly posed the question of the officer's concept of rightful obedience. Emory replied that he had already consulted lawyers on the issue and they had concluded that he was governed by existing army regulations, including Congress's law of 1867 which specified that all orders to army commanders must go through the commanding general. Johnson insisted that army officers had to give precedence to his orders as commander in chief over any legislative enactment. But the general, not totally disagreeing, pointed out that Johnson had approved the army order transmitting the 1867 law to the officers, who therefore assumed he also approved the law. Most officers, Emory asserted, would act on this basis.

Altogether it was a frustrating Saturday afternoon for Andrew Johnson. He soon learned, taking the news with great composure, that the House Reconstruction Committee, after a wild session, had recommended that Congress impeach him, and he told Moore, as the secretary has recorded it, that "he has made an issue demanded by his self-respect, and that if he cannot be President in fact, he will not be President in name alone." Yet the night before, Johnson had assumed that no impeachment would follow his attempt to oust Stanton, that the Senate's resolution declaring that Thomas might not take the war office would end Congress's role in the affair.

It was only after hearing of the impeachment resolution that Johnson tried to secure a judicial decision on the tenure law. Heretofore he had expressed no great interest in Thomas's joust in court that morning. Now he sought to use a court test of the tenure law as a way to keep himself out of Congress's hands.

Soon after news of the impeachment motion reached the White House, Walter S. Cox, a Washington lawyer of note, arrived at the executive mansion in response to a request from Seward. Cox and Johnson discussed the possibility of getting Thomas jailed so that a quick test of the tenure law might result from efforts to get him out, and it was their hope that a favorable verdict would force Stanton to vacate. With Merrick, Cox agreed that Thomas should refuse to continue bail when he faced Cartter the following Wednesday, and should then submit to arrest. Meanwhile, the general must continue to assert that he was the legitimate War Secretary.[6]

In these tense days, as rumors of impending violence unsettled the nation, Stanton remained creditably calm. He secretly ordered that if Thomas tried to take the war office by force, it was to be surrendered at once, so that bloodshed might be avoided.

Sunday, February 23, passed quietly. Johnson spent part of the Sabbath with Stanbery, preparing an objection to the Senate resolution that had denied him the power to discharge Stanton. The President seemed cheerful. He enjoyed controversy and this one promised to overshadow all others in the nation's history. Monday's events added to the excitement.

At nine o'clock the War Department opened for the beginning of the day's work. Armed soldiers near the entrance doors snapped to the salute as General Thomas entered. He went to Stanton's room and repeated the demand for possession. Again Stanton refused. Thomas then went to the offices of Generals Townsend and Schriver, picked up his personal mail, and told them that all Department business must go through him. The officers remained noncommittal and Thomas left the building. Stanton worked on as though nothing untoward was occurring.[7]

The President, meanwhile, got off to the Senate his answer to the Friday resolution denying him the right to oust Stanton, along with the nomination of Ewing to replace him. But the major drama was to occur in the House, where, late in the dark, snowy afternoon, by a party vote, the representatives impeached Johnson, essentially for violating the tenure law; the ousting of Stanton and all it symbolized had thrown the weight of congressional opinion against the President. Everyone was conscious of the fact that this was the first time in the country's history that a chief executive was to face formal legislative condemnation. A sense of drama, of urgency, of crisis, permeated the scene.

---

[6] Senate, *Trial*, I, 164–76, 427–32, 556–7, 605–9, 705; II, 170–1; Townsend, *Anecdotes*, 126–9; Morse, *Welles Diary*, III, 288–90; Boutwell, *op. cit.*, II, 110–11; "Notes of Colonel W. G. Moore," *loc. cit.*, 121–2.

[7] "Notes of Colonel W. G. Moore," *loc. cit.*, 122; Townsend, *Anecdotes*, 129; Senate, *Trial*, I, 215; Washington *Intelligencer* and *Evening Express*, both Feb. 27, 1868.

Johnson received the news calmly. But nerves were raw. Rumors of clashes of armed men and of the theft of a stock of nitroglycerine in New York City, perhaps to blow in the locked doors of Stanton's office, received ready credence. Senator Chandler and Representative Logan hand-picked more than a hundred armed men and stationed them in the basement of the building, and almost each night thereafter Stanton shared his siege with volunteer partisans.[8]

Democrats chortled at these precautions and scorned Stanton as a frightened mouse obsessed with maidenish fears. Welles gloated that "this ridiculous conduct makes Stanton a laughing stock. He eats, sleeps, and stays cooped up in his entrenched and fortified establishment—scarcely daring to look out of the window." General Sherman, reporting later to Washington to testify at the impeachment trial, was amused when he saw armed sentries barring all War Department entrances but one, where visitors were carefully checked. "Why," Sherman laughed to Moore, "the Secretary takes more precautions for his protection than I . . . when travelling through Indian country."

Stanton was behaving ridiculously, even though millions of Americans believed as he did that physical violence was not only possible but probable. He was hurt when an old friend, Roswell Marsh, chided him for the security preparations around the War Department: "No one will steal it now." But Stanton also knew that in the eyes of most persons he respected, his holdout was heroic rather than burlesque. Mrs. M. L. Pomeroy, the wife of the Kansas senator, depicted him as a valiant defender of human rights against executive tyranny, and asserted to Stanton that congressmen, generals, and journalists were behind him. Cabinet officers such as Browning shared his fears that "danger of a civil war seems imminent." Moderate men such as George Templeton Strong and John Sherman agreed that Johnson had brought crisis to a country which, still recovering from the strains of the war years, might not be able to endure the new test. So Stanton found the courage to wait.[9]

[8] DeWitt, *Impeachment*, 358; Morse, *Welles Diary*, III, 292, 297; Detroit *Post, Chandler*, 296; "Notes of Colonel W. G. Moore," *loc. cit.*, 122.

[9] Gideon to John Welles, March 1, 1868, Welles Papers, LC; April 7, 1868, Moore notebook, Johnson Papers, LC, on General Sherman; Marsh to Stanton, March 9, 1868, Stanton MSS; Mrs. Pomeroy to Stanton, *ca.* March 1, 1868, owned by Mrs. Van Swearingen; Browning, *Diary*, II, 182; Strong, *Diary*, IV, 193; Thorndike, *Sherman Letters*, 313–14; W. A. Russ, Jr., "Was There a Danger of a Second Civil War during Reconstruction?" *MVHR*, XXV, 39–58.

CHAPTER XXIX

CLING TO THE OLD "ORIFICE"

Mᴏʀᴇ ᴛʜᴀɴ anything else, Stanton was concerned about Ellen's reaction to all this. He feared that her strong views might find expression in some way permanently damaging to their life together. This was the one price which he would not pay for continuing on at the war office.

On Monday night, the twenty-fourth, Stanton realized that he might be in for a long siege and that he must make some housekeeping preparations. He sent Sergeant Koerth to the Stanton home for a supply of food, clothing, blankets, and pillows. The sergeant, arriving there, received an unexpected reception. In her anger with her husband for disregarding his personal and family interests, and from her frantic fear for his safety, Ellen refused to send the linens and food. She told Koerth to convey her insistence to Stanton that he quit the Department, resign the disputed portfolio, and come home.

Koerth returned empty-handed. When he reported to Stanton on Ellen's reaction, the Secretary smiled and said: "Koerth, go to your own house and bring blankets, pillows, and such cooking utensils as we may need." In the predawn darkness Koerth fulfilled his mission. He then stopped at a farmers' market near the Capitol to purchase meat and vegetables.

Stanton was delighted when he saw the food. Suddenly ravenously hungry, he prepared an Irish stew. The sun rose as he put it over the fire which had been burning all night. Watching the flames, Stanton and the sergeant succumbed to the exhaustion that gripped them both and fell asleep. In the full light of the morning Stanton suddenly wakened. "Koerth! Koerth! Wake up, man," he shouted, "the stew is burning!" But they were too late to save the meal. Ruefully the Secretary rolled himself up in a blanket and returned to the couch, where he wrote a note to Ellen pleading for her understanding.[1]

The Stantons' oldest son and Senator Sumner became intermediaries between the beleaguered Secretary and his distressed, stubborn wife. They softened Ellen's bitterness at her husband's self-destructive course of action, and on Tuesday afternoon, which for Stanton had already been highlighted by a brief visit from Grant, a clerk informed him that Ellen was waiting outside in their carriage.

Leaping up from his desk, Stanton rushed out into the chill street without bothering to don a coat, pushed past the surprised sentries and the crowding reporters, and sat with Ellen for an hour. They quarreled, he defending the rectitude of his course, she seeking to persuade him to give up. But he would not. When Ellen drove off she was angrier than ever before in their marriage. Stanton returned sadly to the dreary office where he must spend an unknown number of weeks to come.

A few days later he was overjoyed when a note from Ellen admitted that she was resigned to his continuing the struggle. He answered in a grateful mood: "My Dear Wife. Your very kind note of this evening gives me great comfort. Harassed with care and earnest responsibility, suffering in health, and with no chance for immediate release, . . . I have longed much to see you during the past week, but knowing your aversion to the War Office, I have not asked you to come while hoping your love might draw you hither. If in a moment of disappointment and suffering I said anything to occasion you pain, or do you injustice I humbly crave your forgiveness." At least Stanton had Ellen's acquiescence if not her complete backing in his perilous adventure.[2]

Stanton's concern over Ellen did not diminish his awareness of the legal and political dangers in which he was involved. Soon after Ellen had left on Tuesday, Stanton received a note from Congressman William Pile, who had learned that General Thomas, due to appear before Judge Cartter the next day, was going to refuse to continue bail and then seek a writ of habeas corpus should Cartter order his imprisonment. It seemed probable that, if the general was refused by Cartter and then appealed to the Supreme Court, the judges would declare that he was illegally in arrest and that Stanton was guilty of felonious

---

[1] Koerth, in New York *Commercial Advertiser*, March 24, 1903, describes this incident correctly except that he misdates it as of the preceding Saturday; see Benjamin P. Thomas's note on Stanton's letter to Ellen, dated Feb. 25.

[2] To Ellen, *ca.* March 2, 1868, owned by Gideon Townsend Stanton.

misconduct. Thus the war office fortress might be breached, which was what the President most wanted.

As Colfax later expressed it, the Republicans believed that "a Majority of the Supreme Court are evidently determined to overthrow all our Reconstruction laws." To be sure, Congress had already overridden adverse Court judgments. But if Stanton's case against Thomas served the President's interests, then Stanton had opened a way for Thomas to win the war office. If Stanton refused to answer a summons from the Court, he would be involved in a gesture of open defiance against the high tribunal, an act that was personally and professionally repugnant to him. In the frenzied atmosphere of the moment, either course might precipitate the violence that everywhere threatened. Unlike the President, Stanton did not permit his emotions to oversway his better judgment. He called Cartter in and acted to avoid spreading the conflict to the courts.[3] Stanton gained a great advantage from his careful, lawyerlike preplanning.

On Wednesday, February 26, during the same hours when the House decided to impeach the President, Thomas appeared in Cartter's chambers accompanied by his counsel, Cox and Merrick. Stanton was represented by his friends Riddle and Carpenter, and his son, now in training for a law career, served them as clerk. Carpenter first tried for a postponement, which Thomas's counsel prevented. Then Judge Cartter asserted that no trial was in progress; he was merely serving as a magistrate to inquire whether a crime had been committed.

Merrick took alarm at this. He asked Cartter for a writ of habeas corpus to release Thomas from the nominal imprisonment that he was theoretically suffering. Carpenter countered that the application for the writ was out of order. As Thomas no longer threatened violence against Stanton, the Secretary wished to drop the charges.

No, thundered Cox. His client, Thomas, had committed a crime, was under arrest, and now wished to refuse bail. Cartter dryly remarked that his knowledge of the general's high character would not allow him to deprive Thomas of his liberty. The judge declared that he would report the offense that had occurred to the forthcoming term of the District grand jury the following December. That body would decide whether an indictment and a trial should follow.

It took less than twenty minutes. Claiming that he had been "eu-

[3] Pile to Stanton, Feb. 25 (misdated Feb. 26), 1868, and Stanton to Sen. Howard, Feb. 25, 1868, Stanton MSS; Colfax to John Russell Young, March 11, 1868, Young Papers, LC. Note that Stanton's concern was not with a possible court test of the tenure law, but with a criminal action against himself.

chred," Thomas and his disgruntled counsel left the courtroom after lodging a countersuit against Stanton, claiming false arrest and malicious prosecution—a suit that Thomas never carried through. The general's lawyers had played into Stanton's hands and lost their gamble because of inferior planning and contempt for the prowess of the opposition. Stanton was rarely guilty of these failings.[4]

Stanton, like Grant, believed that the campaign against Johnson would be brief. But the hectic February days settled down to long weeks of barely lessened tension. This unexpected extension of uncertainty, and the boredom of his self-imposed incarceration at the war office, added to Stanton's nervous irritability. Rumors that he was giving up were frequent, and they inspired a Stanton supporter in Ohio to plead with him to "never faulter . . . Cling to the old orifice [*sic*] like an eagle doth to her prey. . . . Say Sick Andy is an old s—t. . . . I will assist you as soon as I can get my dog cart I will come to Washington to fight for you." [5]

Although Stanton smiled at such earthy expressions of support, they sustained his conviction that he was again a leader in a vital conflict in which the life of the nation was at stake. While the battle raged, he had to work out with Grant prosaic ways of keeping the Army going although neither man was welcome at the White House. From the last week in February until the impeachment trial should end—and no one knew when that would be—the Army would lack a commander in chief and have two Secretaries of War. Lorenzo Thomas sat in on cabinet meetings and periodically restated his claim to Stanton's place, but no one was paying much attention to the poor old man any more.

Fortunately, most army officers and civilian employees assumed that Grant and Stanton were running things. Townsend relates that Johnson, Stanton, Thomas, and Grant sent him orders for execution, "and by a little tact I managed to avoid any question of jurisdiction or other difficulty." Equally important, the Treasury Department continued to honor Stanton's drafts and bills and the President never permitted Thomas to sign any warrants for public funds. On the other hand, Johnson took to corresponding directly with general officers on duty in the South and elsewhere. Some, like Hancock, responded to the gam-

---

[4] Senate, *Trial*, I, 597–8, 605–9; DeWitt, *Impeachment*, 376–7; Morse, *Welles Diary*, III, 294; "Notes of Colonel W. G. Moore," *loc. cit.*, 122; Townsend, *Anecdotes*, 130.
[5] "Gideon" to Stanton, April 23, 1868, Sec. War Correspondence File, Box 333, RG 107, NA; Grant to Sheridan, March 1, 1868, Sheridan Papers, LC.

bit and replied to the White House. Most others, like Meade, sent answers to the President's inquiries through the army channels centering in Grant's and Stanton's offices.[6] The net result of these pragmatic institutional adjustments was that Stanton remained War Secretary in title and in fact so far as the Army and the War Department's functions were concerned.

A triangular command structure emerged, in which two points, army headquarters and the war office, possessed the power to run the Army, and the third, the White House, was blunted. Remarkably, none of the triad threatened this precarious equilibrium by trying to reinstate or to transfer army commanders in the South; undoubtedly all thought that the results of the impeachment trial would provide these partisan laurels in due course. Upsetting the boat now might provoke the crises that each contender in his own way wished to avoid. Meanwhile, for the White House, Stanton and Grant did not exist. Next door, at the War Department, there was nothing for the President to do. One of the essential functions of the American executive was in suspense while the trial proceeded.

The ease with which army headquarters fell in with congressional rhythms of operation indicates that the commander-in-chief function can in our system find a focus other than the President, at least during a nonwar period, and recalls the operations under the Articles of Confederation. For example, the reports that Stanton and Grant would normally have made to the President now went directly to chairmen of congressional committees. The war office sent to Capitol Hill reports on the number of Negro voters in the South who did not cast ballots and the number of disfranchised whites; in another instance they offered conclusions concerning the buoying effects of postwar Supreme Court decisions on intransigent Southern whites and the resulting diminution of the morale of the army officers on reconstruction duty.

Together with Grant, Stanton reviewed army reorganization plans, prepared suggestions for Congress on legislation concerning wartime damage claims against the Army issuing from self-proclaimed Southern Unionists, and sought to untangle the contradictions between the now ratified Fourteenth Amendment's disability clause and Congress's reconstruction laws, so that army officers in the South might follow consistent policies. Grant no longer held that the occupation forces were

[6] Townsend, *Anecdotes*, 131; correspondence, Feb.–May 1868, HQA 109, RG 108, NA; Flower, *Stanton*, 342–3; Benjamin, "Secretary Stanton: The Man and His Work," *loc. cit.*, VII, 239–56.

independent of the war office or of army headquarters, but only of the President, now that Congress had interposed itself between the White House and the military.

Along with these serious matters, Stanton found time to attend to less pressing concerns. His orders closed the Department on the third anniversary of Lincoln's murder and required army posts everywhere to fire salute guns each half hour from sunrise to sunset. He attended to the routine tasks of appointing members to the Board of Supervisors for the Military Academy, and after receiving from the popular sculptor John Rogers a statuette showing him, Grant, and Lincoln in an imaginary "Council of War," Stanton complimented the artist on his sensitive execution of the dead President.

As ever, Stanton was concerned over problems of health. Hearing that Hitchcock was ailing, Stanton sent the aging officer his wishes that "the opening spring would restore your health," along with the admission that his own was none too good. Hitchcock's reply gratified Stanton, for the general, who had sharply criticized him during the war, wrote: "I . . . am glad once more to see your handwriting dated at the War Department."[7] Only the result of the impeachment would determine how long Stanton would stay there.

On March 1, the House managers—Bingham, Boutwell, Butler, Logan, Stevens, Williams, and Wilson—presented articles of impeachment to the Senate. Except for a catchall clause, the eleven-point indictment amounted to restatements that Johnson had illegally ousted Stanton, broken the tenure law, and sought to use the Army for his own purposes. March passed suspensefully in parliamentary technicalities. Doubtless the interval was beneficent in reducing passions, and Storey noted that "Stanton has been known to take a short walk in the grounds of the War Department, ready to run back to his room, if Lorenzo Thomas should show his head around the corner."

Stanton was irked to be a mere spectator of the trial, although daily reports of congressmen and other visitors supplemented the full accounts of the Senate proceedings which filled the public press. He read four newspapers daily during the trial. Still, he wanted more personal estimates. His oldest son became a familiar fixture in the Sen-

---

[7] Grant to Stanton, May 6, and to Wade, May 7, 1868, CG Letterbook, Letters Sent, 1866–8, RG 108, NA; Stanton to Rogers, May 15, 1868, NYHS; same to Prof. N. W. Edwards, May 16, 1868, CHS; same to Hitchcock and reply, March 18, 1868, Hitchcock Papers, LC; Frank W. Klingberg, *The Southern Claims Commission* (Berkeley, 1955), 36.

ate's visitors' gallery, where space was a rare prize, and he was soon joined by Ellen's mother, Mrs. James Hutchison, "that noble woman with the silver hair," who had come to stay with Ellen while Stanton was absent from home but spent almost all her time at the Senate.

In the first weeks of Johnson's trial Stanton helped Grant collect from army records all the information sustaining their position against the President, and sent it on to the impeachment managers.[8] Stanton's son helped Butler keep surveillance over possible prosecution witnesses. Army agents spied on defense witnesses who arrived in Washington and tried to rush them to the Senate before they could be defiled by communication with the White House. Grant openly supported anti-Johnson sentiment among the senators after testifying at the trial. Partisanship was the order of the day.

On the other side, Johnson was indulging in surreptitious surveillance over Stanton. He employed an army officer on War Department duty who, though a radical in politics, was devoted to Hancock and through that medium transmitted full reports on the Secretary's actions to the White House. Johnson knew how strained Stanton's nerves were and believed that the Secretary was cracking as the weeks passed.

Indeed, by mid-April, Stanton had to have a break. He and Ellen slipped quietly out of the capital for a blessedly calm weekend in Baltimore. In his absence Eddie remained in the war office as a kind of deputy. After returning from this stolen interlude, Stanton began to leave the war office each evening to go home for dinner and rest. Eddie held the fort, and he was under orders to send a courier and a carriage to the Stanton home at once if an emergency arose.

Impeachment concerns followed Stanton home. One evening, Butler and Boutwell, needing something with which to frighten doubtful senators, asked for a list of civil and military officers whom Johnson might remove if the impeachment failed. Wearily, Stanton worked through the entire night assembling the list and the next morning put War Department clerks to copying it for the use of the impeachment managers.

Unable by nature to remain a bystander, Stanton wrote anti-Johnson editorials for the powerful New York *Tribune*. John Russell Young, of that newspaper, in his frequent visits with Stanton played the great guessing game that had captured the imagination of the nation—how would the senators vote? Every sort of rumor, any chance remark, shifted the tallying. As by late April the indications grew that the

[8] Howe, *Portrait of an Independent*, 81–2, on Storey; Grant to Bingham, April 1, 1868, HQA, Letters Received, Box 107, RG 108, NA, on records; Emily Edson Briggs, *The Olivia Letters* (New York, 1906), 50, on Mrs. Hutchison.

President would escape conviction by the barest margin because of the "defection" of one or two senators, Stanton grew despondent and angry by turns. Colonel Moore heard Johnson's spy report on April 23 that "Stanton was furious . . . he cursed and swore terrifically, declaring that such men as Fessenden, Grimes, Trumbull, and Sherman had gone back on him."

Through Young he planted an article in the *Tribune* predicting ferocious penalties against any Republican senator "that proves recreant to his country in this hour of its agony," and he applauded Young's essays repeating the theme. To Stanton, the only just verdict the Senate could reach was a conviction of Andrew Johnson. He was no longer the impersonal lawyer. Like Johnson, Stanton was engaged in a crusade.[9]

As the weeks dragged by, every public event was given a significance in terms of the impeachment. A Republican victory in a New Hampshire election early in March inspired Sickles, who, at Stanton's suggestion and with Grant's approval, stumped there for radical candidates, to wire Stanton: "New Hampshire sustains you by a splendid majority."

Stanton had placed a particular importance on the outcome of that state election. For the Supreme Court had before it McCardle's petition alleging that the reconstruction laws were unconstitutional. Along with Colfax, Grant, and others, Stanton believed that if the New Hampshire balloting had favored the Democrats, then the ever untrustworthy Court would have immediately given a verdict in favor of McCardle. The President would then have had Welles send marines to enforce the decision and to oust Stanton from his office at the same time.

Despite their achievement in New Hampshire, Republican strategists still feared that the President was readying a coup through the Court. There were reports that Justices Nelson, Clifford, and Davis were surreptitious visitors at the White House. What if, while the impeachment trial was in progress, the Court did declare that the reconstruction laws were invalid? Then pro-Johnson sentiment in the Senate would rise spectacularly.[1]

Congress side-stepped the dangerous McCardle issue. Late in March

---

[9] Butler to Stanton, April 17, and Young to Stanton, May 6, 1868, Stanton MSS; April 23, 1868, Moore notebook, Johnson Papers, LC; DeWitt, *Impeachment*, 394–5; Bowers, *op. cit.*, 191; E. L. Stanton to Butler, March 11, 1868, Butler Papers, LC.
[1] Sickles to Stanton, March 10, 1868, Stanton MSS; Colfax to John Russell Young, March 11, 1868, Young Papers, LC.

it passed over Johnson's veto a measure retroactively denying to the Court jurisdiction in the kind of appeal that McCardle had lodged. But the possibility still remained that the jurists would not acquiesce in this extraordinary diminution of their power.

The Court also had before it a case that had emerged from Georgia against Generals Meade and Ruger, in which the jurists were petitioned to enjoin those officers from enforcing the assertedly unconstitutional reconstruction laws in that state. But on March 23 Stanton wrote happily to Meade that the jurists had specified "personal service of notice on the defendants" in Washington. This meant that the judges were seeking a way out so as to avoid a direct clash with Congress. Stanton, as anxious as the members of the Court to stabilize the dangerous situation, suggested to Meade: "If you & General Ruger . . . have any business in Florida or elsewhere the notice can not be served personally, & I think the Court will be glad of it, so as to let the matter stand over until December. Can you not take an inspection [tour] immediately . . . & let your destination be known only to yourself?"

Next day he wired Meade even better news. The Court, thoroughly cowed by the ferocity of Republican reaction to the Milligan, test oath, and McCardle cases, had refused to entertain the petition for the injunction. Congress's new law limiting the jurisdiction of the tribunal would be obeyed. The appellant's counsel—Jeremiah Black, Montgomery Blair, and David Dudley Field—were left gasping in outraged helplessness. In effect, Stanton exulted, the Court was out of the reconstruction picture. Congress had only the President left to fight. Impeachment could proceed with far less threat of violence.[2]

Mountains of testimony accumulated as a parade of witnesses offered their observations to the Senate. There were few surprises, and Grant, whose appearance as a witness was anticipated as the spearhead of a spectacular onslaught against Johnson, gave careful, restrained accounts of the facts he knew and refused to deal with inferences. Thus the total testimony amounted to a recital of the bare facts of Stanton's suspension as seen from opposite viewpoints. Johnson's trial became an interminable lawyers' duel after April 20, when the taking of testimony ended.

[2] Stanbery to Grant, Feb. 12, 1868, HQA, Letters Received, Box 107; Grant to Stanbery, Feb. 13, 1868, CG Letterbook, 1866–8, p. 335, RG 108; AGO, RP 670220, RG 94, NA; Stanton to Meade, March 23, 24, 1868, Stanton MSS; Morse, *Welles Diary*, III, 323–4.

Three days later, at the suggestion of William Evarts, one of his counsel, Johnson tried to swerve the Republicans away from carrying the trial through to a verdict. He wrote out a nomination of General Schofield as Stanton's successor, at the same time withdrawing the nomination of Ewing, which was still before the Senate. Johnson told Moore that "the idea was to relieve some of the Senators of the opposition" of the necessity of voting against him in order to uphold Stanton, and to show them that he would not put an extremist in the war office if acquitted. Moore protested that Schofield was at that moment a house guest of Grant's. The President shrugged this off, insisting that Schofield was trustworthy and that if he was Grant's friend, so much the better. But the radical Republican leaders in the Senate put Schofield's nomination aside to await the outcome of the trial.[3]

As April neared its end and the termination of the trial drew closer, speculation on the senators' votes reached new peaks of intensity. Stanton continued to be pessimistic over the probable outcome of the trial. Apparently very few persons, even among the Secretary's friends, spared a thought for the query Lieber addressed to Sumner: What would be the effects on Stanton of a not-guilty vote combined with the President's "ferretlike vindictiveness"?

Grant was taking care of his future by chancing a run for the presidency. If acquitted by the Senate, Johnson merely remained in the White House. But whatever the decision at the impeachment, Stanton's fate and future were undecided.

Waiting quietly at the war office, he kept his uncertainties and fears to himself and remained out of the public eye as much as possible, ignoring the fact that he was again being considered as a possible competitor against Grant for the Republican presidential nomination. "What a president he would make," Lieber mused. "And then the Southerners hate him so delightfully. It makes one's mouth water."

But Lieber concluded that though Stanton, in his opinion, was "by far the fittest" potential candidate, Grant was the one who would win both the nomination and the election. In any case, Stanton made it plain that he was not interested in any elective office. The beleaguered

---

[3] There is evidence that Evarts, changing his mind on the usefulness of the Schofield plan, did not press very hard to have the nomination acted on; see April 23, 1868, Moore notebook, Johnson Papers, LC; Gorham, *Stanton*, II, 450–3; Chester L. Barrows, *William M. Evarts* (Chapel Hill, 1941), 150–1. Chauncey M. Depew, in New York *Herald*, Oct. 24, 1885, claimed that Grant told him that he had proof of the President's plan to revolutionize the government but withheld it for fear of initiating violence.

Secretary just had no self-serving ambition, Lieber concluded, even though "he could easily turn his semi-dismissal into a very proper lever to be lifted into the place where now the incorrigible trickster sits."

Lieber's estimate of Stanton's determination to leave political life permanently is convincingly sustained by Stanton's own statements and the opinions of other informed persons.[4] Nonetheless, Johnson and his supporters and other presidential aspirants, such as Chase, continued to depict Stanton as a man of overweening ambition for office as well as power.

But while men fought the phantom of Stanton's supposed availability, he was squelching a move originating in Ohio to enter him as a vice-presidential nominee. Further, when Ben Wade, who as President of the Senate would step into the White House if Johnson was convicted, confidently announced a cabinet slate in which Stanton was kept on as War Secretary, Stanton stated for publication that he was out of the running for any post. "Enough of my life has been devoted to public duties," he said. "No consideration can induce me to . . . continue in the War Department longer than may be required for the appointment and confirmation of my successor."

Meanwhile his friend Pierrepont was touting him for a diplomatic appointment under Wade, but Stanton pushed away this suggestion too. He had already prepared his letter of resignation from the war office, and he was determined to submit it once the Senate's verdict was in, no matter how it went, thereafter to be free of all public office. This was known at the White House, for on April 25 one of the President's spies reported to Moore that "Mr. Stanton had written to his old home at Steubenville, Ohio, asking that preparations be made for the return of himself and his family there in two weeks' time."

Yet historians DeWitt and Bowers assert that up to the last minutes of the trial Stanton was determined to stay in office and in politics and so exerted efforts to sway doubtful senators against Johnson. They accept as their total evidence a reminiscence of Sickles that on May 15, at Stanton's behest, he camped all night in Senator Ross's apartment to overawe that wavering man to a stern course when the vote came due the next day. But Stanton intended to return to private life whatever the outcome of the impeachment. He was despondently

[4] Lieber to M. R. Thayer, Aug. 19, March 2, and to Sumner, May 4, 1868, HL; Thomas Sergeant Perry (ed.), *Life and Letters of Francis Lieber* (Boston, 1882), 381; Boutwell, *op. cit.*, II, 89–90; Forney, *op. cit.*, 189.

sure that Johnson would escape conviction. Considering Stanton's nature, it is doubtful whether he would continue to seek a conviction after deciding that it was impossible to obtain one. In addition, Sickles's recollection dates from years after the event. Evidence from sources much closer in time fails to sustain the general's memory.[5]

"The hour of judgment is nigh at hand," Stanton wrote Young on May 10, when "the great criminal" should be condemned if justice was to be done. But, he admitted sadly, "I do not hear that Fessenden & Trumbull have shown any improvement." Stanton deeply regretted the fact that the impeachment crisis was impairing his close associations with several of his friends among the senators who believed that Johnson, though derelict in his policies, was not guilty of the charges facing him. As each day passed, Stanton's hopes lessened that his erring friends would realize that they were on the wrong path. And he predicted that their defection might swing the scales.

On May 16, two hours before the senators were to cast their fateful ballots, Garfield wrote that "it hangs in almost an even balance. There is an intensity of anxiety here, greater than I ever saw during the war." The tension pervaded the White House, where McCulloch, Welles, and General Thomas joined the President and Colonel Moore in a quiet group. Their irrelevant conversation failed to disguise the nervous expectancy each man felt. Seward was so sure of a conviction that, the week before, he had submitted his resignation, to take effect when the Senate voted the President guilty.

Near by, at the War Department, Stanton was alone, at his own request. He opened the windows of his office to enjoy the warm breeze, and like the nation, he waited.

At noon the senators convened to vote. The hours dragged slowly by until Republican strategists forced the balloting first on the eleventh article of accusations, designed as a catchall to entice any hesitant senator's vote of guilty. Thirty-five voted to convict; thirty-six votes were needed to carry this verdict.

Messengers rushed the news to the White House. Later that afternoon the President learned that the impeachment managers had not given

[5] See Charles A. Jellison, "Ross's Impeachment Vote: Need for Reappraisal," *Southwestern Social Science Quarterly*, XLI, 150–5; J. F. Oliver to Stanton, April 8, Pierrepont to same, April 15, Deming Duer to same, May 16, and resignation draft, May 11, 1868, Stanton MSS; Schuckers to John Russell Young, May 11, and Stanton to same, May 13, 1868, Young Papers, LC; April 25, 1868, Moore notebook, Johnson Papers, LC; Flower, *Stanton*, 341; DeWitt, *Impeachment*, 544; Bowers, *op. cit.*, 195.

up, but had secured a ten-day adjournment, after which voting on the other charges would commence, and his jubilation lessened.

Stanton received the news from the army telegraph. A hot flush mottled his cheeks. For a moment he felt almost feverish with disappointment. Although he had expected the verdict, he had still hoped that the senators would condemn the President. Then, refusing to give any comment to the crowding journalists who sought a statement from him, Stanton ordered his office door locked and took from the files his prepared letter of resignation. But he did not send it on to the White House.[6]

After the first jolting shock lessened, Stanton, like most Republicans, hoped that the President might still be found guilty when the trial resumed ten days hence. He decided to wait it out that long. It seemed a good omen that midway through that waiting period, on May 21, the Republican convention at Chicago named Grant as its presidential candidate.

As soon as this information came in on the wire, Stanton ran to Grant's office to tell him the news and, as Badeau described it, was "panting for breath lest some one else should precede him." Stanton's joy was sincere. He was now sure that Grant and he were as one on reconstruction, and he felt that Grant could defeat any Democrat. His pleasure increased when his friend Colfax secured the vice-presidential nomination. Commenting to Sherman, Grant reflected the reasons for Stanton's satisfaction over the choice of the general as Republican standard-bearer. It had prevented the Democrats from choosing Johnson, Grant asserted, or other "mere trading politicians, the elevation of whom, no matter which party won, would lose to us, largely, the results of the costly war which we have gone through. Now the Democrats will be forced to adopt a good platform and put upon it a reliable man who, if elected, will disappoint the Copperhead element of their party. This will be a great point gained if nothing more is accomplished."

However Grant may have been rationalizing personal ambitions, his patriotic motive for seeking the presidency was genuine. Johnson had secretly wanted the Democratic party nomination, but with Grant running on the opposition ticket this was impossible. Grant was sure that even if Johnson again escaped conviction when the senators voted on May 26, the people would counterbalance this verdict when they bal-

[6] Young, *Men and Memories*, I, 152; Benjamin P. Thomas's notes on Stanton's memo of war office scene, dated May 16, 1868; May 15, 16, 1868, Moore notebook, Johnson Papers, LC; Garfield to Prof. C. L. Loos, May 16, 1868, Garfield Papers, LC.

loted in November.[7] Stanton could share the sense of substantive victory whatever the final verdict of the impeachment.

May 26 came, and early in the afternoon the Senate, now voting on the second and third articles of the impeachment list, again failed by one vote to convict, and adjourned the trial proceedings. The game was over; the tension finally ended. Although the Senate vote did not require that Stanton give up the war office, most commentators assumed that he would.

Shortly before three o'clock, Stanton had his son deliver a note to Townsend ordering him to take charge of the Department "subject to the disposal and directions of the President." "Eddie" Stanton told the general that the Secretary had also entrusted him with his letter of resignation, which he was personally going to deliver to the White House along with a notification of Townsend's temporary assumption of responsibility. But soon after young Stanton left for the executive mansion, he returned to Townsend's office. A messenger from his father had intercepted him, with instructions to have Townsend deliver both messages to the President. The elder Stanton wanted no more outbreaks of temper from Johnson, and one might be provoked if a member of the family appeared in his presence.

Having heard the news of the Senate's favorable verdict, Johnson was calm and happy when Townsend arrived. The general produced the note that he had brought, sealed, from Stanton. As Johnson read it his features took on "an expression of marked displeasure," Townsend recalled, for in surrendering the war office Stanton bitingly alluded to the Senate's resolution of the past February 21, which had forbade the President to remove or replace him. Now that the Senate had failed to support its earlier resolution by the needed two-thirds vote in the impeachment trial, Stanton therefore "relinquished" the War Department's records in care of Townsend.

Observing Johnson's angry reaction to Stanton's impudent note, Townsend hastened to assure the President that he had not known the contents of the message he had delivered. Then the general handed over the first note Stanton's son had given him, which placed Townsend in charge at the war office. After reading it, Johnson at once became genial and pleasant, asking Townsend only inconsequential questions. The general, rising to leave, asked: "Have you any orders

[7] Badeau, *Grant*, 144; Buckingham to Stanton, May 21, 1868, Stanton MSS; Grant to Sherman, June 21, 1868, W. T. Sherman Papers, LC; July 6, 9, 1868, Moore notebook, Johnson Papers, LC.

to give me, sir?" Johnson answered: "None." Townsend concluded that Johnson did not want Lorenzo Thomas to take over the war office despite his retention of the interim title, and departed with the key to the Secretary's door.

By specifying in the second note to the President that Townsend should maintain temporary charge at the War Department, Stanton had done a large service in keeping the unstable situation from exploding anew. Had the President sent Thomas to take over, the bitter Republicans in Congress might have felt themselves forced to take action once more. Stanton's motive could only have been to keep alive a remnant of stability. Johnson, however, though telling Townsend that there was a reciprocity of trust between them and that he was confidently in control of the situation, actually mistrusted him, and declined to give Townsend any orders, "seeming to think," Moore guessed, "that a trap was laid into which he might be inveigled."

There was no trap. But Johnson's suspicious reticence made possible a situation which almost provoked another crisis.

After leaving the White House, Townsend stopped at Stanton's home to reassure himself that the former Secretary was still determined to give up the contest, for there were rumors that he intended to hang on. Stanton, haggard, ill, and appearing far older than his years, told the circumspect officer that he could no longer sacrifice himself or his family's interests by "contending longer for the possession of the [war] office." [8]

Assuming that with Stanton's resignation he had the President's automatic permission to take over, Thomas the next morning asked Townsend for the keys to the Secretary's room. Townsend told him, however, that Johnson, at the meeting of the day before, "had tacitly confirmed" Stanton's order to Townsend to hold the keys subject only to a presidential order. Thomas proposed that he would write out the order himself as War Secretary ad interim, but Townsend insisted that it come directly from the President. Rebuffed, poor Thomas went on to the White House to learn that Johnson "would not touch the thing."

It was an amusing situation. As one of General Sherman's friends

---

[8] Townsend, *Anecdotes*, 132–3; May 23, 26, 1868, Moore notebook, Johnson Papers, LC; Browning, *Diary*, II, 199. Recent scholarship on the causes of the impeachment's failure and on the fate of the Republicans who voted not to convict the President is in Hans L. Trefousse, "Ben Wade and the Failure of the Impeachment of Johnson," *Bulletin* of the Historical and Philosophical Society of Ohio, XVIII, 241–52, and Ralph J. Roske, "The Seven Martyrs?" *AHR*, LXIV, 323–30.

set the tone of reaction: "Townsend held the Keys, & no one dared to approach it—not even the 'ad interim'!" But the President was not amused. Once again he did not know whom to appoint to this touchy office. Obviously Thomas was a useless liability, and without forewarning that hapless officer, Johnson sought to supersede him.

On May 27 he named Seward to hold the war portfolio on an interim basis, in addition to his diplomatic chores, "according to law." After writing out this commission, Seward joked to the President: "Now, if they choose, they can find out to what law we refer." Then caution moved Seward to check first with Senator Conkling "and see what he will have to say about it. No mischief can go on without him." Conkling warned Seward not to play games with Congress. Tempers were high and Seward was no more acceptable for the war office than Thomas.[9]

If it had slipped through, the "interim" appointment of Seward undoubtedly would have lasted the remaining nine months of Johnson's term. At the least the President would have won a symbolic victory in replacing Stanton with a man much closer to the White House's views on the South. He would also have chanced new clashes with Grant, now wearing the added prestige of being a presidential nominee, on reconstruction matters. Almost certainly Republican congressmen would have been exacerbated once again, for Seward was anathema to a large portion of that party's membership. The Seward plan was thoughtlessly dangerous. It was to his credit that he, not Johnson, sought out a realization of the potentialities and withdrew his name.

Some appointment, however, had to be made, for in the absence of a Secretary the War Department machinery was grinding to a halt. Since Stanton's unceremonious departure from the office, Townsend, refusing to do anything that might be misconstrued as an assumption of top-level duties, had even ordered incoming mail addressed to the Secretary to remain unopened. The President, informed of this by Townsend, admitted that "there might be some business that ought to be transacted," commended him for refusing to turn over the keys to "Ad Interim" Thomas, and asked him to retain charge of the Department for the present. Johnson was still expecting the Seward scheme to succeed. But it fell through even while he was speaking so confidently to Townsend.

[9] Townsend, *Anecdotes*, 134; S. Van Vleit to W. T. Sherman, May 29, 1868, Sherman Papers, LC; May 27, 29, 1868, Moore notebook, and Seward's commission and memoranda, Johnson Papers, LC.

For once, however, the three major actors in this complex drama worked toward the same end. The President dropped the dangerous idea of pushing Seward and decided to accept Schofield; his nomination had been in suspense before the Senate since April 23. Grant convinced doubtful legislators that he could control Schofield, and from the seclusion of his home Stanton let it be known that he was in favor of that officer "to succeed" to his place.

On May 30, after a daylong session of heated, partisan debate, the Senate confirmed Schofield as War Secretary in a curious manner. The resolution stated that Stanton had not been legally removed from his office, "but inasmuch as . . . Stanton has relinquished his place as Secretary of War," the Senate accepted Schofield. The word "relinquished"—a carefully chosen, lawyerlike phrase—had angered the President when Stanton used it in his letter resigning the war portfolio. It now provided the Senate with a way to get off the hook, for Congress had impeached and almost convicted Johnson for violating a law designed to prevent the President from removing Stanton, and now, by approving Schofield, the Senate was acquiescing in Johnson's choice of his successor.[1]

Thus the President and Welles felt that even in retreat Stanton had scored a point on them. "He goes out without respect," Welles believed, "except on the part of ignorant and knavish partisans." But a few days later the Senate passed a resolution, in which the House subsequently concurred by a vote of 102 to 25, praising Stanton's wartime services and postwar efforts to enforce the laws "provided by Congress for the restoration of a real and permanent peace."

Despite these gripings the President was happy to have won the war office fortress. On June 1 he and Schofield walked there together from the White House. Townsend gave the new Secretary the coveted key to the rooms Stanton had labored in for six years. As Johnson entered the Secretary's office, he laughed aloud, and turning to Townsend, remarked: "It is some time since I was in this room before!"

It was a Pyrrhic victory. Johnson won only a shell, a powerless symbol. For the brief months remaining to him in the White House he would not interfere again in army policies or with army personnel. Grant would remain effectively in charge of the execution of the reconstruction laws, and he ran the Army almost as if the White House did not exist. President and commanding general were now admittedly

---

[1] Morse, *Welles Diary*, III, 371; May 27, 29, 1868, Moore notebook, Johnson Papers, LC; Townsend, *Anecdotes*, 135; Flower, *Stanton*, 344, has the resolution.

personal enemies; Grant despised everyone in the cabinet, kept his official communications with them to an absolute minimum, and cut himself off from all social intercourse with the White House and the cabinet, except for Seward. Schofield performed in the tradition of prewar Secretaries: as a glorified clerk transmitting papers from army headquarters to the White House and back again. By the end of 1868, the centrifugal tendencies inherent in the Army's administrative structure became evident when the bureau heads published their annual reports without even referring them to the Secretary of War's office.[2]

This inefficient equilibrium between White House, Congress, and war office did maintain peace until Grant took over the presidency. It was precisely such a caretaker stability that he and Stanton had sought since mid-1866 and that Johnson had refused to accept until impeachment frightened him off from his quest for domination. Considering the corrosive effects of the war years, it is doubtful whether the country could have survived much more strain had not some compromise, however acrimonious, been achieved. Impeachment not only climaxed and decided the dangerous debate concerning reconstruction policy. It also subdued the President, so that stability of a sort became possible. In losing his office, Stanton had helped the nation win the larger game.

Johnson, mistaking the Senate's narrow verdict as being heavily in his favor, never realized that it signified a defeat, however temporary, for his cherished principles of white supremacy and state autonomy regarding the suffrage. He always insisted that he had been the victim of a conspiracy by which Stanton and Grant, in company with the Republican congressmen, had upset the unchangeable constitutional fabric woven by the Founding Fathers. The President could not conceive that his rigid constitutionalism had set up such strains in the fabric of the dynamic federal system that the intrusion of Congress had been necessary to prevent a rupture.[3]

There had been no conspiracy. But Johnson's insistence on the existence of a plot has helped to set the character of Stanton in history.

"Stanton's reputation rests a good deal on his quarrel with President Johnson, and in this his character is treated unfairly," Grant confided years later to his friend Young. "Stanton's relations with John-

---

[2] May 29, Aug. 5, 7, 1868, Moore notebook, Johnson Papers, LC; Morse, *Welles Diary*, III, 370, 377; Townsend, *Anecdotes*, 135–6; Gorham, *Stanton*, II, 456–7; Ben. Perley Poore to E. W. Clapp, Nov. 17, 1868, Clapp Papers, LC, on annual reports.
[3] McKitrick, *op. cit.*, 506–9, suggests that the impeachment was a psychological release for the nation. It would seem more logical to judge the trial as an institutional readjustment between the contending branches of the government.

son were the natural result of Johnson's desire to change the politics of his administration and Stanton's belief that such a change would be disastrous to the Union. . . . Of course a man of Stanton's temper, so believing, would be in a condition of passionate anger. He believed that Johnson was Jeff Davis in another form and he used his position in the Cabinet like a picket holding his position in the line." The general did not see fit to expose the fact that he had secretly used his position as head of the Army for the same purpose and because of similar convictions.

Grant's analysis is convincing. It seems clear that from his nightmare memory of the assassination night, Stanton drew the conclusion that the South as a region was irrevocably tarred by the deed. What followed, however, was not an unbalanced search for vengeance, but rather a dedicated insistence that a reconstruction bring forth the results for which Lincoln and thousands of blue-clad martyrs had died. Stanton could never forget "the starvation of 100,000 men at Andersonville under the orders of Jeff Davis," said General Meigs, who knew the Secretary well.

"We were all under deep feeling at the time," Grant recalled, and remarked that Stanton "required a man like Lincoln to manage him." [4]

Stanton did have a man able to manage him. His name was Ulysses Grant.

[4] Young, *Around the World*, II, 358–9; Weigley, *Meigs*, 325.

CHAPTER XXX

CAMPAIGNING FOR GRANT

$\mathbb{S}$TANTON CONDEMNED!" thundered Johnson's spokesman, the Washington *Intelligencer*, setting the theme that the impeachment results not only vindicated the President, even if only by one vote, but proved all his opponents guilty. The fact is, however, that Stanton was far from being as isolated and unpopular as administration spokesmen asserted.

It was only to be expected that Republicans publicly lauded him. More significant, and to Stanton far more warmly sustaining, were the private estimates of his government service that came to him from individuals whose opinions he treasured. Some of the Republican senators who had voted to acquit Johnson now sought to regain their former friendship with him. But Stanton was too hurt at first to forgive, although Fessenden, who had hated most "the necessity of grieving Mr. Stanton" by his vote in favor of Johnson, made what amends he could by going along with Grimes, Trumbull, and Van Winkle on the congressional resolution of thanks to the former War Secretary.[1]

Stanton had more to worry over than his own hurt feelings. His secretary described him as "a wreck, not so much from the result of his ceaseless energy in the . . . war, as from his ceaseless watching of the doings at the White House under President Johnson." Despite this, Stanton was determined to resume private law practice as soon as possible. First, however, he planned to rest and then visit his mother and sister in Ohio before commencing his new career.

Packed and ready to start westward, Stanton abandoned the trip at the last minute, for the children came down with the measles and he

---

[1] *Intelligencer*, May 27, June 30, 1868; William Salter, *The Life of James W. Grimes* (New York, 1876), 361; Fessenden, *op. cit.*, II, 221.

would not leave Ellen, herself unwell, to bear the total weight of their care. Meanwhile he tutored young Eddie in the law. Soon, the father hoped, the two Stanton men would bring the family out of its financial difficulties.

It would have to be soon. Stanton was almost without funds, and when the Riggs National Bank, whose president was a warm Johnson supporter, refused him a small loan though the Stanton family had banked there for a decade, his anger was understandable. Securing $500 from another bank, Stanton had only this and what remained of his salary to see him through until money came in from law work. It was not enough.

Ellen began to dispose of her government bonds, their only wartime investment. They discharged their driver, whose salary had come from the family purse all through Stanton's years in office though cabinet members usually placed such retainers on the government payroll.

Still he would not consider politics. Pennsylvania Republicans and his friend Young, of the *Tribune,* offered to back him if he would seek a United States Senate seat from the Keystone State. It would have been a sweet morsel of revenge for Stanton to gain this expression of public support had it been forthcoming, but that was not what he wanted. "I am not a candidate . . . under any circumstances," he wrote Young. "No public or official station presents any temptation— I covet only rest, & the restoration of health to pursue my profession." [2]

Politics in this presidential year would not leave the Stanton family alone, however. His name kept appearing in the public press. When the Democratic nominating convention picked Seymour and Montgomery Blair to head its ticket, Stanton was delighted to see that Johnson had been passed over, and relished the rumors of the President's fury at the slight. Still, Stanton feared that if the Democrats won the White House and Congress, then "the Rebels need no longer mourn about the 'lost cause.' "

The only direct political action Stanton felt inspired to take that summer involved a hang-over from his war office years. Early in July, Republican national committeeman and former Assistant Treasury Secretary William E. Chandler wrote to him telling of his fear that, with the failure of impeachment, many Southerners would claim damages for wartime property losses and again use the courts to harass

[2] Johnson, "Reminiscences of Hon. Edwin M. Stanton," *loc. cit.,* 87; Ellen to Bessie Stanton, Sept. 13, 1868, owned by Mrs. Van Swearingen; Flower, *Stanton,* 344, 350; Stanton to Young, June 24, 1868, Stanton MSS.

the execution of the reconstruction acts. Stanton had always had intense feelings on this matter, and the Smithson damage suit was still hanging over his head. Chandler asserted to Stanton that "a quiet word from you to Edmunds, Conkling, Stewart, & any others will help very much & there is no knowing how soon after the Chief Justice's Magnificent Apostasy . . . there may be need of it." Of course Stanton gave his full support, and improved legislation went into effect within a year.

Then, instead of father and son beginning law practice together as planned, Stanton permitted Eddie to tour with Congressman Bingham, who had so often sustained the War Secretary, to help win Ohio for Republican candidates. All the younger children except little Bessie went off to Ohio to visit their grandmother there, in anticipation that their parents would soon join them. Filling in the empty midsummer days working on the neglected lawns and garden, Stanton found the big house very lonely, especially at the dinner hour. In the eternal manner of parents, Ellen passed on her husband's advice to the children, especially to read with care, and she demanded two letters a week from the children, who never managed to obey this injunction.[3]

The political magnet soon reached out more strongly to attract Stanton to action, although he continued to be resentful because he had not received a word directly from Grant since the impeachment ended. In the first days of August, Stanton felt impelled to overcome his irritation and to become personally involved in furthering the Republican campaign. The wartime copperhead Vallandigham was announced as the Democratic candidate for a Senate seat from Ohio. His Republican opponent, Robert Schenck, asked Stanton to support him and the Republican ticket. Stanton could not resist a chance to strike again at men whom he still considered to be the nation's foes. He sent Schenck a copy of an 1863 provost marshal's report on the Democrat and promised that he would stump for Schenck and others in Ohio late in September.

When the news got out, few persons thought that Stanton would add much weight to the Republican candidates, though the mere announcement helped to quiet rumors of discord in the Republican ranks which Democrats were spreading. Stanton planned to follow an itinerary that would include Ohio's major cities, if his health permitted, and Sickles promised to join forces with him in Cleveland. He arranged with

[3] Ellen to "My dear little Daughters," Sept. 13, 1868, owned by Mrs. Van Swearingen; Pierrepont to Stanton, June 24, July 12, and Chandler to same, July 8, 1868, Stanton MSS; Flower, *Stanton*, 394.

Young for a reliable reporter to accompany him, "as there will be great disposition to pervert . . . what I may say. I have not prepared any speech, & shall talk to the occasion & audience as may appear proper at the time." Readying excitedly for the trip, Stanton wrote to the children at Gambier to expect him soon, and to check on the whereabouts of young Eddie, who, still campaigning with Bingham, was remiss about writing to his parents.[4]

Eddie suddenly showed up in Washington, excited over his experiences as a stump speaker and by his admission to practice before the Supreme Court. Ironically, this brilliant young man's first case was a claim against the War Department for the wartime services of an Ohio River bargemaster. Knowing that his father would not help him prepare his argument, the new lawyer worked it out alone, and after he submitted it to Secretary of War Schofield, the Stanton men set out for Pittsburgh.

In the familiar surroundings of the Golden Triangle, Stanton offered a short testimonial on behalf of local Republicans. Immediately, Democratic spokesmen began to vilify him. Reminiscences of Union veterans were now popular, especially those which described the horrors of imprisonment in the Confederacy, and some resurrected the old assertion that Stanton was responsible for halting the prisoner exchanges. Again the charges were rung on his "atrocious inhumanity." Ignoring these barbs, Stanton continued on to Steubenville.

He arrived at his old home on September 23, and as soon as a furious rain lessened, visited the grave of his first wife, Mary, where he sat silently for a long hour on the sodden earth. He renewed acquaintance with old friends and with places he had known and loved as a youth; walked again along the swollen Ohio's shore, and then climbed to the high ledge, already known as "Stanton's Rock," where he had often, years before, dreamed of the future he wanted. Now he was ailing in body if not old in years, almost completely without money, spending time and energy politicking though no rewards would come from it, when self-interest required him to be starting a new life as a private lawyer. He decided that he would make only this one Steubenville speech and then go home, for suddenly he was too tired to do more.

The day for his address dawned bright and lovely, and Steubenville became so crowded with persons seeking admission to the auditorium

[4] Schenck to Stanton, Aug. 27, 1868, Stanton MSS; W. H. Hudson to Sickles, Sept. 16, 1868, Sickles Papers, LC; Stanton to Young, Sept. 19, 1868, Young Papers, LC; Stanton to Ellie Stanton, Sept. 19, 1868, owned by Mrs. Van Swearingen.

where Stanton was to speak that the seats were removed to increase its capacity. As the autumn twilight deepened into night, Stanton made his way to the platform, was introduced, rose to speak, then sat again, too weary to remain on his feet.[5] The chairman suggested that he continue while seated, and Stanton, though sometimes coughing painfully, spoke out clearly and effectively. Except when moved to excitement he seemed old and ill. But when he came to a point he wished to stress, his voice boomed out, so that it roared over the hall, and he briefly took on the characteristics of youthful vigor.

It was a vote-as-you-shot speech, linking Grant with Lincoln and Democrats with disloyalty. A victory for Seymour, Stanton insisted, must overturn everything that had been gained from seven awful years of war and reconstruction, and let the country fall prey to wild, sinister schemes of debt repudiation and paper-money panaceas such as Democratic Senator Pendleton proposed. He never mentioned his own record, but when he spoke of Grant's martial accomplishments, of Lincoln's shrewd, tender, guiding hand, of Buchanan's lame-duck panic and Sheridan's Valley campaign, Stanton struck fire again and again. Dana was sure that he was appealing from the heart as well as asking for votes, and he and other editors noted that Stanton was the first Republican campaigner willing to take on the paper-money issue.

Satisfied with the reception his speech received, and with the "closely packed attentive audience," Stanton wrote Ellen that "my political labors are over. Scores of invitations and urgent entreaties still come every day." But he intended only to go to Gambier to see his mother and Pamphila, then to return to Washington. "I . . . will make no more speeches." [6]

Unless Stanton's letter to Ellen, showing his determination to give up all further activity in favor of Grant and to begin private law work, is taken into account, the Steubenville speech can be misconstrued as the first of a series of baited hooks cast into the turbulent pool of Ohio politics so that Grant might notice them and reward the angler with a

---

[5] E. L. Stanton to Schofield, Sept. 26, 1868, WD, Letters Received, XCIII, S358, RG 107, NA; Stanton to Ellen, Sept. 27, 1868, owned by Edward S. Corwin; A. D. Sharon in Washington *Evening Star*, March 16, 1900; Dr. Alexander M. Reid ms reminiscence, owned by Alexandra Sanford; Shotwell, *op. cit.*, 100; Doyle, *op. cit.*, 26.

[6] Speech in Doyle, *op. cit.*, 304–7; other data in Flower, *Stanton*, 396; *Nation* (Oct. 1, 1868), 262; Stanton to Ellen, Sept. 27, 1868, owned by Edward S. Corwin. In 1872, Sumner asserted that on his deathbed Stanton told him that out of distrust for Grant he had never supported the general's candidacy. Either Sumner was in error or Stanton's mind was playing him false; probably the former, for Stanton was always proud of this Steubenville speech. See Pierce, *Sumner*, IV, 526; Everett Chamberlain, *The Struggle of '72* (Chicago, 1872), 555–6.

government post after the election. This was the inference drawn by some commentators. But Stanton, wanting no government favors, intended to make no more speeches, and General Sherman's hope that Grant "will shake himself free from the evil counsellors—Stanton, Wade & Co who led him astray"—was misdirected. Grant, far from being under Stanton's counsel, had totally ignored him since May.

Nevertheless, between September 27, when Stanton wrote Ellen of his intention to curtail further political activity, and October 1, Stanton changed his mind and embarked on a rigorous speaking tour on Grant's behalf. This is even more remarkable considering that Stanton was suffering from an extraordinarily severe asthmatic paroxysm induced by his fatigue and by the effects of crossing the mountains. Yet he accepted further campaigning commitments in response to pleas for aid in Michigan and for assistance to other Republicans in Ohio. Though Stanton rejected the Michigan assignment as being beyond his strength, taking on more work in Ohio was an adequate testimony to his sense of duty.

Two reasons serve to explain his change in plans. The first was his fear that the Democrats were winning; he felt that a Democratic victory would be a condemnation of all he had done in the war office. He was immensely gratified by the plaudits his Steubenville speech evoked, and Republican managers, impressed by the impact Stanton's criticisms of Pendleton were making in Ohio, redoubled their efforts to keep him active.

The second reason was probably more decisive. He received a letter from Conkling describing a meeting between the senator and Grant in which the general "asked where you were." "He spoke of you," Conkling reported, "with strong feeling of friendship, and said he wanted to write to you also." Stanton also learned that Grant was refusing to aid the election campaign of any Republicans who had sustained Johnson in the impeachment controversy.[7]

Thus encouraged, Stanton spoke at Carlisle, reiterating his praises of Grant and stressing the evils of war-debt repudiation. Stopping at Gambier, Stanton shocked Pamphila by his appearance. Later that day he attended a meeting of his college literary society, the Philomathesian, and spoke tenderly and optimistically to the young men who

---

[7] On Sherman, T. Ewing, Sr., to Jr., Ewing Papers, LC; Stanton to Chandler, Oct. 1, 1868, Chandler Papers, LC; Conkling's letter, in Gorham, *Stanton*, II, 468, was probably inspired by Pierrepont; see Morse, *Welles Diary*, III, 452. On Grant and Republican candidates, D. A. Ward to Doolittle, July 14, 1872, Doolittle Papers, LC.

gathered to hear him of the grand future that was theirs. There was none of the imperious harshness about him which the youths had expected to observe. Instead, there was weariness and evident illness.

By October 9 he was in Cleveland, where the Republican newspaper, the *Leader*, reported that the city was jammed with spectators. After a flag-waving speech by Rutherford B. Hayes, Stanton castigated all Democrats for their party's "evils and cruelties." He brought the crowd to its feet when he asked the presiding officer to read Lincoln's Gettysburg speech, and then concluded by saying that Grant would harmonize the dead President's merciful plea with the need for intelligent sternness toward the South.

It was an immensely effective performance. Although Stanton had not played the role of campaigner before, he was proving himself a sensitive, powerful public speaker, and the *Leader* extolled the speech as the best one made in the whole Ohio campaign.[8]

Backtracking through Steubenville, Stanton spoke of the 1864 election night, when Lincoln had expressed gratification that "Stanton's town" had voted the Union ticket. On October 29 he was in Pittsburgh again, carefully scheduling his appearance there to follow speeches by Seymour. Then, weary almost to the point of collapse, he went on to Philadelphia, again trailing Seymour, where the Union League had reserved the Academy of Music. Later he wrote to Watson that the "Philadelphia reception would have been highly gratifying to a person who prizes such displays. The monster building . . . was jammed from roof to foundation by a throng of ladies and gentlemen and thousands were outside, waiting for an address to them."

Using a sketchy outline that he had prepared that morning, Stanton developed it on the platform into a defense of his administration of the War Department during the rebellion. It was the first time in the tour that he had troubled to answer the attacks on himself which the Democratic press, responding to the threatening popularity of his speeches, had been launching. Stanton cleverly linked Seymour with the draft riots and defeatism of the 1864 period.

While Stanton spoke, a doctor was seated next to him holding a watch, for the physician had forbidden him to speak at all unless he promised to end within twenty minutes. Publisher McClure visited Stanton at his hotel room immediately after the speech and "found him very feeble, suffering very greatly from asthmatic disorders, and in his public address he was often strangely forgetful of facts and

[8] Wolcott MS, 209; Bodine, *op. cit.*, 286; *Leader*, Oct. 9, Nov. 12, 1868; Flower, *Stanton*, 396, confuses the Steubenville speech with this one in Cleveland.

names, and had to be prompted by gentlemen on the stage." [9] Stanton had indeed reached the end of his strength, and in the first week of November returned to Washington, as he later admitted to Watson, "in a state of great exhaustion from the fatigue and excitement."

Stanton's exertions had sorely taxed his slim store of health, but they had also been therapeutic. He snapped out of the lethargy that had marked his behavior during the past summer and autumn, now took the keenest interest in following the campaign in the newspapers, and was exultant at the Republican victory, boasting to Watson of "an increased [Republican] vote of 5,000 . . . [in Philadelphia] and nearly 9,000 in Pittsburgh [which] shows that the throttling of Seymour did not prejudice our cause, and he was pretty thoroughly skinned from snout to tail." Welles, characteristically, felt that Stanton had not had influence enough to gain a vote for anyone. The fact remains, however, that Stanton was eagerly sought after as a speaker, and that he had discerned the immensely useful path of attack on Seymour—stressing Grant as a war hero rather than arguing the postwar cabinet controversies which the Democrats sought to exhume, and injecting the war-debt-repudiation and paper-money issues into the Republican campaign for the first time. Stanton felt that he had contributed something useful. This conviction of rectitude was always necessary for his happiness.

Ellen's health, as well as his own, concerned him. She was still suffering intensely from the dental disorder that had plagued her since the summer. Together they went to Baltimore and sought aid from highly recommended specialists there, but his condition worried his friends more than Ellen's annoying but obviously superficial ailment. Congressman Hooper visited the Stantons in mid-November and reported to Sumner that he "is not well, and does not go out. He seems to think Wendell Phillips is the only true man we have in New England."

Hooper realized that Stanton was disgruntled because Grant had not visited his home except for one time when he had been too ill to receive callers; he and the President-elect had held only a brief conversation the day after the elections, when they chanced to meet on the street. But politics could hold only a back place now in

[9] Doyle, *op. cit.*, 308; Steubenville *Daily Chronicle*, Oct. 30, 1868, and Wolcott MS, 215, on details of second speech there. The Philadelphia speech and the letter to Watson are in Flower, *Stanton*, 396–9. The outlines of the Pittsburgh and Philadelphia speeches, in Stanton's hand, in Stanton MSS, and see McClure, *Lincoln*, 172.

Stanton's thoughts; his health, money problems, and the preparation of law cases took precedence. It was sure, Hooper reported on December 1, that "he has not improved in health since I saw him." [1]

Ignoring his unceasing illness, Stanton was preparing to plead a case which necessitated hard work and travel, assiduous research, and imaginative argumentation. It involved disputed land titles to more than two million dollars' worth of coal and timber lands in West Virginia. The records were confused and deficient owing to the ravages of war and the dislocations involved in the creation of the new state. Ironically, one of Stanton's clients was R. M. T. Hunter, of Virginia, a prominent officeholder in the Confederate government. Like any private lawyer, Stanton was apolitical where a case was concerned; his antipathy toward former rebels could not interfere with his profession.

Asserting to Watson that he was feeling "as strong and vigorous as at any time within two years," Stanton pleaded the case, with Eddie serving as companion and assistant, at the Wheeling federal court, and claimed that he "never made an argument with more ease and effect and success." But men who heard him at Wheeling had reactions different from his own. The judge on the case recorded that he had expected to see "an immense, burly, rough, and resistless man, full of health and power and ready for any emergency. Instead of my ideal, there came in, walking slowly and wearily, a feeble and exhausted invalid, whose death-like pallor shocked all beholders. His argument was delivered in low conversational style, but with wonderful clearness, directness, and completeness." Some men there thought he would die before leaving Wheeling. One visitor had the tactless temerity to tell him that he was "failing." "Do you think so?" was Stanton's only response.

The journey home further weakened him. Stanton admitted to Watson that he sickened whenever he crossed the high Alleghenies, and this time "special circumstances contributed . . . so that I have been without voice from sore throat and without breath from spasms of asthma." Despite his condition, Stanton appeared at the United States Supreme Court on December 12 to lodge an appeal from the adverse decision of the lower federal tribunal at Wheeling. Three days later he was so ill that the marshal of the court, with the special permission of Chase, delivered new papers in the matter to him at his

[1] Stanton to N. W. Brooks, Dec. 12, 1868, Chandler Papers, LC; Hooper to Sumner, Nov. 17, Dec. 1, 1868, Sumner Papers, HU; Pierce, *Sumner*, IV, 369; Flower, *Stanton*, 399; Morse, *Welles Diary*, III, 508.

bedside. His legal acumen undiminished, Stanton was able to counter the opposition attorney's move to dismiss the case with a request to remand it back to Wheeling for certification of the record.[2]

With the Christmas season approaching, the Stantons prepared for their first family holiday together since 1861 with the father not in public office. Pamphila arrived in Washington for the seasonal celebration, but because she and Ellen did not get along well, she took rooms near by. On Christmas Eve, Stanton was too ill to come downstairs; so the family went to his bedside. In the early morning hours of Christmas Day, long after the children had retired, "Kris Kringle" dictated to Ellen a letter to them:

> I have just come from beyond the Rocky Mountains and arrived here at your home. I have a long journey yet to make before daylight, and many things to distribute among the good children between here and the Atlantic, so that I have time only to say a few words of love to you, and leave in your stockings, the gifts intended for you this Christmas.
>
> I am glad to see that you are all growing finely, and during the past year have been good children.
>
> Ellie, I am afraid, is growing too fast for me to make her any more visits, unless she turns out to be an uncommon good girl. She must learn to govern her temper and be patient to her brother and her little sister, and if she is so, I shall always be glad to stop and make her a Christmas visit.
>
> Lewis has been a very good boy and minds his mother very well. I hope he will continue to do so, and that when I come again, he will have learned to read very well.
>
> Bessie has generally been as good as any little girl that I have seen on my journey, but she cries too much when she gets angry; if she quits that, she will be a great favorite of mine.
>
> And now, my dear children, it is time for me to be going. I give you all a kiss, wish you a Merry Christmas, and hope to see you all well and that you have been good during the year, when I make my next visit.
>
> Good Bye
KRIS KRINGLE

Kris Kringle never returned to write another Christmas letter.[3]

---

[2] Flower, *Stanton*, 400; ms record of *James Evans* v. *Samuel McClean, Jr.*, #5254, U. S. Supreme Court. Stanton subsequently secured a favorable verdict from the Wheeling court.

[3] Kris Kringle letter, with Ellen's notation that Edwin dictated it, owned by Mrs. Van Swearingen; Pamphila to Holt, *ca.* Dec. 24, 1868, Holt Papers, LC.

With the new year, Stanton took stock of his situation. His earlier estimate of his earning power had proved to be excessively optimistic, he now realized, in part because of the time and energy he had invested campaigning for Grant but mainly because of his uncertain physical condition. Casting about now for some sources of income with which to keep going until he was able fully to resume law practice, Stanton was forced to a personally distasteful step.

Just before taking on the war office responsibility for Lincoln, Stanton had loaned Watson $30,000. Obviously detesting the necessity that forced him to the move, Stanton wrote Watson on January 10 stating that "my health continues to improve, and I am busy with the cases, but straitened for money. Can you do anything for me, or must I look elsewhere?" When Watson received Stanton's letter he was in conference with railroad contractor Stillman Witt, of Cleveland, who had worked with him and Stanton during the war. Witt immediately wrote out a draft for $5,000 in Stanton's favor.

The sick man in Washington was astounded upon receiving this check, which Witt obviously intended as a gift. He gratefully acknowledged "the first and only practical appreciation, among many thousand verbal and sincere words of affectionate respect that I have received." He admitted that he could not resume law practice without a few months' rest and that money must be obtained to finance this respite, but he accepted the money only on condition that Witt sent it as a loan for one year, with 10 per cent interest to him.[4]

Just at this time the rumor was abroad in Washington that Grant had slated Stanton for a cabinet post. Democratic spokesmen, still sour over the impeachment and the election results, launched a counter-attack on Stanton by asserting that in 1863 he had been so impatient with Grant's slowness in capturing Vicksburg that he had ordered Banks to succeed him in command. For once Stanton retorted publicly, and asserted that he had never thought Banks fit for any military command, much less over Grant.

So far as Grant's cabinet choices were concerned, Stanton insisted to Congressman Shellabarger, of Ohio, a frequent visitor, and to others, that he would never go into Grant's cabinet even if invited; "says he has not a great while to live & must devote that to his family —spoke of the cuffs and knocks he had recd in official life as . . . a

---

[4] Ellen to Alexander Wylie, April 9, 1870, on Watson's debt, and note of indebtedness to Witt, Feb. 1, 1869, in Stanton's hand, owned by Craig Wylie; Stanton to Witt, Jan. 29, 1868, Stanton MSS, which is more complete than the version in Jones, *op. cit.*, 140–1.

great boon," Shellabarger wrote, the memories of which "he could not now afford to part with." [5]

Stanton was sincere concerning his lack of interest in a cabinet post, but in romanticizing the benign memories he retained of his public career, he was trying to cloak his deep disappointment over the fact that Grant was still ignoring him almost entirely. Ellen realized how utterly despondent her husband was when he sent for Reverend William Sparrow, who had taught Stanton at Kenyon and now led a congregation at nearby Alexandria, to baptize him into the Episcopal Church, and brought Surgeon General Barnes to his bedside to confer concerning a burial plot. She desperately sought to lift his failing spirits, and held a series of small dinners and receptions at the Stanton home, inviting persons of status such as Justice Swayne, in order to impress her husband with the continued high regard in which he was held by the social leaders of the capital. For whatever reason, his condition improved.

Against the advice of Barnes, who was treating Stanton as a private patient, Ellen permitted her husband an unlimited number of visitors, and the result was beneficent. The man required activity and stimulation. His inner resources were too few to sustain loneliness. A lifetime of ceaseless expenditure of energy in work and in public office could not so quickly come to a halt. Since his youth he had rushed through life in a tireless search for wealth, success at the bar, and concrete results as a public official. Now he could not rest though he knew that his life literally depended on it.

During the last weeks of 1868, news of election riots, lynchings, and murders in the South filled the newspapers. Stanton's reaction was to nurture his distrust of Grant. He was again uneasy concerning the President-elect's views toward the Negro; unsure of his willingness to suppress the upsurging Klan organization and to check the increase of Democratic strength in a Dixie that would not admit that its cause was lost.

"I am sorry to know that Stanton has not seen Grant since the election," Sumner noted to the poet Whittier late in February 1869; the senator marveled that Stanton still asserted confidence in Grant's plans for economy in government, "but nothing about the rights of man to be maintained in all their fullness." With Sumner, Stanton hoped for the best, and his son Eddie echoed these mixed feelings: "Events here

[5] To Watson, Flower, *Stanton*, 401; to Witt, Jan. 29, 1869, Stanton MSS; Shellabarger to James Comly, Feb. 20, 1868, Comly Collection, OHS.

seem to be in a transition stage," he advised Rutherford Hayes. "No one seems to know what will be the definite form of the outcome, but Republicans are confident of the future." [6] Not all Republicans; not his father.

[6] Swayne to Ellen, Jan. 22, 1869, owned by Mrs. Van Swearingen; Edward S. Jerome, *Edwin M. Stanton, the Great War Secretary* (n.p., n.d.), 14; Flower, *Stanton*, 402; Pierce, *Sumner*, IV, 369; Eddie to Hayes, Jan. 8, 1869, HML.

THE OBSEQUIES HAVE BEEN
ENLARGED

𝔸 S THE milder mood of spring replaced the dour gray of the winter months, there was improvement in Stanton's health. He still felt it necessary to decline to serve as leading orator at a forthcoming Gettysburg memorial meeting, but he was pleased that he had been invited before Colfax, the Vice-President-elect. He summoned enough energy to appear before a congressional committee inquiring into wartime ordnance practices; out of this inquiry there emerged plentiful evidence from other witnesses that Stanton had wrought miracles of co-operation from manufacturers and given the Union troopers a flow of weapons greater than any army in the history of the world had known.

His obvious improvement in health and reappearance in public revived rumors that Stanton was due for recognition from Grant, now in the White House. Stanton had outspokenly criticized the trend of negotiations with England concerning American claims for damages done to Union shipping during the war by raiders built in British yards. Republican leaders saw this approach as an opportunity to sway Anglophobe Irish Americans away from their traditionally Democratic party allegiance, and began to tout Stanton as Grant's logical choice for the significant English mission.

But instead, the White House tendered him an unimportant scraping from the diplomatic barrel: an assignment to Mexico to deal with claims arising from wartime border depredations. This was less exalted a post than Buchanan had provided Stanton a decade before, when he was a relatively young, untried man. Since then Stanton had helped to preserve a nation, and only recently had campaigned effectively to put Grant into the presidency. Now the Mexican mission, without prestige or security, was his reward.

Hurt, Stanton curtly rejected the offer. He felt ill treated and was again despondent. Hooper, after talking with Grant in June, advised Sumner: "I am sorry Stanton takes things so much to heart, as it seems to me he would do better to keep his mind at ease—but I fear there is too much reason for him to feel as he does." [1]

Feeling that Grant had rebuffed him unjustly, Stanton tried to immerse himself in the few cases he had taken on and in studying others which he was contemplating accepting. But by the end of June he felt constrained to return the papers in several cases he had under consideration, admitting that his health could not stand the strain and that it was unfair to hold off the pleading because of his weakness. Although he asserted to Watson at this time that he had "hope now for a full recovery," Stanton also admitted that his wife and Barnes were waging a campaign to get him out of Washington during the approaching summer heat. Stanton did not want to leave Washington, however, and the reason he gave to Ellen—that he needed to prepare arguments in cases already committed to his care—was not the whole story.

Stanton's political stock had begun to rise as Sumner and other Republican leaders followed his line and hammered on the developing negotiations with England. Grant's Postmaster General, J. A. J. Creswell, welcomed patronage recommendations from the former War Secretary, which would receive "favorable reception." Best of all, word came from Pierrepont, who, after dining with the Grants, wrote Stanton that the President had taken him aside, and while the other guests grew feverish with curiosity, "spoke several times of you with *marked* favor." Mrs. Grant was even more enthusiastic, Pierrepont reported, "saying how much was due to you & that the General had made a mistake in not giving you a place of the highest grade &c, & that it ought to be done now. This was repeated over & over by her in a way so marked and unusual that I of course knew it had some special purpose, being . . . directed to me, when our relations were by her so well known." And so for Stanton there was the expectation of better things to come from the enigmatic, taciturn hero in the White House.[2]

---

[1] Testimony, March 16, April 22, 1869, Dyer Court of Inquiry, II, 127, 140, RG 153, NA; Hooper to Sumner, Nov. 17, 1868, June 13, 1869, HU; Stanton to Hamilton Fish, April 15, 1869, Fish Papers, LC.

[2] To Watson, Flower, *Stanton*, 403; to D. P. Brown, July 6, and Pierrepont to Stanton, June 23, 1869, Stanton MSS; E. L. Stanton to Creswell, June 16, 1869, owned by Ralph Newman.

A second reason was his worry over the Smithson lawsuit against him, now due in the District Supreme Court. Young Edwin represented his father, claiming that as War Secretary the elder Stanton was immune from private suits as an agent of the President, as specified by the terms of the 1863 act on habeas corpus suspension and the 1867 reconstruction law. All through July 1869, Stanton waited to hear the verdict of the court concerning the acceptability of this defense. Now he learned that the judges very reluctantly had decided that Smithson's plea might not be ruled out on those grounds. However, his friend Cartter placed the hearing of the case proper as far back as possible on his calendar, scheduling it for a hearing in the 1870 term; it was never to be pushed to a decision.

This was some comfort to Stanton, but the weight of the Smithson case hung over his spirits like a cloud. In his mind the suit was another symptom of the ingratitude of a nation which he had helped to save, now casting him indifferently aside to receive the rebuffs of unworthy and vicious men. While the Smithson plea was being argued, he could not leave Washington.

Faith in the possibility of a cure was the third reason. For years Stanton had known Dr. John Bayne, a Maryland medical practitioner with novel ideas on the treatment of respiratory ailments. Because his physician, Barnes, was unsympathetic to these theories, Stanton kept secret the fact that he was following dietary modes based on vegetables supplied from Bayne's farm. By the end of June, Stanton reported to Bayne a general improvement in his health "but the paroxysms of asthma still continue, sometimes lasting all day. General Barnes has at my request and apparently with pleasure, determined to invite you to consult with him & examine my case. . . . He knows nothing of your having seen me nor is there any necessity for communicating the fact."

But late in July a relapse occurred; Barnes suggested that Stanton draw up his will. Then, somewhat recovered, and with the Smithson case in suspense, Stanton wearily acceded to Ellen's demands that he leave the city for a more healthful climate.[3]

He wrote to his mother that he and Ellen had considered spending the summer touring the Rocky Mountains country, "but the distance is too great I fear for either of us to undertake it now, and the Indian troubles are not over." Stanton was dissembling here out of concern

[3] *Smithson* v. *Stanton*, Records of the Supreme Court of the District of Columbia, RG 21, NA; Stanton to Bayne, May 17, June 26, 1869, Stanton MSS; Flower, *Stanton*, 403.

that his mother should learn how ill and penniless he was. At the time he wrote his mother he had already heard from General Sherman, who was in Washington and was willing to end in amity the feud that had festered between them, and he knew that Indians were no problem to a traveler protected by cavalry escort, as he could have been.

Sherman, offering his friendship and aid to the sick man, mapped out a detailed route entailing "as little fatigue as [going to] Ohio by dividing up the country according to your strength." The western trip would prove beneficent, Sherman cajoled. "Atmosphere purity itself, and one that I think offers a better chance to suit your particular state than any I know — Say the word and I will call to see you, and elaborate the details."

It was a generous gesture, but Stanton could not afford the trip, and so the two men did not meet. But Sherman's letter was a harbinger of hatchet burying. Hearing that Jeremiah Black had suffered an accident, Stanton had rushed off an inquiry concerning the health of his long-time friend and erstwhile enemy. Black responded with cautious cordiality, and in like spirit Stanton sent him his best wishes for a speedy recovery. The accord between Sherman and Stanton was to be permanent for both men. Black, however, was to show himself as an unconverted enemy.[4]

Meanwhile, Ellen had to stay in Baltimore to continue dental treatments. "Everything about town & in the house is so still and quiet that there is scarce material for a daily letter," Stanton wrote her; the boys playing croquet, Ellie involved in a girlish feud with her friends, "and this affords all the excitement that is going on K Street." Each evening he sent Eddie to the depot in the hope that Ellen might return on the last train. But though he missed her intensely, he hoped she would stay on to complete the treatment. For himself, he asserted his health was no worse. "Last night I had too much company," Stanton admitted, "& had to take the potash but it did not do as well as heretofore & I have been in bed all day."

She returned home as July ended; on August 3 he wrote to his friend Hooper that "under her escort" he was departing that day for New Hampshire. "I am suffering so much," he admitted, "as to require me to leave without delay." But unlike his experience two years earlier, the mountain weather now proved unsuitable for his condition; he sat immobile on the piazza of a hotel, gazing vacantly

<hr/>

[4] Wolcott MS, 220–1, to Stanton's mother; Sherman to Stanton, July 28, 1869, owned by Gideon Townsend Stanton (misdated 1867 in LC copy) ; Stanton to Black, July 17, 1869 (misfiled under 1857), Black Papers, LC.

at playing children, a "wreck" of a man according to the description of a journalist who observed him. Ellen decided against their remaining there, and they moved on to Boston, where they were guests of wealthy friends through the remainder of August.

They intended to return to Washington at the end of the month, but Hooper came to Boston with Eddie Stanton at this time, and Ellen wrote to the younger children that "as soon as Mr. Hooper saw us . . . he persuaded your Father to try Cotuit [Point] and see what effect the sea air would have." Ellen and Stanton arranged for Anna Barnes, the wife of the Surgeon General, to care for the younger children in Washington now that the reopening of the schools was at hand, and Ellen's mother and sister came from Pittsburgh to lend their assistance.

Stanton could not help knowing that he was in the position of being dependent upon the charity of friends and the co-operation of relatives. Sickness of spirit and shame added their weight to the deterioration of his body. Once at Hooper's Cape Cod home, he tried to isolate himself from the outside world, hoping to cut himself off from communication with everyone but his children, his mother in Gambier, and a very few trusted intimates.[5] Roscoe Conkling, wanting the Stantons to visit at his home next, and offering "all belonging to me" to aid in the sick man's recuperation, had to send a dozen telegrams to locate them.

Good news came in from Wheeling of the favorable verdict in the land claim which he had pleaded earlier that year. But his bodily sickness was not routed. For the first time, Stanton admitted to his mother how unwell he was. "I have this summer been diligently seeking health on mountains and the seashore," he wrote her on September 18, "hoping to find some place where we could be free from asthma. But my search has been in vain and tomorrow I start home scarcely as well as when I set out." The next day, however, Stanton seemed close to death. Remaining of necessity at Hooper's home, he commenced a slow recovery and attributed his retention of life to the "pure air and fresh surroundings" of this "sweet oasis."

The crisp autumn days passed slowly for him as he lay, almost a complete invalid, near a warm hearth, listening to the surf. On fine days Ellen sat with him on the porch overlooking the ocean as he watched the patient maneuvers of sea birds and breathed deeply of the inspiriting breezes wafted inshore from tidal flats. In the evenings,

[5] Stanton to Ellen, July 8, *ca.* July 16, and to Hooper, Aug. 3, 1869, owned by Edward S. Corwin; Mary Bailey to Ellen, Dec. 28, 1869, Stanton MSS; Ellen to "My dear children," Sept. 10, 1869, owned by Mrs. Van Swearingen. Flower, *Stanton,* 403, is incorrect on the itinerary of the trip.

as strength returned to him, Stanton sat gazing into the flickering pattern of the parlor fire; a rare visitor found him thus one September night.

John C. Ropes was a guest at a neighboring home. Disappointed because he could not fight in the Civil War, young Ropes had conceived an interest in military history. Learning that Stanton was close by, he came to see him, hoping to record some facts about wartime for future use, and to pay his respects to the famed Secretary.

He found Stanton slumped in a chair set by the hearth, flabby limbs and heavy body wrapped in blankets to fend off the autumn chill, seeming to be a decade or even two past the fifty-three years that were rightfully his. Deep lines etched his brow and furrowed from flaring nostrils, set off petulant lips and sagging cheeks, and emphasized broad features framed by thinning gray hair and a scraggly beard. The presence of sickness received testimony from a heavy odor of medicines that lay in the close-shuttered room and from the anxious efforts of his wife to quiet him. But on this night Stanton wanted to talk. The admiring attitude of young Ropes and his intense curiosity concerning past events triggered an unprecedented flow of reminiscences from Stanton.

Words tumbled from his lips as though they had been too long pent up. Stanton pushed aside the medications that Ellen brought and insisted that lamps be placed to relieve the deepening shadows of the room. Hours passed by as his rasping voice cut through the mutter of the nearby surf and the whisper of the wind. Only uncontrollable spasms of asthmatic coughing interrupted him, but they ran their course and he went on.

As Stanton spoke, the shadows of men who had shaped the destiny of the nation since 1860 took shape in the minds of his listeners. But soon after midnight the coughing became too severe for him to continue, and Ropes took his leave. Stanton's declining health prevented another meeting between him and Ropes, which both men wanted.[6]

September drew to a close, and Hooper reported to Sumner that Stanton's convalescence was slow and uneven; he was too weak even to take up a pen. "He gets along well by day but suffers at night,"

---

[6] Ms memo by Ropes, Feb. 1870, of the Sept. 1869 conversation, Woodman Papers, MHS; Conkling to Stanton, Sept. 6, 1869, Stanton MSS; Wolcott MS, 222, to his mother; Flower, *Stanton,* 403.

Hooper wrote, and Stanton later specified to Dr. Bayne that "the cough paroxysm begins about 5 PM, and lasts until 2 in the morning after which hour I sleep well."

Over his host's protests, Stanton, though dreading the journey, decided to start his return to Washington on September 28, for he now professed to feel far better and there was a case pending before the Supreme Court which he dared not drop. Back in Washington after a tedious trip, he lay in a stock of medicines, including the novel oxygen inhalators. There were the unending expenses of his family to deal with as well—dental bills, and tuition for Lewis, Ellie, and Bessie.[7]

Stanton had hoped to be able to handle the defense of the Crédit Mobilier against certain state regulations of Pennsylvania; the corporation had sent him a good retainer, which he desperately needed. But too ill to work on the matter, he returned the money. By late November he admitted to Watson that he was again in need of cash. It was by now obvious that Stanton could not expect any immediate large income from practicing law, and Barnes was insisting that he rest completely. To "drive the wolf from the door," he was therefore forced to ask Watson again for any part his friend could spare of the loan advanced to him years before.

In Washington, Stanton kept a braver face, and almost no one there outside his family knew how straitened his finances were. He asserted to Conkling that his health had improved considerably; although "I shall perhaps never regain my former vigorous strength the improvement encourages me to hope for still further amendment." His appetite was larger, which he attributed to the seaside environment that he had enjoyed in the autumn. Friends were pleased to learn that only the unending coughing remained as a visible symptom of his asthmatic ailment. Stanton had Eddie inquire about reputed cures for asthma, and a number of wonder-working remedies were suggested, none of which seemed to help the ailing man.[8]

It was time for him to take stock. With his mind unimpaired and his

[7] Hooper to Sumner, Sept. 22, 24, 27–9, Oct. 2, 1869, Sumner Papers, HU; Stanton to Bayne, Nov. 27, 1869, Stanton MSS; medical and tuition bills owned by Craig Wylie.

[8] Stanton to Conkling, Nov. 4, 1869, Conkling Papers, LC; George Innis to Edwin L. Stanton, Nov. 2, Stanton to Bayne, Nov. 27, and Watson to Stanton, Dec. 22, 1869, Stanton MSS; same to Gail Sanford, Nov. 7, 1869, owned by the estate of Foreman M. Lebold; Flower, *Stanton*, 403–4; notes of indebtedness Dec. 1, 1869, owned by Craig Wylie.

Stanton : The Life and Times

body evidencing some improvement, Stanton for the first time in his life set out to beg for an official position. He felt, as Robert Anderson of Fort Sumter fame told him, that he had earned it.

Learning from Justice Grier, of the Supreme Court, that he planned to retire, Stanton set out to secure the place. He worked through his old friend Bishop Simpson, whom he knew Grant trusted, asking him to intervene with the President on his behalf, insisting that he was physically able to manage the high judicial responsibility and that his mental resources "are as acute & vigorous as any period of my life— and perhaps more so." This appointment, he felt, would be mere justice to him, and Grant could be sure that as a judge "there is no man who would uphold the principles of the war . . . with more or equal vigor from the Bench." Accurately predicting that the Court would rise in importance from the depths to which it had plunged in the decade spanned by the Dred Scott and Milligan cases, Stanton argued that his appointment would please all Republicans. He had implied nothing of his desire to Grant, and would not. But he hoped Simpson would talk with the President. "To me it may in considerable degree be a question of life—it certainly is of health, for I must go to the Bench or the Bar. His [Grant's] name & fortune he owed at critical moments to me. He can preserve me to my family under Providence."

Grant at first reacted favorably to Simpson's suggestion until George W. Childs, a Philadelphia banker with whom the President was now on intimate terms, discouraged him by implying that Stanton's health was inadequate to sustain him on the Court. Stanton wrote Simpson to thank him, and said that he wanted no more efforts made on his behalf. He noted that soon after becoming War Secretary he had canceled a contract made between Childs and Cameron, and now the financier was achieving revenge. A shaft of bitterness showed through his careful language only at one point; "as respects General Grant he will be influenced by his judgment as to his own interest," Stanton wrote.[9]

Despite Stanton's injunction that his hope for the Court appointment was ended so far as he was concerned, Simpson continued to press Grant, who needed to appoint two judges rather than one because

[9] Anderson to Stanton, Dec. 9, 1869, Stanton MSS; Stanton to Simpson, Oct. 26, Nov. 3, 1869, LNLF. Substantiation of Childs's role as a consistent enemy to Stanton is in Lieber to "My Dear Sir" (probably Benson J. Lossing), Dec. 25, 1865, Lieber Papers, LC.

Congress had reset the total membership of the Court back to nine after having prevented Johnson from naming anyone to its roster. Unknown to Stanton, others of his friends were also trying to obtain for him the Court seat he coveted. Chandler was lobbying among the Republican senators to bring pressure on Grant, and quite independently, Wade was insisting to the President that Stanton was less ill than reports indicated. Grant was pleased to learn this. But Stanton's bitterness increased meanwhile at what he felt was Grant's inexcusable aloofness toward him.[1]

In the first week of December 1869, Stanton put aside the political concerns and against his physician's orders prepared to plead an important patent case before the Supreme Court. He exhibited his old skill and energy, matching and surpassing the legal arguments of his opponent, Benjamin R. Curtis. Returning from the Court building on the twelfth, Stanton stopped at the White House in response to a summons from Grant, and then, jubilant, returned home. The nomination to the supreme bench was his.

Next day he was too weak, from excitement, Barnes believed, to brave the wintry weather and go to court, and Justice Swayne came to the Stanton home to hear his argument. Meanwhile, rumors were abroad that Stanton was due for the Court nomination, and the New York *World*, under the guidance of Manton Marble, who never missed a chance to hit at Stanton, pleaded with the President to pass over this "sick spoilist and asthmatic patriot." Marble crudely and erroneously charged that Stanton's illness was a dodge designed to protect him from damage suits for excesses committed as War Secretary: "Now when a life office is vacant, his health is all right."

Stanton's friends rallied. In the Senate, Carpenter secured in less than twenty minutes the signatures of 38 colleagues to a petition for Stanton's nomination; 118 representatives added their signatures to the appeal. Carpenter and Chandler brought the document to Stanton. The sick man was unable to speak. Tears coursed from his eyes. The senators withdrew to take the petition to Grant, who promised to send in Stanton's name the next day.

On December 19, Stanton's fifty-fourth birthday, Ellen was at her husband's bedside when a servant announced a visitor and presented a card, graciously inscribed: "Mrs. Judge Stanton, with compliments

[1] Pierrepont to Hamilton Fish, Nov. 18, 1869, Fish Papers, LC; same to Stanton, Nov. 21, 1869, Stanton MSS; Detroit *Post, Chandler,* 299–300; Colman, *op. cit.,* 54; Pierce, *Sumner,* IV, 526.

of Gen. U. S. Grant." The President was there with Colfax to inform them officially of the nomination.[2]

Over the country, the reports of Stanton's nomination received mixed reactions. Pierrepont was naturally enthusiastic, and he makes it clear that Grant had not appointed Stanton merely as a gracious gesture to a dying man, in the expectation that Stanton would probably never take his seat on the Court. In Pierrepont's view, and he was close to the White House, Grant planned for Stanton to become Chief Justice if Chase later stepped down to run in 1872 for the presidency as a Democrat.

Another indication of the seriousness of the nomination is evident from the cases the Court had at hand for decisions. The first major question Stanton would face on the bench involved the legitimacy of the government's wartime paper-money issues; indeed, Grier's instability on this matter was part of the reason for the pressure for his resignation. In view of the fact that Stanton had taken a cabinet post under Lincoln as a means of halting the government's descent to bankruptcy, and that his view on the nation's power to protect itself from rebellion was of the most expansive kind, his position on the money-issue question would undoubtedly be to sustain the greenbacks as legal tender, and this was one reason why Grant chose him. At least this was Lieber's view as expressed to Sumner; Lieber had agreed with Stanton in every instance where the lives of the two men had crossed, and Sumner was now Stanton's closest friend. Probably Stanton had expressed this opinion to his intimates.

Agreeing with the sense of Lieber's conviction that Stanton was "a potent element" as a jurist, Justice Joseph Bradley recalled that his new colleague had been an outstanding private lawyer, Buchanan's Attorney General, and "the great War Secretary." Stanton, Bradley believed, "with the exception of Grant and Seward and Sumner and Chase, . . . was undoubtedly the most conspicuous figure in American public life."

Chase himself expected Stanton to be "a great and honest Judge," capable of strengthening the Court in every way. It seems sure that Grant's naming of Stanton to the high bench was the result of the widespread conviction that he was the best man for the place, as well as a gracious though belated acknowledgment of his services and abilities. Certainly it was not a mere gesture.[3]

[2] *World*, Dec. 14, 1869; *Tribune*, Dec. 25, 1869; Flower, *Stanton*, 405–6; Gorham, *Stanton*, II, 471–4; Grant's card owned by Mrs. Van Swearingen.

[3] Pierrepont to Stanton, Dec. 20, 21, 1869, Stanton MSS; Lieber to H. Woodman,

Across town on Capitol Hill, congressmen approved the nomination without the usual committee referrals. A steady stream of callers left cards of congratulation at the Stanton home: old friends Joseph Holt, General "Ed" Townsend, ordnance chief A. B. Dyer, and Senator Edmunds; his new colleagues Justices Swayne and Field; and several of Grant's cabinet. On the twenty-first, after his doctor had firmly refused to permit him to go personally to the White House to thank Grant, Stanton penned a note of acceptance to the President whose key phrase was: "It is the only public office I ever desired and I accept it with great pleasure." Stanton expressed his gratification at receiving the appointment from Grant, "with whom for several years I have had personal and official relations, such as seldom exist among men."

Her husband was happier now than Ellen remembered having seen him in years. She took his note to the White House and then stopped at a bookseller to buy Christmas gifts. Bessie was to get *Baby's Christmas* and Eleanor would enjoy *Our Dumb Companions,* while for her husband, Ellen purchased a lined memorandum pad in leather covers for him to use for taking notes while hearing cases. A new life was to begin for the Stanton family; ease, dignity, security, were to be theirs at last.[4]

But when Ellen returned home she found Edwin complaining of weakness induced by severe coughing. No one was alarmed, for his discomfort had become part of living for them. Next day, Stanton was too weak to write out a note of thanks to a congratulatory telegram he had received and General Thomas Vincent, who was calling on him that morning, had to act as amanuensis. As the afternoon hours passed, his coughing increased in violence, wracking the man's frame almost without cessation. His mother and sister, in Washington to celebrate the Christmas holiday and the Court appointment, were called from their nearby lodgings and sat in the parlor, while upstairs a group of doctors sought to alleviate his suffering. Midnight came.

Jan. 6, 1870, Woodman Papers, MHS; to Sumner, Feb. 9, 1870, Lieber Papers, HL; Charles Bradley (ed.), *Miscellaneous Writings of the Late Hon. Joseph P. Bradley* (Newark, 1901), 57; Chase to Schuckers, Dec. 27, 1869 (misfiled in 1867), Chase Papers, 2d ser., LC.

[4] Contrary to the statement in Flower, *Stanton,* 406, Stanton did not take the note to Grant and thereby contract the cold that killed him. Calling cards in Stanton MSS; letter of acceptance in Stanton's hand is owned by Gideon Townsend Stanton, from which the printed texts vary in minor ways; on Ellen, see Dec. 22, 1869, memorandum of purchases, owned by Craig Wylie.

Barnes sent for the minister of the nearby Church of the Epiphany, but before the clergyman arrived, Stanton became unconscious.

Ellen, seated next to the bed, watched her husband. The children— tall, mature young Edwin, adolescent Eleanor, whose sophisticated poses now dissolved in tears, nine-year-old Lewis, and untamable little Bessie—huddled on a bench in a corner of the room. Then, at three in the morning, their father died.

Christmas Day passed in preparations for the funeral. Ellen arranged for interment in the Georgetown cemetery where their infant son lay buried. Next day Stanton's body was placed in a casket in the upstairs sitting room.

Ellen was close to breaking. She derived some comfort from a letter which young Edwin read to her, and which both of them came to treasure. It was from Robert Lincoln, who wrote: "I know that it is useless to say anything . . . and yet when I recall the kindness of your father to me, when my father was lying dead and I felt utterly desperate, hardly able to realize the truth, I am as little able to keep my eyes from filling with tears as he was then." [5]

Seeking a last remnant of privacy for a life that for too long had been exposed to public contention, Ellen closed the house before the funeral to all save the family and a handful of intimate friends. Her secretiveness gave credence to rumors circulating almost immediately that Stanton had committed suicide out of remorse for Mrs. Surratt, cutting his own throat as his brother Darwin had done, and that Ellen had sealed the coffin to prevent observation of the wound. These rumors were uncritically accepted by men who hated Stanton, and are still offered as the truth in some accounts of Stanton's life.

But the evidence is absolutely convincing that his death was caused by his asthmatic ailment. Stanton's heart could no longer sustain the strain of a ravaged respiratory system and the effects of years of overwork and worry. Those who were with him only a few hours before the final collapse began saw a happy, confident man in full possession of his mental faculties and expressing thoughts in which the grim specter of self-guilt had no place. On the evening before he died he momentarily roused from his coma and asked when the next Supreme Court session was scheduled so that he could prepare in time. "No

---

[5] R. Lincoln to E. L. Stanton, Dec. 24, 1869, owned by Gideon Townsend Stanton; death scene in correspondence between A. Wylie, Ellen, and Pamphila, owned by Craig Wylie.

one," Hooper recalled, "entertained any serious apprehension of any immediate danger." Life, not death, was on Edwin Stanton's mind.[6]

For the last time Stanton traveled the familiar route from K Street to Georgetown that he and Lincoln had taken together so many times. Now he rested on a somber artillery caisson, and proceeded at the slow pace set by soldiers who, with rifles reversed in the heraldic symbolism of grief, flanked the conveyance. More than one hundred carriages followed in a line so long that sight of the rearmost vehicles was lost in the steady rain that fell all day. His family, high officials of the national government, representatives from the states and from foreign nations, military and naval officers, and delegates from veterans' and Negro welfare organizations were at hand to see Stanton buried. Onlookers crowded the streets as the procession made its slow way through the capital, for Grant had ordered the public offices closed and public buildings draped in the raiments of sorrow. Flags flew half-staffed in Washington, New York, Pittsburgh, and Columbus. At the President's command, salute guns were firing at every army camp in the country, and the sound of these martial compliments echoed from military installations near the path of the funeral procession. In the overwhelming monochrome of mourning created by the sad purpose of that wintry day, only the floral tributes on a carriage behind the hearse provided a flash of color.

Other important men had died recently—General Rawlins, Henry J. Raymond, William Pitt Fessenden, and Edward Bates, who, like Stanton, had served in Lincoln's cabinet. But the unexpectedness of Stanton's death at a moment of triumph for the man inspired spectators and commentators with a feeling of shocked disbelief and a consciousness of analogy to Lincoln's fate, and years later Grant was to say that Stanton "was as much a martyr to the Union as [Generals] Sedgwick or McPherson."

This was the funeral of an important man, and the presence of the President and Vice-President, of Supreme Court jurists and senators

---

[6] Vincent, *Abraham Lincoln and Edwin M. Stanton* (Washington, 1890), 20, and Townsend, *Anecdotes*, 140–2, on refutation of suicide. The best account of Stanton's death is in a ms reminiscence by A. E. H. Johnson, owned by Gideon Townsend Stanton. On suicide rumors, see Eisenschiml, *Why Was Lincoln Murdered?*, 289–90; ms reminiscence by Col. W. M. Nixon in George Fort Milton Papers, LC; Poore, *Trial*, II, 301–5; and Richard Taylor, *Destruction and Reconstruction* (New York, 1879), 294; Hooper to Woodman, Dec. 25, 1869, Woodman Papers, MHS.

and representatives, lent the highest tone of official participation. Beyond this, however, the outpouring of eulogies from Congress, courts, state legislatures, and pulpits, bore witness that death had claimed a part of the history of the nation. Those who bore Stanton's coffin to the grave—Generals Barnes and Townsend, Justice Swayne and Judge Cartter, Senators Sumner and Carpenter, Secretary of War Belknap, and Postmaster General Creswell—had worked with him during a decade of drastic changes, uncertain politics, and frightening dangers. A link to all this was gone.

Grant had wanted a full state ceremony with the body on display in the Capitol Rotunda, but Ellen had insisted on as much simplicity as possible. Now she rode with Eckert and Dana; Hooper, who had quietly made all the funeral arrangements, escorted and comforted the younger Stanton children and the dead man's mother and sister. Vice-President and Mrs. Colfax and Mrs. Grant shared a carriage with Edwin Lamson Stanton, whose grief was mixed with worry over the future of the family for which he was now responsible.

At the grave site Reverend Sparrow conducted a brief service, thinking the while of the youth he had taught years before at Kenyon. The soldiers fired three volleys in final salute, and it was finished.[7]

---

[7] Funeral descriptions in New York *Times*, Dec. 27; *Tribune*, Dec. 29, 1869; *Nation* (Jan. 6, 1870), 1; and see Young, *Around the World*, II, 358–9. Stanton's family was soon faced with actual want, despite the $11,950 insurance, which was spent repaying debts; see Probate File #6255, Old Series, RG 21, NA. Congress thereafter voted Ellen a year's salary of a Justice, perhaps, as James Parton asserts in *Topics of the Times* (Boston, 1871), 9, because the country felt guilty at having worked Stanton to death. John Tappan, Woodman, and Hooper arranged a private subscription—not a public one at Pierrepont's instigation, as stated in *ANJ* (Jan. 1, 1870), 310–11—which realized $111,466.44—not $140,000, as Chandler states in Detroit *Post, Chandler*, 33, or $175,000, the amount accepted in Gorham, *Stanton*, II, 469. The correctives are in Lewis Stanton's memo on the fund raised in his father's memory, owned by Gideon Townsend Stanton, and exchanges in Woodman Papers, Dec. 1869– Jan. 1870, MHS. Ellen gallantly carried out her husband's lifetime program of making his mother and sisters financially secure, but the Stanton women, and the estate's executors, Wylie and Townsend, did not get along, and increasing acrimony marked their relationships. Stanton's family began the process of dissolution which is so common when the strong element that held it together departs. See the exchanges between Wylie, Townsend, Pamphila Wolcott, and Ellen Stanton, owned by Craig Wylie.

A NOTE

ON THE HISTORY OF STANTON
BIOGRAPHIES

Stanton's death, far from quieting his enemies, gave them new voice. They became bitter at the praises lavished on the man in eulogies across the country, and determined, as a friend of Jeremiah Black's stated it, that "the bones of Stanton should rattle in their grave." Manton Marble set the theme in a New York *World* obituary on Stanton: "All men die and death does not change faults into virtues."

Black took on the role of architect of an anti-Stanton tradition. Within weeks after Stanton's burial, he published a series of articles which questioned his former friend's veracity, integrity, and consistency. These articles, wrote Ward Hill Lamon, were "such a portrayal of vice, corruption, and sycophancy, that it sickens the heart to contemplate the state of morals in high places." [1]

The abuse being heaped on the memory of his father sickened the heart of Edwin Lamson Stanton. This brilliant young man was emulating his father in his swift advancement in the law. Grant favored him with a federal attorney's commission, and by the early 1870's he numbered even Andrew Johnson and Montgomery Blair among his private clients. Knowing the truth of his father's relations with Black, and wanting to correct the errors that General Sherman broadcast in his published memoirs, young Stanton decided to write a life of his father.

But like his famous parent, Stanton's son devoted himself to material advancement ahead of almost any other consideration. Although he collected as many of his father's papers as he could in preparation for

[1] *World*, Dec. 25, 1869; Lamon to Black, Jan. 31, and J. Harvey to same, Oct. 2, 1870, Black Papers, LC.

641

advancing a biography, business cares kept intruding. The book never materialized, and less than a decade after Edwin McMasters Stanton died, his promising oldest son followed him to the grave.[2]

The documents that he had laboriously assembled were scattered anew. Descendants of the Lamson branch of the family kept a portion. Some went to Lewis Hutchison Stanton, the younger son, and after much acrimony, a group came into Pamphila's possession. As the years passed, and the chorus of criticism of her late brother increased in volume and intensity, Pamphila tried unsuccessfully to reassemble all the dispersed papers so that she could commission a biography. She then decided to go ahead on her own and prepared a "sketch" of his life, but found that "a strange fatality" attended her efforts to gain publication for the composition. Pamphila supposed that Stanton relatives, unwilling to contribute to the endless debate over his controversial career, exerted influence to prevent its appearance in print. According to a third-generation Stanton descendant, Willis Weaver, the family's feelings did run "pretty high" concerning Pamphila's memoir. It remained unpublished.[3]

Meanwhile Lewis Stanton had commissioned his father's friend George C. Gorham, former Secretary of the U. S. Senate, to write a biography. An intimate of the Stanton family, G. A. Mendall, confided to Frank A. Flower, a young Wisconsinite who was also interested in preparing a life of Stanton, that "Gorham is a pungent, bitter writer. . . . [There will be] a good deal more Gorham than Stanton in it." And so it proved to be. When the two-volume Gorham book appeared in 1899, it fell far short of the hopes of the Stanton family and admirers, though it was a totally favorable view of its subject. In a review, George W. Julian unhappily admitted that "this is not the final Life of Edwin M. Stanton," and concluded that Gorham had prepared "a healthy and inspiring story" for young people. Gorham's *Stanton* remains, however, an indispensable source collection, for the author never returned to the Hutchison branch of the Stanton family the large number of manuscripts he had received from them to aid him in his task, some of which appear in the book.

In 1905, using materials supplied by the Lamson members of the family, Flower published a Stanton biography. Stanton's cousin, the wartime Ohio legislator Benjamin Stanton, after reading some of

[2] E. L. Stanton to John Schuckers, July 13, 1874, Schuckers Papers, LC; to Whitelaw Reid, May 24, 1875, Reid Papers, LC.
[3] Pamphila to J. A. Howells, March 28, 1897, Howells Papers, HML; Weaver to E. S. Corwin, Dec. 29, 1927, owned by Prof. Corwin.

Flower's manuscript, was sure that "you hit the character of Stanton exactly." But Flower was no more capable than Gorham of delineating character or of constructively balancing conflicting pieces of evidence. He was a warm admirer of the War Secretary, and his book is as one-sided a defense of its subject as its predecessor. Also, like Gorham, Flower failed to return to the Stanton family the papers he had received from them.

Six years later, the diary of Gideon Welles went into print. Its caustic assertions concerning Stanton's role in public affairs and his alleged inadequacies in matters of character made an immediate and lasting impression. Jesse Weik admitted that it had "completely upset my notion of Seward, Stanton, and Grant. I have always been such an admirer of all three that I sometimes regret that I ever read Mr. Welles' estimate. But the great thing is his vindication of Andrew Johnson." [4]

The vindication of Johnson continued for the next forty years, almost without contradiction. Then, in 1953, Fletcher Pratt published his study of Stanton, which, although it corrected some tenacious misapprehensions, did not provide the needed full study of his life. There, until now, the Stanton story has rested.

[4] B. J. Stanton to Flower, Nov. 29, 1887, and Mendall to same, Feb. 23, 1888, WSHS; Julian in *Dial*, XXVII, 48–52; Weik to Horace White, *ca.* Nov. 1911, copy owned by the estate of Benjamin P. Thomas.

INDEX

A NOTE ON THE TYPE

THE TEXT of this book was set on the Linotype in BODONI BOOK, a printing type so called after Giambattista Bodoni (1740–1813), a celebrated printer and type designer of Rome and Parma. Bodoni Book as produced by the Linotype company is not a copy of any one of Bodoni's fonts, but is a composite, modern version of the Bodoni manner. Bodoni's innovations in printing-type style were a greater degree of contrast in the "thick and thin" elements of the letters and a sharper and more angular finish of details.

Composed, printed, and bound by
Kingsport Press, Inc., Kingsport, Tennessee.
Typography and binding design by
J A M E S   H E N D R I C K S O N

A NOTE ABOUT THE AUTHORS

BENJAMIN PLATT THOMAS is generally considered to have been one of our nation's leading authorities on Lincoln. He was born in Pemberton, New Jersey, in 1902, and attended Johns Hopkins University, where he received his A.B. degree in 1924 and his Ph.D. in 1929. After teaching history for three years at Birmingham-Southern College in Alabama, he served as executive secretary of the Abraham Lincoln Association from 1932 to 1936, was associate editor of the *Abraham Lincoln Quarterly* from 1940 to 1953, and, until his death in 1956, was a trustee of the Illinois Historical Library. Before doing his own biography of Lincoln, Thomas wrote five books, of which perhaps the most outstanding was *Portrait for Posterity: Lincoln and His Biographers*, published in 1947. He was also the author of *Lincoln's New Salem* (1934), *Lincoln, 1847–1853* (1936), and *Theodore Weld, Crusader for Freedom* (1950), and edited *Three Years with Grant*, recollections of war correspondent Sylvanus Cadwallader (1955). Mr. Thomas had also been an editorial adviser for the Abraham Lincoln Association's "Collected Works of Lincoln."

HAROLD M. HYMAN was born in New York City in 1924. After taking his A.B. degree at the University of California at Los Angeles, he did graduate work at Columbia University, and his doctoral dissertation, *Era of the Oath: Northern Loyalty Tests during the Civil War and Reconstruction*, won the American Historical Association's Albert J. Beveridge Award in 1952. He has taught at Earlham College in Indiana and at Arizona State University, and is presently an associate professor of history at U.C.L.A. In 1959 he received the Sidney Hillman Award for his *To Try Men's Souls: Loyalty Tests in American History*.

Mr. Hyman is married, and the father of two daughters and a son.

January 1962